Thirty-Five Years of Archaeological Research at Salmon Ruins, New Mexico

Volume Two: Ceramic Studies

Thirty-Five Years of Archaeological Research at Salmon Ruins, New Mexico

Volume Two: Ceramic Studies

edited by Paul F. Reed

Contributions by

Hayward Franklin
Tori L. Myers
Lori Stephens Reed
Dorothy K. Washburn
C. Dean Wilson

Center for Desert Archaeology, Tucson
and Salmon Ruins Museum, Bloomfield, New Mexico
2006

Center for Desert Archaeology
Tucson, Arizona 85705

Salmon Ruins Museum
Bloomfield, New Mexico 87413

Volume II
ISBN 1-886398-53-4
$24.95

CONTENTS

FIGURES

TABLES

Chapter 18

GENERAL INTRODUCTION TO THE SALMON CERAMIC VOLUME

by Lori Stephens Reed

This ceramic volume represents an amalgam of the work completed over the last 35 years. The Salmon Ceramics Laboratory undertook ceramic analysis between 1972 and 1980 under the direction of Ann Bennett (1972–1974) and Hayward Franklin (1975–1980). Following a more than 20-year hiatus, in 2002, I began Salmon ceramic studies anew with my colleagues at Animas Ceramic Consulting. Approaches to the study of ceramic artifacts have evolved considerably over the last two decades, and these changes are reflected in the methodological differences between the original Salmon ceramic analysis and the newer studies. In particular, the basic approach to ceramic typology has changed dramatically. In the 1970s, ceramic analysts typically assigned ceramics to diagnostic types (e.g., McElmo Black-on-white) through an examination of surface attributes, such as design, slip, and paint type. Although analysts were aware of the need to examine temper and paste to confirm assignment to a specific ceramic tradition, series, and type, this was not the standard practice. Thus, the Salmon rough-sort analysis made tradition, series, and type assignments for thousands of sherds without examination of the critical attributes of paste and temper (see Franklin, Chapter 19). To be fair, the Salmon rough-sort analysis was primarily intended to rapidly assess ceramics to provide feedback to field crews and provide initial ceramic dates for strata. It was not intended to be the only nor the most detailed analysis undertaken on the project. Two attribute-based studies were completed (as detailed by Franklin in the chapters that follow) and these studies examined paste and temper. Additional discussion of the methodology of the Salmon Ceramic Laboratory follows in Chapter 19.

Ceramic studies conducted these days are more sensitive to subtle differences in paste and temper, and are more concerned with identifying source areas for the ceramics found at particular locales. The primary concern with using data from the earlier Salmon ceramic studies relates to the accuracy of type designations. As noted, many sherds were typed solely on the basis of visual criteria. Given the complexity of ceramic production and use in the Salmon area, many of these assignments are probably incorrect; thus, we must be very careful when using data derived from these studies. For example, a finding that 75 percent of the McElmo Black-on-white pottery from Salmon was imported from the north should be viewed with caution. Recent work has revealed that local potters experimented with a number of clays, slips, and tempers, essentially producing ceramics that were very similar to those made in the Chaco-Cibola and Northern San Juan–Mesa Verde areas. Detailed analysis has shown that many of the Salmon items were in fact made locally, although they emulate intrusive ceramics. Depending solely on visual criteria would not have revealed these patterns and the ceramics in question would have been combined into imported categories.

In a clay reconnaissance and refire analysis of the ceramics from Salmon, Franklin and his colleagues (see Wilson, Chapter 27) noted distinctive differences between the Middle San Juan resources and those to the north and south. Systematic examination of temper and paste characteristics and confirmation of local production signatures unique to the Middle San Juan and Salmon are required to accurately identify locally produced ceramics. As discussed in Chapter 31, the distinctiveness of Middle San Juan pottery is evident in the type of crushed rock temper used compared to ceramics produced to the north, and the silty, brownish to yellow discolored pastes (most likely resulting from lower firing conditions) produced in areas to the north and south.

Local Northern San Juan Animas Variety ceramics were identified through a detailed examination of paste, temper, and slip. These local ceramics comprise the majority of pottery produced at Salmon and other sites in the Middle San Juan, including Aztec Ruins (L. Reed and Myers 2005). Washy slips, a characteristic traditionally associated with Cibola pottery, were noted on Northern San Juan Animas

Variety ceramics and also on a smaller number of sand-tempered ceramics with local paste characteristics. Local production of ceramics similar to those made in the Chaco-Cibola area prompted classification of a Cibola Animas Variety. Thus, the variability in the local assemblage, the distribution of imported wares based on temper identification, and the recognition of local production of Chaco-Cibola White Ware could not have been accurately identified or interpreted without a renewed analysis methodology for the Salmon ceramic assemblage.

The Salmon ceramic assemblage is one of many large ceramic collections that merit additional work in light of recent findings. Our work on the Salmon ceramic collection certainly benefited from the prior efforts of Hayward Franklin and the Salmon Ceramic Laboratory; the 1970s ceramic database was available for limited examination and query. Many sites in the Southwest and the Middle San Juan—Aztec Ruins in particular—were excavated in the early decades of the twentieth century and ceramic analyses were never conducted. Thus, this initial work at Salmon on a preliminary sample of six rooms and kivas (see Chapters 30–33) represents the beginning of significant new research that could shed light on many of the mysteries of ceramic production and use in the Middle San Juan region.

Chapter 19

1980 INTRODUCTION TO THE SALMON CERAMIC ANALYSIS

by Hayward Franklin

The initial archaeological testing at Salmon Pueblo in 1970 and 1971 produced a considerable ceramic assemblage; a ceramics laboratory was therefore established in 1972, directed by M. Ann Bennett. Under her direction, the lab began an ambitious program of detailed attribute analysis, based on Bennett's methodology (developed in her *Basic Ceramic Analysis,* 1974). This approach guided analysis procedures for the following 2 years, and indeed formed the methodological basis for all subsequent attribute-based analyses at Salmon. Between 1972 and 1974 the laboratory analyzed 1591 sherds using standardized forms. Computerization of the data also began at this time, with the aid of computer specialist Zoe (Paddy) Johnson.

Typological identification of ceramics according to traditional Southwestern taxonomy was also initiated between 1972 and 1974, as well as a reference collection of ceramic types found at Salmon. Type identification had not been undertaken on a large scale before 1974 due in part to the emphasis on establishing the attribute-based system. The delay in initiating type analysis was also due to discussion and doubt regarding the typological definitions to be used. The better-preserved ceramic vessels formed the basis of the museum display collection during this period. Petrographic analysis (Helene Warren) and symmetry analysis of design (Dorothy Washburn) were also begun at this time.

In the fall of 1974, the author assumed direction of the ceramics laboratory and immediately made several changes in methodology. The procedures used for attribute analysis were extremely time consuming, with a wide range of detailed information recorded for a very limited sample of sherds. A large and spatially representative sample of sherds from Salmon had not been analyzed on the existing forms, and it appeared unlikely that sufficient samples from a variety of proveniences would be analyzed unless the format was changed. Consequently, a more streamlined version of the original attribute form was designed, which encoded much of the same information but allowed the analysis to proceed more rapidly.

It was apparent that one of the most important sources of variation in the ceramic assemblage was the distinction between the common San Juan Series ceramics and the many intrusive series and types present, especially in the Primary or Chacoan occupation. Further, an increasingly large backlog of unanalyzed ceramics was being generated by the large-scale excavations in the ruin itself. Typological analysis or rough-sort analysis was therefore undertaken on a separate form designed to be used on large samples of sherds rapidly as they were excavated. Basic ceramic information was thus provided for all strata excavated, preventing a further backlog from accumulating and providing quick feedback to excavators on the ceramic content, cultural affiliation, and rough temporal position of the strata currently being excavated. The field procedures could thus be made more effective through ceramic monitoring, with results usually obtainable within 1–3 days after the ceramics had been removed from the ground. Basic temporal and cultural affiliation information necessary for cross-dating rooms and strata and for determining ceramic contact with other areas was now available through the identification of the many intrusive ceramic types present, and this also allowed comparability with the ceramic identifications and dated associations of these ceramic types with earlier investigations in the region. Although sorting differences between investigators would always pose a problem, the great amount of prior work in the area and the relatively well defined ceramic types, together with the availability of tree-ring dated ceramics at other localities, made the comparable analysis of Salmon ceramics highly desirable.

---

* The chronology and stratigraphic assignments used in Chapters 19–28 follow the original Salmon sequence developed by Rex Adams. See Reed (Chapter 12) for the new Salmon chronology and differences-similarities in the sequences.

Other work initiated in 1974 included refiring analysis (by Lynne Arany and Franklin) to determine clay usage and to help documentation of types thought to be intrusive, as well as identification of tempering materials by microscopic and petrographic methods (Helene Warren). An intensive analysis of a portion of the west wing of the pueblo involving reconstruction of Mesa Verde Black-on-white vessels was undertaken by Suzanne Bradley (1979). In 1975, Steve Lekson and Cathy Cameron (1975) completed a pilot study of floor-related materials (lithics and ceramics) from across the pueblo.

Starting with the summer field season in 1974, all ceramic materials were rough sorted in the field laboratory, after the washing and numbering process. This program was successful in analyzing all ceramics collected from Salmon in 1974 and thereafter. In addition, considerable progress was made in rough sorting the backlog of ceramics collected before that date. Only the ceramics from the most important behavioral strata were completely analyzed from this backlog, but upon completion of the analysis, roughly 90 percent of all ceramics from Salmon had been rough sorted. An inventory of whole or restorable vessels was used to keep track of the more complete ceramic specimens, with nearly 300 items recorded.

In 1974, data retrieval from the computer system began in earnest, oriented at first toward stratigraphic changes in ceramic type frequencies in some of the rooms already excavated. Summaries for a number of rooms (6A, 6W, 31W, 93W, Plaza Trench 13P, 100W, and 102W) were used to produce a general picture of the Salmon ceramic sequence, as well as the associated ceramic complexes for each major period of occupation.

About this time the discovery of long, uninterrupted sequences of deposition in certain rooms indicated that the site had not been abandoned in the middle 1100s, as previously thought. The appearance of McElmo dominant strata above the Primary and below the Secondary levels in Rooms 33W, 100W, and others provided the basis for the definition of an Intermediate occupation. As it later appeared, this period was probably not a separate reoccupation of the site, but was a continuation of the San Juan element from the Primary occupation, following the departure of the Chacoans, and continuing into the later Secondary occupation. This interpretation—of a short Primary/Chacoan occupation (AD 1090–1120) followed by an extended Secondary occupation (AD 1120–1280s)—also emerged from Reed's new look at Salmon's chronology (Reed, Chapter 12).

Individual room studies also provided valuable information regarding the long uninterrupted San Juan White Ware sequence at Salmon, and the attribute changes that occurred in this series over about 200 years. The long Pueblo II–III sequence of San Juan types helped solve some persistent problems in our understanding of prehistoric ceramic change in the San Juan types for this time period.

Data manipulation and statistical work were begun in 1976 with an extensive factor analysis program that used typological data from all rough-sorted strata to reveal consistent ceramic associations within Salmon strata. It appeared from the stratigraphic position and cross-dating of these strata that the major source of ceramic variation produced by factor analysis was temporal. Therefore, a technique was developed for assigning factor scores to each stratum; these were derived from a scattergram plot illustrating a parabolic curve of the positions of strata relative to factor loadings on the first two temporal factors, which contained most of the ceramic variation. The technique of factor scores proved to be a useful tool for characterizing the ceramic contents of a stratum, and could thus be used in conjunction with stratigraphic position to determine room chronology. In addition, factor scores provided a basis for all laboratories to select strata belonging to a given period (Primary, Intermediate, Secondary) for temporal control in synchronic studies. Rex Adams's Codex (R. Adams 1980), which gave all strata designations by room, stratigraphic position, and factor score, helped to determine which strata belonged to each period. Discriminant analysis showed that factor analysis results often coincided with Rex Adams's stratigraphic evaluation—that is, Secondary strata (ceramically) were usually positioned above Primary strata. Conditions such as redeposition and mixing, and Secondary contamination of Primary strata could also be viewed using the contrast between a stratum's position or context and its ceramic content.

Between 1976 and 1979, studies of Secondary ceramics in the East and West Wings were undertaken by Suzanne Bradley and Penelope Whitten. Reconstruction efforts with Mesa Verde Black-on-white proved successful in reducing the sherd totals for several rooms into vessel units. Bradley's work was reported in her master's thesis (1979) on the West Wing of the pueblo. Studies by Linda Linnabery on Chuskan ceramics and Lynne Arany on refiring corrugated ceramics were also completed about this time. Attribute analysis continued, recording all decorated assemblages in six rooms onto standardized forms. Symmetry analysis of decoration on Salmon ceramics also continued, by Dorothy Washburn and Emily Garber.

With the completion of excavations at Salmon in 1978, the focus of the project turned nearly exclusively to the Primary occupation, and to the testing of specific research hypotheses developed by Irwin-Williams that involved the Chacoan occupation of the site. Spatial studies of Chacoan strata across the site were begun, using factor analysis and stratigraphic context as guides for temporal control. Considerable attention was paid to temporal control of the sample to Primary occupation strata and to conditions of mixture of floor and trash strata. These studies showed, at the least, the degree of expectable error in synchronic studies of the Primary occupation. The first large project involving spatial distributions was undertaken by Jim Priesnitz, who assessed intrusive versus local San Juan ceramic variation in the Chacoan occupation during the earliest building period. His master's thesis (1979) formed the foundation for similar distributional evaluations on a wider scale for the Chacoan occupation, attempting to locate foci of Chacoan residence and special function rooms within the Primary period. The contrast between high and low intrusive rooms held considerable potential for studying aspects of Chacoan room usage and localization of Chacoan activities.

In another realm, the problem of locating source areas was addressed with an expanded refiring analysis program. Refiring of suspected intrusive white ware and gray ware types from the Cibola and Chuska Series (by this author) confirmed the nonlocal nature of types from these two regions. A more extensive testing of the types in the San Juan White Ware at Salmon by Dean Wilson produced very informative results. By comparing San Juan types to refired raw clays found in the environment of Salmon as well as to unfired clays from an archaeological context within the site, Wilson defined temporal patterns of clay usage in San Juan White Ware through time. There was frequent ceramic exchange of San Juan White Ware in the Primary period, compared to the nearly exclusive use of locally available clays in the Secondary occupation. Clays and ceramics from tested sites on the San Juan, La Plata, and Animas Rivers provide comparable data from other related drainages.

All Primary strata were reanalyzed on a limited-attribute form to encode information on type, series, ware, temper, and vessel form. These data, initially utilized by Priesnitz (1979) and subsequently augmented with additional samples, have been subjected to a variety of statistical manipulations, including cluster analysis, multidimensional scaling, SYMAP, and analysis of variance. Although the ultimate reconstruction of Chacoan social organization through localization of activities must await the integration of all types of data (e.g. ceramics, lithics, botanical, osteological), the ceramic data suggest that certain areas in the site were occupied by or intensively used by mostly Chacoan residents. Rooms with high intrusive ceramic counts are nonrandomly distributed across the site, implying differential spatial use of rooms and blocks of rooms for residences or other functional purposes.

Not all planned investigations and interpretations of Salmon ceramics have been completed; due to the emphasis on the Primary occupation, many aspects of the Secondary occupation have not been investigated. A comparison of Primary to Secondary social organizations, and a comparison of both ceramic assemblages to other sites in the region, constitute incomplete aspects of the ceramic interpretation. These chapters therefore present the results of the several Salmon ceramics projects that were completed; this is not a final synthetic ceramic report. Some of the 62 reports written for the project appear in master's theses or other completed major works, and some of the smaller preliminary reports have appeared in the progress reports of Salmon Ruin from 1975 through 1980 or are presented in the chapters in this volume.

SALMON CERAMIC LABORATORY PERSONNEL

Ceramic analysis for the Salmon Project benefited from the inspiration and hard work of many individuals. Laboratory members associated with ceramics at one time or another during the project include Keith Adams, Lynne Arany, Barbara Beck, M. Ann Bennett (laboratory director 1972–1974), Heidi Blake, Suzanne Bradley, Bruce Burns, Leigh Caskey, Hayward Franklin (laboratory director 1974–1980), Emily Garber, Stephen Lekson, Tim McNiven, James Priesnitz, Karl Reinhardt, Donna Reinhardt, Lucy Whalley, Penelope Whitten, and Dean Wilson. Many others, including work study students at ENMU, helped in various ways. In particular, Jim Carroll, accounting student at ENMU, checked printouts and prepared raw data for statistical manipulations. In addition, ancillary studies using Salmon ceramic data were completed by Peter McKenna, Linda B. Linnabery, and Michelle Snider. Specialists in several areas provided consultation and information in petrography and temper studies (Helene Warren), mineralogical and geological information (Leroy Corbitt and Fred Nials, ENMU Geology Department), and symmetry analysis of design (Dorothy Washburn). Master's theses using Salmon Ruin ceramics have been written by Bradley (1979), Priesnitz (1979), Whalley (1980), and Wilson

(1985). Everyone connected with the Salmon Ruin ceramics laboratory over the years deserves credit and thanks for their contributions. The results are due to the cooperative efforts of many individuals, not only of the ceramics laboratory, but also of the other Salmon laboratories and the Salmon Ruin Museum staff, and the overall direction of the late Dr. Cynthia Irwin-Williams.

Chapter 20

SALMON CERAMIC LABORATORY METHODOLOGY

by Hayward Franklin

The Salmon ceramic methodology began with the establishment of provenience for all ceramic artifacts. Sherds from each grid unit and 10 cm level were collected in a bag, and the room, room quad, grid, stratum, depth, and date were marked on its tag. Except for postoccupational fill and unstructured roofs or trash, provenience was controlled by 10 cm depths within 1 x 1 m grid squares—"tight" provenience control by most standards. Large pieces of vessels or whole vessels were provenienced similarly, but also received a significant artifact (SA) number. Those found on roofs or floors were provenienced to the exact location within the grid. Field forms recorded the presence and location of whole or restorable vessels, and black-and-white photos were taken for inclusion in the field notes. In situ ceramic vessels were photographed by the field photographer, Peter B. George.

In the field laboratory, ceramic materials were washed with water and lightly brushed to remove soil. No other washing solutions or acids were used. Whole vessels were first sent to the ethnobotanical laboratory, where the soil contents were removed for analysis prior to the washing process. After washing, the sherds were given individual identification numbers (PO numbers). These numbers were sequential throughout the entire excavation, so that no two sherds received the same number. The PO number was written on each sherd with India ink, and sherds were placed back in the original bag with its provenience tag. PO numbers were necessary for attribute analysis, where each sherd was analyzed separately; they were not needed for analysis by bag lots as in rough-sort or limited-attribute analysis. For some reason, a bag numbering system was not used on the project until the fall of 1974. In 1975, a record key number that matched the field forms for that same provenience was placed on each bag of ceramics, serving as a bag identification number. Ceramic bags from before this date had no bag number, and because no record key number could be retroactively assigned to these early years, a different bag numbering system had to be used, which consisted of a sequential series of numbers assigned within each room to these early recovered ceramic collections. For example, 37-12 represented bag number 12 from Room 37; the numbering sequence began anew with each room. All ceramics analyzed from Salmon thus have either a bag number or a record key number that is used to identify the bag on rough-sort and limited-attribute forms. Some samples that were not analyzed between 1972 and 1974 have never received a bag number.

After washing and numbering, ceramics were ready for analysis in the field laboratory within 1–2 days after excavation. At that point, all ceramics were rough sorted by bag (1975 summer and later); the provenience was copied from the original bag tag onto the analysis form. Whole or restorable vessels were rough sorted, entered on the inventory of whole or restored vessels, and stored in the museum collections. Some vessels were put on display in the museum and some were taken to Portales temporarily for study. Rough sorting of ceramics occupied three to five full-time laboratory personnel during the field session. Vessels were reconstructed and design symmetry was recorded. Limited analysis of the collections at Aztec Ruins was conducted using Salmon rough-sort and attribute forms (Franklin 1978). Samples were collected at localities in the Salmon vicinity that exhibited good-quality clays, and wider ranging trips for clay collection were also taken later by Dean Wilson and Fred Nials. Possible tempering materials were also collected; these were analyzed by Helene Warren in the field laboratory. Evening instruction sessions in ceramic identification and analysis methods were provided for field personnel, and public lectures were held in the museum rotunda.

Sherd collections, a few whole vessels, and the samples of clays and tempers were all taken to the archaeological laboratory at Eastern New Mexico University in Portales at the end of each field season for study during the winter months. Analysis of the backlog of unsorted ceramic materials from the early years was conducted there, together with all attribute, temper, and past clay analyses.

All three types of analysis forms (attribute, limited attribute, and rough sort) were key punched at Salmon or Portales, and entered into the SELGEM storage and retrieval system; the original forms were retained as a cross-check against printout results. Occasional errors in transcribing provenience information were detected, as well as changes in strata nomenclature (i.e., multiple aliases for the same strata). Printouts showing bag numbers and provenience information were checked several times against the stratigraphic guide—the Codex—compiled by Rex Adams, and sometimes against the original forms to clean the computer files of transcription errors or multiple stratum names assigned within the field to the same excavation level (i.e., aliases). Aliases were a constant problem because some strata were excavated over a period of years, resulting in multiple designations. In the end, all such multiple names were converted to the single legitimate stratigraphic designation provided in the codex.

After analysis, sherd collections were returned to their original bags and the analysis type and date were marked on the bag tag. Sherd collections were stored in boxes identified by room number and these boxes were inventoried. Whole or restorable vessels were returned to the museum collection at the site. Black-and-white photos and color slides were taken of ceramic artifacts by Jeff Scovil.

ANALYSIS METHODS

The three kinds of analysis conducted by the Salmon ceramics laboratory are described here. Specific methods used in technical studies are provided in the chapters on analysis of tempers and clays.

Rough Sort

Typological identification of sherds—a rough-sort analysis—was conducted on a large sample from Salmon. (The rationale for this was presented in the introductory section.) All sherds collected in the summer of 1975 and later were rough sorted, and most samples collected before that date have also been rough sorted. Nearly 400,000 sherds, an estimated 90 percent of all ceramics recovered from Salmon Ruin, have been recorded on rough-sort forms. Only a few Secondary strata excavated prior to 1975 were not analyzed in this way. Portions of this total have also been analyzed on attribute or limited-attribute forms.

A rough sort consists of recording the provenience information from the bag tag onto the form, then opening the bag and sorting all sherds (decorated and utility) by pottery type. Sherds smaller than a nickel were not recorded, because they were usually too small to reveal diagnostic design elements. Tests showed that this size limitation did not discriminate against any particular pottery types. The frequency of each type in the bag was entered on the form, which could accommodate eight bags. Due to the large number of ceramic types present, only the more common were printed on the form. The rarer ones received code numbers that could be entered in the other boxes at the end of the form, along with the frequency data for those types.

The San Juan Series types were subdivided into several stylistic variants, which were recorded separately. Mancos and McElmo Black-on-white were each divided into Sosi (wide-line), Dogoszhi (hatched panels), and other or miscellaneous styles. In addition, Mancos B/w included a pseudo-Chaco B/w decoration (Aztec style), and the late McElmo banded style was a further subdivision within McElmo B/w. In Mesa Verde B/w, the major divisions of banded, all-over, and undifferentiated were used. The undifferentiated class was not a separate style, but was a combination of banded and all-over sherds that could not be specifically identified as such. In the later forms, Mesa Verde was further subdivided into hachure, solids, and hachure-solid subvariants within the three major design layout classes. The major stylistic variants of the San Juan types were monitored to evaluate chronological and spatial changes in major design classes. The stylistic variants recorded do not represent a complete inventory of design for each San Juan type; they are simply the most common stylistic variants. Because these are readily visible on the surface of decorated sherds, identification to style group for each type did not require additional analysis time over the recording of the type identification alone. As it later appeared, the stylistic variants of San Juan types proved useful in temporal evaluation (e.g., banded McElmo began later than other McElmo styles), and also in spatial assessment (e.g., Mesa Verde B/w banded and all-over designs show a nonrandom distribution within the Secondary strata).

The rough-sort analysis form evolved through several modifications between 1974 and 1978. A distinction between Pueblo II and III corrugated was employed on earlier forms (until July 1976) to monitor temporal changes in corrugated pottery. The Pueblo II style of corrugated (e.g., Mancos corrugated in the San Juan) employed wider coils, deeper indentations, alignment of corrugations, and a globular vessel form with a moderately flared rim. The

Pueblo III style (e.g., Mesa Verde corrugated in the San Juan Gray Ware) had narrower coils, shallower indentations, greater obliteration of coils, and a more egg-shaped vessel form with a sharply everted rim. Breternitz et al. (1974) defined the distinction between Mancos and Mesa Verde corrugated in similar terms. Stratigraphically, a chronological change from Pueblo II to III styles seemed present at Salmon, confirming the sequence of Mancos to Mesa Verde corrugated in the Mesa Verde area. However, utility ceramics displayed only a gradual change in this respect, with extensive stratigraphic overlap between the two styles. Because change was apparently slower for utility ceramics than for decorated, the latter would provide much better temporal assessment. Further, considerable analysis time was required to differentiate between the Pueblo II and III styles, as corrugated ceramics comprised most of the ceramics (as is usual) for all occupational periods. For both reasons, no distinction was made between the two kinds of corrugated in later analysis. The identification of Mummy Lake Gray was maintained throughout; it was more common in the Primary and Intermediate periods than in Mesa Verde times. Except for the complete obliteration of the coils, plain gray did not differ from Mancos corrugated.

Wetherill Black-on-white (Hayes 1964) was added as a sorting category in 1975, but it proved to have little typological or temporal significance. Stratigraphic plotting of San Juan types in several rooms showed that Wetherill B/w occurred randomly throughout the time span of McElmo B/w, and not as a discrete, coherent temporal marker. Although Wetherill B/w theoretically marked a period of experimentation with carbon painting by Mancos B/w potters, at Salmon Ruin, sherds typed as Wetherill B/w occurred throughout Mancos and McElmo B/w time spans. Indeed, more recent work at Mesa Verde has tended to treat Wetherill B/w as a carbon-painted variety of Mancos B/w, or has combined it with McElmo B/w. Although the category of Wetherill B/w was maintained analytically, in the end, early carbon-painted ceramics (including Wetherill and McElmo B/w) were combined for data manipulation under the overall type category for McElmo B/w. In practice, it was difficult to distinguish Wetherill from fully developed McElmo B/w. Another problem was that the earliest experiments with carbon painting had already occurred by the AD 1090 initiation of the Primary occupation. By AD 1090, a fully developed McElmo B/w type was present alongside mineral-painted Mancos B/w. In fact, the two types apparently overlapped by 50–60 years, from 1090 to 1150. Thus, if Wetherill represented a stage of development before the fully developed McElmo B/w, it occurred earlier than the first occupation of Salmon. Alternatively, it may have been just a sporadic variant of carbon painting, contemporary with fully developed McElmo B/w.

The stylistic variants of the three major San Juan decorated types were added in 1976, and were maintained thereafter. In the summer of 1977, Mesa Verde B/w was further subdivided by hachure versus solid versus solid-hachure within the banded, all-over, and undifferentiated groups. These finer distinctions proved to have little temporal or spatial validity, although the banded versus all-over distinction had at least spatial meaning within the Secondary occupation.

Finally, during the last summer of excavation in 1978, corrugated pottery was separated according to temper groups, which had not previously been done on rough-sort forms. Whereas temper distinctions had been recognized as a source of useful information all along, and were employed as an aid in identifying decorated types in rough sort, the time-consuming task of temper group identification in utility ware had not been considered practical during rough-sort analysis. Despite this, corrugated ceramics were satisfactorily separated into major temper groups during the last season with some loss of analysis time.

These changes in procedure involved both advantages and disadvantages. The final form contained more information and was probably more sensitive to major sources of ceramic variation than the earlier forms, but every improvement also carried with it the introduction of incompatibility with data recorded earlier. Thus, the Pueblo II–III separation in corrugated ceramics can only be used in rooms and strata analyzed with that format (i.e., until July 1976). Similarly, Wetherill Black-on-white can only be examined in rooms analyzed after February 1975. Stylistic variations of San Juan types were first introduced in 1976; before that only the types as a whole were recorded. Therefore, only certain rooms and strata can be used for spatial and temporal evaluation of data classes that were not present on the forms throughout the history of the Salmon project. Such evaluations were made for the Pueblo II and III corrugated and for Wetherill B/w on the basis of the rooms and strata where these were employed, and probably as much information was derived from these samples as would have been obtained if such distinctions had been recognized on all editions of the form. It is also important to realize that the types themselves did not change in the process. For example, Mesa Verde B/w has the same identity on all forms, although the design varieties are subdivided on later editions of the rough-sort form. Identification of types was therefore consistent through all rough-sort forms used on the project.

Consistency was maintained by using a reference collection of types and wares and by frequent communication among the analysts. Numerous references, listed in Table 20.1, were consulted to build ceramic type definitions for the laboratory. All beginning analysts spent several weeks familiarizing themselves with the system before beginning work on their own. Comparability between analysts was occasionally tested to check for consistency, although total consistency is probably never attained in a situation involving several analysts and an analysis period spanning several years. Even a single individual is likely to vary slightly as new insights are acquired through practice. Further, there are likely to be slight variations spatially or temporally within named types from the standard definitions.

Despite some variation, the approach taken by Salmon analysts was sufficient to maintain a high degree of consistency in procedures. If a particular specimen was in doubt, the opinions of several laboratory members were sought before completing the form. When in doubt as to the series or regional identification, it was standard practice to clip the sherd and examine the paste and temper, which usually confirmed the sherd's identity. This approach allowed for the possibility that the series (e.g., San Juan, Chuska, Cibola) could be identified, but not the specific type. Thus, unidentified carbon-painted San Juan pottery could be entered as such when the exact type was in doubt. Borderline cases between two sequential types in the same series (e.g., McElmo-Mesa Verde B/w, Gallup-Chaco B/w) are always to be expected; such instances were handled by consultation among several laboratory members. The vast majority of sherds could be identified using the visible attributes of slip, polish, vessel form, and decoration. In a few cases, however (e.g., Chuska White Ware), a check of the temper was required for certainty. An examination of all sherds (including corrugated) for temper would have greatly extended the rough-sort phase so that fewer proveniences could be analyzed. Overall, the compromise worked well; speed was maintained for common types, and rare or questionable examples were tested for paste and temper characteristics. The identification of decorated types and series was thus essentially accurate, given the purposes for which these data were to be used. The greatest absence of information lies in the utility assemblage, for which the temper analysis required for identification to series or ware (e.g., Chuska, Cibola, San Juan Gray) was not undertaken during the rough sort. However, such distinctions could be made during more intensive analyses using attribute or limited-attribute procedures, in which all sherds were examined for paste and temper aspects. The overall success of rough-sorting procedures was due to the presence of well-defined ceramic types that had been described (sometimes repeatedly) in the course of earlier work in the region, and the controls for consistency employed by the laboratory analysts.

Attribute Analysis

The original attribute analysis for Salmon Ruin ceramics was designed by Ann Bennett. The forms and procedures are presented in her *Basic Ceramic Analysis* (1974), which provides the basis for recording a variety of ceramic data in a format compatible with the SELGEM system of data storage and retrieval. *Basic Ceramic Analysis* offers a very ambitious program for encoding some 23 attributes of a nondecorative nature, and about a dozen attributes related to painted decoration. Each of these attributes consists of multiple attribute states; for example, for paste texture there are several degrees of coarseness. The number of discrete pieces of information on each specimen is thus very large. Essentially, this exhaustive program records objective data on every major aspect of the ceramic specimen. From a theoretical standpoint, this method is well constructed, and very comprehensive. This format was used in attribute analysis through the summer of 1974. In all, 1491 sherds (or sherd combinations) were recorded on the attribute forms. This very detailed approach was however quite slow—analysts required at least 15 minutes per decorated sherd to complete the forms. It became clear that such an extensive recording system would only be useful on small samples of pottery, so the attribute form was streamlined. The number of attributes recorded was reduced to 19 nondecoration attributes and 6 basic design aspects. More important, though, was a reduction in the number of attribute states within each category. Thus, for example, under carbon streak, the original form encoded the color, thickness, definition, and position; the new form simply noted the presence, absence, and number of carbon streaks present in the cross-section. Further, the codes for simpler attributes were placed directly on the form itself, so that the analyst would not have to look up the correct code in the manual. A code list was still required for the complexities of painted decoration. The attribute form underwent several minor changes between 1974 and 1980, without materially altering the data

Table 20.1. Reference sources for Salmon's common ceramic series and wares.

Ceramic Series / Tradition	Reference
San Juan White and Gray Ware	Abel (1955), Breternitz et al. (1974), Hayes (1964), Hayes and Lancaster (1975), Morris (1939), Rohn (1971), Swannack (1969).
Cibola White and Gray Ware	Hawley (1936), Judd (1954, 1959), MNA Cibola White Ware Conference (1958), Vivian and Mathews (1964).
Tusayan-Kayenta White and Gray Ware	Colton (1955), Colton and Hargrave (1937).
Chuska White and Gray Ware	Peckham and Wilson (1965), Windes (1977).
San Juan Red Ware	Colton (1956), Abel (1955), Breternitz et al. (1974).
White Mountain Red Ware	Carlson (1970), Second Southwest Ceramic Seminar, MNA (1959).
Tsegi Orange Ware	Colton (1956), Colton and Hargrave (1937).
Northern Mogollon Red Ware	Colton and Hargrave (1937).

This list is not exhaustive. It contains the major references used for reference and type in the ceramics laboratory.

recorded. In essence, the changes made the original format more practical to use and still allowed for documentation of a wide-ranging list of ceramic aspects about each specimen.

Ultimately, analysis time was reduced to about 5 minutes per sherd, and sometimes less for undecorated sherds. The updated form was used for all sherds from 13 rooms, for a total of 6814 sherds. Even with the shortened form, attribute-based analysis was not possible for large sherd samples. After the analysis of Room 93W (all ceramics), the attribute form was confined to the analysis of decorated ceramics in the remaining rooms. With half a dozen rooms on the attribute form, the samples were large enough to use for objective descriptive analysis of the attribute composition of typological classes and the variation therein, but the sample of rooms and strata on attribute forms was still too limited to provide much information on spatial variation among ceramic attributes. The attribute data were most useful for the Secondary occupation, because most ceramic variation is in the subtype level within Mesa Verde Black-on-white. Nevertheless, variability at the series, ware, and type level for Primary occupation ceramics was monitored via rough-sort and limited-attribute analyses.

In retrospect, a complete attribute analysis, although theoretically ideal for all excavated ceramics, suffers from several problems. First, the quantity of information recorded makes the possible attribute and attribute-state combinations enormous. One purpose for such analysis is to produce new types or at least new varieties on the basis of clusters of co-occurring attributes. To do this using the computer became an impossible programming task, and in fact, the computer available could not handle the permutations of the total attribute file.

Also, because large quantities of specimens were beyond the scope of any intensive analysis, it was necessary to select carefully the samples analyzed in relation to particular problems. Unfortunately at Salmon, attribute analysis was not designed to attack particular problems with specific samples. As a shotgun approach, full attribute analysis provided tremendous information about a very small sample of ceramics. With some knowledge about ceramic variation and the strata and dating of the site, attribute analysis could have been used to test particular hypotheses on limited samples chosen from a stratified universe. Analysis of 100 sherds each of Mancos, McElmo, and Mesa Verde Black-on-white at Aztec Ruin is perhaps an example of intensive analysis on a limited scale. Conversely, it could be argued that without full attribute analysis, the range of variation of each attribute cannot be assessed in the first place. That is, a shotgun method is needed to define which variables are the most sensitive to time, space, or function. Ideally, however, after this initial evaluation of the sensitivity of each attribute, the form can be shortened to drop out all attributes not sensitive to the problem at hand. For example, the attributes recorded on the form for Mesa Verde B/w at Salmon were consistent: all examples have squared rims, thick slips, rim decoration, high polish, and so forth. Knowing this, a more limited form could be devised to record only the variables that display internal variation within this restricted class of ceramics for an in-depth study of the spatial or microtemporal variation in the Secondary occupation. A preliminary evaluation of Mesa Verde B/w attributes, as well as the personal experience of several analysts, has in fact suggested a number of variables that could be monitored in the Secondary occupation, deleting the redundant or complacent variables from the existing attribute form.

In sum, the question of a general versus detailed and specific type of analysis is actually a decision as to whether we want to know "a lot about a little" or "a little about a lot." At Salmon, we have attempted to do both, although any future attribute analysis could benefit from the experience of the Salmon laboratory, and perhaps focus on specific problems with a limited range of the more productive attributes.

Limited-Attribute Analysis

The concept of a limited-attribute analysis as a compromise between a rough sort and a complete analysis is an appealing one. Registry of a few major attributes of special significance broadens the scope of a rough sort while maintaining relative simplicity and ease of recording. At Salmon an Intensive Rough Sort (IRS) analysis was conducted for ceramics from Rooms 33W, 64W, and 100W in 1976; this included information on ceramic type, series, ware and variety, the vessel form, the portion of the vessel present (rim, handle, base), and their frequency by bag. This information proved useful in revealing vessel form–type correlations and temporal changes in vessel forms in these three rooms.

The idea was then revived for a limited-attribute analysis specifically for the Primary occupation. The Ceramics Limited Attribute Program (CLAP) recorded series, type, ware and variety, vessel form, temper, and the frequency of each of these combinations by bag. It was essentially the same as the IRS form, but the kind of sherd was deleted in favor of recording temper classes.

The recording of series, ware, type, and variety is handled on the limited attribute form and the more recent attribute forms by way of a four-letter code system developed by Bruce Burns. In this system, the first letter refers to the series (e.g. San Juan, Cibola), the second letter refers to the ware and paint type (e.g. carbon, mineral, plain white, red ware, polychrome), the third letter code refers to the type (e.g., Mancos B/w) in time sequence within the series and ware, and the final box is used to record varieties within the types at Salmon; San Juan types have named stylistic varieties that received a letter code. For the other series, the types do not have named varieties, so a "9" is entered in the last box. An example would be McElmo B/w, banded variety (EBBA): E (San Juan Series), B (carbon painted), B (McElmo B/w), A (banded variety). This system is very useful because it is hierarchical, it taxonomically records several levels of identification, it is expandable in all four codes, and it allows identification of a series or ware even when the exact type or variety is unknown. For example, "AE99" refers to a Cibola Series White Ware sherd that does not display painted decoration (hence the type and variety are listed as "9"). In this way, the more general aspects of series and ware can be recorded, instead of disregarding the specimen because the exact type is uncertain.

A letter code is used to record vessel form, together with a list of portions of vessels minimally present for identification of a given form. The second box under form provides the size range of rim sherds as measured on a template of concentric rings to which the rim sherd is matched. This is left blank if the sherd is not part of the vessel rim.

Temper, as recorded on both the attribute and limited-attribute forms, refers to broad temper classes. At Salmon these classes included San Juan crushed rock, sand or sandstone, sherd temper, and sanidine basalt (trachyte) tempers. All combinations of these filler materials were also coded. Identification was made by viewing a clipped cross-section of the sherd under a binocular microscope at 15–30X. The attribute form requires evaluation of the relative amount and size of the tempering material, whereas the limited attribute does not. There is space on the attribute form for a more precise definition of the mineralogical constituents, but precise mineralogical information was difficult to obtain, due to either the inexperience of most analysts with mineralogy and/or the difficulty of making precise determinations with the equipment at hand (binocular microscopes). It was redundant to specify mineral constituents of rock tempers when the rock source was employed repeatedly as tempering material, so in the end, major temper groups and their combinations were coded; these could be recognized by analysts with some practice. A reference collection was kept of examples of each temper. The more precise mineralogical content of the rock materials was identified through published literature, or through consultation with geologists Helene Warren, Fred Nials, or Leroy Corbitt.

The ceramic limited attribute analysis (CLAP) was completed for nearly all Primary occupation strata at Salmon, as well as for a few Intermediate and Secondary strata. In total, 46,239 sherds were analyzed; all were previously rough sorted. The CLAP form was designed particularly for the Primary occupation, because of the considerable variety in the series, ware, type, and temper of Primary assemblages. Further, the spatial patterning of intrusive versus local types and wares was viewed as a culturally important variable. The form would not be suitable for spatial studies in the Secondary occupation because most of the variability in the Secondary assemblages occurs at a subtype level within the Mesa Verde Black-on-white type. In its application to Primary levels, however, the CLAP approach proved very suitable. Recording a few of the major variables over essentially 100 percent of the Primary proveniences available has provided a broad and representative spatial sample for use in statistical manipulation and distributional analysis for testing intrasite hypotheses regarding the Chacoan occupation.

In general, analysis of ceramics at Salmon has spanned the gambit from rough-sort to full attribute analysis, all on standardized forms that were computerized by the data processing laboratory. Whereas philosophies of analysis may differ, the theoretical ideal of obtaining detailed information on all Salmon ceramics was clearly impossible, as with any large project, due to limitations on time, money, and manpower. For this reason, there is an effective limit to the number of ceramic variables monitored and the number of samples analyzed. With the approaches taken here, we believe that the analyses fully attained the objectives for which they were intended. Full attribute analysis, while providing some useful information about variation within ceramic classes, has not realized its potential due to the weakness in spatial representation of the analyzed samples and the absence of clear research objectives inherent in the approach. Limited-attribute analysis, based on some minimal prior knowledge of the nature of ceramic variation and on some concept of the cultural implications or meanings of attributes chosen, appears to be the most satisfactory compromise solution to the problem of gathering the most meaningful information for the least effort, especially when applied to a stratified sample for limited research objectives.

Chapter 21

CERAMIC ASSEMBLAGES AND SHERD COUNTS

by Hayward Franklin

Ceramic series and types can be assigned to the three occupational time periods at Salmon using evidence from cross-dating, stratigraphy, and ceramic associations (Table 21.1). Most such assignments at Salmon are fairly secure. Several pottery types spanned more than a single occupation, although they are much more common in one. For instance, McElmo Black-on-white spans the Primary, Intermediate, and early Secondary periods, although it is much more common in the Intermediate. Wingate Black-on-red and Citadel Polychrome types are found mainly in Primary period assemblages, but they do extend somewhat into the Intermediate. Wingate Polychrome (and perhaps early St. Johns Polychrome) began during the Intermediate shortly before AD 1200 and extended into the Secondary. After AD 1200, St. Johns Polychrome replaced Wingate Polychrome entirely as the White Mountain Red Ware intrusive. All other types are assigned to a single occupational period. Table 21.1 also indicates types belonging only to a portion of an occupation. For instance, Puerco-Escavada Black-on-white is assigned to the early Primary only; banded McElmo Black-on-white is assigned to the Intermediate and very early Secondary only.

Considerable differences exist between the Primary and Secondary occupation in the nature of types and varieties present. Although it contains fewer ceramics than the Secondary, the Primary assemblage is much more diverse, with more series and types than the later periods. Eight major series of decorated types (including white ware and red ware) are represented in the Primary, as well as ceramics belonging to the San Juan, Chuska, and Cibola utility ware traditions. The Primary decorated series contain 16 types represented by more than 100 sherds apiece; an additional dozen types are represented by fewer than 100 sherds apiece. By contrast, the Intermediate and Secondary occupations are dominated by vast quantities of San Juan ceramics. There are very few intrusive ceramics in the post-Primary period assemblages; most are White Mountain Red Ware. No other major ceramic series are present in the assemblage from after about AD 1130—the insignificant amounts of Chuska and Tsegi types may represent holdovers of ceramics imported during the Primary period. Although the San Juan series is the most frequent in the Primary (72% of the decorated assemblage), types of this white ware series increase to more than 90 percent in the post-Primary period. The utility assemblage is also nearly exclusively San Juan Gray Ware by the time of the Secondary occupation at Salmon. The previously large amounts of intrusive utility ware from the Chuska and Chaco areas declined dramatically by the mid-1100s, along with white ware imports from those regions.

There was a clear temporal trend toward uniformity and a decrease in ceramic imports in the Intermediate and Secondary periods. The Primary collection, containing only an estimated 25 percent of the ceramics from Salmon, contains four times the number of decorated series as the Secondary, eight to ten times the number of decorated and identified types, and three times the number of utility ware series. Of the named stylistic varieties of San Juan White Ware at Salmon, the Primary contains all the varieties of Mancos Black-on-white, as well as all the McElmo Black-on-white varieties except banded. Even within the San Juan White Ware, there is more variation in the Primary than in later periods. The reason for the greater variety of ceramics in the Primary is related to cultural trends on a regional scale, and is therefore not fully discussed in this chapter. In general, however, the Chacoan trading network was largely responsible for the widespread ceramic contacts of Salmon Ruin with other regions during the Primary occupation. In the Secondary the absence of intrusive wares, except for White Mountain Red Ware, is a reflection of the collapse of that network in the middle AD 1100s and a corresponding lack of communication (at least ceramically) with most other Puebloan areas. Suffice it to say that at Salmon, there was a distinct decline in variation of the ceramic

Table 21.1. Ceramic associations of the three occupations at Salmon Pueblo.

Primary Occupation
San Juan Series White Ware
Mancos B/w (all varieties)
Cortex B/w*
Weatherill B/w
McElmo B/w (all but banded)
Cibola-Chaco Series White Ware
Red Mesa B/w* (early Primary only)
Puerco-Escavada B/w (early Primary only)
Gallup B/w
Chaco B/w
Chaco-McElmo B/w
Chuska Series White Ware
Brimhall B/w*
Taylor B/w*
Newcomb B/w*
Chuska B/w
Toadlena B/w
Nava B/w
Tusayan Series White Ware
Black Mesa B/w*
Sosi B/w
Dogoszhi B/w*
Tsegi Orange Ware
Medicine B/r*
Tusayan B/r
Citadel & Cameron Polychromes (late Primary only)
White Mountain Red Ware
Puerco B/r (early Primary only)
Wingate B/r
Mogollon Red Ware
Forestdale Smudged
San Juan Red Ware
La Plata (Deadmans) B/r*
"Intermediate" Occupation
San Juan Series White Ware
Mancos B/w (minor amounts)
McElmo B/w (all varieties, especially banded)
Chuska Series White Ware
Nava B/w*?
Tsegi Orange Ware
Citadel and Cameron Polychromes*
White Mountain Red Ware
Wingate B/r
Wingate Polychrome
Secondary Occupation
San Juan Series White Ware
Mesa Verde B/w (all varieties)
McElmo B/w banded*? (early Secondary only)
Chuska Series White Ware
Crumbled House B/w*?
White Mountain Red Ware
St. Johns Polychrome

*Minor amount only (less than 100 sherds).
?Assignment of period is questionable.

assemblages through time, as judged both by the number of types and series represented and by their quantities.

CERAMIC COUNTS FOR SALMON'S OCCUPATIONAL PERIODS

The total sherd count for Salmon Ruin (all components) is provided in Table 21.2. White ware is 31.4 percent, red ware 1.4 percent, and utility ware 67.2 percent of the total number of sherds. These figures are based on total rough-sort counts amounting to 260,106 sherds. An estimated 90 percent of all sherds recovered from Salmon were rough sorted. A few upper portions of rooms, test trenches, and search areas collected between 1971 and 1974 were not analyzed. Several rooms were not excavated to Primary levels, so the count for Secondary types may be slightly inflated; this is probably offset by the lack of analysis of some mostly Secondary strata that were excavated early in the project. In any case, the numerical dominance of Secondary ceramics is clear; Mesa Verde Black-on-white by itself amounts to about half of all the San Juan Series White Ware and about 45 percent of all the white ware at Salmon Ruin.

The overall ceramic assemblage from Salmon includes large samples from every area of the site excavated. However, several sources of possible bias should be mentioned. For example, rough-sort data were generated by a total of eight people from 1974 to 1978. Although every effort was made to keep sorting categories consistent between individuals and through time (see Chapter 20), we must assume some amount of sorting bias due to personnel and temporal factors.

Also, rough-sorting procedures did not specify temper assessment for every sherd, which would have required considerably more analysis time. Temper was checked in cases of questionable identification only, so identification of certain series whose criteria depend heavily on temper (e.g., Tusayan Series or Chuska Series) may not be accurate. Counts for these wares should be considered minimums. Sufficiently clear diagnostic criteria are visible on the surfaces of most types and series to make identification generally secure. Problems with identifying adjacent sequential types in a single series (e.g., McElmo vs. Mesa Verde B/w; Gallup vs. Chaco B/w) were handled by reference to the established type definitions. The inevitable borderline cases cause few problems when clearly defined criteria are established. At the least, this kind of error is probably randomized across rooms and strata, and is a small but constant source of error.

Table 21.2. Total sherd counts for all occupations.

Type	Number	Percent in Type	Percent in Series	Percent in Ware	Percent in Ware w/o Unidentified
San Juan White Ware					
Mesa Verde general unidentified	13567	50.0	–	–	–
Mesa Verde general hachure	461	1.7	–	–	–
Mesa Verde general hachure-solid	512	1.9	–	–	–
Mesa Verde general solids	1064	3.9	–	–	–
Mesa Verde banded unidentified	5095	18.8	–	–	–
Mesa Verde banded hachure	197	0.7	–	–	–
Mesa Verde banded hachure-solid	799	2.9	–	–	–
Mesa Verde banded solids	3608	13.3	–	–	–
Mesa Verde all over unidentified	535	2.0	–	–	–
Mesa Verde all over hachure	115	0.4	–	–	–
Mesa Verde all over hachure-solid	888	3.3	–	–	–
Mesa Verde all over solids	289	1.1	–	–	–
Mesa Verde mineral paint	2	0.0	–	–	–
Total Mesa Verde Black-on-white	27141	100	49	33.3	45.6
McElmo B/w other	10921	67.8	–	–	–
McElmo B/w banded	1505	9.3	–	–	–
McElmo B/w Sosi style	2129	13.2	–	–	–
McElmo B/w Dogoszhi style	1425	8.8	–	–	–
McElmo B/w Sosi-Dogoszhi	138	0.9	–	–	–
Total McElmo B/w	16188	100.0	29.1	19.8	27.1
Mancos B/w other	3567	62.4	–	–	–
Mancos B/w Dogoszhi style	1227	21.5	–	–	–
Mancos B/w Sosi style	593	10.4	–	–	–
Mancos B/w Aztec variety	312	5.5	–	–	–
Mancos B/w banded	15	0.3	–	–	–
Total Mancos B/w	5714	100.1	10.3	7.0	9.6
Wetherill B/w	671	–	1.2	0.8	1.1
Cortez B/w	63	–	0.1	0.1	0.1
Peidra B/w	1	–	0.0	0.0	0.0
San Juan B/w corrugated ext. general	36	21.2	–	–	–
McElmo-M.B. corrugate. ext.	44	25.9	–	–	–
Mancos B/w corrugated ext.	90	52.9	–	–	–
Total corrugated ext. B/w	170	100.0	.3	.2	.3
San Juan B/w with basket imp.	3	–	0.0	0.0	0.0
Unidentified San Juan B/w	54	2.4	–	–	–
Unidentified San Juan carbon paint	1882	82.4	–	–	–
Unidentified San Juan mineral paint	300	13.4	–	–	–
Total unidentified San Juan	2236	100.0	4.0	2.7	3.8
San Juan plain white sherds	3361	–	6.1	4.1	5.6
Total San Juan White Ware	55478		100.1	68.0	93.2
Cibola White Ware					
Chaco McElmo B/w	498	–	15.6	0.6	0.8
Chaco B/w	1561	–	48.8	1.9	2.6
Gallup B/w	501	–	15.7	0.6	0.8
Escavada B/w	180	–	5.6	0.2	0.3
Puerco B/w	210	–	6.6	0.3	0.4
Sosi-style Cibola	13	–	0.4	0.0	0.0
Red Mesa B/w	65	–	2.0	0.1	0.1
Kaituthlanna B/w	1	–	0.0	0.0	0.0
Reserve B/w	8	–	0.3	0.0	0.0
Tularosa B/w	21	–	0.7	0.0	0.0
Socorro B/w	2	–	0.1	0.9	0.0
Unidentified Cibola White Ware	137	–	4.3	0.2	0.2
Total Cibola White Ware	3197	–	100.1	3.0	5.4

Table 21.2 (continued)

Type	Number	Percent in Type	Percent in Series	Percent in Ware	Percent in Ware w/o Unidentified
Tusayan White Ware					
Sosi B/w	74	–	49.7	0.1	0.1
Black Mesa B/w	27	–	18.1	0.0	0.0
Holbrook B/w	1	–	0.7	0.0	0.0
Unidentified Tusayan Series	47	–	31.5	0.1	0.1
Total Tusayan White Ware	149	–	100.0	.2	.2
Chuska White Ware					
Brimhall B/w	12	–	1.6	0.0	0.0
Taylor B/w	8	–	1.1	0.0	0.0
Newcomb B/w	6	–	0.8	0.0	0.0
Burnham B/w	1	–	0.0	0.0	0.0
Chuska B/w	234	–	31.1	0.3	0.4
Toadlena B/w	184	–	24.5	0.2	0.3
Nava B/w	35	–	4.7	0.0	0.1
Crumbled House B/w	12	–	1.6	0.0	0.0
Unidentified Chuska mineral paint	5	–	0.7	0.0	0.0
Unidentified Chuska carbon paint	77	–	10.2	0.1	0.1
Unidentified Chuska unidentified paint	178	–	23.7	0.2	0.3
Total Chuska White Ware	752	–	100.0	0.9	1.2
Total Identified White Ware	59576	–	–	–	–
Unidentified B/w carbon	3420	–	4.2	–	–
Unidentified B/w mineral	829	–	1.0	–	–
Unidentified B/w unidentified	2554	–	3.1	–	–
Total unidentified B/w	6803	–	8.3	–	–
Unidentified plain white	15196	–	18.6	–	–
Total White Ware	81575	–	99.9	–	–
San Juan Red Ware					
La Plata B/r	30	–	44.8	0.8	1.0
Deadmans B/r	2	–	3.0	0.0	0.1
Abajo Red-on-orange	7	–	10.4	0.2	0.2
Unidentified San Juan Red Ware	28	–	41.8	0.8	1.0
Total San Juan Red Ware	67	–	100.0	1.8	2.3
Tsegi Orange Ware					
Tusayan B/r	106	–	42.9	2.8	3.6
Medicine B/r	21	–	8.6	0.6	0.7
Citadel Polychrome	64	–	25.9	1.7	2.2
Cameron Polychrome	3	–	1.2	0.1	0.0
Tusayan Polychrome	4	–	1.6	0.1	0.1
Unidentified Tsegi Orange	49	–	19.8	1.3	1.7
Total Tsegi Orange Ware	247	–	100.0	6.5	8.4
White Mountain Red Ware					
Puerco B/r	215	–	9.6	5.8	7.4
Wingate B/r	1016	–	45.2	27.3	34.8
Wingate Polychrome	335	–	14.9	9.0	11.5
St. Johns Polychrome	424	–	19.2	11.6	14.8
St. Johns B/r	114	–	5.1	3.1	3.9
Pinedale B/r	1	–	0.0	0.0	0.0
Unidentified White Mtn Red Ware	135	–	6.0	3.6	4.6
Total White Mountain Red Ware	2248	–	100.0	60.4	76.9
Smudged Red Ware	361	–	100.0	9.7	12.4
Total Identified Red Ware	2923	–	–	–	100.0
Plain red (no decoration)	221	–	–	5.9	–
Unidentified B/r	442	–	–	11.9	–
Unidentified Polychrome	128	–	–	3.4	–
Red Ware corr. ext.	9	–	–	.2	–
Total Red Ware	3723	–	–	99.9	–

Table 21.2 (continued)

Type	Number	Percent in Type	Percent in Series	Percent in Ware	Percent in Ware w/o Unidentified
General Utility					
Pueblo II style corrugated	1151	–	–	0.8	–
Pueblo III style corrugated	18537	–	–	12.5	–
Corrugated (no style)	118616	–	–	80.2	–
Plain gray ware	9540	–	–	6.5	–
Plain brown ware	31	–	–	0.0	–
Corrugated brown ware	10	–	–	0.0	–
Los Lunas Smudged	3	–	–	0.0	–
Total Utility	147888	–	–	100.0	–
Utility Analyzed by Temper					
San Juan Corrugated (crushed rock)	21972	90.8	–	81.6	–
San Juan plain gray ware	2226	9.2	–	8.3	–
San Juan basket-impressed	1	0.0	–	0.0	–
San Juan gray tool incised	4	0.0	–	0.0	–
Total San Juan Utility	24203	100.0	–	89.9	–
Utility Analyzed					
Chuska Series corrugated (trachyte)	1930	–	99.7	7.2	–
Chuska Series plain gray	6	–	0.3	0.0	–
Total Chuska Utility	1936		100.0	7.2	–
Cibola Gray Ware?	6	–	–	0.0	–
Tusayan Gray Ware?	2	–	–	0.0	–
Unident. corrugated (sandstone & sherd)	55	–	–	0.2	–
Unident. corrugated (sandstone temper)	607	–	–	2.3	–
Unident. corrugated (sherd temper)	96	–	–	0.4	–
Plain gray ware (sandstone temper)	15	–	–	0.0	–
Total Utility analyzed by temper group	26920	–	–	100.0	–
Total White Ware	81575				
Total Red Ware	3723				
Total Utility	174808				
Grand total	260106	As of printout 3/15/79			

Note: This is essentially the complete rough-sort count. Counts on Tusayan and Chuska Series White Ware represent the minimum count for these series because some may have been misidentified as other series when sherds were not always inspected for temper. Corrugated and gray ware counts are split into two groups: (a) counts from early forms on which temper was not checked and (b) utility counts from the latest edition of the form on which temper of utility ware was recorded.

The rough-sort forms underwent changes over time. The major difference involved increased detail for recording styles within the San Juan White Ware types. Whereas the early rough-sort forms merely recorded these as types, they were increasingly subdivided into stylistic variants on later forms (see Chapter 20). More pottery over a longer analysis period was recorded by the single type designations, instead of by variety, so the amounts of undifferentiated or other Mancos, McElmo, and Mesa Verde Black-on-white sherds are high relative to their respective varieties. The ratio between the named style varieties (e.g., Mancos, Sosi, or Dogoszhi), however, should be valid. Aside from the varieties of San Juan types, the recording system remained unaltered through the course of analysis; changes in form editions, then, could not have been a biasing factor for non-San Juan decorated types.

Procedural bias also affects the subdivision of utility ceramics, similar to the case with San Juan White Ware. Intrusive utility ware was not monitored on the rough-sort form because ordinarily its identification requires examination of tempers under a microscope, which time did not permit at this level of analysis. Early analysis forms did record the difference between Pueblo II and III styles of surface treatment on corrugated pottery, which did have temporal stratigraphic validity, as outlined above. However, the complete continuum between the two styles made it difficult to assign many sherds to one or the other of these classes. Because decorated types had greater potential for temporal sensitivity anyway, the time-consuming analysis of corrugated by style was deleted from the later rough-sort forms. Hence the ratio of Pueblo II to III corrugated in Table 21.2 has validity for the forms where this distinction was made, but the named styles cannot be compared to the unidentified corrugated category. The dominance of the unidentified category merely reflects the fact that all corrugated sherds were classed this way on the later forms.

Finally, there is a residual category of undefined or partially defined ceramics not assignable to any particular type. Such unknowns are common with rough-sort analyses that allow only cursory examination of sherds. In many cases the absence of certain attributes on a specimen limits the identification to the series and ware only; this accounts for the 2236 sherds of San Juan White Ware identified as San Juan Black-on-white without determination of the type. Another large group consisted of 6803 black-on-white sherds of unknown series or type. The approximately 15,000 sherds of plain white ware lacking any decoration could not be assigned to types, but in many cases it was possible to at least assign them to series.

QUANTITATIVE SHERD COUNTS FOR EACH OCCUPATION

The actual numbers of types for each occupation can be estimated either by using the time spans assigned to types in conjunction with their degree of interassociation as shown by correlation and factor analysis, or by deriving a count from stratigraphically verified Primary, Intermediate, and Secondary strata. Each method has its advantages and disadvantages.

Estimating the relative importance of ceramic series in each occupation by subdividing the total sherd count (see Table 21.2) by time spans and associations within the site was attempted first. The results are provided in Table 21.3. Where pottery types are associated with a single occupation only, there is no problem in occupational assignment. Where types such as McElmo Black-on-white span more than one occupation, portions of the type were assigned to respective occupations on the basis of the degree of association with other unequivocally assigned ceramics of the period. In these cases of overlap between occupational phases and ceramic types, the amount ascribed to each phase cannot be completely accurate with this method. Whereas the major quantitative relationships of series can be made in this way, the exact amount for each type could not be determined. The estimation of relative frequency of types and series without reference to stratigraphy avoided the contextual problems of mixing, reuse, and redeposition which in many cases at Salmon considerably altered the original use associations and sequence of types.

Derivation of ceramic counts by stratifying the sample according to R. Adams's context evaluation and the use of factor scores was also attempted. Although there is, in general, good agreement between factor score, stratigraphic position, and Adams's evaluation of context, the match is not universally good enough to derive an accurate count of each ceramic type. There are too many examples of types with substantial frequencies outside their true occupation phase (Secondary sherds in Primary strata, and vice versa). For example, of 1129 Chaco Black-on-white sherds found in strata evaluated for stratigraphic position, 26.5 percent were found in strata that were evaluated as Secondary in depositional context. A similar result was seen with the early Cibola Black-on-white group. Although theoretically the earliest pottery at Salmon, 24.9 percent of the sherds of this group were found in strata evaluated as Secondary. Thus, if ceramic counts were compiled strictly from the depositional context of strata alone, the results would be quite misleading. From other lines of evidence (cross-dating, absolute dates, ceramic associations, and factor analysis), we know that Primary occupation types were not entering the site or being used at Salmon throughout the entire occupation including the Secondary. In fact, the spurious sherd counts by occupation obtained from the stratigraphic evaluations and factor scores are ascribed to several factors:

1. Factor scores, used as part of the evaluation procedure, are only an approximation of and brief designation for the ceramics in a stratum. Factor scores yield a convenient approximation of the ceramic content of a stratum, and do not account for minor amounts of mixture. For example, a level may score A and yet contain some amount of Mesa Verde Black-on-white from the Secondary period. It would clearly be an error to assign this Mesa Verde Black-on-white to the Primary period. Because of the averaging effect of factor scores, the approach characterizes the entire ceramic assemblage of a stratum, and tends to correct for small amounts of mixture.

2. Some strata were classified as Secondary, which they are in deposition, but they contained mostly redeposited Primary materials.

3. Many strata were mixed, redeposited, or reused by Secondary occupants.

4. Mixing between strata due to natural causes as well as to excavational misassignment of cultural materials must also be taken into account.

Table 21.3. Estimated ceramic percentages for major occupational periods by series.

Series	Primary	Intermediate	Secondary
San Juan White Ware	72.1% (Cortez B/w, Mancos B/w, McElmo B/w [Sosi & Dogoszhi styles]; 1/2 of McElmo, other styles)	94.7% (McElmo banded, 1/2 of McElmo B/w)	97.6% (Mesa Verde B/w, all styles)
Cibola White Ware	14.0% (all types)	0.0%	0.0%
Chuska White Ware	3.1% (all types, except 1/3 of Nava B/w)	0.2% (2/3 of Nava B/w)	0.001% (Crumbled House B/w)
Tusayan White Ware	0.7% (all types)	0.0%	0.0%
Tsegi Orange Ware	1.1% (all B/w; 1/2 of Citadel Polychrome)	0.4% (1/2 of Citadel Polychrome)	0.0%
San Juan Red Ware	0.3% (all types)	0.0%	0.0%
Mogollon Red Ware	1.6% (Forestdale Smudged)	0.9%	0.0%
of White Mountain Red Ware	7.1% (Puerco B/r, 2/3 of Wingate B/r)	4.6% (1/3 Wingate B/r, 2/3 of Wingate Polychrome)	2.4% (1/3 of Wingate Polychrome, all St. Johns Polychrome)

See Table 21.2 for total types in each series present at Salmon Ruin derived from total rough-sort count by temporal span and associations between types. Types assigned to a single phase included as total; types spanning occupational phases are portioned by probability amount assigned to each component (e.g., McElmo B/w, Citadel Polychrome, Wingate B/r, and Polychrome.)

5. There is always the possibility that the same vessels were reused or kept in continued use for a long time after manufacture.

Of these variables, by far the most pervasive is the condition of mixing and redeposition by Secondary inhabitants. These processes can be seen in the Salmon stratigraphic sequences at several locations, resulting in ceramics displaced from their original temporal position of import, manufacture, or use.

For the above reasons, the ceramic content of strata may deviate from the logic of their stratigraphic position. This prohibits a totally accurate sherd count and arrangement of frequencies into battleship curves by stratigraphic provenience alone. Although the stratigraphic changes in ceramics are certainly useful indicators where a long undisturbed sequence occurs (as in the particular instances of Rooms 100W, 82W, 31W, 33W, and 93W), stratigraphic position in the site as a whole is insufficient to produce the desired ceramic count for particular occupations. In many instances, the frequency of types by strata would indicate the position and sequence of ultimate deposition, but not necessarily the original time of usage, manufacture, or import of ceramic types.

PRIMARY OCCUPATION COUNT FROM LIMITED-ATTRIBUTE DATA

Because the focus of the project was the Primary occupation, it was necessary to determine a reliable sherd count for the early occupation. Unfortunately, the contrast between original temporal association of manufacture (or import) and the ultimate depositional position of Primary ceramics is particularly acute with the Primary occupation materials. Some Primary materials were subject to mixture and redeposition due to the cleaning of rooms by Secondary occupants. To a limited extent, of course, the reverse was also true—these processes have also affected Secondary materials, which may be found out of context due to downward mixing, erosional forces, and the reuse of Primary surfaces by the later inhabitants.

To obtain the most reliable quantitative estimate of Primary occupation types, data were used from the limited-attribute analysis that included all excavated Primary strata. The count was compiled from strata that are stratigraphically early and uncontestably Primary, excluding all Primary-Secondary materials, questionable strata, and stratigraphically

Table 21.4. Ceramic totals for Primary strata at Salmon.

Pottery Type	N	Percent of Series	Percent of Ware	Percent of Total Decorated
Red Mesa Black-on-white	27	2.1	0.3	0.3
Puerco-Escavada B/w	176	13.5	2.2	2.1
Gallup B/w	128	9.8	1.6	1.5
Chaco B/w	659	50.5	8.2	7.7
Chaco-McElmo B/w	124	9.5	1.5	1.5
Unidentified Cibola mineral paint	63	4.8	0.9	0.7
Cibola Series plain white	128	9.8	1.6	1.5
Total Cibola	1305	100.0	16.2	15.3
Cortez B/w	27	0.4	0.3	0.3
MancosB/w	2021	32.7	25.1	23.7
Wetherill B/w	92	1.5	1.1	1.1
McElmo B/w	1485	24.0	18.4	17.5
San Juan mineral paint	150	2.4	1.9	1.8
San Juan carbon paint	493	8.0	6.1	5.8
San Juan plain white	1917	31.0	23.8	22.5
Total San Juan	6185	100.10	76.7	72.7
Chuska Series mineral types	16	3.3	0.2	0.2
Newcomb B/w	7	1.4	0.1	0.1
Toadlena B/w	108	22.2	1.3	1.3
Chuska B/w	101	20.6	1.3	1.2
Nava B/w	35	7.1	0.4	0.4
Crumbled House B/w	3	0.6	0.0	0.0
Unidentified Chuska carbon paint	104	21.2	1.3	1.2
Chuska Series plain white	116	23.7	1.4	1.4
Total Chuska	490	100.0	6.1	5.7
Sosi & Black Mesa B/w	52	67.1	0.7	0.6
Dogoszhi B/w	15	19.0	0.2	0.2
Tysayan Series carbon paint	8	10.1	0.1	0.1
Tusayan Series plain white	3	3.8	0.0	0.0
Total Tusayan	79	100.0	1.0	0.9
Total White Ware	8059		100.0	94.7
La Plata, Deadmans Black-on-red	16	100.0	3.5	0.2
Total San Jan Red Ware	16	100.0	3.5	0.2
Puerco B/r	53	33.1	11.8	0.6
Wingate B/r	28	17.5	6.2	0.3
St. Johns B/r	3	1.9	0.7	0.0
Wingate Polychrome	3	1.9	0.7	0.0
St. Johns Polychrome	2	1.2	0.4	0.0
Unidentified White Mtn Red Ware B/r	37	23.1	8.2	0.4
Unidentified White Mtn Red Ware	34	21.3	5.5	0.3
Total White Mountain Red Ware	160	100.0	17.1	0.9
Medicine, Tusayan B/r	60	77.9	13.3	0.7
Citadel, Cameron Polychrome	8	1.0	1.8	0.1
Unidentified Tsegi Orange Ware	9	11.7	2.0	0.1
Total Tsegi Orange Ware	77	100.0	17.1	0.9
Forestdale Smudged?	207	100.0	45.9	2.4
Total Mogollon Red Ware	207	100.0	45.9	2.4
Total Red Ware	460		100.0	5.3

Table 21.4. (continued)

Pottery Type	N	Percent of Total Utility Pottery
Utiity Ware		
Plain Gray (San Juan)	1274	8.5
Plain Gray (? series)	66	0.4
San Juan corrugated	10754	72.0
Chuska corrugated	2104	14.1
Cibola corrugated	100	0.7
Unidentified corrugated	632	4.2
Total Utility Ware	14930	99.9
Total White Ware Count	8059	
Total Red Ware Count	460	
Total Utility Ware Count	14930	
Grand Total Count	23449	

Derived from limited-attribute data on stratigraphically defined Primary strata with Primary factor scores. No redeposited, questionable, or mixed Primary strata are included. Small amounts of Mesa Verde Black-on-white are excluded.

mixed strata. Even with these constraints, about 100 sherds of Mesa Verde Black-on-white were still present in the best Primary strata. These were excluded from the list for obvious reasons.

The results of this procedure are shown in Table 21.4. Also included are the frequencies of utility ware types from the Primary period. Because limited-attribute analysis involved the examination of temper on every specimen, identification of intrusive ceramics from the Chuska and Cibola-Chaco areas could be made. We should observe that the totals for each Primary type or series are considerably lower than the rough-sort totals for those categories in the site as a whole (see Table 21.2). The difference is due to sherds in redeposited or mixed conditions, which were eliminated from consideration.

The percentages of types and series in Table 21.4, derived from stratigraphically "pure" Primary levels, were compared to an estimated count for the Primary occupation made by deleting Secondary ceramic types from the overall ceramic count for the whole site (see Table 21.2). The comparison shows a close correspondence. Most relative frequencies of ceramic series were estimated correctly within two percentage points, when compared to the more accurate, stratigraphically controlled ceramic count. Chuska White Ware had been slightly underestimated, whereas White Mountain Red Ware during the Primary had been slightly overestimated, due to the fact that types from both series were not confined to the Primary period. Further, it was difficult to estimate how many of these series were assignable to just the Primary. McElmo Black-on-white, in particular, was a problem because it spanned parts of three occupations, and several types of White Mountain Red Ware spanned the entire Salmon occupation. In general, the Primary sherd count, from the most reliable strata (see Table 21.4), confirmed the basic character of the Primary ceramic assemblage as estimated without regard to stratigraphy. It also tends to substantiate the relative and absolute dating of these types at Salmon and elsewhere.

TEMPORAL CONTROL

The degree of temporal control achieved allowed assignment to a range of about 40 years for the Primary occupation, 50–60 years for the Intermediate, and 60–75 years for the Secondary. By comparison to most studies of prehistoric pueblos with long single occupations or with several components, the degree of temporal control is considered rather good at Salmon. The early Primary group of Puerco-Escavada Black-on-white, Red Mesa Black-on-white, and Smudged Red Ware and Puerco Black-on-red has already been mentioned, and there is also evidence of microtemporal change in the ratio of local San Juan White Ware (Mancos and McElmo B/w) relative to intrusive ceramics through time within the Primary (see discussion in a later section). The use of varieties of McElmo Black-on-white has proven useful in the distinction between Primary McElmo styles versus Intermediate period McElmo with the addition of the banded style. The Secondary is not easily subdivided typologically because the period is characterized by only two decorated types—Mesa Verde Black-on-white and St. Johns Polychrome. Here, temporal (and spatial) variation will have to be assessed at a future time on a subtype or variety level within Mesa Verde Black-on-white through analysis of its attributes and design styles.

Although subdivisions of the three major periods were suggested by analysis of types and varieties, the problems of context with mixing and redeposition are obviously even greater between strata that are temporally very close to each other, and the temporal spans of pottery types, and even of stylistic varieties, are too long to permit assignment of strata within a minimum of about 25 years. Temporal specificity to a 40–50 year period for the Primary, nevertheless, represents only two generations of potters. Additional temporal subdivisions based on ceramics alone would necessarily involve complete attribute analysis and seriation at the subtype level.

Consequently, microtemporal stratification of sample sets was not attempted with typological data alone. Instead, stratigraphic sequences and strata types (e.g., floors and roofs) within each occupation were the most adequate basis on which to subdivide the major occupations. Hence, for analysis of synchronic variation across the site within the Primary occupation, the category of floors, or of lowest Primary floors, or lowest trash deposit provided the basis for further temporal control. In the Secondary also, there are a number of rooms in which early Secondary may be stratigraphically separated from late Secondary. The major problem in achieving such fine temporal control within each occupation is that relatively few rooms produced a contrast between early and late strata. For the majority of rooms, such fine subdivisions were not apparent in the stratigraphy.

Chapter 22

PRIMARY OCCUPATION CERAMICS

by Hayward Franklin

Chaco Canyon has been the focus of much attention by archaeologists, including the Chaco Project of the National Park Service, which investigated some of the most persistent problems of Chacoan prehistory. In particular, attention has focused on the nature of the highly developed Chacoan organization and administration, which was responsible for the construction and maintenance of large town sites in Chaco, as well as the establishment of outlying colonies of Chacoan culture in the San Juan Basin, tied by roadway links to the Chacoan heartland. The florescence of Chacoan culture in the AD 1000s and 1100s has been the subject of various models, with explanations for this phenomenon provided by Judd (1954, 1959, 1964), Vivian (1970), Grebinger (1973), and Judge (1979). These models concern Chacoan society and internal variation in Chaco Canyon and can be tested only indirectly using data from outlying settlements such as Salmon Ruin. Chacoan society at Salmon, however, presumably reflects segments of the larger Chacoan pattern, so knowledge gained from Salmon has great relevance for the reconstruction of Chacoan society in general.

Interpretating Salmon's Primary occupation was the main focus of attention for Cynthia Irwin-Williams from the beginning of the project (Irwin-Williams 1972, 1977). Irwin-Williams's primary goal was to understand Salmon as a living town in terms of the sociopolitical, religious, and other organizations that allowed it to function, and with particular attention to aspects of social control that permitted the massive coordinated effort responsible for its initial construction (Irwin-Williams 1977:7–8).

Irwin-Williams presented a model of Chacoan society (of which Salmon Ruin was a part) using a theoretical framework of general systems theory. A major aspect of the Salmon excavation and analysis program involved tests of specific hypotheses generated by the principal investigator, as well as an investigation of the general organizational, institutional, and functional parameters of Salmon Ruin's Primary, Chacoan occupation. This chapter addresses the testing of hypotheses that relate to the internal organization of the Salmon Primary occupation, and that can be explored with ceramic data. Naturally, there are other hypotheses that could not be tested with ceramics, and there are those that can utilize ceramic data but must also rely on other data classes for complete testing. This chapter is thus a partial and exploratory investigation of some of the project hypotheses.

IRWIN-WILLIAMS'S MODEL OF CHACOAN SOCIETY AT SALMON RUIN

Hypotheses relating to the nature of Chacoan economic, social, and ideological subsystems at Salmon are provided in detail by Irwin-Williams (1977). The general model for Salmon Ruins developed by Irwin-Williams (1977:38–68) is summarized here in the form of several postulates:

1. Chacoan society at Salmon was a highly organized system with centralized sociopolitical control which enabled it to efficiently undertake large-scale town planning and construction activities, intensive agriculture and other economic functions, trade relations with other Puebloan groups that channeled resources to and from the Chaco Canyon heartland, and regulation and control of religious and ideological information.

2. Chacoan society at Salmon was organized socioreligiously at a number of levels, superimposed upon each other. Irwin-Williams (1977:87) summarized some of the suggested integrative mechanisms that could have been used by Chacoan society. In the model, the social base was the kin or residence-based group, which corresponds to the widespread familial organizations of pueblo groups. Superimposed over this basic level of Puebloan organization were a series of higher level groupings that probably cut across kin groups. Such groupings may have included dual organizations (moiety), kiva-affiliated groups, higher status socioreligious officials in charge of religious, political, and economic functions, or groups of specialists in charge of specific

task functions. The heads of such organizations had some degree of socioreligious authority and control, possibly including greater access to luxury items. However, a true ranked society was not envisioned (Irwin-Williams 1977:89).

3. Chacoan society differed from typical Puebloan societies (as exemplified by the Secondary period occupants) in that ordinary pueblo societies lacked the incipient social stratification and the degree of centralized control and specialization characteristic of Chacoan society. As such, ordinary pueblo society was limited in its growth potential, being essentially egalitarian and integrated by various society memberships that cut across the kin groups. Chacoan society, on the other hand, had greater potential for social and environmental control and manipulation due to a more centralized socioreligious leadership and a greater degree of specialization in personnel and activity locales. Inevitably, social stratification led to unequal access to luxury or exotic items and resources, which were regulated by or used by higher status individuals or groups who also maintained exclusive rights to esoteric knowledge of religious, and perhaps of political and economic matters.

Testing the Model with Ceramic Data

Using her systems model, Irwin-Williams generated a number of specific hypotheses concerning economic, social, and ideological subsystems. Many of these were not testable using ceramic data, but some can be tested using the same data and the same statistical techniques. Essentially, ceramic tests rest on the nature and variability of the Primary occupation ceramic assemblage, as well as on the spatial distribution of ceramic variables across Salmon Primary occupational rooms and strata. Comparison of ceramic patterns to the architectural patterns of room size, shape, and placement should yield architectural-ceramic correlates interpretable as confirmation or refutation of the model outlined above, and the specific research hypotheses based on them (Irwin-Williams 1977).

More complete testing of many of the aspects of the model (especially involving room function) is not possible until complete integration of other material culture categories (e.g., lithic, botanical, osteological) into functional assemblages is undertaken. Ideally, entire functional associated assemblages would be reconstructed and spatially patterned as a complete testing of the model. However, the ceramic expectations and results provided here constitute a portion of the ultimate goal of complete reconstruction. These tests concern the nature of Chacoan society within Salmon; exterior comparisons are made elsewhere. Also, these do not facilitate Primary versus Secondary comparisons, but they do form a basis for doing so when equivalent data are available on the Secondary.

Hypotheses

Review of the model and the corollary hypotheses of Irwin-Williams, summarized above, reveals several organizational features expected in Primary period Chacoan society. Groupings or institutions that left material remains, especially if they had ceramic correlates, may be analyzed using ceramic data. Ceramic variables should then be spatially patterned in accordance with the social and functional use of space within the Chacoan community. The major facets of the model are listed here, together with the ceramic correlates that could be expected as a result (i.e., test implications).

1. Chacoan society provided access to a variety of exotic (not available locally) and luxury items by virtue of centralized authority and integration into the widespread Chacoan trade network.

Test Implication: Although better tested by studies of ornaments, ceramics may be expected to include exotic or rare examples from a variety of areas, brought to Salmon via the widespread trade network. Whether or not these were treated as luxury items, exotic and intrusive ceramics were certainly rare, and therefore potentially more valuable than local wares.

2. Uneven access to or use of exotic or rare ceramic vessels, as with other luxury goods, was concomitant with socioreligious control concentrated in the hands of a theocratic minority. Such activities were restricted to certain loci.

Test Implications: Intrusive ceramics, especially Chacoan ceramics, should be concentrated in rooms of known religious function, especially the Tower Kiva and the Great Kiva. Intrusive ceramics should also be concentrated in special (nonkiva) rooms having a placement or internal features suggesting particular socioreligious functions. Specifically, the rooms surrounding the Tower Kiva (Rooms 81, 82, and 62) should contain such things as unusual post and roof-support arrangements, which would indicate special activity of a primarily ceremonial nature. Their proximity to the Tower Kiva, presumably a major center of religious activity in Chacoan times, also suggests that these rooms would have special significance.

3. One higher level integrative mechanism may have been a dual organization (moiety) dividing the pueblo spatially into two equal parts. Exogamous moieties are in evidence today among the eastern

pueblos, particularly the Tanoan pueblos of the Rio Grande drainage.

Test Implication: If a dual division existed, and if it was localized spatially and contained ceramic correlates (both of which conditions are debatable), ceramic variables should demonstrate this subdivision. This should take the form of an east-to-west pattern, with the rooms east of the Tower Kiva containing a different ceramic assemblage than those west of it—the Tower Kiva represents a major dividing line in the settlement layout.

4. Residence or kin-based groups will continue to exist despite the overlay of higher level integrating mechanisms.

Test Implication: Ceramic patterning should reveal an association of ceramic variables in accordance with room blocks or suites of contiguous rooms. At Salmon, these take the form of front-to-back alignments of rooms interconnected by doorways. The site map clearly shows a number of such units, not all of which have been excavated. The accessibility is front to back (i.e., plaza-facing to back-wall rooms), with very few lateral doorway positions. Along the main back part of the pueblo, including the east and west arms, these alignments run north to south; in the wings the same alignments are present but the orientation runs east to west. Ceramically, these should be more homogeneous internally and should show greater heterogeneity between members of different suites, if residence groups were localized and each produced different pottery.

5. Under the general model, residence units also reflected the differential status of their occupants within the total Primary occupation population. This would result from either the differential access to rare items among the Chacoans themselves, or possibly the incorporation of local, Middle San Juan population groups into the community (Irwin-Williams 1977:90). The latter would presumably have had less access to rare ceramic wares than Chacoan administrators.

Test Implications: There should be substantial amounts of local San Juan White Ware and Gray Ware pottery in the Primary assemblage, which may be assumed to represent ceramics produced by a local population in the community or in the general vicinity of Salmon. San Juan pottery should have been less valuable, due to its ready availability. There should be considerable differences between residence units (suites) in the presence of local versus rare or exotic (intrusive) ceramics. These tests would illustrate whether the distribution of intrusive versus local types is nonrandom, indicating differential use. It would not however distinguish between differential use of San Juan ceramics by the Chacoan occupants and incorporation of San Juan potters into the Salmon community. To decide this question, further tests would be necessary:

If there were San Juan populations resident at Salmon and if their residence was localized (by room locus or suite), then a whole complex of northern San Juan Puebloan material culture should be found associated with such residence units. That is, not only would San Juan ceramics be localized, but lithic, botanical, and other items associated with northern San Juan Puebloan groups should also be localized in the same portions of the pueblo. Final testing of this hypothesis would thus involve multiple artifact types; ceramics alone provides an insufficient basis for identification of populations. Alternatively, if San Juan Puebloan products are present but not localized by suite, or if different classes of San Juan Puebloan material culture do not coincide in their spatial distribution, the alternative of Chacoan use of San Juan items obtained from other local communities would be favored. In this case, spatial differences in local versus nonlocal ceramics would be explainable as a result of social or functional correlates within the Chacoan population itself.

Source identification of Mancos and McElmo (San Juan Series) pottery by means of refiring analysis (undertaken by Dean Wilson) will indicate how much of this local pottery could have been produced from clays available nearby, versus imported examples of the same types made farther afield within the geographic area. The distribution of the locally made Mancos and McElmo compared to pottery from other northern San Juan areas (e.g., from the Animas, lower San Juan, or La Plata drainages) could also be used as a test of this hypothesis. Specifically, if there are considerable amounts of nonlocal Mancos and McElmo at Salmon, and especially if they are associated with residence units that have many intrusive ceramics, the hypothesis of Chacoan use of San Juan ceramics would be supported. On the other hand, if most Mancos and McElmo during the Primary occupation could have been made at Salmon from locally available clays and tempers, and if proven locally made San Juan pottery correlates with low intrusive rooms, the alternative of a resident San Juan population could be strengthened.

If there is evidence for actual ceramic production at the site during Primary times that can be related to the production of San Juan types such as Mancos and McElmo Black-on-white, or San Juan Gray Ware manufacture, the concept of a resident San Juan population would also be supported. Evidence of ceramic manufacture during the Primary occupation would probably relate to the production of San Juan wares, on logical grounds alone. There is good evidence that all other types and series represent imports that were not produced from local materials. In any case, the San Juan Series ceramics were being produced along the drainages north of the San Juan River, and it is therefore likely that evidence relating to ceramic production would imply manufacture of San Juan White and Gray Ware (additional evidence to this effect is reviewed below). On the other hand, if there is no evidence of manufacture of San Juan ceramics during the Primary occupation, then San Juan ceramics would have been obtained by exchange with other communities in the area. It is possible, of course, that both conditions existed—that there was a resident San Juan population at Salmon as well as exchange with other groups.

6. The differentiation in function implied by the model could include specialization in activity locales, manufacture of tool kits, and/or the presence of craft specialists. Such specialization may have been part time or full time. The term "function" potentially includes all aspects of the use of locales such as rooms and plaza surfaces. The term as used here refers to general use categories (e.g., living, storage, ceremony, food processing) and not to residence groupings, or the potentially specialized production of material culture classes or the associated craftspeople. Room functions, which are in some cases very specific, may be expected to overlap with each other, with most rooms used for several purposes, much as rooms in modern houses are multifunctional. Distributional mapping will therefore specify not one function of a locus, but rather a range of probable functions.

In general, each suite contains a large square room facing the plaza, followed by successively narrower rooms toward the back. The large square rooms in the front are single storied only; rooms to the rear have two stories. Each suite has the same range of rooms in terms of size, shape, and placement, just as modern houses contain an equivalent group of living rooms, dining rooms, bathrooms, and storage rooms. Room function is thus likely correlated with similarities in size, shape, and position in the pueblo, but not with residential suites.

Test Implication: If the above is true, ceramic attributes relating to function (vessel form and ware) should display a spatial pattern corresponding to room size, shape, and placement; that is, these attributes should be less variable within these room types and more variable between them. Thus, large square rooms should have more in common with themselves than with narrow back-wall rooms or with kivas, for example.

The above hypotheses can be tested with data concerning the nature of the ceramic assemblages of the Primary occupation, assessment of the variability in those assemblages, and the spatial patterning of this variation. Ceramic spatial patterning can then be compared to the spatial patterning of other artifact classes, although that is beyond the scope of this report. As Binford stated: "Processual change in one variable can then be shown to relate in a predictable and quantifiable way to changes in other variables, the latter changing in turn relative to changes in the structure of the system as a whole (1962:217)."

The ceramic attribute variables of type, series, and temper (and the distinction between local vs. nonlocal production) are thought to be sensitive not only to temporal changes and cultural affiliation, but also to within-site social differentiation and residence patterns. These variables may reflect social processes if there was a distinction between the uses of local and intrusive (rare) ceramic types, and if the rare types were the property of high-status population groups, which would indicate specialized Chacoan use, if they were used in Chacoan residences or for certain specific purposes (e.g., in ceremonial contexts). In other words, differential access to exotic ceramic types should be expressed by their presence in blocks of rooms occupied by administrative Chacoan officials or used for ceremonial purposes.

Vessel form and ware (white ware, red ware, gray ware) probably relate to cooking, food preparation, storage, living, and ceremony. It must again be emphasized that adequate reconstruction of room function must depend on interpretation of the entire artifact assemblage, not on the ceramics alone. This is especially necessary for functional interpretations, because functional complexes usually involve more than one artifact or material type.

It is also important to note that the functional implications of ceramics have not been well studied. Ceramics even in an area such as the Southwest, where much research has been undertaken, have been used mainly for chronological and regional interpretations. Several studies have used ceramics to interpret social organization, but the implications for function have not been thoroughly explored. In fact, at present, botanical and lithic objects carry greater functional implications than do ceramics. Indeed, ceramic functions need to be investigated by their association with other classes of objects of known function. In this sense, ceramic data are in some respects on the receiving end of a functional study rather than providing input to it.

Despite these problems, certain aspects of ceramics are thought to be more indicative of function than others. In particular, the distinction between wares (e.g., white, red, utility) carries functional overtones. Decorated ceramics may be assumed to have been used for food preparation, serving, and limited transfer or storage of contents. Utility ceramics are assumed to have been used for cooking and to some extent for storage and transport (Rohn 1971). The distinction between white ware and red ware was maintained, although both are decorated, because all red ware is intrusive and hence rare at Salmon, and because factor analysis at Broken K Pueblo separated white ware from red ware even when the same design elements were common to both (Hill 1970:28). The two wares thus may have had different social and functional referents.

A vessel's form also has functional implications. Vessels are created for specific purposes, but there is probably not a one-to-one relationship between vessel form and function. Realization of the varied uses of ceramic bowls and plates, as well as pots and pans in our houses today provides a hint of their multifunctional nature. Although there are certain practical and logical limitations on the uses of vessel form classes, there remains a broad spectrum of potential functions for any particular vessel form class. To take an extreme example, the carrying of water would probably not have been accomplished satisfactorily with a ladle or small bowl, but that does not specify the exact uses for ladles and bowls. The theoretical limits of vessel forms are so broad that the precise purpose of the vessel forms cannot be judged without other sources of data, especially associated items in context. It may be assumed that bowls, pitchers, mugs, and ladles relate to food preparation and consumption, whereas decorated jars relate to storage and transport. Utility jars were probably used for cooking and/or storage and transport. Special forms (effigies, canteens, kiva jars, cylindrical jars) are assumed to have had equally specialized functions, primarily socioreligious in nature.

Conceptually distinguished in this way, the two groups of ceramic attributes have different meanings and their distributions are therefore considered separately in this report. However, there is considerable overlap in the behavioral referents of attribute use. For example, the distribution of red ware relates not only to function but possibly to social and residential variables as well, again because all red ware is intrusive and hence rare at Salmon. Although the two classes of attributes monitored here are theoretically sensitive to different kinds of behavior, it may not be possible in many cases to separate the social framework. As pointed out by Priesnitz (1979:29), "predictions and tests for one culture 'subsystem' or 'class' of artifacts will undoubtedly have relevance for other components of the system." Due to the overlap of economic, social, and ideological subsystems, as well as to the multifunctional nature of ceramic vessels and of the loci in which they were used, it is impossible a priori to predict the precise cultural implications of each ceramic attribute. The choice and implications of the attributes monitored in this study thus rest on logical behavioral referents, previous use of such variables, and assumption.

Some of the most obvious preconditions that must be met by this or any other intrasite study are listed below. Considerable time has been spent in verifying that some of these preconditions have in fact been met by the Salmon stratigraphic and ceramic sample; others are merely assumptions.

1. The sample of rooms and strata available from excavated portions of Salmon Ruin must be representative of the whole. Despite some gaps in the excavational sample (e.g., no complete suites have been excavated along the west arm of the site), there is much variety in the size, shape, and position of rooms excavated. By the close of excavations in 1979, 36 percent of the ground floor rooms at the site, about 40 rooms, had been completely excavated through the Primary levels. This sample, then, is assumed to be sufficient for a study of Primary room usage.

2. It must be assumed that temporal control is sufficient to narrow the sample of rooms and strata to those which are essentially synchronous. Control of time to the Primary occupation (about 50 years long at the most) has been accomplished (see Chapter 22). A discussion of microtemporal change in the frequency of ceramic types within the 50 or so years of the Primary period is provided below.

3. It is assumed that the social, institutional, and functional aspects of Salmon Chacoan society as hypothesized contained ceramic correlates, and that these remain essentially in situ where the activity occurred. Naturally, if a social group or a range of activities did not involve ceramics, or if the ceramic correlates of behavior have been removed or disturbed by human or natural agencies, attempts at ceramic patterning cannot elucidate behavior.

4. The ceramic variables chosen to monitor social and functional activity across the Primary period must be reflective of those social and functional activities. Specifically, the dimensions of series, type, ware, and variety should be sensitive to social and cultural distinctions based on residence and status, whereas vessel form and ware should be sensitive to

room function. It is also assumed that the contrast between local and intrusive ceramics corresponds to the differential degrees of common to rare, and therefore translates into the degree of value placed on ceramic items (Priesnitz 1979:37). Chacoan pottery should have been of elevated value especially because of its rarity as a result of distance from the source, but also because this ceramic class was the accustomed ware of the Chacoan immigrants. Of course, other attributes may also reflect social and functional variables, but because time did not permit complete attribute analysis of all Primary period ceramics, a complete assessment of the potential of all attributes could not be made. The attributes chosen for analysis are theoretically sensitive to the range of social processes being examined; other attributes (especially design) could potentially also have social-functional implications.

5. Finally, it must be assumed that statistical manipulations and the results thereof reflect cultural factors—that is, that numerical treatment and relative quantity is culturally meaningful, that representative sherd populations are present, and that sample sizes are large enough to avoid sample error problems. There is no doubt that quantitative treatment is applicable in this situation and that it could reveal culturally meaningful patterns of behavior and deposition. The entire sample (100%) of sherd materials available was analyzed and used in statistical work for the Primary stratigraphic units chosen, so that the maximum possible sample of both strata and ceramics was included. Also, there are strata (especially floors) that—despite the 100 percent sample used—contain so few ceramics that using their counts is problematical. Some stratigraphic units (e.g., some floor pits) contained no ceramics at all. Absence can be as culturally meaningful as presence, but a total lack of data or having very small quantities of data certainly frustrates statistical treatment. Units with small sample sizes were usually included to avoid severely limiting the room and stratigraphic representation, but small sample sizes were taken into consideration in the interpretation of results.

Several of the preconditions—temporal control, sample sizes, and stratigraphic contextual evaluation of association—were studied closely to provide some assurance that minimum conditions were met. This is discussed at greater length in the following sections. Regarding the representativeness of the excavational sample, the choice of ceramic attributes to be recorded, and the ability of ceramics to reflect social-functional behavior, the preconditions are either untestable assumptions or are considered essentially satisfied on logical and theoretical grounds. The acceptance of some of these preconditions remains in the realm of assumption, despite testing to assure compliance with the basic prerequisites.

I nevertheless believe that the prerequisites have been met here as well or better than in comparable studies of this nature at other sites. In most studies, these preconditions have been assumed from the outset. For this reason, also, the substantive results were approached somewhat inductively, in case other variables could account for the observed results besides the hypothesized ones. That is, the descriptive results were used as an exploratory vehicle within which confirmation or denial of hypotheses could be approached.

COMPARISON TO OTHER INVESTIGATIONS

Other studies at Salmon Ruin have used the distributions of typological and attribute data from restricted portions of the pueblo to investigate certain social aspects. Lekson and Cameron (1975) examined floor-related ceramics samples using weight as well as sherd count. Suzanne Bradley (1979) studied both the Primary and Secondary ceramics in the West Wing of the site (Rooms 6W, 6A, 4A, 4B, 4W, 7W, 5A, 5W, 1W, 2W), and assessed the distribution of ceramics as well as lithic and botanical data in two suites of rooms for both major occupation periods. Also, Priesnitz (1979) investigated the distribution of intrusive versus local San Juan ceramics in a study designed to test several hypotheses regarding the use of intrusive ceramics in the first construction phase of Salmon, including the east and west arms, and the central Tower Kiva area.

Studies undertaken in late Mogollon pueblos represent earlier attempts at intrasite interpretations of social-functional systems. These include work by Freeman and Brown (1964), Longacre (1966, 1970) at Carter Ranch, Hill (1968, 1970) at Broken K Pueblo, and also Cronin (1962). Together with the study of Deetz (1965) on Arikara ceramics, these works have demonstrated the possibility of using archaeological data to study certain facets of the social organization of communities from spatially patterned ceramic data. Later studies, such as those of DeGarmo (1975), addressed intracommunity, societal aspects of behavior.

A comparison may be made between the approach taken here and the pioneering studies of Longacre and Hill. These studies broke new ground in the interpretation of untapped aspects of prehistoric social behavior. Discussion and criticism of the studies at Carter Ranch and Broken K Pueblo are provided in Dumond (1977). The major resemblance between this study and those of Longacre and Hill is, of course, the goal of revealing aspects of social behavior in a synchronic, intrasite framework. The ceramic data used in this and most other works are considered reflective of loci of organized activity; nonrandom distributions of ceramic variables are considered indicative of localization of patterned social behavior, including inference of residential or functional patterns.

A major point of difference between this study (and that of Priesnitz) as compared to the Longacre and Hill studies lies in the kind of organization hypothesized. Longacre and Hill searched for ceramic distributional evidence to support the hypothesis of matrilineal-matrilocal residence units, using stated assumptions about female production of ceramics and transmission of ceramic knowledge through female lineages. It was assumed that the ceramics represented a closed system—that the ceramic variables represented ceramic manufacturing activity within the community. At Salmon Ruin, however, the model to be tested proposes several levels of organization, only one of which may be the residential unit. Moreover, the Primary ceramic complex is definitely not a closed system; a considerable portion of the pottery from the Chacoan occupation is intrusive. Although there may be spatial differences in the attributes of locally produced ceramics at Salmon, the major source of internal variation in the Primary occupation ceramic assemblages lies in the contrast between the local San Juan pottery and the many intrusive types and series in the Chacoan occupation. Whereas earlier studies focused on decorative variation within a limited typological range of ceramics thought to be locally produced, at Salmon the great variation of series and types, many not made in the vicinity, facilitates distributional analysis on a typological level rather than a design element level of analysis.

Due to the differences in initial hypotheses as well as the nature of the internal variability of the ceramic complexes, the ceramic data collected from the Primary occupation at Salmon were quite different from the decorative attributes used at Carter Ranch and Broken K. At Salmon, the attributes of type, series, ware, and vessel form used for this study as well as that of Priesnitz (1979) were designed to test a broad spectrum of activities and ceramic functions. In the Longacre and Hill studies, the stylistic and decorative aspects of a more limited range of types were chosen to reveal a nonrandom pattern inferred to be the result of localization of a female-related process of ceramic manufacture. At Salmon, a complete design element analysis was not attempted due to the large sample size of ceramics and the large sample of strata to be analyzed for the Primary occupation. However, design data are indirectly incorporated as part of the ceramic data, because design style variants in San Juan White Ware were recorded, and because an independent full attribute analysis was completed on several rooms. The point to be made, however, is that the nature of ceramic data at Salmon and the social institutions to be reconstructed from ceramic data are quite different from Carter Ranch and Broken K Pueblo.

The sample sizes at Salmon, of strata analyzed and of the ceramic population, are larger than those used in the studies at Carter Ranch and Broken K. As a basis for comparison, during the Primary occupation at Salmon a total of 281 Primary floor-related strata from 33 rooms were available from the excavated portion of the pueblo. These are grouped into 63 floor units, including occupation fill, floor surface, structural floors, and the fill of associated pits. At Carter Ranch, the floor sample numbered 14 (Longacre 1970:38); at Broken K Pueblo, 38 floors were studied (Hill 1970:25). At Salmon, an additional 38 Primary trash strata and several Primary roofs were also analyzed. Total ceramic samples analyzed are therefore correspondingly larger than in the earlier studies. The relatively large sherd and stratigraphic samples at Salmon precluded a full-scale attribute analysis, the recording of all design elements, or a comprehensive reconstruction of all vessels during the Primary occupation.

Methods of statistical treatment of Salmon data also differ somewhat from the statistical treatment of the Carter Ranch and Broken K ceramics. At Carter Ranch, data were entered into a multiple regression program (Longacre 1970:35), whereas factor analysis of ceramic types as well as design elements was used at Broken K (Hill 1970:24). At Salmon, a number of techniques have been used, including information derived from factor analysis (designed mainly for temporal control), multidimensional scaling, cluster analysis, and the visual mapping of the SYMAP program. It may also be noted that Longacre used frequencies as input data (Longacre 1970:38); at Broken K, both frequency and proportional data were used, with little difference in the results (Hill 1970:25). At Salmon, computer entry data consisted of proportional data, expressed as percentages of the totals within the stratum, or in the case of floors, the floor unit was a combination of several floor-related strata. Both raw counts and percentages contain potential biases. However, the advantages of proportions, as in correcting for differences in sample sizes, probably outweighed the disadvantages.

Finally, considerable time at Salmon was devoted to testing the validity of the preconditions and assumptions underlying a synchronic intrasite study (e.g., temporal control, sample sizes, problems of mixing, and reliability of association). These aspects remained largely in the realm of a priori assumption at Carter Ranch and Broken K Pueblo. At Salmon, Priesnitz (1979:40–58, 117–125) addressed these problems at the site; problems of sample size and stratigraphic context are addressed below.

As an illustration, sherds were the unit of analysis in the Longacre and Hill studies as well as at Salmon, but limited reconstruction (Priesnitz 1979) and typological and stratigraphic comparison of floors to strata resting upon them was undertaken only for the Salmon Primary occupation; this was not attempted in the other studies. Consideration of mixture visible through reconstruction has also taken place at Coyote Creek (DeGarmo 1975) and for the Chaco Project.

Contemporaneity of stratigraphic units used for synchronic comparison, often assumed, received considerable attention for the Salmon Primary period. Temporal control to a period of about 40–50 years was accomplished, whereas microtemporal controls in the form of building phases, ceramic trends, and stratigraphic position provided a finer microtemporal evaluation (if not complete control) within the Primary time span itself.

All ceramic data used in this report are from the ceramic limited-attribute analysis program (CLAP; see Chapter 20), which was conducted on all Primary strata during the last 2 years of the project. This limited-attribute analysis was designed specifically for the Primary period; it monitored series, ware, type, and variety, as well as vessel form and temper for all sherd samples. All sherds were examined in cross-section under a binocular microscope for temper types and combinations of tempers. Out of a practically unlimited number of possible ceramic attributes, the variables of series, type, and variety were chosen as sensitive to factors of cultural affiliation and locality of origin, with implications within the site for Chacoan versus local population affiliation, status, and specialization of activities as measured against nonceramic data. Vessel form and ware were recorded with a consideration of their probable utility in analysis of room function.

The ceramic samples available within the Primary occupation at Salmon do not form an ideal database for distributional work for several reasons: ceramics and other material culture items were likely removed by the original occupants, reoccupation by Secondary people resulted in further discard or redeposition of Primary materials, and many behavioral surfaces were also reoccupied. Of a grand total of 260,106 sherds (decorated and utility) recorded on rough-sort forms from Salmon Ruin to date, only 23,449 are from Primary occupational strata. In other words, only about 10 percent of the recovered ceramics are of Primary types, and are also from Primary occupational strata. The totals for all Primary types, regardless of stratum, would be somewhat larger because Primary materials were often redeposited or mixed with Secondary materials in post-Primary strata. Such strata were not used in this study, however. Although the sample of types from in situ Primary stratigraphic contexts is only an estimated 10–15 percent of all pottery sherds recovered, the actual number of Primary sherds (more than 23,000) is certainly adequate.

The same situation holds for the category of whole or restorable vessels. Of more than 300 whole or mostly restored vessels at Salmon, only 35 are of Primary types, and most of these are badly fragmented and incompletely restorable. In fact, the number of whole (unbroken) decorated vessels from the Primary period amounts to no more than half a dozen. Analysis of the distribution of whole or even partial ceramic specimens is thus impossible for the Primary, although experimentation with partial reconstruction for monitoring stratigraphic mixing was undertaken as reported in the discussion of context in this report. In sum, the total sample of sherds from the Primary strata was considered adequate for distributional analysis, but samples of vessels were not.

Fifteen white ware types and six red ware types are present in amounts of more than 10 sherds each (and several additional types are represented by smaller figures) from four white ware and four red ware series. Primary utility ceramics include approximately six to eight recognized types, grouped into four series. Although quantitatively there is great variation in the Primary ceramic assemblage, it is well to point out that the San Juan ceramics dominate. Tables 22.1 and 22.2 show that in stratigraphically "pure" Primary strata the San Juan decorated types (Mancos and McElmo Black-on-white) comprise 72.6 percent of the total decorated assemblage. In the utility ceramics, San Juan plain gray and corrugated types amount to 8 1 percent of the total utility assemblage. The dominance of San Juan ceramics reduces the overall quantitative variability of the Primary complex, but is of great interest in itself. The possible reasons for the dominance of San Juan ceramics in the Chacoan occupation are discussed further below.

Table 22.1. Ceramic counts by decorated series from Primary strata, by stratum type.

Stratum Type	San Juan WW	Cibola WW	Chuska WW	Tusayan WW	White Mtn Red	Tsegi Orange	Smudged Red	San Juan Red	Total
Trash	2705	570	221	16	78	29	76	5	3700
Nonfloor Behavioral	1010	169	88	23	6	7	38	6	1347
Floors	2131	461	159	38	76	38	80	5	2988
Subfloor Pre-Primary	339	105	22	2	3	3	4	0	476
Total	6185	1305	490	79	163	77	198	16	8513
Percent	72.6	15.3	5.8	0.9	1.9	0.9	2.3	0.3	100%

Data derived from limited attribute data. Strata all have Primary factor scores. No redeposited, questionable, or mixed Primary strata are included. Small amounts of Mesa Verde B/w excluded. Includes plain white and red sherds.

Table 22.2. Ceramic counts by utility series from Primary strata by stratum type.

Stratum Type	San Juan plain gray	San Juan Corrugated	Chuska Corrugated	Cibola Corrugated	Unidentified Utility	Grand Total
Trash	749	4671	590	27	319	6356
Nonfloor behavioral	115	2013	728	21	101	2978
Floor	410	3557	713	43	171	4894
Subfloor (pre-Primary)	66	513	73	9	41	702
Total count	1340	10754	2104	100	632	14930
Percentage	8.9	72	14.1	0.7	4.3	100

The regional series, and not their constituent types, form the analytical base for distributional analysis in this report. One reason for this is the focus on the differential usage of ceramics from different Southwestern regional traditions; thus, the series rather than the type is the logical frame of reference. Second, many of the individual types are represented by small samples, either in the Primary strata as a whole, or on many individual behavioral surfaces. Many are too poorly sampled to use in statistical analysis. Combined and treated as series, however, the sample sizes for each ceramic analytical unit become much larger. Table 22.1 shows that the decorated ceramic series all contain 77 or more sherds in the Primary as a whole, except for the rare San Juan Red Ware sherds, which were not included in statistical treatment due to small sample sizes. Among utility ceramics, all four series are represented by large sample sizes; the smallest is 100 sherds for Cibola Corrugated. In total 8513 decorated sherds and 14,930 utility sherds were collected from Primary strata with no mixture with Secondary materials.

The total samples available were considered acceptable, although the variation in sample size between strata is quite large. The sherd samples for stratum types used in cluster analysis and the mean number of sherds per stratum are provided in Table 22.3. This table reveals that both the total sample sizes and the average number of sherds per stratum are adequate for distributional analysis. Where only decorated pottery was used in distributional work, the total count and mean sherds per stratum are correspondingly smaller than where all pottery or just utility ceramics were used. This is expectable because about two-thirds of the sherds are utility ware. Even without utility ceramics included, the floor strata averaged 53 sherds per floor unit. There was, however, considerable variation in sample size available from particular proveniences.

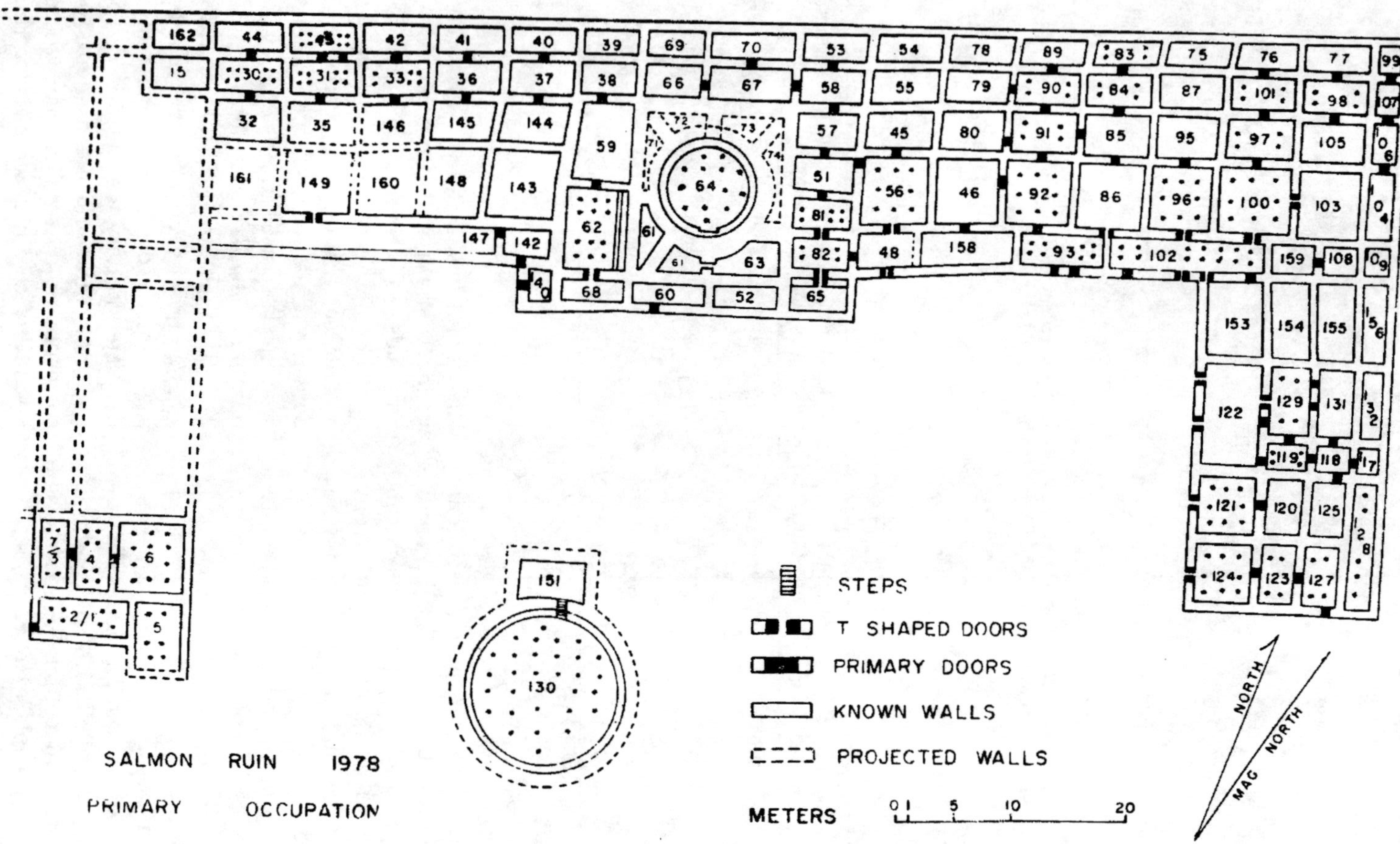

Figure 22.1. Rooms excavated to Chacoan levels that produced Chacoan ceramic assemblages.

Table 22.3. Ceramic sample sizes for cluster analysis.

Ceramic Units	Data	Strata	Total Sample Size	Mean Count/ Stratum
5 vessel form-ware categories	All ceramics	51 Primary floor units (no G strata)	4171	82
7 ceramic series	All decorated	43 Primary floor units (with G strata)	2276	53
7 series, in 3 groups	All decorated	43 Primary floor units (with G strata)	2276	53
7 ceramic series	All decorated	12 roofs and roof-like features	1271	106
7 ceramic series	All decorated	22 lowest Primary trash levels	2234	102
5 utility series	All utility	42 Primary floor units (with G strata)	4934	119

SAMPLE OF EXCAVATED ROOMS

Field research at Salmon has resulted in the excavation of approximately 40 percent of the ground floor rooms at the site. Not all of these have been excavated to the lowest Primary levels, however, and just a small number have been tested below the lowest floors. Figure 22.1 illustrates the rooms at Salmon excavated to Primary levels that also contain Primary in situ strata with associated ceramics.

The room sample is the result of the excavational strategy developed by Cynthia Irwin-Williams and Lonnie Pippin, which lasted for an 8-year period; it is considered adequate. Spatially, the excavated rooms are spread fairly evenly across the pueblo. All major sections of the pueblo except the extreme northwest corner have at least some representation. The eastern side of the pueblo has greater excavational representation; only 9 of the 33 rooms shown in Figure 22.1 lie to the west of the Tower Kiva area. It is unfortunate, also, that more complete blocks and suites (front-to-back transects) were not excavated, because one of the principal ways in which rooms are structured within the pueblo is along front-to-back lines. Although distribution of artifacts by suites is a major focus of this report, only three suites have been fully excavated to Primary levels, an additional two are nearly complete but for the back-wall rooms, and another three are represented by two excavated rooms each. In some cases, the problem lies in the lack of Primary materials remaining in the rooms, rather than a lack of excavation. Several other blocks of rooms (not front-to-back suites) are included in the sample: 92–102, 129–119, and the Tower Kiva area (Rooms 64, 62, 81, and 82). The Tower Kiva and the Great Kiva have both been excavated, although the former contained little evidence of use in Chacoan times, and the latter is incompletely excavated. Several other rooms could be included for comparisons, but they are excavationally isolated from the other rooms of the suites or blocks of which they are a part (Rooms 30, 33, 56, 96, 98, and 121). It must be assumed that the room sample available for study is representative of the site as a whole. Despite noncompletion of some blocks of rooms, the approximately 40 percent sample included here is broadly based, and likely includes a representation of major kinds of residential and functionally oriented loci in the Primary occupation.

The 64 primary excavated floor units used in this study consisted of associated occupational fill (G), floor surface (H), structural floor (I), and associated pit fill (L) strata. Several O strata and S strata were also considered as floors although they lacked the visible structure or thickness usually present with floor units (see R. Adams, Chapter 6, for strata letter codes and definitions). Not all strata types were present for all floor units; some lacked occupational fill levels, whereas in other cases there were no pits (L) in the floor. Sherd counts were combined for all available associated strata of these code types, thus making up the floor unit.

In considering the distributions of only decorated ceramics, the G (occupational fill) levels were included where present, in order to augment the sometimes small samples of decorated pottery on floors. For analysis of wares and vessel forms, however, the G strata counts were deleted because they were not considered as well associated with the floor as floor contact sherds (H), and also because the sherd samples were much larger when the utility ceramics could be included. Of a total of 63 Primary floor units, 51 had decorated or utility ceramics, or both, and could be used for analysis of ware and vessel form distributions.

Statistical treatments, of course, require large independent sample sizes. When the strata sample has been narrowed to certain strata types (e.g. floors and roofs), and further to those which are as contemporaneous as possible, unmixed with later components and stratified by ceramic analytical classes, the sample sizes dwindle appreciably. This is why at Salmon, a study using only floor surface (H) strata and ceramic types, for example, would not have been feasible distributionally. Too many stratum-ceramic class samples would be numerically minimal or nonexistent. The methods adopted here represent a compromise between (a) sample size adequacy and the necessity to impose strict micro-temporal controls, and (b) sample size availability and the number of ceramic analytical classes used. Combining floor-related strata into floor units but at the same time reducing the analytic classes to seven series and five vessel form-ware combinations helped to assure that each provenience–data class combination would be as large as possible. Although these problems are especially critical on floors where artifact samples tend to be small, they are also present to a lesser extent in Primary trash and roof levels. It is undoubtedly true that the incongruity between the desirability of large sample sizes and stratigraphic-analytical class controls is not unusual at archaeological sites; Salmon Ruin is certainly not unique in this regard.

Primary trash strata available from the excavations to date include approximately 35 major C or M strata that pertain to the Primary period. Several other J and D strata are probably in fact trash although not labeled as such in the field. Of these, the 22 lowest trash strata just above Primary floors were chosen for distributional evaluation, because they can be determined to be relatively contemporaneous. Upper Primary trash was more likely to be affected by mixture from later periods, and in rooms with multiple trash strata, the refuse levels continued uninterrupted into the Intermediate period after AD 1130. Although at one time it was believed that the Primary period contained little or no refuse, and searches for an extramural refuse mound proved fruitless, it later became clear that considerable amounts of residential trash from the Primary occupation had been deposited in a number of rooms.

As a stratum type, Primary roofs (mostly second-story floors) presented the greatest problem of all. In an evaluation of roofs at Salmon, R. Adams found (from tree-ring dates) that there were 43 excavated roofs that were constructed in Primary times. Of these, 40 were either reused by Secondary occupation people in the Secondary as living surfaces, or were heavily contaminated by Secondary refuse. Primary materials thus either were totally removed or were disturbed and mixed with massive amounts of Mesa Verde Black-on-white. Only three Primary construction roofs had not been affected by Secondary materials; this sample was clearly too small to work with distributionally. An attempt was made to determine how much Primary ceramic material remained on the affected roofs, and in some cases Primary materials still existed, but in most cases sample sizes were quite small. Furthermore, it could not be assumed that the Primary sherds from Primary roofs were the residual remnant of activities that took place on them because of Secondary disturbance and because all Primary roofs have fallen from their original wall sockets. Although much activity during the Primary occupation must have taken place on second-story floors and the upper roofs forming the top of the pueblo, very little material culture remained of the Primary usage of roofs. There were, however, 17 "roof-like features" that were Primary in date and not affected by the Secondary materials. These included problematical roofs, roof remnants, possible repair of rooms, and construction of roofs. Probable platforms in two rooms were also included in this category. Fortunately, some of these retained Primary ceramics unmixed with Secondary ceramics. In total, 12 roofs and roof-like features containing Primary ceramics were used in distributional assessments as a comparison to similar treatment of floor units and lowest Primary trash levels. Whether these strata represented true roofs or not, at least they related to activities that took place in those rooms.

After completed limited-attribute forms were entered into the SELGEM storage and retrieval system, statistical analyses were accomplished using the SPSS statistical package or cluster analysis (with the HCLUS program). Data reorganization and grouping for noncomputerized preliminary comparisons and for cluster analysis was accomplished by James Carroll, drawing upon a raw data printout of ceramic classes crosstabulated by room and stratum. Data manipulations requiring a computer were completed by Paddy Johnson, using the IBM 4031 computer at ENMU.

For the distributional work required, it was necessary to determine the variability of the discrete analytical classes, ensure that the spatial arrangement of the variability was nonrandom, and employ an appropriate technique to illustrate spatial patterning of the ceramic variables. As such, it was the spatial patterning of the Primary ceramics that was of paramount importance, not the statistical significance of the differences per se. As it turned out, many of the patterns produced also involved differences that were statistically significant; however, it was not assumed that statistical significance could be equated with cultural significance. An attempt was made to grasp the basic, large-scale (and sometimes obvious) patterning of the data by inspecting the percentage data, or broad-based nonparametric statistical methods prior to employing computerized analysis. In this regard, the commentary of David Hurst Thomas (1976, 1978) about statistical versus cultural significance and adherence to set levels of statistical significance was considered well advised. Essentially, then, we were searching for patterned distributions reflective of patterned activities of loci, not necessarily statistical significance.

Computerized cluster analysis was chosen to reveal spatial patterning, and multidimensional scaling (Kruskal and Wish 1978), which has also been used on Salmon ceramic data with equally good results (Priesnitz 1979), was used to cross-check the result. Six cluster analysis computer runs were used to differentiate the strata sample by stratum type (roofs, floors, trash) and into analytic classes using seven ceramic series or five vessel form-ware combinations. Ceramic data were entered as percentages within each stratigraphic level or combination of strata units (for floors).

The use of cluster analysis is described in Anderberg (1973) and Hodson (1970). We used John J. Wood's (1974) HCLUS program, which is a form of hierarchical cluster analysis that uses a matrix of coefficients of similarity as a basis for producing cluster diagrams or dendrograms by eight optional methods. The choice of cluster method is somewhat arbitrary (Wood 1974:5), but we found that Method 2 (complete linkage or furthest neighbor) and Method 7 (flexible, using both single and complete linkage methods) were the most useful in interpreting results. Bradley (1979:83) also found Methods 2 and 7 to be the most suitable in her work with ceramics at Salmon. In practice, the results from the two methods were quite similar, although the ordering of the clusters in the dendrogram was sometimes shifted. The choice of method for illustration here was simply a matter of whether Method 2 or Method 7 gave the clearest visual representation of the spatial patterning.

As used here, the dendrogram, a tree-like diagram produced by cluster analysis, indicates the relative degree of similarity or distance between proveniences in terms of the ceramic classes (as percentages by stratum). The merge sequence and closeness of joins between proveniences on the dendrogram provides a visual representation of the relative similarity or dissimilarity of strata and proveniences in terms of ceramic content. Close joins, or proveniences linked tightly toward the right side of the dendrogram, differ only slightly in ceramic percentages; the magnitude of difference increases for joins toward the left of the diagram. Because in cluster analysis all units must be joined ultimately to all others, connections to the extreme left of the dendrogram have little consequence. As a general rule of thumb, joins left of the two-thirds point on the cluster dendrogram scale are considered of little cultural significance. Major clusters were identified by viewing the merge sequence; major dividing points were identified by breaks between major clusters, and were labeled accordingly. Subclusters having some relevance within the major cluster groups were also labeled (e.g., Cluster 1A, B, etc.). Minor subclusters were not interpreted because their differences ceramically were minor and subject to small deviations in percentages, as well as sampling error. For ease of interpretation of the ceramic contents of each cluster, the percentages of the ceramic classes used were then manually written onto each line of the dendrogram. In this way, an idea could be gained of the ceramic similarities or proveniences clustered together. Finally, the spatial meaning of the cluster patterns was assessed by referring to the stratigraphic and spatial parameters (room size, placement, features) of proveniences grouped together by cluster analysis. Cluster analysis was found to be a most productive means of discovering spatial patterning in ceramic data. Although by itself the technique does not provide a statistical measure of the strength of cluster divisions or of the discriminatory power of each variable, discriminant analysis (Klecka 1975; Hill 1978) could have been used to further validate the cluster groups. Even without a formal statistical validation, however, a satisfactory evaluation of the ceramic variables for the major cluster divisions was gained by examining the analysis class percentages for each cluster as described above.

PROBLEMS OF CONTEXT AND RELIABILITY OF ASSOCIATION

One of the prerequisites for a study of this nature is the presence of uncontaminated deposits remaining within or near their original locus of use. Only if this is true can distributional patterning reflect behavioral patterns. It is necessary to consider, then, whether the data considered here for the Primary occupation meet this requirement.

A distinction is usually made between occupational surfaces where activity occurred and refuse or trash deposited away from original points of usage. Theoretically, floors, roofs, and plaza surfaces are behavioral strata, in that they represent occupational surfaces used for specific purposes. The materials on behavioral surfaces are usually thought to be the most important source of information because they represent a behavioral complex of material culture associated with a specific locus, and they may be correlated with architectural boundaries within which such behavior occurred. Refuse, on the other hand, is assumed to have been transported away from its original behavioral context, so articles in it are not functionally associated with the spatial or architectural boundaries within which they are found. Ultimately, of course, disposal is behavioral too, and trash may provide information about patterns of refuse dumping. However, the basic contrast between behavioral surfaces and the discard of objects in refuse piles some distance away is a useful dichotomy. Distributional patterns should therefore be based on behavioral strata for the most part, because such patterning would reflect differential use of space. Spatial patterns using trash strata reflect patterns of refuse disposal instead of utilization in a functional context.

Because of the importance of behavioral strata, it is essential that the materials connected with them be not only excavationally or depositionally associated with these levels, but also functionally associated. Schiffer (1976) has discussed problems of contextual association in greater detail.

Although cultural materials are often assumed to remain in their original place of usage, especially on behavioral surfaces, there are a number of mitigating factors, including both cultural and natural processes, that serve to mix, remove, or relocate materials, destroying or at least modifying the original association of locus and cultural assemblage. Cultural processes include trash dumping, removal upon abandonment, or removal for storage, reoccupation, and reuse of strata and/or the material remains of the earlier component. Natural, geological forces include the collapse of walls and roofs and settling of strata due to gravitation; erosional forces cause lateral and vertical movement. A third category is excavational—mixing due to the inadvertent misassignment of association provenience during excavation. These processes of disturbance are always present to some degree, but the amount of disturbance can be tested to determine reliability of associations.

At Salmon Ruin, the degree of reliability of associations with occupational surfaces was tested by stratigraphic evaluation, limited reconstruction of vessels to show the extent of cross-cutting of sherds to a single vessel between adjacent strata, and statistical comparisons of sherd type populations between occupational surfaces and the strata adjacent to them. At least some idea of the extent of mixing, and therefore the degree of reliability of association may be gained in this manner.

Nonbehavioral levels, however, are not thought to represent in situ manufacture or use behavior to begin with. Nevertheless, patterns of trash disposal can be examined to determine how widely trash was dispersed, or whether it remained near the original locus of use. It is not usually possible to determine the exact stratum or locus of origin of refuse materials, although it may at least be narrowed to an area or a range of possible strata. In the Primary occupation at Salmon, there is stratigraphic and distributional evidence that refuse, although moved, was not transported randomly across the site. In many cases, it appears that Primary trash came from adjacent rooms or from higher portions of the same rooms (second and third stories).

In any case, trash should produce information about assemblages of tools, and about relationships between lithic, ceramic, botanical, and faunal data, even where the point of origin cannot be determined. Assuming that trash deposition included all types of material culture originally in use somewhere else (barring selective dumping of one artifact category), the original relationship between ceramic types, or between ceramics and other artifact classes, should remain unaltered. The structure of the activity complex thus need not be destroyed, but merely transposed into a new depositional environment.

In any multicomponent site the later occupations are likely to disturb or remove evidence from earlier occupations. Salmon Ruin is no exception. The Secondary occupants affected Primary occupation remains by reusing Primary rooms, sometimes down to the original Primary floors, by redepositing Primary strata in other rooms in the process, by placing burials into pits dug into the lower Primary fill of rooms, and by constructing subdivisions within Primary structures, in the form of partition walls and insertion of small kivas into formerly large square rooms. These processes resulted in the removal of all Primary strata in some rooms, especially those of just one story. In two-story sections of the pueblo, Secondary modifications often extended down only through the second-story level, leaving Primary strata intact beneath. In such instances, however, the Primary materials did not always remain unaffected, because some Secondary refuse was discarded down below the reoccupied second-story floors, and some burials were placed into the Primary strata of the lower story. Primary strata, then, were subject to complete removal where Secondary reuse penetrated to the original floor, partial removal in other cases, contamination of remaining Primary materials by downward mixing, and redeposition of some Primary materials into other rooms not reoccupied by Secondary inhabitants. The processes of abandonment, trash disposal, and reuse are documented ethnographically. Stanislawski indicated (1973:117–118) that after rooms were occupied "within a few years contiguous room units are abandoned, refuse is deposited and fills the rooms, and then the refuse is thrown elsewhere as the rooms are cleared and re-used." In fact, 26.5 percent of the Chaco Black-on-white pottery at the site was located in strata evaluated by Rex Adams as Secondary in terms of depositional period. The early Cibola group of types suffered the same fate; 24.9 percent of these sherds were also in Secondary period strata.

Secondary reuse and contamination also reduced the number of behavioral strata that could be analyzed. Of approximately 80 total Primary floors, 23 had been reused or contaminated by Secondary occupants. Of a total of 40 roofs (mostly second-story floors), only 3 escaped Secondary reuse or contamination. The Secondary intrusion affected rooms and strata differently across the site. Each stratum was therefore evaluated stratigraphically and typologically in order to exclude Secondary strata, extensively mixed strata, and redeposited Primary strata from the Primary sample. In some Primary strata eventually included for analysis, small amounts of contamination were recognized typologically and eliminated from tabulation of the sherd counts for each of these stratigraphic units.

Mixture Within the Primary Occupation

Temporal control for strata associated with the Primary occupation was achieved using the methods of stratigraphic evaluation and factor analysis previously discussed. By these means, the sample was narrowed to Primary strata unaffected by the Secondary occupation. There remained, however, the possibility of mixture within the Primary strata. In particular, the reliability of Primary floors was assessed by examining the strata types immediately above the Primary floors, reconstructing some ceramic vessels between Primary floors and overlying strata, and statistically comparing the ceramics from floor units to overlying strata.

Mixture between nonbehavioral levels presumably occurred because of cultural, natural, and excavational processes. Mixture between trash strata was not assessed in detail, however, because the assumption (usually made for occupational surfaces) that materials represent in situ behavior is not made for trash strata. In his study of Primary period behavioral loci at Salmon, Priesnitz (1979:117–133) faced the problem of reliability of sherd-floor associations for a number of Primary strata. Exclusion of Secondary strata and Primary strata contaminated from later periods was made by the same methods used here (i.e., factor scores, stratigraphic position, and typological evidence of mixture from the Secondary as seen by Mesa Verde Black-on-white sherds in Primary strata). Priesnitz concluded that the extent of mixture between floor and above-floor strata was quite variable from room to room, that the strata type overlying the floor (roof, trash, occupational fill) was an important factor in the amount of mixture present, that some mixture of floors and the strata lying on them was almost always present, and that the observed similarity in series count between floor and trash levels could be due to mixture or to actual cultural-behavioral similarity between trash and floor units, unrelated to the mixing of strata. The ultimate conclusion was that mixing within the Primary strata was indeed a problem.

"Because reliable data for in situ behavior has not been accumulated for the majority of cases discussed above, only general conclusions can be reached" (Priesnitz 1979:133). Despite the additional evaluation of floor associations discussed below, the cautionary note raised by Priesnitz must apply equally to this study, which is based on a larger sample of the same kinds of strata used in his study. Material remains of Primary social-functional behavior are present in some rooms at Salmon. Nevertheless, the degree to which these may be localized to a particular room and stratum requires further consideration.

Strata Types

The floor-related strata of occupational fill (G), floor contact (H), floor structure (I), and pits articulated with the floor surface (L) were typically combined into a "floor unit" as a behavioral complex in this study and in Priesnitz's work. However, the assignment of the occupational fill (G) stratum to the floor unit was questionable in some instances, and therefore was not always included in the floor units with the other floor-related strata. Stratigraphically, these floor units are generally situated above artificial fill (D), construction debris (T), or other floor units. Artificial fill (D) strata are located immediately below or between adjacent floors.

The classification of Primary floors by the strata immediately overlying them is provided in Table 22.4. Of about 80 Primary floors, 20–23 were rendered unusable for ceramic distributional work due to reuse or mixture with Secondary materials. Of the

Table 22.4. Strata classes overlying floor units of the Primary occupation.

Floor Context	Number of Floors
Primary floors reused or "contaminated" by Secondary occupation	ca. 23
Primary floors not ceramically mixed with Secondary occupation	63
Top Primary floors overlain by Secondary, but not contaminated or reused	13
Top Primary floors overlain by Primary trash	13
Top Primary floors with roofs over them	7
Lower Primary floors with Primary trash, roofs, or construction debris between them and floors above	12
Lower Primary floors immediately under other Primary floors, or with only thin artificial fill strata between them and the floors above	18

63 Primary floors not extensively reused in the Secondary, some were overlain by Secondary floors, others by Primary refuse, and some by other Primary floors. Because the stratum type overlying a floor largely determines the source of admixture for a floor, an idea can be gained of the number of floors that potentially received the greatest amounts of mixture. Floors that are sealed beneath other floors are the most reliable, because deposition of materials not originally use-associated with such floors would presumably be minor. On the other hand, the uppermost Primary floors tended to be subjected to contamination to a greater degree because they were not sealed from overlying strata. The potential for mixture is greatest where mounded trash lies on a floor, in which case the floor may display nonbehavioral material from multiple trash strata contacting its surface.

Statistical Measurement of Mixture Potential of Primary Floors

Although the stratum type overlying the floor and the position of the floor showed which strata were most likely to have nonbehavioral material on them, a further test was needed to determine the amount of mixture. First, the Primary floor sample was derived by selecting only those with decorated ceramics that had not been reused or contaminated by Secondary pottery (i.e., with factor scores of A or B). Floors with mixed Primary-Secondary assemblages were likewise eliminated. Next, the amount of mixture between these floors and any Primary strata above them was assessed by comparing the typological frequencies between floor units and the strata immediately above them. Initially, factor scores of floors were compared to those of strata immediately above them for similarity or difference in overall ceramic content. Then, a chi-square test for difference was used to compare frequencies of ceramic series between the contiguous behavioral and nonbehavioral strata. Ceramic series were the basis of measurement because individual types were often too few in number to use as separate variables. At least, it could be seen whether a floor was similar or different from overlying strata in terms of the ceramic series (including San Juan, Cibola, Tusayan, and Chuska White Ware, and White Mountain, Tsegi, and Smudged Red Ware). Utility ware was not used in the comparison. In some cases the floor sample had to be compressed by combining adjacent floors due to small samples on each. Some floors could not be compared to the overlying strata due to an absence of decorated ceramics or decorated samples too small for comparison.

We assumed that if the comparisons showed a difference using the factor analysis score and the chi-square test, then the floor material was from a different population from the stratum above it. This would suggest that if mixture had occurred, it was relatively minor and not sufficient to affect the statistical result. If the tests showed similarity, the possibility existed that the contiguous strata contained similar frequencies of ceramic series due to mixture. However, the result of similarity could also be a result of cultural activity similar to the overlying stratum, and not the result of mixture. If a fallen roof contained the same ceramic assemblage as the floor surface beneath it, for example, either the same activities were carried out on both the floor and roof, or the contents of the two had become mixed. Due to the nondiagnostic result of similarity, only the condition of difference could be used to identify floor surfaces that showed the least probability of contamination. It was also anticipated that the same comparisons would be made using lithic data, and we could compare the results of ceramic and lithic similarities and differences between the same sets of strata. This might lend strength to the conclusion of nonmixture. A limited number of strata were in fact tested both ways, and the results noted from ceramic evidence were largely substantiated with the lithic data.

Table 22.5 provides a list of the Primary floor units with decorated Primary period ceramics unmixed with Secondary materials, and the strata immediately above them. The list does not show floors that had no ceramics or floors that were contaminated by Secondary mixture. In several cases adjacent Primary floor units had to be combined for comparison to the overlying strata because the samples were otherwise too small for statistical manipulation. Of a total of 63 Primary uncontaminated floor units, 44 floor units or combinations of units were checked against the strata immediately above them. All Primary floors with Primary ceramics on them, having strata above them also containing ceramics, were tested.

To summarize Table 22.5, of the 44 floor units tested, 23 showed a difference from the overlying stratum in both factor score and chi-square test, 9 were different in either factor score or chi square but not both, and 12 were the same in both respects. The chi-square test was a more powerful measure of difference than factor scores; if factor scores were different, the chi-square test always showed a difference, whereas strata with identical factor scores sometimes produced significant differences in the chi-square test.

In sum, Secondary reuse or contamination of Primary floors could be monitored using the frequency of Mesa Verde Black-on-white intrusion onto stratigraphically Primary surfaces. After elimination of those floors, however, there remained the possibility of ceramic mixture within the Primary, which could not be monitored via typological qualitative differences. Instead, the relative frequency of ceramic series on floors was compared to the stratum above the floor, using factor scores and chi-square tests. The majority of Primary floors are different in overall typological frequency from the strata immediately over them, and if mixture did occur between those contiguous strata, it was not sufficient to alter the conclusion of essential difference. The nine floors that showed some difference have the possibility of slight mixture; the 12 that showed no comparative difference have the potential for contamination, but the result of similarity could be caused by factors other than mixture.

The actual number of differing strata (relatively uncontaminated strata) is probably greater than 23, because in some cases several superimposed floors in multiple floor rooms had to be combined for statistical treatment. In these situations, the upper floors normally seal off the lower floors from mixture by Secondary or Primary trash. Lower floors in Primary rooms are thus more reliable than upper floors, as a rule. An additional 16 floor units from Rooms 93W, 121W, 124Z, 123W, 127W, and 119W are probably reliable strata, because they are the lower Primary floor units of these rooms, separated usually only by a narrow artificial fill stratum, or with no intervening strata at all. These floors could not be tested for mixture separately because the decorated ceramics on them were either nonexistent or so few that they had to be combined with the adjacent floor for statistical results to be meaningful. If all the Primary and separate floors are counted, 39 (65%) are different from overlying strata, out of a grand total of about 60 floor units that were unaffected by Secondary intrusion.

Reconstruction of Vessels

Reconstruction of vessels may be undertaken for two interpretive purposes: to evaluate the extent of mixture between strata or to reduce sherd counts within strata to vessels and thus provide a better indicator of vessel numbers. Despite its appeal for these purposes, however, the method has limitations. For example, to reconstruct relatively complete portions of vessels, the sherd samples should be fairly large, and sherds from a single vessel must be found in close horizontal or vertical proximity to enable successful reconstruction. The sherd samples should have a high degree of reconstructibility; that is, most of the sherds should be matchable to one or another of the vessels. Vessel reconstruction does not necessarily imply anything about original use. Large portions of broken vessels may be discarded in trash and fall onto a floor surface just as easily as small sherds. Conversely, portions of a vessel originally used on an occupational surface may be removed for disposal elsewhere during cleaning activities, or may be used for example as spindle whorls or scoops. In this case, individual sherds may in fact represent the only remaining parts of vessels originally used in connection with that surface. Also, reconstruction requires a tremendous amount of time and skill. Even when the constituent sherds are not glued together, simply collecting all relevant sherd materials across many proveniences is a tedious task. Success often depends on the ability to recognize and remember vessel portions across large samples of sherds that contain numerous examples of similar ceramic types and vessel forms.

Table 22.5. Evaluation of mixing between Primary floors and the strata above. Table includes only Primary floor units that have Primary ceramics on them, not reused or contaminated by Secondary materials.

Primary Floor		FS	Strata Above	FS	Ceramic Period	Chi Square	Mixture Eval.
1W	G-5-53 H-5-54 I-5-55	A A C	N-5-52	A	P	Not significant at .05	?
1W	G-6-57 H-6-58	A A	N-6-56	A	P	Sample too small for chi square	?
7,3W	G-1-04 I-1-05	B B	F-1-02 (N-1-03)	A	P	Significant difference at .05	*?
4W	G-2-07 H-2-08 I-2-09	B B C/2	F-1-06	A	P	Samples on F-1-6 too small for chi square	*?
4W	H-3-12 I-3-13	3/F 1/A	F-3-11	B	P	Significant difference at .250 only	*?
5W	G-2-06 H-2-07	A B	Kiva Floor of 5A	C	S	Primary sealed off by Secondary strata	*
6W	G-1-01 O-1-01 L-1-04 L-2-05 L-3-06 L-5-08	A A A B A	6W C-1-02 Kiva floor 6A	A E	P S	Except for the small C-1-2 Primary floor sealed off by Secondary strata	*
30W	H-2-12	B	F-2-11 C-3-09 C-4-10	B B/F F	P P, mix P, mix	Significant difference at .10 only	?
31W	H-2-11	A	G-1-10 C-3-08 C-4-09	B/C B A	P P P	Significant difference to .025 only	*?
33W	G-1.5-14.5 S-1-14.6	A	C-4-14 F-3-13	S S	P P	Significant difference to .001	*
33W	H-2-17 L-2-17.1	A	C-5-15 F-4-15	A A	P P	Sample too small for chi square	*?
43W	G-1-10 G-1.1-10.1 G-1.2-10.2 H-1-041	B B B	B-4-09 C-2-12 B-3-13	C B B	I? P P	Significant difference at .005	*?
62W	G-1-40 H-1-41	A A	C-37-37	C	P/I	Significant difference at .025	*
62W	O-1-44 L-7-44.5	A	D-1-43	A	P	Sample too small but sealed floor	*
62W	G-2-47.5 O-2-48 L-8-48.5	A A B	CT-45-45 CT-45.55-45.5 C-47.7-47.4	A A A	P P P	No significant difference but strata sealed from above by O-1-44	*?
81W	H-1-14	A	F-2-13	A	P	Sample too small	?
82A	G-1-23 H-1-26 L-1-28 L-6-30	A C	C-9-21 C-10-22	B B	P P	Significant difference to .001	*

Table 22.5 (continued)

Primary Floor		FS	Strata Above	FS	Ceramic Period	Chi Square	Mixture Eval.
82W	G-1.5-23.5 H-2-24 I-2-24 L-17-45 L-19-48	 A A A A	C-9-21 C-10-22	B B	P P	Significant difference to .001	*
56W	H-1-05	A	F-1-04	3/F	P/I?	Sample too small	*
83W	H-1-07	A	C-1-04 C-1-05 C-1-06	9/E	S, mix	Overlain by Secondary strata – no chi square	*
84W	G-1-06 H-1-08	 A	C-1-05	2/A	P	Significant difference at .05	*
90W	H-1-12	B	C-4-11	E	S	Overlain by Secondary strata – no chi square	*
92W	L-1.1-10.1 L-1.3-10.3 L-2-11 1-2.2-13.2	 B E?		Reused P. floor	P	No chi square	*For L's only
93W	H-4-28 H-5-33 I-4-29 I-5-34 L-4-30	1/B A 2 	F-2-27.7	1/B	P	No significant difference	?
93W	H-6-36 H-7-39 L-13.4-36.4 L-14.5-36.5 L-18-7-36.7 L-7-37 I-7-37 L-19.6-41.6 L-20.7-41.7 L-9.1-43.1 L-10-.4-47.4	 A/B B A B F A A	D-2-35.5	B/C	P	Sealed floors by upper Primary rooms	*
96W	I-1-08 L-1, L-6 L-9, L-11 L-14, L-6 L-18-30	A C A/B A B	H-1-05 I-1-06	5/6 D/E	S Reused P. floor	Overlain by Secondary strata – no chi square	*
97W	H-2-14 L-3-08 L-4-08	B B	D-2-13 D-1.5-11.5 H-1-05	B E	P S	No chi square	*
98W	G-1-07 H-1-08	A A	C-1-06 B-1-05	B E	P S	No chi square	*
100W	H-1-19 H-2-22 I-1-19.4 I-1-19.5 I-2-22.4 I-2-22.5 L-4-24 L-5-25 L-7-27 L-22-46 L-8-28 L-10-30 L-13-33	1/B B/A A B A B A	C-13-18 C-12-17 and other trash in mounds	B B	P P	Several trash strata touch floor	?

Table 22.5 (continued)

Primary Floor		FS	Strata Above	FS	Ceramic Period	Chi Square	Mixture Eval.
101W	G-1-08 (H-1-09 & I-1-10 = no decorated ceramics)	B	C-2-07 C-1-06	B E	P S	Sample too small for chi square	?
102A	(C) H-1-25 (H-2-25) I-1-30 (I-2-30)	1/B	C-2-24	A	P	Significant difference at .05	*
119W	I-8-26 H-9-32 I-10-36	B B A	X-8-25	E	S	Primary strata are sealed from Secondary; sample too small for testing between floors	* for Primary strata
121W	H-1-05 L-1-06 L-1-09 L-2-07 I-1-12 L-12-23 I-4-24 L-9-18	 F E? A A	D-1-03	C	I?	No significant difference; mixing between floors not testable	? – from I-1-12 down is probably okay
123W	I-1-06 I-2-05 I-3-07 L-1-08 L-4-15	B B B	G-1-01 (G-1-09)	C	I?	No significant difference; mixing between floors not testable	?
124W	G-2-08 H-2-09 L-2-12	A B/C	Kiva floor 124A	D/E	S	Primary sealed by Secondary floor, but for small, localized contamination	*
127W	L-10-22 L-15-30 L-16-31 I-3-32 L-9-21 L-14-29 L-17-34 L-19-39	E? C E? B B/C	H-2-17 H-1-05 I-1-06	 F C	S S I/S	Primary as a whole sealed off by Secondary	*
128A	H-2-07 (H-2-05) G-1-06 L-4-09 L-5-10 L-7-12		I-1-04 I-1-05 (upper Primary floor, H-1-01, resued by Secondary)		 S S	Primary strata are sealed off by Secondary floor but for a Secondary burial	*?
129W	G-1-92.1 G-2.92.2 H-1.2-92.3 G-0.3-92.3 H-1.4-92.4 I-1.4-92.4 L-3-135	A A A	F-2.5-86.5 C-84-92 G-0.1-92.1 & mixed	A	P	Significant difference to .250 only	?

Table 22.5 (continued)

Primary Floor	FS	Strata Above	FS	Ceramic Period	Chi Square	Mixture Eval.
129W G-1-93	A	H-2-94		P	Significant difference to .250 only, but amount of mixture confined to thin D and M strata only	?
H-2-94		G-0.1-92.1				
H-2.5-94.5		D-1-92.7	A			
I-2.5-94.6		M-2-92.5				
H-2.7-94.7						
I-2.7-94.8						
L-7-143			B			
L-11-147						
L-2-101						
129W G-2-136.8		T-2-136.5	A	P	Significant difference to .05 level	*
G-2-136.9	A	O-1-136				
H-3-137	A	C-112-132	A			
H-3.5-137.5						
I-3.5-137.6	B					
L-6-142						
129W G-3-138.5		D-2-138	A	P	Sample too small, but only mixture could be with thin D strata	*
H-4-139		D-2-138				
I-4-139.1	B	T-2-136.5mix				
H-4.2-139.2		D-2.1-138.1				
H-4.2-139.3						
H-4.4-139.4						
I-4.4-139.5						
L-9-145	A/B					
L-10-146						
129W S-1-150		C-114-140	B	P	Sample too small, but sealed from upper mixing; small mix with C-114-140 possible	*
S-2-151						
H-5-153						
I-5-154						
G-4-152.5						
L-14-152						
L-15-155						
L-16-156						
L-17-157						
L-18-158						
130W H-2-09	A	H-1-05	E	S	Except for slight contamination of H-2-09 by Secondary, all are Primary, and uncontaminated	*?
O-1-10	F	I-1-06	E			
L-6-18	B					
L-7-21	A					
L-8-22	B					
L-10-26	A					
L-11-27	A					
L-12-28						
L-15-31						
L-16-32	B					
L-18-34						
L-19-35						
L-20-36						
L-20-36						
L-20.1-36.1						
Through						
L-20.49-36.49						
L-21-37	B					
L-24-42						
L-26-44						

P = Primary; I = Intermediate; S = Secondary; FS = Factor Score
* = both factor score and chi square indicate difference between floor unit and overlying strata
*? = either factor score or chi square show difference
? = both factor score and chi square show no difference, and contamination by other Primary strata is possible

With these limitations, reconstruction of Salmon Primary vessels hardly seems suitable to the interpretive purpose. Sample sizes on occupational surfaces tend to be small, or at least extremely variable from one floor to the next, and there is little inherent reconstructibility present in these samples. This suggests that reconstruction would not significantly alter the sherd count because most sherds were not matchable within strata, and matching did not succeed in restoring substantial portions of vessels.

As a test of the variation between raw sherd counts and sherd counts reduced through reconstruction, both were compared by ceramic series for a group of 20 Primary floors and roofs using the chi-square statistic. In four cases the raw count remained unchanged (i.e., no reconstruction was possible). In the remainder of the strata the chi-square difference between sherd count and the count reduced by reconstruction was minimal. In no case was the chi-square value found to exceed the .05 level of significance. In fact, in only one instance (81W, F-2-13) did the difference prove to reach the .250 level of significance. That is, either reduction of the sherd count by reconstruction was minimal, or, where somewhat more successful, it did not affect the quantitative relationships between pottery series. Even where sherd counts were reduced somewhat by matching, the process appears to have affected all ceramic series more or less equally. The important point is that reconstruction never altered the essential numerical relationship between decorated ceramic series, which is one of the major analytical groupings used in distributional interpretation.

The fact that 20 Primary behavioral stratigraphic units (mostly floors) were tested from a representative sample of rooms across the site and none showed a significant change in the relations between ceramic series confirms the lack of reconstructibility inherent in Primary behavioral assemblages. A test of sherds versus reconstructed vessels was not conducted for trash strata, but these appear to have the same low reconstruction rate as the behavioral strata. Priesnitz (personal communication, 1979) confirmed that the multidimensional scaling patterns for Primary trash are practically identical whether considering raw count or minimum vessel count. In light of these results, a major reconstruction effort with the goal of using vessel counts rather than sherd counts for distributional data manipulation would not be worthwhile.

Various factors, such as room cleaning at the close of the Primary period or reuse of some Primary floors and redeposition of Primary refuse in other rooms by Secondary occupants, may account for the extreme rarity of whole vessels, or even restorable vessels from the Primary occupation. Therefore, whereas the vessel ideally should be the analytical unit rather than the sherd, the vessel as a unit of comparison could not be used uniformly as a measure of comparison across Primary strata. The low and variable rate of reconstruction of the samples would make conclusions based on hypothesized vessel counts more error prone than conclusions based on sherd counts alone, because the latter do not carry the implication that the original number of whole vessels in use on a living surface is a known quantity.

These conclusions do not hold for sherd sample populations in the Secondary occupation, however, for which samples are much larger, and a substantial number of sherds can be shown to fit to Mesa Verde Black-on-white vessels, reducing the count of sherds considerably. The reconstruction efforts with Mesa Verde Black-on-white pottery undertaken by Suzanne Bradley and Penny Whitten have shown the feasibility of this approach in several Secondary rooms. The reason for the greater reconstructibility of Secondary ceramics may be found in the conditions of deposition and breakage in the Secondary occupation, which resulted in many vessels remaining intact, or at least with the fragments within close proximity in horizontal or vertical space. In sum, whereas successful reconstruction efforts have been made for the Secondary occupation, the lack of success in the Primary reconstruction precludes using the vessel as the unit of analysis for the Primary assemblage. Reconstruction in the Primary succeeded only in reducing the redundancy of the sherd count but did not alter any inherent quantitative relationships.

Even without consistent reconstruction of vessels across Primary strata, limited reconstruction could still be used to measure mixing between contiguous strata, because restoration of vessel portions from sherds provenienced to several strata provides an indication of the amount of mixture between those strata. Priesnitz (1979:122) undertook limited reconstruction for this purpose using several Primary strata in Rooms 62W, 81W, 82W, and 84W, in the area of the Tower Kiva. Priesnitz used two methods of expressing mixture: either as the number of sherds in a stratum that match with at least one sherd in another stratum, or as the number of vessel or vessel portions that contain sherds from different strata. The former method tends to maximize mixing, whereas the latter tends to minimize it. Both methods of expression were used to assess mixture in these four rooms (Priesnitz 1979: 122).

Mixing between Primary strata was extremely variable in this sample. Based on portions of vessels that cut across adjacent strata, the amount of mixture varied from 2 to 80 percent (Priesnitz 1979:123). The average percentage of vessels found in more than one stratum may be calculated from these data at about 26 percent for the 13 strata studied. There did not appear to be any major difference between behavioral and nonbehavioral strata in terms of their mixture with other strata. The mixture observed was ascribed to an inextricable combination of cultural, natural, and excavational processes. From this limited reconstruction effort, it is possible to say only that mixture of floor-related sherds with overlying Primary roofs and trash is a persistent problem. Because it is variable across rooms and strata, it is hard to extrapolate an index of mixture to the Primary occupation as a whole. It was not possible to check the mixture on the more than 60 Primary floors at the site; the four rooms checked by Priesnitz were thus presumed to be representative.

All floors (and one roof) in the test sample were overlain by Primary trash, a situation conducive to mixture, so the degree of mixing in these four rooms may be greater than at least some other Primary floors. On the other hand, many other Primary floors are sealed off from contamination by trash, because they do not contain trash above them. In cases where Primary floors lie beneath a Secondary floor, or below the uppermost Primary floor, mixture with Primary trash was likely minimal. Sample sizes in these cases are no larger or more reconstructible than for floors with trash or fallen roofs on them, but at least they may be less subject to contamination by Primary trash.

Conclusions

In sum, ceramic mixing, as judged by limited reconstruction across several Primary strata, was variable from stratum to stratum and room to room. Much of this variation is probably due to the nature of the strata overlying the floor (whether trash, a fallen roof, another Primary floor, or Secondary strata). Also, in spite of such mixture, statistical comparisons using factor scores and chi-square tests, in conjunction with evaluation of stratigraphic context, suggest that about 65 percent of Primary floor units were different in content from the strata overlying them in terms of typological frequencies. The remainder were similar to overlying strata either because of mixture or because they represent similar behavioral complexes.

With this in mind, the sample of behavioral strata used in distributional analysis could have been limited to only the best or least contaminated Primary floors. Floors contaminated by Secondary ceramics were easily monitored and excluded. However, mixture between Primary strata was more difficult to evaluate. Because such mixture formed a continuum in terms of the potential (and actual) mixture of Primary sherds onto Primary floors, no arbitrary limitation on the amount of acceptable mixture could be made. Instead, the distributional analysis included all Primary floors, but the interpretation of the resultant patterning took into account the qualifying variables of associational reliability as well as the size of the ceramic samples for each of the floor units.

TEMPORAL VARIATION WITHIN THE PRIMARY OCCUPATION

Temporal control is a necessary prerequisite to any synchronic spatial study. To understand ceramic use during the Primary occupation, it was therefore essential to ensure that all rooms and strata compared for functional-social aspects were contemporaneous. Temporal control is a relative concept, and the ideal of assuring contemporaneity within 5–10 years may be unattainable given the methods currently available. Even if this were achieved, the resultant population in terms of strata and sample sizes within an absolutely contemporaneous framework would probably be too small for statistical treatment. Initial time control was achieved by means of cross-dating using the known time spans of ceramic types as dated elsewhere (e.g., Mesa Verde Black-on-white dated to AD 1200–1300), as well as by factor analysis, which yielded the ceramic assemblages assignable to the Primary, Intermediate, and Secondary periods within the site.

The Primary occupation, which is securely dated by means of dendrochronology and archaeomagnetic dating, is also the earliest period stratigraphically. Large-scale construction of Salmon occurred around AD 1090, according to the clustering of tree-ring cutting dates. The end of the Primary occupation is indicated by construction changes in the pueblo and by archaeomagnetic dates between AD 1120 and 1130.

The ensuing discussion represents an attempt to isolate more precise periods within the 30-year Chacoan occupation. The ceramic differences between rooms may be a result of spatial or microtemporal factors, as well as the problem of sampling errors produced by small ceramic samples. Initial analysis of intrasite ceramic distributions (by pottery series) by Priesnitz (1979) and a study of room block differences during the Primary occupation by Franklin both revealed substantial spatial differences in the distributions of pottery series between rooms and room blocks. Thus, it is desirable to control the temporal variable to a finer degree, to ensure that observed spatial variation within the Primary is in fact synchronic variation, and not due to microtemporal variation. This problem was approached through investigation and integration of the following lines of evidence: absolute dating (tree-ring cutting dates and archaeomagnetic date ranges), comparison of Primary to pre-Primary (subfloor) ceramics, study of stratigraphic sequences within rooms containing a series of strata within the Primary, comparison of strata types (e.g. floors vs. trash), and analysis of variance comparing stratigraphic sequence differences within rooms to the variation between rooms.

Stratigraphic Sequences of Rooms with Multiple Primary Strata

Each Primary room was examined for evidence of multiple (i.e., sequential) strata, and the percentages of San Juan White Ware relative to the total decorated assemblage were calculated for each of these strata. A number of conclusions were reached. First, 11 rooms contained Primary materials, but contained no more than two strata within the Primary and pre-Primary periods. These rooms are 13P, 5W, 51W, 53W, 56W, 64W, 83W, 86W, 90W, 92W, 96W, and 98W. Second, 29 rooms were found to contain a stratigraphic sequence of two or more Primary strata within the Primary occupation. Many of these rooms did not have a very long sequence; often the identified sequence consisted of pre-Primary or subfloor strata and the combined Primary floor units. Of these 29 rooms, 16 showed some evidence of a percentage increase in San Juan ceramics through time, from the pre-Primary through the Primary. These rooms are 2BW, 1W, 4W, 6W, 31W, 33W, 82W, 82A, 84W, 97W, 100W, 119W, 121W, 121Z, 124W, 124Z, 127W, 129W, and 130W.

Because of small sample sizes, statistical treatment was not feasible in most cases; even percentages can be misleading when applied to some of the sample sizes in these strata. However, it is clear that a considerable number of the rooms (more than half) with multiple Primary strata demonstrate a trend toward increased San Juan ceramics within the Primary period (and including pre-Primary subfloor strata in some rooms). Larger percentages of San Juan ceramics are interpreted here to indicate slightly later dates for these strata. Not only do 16 rooms show such a trend, but in 12 of them the difference in the percentage of San Juan ceramics of the total decorated assemblage exceeds 20 percent. Furthermore, these rooms were found to have a wide spatial distribution across the site. Rooms that show this trend are not confined to any one part of the site, but include back-wall areas, the East and West Wings, and even test trenches (2BW). Included are the rooms at Salmon with some of the best in situ sequences within the Primary deposits (31W, 33W, 82W, 100W, and 129W). Of the 16 rooms, 8 also showed a vertical trend in factor scores from A to B or C. The distribution of rooms with a definable San Juan trend cuts across room blocks, construction periods, and front-to-back placement of rooms, and is considered an indication of its widespread nature.

Ten rooms have more than one floor level assigned to the Primary occupation with decorated ceramics on them (Table 22.6). Rooms 119W, 121W, 123W, and 128A each contain fewer than 13 sherds on Primary floors, and therefore were eliminated from consideration as evidence for temporal change between floors. Of the remaining six rooms with superimposed Primary floors, three rooms (1W, 4W, and 129W) displayed a trend toward increasing San Juan White Ware (and closely correlated White Mountain Red Ware) from bottom to top Primary floors (Table 22.7). No discernible trend could be seen between the Primary floors in Rooms 33W, 62W, or 93W.

Analysis of superimposed Primary floors provides the same general picture as the analysis of all stacked Primary strata; that is, roughly half the rooms examined show a trend toward increased San Juan White Ware through time.

In summary, about half of the rooms with a multiple-stratum sequence during the Primary occupation demonstrated a trend toward increased San Juan ceramic use through time (16 of 29 rooms). The remainder, however, showed no consistent trend.

Table 22.6. Salmon rooms with more than one primary floor.

Room	Number of Floors
1W	2
4W	2
33W	2
62W	3
93W	2
121W	2
123W	2
128A	2
119W	2
129W	5

Table 22.7. Combined percentages of San Juan White Ware and White Mountain Red Ware compared to all decorated in floor units in rooms with multiple primary floors.

Room	Floor Unit	Combined San Juan White Ware and White Mountain Red Ware Percentages	
1W	Lowest	53.3%	Trend toward San Juan
	Upper	88.2%	
4W	Lowest	57.1%	Trend toward San Juan
	Upper	76.8%	
33W	Lowest	50.0%	
	Upper	39.7%	
62W	Lowest	69.2%	
	Middle	68.2%	
	Upper	63.6%	
93W	Lowest	41.9%	
	Upper	33.3%	
129W	Lowest	36.4%	
	Next	33.0%	Definite trend toward San Juan
	Next	53.0%	
	Next	79.2%	
	Upper	70.0%	

Rooms 121W, 123W, 128A and 119W also have multiple Primary floors, but samples on individual floors are too small (13 or less) for stratigraphic comparisons.

That is, room sequences showed either a San Juan trend or no trend at all. Combined with this is the widespread location of rooms demonstrating such a trend, which implies that it was a site-wide phenomenon. Explaining the absence of a pattern in some of these rooms is difficult. Differences probably relate to the length of time represented by Primary accumulations (different for almost every room), patterns of trash deposition, and the degree of mixing between adjacent Primary strata.

Comparions of Pre-Primary to Primary Strata

Another way to fine-tune chronology is to compare subfloor strata (pre-Primary) to the Primary levels associated with the actual use of the room for habitation or trash disposal (Table 22.8a). A chi-square test for difference compressed the data somewhat (see Table 22.8b), due to small sample sizes for some series from the pre-Primary strata. Chuska and Tusayan White Ware were combined, as well as all the red ware. The result was a value of 19.46 (df = 3), a significant difference at the .001 level. However, the relative amount of San Juan ceramics did not differ from Primary to pre-Primary. The pre-Primary contained a greater than expected frequency of Cibola White Ware, and less than the expected frequency of Chuska White Ware, Tusayan White Ware, and red ware. This difference may be fortuitous considering the sample size problems encountered in the pre-Primary, even when series were combined (as in Table 22.8b). Nevertheless, the comparison indicates that the general nature of the above-floor Primary ceramic assemblage was quite similar to the pre-Primary construction levels, especially in the preponderance of San Juan ceramics. The use of San Juan ceramic material apparently began even with the construction of the pueblo. This should come as no surprise, because the nearby sites of ENM 5107 and 5108 on the terrace west of Salmon also produced a mixture of San Juan and intrusive ceramics at about the same time period. All pottery series present in the Primary occupation are also represented in the pre-Primary strata. The differences noted above, with pre-Primary relatively higher in Cibola and lower in other intrusive frequencies, may relate to the construction or supervision of construction by Chacoans, with a relative absence of other intrusive ceramics until the site was completely occupied and administratively tied to the larger Chacoan trading network. Even this conclusion must be viewed skeptically because Whalley's (1980) work with other sites along the San Juan suggests that there were abundant intrusive ceramics at many sites even before the construction of Salmon Ruin at AD 1090. In other words, an incipient Chacoan trading network was probably already in operation in the San Juan Valley prior to the initial construction of Salmon.

Table 22.8a. Comparison of pre-Primary to Primary occupation ceramics.

	Pre-Primary (Below Lowest Floor)		Primary (Lowest Floor and Above)	
Period	n	%	n	%
San Juan	250	68.9	4600	68.7
Cibola	87	24.0	1185	17.7
Chusk	16	4.4	381	5.7
Tusayan	2	0.6	81	1.2
White Mtn Red Ware	3	0.8	143	2.1
Tsegi Orange Ware	3	0.8	87	1.3
Smudged Red	2	0.6	209	3.1
Total	363	100.1	6686	99.8

Table 22.8b. Condensed version of above table.

Strata Group	San Juan	Cibola	Chuska-Tusayan	All Red Ware	Total
Pre-Primary	250	87	18	8	363
Primary	4600	1185	462	439	6686
Total	4850	1272	480	447	7049

Chi-square = 19.46, df – 3; significant at the .001 level.

An attempt was also made to compare pre-Primary to Primary floor units for percentages of decorated ceramic series on a room-by-room basis. Statistical comparisons were not possible in most instances due to small sample sizes from the subfloor levels, but percentages for most series were approximately the same in pre-Primary and Primary floor strata in most rooms. At the analytical level of ceramic series, then, the pre-Primary does not seem greatly different from the Primary.

Comparison of Strata Types

Primary strata fall into three major categories: floor units (G, H, I, and associated pits, L), trash (C and M), and roofs (F, E, and N). Other strata types (e.g., construction debris, T, and artificial fill, D) account for only a small amount of the Primary ceramics. The major strata groups have temporal implications, because Primary floors tend to be stratigraphically lower (although not exclusively so) than most trash strata. Primary roofs are always stratigraphically above floors. Hence, a comparison of all Primary floors as a unit to strata types found above them should provide additional temporal information. Comparisons of Primary floors to roofs as a whole were not possible because the roof category includes a number of distinct entities such as actual structural roofs, unstructured roofing material, platforms, roof fall, and construction debris. However, Primary floors can be compared to Primary trash layers. Table 22.9 provides the total ceramic series counts for all Primary floors and Primary trash strata from limited-attribute data; pre-Primary levels are also included for comparison. A chi-square test of the data between floors and trash exceeded the value for the .001 significance level. Primary floors exceeded the expected values for Tusayan, White Mountain, Tsegi, and Smudged Red Ware (all intrusive ceramics). San Juan and Chuska Series pottery exceeded the expected values in trash levels. There was essentially no difference between trash and floors in terms of Cibola Series ceramics. Primary trash deposits contained relatively more San Juan Series decorated sherds than Primary floors, which supports the hypothesis of increased use of San Juan ceramics through time during the Primary.

Analysis of Variance

The ANOVA computer program was used to determine whether the stratigraphic position or spatial location of pottery was the more important variable. An analysis of the 10 rooms found to have a stratigraphic trend toward increased San Juan ceramics revealed a significant interaction between

Table 22.9. Total ceramics for all Primary floors and trash strata.

	Primary Floors (Units)		Primary Trash		Pre-Primary	
	n	%	n	%	n	%
San Juan	1470	65.1	1874	66.7	250	68.9
Cibola	430	19.1	534	19.0	87	24.0
Chuska	122	5.4	193	6.9	16	4.4
Tusayan	39	1.7	16	0.6	2	0.6
White Mtn Red Ware	76	3.4	77	2.7	3	0.8
Tsegi Orange	43	1.9	30	1.1	3	0.8
Smudged Red	77	3.4	84	3.0	2	0.5
Total	2257	100.0	2808	100.0	363	100.1

Note: Data derived from ceramic limited-attribute study program (CLAP).

types (San Juan vs. intrusive) and stratigraphic position (to the .052 significance level). That is, there is consistent stratigraphic change in the relationship of San Juan to intrusive ceramics within the Primary strata of the 10 rooms selected for comparison.

Percentage data on San Juan Series pottery from the same 10 rooms were again used to test whether vertical (stratigraphic) or horizontal (spatial) variability was greater. The mean vertical difference within rooms in San Juan White Ware pottery clearly exceeded the mean spatial difference between rooms in the sample, whether across lowest Primary or across upper Primary strata. This suggests that vertical (time) change in San Juan percentages is at least as important as horizontal (spatial) variability in the amount of pottery of this series. It must be recognized, however, that the vertical change measured here would be the maximum, because rooms were chosen that already displayed some evidence of a temporal change within the Primary. Further, in the rooms selected, the uppermost Primary level was compared to the lowest Primary level; adjacent Primary strata in between would not display differences of as great a magnitude—it would be gradational through the succession of Primary strata. This comparison thus produced the maximum vertical contrast between San Juan percentages from the Primary occupation. Although this situation would not hold for many individual rooms, it nevertheless indicates that time change in San Juan pottery may be an important diagnostic variable in the Primary occupation.

It is also interesting to note that the difference across the lower Primary strata is greater than in the upper Primary strata. The increasing uniformity of Primary strata through time relates to the increasing dominance of the San Juan Series to the exclusion of the several intrusive ceramic series. Carried into the post-Chacoan period, after AD 1120, the trend resulted in strata with almost exclusively San Juan ceramic content. In terms of local decorated ceramics, there was greater heterogeneity across the earliest Primary strata (floors and the earliest trash) than in the later Primary strata.

Conclusions

Several lines of evidence support the hypothesis that the use of local (San Juan) ceramics increased through the Primary period (AD 1090–1120). Although this pattern was not found in every Primary room, the trend is indicated in a large proportion of rooms spread widely across the site. Thus, the pattern is not confined to any one segment of the pueblo.

The change toward more San Juan ceramics must be kept in mind when assessing spatial variability and interpreting the associated social or functional interaction. Stratigraphic correlation of multiple Primary strata between rooms is extremely difficult to attain; there is thus no guarantee that the lowest Primary floors are all contemporaneous. However, in addition to the temporal control for the Primary occupation (30–35 years) attained through factor analysis and stratigraphic evaluation, spatial evaluations in the Primary were further controlled by stratum type (floors, trash, roofs) and relative stratigraphic position. Even so, microtemporal change must be considered as a variable in the spatial patterning of Primary occupation ceramics.

DECORATED CERAMICS IN THE PRIMARY OCCUPATION

The Primary assemblage from Salmon contains a wide variety of ceramic types from several major

Puebloan traditions (regional series). For this reason, the first Salmon occupation is here termed Primary because it was not exclusively or even dominantly Chacoan. There are 17 major white ware types and 9 major red ware types in the Primary assemblage; several additional types are present in small amounts only. These types are grouped into several major Southwestern series or traditions: San Juan White Ware, Cibola White Ware, Chuska White Ware, and Tusayan White Ware, in decreasing order of frequency. The red ware types belong to four series: White Mountain Red Ware, Mogollon Smudged Red Ware, Tsegi Orange Ware, and San Juan Red Ware, in approximate decreasing order. Utility ceramics are San Juan Gray Ware, Cibola Gray Ware, and Chuska Gray Ware, including six recognized plain gray and corrugated utility types.

One of the most interesting aspects of the Primary occupation is the great variability in its decorated (and to a somewhat lesser extent, undecorated) ceramics. Whereas ceramic variation in the Secondary assemblage occurs mainly at the subtype level or the attribute level within the ubiquitous Mesa Verde Black-on-white, in the Primary occupation, major differences can be seen at the analytical levels of type and series. The rather large scale and inclusive analytical units of types and series do not reduce each of the Primary types into its constituent attribute clusters, and certainly variation on an attribute level must be recognized in all ceramic types. However, sample sizes for most of the intrusive types in the Primary are too limited for a full assessment of their internal variability. Attribute-level evaluations of internal variability were made, however, for the better sampled San Juan types Mancos and McElmo Black-on-white. Further, these San Juan types were divided into several stylistic variants: wide-line (Sosi style), hatched panels (Dogoszhi style), fine-line hatched panels (Aztec variety), banded, and special or miscellaneous, which were monitored during rough-sort and limited-attribute analysis. Whereas the existence of variability on the attribute or subtype level for each ceramic type cannot be denied, there is no assurance that a reductionist philosophy would be more satisfactory for the problems at hand, which involve differential use of ceramics from spatially distinct sources. For this purpose, the attributes of vessel form and tempering material were monitored during limited-attribute analysis, along with the data on series, type, and ware. In the Salmon Primary, these data classes exhibit great variation, not only in terms of geographical origin, but as we shall see, in differential spatial distribution within the pueblo.

The great variability in Primary pottery is due largely to importation of ceramics (both decorated and utility) from all over the northern Southwest. Geographic regions represented by the ceramic assemblage include the various branches of the Puebloan—San Juan–Mesa Verde, Cibola-Chaco, and Kayenta-Tusayan—as well as ceramics from the Little Colorado and northern Mogollon. White ware and red ware from the San Juan and Kayenta-Tusayan areas are both present at Salmon.

Of the four white ware series present during the Primary occupation, all but the San Juan Series were manufactured elsewhere and brought into the site. Indeed, there is some evidence that even a portion of the San Juan Mancos and McElmo Black-on-white in the Primary period was being made somewhere to the north and imported into the Salmon vicinity (see Wilson 1985; Chapter 27). All of the four red ware traditions or ceramic series present during the Primary occupation were intrusive. There is no evidence that any red ware pottery was produced at Salmon, nor would that have been likely from what is known of the clays in the area. There is some evidence from refiring and temper analyses that the majority of San Juan decorated and utility types could have been, and likely were, made in or near Salmon Ruin (see Wilson 1985; Chapter 27). These locally made San Juan white and utility types comprise the vast majority of Primary occupation ceramics. Fully 72 percent of the decorated and 81 percent of the utility ceramics are San Juan White Ware and Gray Ware, respectively. There is also evidence that ceramic manufacturing implements such as polishing stones and hematite were localized to high Mancos and McElmo Black-on-white contexts during the Primary occupation. Space does not permit a complete discussion of source area analyses at Salmon, but there is evidence for ceramic manufacture during the Primary occupation, but only for the majority of the utility ware (San Juan Gray Ware with crushed rock temper) and most but not all of the San Juan White Ware types of the Primary occupation, Mancos and McElmo Black-on-white.

All other types and series were brought into Salmon from other points of origin. The identification of the three series of white ware and all four series of red ware as intrusive at Salmon is based on detailed comparisons to major literature sources for typological identification as well as on paste and temper studies by various individuals. The studies of tempering materials by Helene Warren and others are summarized elsewhere in this volume; refiring tests of utility pottery have been reported by Franklin (1979d). Petrographic analyses of Cibola and a sample of San Juan White Ware types by Warren, and refiring analyses of Cibola and Chuska White Ware and Gray Ware by Arany (1978) and Franklin (1979b and 1979c), have lent support to the conclusions about geographic origins derived from surface and decorative attributes. Comparative source area work by Warren (1967) and Windes (1977) also helped to confirm areas of manufacture for intrusive ceramics. Also, a microscopic identification of tempers was always made during routine limited-attribute analysis. In other words, the identification of the ceramic types and series, whether local or intrusive, is based on the examination of multiple ceramic attributes, and on technical studies of ceramic materials. In most cases it is clear that the intrusive ceramics could not have been produced in the Salmon vicinity, given the nature of the raw materials (paste clays and tempering materials) known to be available in the immediate vicinity (Wilson 1985; Chapter 27; Franklin, Chapter 26)

In essence, then, both the decorated and utility assemblages of the Primary can be grouped into two major categories: locally made (most San Juan White Ware and probably all San Juan Gray Ware with crushed rock temper) versus intrusive (all other ceramic types and series). Although quantitatively locally produced ceramics are the most frequent, as might be expected, qualitatively there are many more intrusive types and series than represented by locally made pottery, which is confined essentially to the San Juan ceramic tradition.

The magnitude of this basic dichotomy has been made evident during the statistical manipulations of Primary data. Factor analysis, used mainly for temporal assessment, also produced notable contrasts within Primary occupation series and types. The contrast between ceramic series, especially between local San Juan and intrusive decorated ceramics, accounts for much of the variation in ceramic associations. This was also noted in the correlation matrices used as a basis for factor analysis; all intrusive ceramics have high mutual correlations in terms of strata of association. That is, all intrusive ceramics, in general, tended to be found together, especially Cibola, Chuska, and Tusayan White Ware and Tsegi and Smudged Red Ware. Whalley (1980) has noted that intrusive pottery types also tend to be associated with one another at other Chacoan outliers on the San Juan and La Plata Rivers.

Most red ware is also highly correlated (in association) with the intrusive white ware. White Mountain Red Ware however appears to have operated independently of the importation of the other intrusive ceramics in general; types of this red ware series tend to be associated about equally with the local and intrusive groups. They may not have reached Salmon in the same manner, and after the Chacoan occupation, types of this series, especially Wingate and St. Johns Polychromes, continued to be imported while all other intrusive pottery declined sharply, after the end of the Chacoan occupation at about AD 1130. As has been suggested elsewhere (Franklin, Chapters 18–27), the dissemination of White Mountain Red Ware to the San Juan region appears to have been largely independent of, and clearly outlived, the Chacoan trading network.

San Juan Red Ware types (La Plata, Deadmans Black-on-red) produced in the Four Corners area and beyond to the north are so few in number that their association with other Primary types and series could not be assessed. For the same reason, they have not been included in distributional analysis.

The generally high degree of association among the Primary intrusive types (possibly excluding White Mountain Red Ware) suggests that they entered the pueblo as a complex, and perhaps functioned in equivalent behavioral contexts after arrival. A discussion of the processes by which intrusive ceramics reached Salmon is beyond the scope of this chapter, but the presence of documented trade routes between Chaco Canyon and its various outliers certainly facilitated interregional exchange (Hayes et al. 1981; Kincaid 1983; Morenon 1975, 1977; Powers et al. 1983). Additional information on the San Juan and intrusive ceramics for sites in the San Juan and La Plata drainages is provided in Whalley (1980). Salmon Ruin itself is connected to Chaco Canyon via Kutz Canyon, Twin Angels Pueblo, and the North Road to Pueblo Alto—this relatively direct route, giving access to Chaco Canyon over a distance of approximately 45 miles, provided goods and services to Salmon, and from there to Aztec Ruin on the Animas River. It seems highly likely that the Cibola Series ceramics at Salmon arrived from Chaco Canyon (and beyond) via that route. Not only can Cibola Series ceramics be accounted for in this way, but most of the other nonlocal ceramics in the Salmon Primary occupation are also found as intrusive ceramics in Chaco Canyon (Windes 1980). Similar ceramic types and series are also present in collections of ceramics taken from the North Road (Franklin 1975a, 1975b; Morenon 1977). Thus, most of the intrusive complex at Salmon could have been obtained through the Chacoan trading network, or at least as an indirect result of increased regional interaction as initiated or augmented by the existence of the Chacoan exchange system and its outlying "colonies."

Within Salmon Ruin, the spatial distribution of the local and intrusive decorated and utility wares carries two primary implications. First, some portions of the Primary population may have had greater access to or possessed more intrusive ceramics than others. Concentrations of intrusive ceramics, quantitatively dominated at Salmon by Cibola White Ware, probably marked areas of intensive Chacoan (and possibly high-status) activity. Second, the contrast between local and intrusive ceramics should thus shed light on cultural affiliation, on differences in access to rare and Chacoan-derived ceramic items (status), and on specialized functions with which rarer ceramic items are likely to have been associated.

Local ceramics versus several intrusive ceramic series can thus be compared in spatial distribution by room, by stratigraphic type, by groupings of rooms into blocks and suites, and by inferred function(s) of rooms. The basic unit of analysis is the frequency and percentage of the several ceramic series (decorated and utility) across Primary strata. A similar spatial assessment was contemplated at the analytical level of the pottery type, or even variety, but the small frequencies of many intrusive types in strata made this impossible. Consequently, the more inclusive unit of the seven decorated and three utility ware series (all series except San Juan Red Ware) serves as the basis for comparison.

Identification of Blocks and Suites

The settlement pattern of the Chacoan occupation at Salmon Ruin may be divided into a number of blocks of contiguous rooms localized in different parts of the pueblo. Several of these blocks consist of one or two suites, defined as front-to-back alignments of rooms (plaza-facing to back wall) that are interconnected by doorways. Suites are therefore a special class of room blocks with three to four rooms that tend to become smaller and narrower toward the pueblo's back wall. The consistent arrangement of room sizes and positions, as well as the front-to-back connectivity within suites, implies that they may have served as residential units. It is tempting to think of suites as residences for extended families, or at least some form of kin-based social unit.

The definition of a suite of rooms is similar to that used by Rohn (1965:65–66, 1971), in that they contain approximately four rooms, with connectivity between them via doorways, but access to other suites is restricted. Each suite contains a large dwelling space with a hearth, and sometimes has rooms that functioned as either sleeping quarters or storage rooms toward the back of the pueblo. Unlike Rohn's suites at Mesa Verde, however, the Chacoan suites are not arranged into abbreviated "Prudden-units," each with its own plaza. At Salmon, there is none of the evident aggregation of plaza-suite units that is visible at Mesa Verde, where all suites share a common large plaza in the center. Instead of surrounding an open space, Salmon Primary occupation suites form front-to-back alignments of interconnected rooms. However, the basic criterion of contiguous rooms of varying sizes (and function) united through access routes is still the defining characteristic of the suite. And, like Rohn, the assumption is made that such units relate to a societal segment of the community, probably integrated by kinship.

Other blocks of rooms that are not considered suites (e.g., the Tower Kiva area, Rooms 93W–102C, and Rooms 119W–129W), however, form contiguous units presumably not related to residence. Blocks of this type often contain evidence of special functions. Figure 22.2 and Table 22.10 illustrate where these blocks and suites are located, and the individual rooms assigned to them.

Ceramic Differences between Blocks and Suites

Ceramic differences between room blocks for the Primary occupation were revealed using a series of preliminary statistical analyses, followed by more detailed comparisons for all Primary trash and behavioral strata via cluster analysis, thus delineating associations between room blocks, rooms, and strata based on a dissimilarity matrix. Because there are few room blocks or portions of room blocks of the Primary occupation for which we have information, the data are confined enough to be handled manually; when dealing with individual rooms containing Primary data in situ (n = 38) or with all Primary pottery types, however, the database becomes unmanageable using hand-calculator techniques. About all that is attainable, then, on this basis, is a comparison of rooms lumped into blocks, and pottery types combined into series.

Because the early multidimensional scaling results of Priesnitz (1979) indicated that ceramic differences might be organized by room blocks, and because room blocks (or transects) are an architecturally logical way for ceramics to be patterned, some additional room block to series comparisons were attempted. Here, Primary strata data were chosen by factor score and by R. Adams's evaluation of context as actually being Primary. Data for room blocks represent decorated series totals (minus plain white sherds) for all Primary strata in the room

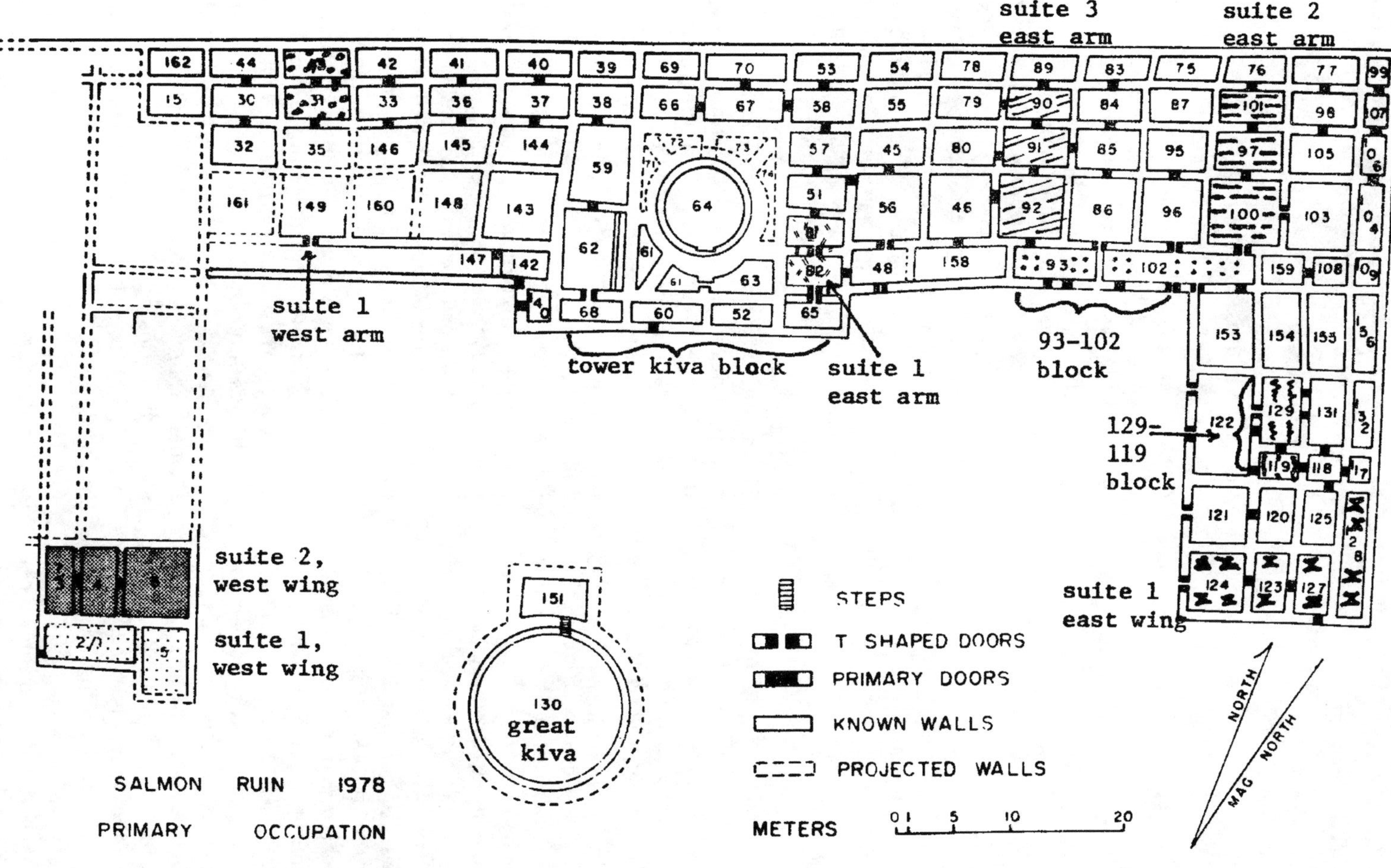

Figure 22.2. Salmon map showing Primary rooms and suites studied during ceramic analysis.

Table 22.10. Rooms grouped into suites. Suites are front-to-back alignments or ranges of rooms interconnected by doorways. Some of these suites are incomplete due to lack of excavation of some rooms; only excavated rooms are included here.

West Wing	
Suite 1	5W, 1W
Suite 2	6W, 4W*, 7/3W
East Wing	
Suite 1	124W, Z, 123W, 127W, 128W?*
Suite 2	119W, 129W
West Arm	
Suite 1	31W, 43W
East Arm	
Suite 1	82W, A, 81W
Suite 2	100W, 97W, 101W
Suite 3	92W*, 91W, 90W*

*This room was not used in cluster analysis of wares and vessel forms due to lack of comparable lithic data on floors.

block, including behavioral and trash strata types; no pre-Primary floors were included. By combining data between rooms in a block and between trash and behavioral strata types, we assume that these differences are relatively minor compared to the differences between room blocks.

There seems to be some justification for combining trash and behavioral levels during the Primary occupation for this kind of a general comparison. Several room blocks were compared internally for a significant difference between Primary behavioral and trash strata. All Primary trash strata were combined within these blocks and compared to all behavioral strata within the same blocks. A Spearman's rank correlation test indicated that trash and behavioral strata types were highly correlated within all room blocks except the 93W-102C block; correlations were all above .83 with this one exception. A chi-square test for differences showed the same thing in reverse as chi-square values tended to be low; four of six blocks showed no significant difference between trash and behavioral strata that exceeded the .05 level. Therefore, the general impression is that Primary trash and behavioral strata, at least when grouped by room block, are not significantly different (by chi square) or are somewhat highly correlated (Spearman's correlation). In addition, Priesnitz has determined that for the 81W, 82W, and 62W room block at least, reconstructed vessels often cut across several stratigraphic units. Whereas no objective measure of the extent of mixing has been developed, the evident mixing across Primary strata and between behavioral and trash strata in the three rooms tested would be another reason to combine all the Primary strata within the rooms for the purposes of a general comparison.

Variability in the Sample

The range of variability in decorated series between room blocks is provided in Table 22.11 and in Figures 22.3 and 22.4. The rank order of these series in each room block is approximately the same: San Juan is the most frequent, followed by Cibola, Chuska-Tusayan, and minor amounts of red ware. Except for the 93W–102C block, San Juan Series pottery comprises more than 50 percent of the assemblage from all room blocks, usually in the range of 60–80 percent of the decorated complex. Intrusive pottery (Cibola, Chuska, Tusayan, and the red ware) as a group exceeds the San Juan Series in only one block (93W–102C). Red ware amounts are always minor, and even when combined do not equal the percentages of Cibola or San Juan in any room block. These conclusions are not necessarily true for every stratum within room blocks, but they hold true for the blocks. However, even at the room level of analysis, San Juan ceramics exceed 50 percent of the decorated pottery in Primary strata (combined in each room) except for 83W (small sample), 93W, and 102C, out of a total of 36 rooms containing in situ Primary strata.

The total range of variability between rooms or room blocks is thus not as great as one would like for analysis of intrasite patterning. The fact that the rank order of pottery series is more or less the same in every case produces a high rank order correlation between room blocks. Although Salmon is thought of as a Chacoan site, there is no individual room or room block in which Cibola pottery in Primary in situ strata exceeds 37 percent; in fact, it typically constitutes only about 10–20 percent of the decorated ceramics. Although there is variability within the Primary rooms and room blocks, it is on a relative scale when considered in the larger perspective. The percentages for pottery series in Primary strata used in this test of room blocks (selected by factor score and stratigraphic situation and based on a total of 6686 sherds) are as follows: San Juan 68.8%, Cibola 17.7%, Chuska 5.7%, Tusayan 1.2%, White Mountain Red Ware 2.2%, Tsegi Orange 1.3%, and Smudged Red Ware 3.1%.

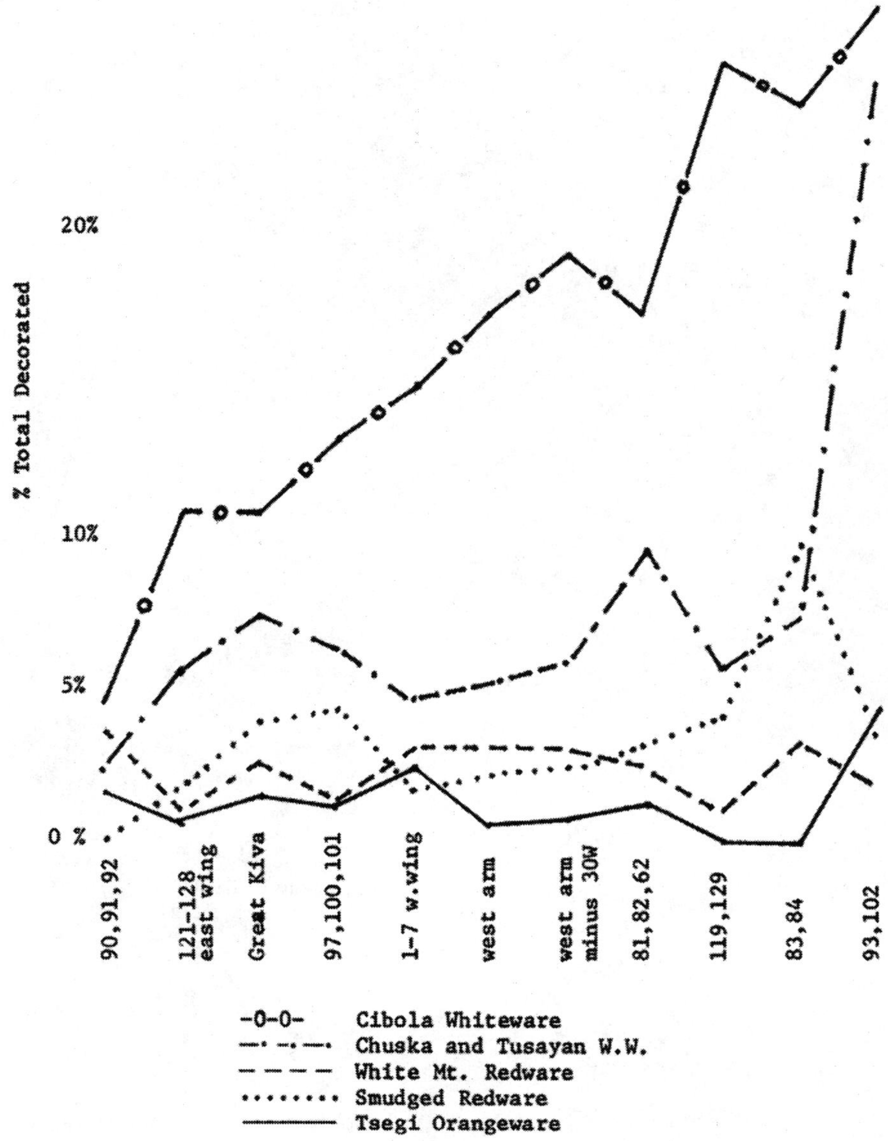

Figure 22.3. Intrusive ceramic percentages in Chacoan deposits at Salmon. Rooms ordered from most San Juan ceramics to least (left to right).

To determine whether or not the total range of variability is organized according to room block (groups of contiguous rooms interconnected by doorways in most cases), an analysis of variance was conducted using the ANOVA program from the SPSS computer package. Six major room blocks that included the total range of variation in the Primary were entered, as well as ceramic series by room grouped into four units: San Juan and White Mountain Red Ware, Cibola, Chuska and Tusayan, and Tsegi Orange and Smudged Red Ware. These groups were produced in order to eliminate small sample

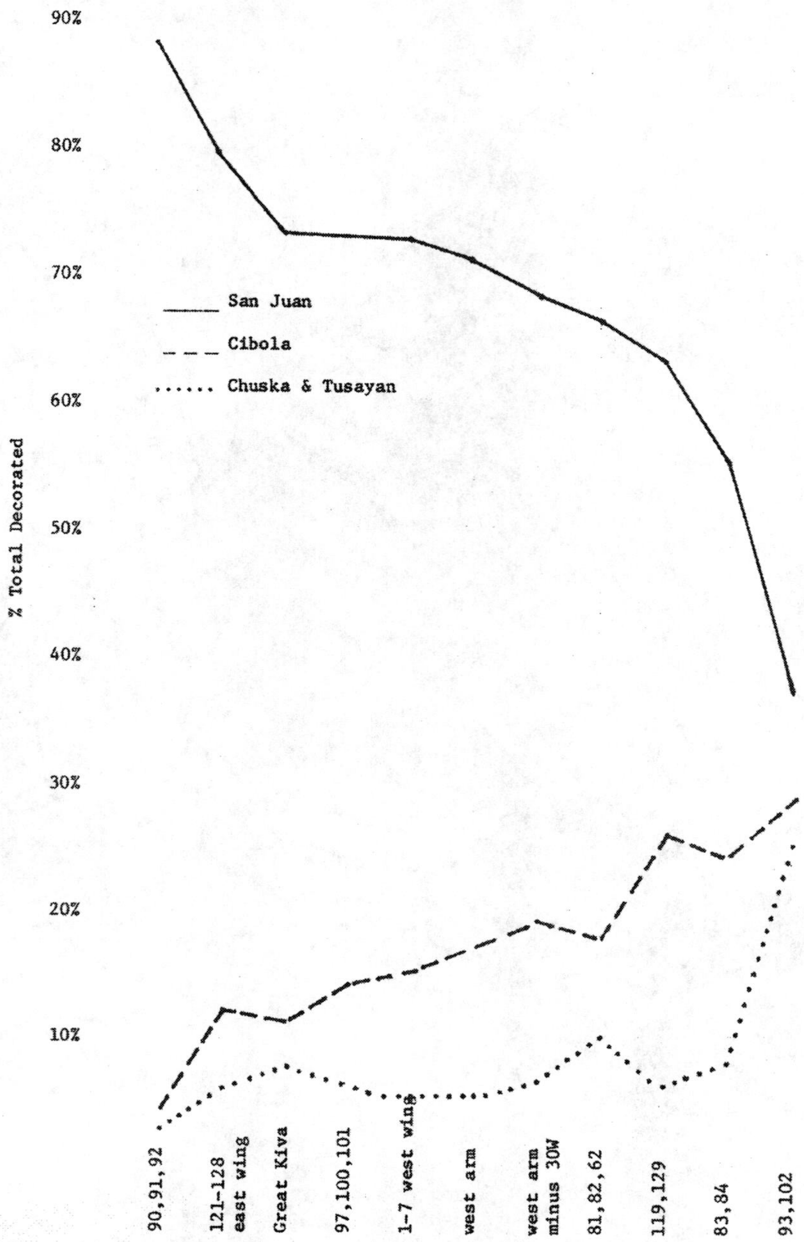

Figure 22.4. Ceramic series percentages in Chacoan rooms and suites at Salmon.

sizes for rarer pottery series, and they combined only the series known to be highly correlated in the Primary. The results showed that the amount of variation within room blocks was less than between room blocks. The interaction between block and pottery series showed significant variance to the .001 level of significance, suggesting that room blocks contain different ceramic assemblages, and verifying that the block is a unit with some ceramic integrity in the Primary.

Comparison of Room Blocks

Initially, a chi-square test was performed on six series compared across eight main room blocks. The result was a value of 405.149 (df = 35); this is a significant difference at the 0.001 level. The contingency table revealed that some blocks exceeded the expected values for San Juan, whereas others exceeded the expectation for Cibola wares and other intrusive ceramics. There appeared to be an inverse relation-

Table 22.11. Decorated ceramic series by room block, trash and behavioral strata combined, and the range and mean of of the ceramic series.

Room Block		San Juan	Cibola	Chuska & Tusayan	White Mtn Red Ware	Tsegi Orange	Smudged Red	Total
West Wing	n:	770	159	52	34	26	19	1060
(1-6W)	%:	72.6	15.0	4.9	3.2	2.5	1.8	100.0
West Arm	n:	1077	260	78	45	9	36	1505
(30, 31, 33, 43)	%:	71.6	17.3	5.2	3.0	0.6	2.4	100.1
West Arm	n:	853	242	75	39	9	30	1248
(minus 30W)	%:	68.3	19.4	6.0	3.1	0.7	2.4	99.9
81, 82, 62	n:	966	256	137	36	22	47	1464
	%:	65.0	17.5	9.4	2.5	1.5	3.2	100.1
90, 91, 92	n:	314	17	9	13	6	0	359
	%:	87.5	4.7	2.5	3.6	1.7	0.0	100.0
83, 84	n:	161	71	22	10	0	29	293
	%:	54.9	24.4	7.5	3.4	0.0	9.9	99.9
93, 102C, D	n:	90	68	62	5	10	9	244
	%:	36.9	27.9	25.4	2.0	4.1	3.7	100.0
97, 100, 101	n:	399	75	35	7	7	25	548
	%:	72.8	13.7	6.4	1.3	1.3	4.6	100.1
119, 129	n:	286	115	25	5	0	19	450
	%:	63.6	25.6	5.6	1.1	0.0	4.2	100.1
East Wing	n:	197	29	14	2	2	5	249
	%:	79.1	11.5	5.6	0.8	0.8	2.0	99.9
130W	n:	234	35	24	9	5	13	320
	%:	73.1	10.9	7.5	0.8	1.6	4.1	100.0

Series	Range (%)	Mean (%)
San Juan	36.9–87.5	67.8
Cibola	4.7–27.9	16.8
Chuska and Tusayan	2.5–25.0	8.0
White Mountain Red Ware	0.8–3.6	2.4
Tsegi Orange	0.0– 4.1	1.4
Smudged Red Ware	0.0– 9.9	3.6

ship between high San Juan frequencies and frequencies of most intrusive ceramics, except White Mountain Red Ware, which more commonly was high where San Juan was high. Table 22.12 lists the series that are above expected frequencies by room block.

This test showed not only that there was a significant difference within the sample, but also that there seemed to be two complexes—high (relatively) San Juan and high (relatively) intrusive ceramics. These results prompted a look at the extent of correlation (i.e., association in the Primary) between these ceramic series across 10 room blocks (Table 22.13). All correlations in this table are positive, because all these series occur with each other often enough to prevent an actual negative correlation. The results confirm the pattern of the chi-square contingency table. The correlation of San Juan pottery is highest with White Mountain Red Ware, higher than with any other decorated series. Inversely, the highest correlation of White Mountain Red Ware is with San Juan ceramics, not with other intrusive series. On the

Table 22.12. Contingency table of series present in higher than expected amounts.

Block	Over Expected Frequency of Series
West Wing (1W–7W)	San Juan, White Mountain Red Ware, Tsegi Orange Ware
West Arm (43W, 33W, 31W, 30W)	San Juan, Cibola, White Mountain Red Ware
Tower Kiva area (81W, 82W, 62W)	Cibola, Chuska-Tusayan, Tsegi Orange Ware,* Smudged Red Ware
90W, 91W, 92W	San Juan, White Mountain Red Ware, Tsegi Orange Ware*
83W, 84W	Cibola, Chuska-Tusayan,* White Mountain Red Ware,* Smudged Red Ware
93W, 102C, D	Cibola, Chuska-Tusayan, Tsegi Orange Ware, Smudged Red Ware*
97W, 100W, 101W	San Juan, Smudged Red Ware
East Wing (121W, 128W)	San Juan

*Indicates that the difference between observed and expected was less than five sherds.

Table 22.13. Spearman's correlation between ceramic series.

San Juan	Cibola	Chuska & Tusayan	White Mtn Red Ware	Tsegi	Sm. Red Ware
San Juan	.70	.61	.76	.54	.57
Cibola	–	.63	.58	.46	.88
Chuska & Tusayan	–	–	.45	.53	.64
White Mtn Red Ware	–	–	–	.53	.64
Tsegi	–	–	–	–	.31
Smudged Red Ware	–	–	–	–	–

Based on CLAP data on Primary occupation in ten room blocks. Correlation between San Juan versus all intrusives combined is .70. Correlation between San Juan and White Mountain Red Ware versus all other Series combines is .60.

other hand, Cibola, Chuska, and Tusayan wares form a highly correlated group of intrusive white ware. Smudged Red Ware and (less strongly) Tsegi Orange Ware appear associated with this group. This confirms the results of factor analyses of the associations of pottery types, suggesting that most intrusive ceramics tend to be strongly associated, as opposed to the San Juan–White Mountain Red Ware group. Two basic ways of combining the data were implied: (a) San Juan versus all intrusive ceramics, or (b) San Juan plus White Mountain Red Ware versus all other intrusive ceramics. Further support for such groupings is seen in the fact that the correlation between San Juan and Cibola (.70) is the same as the correlation between San Juan and all intrusive ceramics combined (see Table 22.13). The correlation (i.e., extent of association) is reduced by adding White Mountain Red Ware to the San Juan category. The correlation between San Juan and White Mountain Red Ware combined, versus the remaining intrusive ceramics, brings the correlation down to .60. This suggests that some of the ceramic series could be combined, due to high mutual association, which would facilitate data manipulations.

Several tests then compared San Juan to all intrusive ceramics combined (Table 22.14). A Mann-Whitney test showed, not surprisingly, that the frequency of San Juan pottery significantly exceeded the "all intrusive" category on the average for the room blocks in Table 22.14. Nevertheless, a Kruskal-Wallis test on the same data set (H-4.8-66, df = 1) exceeded the .05 level of significance, indicating a significant difference in the distribution of San Juan versus intrusive pottery across room blocks; this had also been suggested by the observed versus expected differences in the original chi-square contingency table noted above.

Because there were significant differences across room blocks in terms of the basic San Juan versus intrusive dichotomy, the next step involved ordering the room blocks according to how strongly San Juan or intrusive they were. The data in Table 22.14 were rearranged so that the room blocks were ordered according to percentages of San Juan ceramics (Table 22.15). The table reveals a more or less continuous distribution of room blocks from the most San Juan block of 90W, 91W, and 92W (87.5% San Juan) to the least San Juan block of 93W and 102C, D (36.9% San

Table 22.14. San Juan and intrusive series for Primary strata by room block.

Room Block			San Juan	Intrusive	Total
5	West Wing	n:	770	290	1060
		%:	72.6	27.4	
6	West Arm	n:	1077	428	1505
		%:	71.6	28.4	
7	NW Corner (minus 30W)	n:	853	395	1248
		%:	68.3	31.7	
8	81, 82, 62, 64	n:	966	498	1464
		%:	66.0	34.0	
1	90, 91, 92	n:	314	45	359
		%:	87.5	12.5	
10	83, 84	n:	161	132	293
		%:	54.9	45.1	
11	93, 102C, D	n:	90	154	244
		%:	36.9	63.1	
4	97, 100, 101	n:	399	149	548
		%:	72.8	27.2	
9	119, 129	n:	286	164	450
		%:	63.6	36.4	
2	121, 128	n:	197	52	249
		%:	79.1	20.9	
3	13W	n:	234	86	320
		%:	73.0	27.0	
Avg for blocks		n:	486	217	703
		%:	69.1	30.9	
Total		n:	4600	2086	6686
		%:	68.8	31.2	

Table 22.15. Room blocks arranged by percentage of San Juan decorated pottery.

Room Block		% San Juan Types	Room Block		% San Juan Types
1	90, 91, 92	87.5	Average Primary		68.8
2	121–128 (East Wing)	79.1	7	West Arm minus 30W	68.3
3	130W (Great Kiva)	73.0	8	81, 82, 62	66.0
4	97, 100, 101	72.8	9	119, 129	63.6
5	1–7 (West Wing)	72.6	10	83, 84	54.9
6	30, 31, 33, 43 (West Arm)	71.6	11	93, 102C, D	36.9

Juan). Figure 22.5 plots the same data, revealing a fairly continuous distribution with no large breaks. If such breaks in the continuum are apparent at all, the very high intrusive content of 83W–84W and 93W–102 C, D might stand apart, as would the very San Juan assemblage of 90W-91W-92W and 121W-128W (East Wing) at the other extreme. In the middle are several room blocks (numbers 3–6) that differ by only two percentage points in their San Juan content.

To assess the significance of this ordering, a series of chi-square tests compared each room block to the relative amount of San Juan White Ware in Primary strata for the entire site. The percentage for San Juan and intrusive ceramics for the room blocks is also included for comparison (see Table 22.14). There is less than one percentage point difference between the averages for the room blocks in this sample (69.1%) and all Primary strata in the site as a whole (68.8%), which means that this room block sample is representative of the Primary in total (including rooms not assignable to blocks). The chi-square comparison of room blocks to the average for the blocks, and the same comparison to percentages for all Primary strata, produced an ordering of room blocks identical to that provided in Table 22.16.

The original ranking by San Juan White Ware percentages turns out to be quite similar to the ranking by chi-square comparisons of each block to the percentages of San Juan pottery in all Primary strata, as seen from comparing Tables 5.14 and 5.15. The few reversals of order are explained on the basis that several blocks of rooms (130W, 97W-100W-101W, the West Wing, and the west arm rooms) had values within two percentage points of each other (72% vs. 73% San Juan), and thus are likely to be reversed in different test situations.

Summary and Interpretation

These results tend to support what was anticipated from field observation, along with the initial multidimensional scaling accomplished by Priesnitz (1979). Although all blocks but one have a higher percentage of San Juan than intrusive decorated ceramics, there are nevertheless significant differences between the frequencies of these two major ceramic groups. The chi-square test for differences comparing eight room blocks to six ceramic series, as well as the ANOVA test within and between block rooms, confirmed that there were significant differences between room blocks. The ordering of these room blocks by percentages and by comparisons to the average block and to the total Primary showed that there was essentially the same ranking of room blocks from the most San Juan (90W, 91W, and 92W) to the most intrusive (93W and 102C, D). The room block is at least one of the major dimensions along which ceramic variability in types and series is patterned in the Primary period.

The spatial arrangement of room blocks with high and low intrusive content leads to the following conclusions:

1. The high intrusive blocks are not adjacent to each other. The Tower Kiva area (81W, 82W, and 62W), Rooms 83W and 84W, and Rooms 199W and 129W are all high intrusive blocks, but are not contiguous with each other. In some cases, the physical separation of these blocks also involves intervening blocks of unexcavated rooms, so that a complete pattern is not currently obtainable. However, within the confines of the excavated sample, it is evident that rooms high in intrusive pottery are spatially discrete, and they are often separated by intervening blocks of rooms high in San Juan ceramics. For example, the high intrusive room block of 83W and 84W is adjacent to the highest San Juan block in the site (90W, 91W, and 92W).

2. If this is true, there is little evidence for a hypothesized east-to-west division in terms of the variables of San Juan versus intrusive ceramics. Although it is true that the west arm rooms of 43W, 31W, and 33W are relatively high in intrusive ceramics, 30W, also in this area, is less so. On the east side of the pueblo, there are at least six high intrusive rooms (83W, 84W, 93W, 102C-D, 199W, and 129W), so that the east side of the site is not uniformly dominated by San Juan rooms, either. It would also be difficult to confirm a true east-west division in the current sample of excavated rooms because there are no completely excavated room blocks or suites (front-to-back transects) in the west arm comparable to the three completed (or nearly completed) in an equivalent position in the east arm.

3. The room block differences seen here are correlated with a variety of residential and/or functional differences in the use of ceramic types and series in the Primary. Some of these blocks form suites—groups of rooms in front-to-back (plaza-facing to back wall) arrangements interconnected by doorways. Other blocks are seen to be functionally rather than residentially based. This is true of the Tower Kiva block (81W, 82W, and 62W), the cooking rooms 93W and 102C, and the 119W, 129W group.

4. Several of the nonspecialized residential suites of rooms tend to have higher than average percentages of San Juan White Ware. This is true of the East and West Wings, the suite of 90W, 91W, and 92W, and the one composed of 97W, 100W, and 101W in the east arm. On the other hand, the blocks of rooms

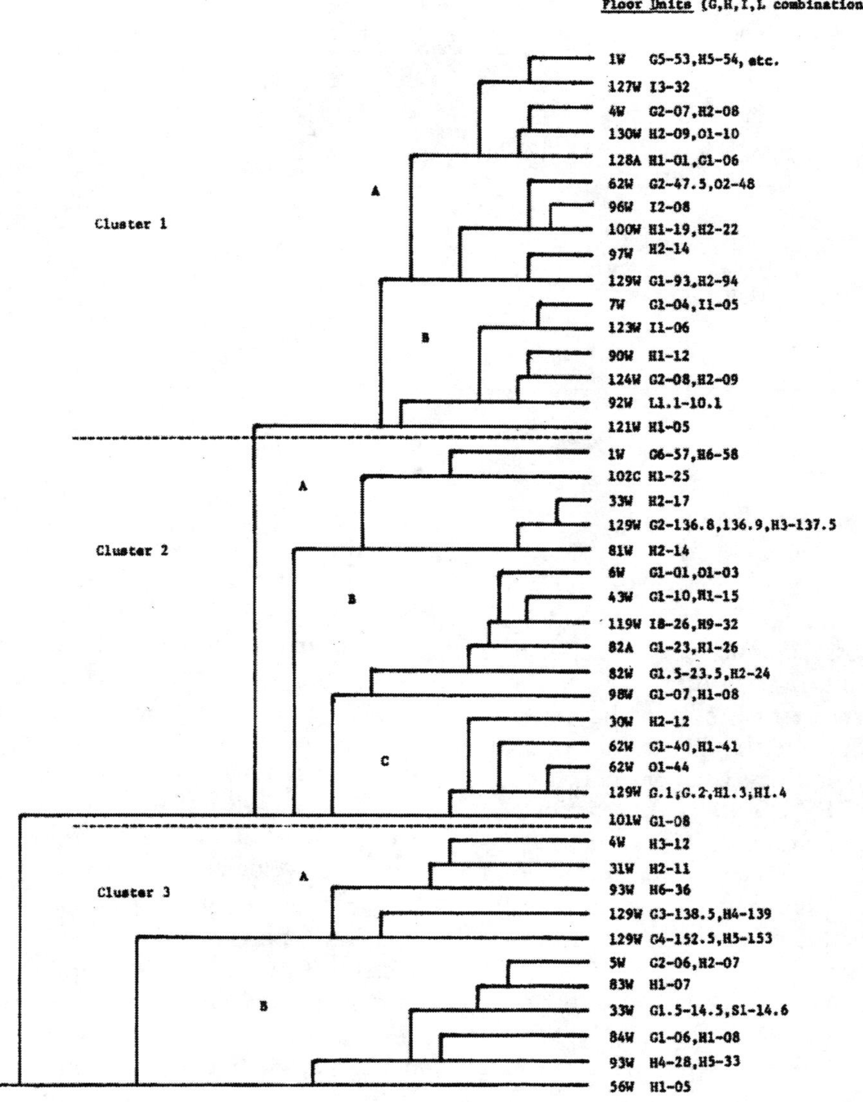

Figure 22.5. Cluster analysis of seven ceramic series from Salmon Primary floors.

low in San Juan percentages are the west arm (Rooms 31W, 43W, and 33W) and Rooms 83W and 84W in the east arm. However, there is some indication of specialized activities even in these rooms. 43W and 83W provided very high cobble-sandstone lithic frequencies on their Primary floors. Butchering and animal processing could have occurred in 31W and potentially in 43W, although the association of the lithic and faunal materials with the actual usage of those floors is questionable.

At least, it may be said that in all rooms and blocks of rooms that contain definite evidence of specialized activities (especially in the areas of food preparation, milling, and ceremonialism), the intrusive ceramics are above the average for the Primary occupation as a whole. The reverse is also largely true: rooms or blocks of rooms with no evidence of specialized activities tend to have a San Juan White Ware percentage that exceeds the mean for all Primary strata. (The northwest corner rooms and 83W and 84W may in fact be parts of high intrusive residential suites.) Without additional excavation it is impossible to determine if the excavated back-wall and next-to-back-wall rooms are representative of the entire front-to-back suite arrangements of which they are a spatial portion.

Table 22.16. Chi-square values of room blocks compared to average for the Primary.

	Block	Chi Square	Level of Significance
Higher San Juan than expected	90, 91, 92	56.9	.001
	East Wing	12.17	.001
	West Wing	6.29	.025
	West Arm	4.42	.050
	97, 100, 101	3.7	.100
	130W	2.58	.250
Average Primary			
higher intrusive than expected	West Arm (–30W)	0.11	Not significant
	81, 82, 62	4.44	.050
	119, 129	5.32	.025
	83, 84	25.01	.001
	93.1-2C, D	109.13	.001

Cluster Analysis of Primary Floors by Ceramic Series

The computerized phase of distributional testing consisted of several cluster analyses: all ceramic series on Primary floors; ceramic series grouped into three major classes on Primary floors; seven pottery series in lower Primary trash strata; the ceramic series on Primary roofs; and the distribution of local and intrusive utility ceramics. Cluster analysis was conducted using the HCLUS program described in Chapter 20. The ceramic data consisted of percentages of each series by stratum or groups of combined strata. Plain white or plain red sherds from decorated vessels were included because they could not be assigned to specific types.

The stratigraphic sample for the first test consisted of floor units as combinations of occupational fill (G), floor surface (H), structural floor (I), and associated pits (L). Occupational fill levels (G) were included with the floor strata where it appeared that the occupational fill level had been accurately identified in the field, and was not excessively thick (see Table 22.17 for a complete list of strata grouped into floor units). This helped to augment the sample sizes available from the floor surfaces themselves. In total, 43 floor units (all floor units with decorated ceramics that could be assigned to series) including a total of 2276 decorated sherds formed the basis of the analysis.

Cluster Composition

The results of cluster analysis of Primary floor units with seven decorated ceramic series are provided in Figure 22.6 and Table 22.18 using Method 2 (furthest neighbor). Three major clusters were produced (Clusters 1–3) on the basis of the percentages of San Juan White Ware (Mancos and McElmo Black-on-white). Secondary or lower level clusters consist of minor differences within the intrusive series percentages within the larger San Juan White Ware based clusters (Table 22.19). There is very little overlap in the percentages of San Juan decorated between the clusters. The relative frequencies of the major series can explain the divisions between first and second order clusters. Table 22.20 provides the mean percentages of San Juan White Ware, intrusive white ware, and intrusive red ware by cluster area. Cluster 1 has the highest San Juan White Ware percentages, followed by Clusters 2 and 3 in that order.

Intrusive white ceramics are lowest in Cluster 1, are 32–36 percent in Cluster 2, and are highest in Cluster 3 (up to 63.8% of the decorated complex). Red ware sherds are never a dominant part of the ceramic assemblages from the Primary. In most clusters, the percentage of red ware amounts to one-half or one-third of the percentages for intrusive white ware. Red ware is low to nonexistent in Subclusters 2C and 3B. There is a general tendency for intrusive red ware to be associated with intrusive white ware (as noted earlier); this is also reflected in cluster analysis, in which the groups with high intrusive white ware percentages also include the higher percentages of red ware. Red ware is especially abundant in Subclusters 2A, 2B, and 3A, which are also higher than the mean in intrusive white ware percentages. On the other hand, red ware never exceeds 13 percent (mean of 5.4%) in Cluster 1, which is dominated by San Juan White Ware. Therefore, red ware tends to be found in clusters with high intrusive white ware frequencies, rather than in those with high San Juan White Ware frequencies. However, within the intrusive white ware Clusters 2 and 3, there are subclusters without the red ware part of the intrusive assemblage (e.g., Subcluster 3B).

Table 22.17. Primary occupation floor units (G, H, I, L strata combinations).

Room	Strata in the Floor Unit
1W	G-5-53, H-5-54, I-5-55
1W	G-6-57, H-6-58, I-6-59
7/3W	G-1-04, I-1-05, O-1-06
4W	G-2-07, H-2-08, I-2-09
4W	H-3-12, I-3-13
5W	G-2-06, H-2-07, l-1-10
6W	O-1-03, L-1-04, L-2-05, L-3-06, L-4-07, L-5-08, L-6-09, L-7-10, L-8-11, G-1-01
30W	H-2-12, I-2-13
31W	H-2-11, I-2-13
33W	G-1.5-14.5, S-1-14.6
33W	G-2-15.1, H-2-17, L-2-17.1, I-2-18
43W	G-1-10, G-1.1-10.1, G-1.2-10.2, H-1-15, I-1-16
56W	H-1-05, I-1-06, L-1-08, L-2-09
62W	G-1-40, H-1-41, I-1-42
62W	O-1-44, L-7-44.5
62W	G-2-47.5, O-2-48, L-8-48.5
62W	H-2-51, I-2-52
81W	H-1-14
82A(W)	G-1-23, H-1-26, L-1-28, L-6-30
82W	G-1.5-23.5, H-2-24, H-1.6-23.5, H-1.8-23.8, I-2-24, L-17-45, L-19-48, and post hole pits
91W	H-1-30, H-0.7-29.7, I-1-15
90W	G-1-11.5, H-1-12, L-4-13, L-5-14, I-1-15
92W	L-1.1-10.1, L-1.3-10.3, L-2-11
96W	H-2-07, I-2-08, L-1-08, L-6-16, L-7.5-17.5, L-8-18, L-9-19, L-11-21, L-14-25, L-16,27, L-18-30
83W	H-1-07, -1-09
84W	G-1-06, H-1-08
93W	H-4-28, I-4-29, L-4-20, L-6-31
93W	H-5-33, I-5-34, L-6-34
93W	H-6-36, I-6-38, L-7-37
93W	H-7-39, I-7-40, L-17.3-39.3, L-8-39.5, L-21.6-39.6, L-23.9-39.9
102C	H-1-25, (H-2-25 in 102A), I-1-30, (I-2-30 in 102A), L-1-26
97W	H-1-06
97W	H-2-14, I-2-15, L-3-08, L-4-09
100W	H-1-19, H-2-22, I-1-19.4, I-1-19.5, I-2-22.4, I-2-22.5, L-4-24, L-5-25, L-7-27, (&27.1, 27.2, 27.3), L-22-46, L:-8-28, L-10-30, :L-13-33
101W	G-1-08, H-1-09, I-1-10, L-1-12, L-2-13, L-3-14, L-7-18, L-4-15
98W	G-1-07, H-1-08, I-1-09
121W	H-1-05, I-1-12, L-1-06, H-1.5-5.5, L-3-08, L-S-10
121W	H-2-13, H-2-11, H-2.4-13.5, H-2.6-13.6, I-2-14, I-2.5-14.5, I-2-5-14.6, L-7-15
121W	H-3.5-16.5, H-3.6-16.6, I-3-20, I-3.5-20.5, I-3.6-20.6, l-8-17, l-9-18, l-10-19, l-11-21
121W	H-4-22, H-4.5-24.5, H-4.6-24.7, I-4-24, I-4.5-5-24.6, I-4.6-24.8, L-12-23

Table 22.17 (continued)

Room	Strata in the Floor Unit
121W	H-5-25, H-5.3-25.3, I-5-25.1, I-5.3-25.4, L-14-26
121W	H-5-27, I-5-28
121W	H-6-30, I-6-32, L-15,31
124W	G-2-08, H-2-09, -2-10, -2-12, -3-13
124W	R-1-07, L-4-08, L-11-08, L-13-09, -10-14, L-15-15
123W	I-1-02, (I-1-06 in 123B, I-2-10 in 123A)
123W	I-2-05, (I-2-09 in 123B)
123W	I-3-07, L-1-08, L-2-09, L-3-14, L-4-15, L-4.5-15.1
127W	H-2-17, I-2-17.5, L-9-21, L-11-23
127W	H-3-24, I-3-32, L-13-27, L-14-29, L-15-30
127W	H-4-33, I-4-38, L-1-7-34, L-18-35, L-19-39, L-20-40
128A	H-2-07, (H-2-05), G-1-06, L-4-09, L-5-10, L-7-12
119W	I-8-26, I-8.5-26.5
119W	H-9-32, I-9-33
119W	H-10,35, I-10-36
119W	H-11-38, I-11-39, I-11.5-39.5, L-13-39.6, L-7-40
119W	H-12-41, H-12.3-41.3, H-12.5-41/5, I-12-42, I-12.5-42.5, L-8-43, L-9-44, L-10-45
119W	H-13-51, I-13-52
129W	G-0.1-92.1, G-0.2-92.2, G-0.3-92.3, H-1.3-92.3, H-1.4-4-92.4, I-1.4-92.4, L-5-135
129W	G-1-93, H-2-94, H2.5-94.5, H-2-7-94.7, I-2.5-94.6, I-2.7-94.8, L-7-143, L-8-144, L-11-147, I-2-101
129W	G-2-136.8, G-2-136.9, H-3-137.5, H-3.5-137.5, I-3.5-137.6, l-6-142
129W	G-3-138.5, H-4-139, H-4.2-139.2, h-4.4-139.4, i-4-139.1, I-4.2-139.3, I-4.4-139.5, L-9-145, L-10-146
129W	G-4-152.5, H-5-153, I-5-154, l-15,155, l-16-156, l-17-157, l-18-158
103W	H-2-09, O-1-10, L-8-22, L-10-26, L-11-27, L-12-28, L-15-31, L-18-34, L-19-35, L-20-36, L-20.1-36.1 Through 36.49 (postholes), L-21-37, L-24-42, L-26-44

Includes all floor units that are Primary in stratigraphic position and have Primary factor scores. Primary floors that were reused or contaminated ceramicallly by Secondary occupants are not included. All strata associated with these floor units are included, regardless of whether they contain ceramics and/or lithics.

San Juan pottery dominates the decorated assemblage (more than half) in all but 11 of the 43 floor units (see Clusters 1 and 2). All strata in Cluster 3 have less than 50 percent San Juan White Ware. However, the mean for all Primary strata is 72 percent San Juan pottery. Measured against this figure, 26 of 43 Primary floors have a San Juan percentage lower than the mean. Included is all but one stratum of Cluster 2, and all of Cluster 3. In other words, about half of the Primary floors are above and about half are below the mean San Juan percentage for the Primary as a whole.

The major break appears to be between Cluster 1 and Clusters 2 and 3 together; this dividing line coincides with average amounts of San Juan White Ware in the Primary (72%). Cluster 1 is above this percentage, whereas Clusters 2 and 3 are below it. Viewing the floor units in this light, the high San Juan Cluster 1 includes several groups of rooms: (a) all East Wing rooms, (b) the Great Kiva, the suite of 97W, 100W and 101W, and the suite of 90W, 91W, and 92W in the east arm, and (c) rooms in the West Wing except for the floors of 6W and 5W (large square rooms). Clusters 2 and 3 taken in combination as lower than the mean in local (San Juan) white ware includes the following groups of rooms:

- Large square rooms in the West Wing (6W, 5W).
- All west arm floors (Rooms 30W, 31W, 43W, and 33W).
- All Tower Kiva area floors (Rooms 81W, 82W, and 62W) except one floor unit of 62W, which is found in Cluster 1 but has the lowest San Juan percentage of any floor in Cluster 1.
- All floors clustered from the block of 119W–129W except for one floor in 129W.
- All floors clustered of 102C and 93W.
- The suite of Rooms 83W and 84W.
- Excavationally isolated Rooms 98W and 56W.

Table 22.18. Percentages of ceramic series on Primary floors.

Floor Unit	San Juan White Ware	Cibola WW	Chuska & Tusayan WW	White Mountain Red Ware	Tesgi Orange	Smudged Red
Cluster 1						
1W:G5-53, H5-54,etc.	76.5	4.4	5.9	11.8	1.5	0
127W:I3-32	75.0	12.5	0	12.5	0	0
4W:G2-07, H2-08	73.5	15.1	2.6	3.4	4.4	1.0
130W:H2-09, 01-10	73.7	10.9	7.5	2.4	1.0	4.4
128A:H1-01, G1-06	76.2	14.2	9.6	0	0	0
62W:G-2-47.5, 02-48	69.2	26.9	0	0	0	3.8
96W:12-08	73.2	19.5	4.9	0	0	2.4
100W:H1-19, H2-22	73.2	18.3	1.2	0	0	7.3
97W:H1-I4	72.4	13.8	0	0	0	13.8
129W:G1-93, H2-94	79.2	8.3	2.1	0	0	10.4
7W:G1-04, I1-05	84.3	9.0	2.2	4.5	0	0
123W:I1-06	86.7	13.3	0	0	0	0
90W:H1-12	100.0	0	0	0	0	0
124W:G2-08	92.4	2.9	4.8	0	0	0
92W:L1.1-10.1	90.9	0	0	0	9.1	0
Cluster 2						
121W:H1-05	72.7	0	18.2	0	9.1	0
1W:G6-57, H6-58	53.3	20.0	13.3	0	13.1	0
1W:G5-53, H6-58	76.5	4.4	5.9	11.8	1.5	0
102C:H1-25	50.0	16.7	0	0	25.0	8.3
33W:H2-17	50.0	40.0	0	0	0	10.0
129W:G2-136.8, 136.9,H3-137.5	53.3	40.0	0	0	0	6.7
81W:H2-13	50.0	50.0	0	0	0	0
6WLG1-01, 01-03	57.5	20.9	14.1	1.9	1.9	1.9
43W:G1-10, H1-26	65.4	21.1	7.0	2.7	1.1	2.7
119W:18-26, H9-26	61.5	23.1	7.7	7.7	0	0
82A:G1-23, H1-26	51.6	23.2	7.1	7.7	5.8	4.5
92W:G1.5-23.5, H2-24	58.3	14.3	7.1	14.3	4.8	1.2
98W:G1-07, H1-08	57.1	11.4	2.8	0	0	28.6
30W:H2-12	76.5	5.9	17.6	0	0	0
62W:G1-40	63.6	13.6	22.7	0	0	0
62W:01-44	68.2	18.2	13.6	0	0	0
129W:G-1, G.2, H1-3, H1-4	68.8	20.0	10.1	1.3	0	0
Cluster 3						
101W:G1-08	58.8	11.8	29.4	0	0	0
4W:H3-12	42.9	33.3	4.8	14.3	0	4.8
31W:H2-11	45.5	18.1	22.6	13.6	0	0
93W:H6-36	41.9	27.9	16.3	0	2.3	11.6
129W:G3-138.5, H4-139	33.3	33.3	33.3	0	0	0
5W:G2-06, H2-07	18.2	36.4	27.4	18.2	0	0
83W:H1-07	26.7	60.0	6.7	6.7	0	0
33W:G1.5-14.5, S1-14.6	39.7	50.7	8.2	0	0	1.4
84W:G1-06, H1-08	28.4	45.3	13.7	0	0	12.6
93W:H4-28, H5-33	22.2	50.0	0	11.1	5.6	11.1
56W:H1-05	14.3	85.7	0	0	0	0

Sequence of strata follows cluster analysis diagram. Complete list of strata assigned to floor units is in Table 22.16. Counts of ceramic series do not include plain white or red sherds.

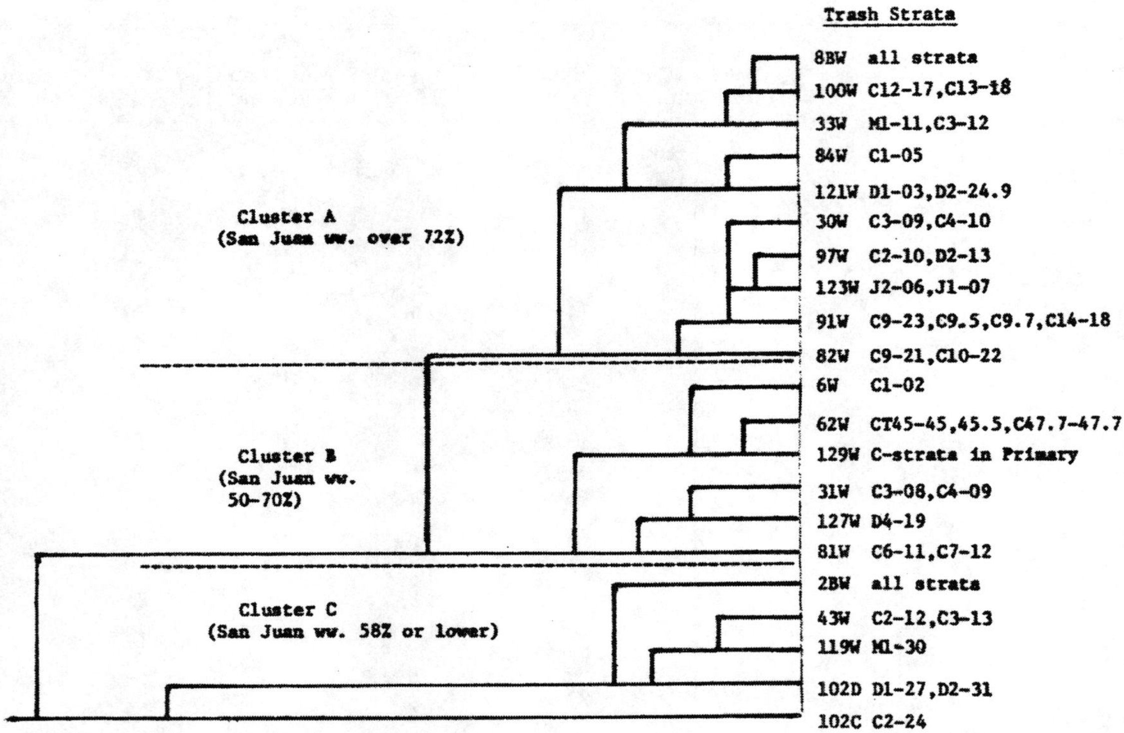

Figure 22.6. Cluster analysis of lowest Primary trash strata by decorated ceramic series.

Blocks and Suites

There is a strong relationship between the dimension of local versus intrusive decorated pottery and the groupings of rooms into blocks and suites of adjacent rooms. Thus, the conclusions derived from the initial comparison of room blocks (including suites) is verified by the cluster analysis. In light of the basic contrast between San Juan and intrusive ceramics, the room blocks may be characterized as follows:

West Wing Block (Rooms 1W through 7W): High in San Juan percentages in all rooms except for the large square rooms.

West Arm Block (Rooms 30W, 31W, 33W, and 43W): Low to moderate amounts of San Juan, somewhat higher in intrusive ceramics. All floor units are in Cluster 2, except one floor found in Cluster 3. All of these rooms have high intrusive white and/or red ware percentages.

Tower Kiva Area (Rooms 62W, 81W, and 82W): Low San Juan percentages. High for intrusive ceramics. Red ware abundant in 82A-82W. Intrusive white ware highest in 62W and 81W.

Block of 93W and 102C: Low in San Juan White Ware, very high for intrusive ceramics (50% or more). Of the two rooms, 93W has higher intrusive ceramics on floors than 102C. Red ware abundant on the two floors of 93W and also in 102C.

Suite of 90W, 91W, and 92W: Highest San Juan White Ware percentages (91–100%). All intrusive ceramics are minor in appearance.

Suite of 97W, 100W, and 101W: Moderate to high amounts of San Juan White Ware. Red ware is low in percentage. San Juan percentages are not as high as in the 90W, 91W, and 92W block. Although this suite is characterized generally as high for San Juan pottery, this may not have been true of 97W, in its earliest Primary usage (see below). Room 101W does not cluster with the other two members of the suite using Method 2 but does using Method 7.

Block of 199W and 129W: Moderate to low San Juan percentages on floors but 129W does contain San Juan dominant trash strata. The five floors of 129W were all included in the test, and although there is no uniformity to their cluster assignments for reasons explained below, it is notable that all floors but one are found in Clusters 2 or 3. The room may generally be seen, then, as having high intrusive counts. Only the uppermost floor is in the high San Juan Cluster 1.

Table 22.19. Description of cluster composition.

Cluster	Description
Cluster 1	69–100% San Juan White Ware
Subcluster A	69–79% San Juan White Ware; intrusive White Ware exceed red ware.
Subcluster B	84–100% San Juan White Ware; all else very low.
Cluster 2	50–77% San Juan White Ware
Subcluster A	50–53% San Juan White Ware
Subcluster B	52–65% San Juan White Ware
Subcluster C	64–77% San Juan White Ware
Cluster 3	15–46% San Juan White Ware
Subcluster A	33–46% San Juan White Ware
Subcluster B	15–40% San Juan White Ware

Table 22.20. Mean percentages of three major decorated classes in cluster analysis of Primary floors by ceramic series.

Cluster	San Juan WW	Intrusive WW	Red Ware
1A	74.1	16.1	8.0
1B	90.8	6.4	2.8
2A	51.2	36.0	12.4
2B	58.7	26.3	15.2
2C	67.2	32.4	0.4
3A	36.4	44.0	19.4
3B	27.2	63.8	9.0

East Wing Block (Rooms 121W, 124W, 123W, 127W, and 128W): The entire suite of 123W, 124W, 127W, and 128W plus the large square room (121W) in the suite next door, are all in Cluster 1, and thus high in San Juan percentages.

The major point here is that there is a great deal of correspondence between the major cluster divisions in cluster analysis of floors, and the grouping of rooms into blocks and suites. Members of suites or blocks are generally clustered together in one of the three clusters. There are several exceptions to this, however. The multiple floors of 1W, 4W, and 129W are found in different clusters. In Room 62W, for example, the floor unit of 0-2-48 is in Cluster 1, whereas the remaining floors in the room are in Subcluster 2C. However, 0-2-48 has only 69 percent San Juan (lowest of Cluster 1), comparing favorably with 64 percent and 68 percent San Juan on the other two floors found in Subcluster 2C. In this room, therefore, there is not much difference in the local to intrusive ratios for the floors, despite the fact that cluster analysis placed one of them in a different cluster from the others. In the case of the suite of 97W, 100W, and 101W, Room 101W is not placed with the other two rooms in Method 2 (as illustrated). Rooms 100W and 97W have floors with close joins in Method 2, with 73 percent and 72 percent San Juan respectively. Whereas 101W has only 59 percent San Juan, the sample comes only from the G-1-08 (occupational fill) stratum, because no decorated pottery was retrieved from the floor surface itself (H-1-09). Further, Method 7 cluster analysis did produce close joins in the dendrogram between the three rooms. All three rooms are quite low in red ware percentages. These results support the initial testing of differences between blocks and suites, suggesting a strong tendency for series to be distributed by blocks of rooms.

Microtemporal Change

The exceptions to the correspondence of ceramic series and block-suite groupings all involve rooms in which there are more than one Primary floor unit (i.e., stratigraphically sequential floors in the Primary period). As noted, the multiple floors of Rooms 1W, 4W, and 129W do not cluster together. Clearly, multiple floors in given rooms may have quite distinct ceramic assemblages. Although the multiple floors in 62W and 93W did not display clearcut temporal changes in ceramic series, the remainder of rooms with multiple Primary floors did.

A preliminary assessment of microtemporal changes in the frequencies of ceramic series showed that the San Juan White Ware tradition became more common through time, a noticeable trend late in the Primary period. The cluster analysis of Primary floors also contains evidence to support this conclusion. Where floors of multiple-floored rooms did not appear in the same cluster together, the stratigraphically higher floors always appeared in the higher San Juan Cluster 1, and the lower ones in Clusters 2 or 3.

The major exception to the clustering of floors of blocks together is in the West Wing. This departure can be explained in light of increasing San Juan percentages through time. Whereas rooms to the back of the large square rooms 5W and 6W may be characterized as high in San Juan pottery in general, the large square rooms apparently contain higher amounts of intrusive ceramics (particularly intrusive white ware), perhaps partly because the large square rooms contain only single Primary floors, whereas those to the back tend to have more than one Primary floor. In large square rooms, the single floors are probably the earlier or only Primary floors, because Secondary kivas were placed into both rooms later, perhaps removing any ceramic evidence from the late Primary period. On the other hand, rooms in back (west) of these large square rooms retain more of the Primary component intact. Multiple Primary floors are present in Rooms 4W and 1W. In each case where there is more than one Primary floor, the upper one contains higher San Juan White Ware percentages than the lower one. This explains why the upper floors in back of large square rooms appeared in Cluster 1 (high San Juan). The lower floors of 1W and 4W are clustered with Rooms 5W and 6W (large square rooms). Thus, the problem in the West Wing involves microtemporal change. The lower floors of 1W and 4W do, in fact, occur in the same cluster as the only floors in 6W and 5W, probably representing the earliest Primary usage of white ware; thereafter, later Primary floors in 4W and 1W (and an Intermediate floor in 7W) were increasingly San Juan in character. Later Primary floors either never existed in 6W and 5W or were removed by later building in those rooms in the late 1100s or 1200s. When separated into its temporal components, then, the discrepancies in cluster placement do not exist. The block was uniformly moderate to low in San Juan at first, altering to increased use of Mancos and McElmo Black-on-white pottery later in the Primary.

Another apparent case of change in ceramic assemblage, and by inference change in function, within the Primary occurred in Room 97W. Although the floor of 97W does coincide with the other two rooms in its suite in ceramic content (see cluster analysis), this may not have been true of the earliest usage of the room. The strata associated with the milling troughs below the H-2-14 floor are very high in intrusive pottery, particularly for Cibola White Ware. This is also true for C-4-17, T-1-18, D-2-16, and D-1-11 near the milling feature, but these strata were not clustered because they were not a part of the Primary floor unit. There may have been a change of function in this room from high intrusive (with the milling activities) to a later Primary floor (H-2-14) dominated by San Juan ceramics. This reconstruction would also accord with the ceramics associated with all other Primary milling loci, which are always of a high intrusive nature.

Microtemporal changes also appear in the cluster analysis for Room 129W. All five Primary floor units included in the analysis fall into different clusters. This can be explained as another example of the change in San Juan to intrusive ratios during the Primary. From top to bottom, these floors contain 79.2, 68.8, 53.3, 33.3, and 18.2 percent San Juan decorated pottery, respectively—a clear trend from intrusive dominant to San Juan White Ware dominant assemblages. Room 129W is useful as a test case because it contains more Primary floors than any other room, and also because it was meticulously excavated. Therefore, although the room is generally characterized as high in intrusive pottery, this in fact is true only of the lower three and possibly four floor units. As in the case of the West Wing rooms, the reason for the nonclustering of multiple Primary floors in the same room can be traced to microtemporal change. In both instances, this takes the form of increasing Mancos and McElmo Black-on-white through time in the Primary.

Two other rooms in the cluster analysis sample contain multiple Primary floors: 62W (three floor units) and 93W (two floor units). Neither shows a microtemporal trend toward San Juan pottery. Both rooms may be termed high intrusive on all Primary floors. Both are highly specialized in terms of function: Room 62W in a ceremonial context near the Tower Kiva, and 93W for cooking and food preparation. These highly specialized activities were accompanied by high intrusive counts throughout the Primary, and were probably foci of Chacoan population activity.

In sum, cluster analysis of rooms with multiple Primary floors illustrates a trend toward increasing

San Juan percentages on the upper (later) Primary floors except for the special cases of Rooms 62W and 93W, which remained high for intrusive ceramics throughout the Chacoan occupation. This is supported by additional data on ceramic changes in the Primary. Unfortunately, most rooms do not contain multiple Primary floors, and the stratigraphic correlation of single Primary floors in some rooms with multiple floors in others is very difficult to achieve. There are several possible reasons for the changes in the ratio of San Juan to intrusive pottery during the Primary: room functions changed; the Chacoan population was receiving less intrusive pottery later in the Primary, and thus had to rely more on the local wares; and/or there was already a San Juan population in residence at the site that was becoming an increasingly dominant part of the Primary population after about AD 1100. Any or all of these possibilities could have been operative. In the latter reconstruction, of course, the San Juan population simply stayed on after the Chacoans left at about AD 1130, whereupon the San Juan White Ware percentages increased to 80–90 percent of the pottery used during the succeeding Intermediate period.

Conclusions

The patterning produced by cluster analysis of Primary floors is the result of two major variables: spatial differences in ceramic usage and microtemporal change. When the microtemporal variable is accounted for, there is surprising uniformity of clustering of rooms assigned to blocks and suites. That is, when small temporal changes are taken into consideration for the multiple-floored rooms, the spatial patterning becomes even cleaner.

Phrased in terms of locations of concentration of the ceramic variables, the cluster diagram demonstrates that (a) areas high in local (San Juan) ceramics include the West Wing (upper Primary floors only), the entire East Wing suite, 96W, the suite of 97W, 100W, and 101W, and the suite of 90W, 91W, and 92W. (b) Areas high for intrusive pottery include the West Wing (lower Primary floors), all west arm rooms (43W, 30W, 31W, and 33W), Tower Kiva area rooms (62W, 81W, and 82W), the blocks of 93W–102C, 83A–84W, 119W–129W (lower floors), and the excavationally isolated Rooms 56W and 98W.

The rooms high in San Juan ceramics all fall into suites (front-to-back interconnected room groups). None are highly specialized in terms of inferred room function, as seen from the integrated ceramic, lithic, and botanical data (see following section). Four suites of rooms, including the upper floors in the West Wing, fall into this category.

The Great Kiva contains series percentages almost exactly on the mean for the Primary as a whole. The 74 percent San Juan pottery on the floor of the Great Kiva makes it about average for the Primary in general. Similarly, the 18.4 percent intrusive white ware and the 1.4 percent red ware figures are not out of line for a generalized Primary occupation floor at Salmon. The rather average nature of the Great Kiva floor in terms of ceramic series may relate to its function as a focus of integration for all of the populace of the pueblo. It thus might be expected to exhibit a wide variety of ceramics, but in frequencies approximating the mean for all Primary strata. This, in fact, is the case as all seven ceramic series are represented, but in amounts similar to the whole Primary occupation. This contrasts with the high intrusive counts found in the Tower Kiva area (Rooms 62W, 81W, and 82W). Although all ceremonial areas are similar in low utility ware frequencies, as discussed below, the two major centers of ceremonial activity differ in terms of ceramic series. The relatively higher amounts of intrusive ceramics in the Tower Kiva area may indicate that these rooms were even more of a Chacoan-related and specialized ceremonial focal point than the Great Kiva, which could have been used for more community-wide integrative ceremonialism.

In the group of rooms with high amounts of intrusive ceramics there are both suites, inferred to be residential, and blocks of specialized rooms. High intrusive rooms in front-to-back suites include the West Wing (two suites, earliest floors only), Rooms 31W and 43W, and Rooms 83W and 84W. Both of the latter are partial suites, because the front two rooms of these suites have not been excavated. However, the data support the existence of suites that may mark residences of Chacoans in the pueblo. As mentioned above, some of these rooms have evidence of specialized functions at least some time during the Primary, for example the lithic debitage and sandstone-cobble features in Rooms 83W and 43W and possible evidence of butchering activity in 31W. Conversely, evidence of high San Juan counts in several residential suites suggests local, Middle San Juan residence. The contrast between high and low intrusive suites in the Primary probably reflects differential use of intrusive versus local ceramics across architecturally similar residential settings. This differential can be explained either as a difference in residential ceramic usage on the part of a single Chacoan population, or as evidence of both a Chacoan and a San Juan population contemporaneously resident at the site in separate residential suites. Additional nonceramic data would have to be brought to bear to distinguish between these two logical possibilities. At this point, suffice it to say that suites, thought to be residential-spatial room groupings, differ greatly in terms of how local or exotic they appear, although they seem to be equivalent in architecture and placement in the settlement pattern.

Finally, all rooms of a specialized nature, judging from architectural features and botanical and lithic data, are in the high intrusive class. These include the Tower Kiva area (ritual-ceremonial), 93W–102C (cooking and food preparation), and 119W–129W (milling and storage). All floors with milling trough evidence (in Rooms 97W, 82W, 93W, and 129W) are in the high intrusive realm. It appears that ceremonialism (aside from the Great Kiva) and specialized cooking and food preparation took place in a high intrusive, and by extension Chacoan cultural context. Additional, though more tenuous associations of high intrusive ceramics with special functions include metate manufacture and discard in 84W and butchering in 31W. All rooms with high frequencies of Washington Pass Chert, an intrusive lithic material from the Chuska Mountains, also contain higher than usual amounts of Cibola and Chuska decorated pottery. In sum, all rooms of a specialized nature (as viewed from nonceramic evidence) have high intrusive white ware and red ware percentages. We may conclude that specialized activities (definitely ceremonialism and cooking and food preparation activities) occurred in a context wherein intrusive ceramics were used frequently—the Chacoan element of the pueblo is very much in evidence in rooms of specialized function. By contrast, high amounts of local pottery are found in rooms with generalized functions, and all fit into residential suites. The intermediate or average ceramic assemblage of the Great Kiva may relate to pueblo-wide integrative functions.

Cluster Analysis of Primary Floors by Grouped Ceramic Series

Cluster analysis was also applied to a more condensed version of the same data. The seven ceramic series were reduced to three major groups: San Juan White Ware (Mancos and McElmo Black-on-white), intrusive white ware (Cibola, Chuska, and Tusayan White Ware), and all red ware (Tsegi Orange, White Mountain Red Ware, and Smudged Red Ware). Stratigraphic groups of floor units remained identical in the two tests. The results were very similar to cluster results with all seven series entered separately; only 2 of 43 floor units changed cluster placement in the three-part test. This is undoubtedly due to the fact that the major distributional distinction lies in the contrast between San Juan and intrusive (white ware and red ware) pottery. The distributions of series within each of these three groups are so similar that including them as distinct data entries did not affect the general cluster pattern. That is, intrusive white ware substitutes adequately for the distributions of Cibola, Chuska, and Tusayan White Ware considered separately; the same may be said of the individual red ware series grouped into red ware. Actually, this was anticipated from the correlations of individual types in factor analysis. Correlations showing the degree of association are high for all intrusive white ware series. They are similarly high for the red ware, which is of course all intrusive. Whereas there is evidence that the White Mountain Red Ware distributions are somewhat different from Tsegi Orange Ware and Smudged Red Ware (i.e., White Mountain Red Ware is associated more strongly with San Juan White Ware), this difference in degree of association is not sufficient to alter the cluster diagrams when each series is considered separately. Part of this result is due to the fact that samples for all red ware series tend to be small, and cluster analysis never produced major cluster divisions on the basis of the smaller samples of ceramic classes. In sum, practically identical results were obtained whether using all seven ceramic series separately, or grouping them into three more inclusive classes. Therefore, only the clustering of the seven ceramic series was chosen for discussion and illustration.

Cluster Analysis of the Lowest Primary Trash Strata

A cluster analysis of the stratigraphically lowest Primary trash strata was used to evaluate the relationship between the floor units and the Primary occupation trash levels that sometimes overlie them. In total, 21 trash strata satisfied the conditions of being Primary stratigraphically by R. Adams's strata evaluations, having Primary factor sores (A or B), and immediately overlying Primary floors. Many Primary floors, or course, did not have Primary trash immediately over them. Some were under other Primary floors, overlain by fallen roofs, or overlain by Secondary occupation behavioral or trash strata. Floors lying beneath other Primary floors had little possibility of mixture with Primary or Secondary trash. Primary floors overlain by Secondary strata could have been, and in some cases definitely were, contaminated by Secondary ceramics. However, this could easily be identified ceramically, and in fact no Primary floors were used in distributional analyses if Mesa Verde Black-on-white was present on them in amounts greater than one or two sherds. The only situation of possible mixture that could not be monitored stratigraphically or ceramically was the case of Primary trash resting on a Primary floor. The great majority of Primary floor units were shown to be reliable due to their stratigraphic position and/or a chi-square test of the floor-related ceramics to the Primary stratum immediately overlying the Primary floor; however, it was still desirable to examine the distribution of ceramic series in lower Primary trash strata to determine whether a distributional pattern emerged that was similar to the floors themselves. Priesnitz (1979) found that trash levels showed a patterning similar to the Primary floors in multidimensional scaling on a smaller sample of proveniences.

Cluster analysis, therefore, was applied to 21 strata representing the lowest Primary trash in the rooms already assessed for floor ceramic distributions. The stratigraphic units included structured trash (C), unstructured trash (M), several artificial fill levels (D) immediately above floors, and in one case (123W) two J strata, which are in this case actually trash levels. In several instances, counts for several small adjacent trash levels were combined. The ceramic input consisted of the percentages by stratum of the same seven ceramic series that were used in the cluster analysis of the floors.

Figure 22.7 illustrates the resultant cluster dendrogram for the lowest Primary trash strata; Method 7 was chosen for this illustration. The three major clusters again coincide with major differences in the percentages of San Juan White Ware (Mancos and McElmo Black-on-white). The relative amounts of San Juan White Ware account for the greatest amount of variation between trash strata, as was true in the cluster analysis of floors. Cluster A consists of proveniences with more than 72 percent San Juan pottery—this is the average percentage of San Juan decorated in the Primary as a whole. Cluster B contains San Juan White Ware in percentages of 50–70 percent, and Cluster C has 57 percent or less of San Juan types.

Cluster A (high San Juan) contains all rooms in which the floors are also high in San Juan White Ware. Included are Primary trash in Rooms 121W, 30W, 97W, 123W, 91W, and 100W. However, there are several rooms in Cluster A with high intrusive floors (33W, 84W, and 82W); in these rooms, the floor levels are more intrusive whereas the trash above them forced them into the high San Juan cluster (Cluster A). This was also noted for Rooms 84W and 82W by Priesnitz (1979). In part, this may reflect the general trend toward an increased use of San Juan ceramics through time in the Primary, because all these trash levels were deposited after the floors had been abandoned.

Clusters B and C, which contain trash strata with less than the mean percentage of San Juan White Ware for the Primary, include rooms in which the floors have also been shown to contain high intrusive counts (Rooms 6W, 62W, 129W, 31W, 81W, 43W, 199W, and 102 C, D). Only one room (127W) is represented in the high intrusive trash clusters that

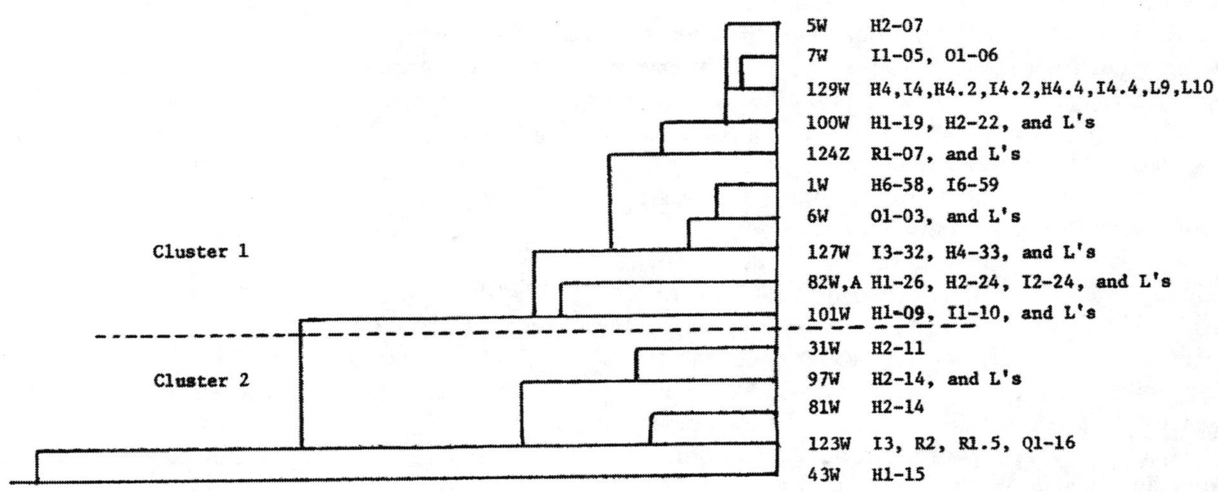

Figure 22.7. Cluster analysis of lowest Primary floors by wares (white, red, and gray).

did not contain large amounts of intrusive ceramics on its floor. In this case, the only trash level was an artificial fill stratum with only nine sherds; hence, sample error could account for the discrepancy. In all, there is a high degree of correspondence between floor units and the Primary trash just above them, in terms of their placement in the San Juan–intrusive continuum. Essentially, all high intrusive Primary trash levels are from rooms with similar percentages on their floors. The reverse is also true with the exceptions of Rooms 84W, 82W, and 33W, noted above. So the original question is answered in the affirmative. The distribution of seven ceramic series in the lowest Primary trash does appear to be similar to the distribution of those series on the floors of the same rooms.

Several factors may be responsible for the general similarities between Primary floors and the lowest Primary trash in rooms where both are present and are stratigraphically adjacent. The one that comes to mind first, of course, is that the adjacent strata may be mixed, at least enough to produce similar-looking cluster analysis results. This could have occurred through the original dumping of trash on an exposed floor surface in Primary times. It could also have been produced during excavation by the inadvertent inclusion of floor-related pottery with the strata lying just over them. Such natural forces as settling could also have served to bring trash materials into contact with the floor surfaces. However, there are other possible solutions to the observed similarities between floors and trash. One is that much of this trash probably was originally located on the upper floors (i.e., roofs) of these rooms and was discarded below them, or slid off the roofs when they collapsed. This possibility cannot be overlooked, because it is likely that rooms that were high intrusive (or high San Juan) on the Primary floor of the first story were likewise on other second-story floors (roofs), all of which have collapsed into lower stratigraphic positions. A second possibility is that the observed results are due to patterned trash disposal in the Primary. That is, the similarity of the floor and trash on the rather gross level of the ceramic series is due to the disposal of trash within the same room blocks or suites of origin. In these cases, trash and floor materials may appear similar in content, without necessarily being physically mixed with each other. The fact that there is a strong correlation of ceramic series with room blocks and suites when all Primary strata are included for each room (see discussion of preliminary tests of room blocks above) lends credibility to this hypothesis. Room blocks and suites tend to have similar ceramic compositions regardless of whether one is dealing with floor units, lowest Primary trash, or a combination of all Primary strata in the rooms. This spatial patterning is probably due to a combination of factors. Rooms within such units were similar culturally or functionally and thus the ceramics in them are similar in terms of original usage. On top of this, trash disposal by human agency apparently was also structured along room block–suite lines, so that the trash was disposed of within the confines of the same architectural units. And finally, the natural processes involved in the postoccupational collapse and settling of Primary materials would also have served to retain cultural materials within the same contiguous room units. Some of the trash, then, represents material originally utilized higher up in the same room. In other cases, the trash levels can be clearly seen to emanate from a neighboring room, coming in through the doorway. Because suites of rooms are interconnected by doorways, the connectivity also served to maintain uniformity of cultural materials within the rooms belonging to suites.

There are several reasons, then, why floor and above-floor trash appear similar in frequencies or percentages of ceramic series with a few notable exceptions. Mixing between strata (prehistorical or excavational), similarity of original behavioral contexts, patterned trash disposal, and natural processes of downward and lateral movement of cultural materials served to produce similar distributional patterns for both Primary trash and Primary floors. Without much more intensive work, including extensive vessel reconstruction, one cannot distinguish between these separate processes. From this point of view, the floor-trash similarities, where they exist in the Primary, do not necessarily invalidate the reliability of the floor-associated materials, especially when the comparison is made on the rather gross level of percentages of ceramic series found in the two strata types. Instead, these data shed light on the interesting facets of patterns of trash disposal and postoccupational natural forces at work in Salmon Primary occupation rooms and strata.

Cluster Analysis of Roofs and Roof-Like Features

A cluster analysis of 12 Primary roofs and roof-like features was also conducted. Recall that most of these are not true roofs, because all but 3 of 40 Primary roofs (second-story floors) contained very high Mesa Verde Black-on-white percentages from reuse by the Secondary occupants. Included in the cluster analysis were the several true roofs that still had not been mixed with Secondary ceramics, as well as several "roof-like features" consisting of platforms and/or roof repair levels.

The resulting cluster dendrogram shows little interpretable pattern. It does not reflect the sort of distributional patterning by room blocks and suites seen from the data on floors, using the same seven ceramic series. There are two possible reasons for the discrepancy: The roof sample included several kinds of strata, although they had all been termed roofs (F) in the field; and roofs (mostly second-story floors) may have been used differently from first-story floors, and thus would contain different percentages of the seven ceramic series also recorded for floor levels. A third possibility is sample error, owing to the small sample of roofs available from the Primary occupation. Without a much larger sample of structural, intact roofs with only Primary ceramics, any conclusions about ceramic distributions on roofs must be deferred. All that can be stated at present is that Primary roofs are often different from floors in ceramic series frequencies, and that no clear distributional patterning emerges from a cluster analysis of the few roofs and roof-like features available from excavations to date.

Cluster Analysis of Utility Ceramics: Intrusive vs. Local on Primary Floors

Utility ceramics, as with decorated ceramics, may be divided into several series, with differing origins of manufacture. Most utility ware on Primary floors is San Juan Gray Ware, including Mancos and Mesa Verde Corrugated and San Juan Plain Gray (Table 22.21). Intrusive utility ware includes Chuska Gray Ware tempered with sanidine basalt (Warren 1967; Windes 1977) and a small amount (49 sherds) of corrugated from the Cibola-Chaco area tempered with sand or a combination of sand and crushed sherd. All data are based on limited-attribute analysis, which required microscopic examination of tempering ingredients for all sherds.

Eighty-one percent of the utility sherds from Primary floors are local ceramics tempered with crushed rock, and only about 15 percent are intrusive, from the Chuska and Cibola Series. Percentages of utility ceramics are nearly the same when all Primary strata are included. It is evident, then, that most of the utility pottery from the Primary occupation was locally produced. The same is true of the decorated ware; roughly 72 percent of the total Primary decorated assemblage consists of Mancos and McElmo Black-on-white. The slightly higher proportion of local utility compared to decorated ceramics reflects the fact that intrusive decorated pottery reached Salmon Ruin in greater amounts than intrusive utility pottery did.

We expected to find intrusive utility pottery in close association with intrusive decorated types; that is, all intrusive ceramics should tend to be associated spatially. A preliminary suggestion of this was found in the overall correlation of Chuska Gray Ware with intrusive white ware from the Cibola-Chuska decorated series; Chuska utility ware tended to be associated with Chuska and Cibola White Ware (i.e., in high intrusive decorated contexts). A test of 27 Primary trash strata with either Cibola or Chuska White Ware, as well as any Chuska utility ware at all, indicated that intrusive white and gray ware sherds are often found together (Spearman's rank correlation exceeded the .005 significance level).

A cluster analysis conducted on the five utility ware series shown in Table 22.21, using 4984 sherds from the same floor units used for the cluster analysis of decorated ceramics (total 42 floor units), confirmed the association of intrusive decorated and utility ceramics. The cluster dendrogram produced a series of well-defined clusters based on the five utility classes. Further examination revealed that clusters with intrusive utility ceramics over the mean of 15 percent in nearly every case were also high in intrusive decorated ceramics. Rooms with Primary floors with large percentages of both intrusive decorated and utility ware include 1W (lowest floor), 93W (all floors clustered), 6W, 98W, 83W, 97W, and 33W (top floor), 62W (two of three floors), 43W, 129W (three floors), 31W, 84W, and 81W. Only 2 of the 19 floors in clusters with over the mean percentages of intrusive utility ceramics could not be considered also high for intrusive decorated pottery (121W, H-1-05 and 101W, G-1-08; the Room 121W floor contained a fairly small sample and had proveniencing problems as well). By way of contrast, the clusters with low intrusive utility ceramics consisted largely of rooms known to have high San Juan decorated ceramics on their floors—for example all rooms in the East Wing, which are quite high in local San Juan decorated types. The upper floors of Rooms 1W and 4W in the West Wing (also with abundant San Juan White Ware) also appear in the low intrusive utility clusters.

Two rooms deserve special mention: the Great Kiva and 102C. The Great Kiva floor assemblage has an average amount of both intrusive decorated pottery and intrusive utility ware. Twelve percent of its utility assemblage is Chuska in origin, which is close to the average of 14.4 percent Chuska for all Primary floors combined. The Great Kiva however is also relatively low for utility ceramics overall. In Room 102C, a cooking room, the floor assemblage contains

Table 22.21. Utility ware from Primary floors.

Series	N	%
San Juan Gray Ware (crushed rock temper)		
San Juan Plain Gray	413	8.3
Mancos and Mesa Verde Corrugated	3628	72.8
Chuska Gray Ware (sanidine basalt temper)	720	14.4
Cibola Gray Ware (sand or sand-sherd temper)	49	1.0
Unidentified Utility Ware	174	3.5
Total	4984	100.0

abundant utility pottery in general, including a whole corrugated jar resting on the floor. Although relatively little of this corrugated ware on the floor proved to be of an intrusive nature, the strata immediately above (C-2-24 and C-1-23), which are probably related to the use of this room, produced higher than usual amounts of Cibola Gray Ware sherds. Together with Room 93W next to it, the frequent intrusive utility ceramics for these rooms probably represent loci where intrusive utility ceramics were used for cooking and food preparation.

DISTRIBUTION OF VESSEL FORMS AND WARES

As previously mentioned, vessel form and ware category are both potentially sensitive to room function. That is, these two aspects are likely to reflect the actual uses of ceramic containers, as opposed to series and types, which are more likely to indicate cultural affiliation, extent of trade or exchange, and residence or status. Although this theoretical division of the cultural implications of ceramic attributes is not mutually exclusive (all ceramic usage is functional in the larger sense), some attributes, such as ware and vessel form, are more indicative than others of the daily uses of ceramic vessels. Indeed, most archaeologists have made the assumption, implicitly or explicitly, that decorated ceramics were used for serving, food preparation, and limited storage, and utility pottery was used for cooking and storage. Likewise, mugs were probably used for drinking, ladles for transfer of food between vessels or containers, bowls for food consumption, jars for liquid or solid food storage or transport, and so forth. With these assumptions, however, must go the recognition that many of the more generalized wares and forms (e.g., jars) may have had multiple uses, precluding a strict one-to-one relationship between vessel form and function. The multiple uses of the cooking and eating utensils in modern homes provides a useful analogy.

Ethnographic evidence from historic Puebloans provides examples of modern uses of ceramics, although such ethnographic analogy has limitations for inferring the uses of ancient ceramic vessels. First, locally made ceramic vessels have played only a peripheral role in most day-to-day domestic activities among the Pueblos during this century. Modern Pueblo ceramics are manufactured almost exclusively for sale, although to a limited extent ceramics continue to function in a domestic and ceremonial context. Second, traditional ethnographers generally did not pay close attention to or describe in detail the behavioral correlates of the various classes of ceramics used; the trend toward production for the outside marketplace was already in progress by the time many ethnographies were written in the twentieth century. A third problem lies in the application of ethnographically documented uses of ceramics to the prehistoric Puebloan, particularly to Chacoan society. If, as many suspect, the Chacoan phenomenon involved greater specialization of room function and division of labor, together with well-organized, long-distance exchange, there may not exist an applicable model for such phenomena among modern Pueblos. On the more mundane level of daily domestic activities, of course, it is probable that ceramic vessels may have continued to be used in much the same way over several hundred years, and as such, would be comparable to the situation in protohistoric time periods. Unfortunately, due to the first two problems, we have relatively little detailed information about specific ceramic-behavioral correlates even in the realm where prehistoric-historic analogies would be most fruitful. Although the fields of ceramic technology (Shepard 1965), ceramic decorative concepts (Bunzel 1929; Guthe 1925; Chapman 1938, 1970), and the learning of ceramic concepts (Stanislawski 1973, 1977) have proven informative, the functions of ceramics in domestic settings have been so altered that ethnographic data are of limited assistance. Therefore, ranges of use for prehistoric Puebloan vessels must be derived either through the logical possibilities inherent in the vessels themselves, and the limitations of given vessel forms, or from contextual-associational information from the archaeological locations of ceramic forms and wares. This section, then, concerns the distribution of the major classes of vessel forms and wares across Primary occupation behavioral surfaces at Salmon, interpreted in light of architectural and limited lithic and botanical evidence from the same proveniences.

Preliminary Tests

Several preliminary tests were used to determine the variability between Primary floors and roofs in terms of white ware, red ware, and utility ware. Totals for these ceramics were compiled for 42 Primary floor units (G, H, I, and L strata) that contained at least two wares. A chi-square test for difference yielded a value of 85 (df = 41), significant at the .001 level, and the rank correlation between the three wares was .55. Variation in the spatial distribution of ceramics was thus significant enough to warrant further study.

The next step was to investigate corrugated frequencies on a larger sample of Primary floors and roofs. A sample of 51 Primary floor (G, H, I, and L) and roof (F) strata that had both decorated and corrugated ceramics was arranged in order of utility ware frequency and percentage, revealing several facts:

1. The mean percentage of corrugated pottery on Primary behavioral surfaces is 61 percent; thus, nearly two-thirds of the ceramics are utility ceramics in general. The floor and roof strata displayed a continuum from 16.7 to 82 percent corrugated.

2. Rooms with high intrusive to local decorated ratios tended to produce relatively little corrugated. Of 17 floors with 55 percent or less corrugated, only 2 are from rooms that are not high in intrusive decorated ceramics. The floors of Rooms 129W, 119W, and 102C are exceptions in that they are high intrusive and yet contained high corrugated counts. These rooms were used for food preparation (102C), grinding (129W), or storage (119W), and thus might be expected to show higher amounts of utility ceramics. In the East Wing, where rooms tend to be low in intrusive ceramics, all proveniences showed 65 percent or greater utility ceramics.

3. Primary roofs are a problem because they were all contaminated by Secondary occupants. There are seven roof-like features, platforms, or roof repair levels, however, that were termed roofs (F) in the field. These were treated for convenience as "roof-like" strata; they all tended to have high corrugated frequencies. All seven of these strata have above 56 percent utility ware. The mean corrugated percent for the roofs is 68.7 percent. This suggests a differential use of ceramics between roofs and floor surface, with more utility ware use on roofs. However, the sample of structural (real) roofs for the Primary is so small that functional differences between roofs and floors could not be pursued further.

4. The two Primary kivas, the Great Kiva (130W) and the Tower Kiva (64W), both have relatively low corrugated frequencies, 50.9 and 53.3 percent, respectively. Although the sample from the Tower Kiva is small, and only from a foot drum, if it is at all representative, it would accord well with the percentage of utility ware from the Great Kiva, where a large sample was available. This suggests that Primary kivas contained relatively little corrugated ceramics, in keeping with their inferred ceremonial functions.

5. The rooms around the Tower Kiva (62W, 81W, and 82W) are all in the low corrugated class. Of eight behavioral levels from these rooms, six are 58 percent or lower in corrugated. The two remaining are in 81A (F-2-13), higher because it is a roof, and in 82W which, as we shall see, contains an internal division with much higher corrugated counts on one floor than the other. Floors in rooms in the Tower Kiva area may be low in corrugated by virtue of the fact that they are high in intrusive decorated ceramics, and/or are associated with ceremonialism, also a functional context of low utility ware usage, as known from the Great and Tower Kivas.

6. Several rooms contain multiple Primary floors (e.g., 33W, 62W, 93W, and 129W) with variable amounts of utility ware. This could reflect functional changes in successive Primary floors, or perhaps only sampling error. No clear site-wide trend emerged of increased or decreased use of utility ceramics on sequential Primary floors through time.

7. Two adjoining rooms with inferred food preparation activities (93W and 102C) contained large percentages of corrugated on their lowest floors.

In sum, it appears from a preliminary ordering of floors and roofs by amounts of utility ware, that there was a nonrandom distribution of utility ceramics. They appeared to be low (under about 55%) in rooms with high amounts of intrusive decorated pottery, such as ceremonial rooms, kivas, or around the Tower Kiva; and higher frequencies of utility ware are associated with low intrusive (high San Juan White Ware) rooms, roofs, and specialized food preparation and food grinding rooms.

Distribution of Wares and Vessel Forms by Suite

One basic hypothesis of this study is that room function, as evidenced by ceramic vessel forms and wares, as well as lithic categories, should not be correlated with suites (front-to-back ranges of interconnected rooms probably for extended family residence). Rather, room function should cut across suite groups and correlate instead with room size and placement—for example large square rooms, narrow back-wall rooms, or special function rooms. In general, room function should be associated with rows of rooms (e.g., across the back wall or front wall) rather than ranges of rooms (front-to-back groupings of interconnected rooms into suites).

Fifteen Primary floor units were used to compare ceramic wares and vessel forms to lithic flaked and ground stone categories (Figure 22.8). These floor units all had both lithic and ceramic artifacts, taken from the lowest or only Primary floors excavated in rooms that fall into suites. Floor units consisted of floor surfaces (H), structural floors (I), and associated pit fills (L). Cluster analyses for the three artifact categories were then compared to determine whether the distributional patterns of the two lithic and one ceramic data categories were similar or different. The diagrams were also studied from the point of view of the settlement pattern. The main question was, did any of the data appear to associate with or contrast with the dimensions of room placement, size, or arrangement into suites?

Hierarchical cluster analysis (Wood 1974) produces a dendrogram based on a dissimilarity matrix, which provides a visual representation of the degree of similarity or dissimilarity between units (proveniences) in terms of another variable (here, vessel form-ware percentages). The position of the joins between units in the dendrogram reflects the relative closeness of the relationship. Joins to the left side are relatively distant; joins to the right side are relatively more similar.

Ceramic Ware and Vessel Form Data

Eleven ceramic classes were used for the cluster analysis: white ware bowls, white ware jars, white ware mugs-pitchers, white ware ladles, white ware canteens, effigies or other special forms, any other white ware forms, red ware bowls, red ware jars and other red ware forms, utility jars, and other utility forms. The program used percentages of each class per stratum (floor unit). Data taken from limited-attribute analyses for all Primary strata were entered into a hierarchical cluster analysis program (Wood 1974).

The cluster analysis of ceramic ware-form classes was conducted in two ways—with and without the occupational fill (G) strata included in the floor unit counts. Each was clustered according to Method 2 (furthest neighbor) and Method 7 (flexible method). The patterns produced both with the G strata and without them were similar; only 3 of the 15 floor units changed cluster assignment when the G strata were added. Methods 2 and 7 produced nearly identical results in the dendrogram patterns.

Results of Cluster Analysis

The cluster analysis of floor units excluding occupational fill strata, using Method 2, is illustrated in Figure 22.8 and Table 22.22. Using relative frequency (percentage) data, the analysis produced two basic clusters showing a contrast between floors with high corrugated percentages (Cluster 1) and low corrugated percentages (Cluster 2). Corrugated was the primary variable used by the computer to cluster floors. Secondary (closer-join) clusters within these were formed in terms of the percentages of white ware and red ware. Although the data consisted of both ware and vessel form data, the resultant clusters can be understood in terms of wares alone; apparently ware differences are a more diagnostic criterion than vessel forms. The minor subclusters within the two major divisions are relatively unimportant because the percentages of red ware are quite small and the positions of their joins to other subclusters is very close.

Table 22.22 reveals that Cluster 1 contains floors with 61–72 percent utility ware, whereas floors of Cluster 2 contain 0–55 percent utility ware. The mean percentage of utility ware in Cluster 1 is 71 percent; in Cluster 2 the mean is only 36 percent. Utility ware, then, accounts for the majority of the patterning present, and displays a clear difference in relative amount between the floors grouped into two major clusters. These clusters may be summarized as follows: Cluster 1 (high in utility ware)—all large square rooms in suites (Rooms 5W, 6W, 100W, and 124Z); several rooms in the third row from the front (Rooms 1W, 7W, and 101W); and Rooms 82A and 82W, and 129W floors. Cluster 2 (low in corrugated)—back-wall (fourth row) and next-to-back-wall (third row) rooms (31W and 43W), and all second row rooms (81W, 97W, and 123W).

Conclusions from the Ceramic Data

1. Corrugated frequencies are highest in large, square, plaza-facing rooms. This probably reflects extensive use of such rooms as living rooms, including activities such as cooking and food preparation

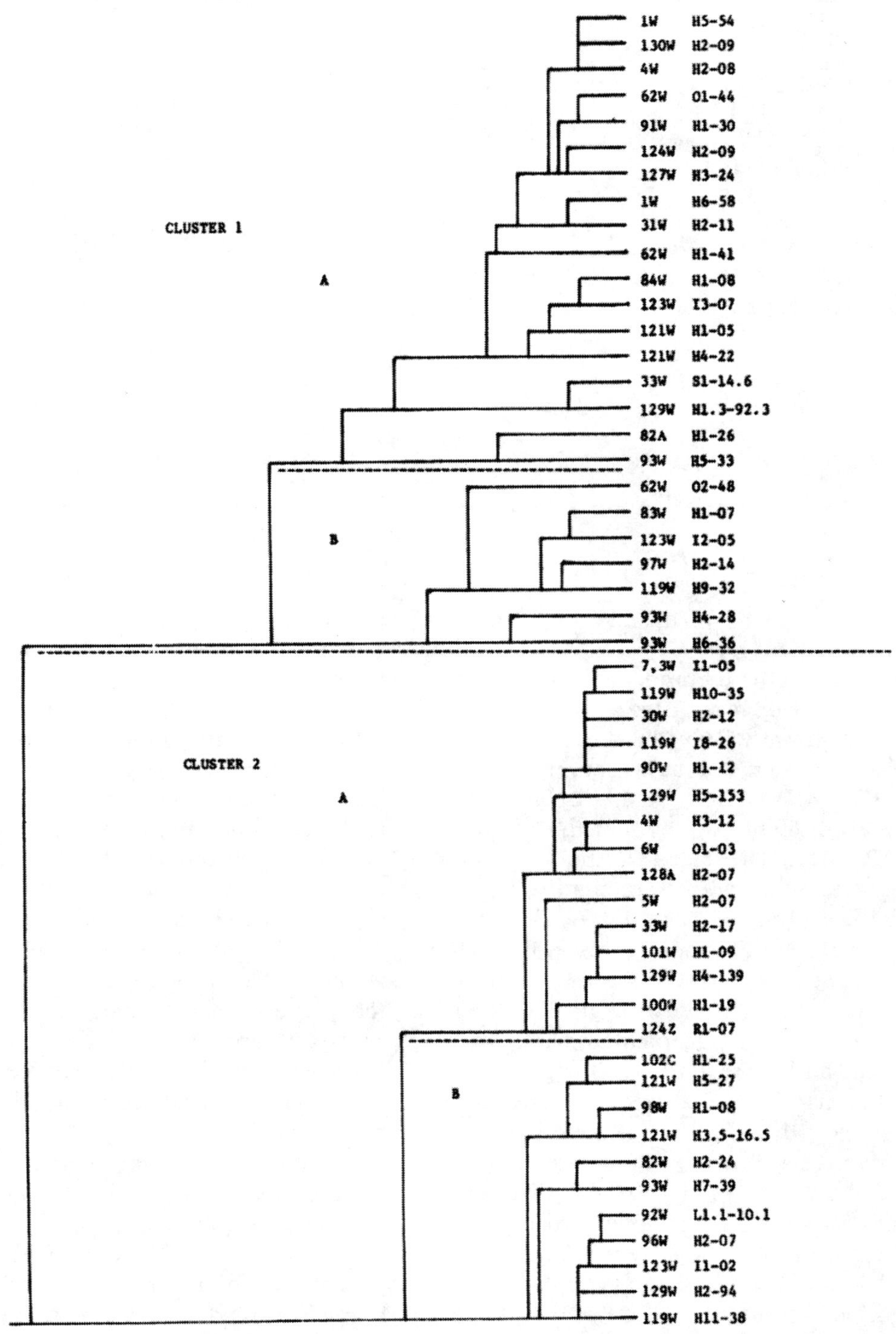

Figure 22.8. Cluster analysis by vessel form and ware for Primary occupation floors, Method 7.

Table 22.22. Ware percentages by stratum for lowest Primary floors in Salmon suites.

Room Floor		% White Ware	% Red Ware	% Utility Ware
Cluster 1				
5W	H-2-07	30	0	70
7W	I-1-05, 0-1-06	28	0	72
129W	H-4, I-4, H-4.2, I-4.2, H-4.4, I-4.4, L-9, L-10	24	0	76
100W	H-1-19, H-2-22, and L strata	24	1	74
124Z	R-1-07 and L strata	22	3	75
1W	H-6-58, I-6-59	37	2	61
6W	0-1-03 and l strata	33	3	65
127W	K-3-32, H-4-33, and L strata	34	3	62
82W, A	H-1-26, H-2-24, I-2-24, and L strata	7	20	73
101W	H-1-09, I-1-10, and L strata	18	9	62
Cluster 2				
31W	H-2-11	39	6	55
97W	H-2-14, L-3, L-4	44	6	50
81W	H-2-14	67	0	33
123W	I-3, R-2, R-1.5, Q-1-16	58	0	42
43W	H-1-15	100	0	0

No occupational fill levels.

on a family level, in which corrugated vessels would have played a prominent role.

2. Second row rooms (behind the large square rooms) are much lower in corrugated percentages than large square rooms. Only three rooms of this placement are present in the suite sample (123W, 97W, and possibly 81W). But there may be a pattern here, because all three of the floors of these rooms are in Cluster 2 (low in corrugated).

3. Third row and fourth row rooms (back-wall and next-to-back-wall rooms) include 1W, 7W, 31W, 43W, 101W, and 127W in the suite sample. Possibly 129W could also be included. All these (the lowest floors of which were clustered) are in Cluster 1, except Rooms 31W and 43W, which are contiguous in the west arm and are found in Cluster 2 (low corrugated). Rooms of this placement category are thus split between the clusters, although on the whole, such rooms tend to have higher corrugated counts than second row rooms (97W, 123W, and 81W). Perhaps the reason for lower corrugated frequencies in Rooms 31W and 43W is related to the general association of low corrugated counts in high intrusive decorated rooms, which 31W and 43W are. Perhaps corrugated is highest in large square rooms (due to cooking activities), low in the next room back, but somewhat higher again in back-wall and next-to-back-wall rooms, wherein the corrugated count is due probably to storage in corrugated vessels rather than to cooking. This conclusion is supported by the fact that large square rooms are plaza facing, spacious, and single storied, and all nine that have been excavated have firepits in their Primary occupation floors. Back-wall and next-to-back-wall rooms are two storied, small, enclosed by upper stories and other rooms to the side, and thus more suitable for storage than for domestic activities. This inference would suggest that corrugated ceramics functioned both as cooking vessels and as storage vessels, but in different loci. The dual role of utility ceramics has also been seen elsewhere (e.g., Rohn's work at Mug House, 1971).

4. Suites of rooms do not cluster together. That is, the rooms in a given suite are split between clusters; instead rooms cluster together on the basis of row (size and placement). This is not surprising because room function should cut across suites, especially if the suites are assumed to form equivalent residential units.

5. Rooms that have a high intrusive (vs. local San Juan) decorated count tend to have smaller percentages of corrugated ware. This is true of Cluster 2 rooms 31W, 81W, 43W, and to some extent 97W. The exceptions to this rule are 129W and 82W. The higher corrugated count of 129W (a high intrusive room) is probably related to food grinding activities (multiple metate rests), and the use of corrugated in conjunction with grinding to hold foodstuffs. The percentage in 82W is actually a combination of the two halves of the room, which are in fact very different within the room, as we shall see below. This count mainly reflects the one high corrugated floor.

Aside from these two special cases, high intrusive rooms appear to lack large quantities of corrugated in this sample. We return to this concept later, using a larger sample of rooms in the analysis.

Comparisons to Cluster Analysis of Lithic Data

The cluster analyses of lithic data (flaked stone and ground stone) reveal several points of comparison. Note that lithic clusters have not been completely interpreted at this point, and the lithic contents of each cluster have not been determined.

1. Ground stone and flaked stone assemblages on these floors have different distributions. This is not surprising given the differential functions implied by ground versus flaked stone assemblages.

2. Rooms in suites tend not to cluster together. Function cuts across residential suites.

3. The ground stone distribution (not including fixed milling troughs) is associated with rooms high in decorated intrusive ceramics—in this sample, Rooms 43W, 81W, 82W, 129W, and 97W. There is however no apparent relationship to the aspect of ceramic ware.

4. Flaked stone does not correlate well with any ceramic clusters based on ware differences. Flaked stone clusters cut across residential suites, but differently from ceramic wares. Flaked stone data from Rooms 43W, 81W, and 82W form a cluster, partly on the basis of relatively high amounts of Washington Pass Chert (an intrusive lithic material from the Chuska Mountains). It is noteworthy that all three of these rooms have high amounts of intrusive ceramics (Cibola and Chuska White Ware).

In summary, vessel wares do not show a distribution that accords well with the cluster diagrams for lithic ground stone or flaked stone. Indeed, there is no reason to suspect that ceramic wares should function in accordance with these basic lithic groups. Instead, the lithic distributions show a greater correspondence to the ceramic dimension of types and series. Specifically, ground stone frequencies and one group of lithic flaked stone materials, including the intrusive Washington Pass Chert, are only found in rooms that have relatively large amounts of intrusive ceramics (Cibola, Chuska, and Tusayan White Ware, Chuska Gray Ware, and red ware). This may indicate that both special grinding activities and the presence of exotic lithic materials are associated with rooms displaying abundant intrusive ceramics; by extension, these were Chacoan activity centers at Salmon Ruin.

This sample was designed to indicate whether functionality was associated with room suites. The one ceramic and two lithic data classes examined indicated no such association. It is unfortunate that the arrangement of the excavated rooms at Salmon resulted in only two complete front-to-back suites and three partial suites available for study.

Cluster Analysis of Wares and Vessel Forms on All Primary Floors

The most complete assessment of the spatial distribution of wares and vessel forms across Primary floor surfaces was gained through a cluster analysis that used all Primary floors in the site excavated to date.

Strata Classes for Cluster Analysis

Only Primary floors (H), structural floors (I), and associated pits (L) were used for the final distributional analysis. Occupational fill levels (G), which were sometimes identified in the field as associated with floor levels, were not included because (a) occupational fill as a class of strata was not always used consistently in the field, (b) these strata are more subject to mixing with overlying strata, and (c) much larger samples were available than in the study of decorated series and types (above) because the entire ceramic assemblage including utility ceramics formed the sample. Primary roofs were not used for cluster analysis because there are no good structural roofs that are ceramically "pure" Primary; 40 of 43 Primary roofs were reused in the Secondary, eliminating or severely reducing their Primary ceramics. Also, the preliminary analysis had shown roofs to be relatively high in utility ceramics.

Sixty-three Primary floor units with ceramics were available for studies; using a cutoff point of five sherds, 12 floor unit assemblages were eliminated from the sample. In total, 4171 sherds from the remaining 51 floors were included in the cluster analysis. Floors had a mean of 82 sherds, but there was considerable variation in sample size, ranging from 5 to 637 sherds. All sherds associated with and collected from these floor units were included in the cluster sample; some floors simply contained many more ceramics than others.

Ceramic Classes

Vessel ware and form data were used from the limited-attribute analysis of all Primary strata. Three categories of wares were recorded—white ware, red ware, and utility ware—and 18 vessel forms were recognized (data on file at Salmon Ruin). Preliminary work with these classes indicated that many of the vessel forms were very rare, and also that several classes could logically be combined. The vessel form classes were thus reduced from 18 to 11. A Spearman's rank correlation of .77 between the number of vessel forms recorded and the total sherd samples of the strata showed that the number of vessel forms (especially the rarer ones) was, in part at least, a function of sample size. Consequently, these data classes were reduced through a further combination of vessel forms, but not wares, into five classes to be used in cluster analysis of all Primary floors. These five are white ware bowls, white ware jars, white ware all other vessel forms, all red ware, and all utility ware. Table 22.23 lists the vessel forms and wares as grouped for cluster analysis treatment. Red ware and gray ware were not separated into vessel form groups because nearly 100 percent of the red ware is in bowl form, and because utility ware consists exclusively of jar forms of varying sizes. In other words, there is such a strong correlation between specific ware and vessel form, that there was no need to include both in the cases of red ware and utility wares.

Description of the Clusters

The dendrogram produced clusters of proveniences based on similarities or differences in ceramic content, as before (Table 22.24). The conclusions derived from Methods 2 and 7 are for the most part the same, although the dendrograms have dissimilar visual appearances. Method 7, visually the clearest, is illustrated in Figure 22.8. Method 7 produced a strong primary cluster divided into two major parts on the basis of utility percentages. Subclusters within these were based mainly on the ratio of white ware bowls to jars. The categories of other white ware forms (all forms but jars or bowls) and red ware did not figure prominently in the formation of clusters in Methods 2 or 7, probably because both categories are normally present in small percentages (with a few notable exceptions) or are nonexistent in most cases. Method 2 produced a more complex configuration of six clusters that appears to use the similarity of white ware jars, white ware bowls, and utility ware more or less equally in producing the cluster dendrogram. Again, the presence of white ware forms other than jars or bowls and red ware did not appear to be a deciding factor in the delineation of major cluster division. The ceramic contents of the clusters produced may be summarized briefly:

Method 2 (furthest neighbor):

Cluster 1: Low corrugated (44–54%), more white ware bowls than white ware jars.
Cluster 2: Moderate corrugated (52–74%), more white ware bowls than white ware jars.
Cluster 3: High corrugated (80–100%), red ware and other white ware forms essentially absent or very low; more white ware jars than bowls or vice versa.
Cluster 4: Low corrugated; more white ware jars than bowls.
Cluster 5: Low corrugated; many more white ware bowls than jars.
Cluster 6: Low corrugated; red ware forms 30–64 percent of the assemblage.

Method 7 (flexible method; see Figure 22.8 and Table 22.22):

- Cluster 1: Low in utility ware (0–65%)
  - Subcluster A: More white ware bowls than jars.
  - Subcluster B: More white ware jars than bowls.
- Cluster 2: Moderate to high corrugated (63–100%)
  - Subcluster A: Moderate corrugated percentages, white ware jars about equal to bowls.
  - Subcluster B: Highest corrugated (80–100%), red ware and other white ware forms very low; more white ware jars than bowls, or vice versa, and all decorated in general very low.

Table 22.23. Salmon vessel forms and wares used in cluster analysis of Primary floor units.

Cluster Analysis Classes	Limited-Attribute Form Classes
1.1 White ware bowls	All bowl forms from San Juan, Cibola, Chuska, Tusayan White Ware.
1.2 White ware jars	All jar forms from the same white ware, including ollas, jars, jar handles, and undifferentiated jar forms.
1.3 White ware other forms	All other forms from the same white ware series. Included are seed jars, canteens, pitchers, mugs, ladles, effigies, cylindrical? Unidentified mug = pitchers, odd-shaped containers, and effigy figurines (not vessels).
2.0 Red ware	Includes Tsegi Orange Ware, White Mountain Red Ware, and Mogollon Smudged Red Ware. San Juan Red Ware not included due to small sample size.
3.0 Utility ware	All utility ware, San Juan, Cibola, and Chuska Gray, including plain gray and corrugated ware.

Table 22.24. Percentages of five ceramic data classes used in cluster analysis of Primary floors.

Room	Floor Unit	% WW Bowls	% WW Jars	% WW Other	% Red Ware	% Utility Ware
Cluster 1A						
1W	H-5-54	29	16	3	3	48
130W	H-2-09	28	16	1	2	52
4W	H-2-08	31	14	1	3	51
62W	O-1-44	33	11	2	0	54
91W	H-1-30	36	9	0	0	54
124W	H-2-09	29	7	2	0	61
127W	H-3-24	24	10	3	3	59
1W	H-6-58	20	16	4	4	52
31W	H-2-11	14	21	4	6	54
62W	H-1-41	22	11	22	0	44
84W	H-1-08	39	15	1	5	40
123W	I-3-07	42	17	0	0	42
121W	H-1-05	36	9	0	0	46
121W	H-4-22	50	0	0	0	50
33W	S-1-14.6	63	13	0	0	25
129W	H-1.3-92.3	63	17	0	0	17
82A	H-1-26	27	9	0	63	0
93W	H-5-33	30	10	0	30	30
Cluster 1B						
62W	O-2-48	4	67	0	2	27
83W	H-1-07	6	28	0	2	65
123W	I-2-05	6	35	0	0	59
97W	H-2-14	10	32	0	6	48
119W	H-9-32	9	46	0	0	46
93W	H-4-28	0	32	32	14	18
93W	H-6-36	21	37	11	11	21
Cluster 2A						
7/3W	I-1-05	13	14	1	0	72
119W	H-10-35	14	14	0	0	71
30W	H-2-12	16	13	0	0	71
119W	I-8-86	16	11	0	3	71
90W	H-1-12	18	13	0	0	68
129W	H-5-153	17	17	0	4	63
4W	H-3-12	22	5	0	4	67
6W	O-1-03	22	11	0	3	64
128A	H-2-07	22	8	0	0	70
5W	H-2-07	7	14	0	0	64
33W	H-2-17	9	13	0	2	75
101W	H-01-09	9	13	1	0	74
129W	H-4-139	10	13	0	0	74
100W	H-1-09	8	15	2	1	74
124Z	R-1-07	13	5	3	3	71
Cluster 2B						
102C	H-1-25	2	4	2	0	93
121W	H-5-27	7	0	0	0	93
98W	H-1-08	0	0	0	0	100
121W	H-3.5-16.5	0	0	0	0	100
82W	H-2-24	12	0	0	8	80
93W	H-7-39	1	0	0	0	86
92W	L-1.1-10.1	7	12	0	2	80
96W	H-2-07	6	12	0	0	81
123W	I-1-02	4	16	0	0	80
129W	H-2-94	4	9	2	3	83
119W	H-11-38	0	12	0	0	88

No occupational fill levels (G) included. Complete strata designations for all strata in these floor units are given in Table 22.17.

It is notable that the major break in Method 7, and to a lesser extent in Method 2 is based on the amount of utility ware present; this appears to have been the most decisive variable in assignment of floor units to clusters. The computer produced the cluster breaks between high and low corrugated groups at about 63 to 65 percent, very near the mean percentage of 62 percent for utility wares on Primary floor strata as a whole.

An examination of the total sherd counts from floors in Cluster 1 compared to Cluster 2 of Method 7 suggests that the total sherd counts were smaller for floors low in corrugated percentages. A Mann-Whitney test for two samples was used to determine if the two populations (high vs. low utility ware) were significantly different. The null hypothesis of no difference between sample populations was rejected at the .05 significance level. Large amounts of utility pottery do, in fact, occur where the total sherd count is high. In behavioral terms, in places where total ceramic usage was heaviest (probably in cooking, serving, and storage areas) corrugated ware was used more extensively.

Conclusions from Vessel Form–Ware Distributions on Primary Floors

Rooms with multiple Primary floors often display considerable differences in vessel form and ware percentages. Most often, multiple floors in a given room do not fall into the same clusters. Regardless of the cluster method used, few rooms with more than one floor have those floors in the same clusters. The only fairly consistent rooms are 1W and 62W. The three floors of 62W are always low in corrugated and high in decorated intrusive ceramics. Further hints of consistency within rooms include 199W where three of four floors are high in utility ware, and 129W where three floors are also high in utility ware. In 93W, three floors are low in utility but high in white ware jars; the other one (H-7-39) is high in utility ware. In other words, 93W is above normal in jar forms, whether white ware or utility. The remaining rooms have floors that are high and some that are lower than the mean in utility ware frequencies. In part, this may reflect sampling error (especially the floors of 129W), but it may also indicate that several of the rooms underwent changes in function during the Primary period.

There is no overall clear temporal trend from lower to upper Primary floors across the site in ware percentages. In some rooms the lowest floor has more utility ware than the stratigraphically highest floor; in others the situation is reversed. There is no evidence that the overall amounts of utility ware in the site as a whole changed materially during the Primary occupation.

High vs. Low Intrusive Rooms

Rooms considered to have above normal numbers of intrusive decorated types in the Primary are 31W, 43W, 33W, 62W, 82W, 81W, 83W, 84W, 93W, 102C, 97W, 129W, and 119W. Rooms containing high intrusive types and series tend to have low corrugated percentages. This is shown by Cluster 1A and B, Method 7, and Clusters 1, 4, 5, and 6, in Method 2. Included in Method 7, Cluster 1 are the only floors or at least one floor (in multiple floor rooms) of all west arm and Tower Kiva area rooms. High intrusive Rooms 83W and 84W are also included in this cluster. Room 43W was not included due to small sample size, but if it had been it would also be in Cluster 1, because its floor had no corrugated pottery. Exceptions to the rule that high intrusive rooms are low in counts of utility ware are 33W (H-2-17), 30W (H-2-12), 82W (H-2-24), three of four floors in 119W, and three of four floors in 129W, which have high or moderate amounts of utility ware despite being high intrusive decorated rooms. Room 30W, in the west arm, is a low intrusive room in any case, so it does not signify a deviation. 82W shows a high corrugated count, but 82A on the other half of the room does not; this is probably a difference in function within this rather specialized room. In 119W and 129W, most of the floors (three of four in each case) are moderate to high in utility ware, although these rooms seem to have a high level of intrusive ceramics in their decorated assemblages. The reason for this is not clear, but it is probably related to their functions as milling and storage loci. In Room 93W two floors are also low in corrugated and a third floor high in corrugated; this room is also high in intrusive sherds of a specialized nature (cooking and food preparation). In 102C, next door, there are abundant intrusive decorated sherds but high corrugated as well, related to cooking and food preparation. Therefore, not all rooms with high intrusive counts are low in utility ceramics, but all those of an inferred residential or ceremonial nature (West Wing and Tower Kiva areas) do conform to this rule. Most red ware is also found in these rooms, as well as the highest percentages of special white ware forms (in 31W, 62W, and 93W).

East-West Division and Comparison

These data provide no evidence for an east-west division separated by the Tower Kiva, but excavated samples of rooms are heavily skewed, with many more rooms excavated on the east side. West Wing rooms all occur in Cluster 2A (Method 7), with moderate amounts of utility ceramics. These rooms are also moderate in intrusive decorated frequencies. East Wing rooms show no clustering by group. In general, wares and vessel forms do not cluster according to the wings of the pueblo. None of the rooms in the east or West Wings suggest specialized functions, by either ceramics or other data.

Large Square Rooms

Large square rooms in the cluster analysis sample include 6W, 5W, 92W, 96W, 100W, 121W, and 124W. All have high corrugated counts on their Primary floors. In Method 2, Clusters 2 and 3 have moderate to high corrugated percentages. All large square room floors except for two of four floors in 121W are in these two clusters. In Method 7, Clusters 2A and B correspond in high counts of utility ware. Again, all floors of all square rooms are in Cluster 2, except for two of the four floors in 121W. (121W has small sample sizes as well as poor proveniencing, so this exception may prove spurious.) Large square rooms all have one story and easy access, and all nine excavated to date contain fire hearths. They are very likely habitation (living) rooms. Thus, one of the major areas where corrugated ceramics are concentrated is in habitation rooms with fire hearths. Utility ceramics were probably used for cooking, among several possible functions. In these rooms, white ware jars and bowls are approximately equal in frequency. Furthermore, these rooms show little or no presence of special vessel forms, in white ware or red ware.

Second Row Rooms (immediately in back of large square rooms)

This sample includes 4W, 1W?, 91W, 97W, 129W, 119W, and 123W, for a total of 14 floors in the cluster analysis. No clear trend is evident. In Method 7 they are split between clusters. However, except for 119Wand 129W, they all have less utility ware than front rooms, and jars exceed bowls in frequency. They clearly have a function different from the large square rooms in front of them.

Back-Wall and Next-to-Back-Wall Rooms

Included in the cluster sample are Rooms 7W, 30W, 31W, 43W, 33W, 90W, 83W, 84W, 127W, and 128A. None of these rooms contain very high corrugated (none in Cluster 2B having 80–100 percent utility ware), but all have moderate amounts of corrugated; these rooms may have been used for storage. Method 2 shows that none of these rooms are in the highest utility Cluster 3. All rooms of this placement occur in Cluster 2, except 84W, which is in Cluster 1 of Method 2, but is also moderate in its utility ware percentage. Many of these rooms have white ware jar counts equal to or greater than white ware bowl percentages, which is in line with their suspected use as storage rooms, at least after the second story was added to the pueblo.

Major Trend in Room Placement

The major trend apparent, then, is between front large square rooms and all rooms to the back of these. Little trend can be discerned within the category of second row versus back-wall or next-to-back-wall rooms. But when these are grouped and compared to large square rooms, a definite difference appears. Large square rooms contain more utility ware, and white ware bowls exceed white ware jars. Rooms toward the back have lower corrugated percentages and a bowl to jar ratio of about 1:1 or in fact more jar forms. This situation occurs in Rooms 83W, 123W, 97W, 129W, 101W, 31W, 199W, and 33W, all second to fourth row rooms. Thus, high corrugated occurs with white ware bowls in large square rooms, and moderate corrugated in rooms behind them, along with higher white ware jar percentages.

Suites and Room Blocks

A separate test of suites found that forms and wares did not correlate with suite groups. The same was found on the larger sample of rooms in this cluster analysis. Suites (front-to-back interconnected groups) thought to represent residential social groupings show no pattern of consistency in vessel forms or wares. Floors of rooms belonging to given suites do not cluster together, contrary to the evidence from types and series where, in fact, such a pattern did emerge. The only hint of a trend is in the fact that some room blocks or suites form clusters by virtue of the fact that they are high in intrusive ceramics, and there is a general tendency for these to have low corrugated frequencies. This explains the fact that Rooms 62W, 82W, 31W, 33W, and 43W (not clustered) in the Tower Kiva area and west arm are found in the same cluster. Other suite units include Rooms 6W, 4W, and 7W; 90W, 91W, and 92W; 100W, 97W, and 101W; and 124W, 123W, 127W, and 128A. These four suites show no pattern of rooms clustering by suite. This confirms the hypothesis that vessel form and ware, indicative of function, should cut across the dimension of residence (suite or room block). It suggests that all large square rooms, for instance, had similar functions in keeping with their consistent size, placement, one-story height, and presence of fire hearths.

The Great Kiva and the Tower Kiva

Several rooms produced architectural, botanical, and lithic data that can be integrated with ceramic vessel form and ware data for functional interpretations. The Tower Kiva and the Great Kiva were both constructed and used during the Chacoan occupation, undoubtedly for ceremonial and possibly other functions. What sorts of ceramics are found in these known ceremonial contexts? The Great Kiva (130W) contains a Primary floor displaying relatively low amounts of corrugated (52%), and a white ware bowl percentage that exceeds that of white ware jars. This conforms to what might be expected in a ceremonial context; corrugated and white ware jars should be low in frequency because presumably little cooking or storage took place in the Great Kiva, although some amount of utility ware would have been necessary to transport food or drink into the kiva, or for very limited storage purposes.

The Tower Kiva (64W) assemblage contains very little Primary ceramic material because the room was extensively reused by Secondary occupation people (it was not included in cluster analysis). However, 15 sherds were recovered from L-6-15, the eastern foot drum, and only 7 of these were corrugated. If this is at all representative of the ceramic complex in Primary times, about half the ceramics used in the kiva were corrugated, which is close to the 52 percent corrugated in the much larger floor sample from the Great Kiva. The two major kivas of the Primary occupation thus both contained relatively low amounts of corrugated ceramics.

Rooms Near the Tower Kiva

Rooms 82W and 82A, which are portions of one original room just east of the Tower Kiva, very likely had a ceremonial-religious function. Room 82 originally had a single floor (H-2-24) across the whole room. Later in the Primary, it was split into two portions by a jacal dividing wall, separating 82A (larger portion on the west) from 82W on the east. A later Primary floor (H-1-26) was placed in the western part of the room, but not in the east. The room contains several unique features: a raised adobe platform or altar with associated heating pits next to the Tower Kiva side on the west, possible milling troughs, a raised platform of wood, perhaps for storage, peripheral post holes arranged in pairs along the north and south walls, a walled-in doorway converted into a niche, and a second-story window. The terms "altar" and "heating pits" are used with caution, because the exact functions of the raised adobe areas and the recessed, stone-lined pits in front of it are not known. Shelley (personal communication) sees some resemblance of floor features in front of this altar to milling troughs elsewhere in the Primary occupation at Salmon. There may have been an altar as well as milling of ceremonial grain in the western half of the room. On the east side of the jacal dividing wall is a series of slabs set into the floor (or just below it), perhaps a form of bin.

After studying the palynological evidence from 82A and 82W, Janet Rose (1979) concluded that there were several forms of evidence for ceremonialism in the room: There were many clumped *Zea mays* pollen groups, especially in the northeast corner pit and in the heating pits near the altar. Clumps were present on the floors of the two halves and in the occupation fill above them. Clumped pollen indicates intentional introduction of tassels by human activity, rather than accidental introduction by wind. There was also a wide variety of wild plant pollen. *Chenopodium* and *Amaranth* pollen occurred in high frequencies near the altar. "This suggests that the altar was an area for collection of food items" according to Rose (1979:30). There was evidence of food preparation in the wall hearth behind the jacal wall in 82W, but not in the large square hearth in 82A, and there was evidence indicating the storage of maize, *Chenopodium*, and Gramineae in the pit in the northeast corner of the room behind the jacal wall. In short, the number of species present, the clumped pollen (especially maize), and the evidence of differential spatial distribution of these pollens all suggest ritual-ceremonial activity in the room. Ethnographic analogy suggests the possible use of 82A-82W as a cacique's room or a medicine society room (Rose 1979:34–35). The room's assemblage also has a high frequency of intrusive ceramics, indicating the relative sociopolitical importance of the room, and perhaps utilization by restricted portions of the Chacoan population.

It is interesting to note the difference in ceramics between the 82W and 82A portions of the room. In 82W on the east side of the partition, away from the altar, there are many more ceramics in general, including 80 percent corrugated ceramics on H-2-24, with only 8 percent red ware. On the other side, on H-1-26 in 82A, although the sample is smaller, there is no corrugated at all, there is 64 percent red ware, the highest relative frequency of red ware on any Primary floor at the site, and bowl sherds are much more frequent than jar sherds. These data may reflect a difference in function for the two portions of the room, as would be suggested by the partition wall and the different kinds of features found on each side of it. The side containing ceremonial features lacks corrugated and has frequent white ware bowl and red ware bowl sherds. The side with the floor slabs and the storage pit looks much more domestic, with no evidence of ceremonialism but rather a storage pit and a hearth used for food preparation (according to botanical evidence). Here, utility ceramics amounting to 80 percent were found on the floor. Perhaps the smaller portion on the east side (82W) was reserved for storage or some domestic type of activity in conjunction with the ceremonial activities that took place on the west side in 82A. The palynological evidence also supports this conclusion; Rose suggests storage of plants in the pit in the northeast corner (82W) and food preparation in the wall hearth on the same side of the room. Conversely, there is no evidence of food preparation at the large square hearth in the west (ceremonial side) of the room. Rose stated that "perhaps the jacal wall served to divide a storage area from the rest of the room" (1979:34).

Room 62W, immediately west of the Tower Kiva, is also associated with the Tower Kiva complex structurally, and undoubtedly functionally as well. As with 82A-82W on the other side of the Tower Kiva, 62W has several interesting features, most notably the spacious size of the room, a masonry bench on the east side toward the Tower Kiva, and a row of large ponderosa pine upright posts set into the floor parallel to the bench, which may have served to help support the roof in this large room. The Primary levels of 62W produced a high intrusive pottery assemblage, like all those in the Tower Kiva area. The three Primary floors of 62W are all below the mean in utility ware, with 54 percent, 44 percent, and 27 percent utility ware.

Palynological evidence for H-1-41 in 62W found by Janet Rose (1979) was similar to Room 82, with the plant pollen indicative of medicinal-ritual practices. The evidence includes high amounts and clumping of maize pollen. "It is entirely possible that corn was used ceremonially in 62W" (Rose 1979:22). Abundant *Pinus* was found in the room, despite the fact that there is no hearth on the floor, which probably is evidence for collection of pine boughs for medicinal or ceremonial purposes. High pollen counts occurred for many other species as well, especially *Chenopodium* and *Ambrosia*, which occur in clumps.

Additional ceramic evidence of ceremonialism on this floor is the relatively great amount of other white ware vessel forms (22%) on H-1-41. This vessel form category includes special forms such as canteens, pitchers, and effigy forms.

There is thus architectural, botanical, and ceramic evidence that Rooms 62A and 82A-82W had ritual-ceremonial functions. Room 81W, next to 82, may also have functioned in this way, but the ceramic floor sample (only three sherds) was too small to assess. The low utility ware frequency, high red ware amounts (82A), high bowl to jar ratios, and the presence of special white ware vessel forms (62W) all support this conclusion. The low utility frequencies are similar to the two rooms of known ceremonial activity, the Tower Kiva and the Great Kiva.

Cooking and Food Preparation Rooms

The two front gallery rooms, 93W and 102C, show abundant evidence for cooking and food preparation. Every floor of 93W contains hearths (Reed, Chapter 8; K. Adams 1980; K. Adams, Chapter 39). The lowest ones contain multiple hearths, including a very large hearth on the lowest Primary floor. It may also be noted that the two adjacent rooms were part of a single long gallery prior to the insertion of the wall dividing them at about AD 1116. The lowest floor of 93W apparently extends under the dividing wall into Room 102C to the east (R. Adams, personal communication). In 102C a grinding slab and a whole small corrugated jar, together with an oxidized partition wall of adobe, suggest activities similar to 93W.

Room 93W's lowest floor contains 86 percent corrugated. The three Primary floors above the lowest floor have successively lower percentages of utility ware, but are high in percentages of white ware jars. The white ware jar percentages in 93W on H-4-28 and H-6-36 are 32 percent and 37 percent respectively; this is very high for Primary floors in general. These same floors have high amounts of special or other vessel forms and red ware. Thus, Primary floors in 93W are high in utility ware jars or high in white ware jars, or both. In 102C there is a very high corrugated count (93%), one of the highest in the pueblo. Both 93W and 102C are classed as high intrusive rooms, so that the cooking and food preparation activities there were probably carried out by the Chacoan element of the pueblo. The decorated assemblage in the two rooms (including the fill above the 102C floor) is heavily weighted toward intrusive ceramics, including Cibola, Chuska, and Tusayan White Ware. Therefore, the high utility counts in 102C and the lowest floor of 93W, as well as the abundance of white ware jars on the higher Primary floors of 93W, together with the relatively few bowls found, help support the conclusion, drawn on architectural, feature, and botanical grounds, of cooking and food preparation.

Rooms With Milling Troughs

According to Shelley (1983; Chapter 48), grist troughs or supports for metates are found in three and perhaps four rooms on Primary occupation floors. The metates themselves were all removed prehistorically, but the support for and depressions of the metates remain as a row or rows of features on these Primary floors. These are found in the following rooms: 129W (H-2-94), 6 or 12 metates (possible double row); 97W (H-2-14), 12 metates; 93W (H-6-36), 6 metates; and 82W (H-2-24), 3–4 metates.

All but the 82W floor had very high jar counts relative to bowls. In 129W on H-2-94, the corrugated jar percentages are high (83%) and the white ware jar percentage exceeds that of bowls. In 97W on H-2-14 and in 93W on H-6-36 the corrugated jar percentages are moderate, but the white ware jar amounts are among the highest for any Primary floor. In other words, all these floors display an extensive use of corrugated and/or white ware jars; white ware jars exceed bowl frequencies on all three floors. These vessels could have been used to transfer grain and plant products into and out of containers at milling locations. The only other places where white ware jars are prominent parts of the ceramic assemblages are the rooms behind the large square rooms, where the white ware jar frequency likely reflects storage of plant products before or after their processing in milling areas. The ware-form counts in 82W on H-2-24 are very different from those in 82A on H-1-26, as noted above. H-1-26 has no corrugated ceramics but abundant red ware, connected with the ceremonial activity occurring on the west side of the room. However, the floor below (and to the east) of H-1-26 (H-2-24) contains 80 percent utility ware. If the milling troughs (if that is in fact what they are) relate to the H-2-24 level, the high corrugated count would place this floor into an agreement with the high utility or white ware jar frequencies noted for the other three Primary floors with milling troughs (above). In this reconstruction, Room 82 may have changed function during the Primary, from a milling location to a focus of ceremonial activity (plus the grinding of ceremonial grain?) later. The position of 82W, once a plaza-facing room before the addition of Room 65 in front of it, would then have been equivalent in position to 93W, also a focus of milling activity. In this regard, it may also be mentioned that 129W, prior to the construction of Room 122 in front of it, also with milling troughs, would have fit into the pattern of Rooms 82W, 93W, and 102C, with food preparation and milling activities in narrow, front row rooms facing the plaza. Room 119W, a small room next to 129W and connected to it via a doorway, also contains floors similarly high in corrugated or white ware jars. Of four floors in 119W, all but the uppermost have jars exceeding bowls; one floor (H-11-38) has no forms other than white ware and utility ware jars. The 129W–119W group, high in intrusive ceramics, may then have formed a food preparation, milling (129W), and storage (119W) unit for the Chacoan population.

All rooms with evidence of milling troughs have high intrusive decorated pottery assemblages. Room 84W, thought to be the locus of metate manufacture and/or discard (Shelley, personal communication), also fits this pattern. The combination of several data classes thus suggests that food preparation and milling activities were concentrated in a few loci falling into a spatial pattern (except perhaps for 97W in the second row back); ceramic evidence suggests that they were areas of Chacoan (high intrusive) activity.

Other Ceramic-Lithic Correlates

Other correlations between ceramic and lithic data include the large amounts of cobble-sandstone lithic materials on Primary floors in 83W and 43W, and the high amounts of Washington Pass Chert on the floors of 43W, 31W (trash), 62W, 82W, 129W, and 102C, in decreasing order of frequency (Shelley, personal communication). All of these rooms and the floors within them are high in intrusive decorated ceramics; the large amounts of sandstone-cobble refuse on the floors, the use of exotic chipped stone materials, and the exotic associated ceramics also imply that these rooms were centers of Chacoan population activity.

Summary

The ceramic variables of vessel form and ware show a nonrandom distribution across Primary floors in a sample that includes all excavated Primary floors with sufficient sample size. The distribution of these ceramic variables, thought to be sensitive to function, is strongly correlated with the size and placement of rooms, the existence of floor features, the presence of lithic milling and exotic flaked stone materials, and various botanical evidence from Rooms 93W, 82W, and 62W. Five ceramic form-ware classes were used in cluster analysis to produce the following conclusions.

1. Utility ware amounts are high in all front row, large square rooms (living), but moderate in all rooms to the back of them (storage). Very high amounts are found in cooking or food preparation rooms—93W (lowest floor), 82W (lowest floor), 102C, and some floors in 129W.

2. White ware bowls exhibit no clear overall trend, but bowls tend to exceed jars in large square rooms, as well as in ritual-ceremonial activity areas.

3. White ware jars are never frequent in large square rooms, but tend to be more prevalent in the rooms behind them. Counts for white ware jars are higher than for bowls in 123W (two floors), 83W, 101W, 119W, 33W (H-2-17), 31W, and 129W (two floors). All of these are in back of large square rooms. White ware jars were used extensively in milling or food preparation rooms—93W (two floors), 97W, and 129W.

4. White ware forms other than bowls or jars are never a dominant part of the assemblage on any floor, but are most abundant in 93W (two floors), 62W (H-1-41), and 31W, all high intrusive rooms. Elsewhere, the amounts on Primary floors are quite small.

5. Red ware likewise forms only a small percentage of the assemblage in most cases, often occurring where bowls exceed jars; almost all red ware consists of bowls, and may have functioned much the same as white ware bowls. Red ware also occurs where corrugated frequencies are low, and in high intrusive white ware rooms. Red ware is the most prominent (more than 5%) in floor assemblages from Rooms 31W, 82A, 82W, and 93W, which are all high intrusive rooms in other respects (i.e., high in Cibola, Chuska, and Tusayan White and Gray).

Ceramic, botanical, and lithic evidence revealed the following trends with regard to room size and placement:

1. Vessel form and ware distributions, as well as lithic flaked and ground stone, cut across room organization by suites, suggesting that each suite contained rooms of different functions (going from front to back), and that rooms of similar size and row placement across the site had similar functions. This confirms the hypothesis that room function should cut across suites (residences).

2. Rooms with high amounts of decorated intrusive ceramics are lower than the mean in utility ceramics (west arm, Tower Kiva area, and 83W-84W). This does not hold true of high intrusive rooms exhibiting evidence of cooking or food preparation (e.g., 93W, 102C, 129W–119W) wherein abundant intrusive (i.e., Chacoan activity) is associated with high utility wares, including relatively high (for Salmon) frequencies of intrusive ceramics from the Cibola and Chuska Gray Ware.

3. Large square rooms have higher than average utility ware percentages, contain hearths, are spacious, have a single story, and are easy to access. Multiple usage is implied, consistent with their identification as living or habitation rooms.

4. Two-storied rooms toward the rear (second, third, and fourth row rooms) generally contain few hearths on the ground floors and were difficult to access. These contain moderate amounts of utility ware and high white ware jar counts. The inferred function for at least some of these is storage.

5. Ceremonial rooms including the Tower Kiva (64W), Rooms 62W and 82W on either side of it, and the Great Kiva (130W) have architectural shapes and internal features suggestive of ceremonial activities; these tend to be quite low in utility ware percentages. High red ware (82A) and high special white ware vessel forms (62W) are noted for some of these rooms. Palynological evidence for ritual and ceremonial activity occurs in 62W and 82W, along with concentrations of Washington Pass Chert (intrusive). Rooms in the Tower Kiva area are all classed as having higher than normal frequencies of intrusive decorated ceramics, indicative of extensive Chacoan usage.

6. Rooms with evidence of milling activities (82W, 97W, 93W, and 129W) or specialized food preparation (93W and 102C) are also situated toward the front of the pueblo (except 97W). Rooms 82W and 129W may have been in a plaza-facing position prior to later Primary construction in front of them. Room 93W exhibits evidence of milling and food preparation (K. Adams 1980; Chapter 39). Food preparation also occurred next-door in 102C. All of these floor assemblages have either high corrugated or high white ware jar frequencies; white ware jars always exceed the white ware bowls in these areas. Bowls, by contrast, are rare. Extensive use of the jar form in these locations is related to storage and transfer of processed (milled or prepared) and unprocessed foodstuffs. All of these rooms also contain abundant intrusive ceramics, implying that specialized milling and food preparation were associated with the Chacoan element of the population.

Although full integration of the ceramic, lithic, and botanical data from Primary floors has yet to be achieved, there appear to be noticeable trends and correlations, several of which have been presented in a preliminary fashion here. Ceramic evidence of room function is often subordinate to the evidence from lithic, botanical, and osteological data, which often provide more powerful and direct functional evidence. The strong mutual support found between the several data classes thus far lends support to the conclusions derived from ceramics alone. These mutually reinforcing relationships also tend to reinforce the probable functions of ceramic wares and vessel forms deduced from their limitations and capabilities, as hypothesized earlier.

These data may suggest that the functionality of Primary rooms may have been either general (e.g., large square rooms for living or habitation) or very specific (e.g., 93W or 82W). The best recognized specific functions appear to relate to either ritual/ceremonial usage in the Tower Kiva area and the Great Kiva, or milling and food preparation rooms. Because all of these specialized localities have high frequencies of intrusive ceramics (assumed to represent possessions of the Chacoan population), it may well be that Chacoan inhabitants held a prerogative on these activities. At least, it may be said that the Chacoans maintained a distinct spatial division of activities within the pueblo, especially in the ceremonial and food preparation realms. Potentially, their societal constitution involved an equally distinct division of labor. Although specialization of room function does not necessarily imply a strict division of labor (by sex, cultural identity, Chacoan vs. local populations, or status), the existence of specialized localities devoted to at least two broad categories of activities at Salmon does point toward such a conclusion. It is certainly apparent that the use of space was structured, and for some activities at least, highly organized. The relationship between architectural placement, together with size and shape of rooms and their internal features, and the artifactual contents (ceramics, lithics, and botanical remains) found on the floors, is a mutually supportive one. This implies specific concepts regarding the utilization of space in the Chacoan occupation, and premeditated planning with such functions in mind.

Chapter 23

RELATIVE DATING WITH SALMON CERAMICS USING FACTOR ANALYSIS

by Hayward Franklin

Factor analysis is a widely applied statistical technique that has been used in archaeology since at least 1970. It is most commonly used for ordering and grouping ceramic data within sites to solve spatial and synchronic problems. Longacre (1970) and Hill (1970) used the technique to elucidate spatial patterning of ceramic design attributes to test hypotheses involving internal social organization at Carter Ranch and Broken K Pueblos. On the Salmon Project, factor analysis was used primarily for chronological control. Used on typological data, it has provided the chronological control necessary to stratify ceramic samples by occupational periods, rather than to directly elucidate spatial differences within each component. The latter problems were addressed via other techniques (multidimensional scaling, cluster analysis, SYMAP) after factor analysis was employed to ensure contemporaneity of sample sets.

The type of factor analysis used—principal factoring with iterations—was applied to the rough-sort data at Salmon with the aid of Zoe (Paddy) Johnson. The goal was to investigate the cooccurrence of groups of variables (whether attributes, types, or proveniences). Based on a correlation or partial correlation matrix, factor analysis produced the initial factor scores, which were then rotated to produce equivalent but different solutions. The matrix factors included variables that were consistently associated with each other. In each factor, each variable has a certain loading or degree of strength within that factor. The number of factors varies with the type of factor analysis used, but the first factor always accounted for the majority of the variability in the sample, with decreasing amounts of variability accounted for by succeeding factors. The eigenvalue of each factor gives an idea of its relative strength. The cumulative percentage of variability accounted for by each factor was also determined.

Several methods of rotation are available, either orthogonal or oblique. Orthogonal rotations, which rotate the matrix into a vertical or horizontal plane, include varimax and equimax methods. Oblique rotation methods pass the data through planes other than vertical or horizontal. Image factoring produces more factors than principal factoring, and spreads the variability out over the factors more evenly. Its special usefulness lies in assessing the finer and more subtle sources of variation in the sample, compared to principal factoring, wherein the first two factors typically account for 70 to 80 percent of the variability in the sample.

FACTOR ANALYSIS OF SALMON CERAMICS

Factor analysis was used at Salmon to investigate which pottery types occurred consistently together. This information was then used to identify temporal and spatial variability within the site. The technique merely demonstrates the extent of association of the major pottery types within stratigraphic units; the interpretation of temporal or spatial correlates rests on stratigraphic and other grounds.

All factor analysis at Salmon was based on a first-order partial correlation matrix, correcting for variation in sample sizes (controlling for total decorated). The final scattergrams were based on principal factoring with iteration, and additional rotation of that matrix by orthogonal and diagonal methods produced the factor structures more easily examined for substantive content.

The first use of ceramic factoring was in September 1976. After stratigraphic corrections, it was used again in July 1977 on the 633 strata analyzed to that point. In addition to all strata present at that time, input data also consisted of a list of 16 of the best-sampled pottery types at the site (with a minimum of 100 sherds each in the site as a whole). Utility wares (plain gray and corrugated) were included among the types entered because their association with other types had potential chronological or spatial significance. The analysis produced three factors, the first two of which accounted for 85 percent of the variance in the sample; that is, they had eigenvalues of greater than 1.0. These two factors, summarized in Table 23.1, had obvious temporal implications. The

Table 23.1. Factor matrix using principal factor with iterations as basis for scattergram .

Type or Ware	Factor 1	Factor 2
Escavada B/w	.27	.11
Puerco B/w	.36	.12
Gallup B/w	.17	.49
Chaco B/w	.48	.60
Chaco-McElmo Black/w	.40	.15
Mancos B/w	.77	.20
McElmo B/w	.77	.20
Mesa Verde Black/w	–.92	.31
Puerco B/r	.43	.21
Wingate Polychrome	.21	–.30
St. Johns Polychrome	–.08	–.12
Tusayan B/r	.31	.05
Citadel Polychrome	.28	–.03
Smudged Red Ware	.34	–.02
Plain Gray	.24	–.04
Corrugated	–.48	.16

Factor loadings were rounded to two decimal places.

first factor (accounting for 60.8% of the variability), included high positive loadings for all intrusive types known to be Primary, as well as high loadings for Mancos and McElmo B/w. Negative loadings were apparent for Mesa Verde B/w, St. Johns Polychrome, and corrugated ware. This factor was interpreted as a contrast between Secondary ceramics versus all Intermediate and Primary ceramics, because it was known from stratigraphy and cross-dating that the Secondary occupation ceramics consist mainly of Mesa Verde B/w, St. Johns Polychrome, and high amounts of corrugated pottery. The second factor, accounting for about 15 percent of the variability, showed positive loadings for both Primary and Secondary types. It contained negative loadings for McElmo B/w, Wingate Polychrome, and St. Johns Polychrome. In essence, Factor 2 presented an opposition between McElmo B/w and Wingate Polychrome versus all Primary and Secondary types. Factor 2 also had temporal implications because we know that there were strata in the site in a position between Primary and Secondary strata (i.e. Intermediate) that contained McElmo B/w as the major associated ceramic type. Therefore, the first two factors produced groupings of associated types that could be interpreted from cross-dated ceramics of the region, as well as from stratigraphic sequences that have temporal meaning. Factor 1 opposed Secondary ceramic types to Primary and Intermediate ones. Factor 2 opposed Intermediate to both Primary and Secondary types. Between the two factors, then, the three ceramic complexes belonging to Primary, Intermediate, and Secondary time periods were represented. Types in opposition to each other in the same factor (e.g., positive versus negative loadings) were invariably of different time spans according to the time periods attached to them by earlier research in the region. Because the factor loadings in the first two factors opposed types of different time periods, and because these two factors accounted for 85 percent of the variance in the sample, the conclusion was that temporal factors accounted for the majority of the variability in the ceramic associations in Salmon strata.

Production of Scattergrams

Due to the predominance of temporal variability in the ceramics, factor analysis results were then employed to aid in stratigraphic and temporal control across the site. This was accomplished initially by producing a scatter plot of all strata in relation to their position vis-à-vis Factors 1 and 2. Figure 23.1 illustrates the first scattergram plot of all strata (through 1976). The plots form a parabolic curve (or a twisted one-dimensional object), indicating a linear relationship between the dimensions and the strata plotted. On this graph, the vertical axis measures a stratum's Factor 1 score, contrasting Primary to Secondary. The horizontal axis locates the stratum's Factor 2 score. The scattergram thus incorporates three dimensions, and a particular stratum's ceramics can be plotted by reference to its association with the three major time periods. Consequently, plots in the upper right corner are high on Factor 1 and low on Factor 2 (i.e., with abundant Primary ceramics). Plots toward the middle left of the plot are high on Factor 2 but low on Factor 1. These strata are high in McElmo B/w, and are usually assignable to the Intermediate time period. Strata found toward the lower right corner scored negative on Factor 1 (i.e., high in Mesa Verde B/w), and thus correspond to the Secondary time period. The area in the middle of the parabolic shape contains strata that do not score strongly to any period; they consist of mixed assemblages of types belonging to all three. Fortunately, there are relatively few plots in this central area as compared to those in the linear structure. The plotting of the ceramics of each stratum against the axes of Factors 1 and 2 was considered successful, since it produced the desired parabolic form; in addition the pattern is tightly packed. There are relatively few plots scattered outside of the main area of concentration, and only a few lying within the arms of the parabolic curve (i.e., mixed Primary, Intermediate, and Secondary ceramics).

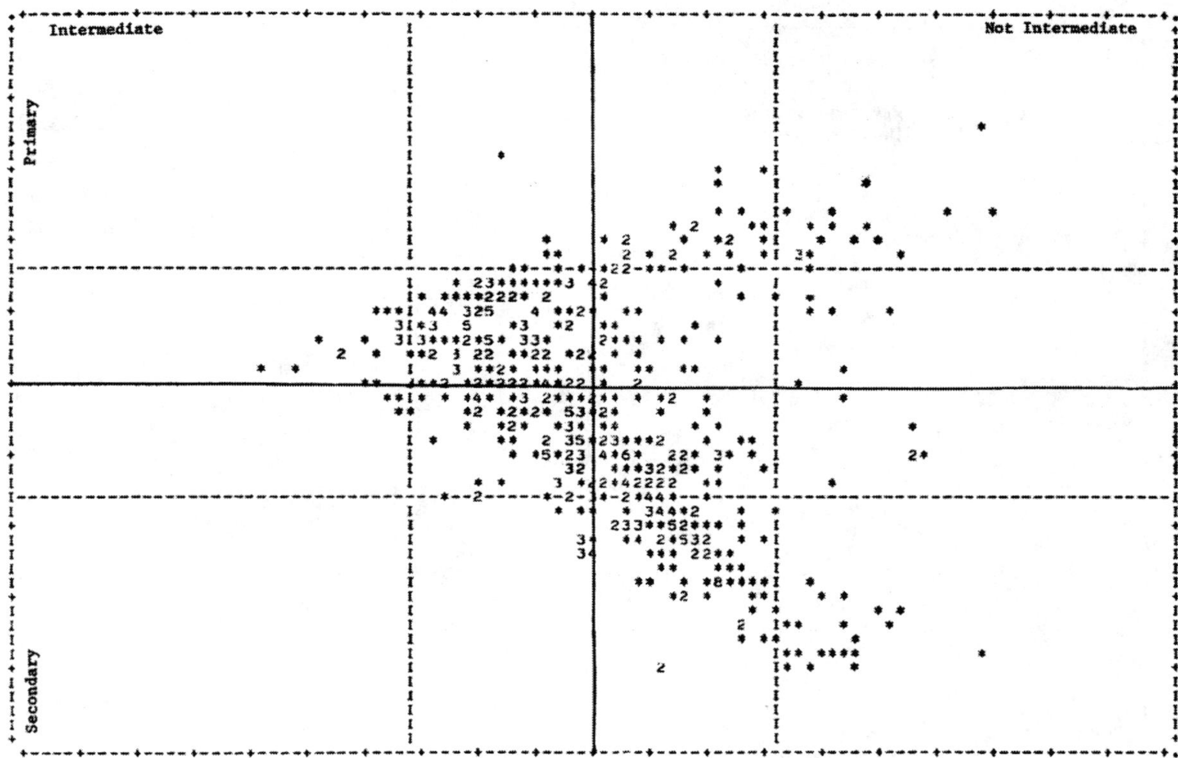

Figure 23.1. Factor analysis scattergram (7-31-1977)

Although the scattergram plots apparently formed an unbroken continuum from Primary to McElmo B/w dominant to Mesa Verde B/w dominant strata, this continuum was further subdivided into several sections by examining the ceramic content of a sample of strata plotted on the scattergram. This identified the ceramics present in every one of the plotted strata (i.e., for every point on the scattergram). In this way the relative amounts of different classes of ceramics could be determined for any stratum. The ceramic contents of strata graded from those with abundant Primary intrusives (especially Cibola Series) on the upper right, to increasing amounts of Mancos B/w toward the upper left. At the left end of the parabola, strata contained mostly McElmo B/w, and toward the lower right corner strata had increasing amounts of Mesa Verde B/w. These pottery types are not totally mutually exclusive within strata in the site due to mixing, and this is reflected in the scattergram, but a trend across the parabola is nonetheless apparent. A stratum in the lower right corner does not necessarily contain only Mesa Verde B/w, but that type would by far be numerically dominant. Ceramic contents become increasingly mixed for strata plotted toward the central area in the middle parabola.

Lines were then drawn across the parabola roughly demarking the boundaries between strata containing major ceramic groups. Figure 23.2 shows the same scatter plot with the dividing lines superimposed. Points (strata) falling within each of these areas are characterized by a general uniformity of ceramic content.

New strata were added to the file as more rough sorting was completed, and three more factor analyses were conducted; the earliest run (described above) used 633 strata and the latest one in 1979 used 1493 strata. The conditions of data entry changed only slightly. The early (for Salmon) Cibola types of Puerco, Escavada, and Red Mesa B/w were combined because of small sample sizes into a category labeled Early Cibola. The selection criteria for data input were also slightly altered so as to eliminate all strata with only corrugated or plain gray utility wares, all strata with only one decorated type, and all excavationally mixed strata (not securely provenienced to a single stratum). The number of pottery types entered into the program changed only slightly; the final analysis used a list of 17 types and series. The better-sampled types were used as discrete entities; the rarer intrusive types remained grouped by series (e.g., Chuska, Tsegi, Tusayan). A

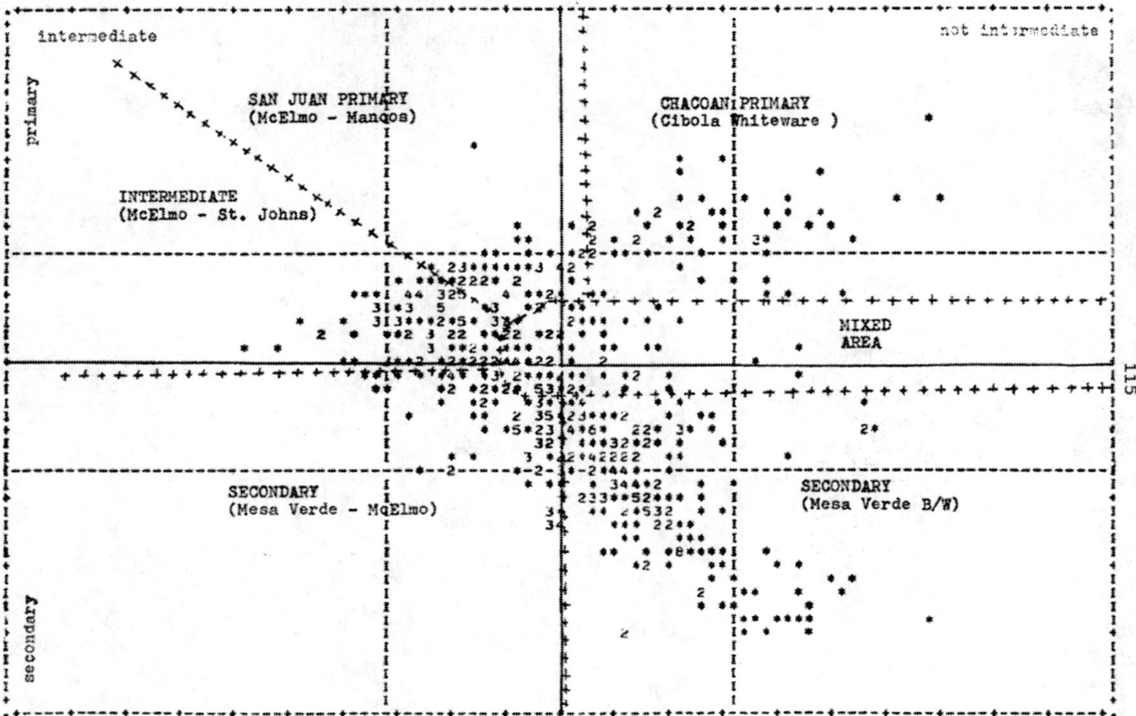

Figure 23.2. Factor analysis scattergram (7-31-1977), with divisions.

fine-grained factor analysis was also conducted using identified stylistic subdivisions within the San Juan types of Mancos, McElmo, and Mesa Verde B/w, and with White Mountain Red Ware types entered as discrete classes instead of the somewhat condensed black-on-reds versus polychromes.

Factor Scores

A method of scoring strata according to the areas of the scattergram they fell into was developed in November 1977 with the second factor analysis. Because the same parabola pattern was reproduced with every factor analysis, with the addition of more strata points, the same divisions of the parabola could be superimposed onto succeeding parabolas. The basic visual pattern did not change with the addition of new data, so we subdivided the later factor parabolas in the same way. Six divisions in sequential units across the parabola were delineated: (1) strata dominated by Cibola White Ware, (2) strata dominated by Mancos and McElmo B/w, (3) strata dominated by McElmo B/w alone, (4) strata with Mesa Verde B/w as 20–30 percent of the decorated ceramics, (5) strata with Mesa Verde B/w as 50–70 percent of the decorated sherds, and (6) strata with Mesa Verde B/w as more than 70 percent of the decorated assemblage. The mixed area in the center was given code 9 (see Figure 23.3). This numerical score could be given to every stratum that produced a factor score of 1 through 6 (or 9 if ceramically mixed) for all strata that met the initial criteria for entry into the factor program. Naturally, there was a residual batch of strata that received no factor scores because they did not meet the necessary criteria. Such strata were, however, easily evaluated because they contained only one pottery type and thus were very obviously assignable to an occupational period. Those containing only utility pottery were not easily assigned to time period on ceramic data alone, however, because corrugated wares are not as temporally sensitive as decorated wares.

The factor scores assigned to each stratum (codes 1–6 and 9) provided a convenient brief numerical designation for ceramic content. Factor scores, as a characterization of the ceramic content of a stratum, could thus aid in the evaluation of ceramic content versus stratigraphic position (accomplished by R. Adams). The rate of success of factor scoring in terms of stratigraphic superposition or stacking of factor scores is illustrated below. These factor scores also allowed selection of samples that were of similar time period for further analysis; the selection of Primary occupation strata for more intensive analysis on the limited attribute form was based in part on

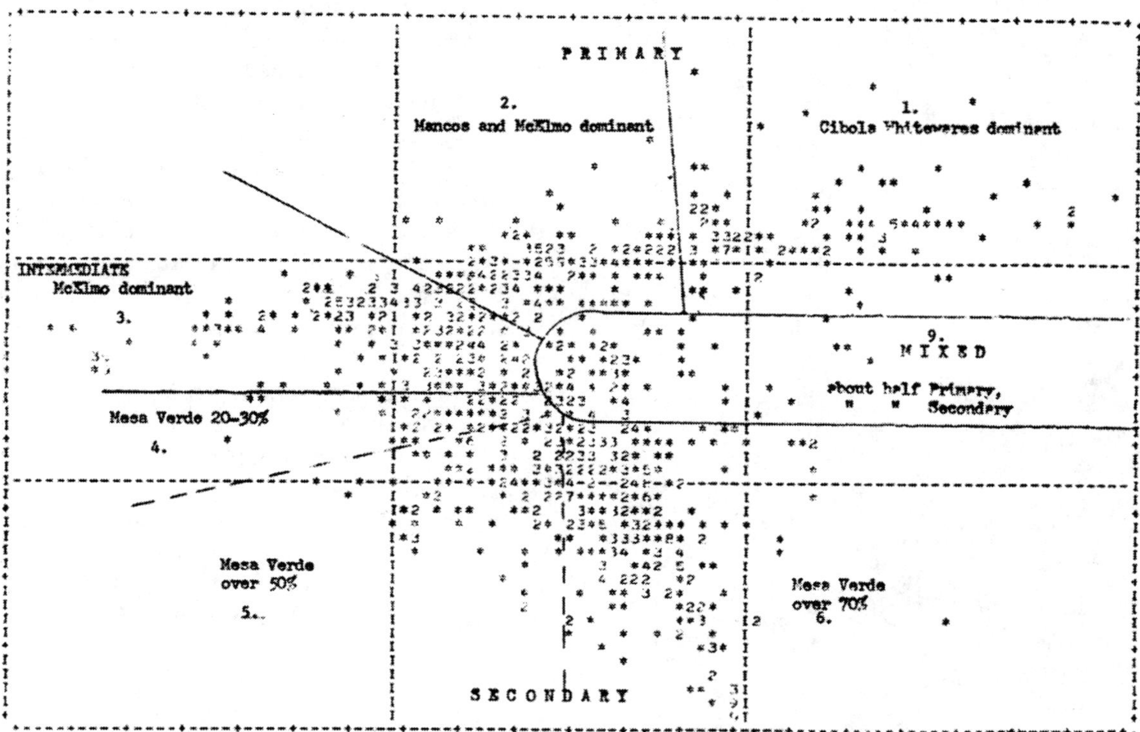

Figure 23.3. Factor analysis scattergram (November 1977) used as basis for first factor scores.

these scores. It also allowed other laboratories dealing with data sets not as temporally well known as ceramics (e.g., lithic and botanical data) to determine temporal assignment of nonceramic materials associated with strata according to their factor scores.

To subdivide the later factor parabolas in a way compatible with the first set of analyses, several techniques were developed in conjunction with members of the data processing lab. The last two factor parabolas were subdivided much in the same way as before, so that strata with a score of 1 in the early factor score system would remain in the same factor area in later analyses. One way of handling this was to redefine the original divisions according to ratios between decorated series rather than the more vague "dominance" method used originally. Once defined in this way (e.g., the ratio of Cibola to San Juan Primary ceramics), the division lines could be transposed more readily to a new scattergram. There was always a back-check to the ceramic contents of a selected sample of strata in each factor area to ensure the comparability of divisions. For the last factor scattergram a further check was included: The original strata in the early factor analysis were plotted according to the location of their points on the final scattergram. A set of clear plastic overlays was made of the distribution of the strata in each of the original factor areas as they appeared on the final scattergram, and dividing lines were then drawn on the final scattergram so as not to alter the factor areas assigned to the original 633 strata. Although some change in plot position is inevitable with every addition of new data, it was encouraging to find that the original strata retained their spatial unity and integrity even in the final scattergram. This was true despite the fact that the final data set included more than twice the number of the original strata entries. Apparently the original sample of 633 strata was sufficiently representative of the site as a whole that the addition of more strata as they were excavated did not materially alter either the visual form as a whole or the position of particular strata within the pattern.

The final factor analysis was completed in 1979, based on the factor matrix in Table 23.2. It contains dividing lines between areas that are as close as possible to the original ones of Figure 23.2. Letters were used to designate the final factor areas to keep them distinct from the factor score numbers assigned in the earlier analysis. Only five factor areas are designated on the final map (excluding the mixed region), however, as opposed to six in the earlier factor analysis. The mixed area, a 9 in the early scattergram, became F in the last scattergram. Areas 4 and 5 in the

Table 23.2. Final factor matrix used as basis for final scattergrams.

Ceramic Class	Factor 1	Factor 2
Early Cibola Black/w (Puerco, Escavada, & Red Mesa Black/w)	.42	.14
Gallup B/w	.26	.02
Chaco B/w	.53	.10
Chaco–McElmo B/w	.54	.10
Mancos B/w	.81	.05
McElmo B/w	.38	–.72
Mesa Verde B/w	–.89	.33
Tusayan Series White Ware	.44	.30
Chuska Series White Ware	.62	.47
Puerco B/r	.21	–.11
Wingate Black/r & Polychrome	.12	–.23
St. Johns Black/r & Polychrome	–.31	.29
Tsegi Orange Ware	.37	–.09
Corrugated Ext. San Juan WW	.55	.30
Smudged Red Ware	.45	.10
Plain Gray Utility	.28	–.41
Corrugated Utility	–.30	.01

Analysis used principal factoring with iterations, controlling for total decorated; first two of six factors.

older run were combined because their difference rested only on a small and difficult to identify difference in the percentage of Mesa Verde B/w. Areas 4 and 5 in the old system thus correspond to area D in the final system. Most strata, in the end, received two factor scores—a number and a letter. Naturally, the latest excavated strata received only a letter score. The degree of correspondence between the two systems is quite high; for example, a stratum that scored 1 in the older system is likely to score A in the new one. Where discrepancy exists, it involves only a shift into an adjacent area. As far as could be determined, there was never a stratum that originally scored 1 (Cibola Primary) but later crossed any significant amount of space across the parabola (e.g., to score E with Mesa Verde B/w dominant). A small amount of cross-over between adjacent factor areas was entirely expectable given the addition of new data along the way, as well as the fact that a continuum had been somewhat arbitrarily divided into discrete groups.

Interpretation

Although the subdivision of a continuum into discrete units may be seen as somewhat arbitrary, the classification of strata requires discrete entities. It is essentially no different from the arbitrary division of a temporal continuum into a series of phases, a practice archaeologists have employed for a long time. Classes of artifacts may also frequently involve the somewhat arbitrary division (and subdivision) of a continuum of attributes into a typology. The point here is that, in order to conceptually handle an uninterrupted continuum of any sort of data, we find it convenient to mark off portions and label them appropriately. In this case, though the continuum of scattergram plots could theoretically have been divided in an infinite number of ways, it was logical to base divisions on the relative frequency of the major pottery types that account for most of the variance in the sample (i.e., White Ware, Mancos, McElmo, and Mesa Verde B/w of the San Juan White Ware). Indeed, inspection of the ceramic contents of strata along the continuum did confirm that the relative frequency of these types was the most obvious dimension responsible for differences in placement along the parabola. Further, after criteria were established for the division of the scattergram, they proved repetitively observable in later editions of factor analysis. The major divisions between the three occupational periods were also drawn in the final scattergram with the aid of the more objective method of discriminant analysis. Thus, division of a continuum is a justifiable procedure, and the present scattergram divisions are logical from the points of view of major causes of variation in the ceramic sample, objective definition for scattergram areas, and repetitive duplication of similar divisions in a series of scattergrams.

Interpretation of the scattergram as a time sequence requires some explanation. It is a temporal curve to the extent that the factors on which it is based are reflective of temporal change (and not of some other source of variability). The interpretation of Factors 1 and 2 as temporally related is based on prior knowledge of pottery type sequences in the region, absolute dating associations, and prior information as to the stratigraphic change in Salmon's ceramics. There is thus some assurance that the scattergram plots are arranged in essentially a temporal order. This applies only to the general comparisons of scattergram areas; it does not necessarily mean that two plots immediately next to each other in the parabola are temporally ordered. In the larger sense, however, strata in the top right corner (area A) do tend to be earlier than those of area C, which are in turn earlier than those in factor area E. Naturally, strata falling within the same factor area are not necessarily temporally ordered relative to each other. The closer two strata are together, the less likelihood of a temporal sequence being involved.

The final scattergram shows the five factor areas plus the mixed area in between. Although these are essentially in temporal order from area A through E, the three basic and more reliable divisions are between A and B (together) versus C versus D and E (together). This basic three-part division stems from the contrast between the spatial dimensions of the two factors, verified by discriminant analysis, and thus contains a measure of objective reality. These three divisions do, in fact, contain strata that may be referred to as Primary, Intermediate, and Secondary, respectively. The first and third areas have subdivisions (A, B/D, E) that are somewhat more arbitrary in the sense that although they reflect ceramic differences between them, they are not necessarily indicative of major temporal change. As we now know, areas A and B, for example, both contain Primary occupation strata. Essentially, areas A and B reflect internal spatial differences in the ratio of San Juan types to intrusive types synchronically across the Primary strata. The A-B contrast is also somewhat reflective of temporal change within the Primary, since we now know that the San Juan types of Mancos and McElmo B/w increased in frequency microtemporally within the Primary occupation. There are even a few Primary strata that are McElmo B/w dominant (C), and it is now realized that McElmo B/w was present from the earliest occupation of Salmon. However, due to the quantum increase in McElmo B/w frequencies after the end of the Primary (i.e., in the Intermediate between ca. AD 1130 and 1190), most of the McElmo B/w dominant strata are actually later than the A and B scoring strata. Finally, the contrast between areas D and E relies basically on the relative frequency of Mesa Verde B/w. Mesa Verde B/w replaced McElmo B/w as a style only gradually (the estimated overlap is between AD 1190 and 1230) and the period of overlap is represented by area D. So from area C through E we see increasing amounts of Mesa Verde B/w compared to McElmo B/w, which is inferred to be a temporal change. Thus, the scattergram represents a temporal ordering of strata based on ceramic types, though only in a very general sense. Many strata in close proximity on the scattergram are in fact contemporaneous.

Evaluation of Results

In retrospect, factor analysis and scattergrams have been extremely useful tools for temporal control. Obviously, temporal control is only as good as the accuracy of our knowledge of the time spans of ceramic types and the degree to which the first two factors with most of the variability in them are indicative of temporal variability. Clearly, a factor program arranged on a complete seriation of ceramic attributes would have provided a finer degree of temporal control. The present system worked well in an area where ceramic types were well defined and previously dated; it is certainly sufficient for subdivision of the Primary, Intermediate, and Secondary components, and probably could be extended to somewhat finer detail than that as well. Using this kind of data, the technique would have been somewhat more accurate by excluding strata with small sample sizes in addition to the other criteria for exclusion mentioned above. Of course, this would have resulted in fewer strata receiving factor scores. Exclusion of utility wares might have also been desirable, as many strata received factor scores based in large part on their utility frequencies. No strata with only one type were included; however, a stratum with only one or two decorated sherds and a quantity of utility ware did receive a factor score. The temporal sensitivity of corrugated and plain gray utility ware is probably not sufficient at this level of analysis for precise temporal assessment without accompanying decorated ceramic data. This holds true despite the very general trend from plain gray to corrugated preference through time as well as the increase in utility wares relative to decorated through the entire occupational span of Salmon Ruin. In sum, however, the several factor analyses with the addition of more data as excavation proceeded provided an abundance of associational information. This information was then used to characterize ceramic contents in a temporal context via factor scores, to compare factor-scored strata to the stratigraphic sequence, and to evaluate the cultural implications of ceramic associations and assemblages assignable to each occupation.

STRATIGRAPHIC AND CONTEXTUAL RELATIONSHIPS OF STRATA TO FACTOR ANALYSIS

If factor scores are indeed reflective of ceramic and temporal changes, they should display a general pattern of stratigraphic superposition, or stacking in the site as a whole. Given the problems of ceramic mixing from different periods, reuse of Primary surfaces by Secondary occupants, and redeposition of Primary materials, we would not always expect to find stratigraphically superimposed sequences of factor scores running sequentially from 1 through 6 (old system) or from A through E (new system). However, if factor scores do reflect the temporal nature of ceramic assemblages and if stratigraphy is more often than not a reliable measure of relative time, there should be a general correspondence

Table 23.3. Stratigraphic superposition (stacking) of factor scores.

	Concordant* Strata		Discordant** Strata		
	n	%	n	%	Total Strata
Primary					
A Intrusive dominant	115	85.2	20	14.8	135
B San Juan dominant	135	66.8	67	33.2	202
AB Mixed A and B	6	75.0	2	25.0	8
Intermediate					
C McElmo Black-on-white dominant	155	73.8	55	26.2	210
Secondary					
D McElmo & Mesa Verde B/w mixed	115	74.2	40	25.8	155
E Mesa Verde Black-on-white dominant	332	100.0	0	0.0	332
Total Black-on-white	858	82.3	184	17.7	1042

*Concordant: Strata with factor score stratigraphically above other strata with the same or "earlier" scores.

**Discordant: Strata with a score stratigraphically above strata with "later" factor scores (i.e., out of expected position).

Note: Mixed strata (factor score F) are not included as they are neither concordant nor discordant and because they occur randomly with regard to other factor scores. All strata not assigned factor scores are also eliminated as they can be neither concordant nor discordant with other strata that received a factor score.

between the stratigraphic position of a level and the factor score assigned to it.

A computer printout was produced showing how many strata with a given factor score occurred stratigraphically above all other strata with the same or different factor scores. This information was simplified by grouping all strata as concordant or discordant relative to a given factor score. That is, strata of a given factor score should theoretically always occur above strata having the same or earlier factor scores. The only exception would be the relationship between factor scores A and B, because although the ceramic content is different, strata with both of these scores are Primary in time so no temporal separation is implied. Strata were grouped into the concordant or discordant classes relative to a given factor score; that is, they either conformed to the expected vertical stacking or they reversed the expected relationships due to a multitude of variables, such as mixing, reuse, or redeposition (Table 23.3). Strata that did not receive factor scores, or strata with ceramically mixed assemblages (factor score F) were eliminated from consideration, because they could not be rated as either concordant or discordant relative to other strata with factor scores.

The percentage of factor scores that stratigraphically follow the same or earlier factor scores is quite high. The success rate expressed as the percentage of concordant relative to total strata with a given factor score ranges from 66.8 to 100 percent. The total success rate is measured by the total of all concordant strata relative to the total strata. The overall success rate for all factor scores combined is 82.3 percent, quite high considering the multitude of reasons for possible reversals of stratigraphic sequences at Salmon. The results may be interpreted as indicative of the general association between factor score (i.e., ceramic complex) and stratigraphic position. It means that, on the whole, Primary factor scores (i.e., Primary ceramic types) are found stratigraphically below those of the Intermediate and Secondary periods. Thus the stratigraphic relationships across the whole site support the ceramic sequence and also validate the use of factor scores as a temporally sensitive indicator.

This does not mean, of course, that every room or locus contains a perfect sequence of stacked strata. There are often gaps in the sequence of particular rooms; for example, some rooms lack Intermediate (C scores) strata, and some lack either San Juan or intrusive dominant Primary strata (A or B scores). This is expectable, and does not contradict the correlation of strata and factor scores. Actual reversals of stratigraphic versus factor score relationships (i.e. discordant) are relatively rare. There are certain rooms with long and relatively undisturbed stratigraphic sequences that do in fact produce an essentially unbroken range of factor scores without gaps in a superimposed arrangement—these include 31W, 33W, 62W, 82W, 100W, and 129W.

Table 23.4. Strata evaluations by Rex Adams (condensed).

Codex Evaluation	Number of Strata	Percent of Strata
Pre-Primary	3	0.2
Pre-Primary?	6	0.5
Primary	287	23.9
Primary?	76	6.3
Primary / Intermediate	8	0.7
Primary / Intermediate?	40	3.3
Primary / Secondary?	4	0.3
Redeposited Primary	35	2.9
Primary contaminated	5	0.4
Intermediate	8	0.7
Intermediate?	23	1.9
Intermediate / Secondary	23	1.9
Intermediate / Secondary?	25	2.1
Secondary	501	41.7
Secondary?	39	3.2
Secondary Redeposited	22	1.8
Secondary contaminated	16	1.3
Post Secondary occupation	53	4.4
Unplaced strata	27	2.2
Total	1201	99.7

Relation of Factor Scores to R. Adams's Evaluation of Context

Rex Adams (Chapter 6) evaluated the stratigraphic position or context of essentially all excavated strata at Salmon—more than 1200 strata (Table 23.4)—as well as the condition of the deposit (e.g., in situ, redeposited, or contaminated). Questionable evaluations are indicated in the table, as are strata that lie between each of the major occupation phases or that could be one or the other (e.g., Primary/ Intermediate). Of the more than 1200 strata, 41.7 percent are Secondary and only 23.9 percent are Primary. Intermediate strata were difficult to define, and include only eight definite ones, though 23 are probable Intermediate strata. This gives an impression of the relative frequency of strata assignable to each of the three periods. Also, 35 strata were Primary, but in a redeposited condition (i.e., displaced by Secondary occupants and found in a state of reverse stratigraphy). Post-Secondary occupation strata refer to strata of noncultural deposition, usually in the upper part or postoccupational fill of rooms.

Table 23.5 gives the average number of sherds per stratum by time period on the basis of an earlier sample of 717 evaluated strata. Secondary strata far outnumber Primary and especially Intermediate strata. The mean number of sherds per stratum demonstrates a clear difference between Primary and later strata. The greatly increased mean number of sherds per stratum in Intermediate and Secondary strata is due in part to thicker and deeper strata in the later periods, as well as the probably greater density of pottery in each Secondary level. The Primary strata are not only thinner, but contain relatively fewer sherds, due to cleaning of rooms by Primary occupants during and at the end of their occupation, as well as to the removal or redeposition of Primary ceramics during later occupations.

When these data are separated into means per stratum for decorated versus undecorated sherds, the same trend persists: Primary strata have fewer sherds per stratum of both decorated and undecorated wares, and, of course, the average for utility wares always exceeds that for the decorated wares. However, the mean number of utility sherds per stratum increases more rapidly through time than does the figure for decorated pottery, going from Primary to Secondary strata. That is, the ratio between decorated and utility sherds changes through time, with relatively more utility sherds to decorated sherds in the Secondary occupation. Increased utilization of corrugated pottery is probably related to a decline in the function of decorated forms, and the relative decline of decorated jars in particular.

The distribution of strata by context evaluation versus factor score is given in Table 23.6. Theoretically, Primary strata should have a factor score of A or B (Cibola or Mancos dominant), with a few C scores. Intermediate strata should consist mainly of C scores (McElmo B/w dominant), and Secondary strata should score D or E (Mesa Verde B/w dominant). The factor score of F indicates a mixed stratum (ceramically), which could theoretically occur in any period. Table 23.6 does in fact indicate a general relationship between context evaluation and factor score (or between stratigraphic placement and ceramic content). Primary and before-Primary strata fall mainly into A and B factor scores, and Intermediate and Primary/Intermediate strata are mostly B and C in score (i.e., increasingly dominated by San Juan Series ceramics). Intermediate/Secondary and Secondary position strata have a ceramic content high in Mesa Verde B/w; in fact, 79.3 percent of Secondary strata fall into factor areas D and E. The median percentage clearly shows a trend from upper left to lower right in Table 23.6. To test the strength of this relationship, a condensed version of Table 23.6 was derived (Table 23.7), in which only Primary, Intermediate, and Secondary strata were used. No marginal identification strata (between periods) were used. Factor score dimensions remained the same except for the mixed (F) factor score, which could not

Table 23.5. Average number of sherds per stratum for each occupation.

	Sample Sizes	Mean Number Sherds/Stratum	Number of Strata
Total Sherds			
Primary	7934	87	206
Intermediate	6914	238	29
Secondary	115,171	239	482
Total Decorated			
Primary	5305	25	206
Intermediate	1900	66	29
Secondary	27,082	56	482
Total Undecorated			
Primary	12,629	62	206
Intermediate	5014	172	29
Secondary	88,089	183	482

Table 23.6. Relationships of factor scores to strata evaluations.

	BP		P + P?		P/I = P/I?		I + I?		I/S + I/S?		S + S?	
Scores	n	%	n	%	n	%	n	%	n	%	n	%
A + AB	2	28.6	109	38.8	8	17.4	3	10.3	1	2.4	1	0.2
B + BC	1	14.3	113	40.2	16	34.8	10	34.5	4	9.5	1	0.2
C	2	28.6	42	41.3	19	41.3	14	48.3	23	54.8	61	12.9
D + E	1	14.3	11	3.9	2	4.3	2	6.9	10	23.8	376	79.3
F	1	14.3	6	2.1	1	2.2	–	–	4	9.5	26	5.5
Total	7	100.1	281	126.3	46	100.0	29	100.0	42	100.0	474	98.1

BP = before Primary; P = Primary; I = Intermediate; S = Secondary; ? = uncertain evaluation.

Table 23.7. Condensed distribution of Rex Adams's strata evaluations by factor scores.

Evaluations	A & AB	B & BC	C	D & E	Total
Pre-Primary-Primary-Primary?	111	114	44	12	281
Intermediate-Intermediate?	3	10	14	2	29
Secondary-Secondary?	1	10	61	376	448
Total	115	134	119	390	758

Chi square significant to .001; Kruskal-Wallis significant to .01; borderline evaluations between occupations have been eliminated.

be expected to associate with any particular time period and was deleted. A chi-square test for independence resulted in a value significant to over the .001 level of significance. A Kruskal-Wallis test on the same matrix was significant to the .10 level. Both tests indicated a condition of nonrandomness in the distribution; there is thus a strong association of certain factor scores with certain stratigraphic placements. As anticipated, the frequency of A and B factor scores in Primary strata greatly exceeded the expected amount in the contingency table, and the amount of D and E factor scores in Secondary strata also greatly exceeded the expected value.

Discriminant Analysis

Discriminant analysis was used to answer the question, how well could the major pottery types discriminate between Primary, Intermediate, and Secondary strata as evaluated for context by R. Adams? In other words, how well do pottery types accord with stratigraphic position as evaluated by R. Adams and is there a consistent ceramic group for each period? The discriminant analysis program used was the step-wise version of Klecka (1975) in the SPSS computer program package. The relation between context evaluation and factor scores suggested in a gross way that types should have stratigraphic predictability. Although some strata were questionable as to relative position, only the most securely assigned were used in discriminant analysis. These included three groups: Group 1 strata including all before-Primary (sub-lowest floor) and all Primary context strata; Group 2 including all strata that are Intermediate in context (above Primary and below Secondary strata); and Group 3 including all Secondary strata. Ceramic types used to discriminate the three stratigraphic groups were the same ones used in factor analysis, as they are the best sampled (with a minimum of 100 sherds of each type)—Early Cibola (Puerco, Escavada, and Red Mesa B/w), Gallup, Chaco, Chaco-McElmo, Mancos, McElmo, and Mesa Verde B/w, Tusayan Series White Ware, Chuska Series White Ware, Puerco B/r, Wingate B/r, St. Johns Polychrome, Tsegi Orange Ware, Corrugated Exterior B/w, Smudged Red Ware, plain gray ware, and corrugated.

Discriminant analysis (in the SPSS computer package) uses a correlation matrix to measure the discriminating ability (by stratigraphic time period) of each variable (ceramic type). Five methods of discrimination were used: (1) Select the variable that maxims minimum mahalanobis distance between group pairs. (2) Maximize Rao's V. (3) Minimize Wilkes's lambda. (4) Minimize residual unexplained variation. (5) Direct solution. The first four are step-by-step solutions that yield a summary table with the types found to have the best discriminatory ability. The direct method forces all the data into the solution in one step, and does not provide a summary list of the best variables. For each method the prediction results give the actual groups against the predicted groups, and the percentage of correct prediction (of types against stratigraphic evaluation).

This program was used to evaluate (a) all strata already evaluated by R. Adams (717 strata) with the further stipulation that each stratum must contain at least one sherd from at least one pottery type to be entered; (b) trash strata only, with a minimum of two pottery types present to use the stratum (202 strata); and (c) all strata with a minimum of two pottery types present in the stratum (590 strata). The latter analysis (c) was the most successful. Success rates of prediction by the direct method were as follows: All strata (minimum 1 sherd, 1 type) – 73.36 percent; trash strata (minimum 2 types) – 69.31 percent; and all strata (minimum 2 types) – 76.44 percent. Use of all strata with a minimum of two types thus had a slightly better prediction rate than the other data sets. One reason for this is that since the technique is based on a correlation matrix, the input sample should include only levels having two or more pottery types present; otherwise the degree of association cannot be accurately measured. This condition also ensures inclusion of strata with larger sample sizes. It is not clear why trash strata did not produce better results; trash (with larger average sample sizes) should provide a better sample population. Clearly, pottery in trash in particular is no better at discriminating stratigraphic position than all strata in general.

Since the analysis using all strata with a minimum of two types present had the best success rate, it was examined for further information. All the stepwise solutions were equally successful in matching pottery types to the three stratigraphic periods (Primary, Intermediate, and Secondary). Further, all methods selected the same nine ceramic types as the best predictors of time: Early Cibola, Chaco, Chaco-McElmo, Mancos, McElmo, and Mesa Verde B/w, Puerco B/r, Tusayan White Ware, and Tsegi Orange Ware. Among these nine, several were shown to be more useful than others. Judging by the F value (discriminating ability) of each of the nine types, the following types were the best for distinguishing the three time periods: Chaco, Mancos, McElmo, and Mesa Verde B/w. This is not surprising, as these types span the entire occupation(s) of the site, and are also present in larger quantities than the other types. Indeed, the paucity of such entries as Tsegi Orange Ware and Puerco B/w probably limited their time discrimination abilities even though they are confined nearly exclusively to the Primary occupation. The three sequential types in the San Juan Series are among the best predictors of stratigraphic time, as well as the most common of the Primary occupation intrusive types, Chaco B/w.

The success rate of prediction for the direct method is given in Table 23.8. The success rate of 76.44 percent is the highest obtained in discriminant analysis; all the other methods produced success percentages of 76.1 percent. In other words, ceramics were successful in predicting stratigraphic position more than three-quarters of the time. This is considered a rather good result for archaeological data (P. Johnson, personal communication 1980). Further indication that the result was a good solution is the fact that all four step-wise methods produced the same percentage of success, and chose the same set of pottery types as being the best predictors of time period.

Examination of the prediction success (see Table 23.8) reveals why the percentage was not higher. Although 47.4 percent of the Primary context strata were correctly predicted, a nearly equal percentage were classified into Group 3 (Secondary) by discriminant analysis, because many stratigraphically Primary levels were reoccupied during the Secondary occupation, or were subject to a downward mixing of Secondary ceramics (Mesa Verde B/w).

Thus, although R. Adams's contextual evaluation for 71 strata was Primary, they contained enough Mesa Verde B/w to be classified as Secondary in the discriminant analysis. A similar problem is seen in the Intermediate strata, where the Mesa Verde B/w content was sufficiently high for the computer to place 15 strata (55.6%) into the Secondary. The reverse discrepancy occurs with 21 strata, which were evaluated as Secondary but are Primary ceramically. This is due to Secondary redeposition of Primary strata during cleaning of some rooms by the Secondary occupants. In actuality, Secondary contamination of Primary strata is evidently a greater problem than redeposition of primary materials into Secondary strata; 46.7 percent of the Primary strata were classed as Secondary by the computer, and 5.1 percent of R. Adams's Secondary strata were classed as Primary by the discriminant analysis.

An illustration of the degree to which vertical mixture of ceramics between phases, as well as redeposition, can affect the concordance of stratigraphic placement vis-à-vis ceramic content is found in Table 23.9. Here, the average number of sherds per stratum by type was calculated for each major time block. Primary types should have a larger sherd per stratum count in strata evaluated as Primary, as shown in the table. For example, Chaco B/w is more numerous in the Primary occupation, McElmo B/w has a larger count per stratum in the Intermediate, and Mesa Verde B/w is greatest per stratum in the Secondary. Of 10 types commonly occurring in Primary strata, 7 do in fact have higher sherd per stratum counts in Primary context strata than in later periods. Puerco B/r, Wingate B/r, and Tsegi Orange Ware actually have slightly higher frequencies per stratum in the Intermediate. This may be a reflection of continual import of red ware of the Tsegi and White Mountain Series into the site after the Primary period, but it also is affected by the small sample of these from the Intermediate period available for study.

Even with types such as Chaco and Mancos B/w, which do have their highest sherds per stratum count in Primary strata (as expected), there are also smaller counts per stratum into the Intermediate and Secondary, reflecting redeposition, and perhaps limited reuse of Primary occupation vessels or sherds. Mesa Verde B/w, clearly the dominant decorated type in Secondary strata, is also present in small amounts in strata assigned to the Intermediate and even Primary periods, as the result of reuse of Primary occupational surfaces or downward mixing.

Table 23.9 also illustrates the relative frequency of each of these types within each phase (by reading down each column). The average per stratum supports the evidence of overall sherd counts and factor analysis as to the relative abundance of each type in each occupation. It is not surprising, for instance, to find that Mancos and McElmo B/w have more sherds per stratum in the Primary than do any other types in that occupation. The highest count for any intrusive type is Chaco B/w, with an average 3.1 sherds per stratum in the Primary.

The increased reliance on corrugated ceramics through time is illustrated by the fact that it increases from 66.4 sherds per stratum in the Primary to 187.0 sherds per stratum in the Secondary, a greater than two-fold increase in frequency per stratum.

Aside from mixing and redeposition, another source of error lies in the numbers of strata of each time period available in the sample. Of the 455 strata predicted as to time period by discriminant analysis, 81 percent were Secondary strata, 3.3 percent were Intermediate, and 15.6 percent were Primary in context. The number of strata pertaining to each component is clearly unequal; this is unavoidable, however, as it reflects the relative quantities of strata in the

Table 23.8. Prediction results of discriminant analysis. Percent of grouped cases correctly classified = 76.44%.

		Predicted Group Membership		
Actual Group	Number of Cases	Group 1	Group 2	Group 3
Group 1 (Primary)	152	72 (47.4%)	9 (5.9%)	71 (46.7%)
Group 2 (Intermediate)	27	2 (7.4%)	10 (37.0%)	15 (55.6%)
Group 3 (Secondary)	411	21 (5.1%)	21 (5.1%)	369 (89.8%)
Ungrouped Cases	628	62 (9.9%)	54 (8.6%)	512 (81.5%)

This is the direct method of discriminant analysis, here including all strata (590) with two or more ceramic types present.

Table 23.9. Average number of sherds of each type per stratum in Primary, Intermediate, and Secondary strata.

Ceramic Class	Group 1 Primary	Group 2 Intermediate	Group 3 Secondary	Total
Puerco/Escavada B/w	0.8	0.9	0.2	0.4
Gallup Black-on-white	0.6	0.4	0.4	0.4
Chaco Black-on-white	3.1	1.5	0.9	1.4
Chaco-McElmo Black-on-white	0.5	0.7	0.5	0.5
Mancos Black-on-white	8.2	8.0	3.2	4.7
McElmo Black-on-white	8.8	38.5	14.3	14.0
Mesa Verde Black-on-white	1.3	7.6	36.6	26.2
Tusayan Series White Ware	0.4	0.0	0.0	0.1
Chuska Series White Ware	1.5	0.3	0.3	0.6
Puerco Black-on-red	0.2	0.5	0.1	0.2
Wingate Black-on-red	0.3	2.7	1.4	1.2
St. Johns Polychrome	0.0	0.2	0.7	0.5
Tsegi Orange Ware	0.2	0.8	0.1	0.2
Smudged Red Ware	0.7	0.4	0.2	0.3
Plain Gray	7.0	20.8	9.1	9.1
Corrugated	66.4	139.1	187.0	153.7
Strata frequency	152	27	411	590

whole site. This is also shown from the entire sample evaluated by R. Adams of 717 strata: 206 were Primary, 29 were Intermediate, and 482 were Secondary. No matter how measured, Secondary occupation strata are obviously more numerous than those of any other period. In part, this relates to the fact that a few rooms have not been excavated deeply enough to reveal Intermediate and Primary strata, but the phenomenon is more reflective of the extent to which Secondary occupation people reoccupied and modified the Chacoan pueblo.

In sum, discriminant analysis illustrates that pottery types are good predictors of stratigraphic position and cultural occupation in more than three of every four cases. The computerized solution was considered successful in terms of the consistency of the results between methods, as well as in the satisfactory confirmation of the sensitivity of ceramics to stratigraphic and phase changes within the site.

Analysis of Variance

The degree of success was also evaluated by placing the results into an analysis of variance program (ANOVA), which determined the ceramic variation within and between Primary, Intermediate, and Secondary strata. When using a total of 717 strata (the entire evaluation file at that time), the result was significant to the .0036 level. That is, there was significantly less variation within the time periods than between them. A similar test using only decorated pottery from the same sample set of 717 strata was significant to the .0064 level. That pottery types produced more interaction within groups than between them indicates that the ceramic assemblages of each time period are, by and large, internally cohesive, with greater variance between than within the major time blocks. The success rate of discriminant analysis is therefore significant, which supports

Table 23.10. Correlation coefficients for major ceramic types (entire site) showing relative degrees of association between types.

	Early Cibola	Gallup B/w	Chaco B/w	Chaco-McElmo B/w	Mancos B/w	McElmo B/w	Mesa Verde B/w	Tusayan White Ware	Chuska White Ware	Puerco B/r	Wingate B/r Poly	St. Johns B/r Poly	Tsegi Orange Ware	Corr. Ext. B/w	Smudged Red	Plain Gray	Corru-gated
Early Cibola																	
Gallup Black-on-white	.09																
Chaco Black-on-white	.36	.37															
Chaco-McElmo B/w	.16	.08	.20														
Mancos Black-on-white	.35	.28	.53	.43													
McElmo Black-on-white	.03	-.04	.06	.19	.22												
Mesa Verde B/we	–.29	–.22	–.34	–.45	–.67	–.59											
Tusayan White Ware	.16	.09	.22	.30	.37	–.03	–.35										
Chuska White Ware	.26	.02	.18	.45	.43	–.03	–.46	.45									
Puerco Black-on-red	.15	.02	.07	.09	.17	.17	–.18	.08	.04								
"Wingate B/r, Polychrome	.03	–.03	–.07	.12	.06	.18	–.26	–.08	.03	.03							
"St. Johns B/r, Polychrome	–.03	–.16	–.22	–.12	–.25	–.32	.29	–.05	–.05	–.10	–.08						
Tsegi Orange Ware	.23	.03	.13	.12	.30	.23	–.37	.13	.24	.09	.01	–.15					
Corrugated Ext. B/w	.25	.09	.23	.41	.43	.03	–.39	.30	.59	.07	.00	–.10	.17				
Smudged Red	.31	.10	.36	.18	.45	.11	–.30	.24	.21	.21	–.05	–.09	.12	.20			
Plain Gray	.07	.10	.12	.11	.23	–.38	–.36	–.06	–.02	.12	.11	–.24	.15	.06	.06		
Corrugated	–.11	–.07	–.13	–.18	–.26	–.06	.36	–.11	–.18	.01	–.12	.02	–.15	–.14	–.02	–.05	

Table 23.11. Factor analysis, varimax rotated factor matrix.

Type	Factor 1	Factor 2	Factor 3	Factor 4	Factor 5
Early Cibola	.20	–.02	.48	.13	.13
Gallup Black-on-white	.05	.06	.02	.57	.04
Chaco Black-on-white	.17	.07	.41	.62	.03
Chaco-McElmo Black-on-white	.53	.19	.09	.08	.15
Mancos Black-on-white	.46	.25	.45	.41	–.22
McElmo Black-on-white	.02	.81	.13	–.13	.15
Mesa Verde Black-on-white	.45	–.58	–.29	–.17	–.55
Tusayan White ware	.48	–.05	.21	.11	.04
Chuska White ware	.86	–.06	.13	–.04	.11
Puerco Black-on-red	.04	.19	.29	–.03	–.05
Wingate Black-on-red, Polychrome	.01	.20	–.06	–.08	.28
St. John Black-on-red, Polychrome	.08	–.44	–.03	–.23	.05
Tsegi Orange Ware	.20	.21	.22	.01	.18
Cor. Ext. Black-on-white	.65	.05	.14	.10	.04
Smudged Red Ware	.19	.07	.60	.14	–.07
Plain Gray	–.02	.46	.08	.10	.10
Corrugated	.15	–.00	–.03	–.12	–.49

Based on partial correlation coefficients, corrected for total decorated.

the conclusions derived from factor analysis that the major determinant of ceramic variability at Salmon is temporal.

DATING CERAMIC TYPES AT SALMON USING FACTOR ANALYSIS

The following conclusions are based on the several lines of evidence discussed above—primarily associational evidence (correlations, absolute dates, and R. Adams's contextual evaluation of strata and factor scores). The high degree of substantiation between the several lines of evidence lends a degree of reliability to the typological sequence and synchronic assemblages outlined here.

Factor analysis was especially useful because it produced a factor score for each stratum and also provided additional information about both the diachronic and synchronic relationships of pottery types at Salmon. Factor analysis based on the final total of about 250,000 sherds also produced a factor structure via the varimax and image rotation methods, which together with correlation matrices provided considerable information regarding the sequence at Salmon. The following conclusions are therefore based mainly on associations including correlation coefficients (Table 23.10) and factor analysis (Table 23.11), along with other sources of information. The degree of association between types, as shown by correlations and factor analysis, may be indicative of temporal placement and/or degree of association produced by synchronic social-functional causes. At Salmon, all types belonging to the same period have positive correlations; negative correlations are only produced between nonsynchronous ceramic types. Within the major temporal periods, associations display minor differences between types of that phase, due to either microtemporal changes or differences in spatial frequency as a result of use patterns. Variations due to social-functional causes are never as strong as those produced by temporal variation, because there are never negative correlations between types of the same phase. Thus, the strongest positive correlations occur between types that are of the same time period, and that also have similar distributional patterns across contemporaneous strata. High negative correlation is produced by noncontemporaneity, and to a lesser extent by spatial differences.

The major determinant of variability is time. This has already been seen in the first two factors (principal factoring unrotated matrix with iteration) used for factor scoring. The same conclusion is quite apparent from the correlation matrix itself and the varimax rotation (see Table 23.11). In the latter, the first two factors, accounting for 76 percent of the variation, involve the same contrast between Primary, Intermediate, and Secondary ceramics as in the unrotated matrix used for factor scores. Table 23.11 clearly shows a Secondary versus Primary and Intermediate contrast in Factor 1, and a late Primary-Intermediate complex in Factor 2 (McElmo B/w, Wingate B/r, Wingate Polychrome, Tsegi Orange Ware, plain gray complex). The Secondary assemblage is particularly salient in correlations and factor analysis, with an associational complex of Mesa Verde B/w, St. Johns Polychrome and corrugated distinctly separated from all other ceramics. In the correlation matrix, Mesa Verde B/w has negative correlations with all other types except St. Johns Polychrome and corrugated, both of which are strongly positive.

The Primary occupation ceramic assemblage is defined by Factor 3 (see Table 23.11), and by positive correlations between the following types: Puerco, Escavada, Gallup, Chaco, Chaco-McElmo, and Mancos B/w, Chuska White Ware, Tusayan White Ware, Smudged Red Ware, and Tsegi Orange Ware. In a general sense, all these are associated due to their presence in the Primary occupation, although there are some intriguing variations in the associational relations between them due to synchronic variables of a social-functional nature.

Another source of variation within the Primary complex is due to microtemporal factors. Evidence of the increased use of San Juan Series pottery during the Primary period is discussed elsewhere. Typologically, the early Cibola group of Puerco, Escavada, and Red Mesa B/w, although numerically small at Salmon, should be early. Presumably these types are poorly represented because they were already declining in popularity when the site was built in AD 1088. As such, this complex should be present in the earliest occupational strata, or where the earliest ceramic complexes have been preserved (e.g., the lower stories of back-wall rooms and the lower strata of the plaza). Indeed, these are precisely the localities where this early complex is found, confirming the early identity of this complex (plus Smudged Red) in the correlations and factor analysis. The strongest associations of this complex are with Chaco B/w, Mancos B/w, and Smudged Red. In factor analysis, the early Cibola and Smudged Red types appear in only one factor together with high loadings, not in other factors with Primary types. It should be stressed that at no time (at Salmon) does this early complex appear without other types such as Chaco and Mancos B/w. But the reverse is not true; the later or more long-lived Cibola types at Salmon of Chaco and Chaco-McElmo B/w do occur without the early complex of Puerco, Escavada, and Red Mesa B/w and Smudged Red. The distribution of the early Cibola group is largely a result of its location in areas that have not been disturbed by later occupations—in the lower levels of back-wall rooms, in the lower levels of some plaza trenches, and in parts of the ruin associated with the earlier building construction. In all such cases, the early group appears associated with other Primary types, not alone or stratigraphically below them. These data suggest a temporal shift from the early Cibola group, Smudged Red, plus Chaco B/w, Chaco-McElmo B/w, and other Primary types to the later Cibola types without the early group, along with increased amounts of Mancos and McElmo B/w toward the end of the Primary occupation.

On the other hand, Chaco-McElmo B/w would be expected to represent a late Primary Cibola type because carbon-painted Cibola ceramics are a relatively late evolutionary development within the Cibola area. As such, Chaco-McElmo B/w should theoretically reflect late Cibola aspects of Salmon Ruin. Stratigraphic evidence is not very conclusive on this point. Apparently the type was present in at least small amounts from the very first occupation of the site in AD 1088. It thus overlaps in time with Chaco B/w in the same way that the early Cibola group does on the early end of the sequence. There is, though, some indication from factor analysis of an increasing use of this type during the Primary occupation. It has a relatively low positive correlation with the early Cibola group of types. In factor analysis it has a very low loading of .09, which is the highest in the early Cibola group (Factor 3). There is no stratigraphic evidence that Chaco-McElmo B/w as an imported type survived any longer than Chaco B/w itself (i.e., to the end of the Primary), but it may have become more popular during the time span of the Primary until the abrupt cessation of all Cibola Series imports at about AD 1130. Other areas (Chaco Canyon, Puerco River Valley) exhibit evidence of a subsequent evolution of Cibola carbon-painted ceramics, but this is not evident at Salmon due to the abrupt truncation of contacts with Chaco Canyon and a lack of Cibola intrusives after about AD 1130. The associations of Chaco-McElmo B/w within the Primary do not uniformly match other Cibola White Ware types, but are actually stronger with some other intrusives (Tusayan and Chuska White Ware), which points to differential usage of the mineral and carbon painted Cibola types.

In the San Juan Series, Mancos B/w is exclusively Primary in time period, probably lasting no later than AD 1150. There is no indication of temporal overlap between Mancos and Mesa Verde B/w, and there is only a partial overlap with Mancos and McElmo B/w.

Despite the typological and longevity difficulties with McElmo B/w, which is associated with both Primary and Intermediate strata until about AD 1200, the type is not randomly associated with all other types. Its correlation with Mesa Verde B/w, the type with which it should be most easily confused, is –.59; this negative correlation indicates that McElmo B/w is both typologically and associationally distinct from its succeeding type in the San Juan White Ware. Because Factor 2 (see Table 23.11) has its highest loading for McElmo B/w (.81), and because the major determinant of variability in the sample is temporal, McElmo B/w has a temporal assignment that differs from the basic Primary versus Secondary occupation. Although the type was present in Primary, Intermediate, and Secondary strata, its greatest relative frequency was in Intermediate times, between AD 1130 and 1200. McElmo B/w is so nearly absent in the Secondary as a whole that it never appears with factor loadings similar to Mesa Verde B/w, and in fact it has a negative correlation with Mesa Verde B/w. McElmo B/w associates to a somewhat greater extent with Mancos B/w (correlation –.22), as might be expected from its presence in Primary strata. Even though it has a somewhat greater association with the Primary than with the Secondary period, McElmo's association tends to be correlated only with Mancos B/w to any great extent. So, although present for a considerable period, McEmo B/w is negatively associated with the Secondary types and only somewhat associated with the Primary Mancos B/w. Aside from its moderate correlation with Mancos B/w, the highest correlations of McElmo B/w are with Tsegi Orange Ware (.23), Wingate B/r (.18), and plain gray (0.38). In part, the high association of McElmo with Tsegi and White Mountain Red Ware types is a reflection of the continued import of these into the Intermediate occupation, when McElmo was most dominant. Although Tsegi wares ceased in importation sometime during the Intermediate, White Mountain Red Ware continued unabated through the Intermediate and Secondary. Thus, the Intermediate complex consists of McElmo B/w, with small amounts of late Mancos B/w (?), White Mountain Red Ware types, a small amount of Tsegi Orange Ware Polychrome, and utility wares—a small assemblage compared to that of the Primary occupation.

Chuska and Tusayan White Ware intrusives are nearly exclusively Primary in their temporal association; this is evident from the types' appearance at Salmon and their time spans alone. In the Chuska Series, the vast majority of intrusive white ware is Chuska B/w and Toadlena B/w, carbon-painted types contemporaneous with Primary occupation. These late Pueblo II types display the same hatched panel (Chuska B/w) versus wide-line or Sosi style (Toadlena B/w) contrast so evident in the contemporaneous and analogous Mancos and McElmo B/w varieties at Salmon. The use of hatched panels or wide-line decoration contemporaneously is a phenomenon of ceramic decoration across the entire northern Anasazi area at this time, encompassing types in the Tusayan, Chuska, Cibola, and San Juan Series White Ware.

There is no evidence that the import of the most popular Chuska types of Chuska B/w and Toadlena B/w continued past the end of the Primary occupation. The two succeeding types of the Chuska Series (carbon painted)—Nava B/w (analogous to McElmo B/w) and Crumbled House B/w (analogous to Mesa Verde B/w)—are much rarer at Salmon than the preceding Chuska types. Nava B/w would logically be associated with the late Primary and Intermediate periods, while Crumbled House B/w should associate with Mesa Verde B/w of the Secondary. In fact, the small amount of Nava B/w present is mostly in Primary contexts, and Crumbled House B/w is extremely rare. Essentially, then, Chuska White Ware imports were confined to the Primary occupation, with only minimal importation after about AD 1130. Undoubtedly the loss of contacts with the Chuska area, as with many other ceramic traditions of the northern Southwest, was due to the demise of the Chacoan trade network.

Tusayan White Ware at Salmon consists exclusively of Sosi, Black Mesa, and Dogoszhi B/w, all found in the Primary occupation. Of these, Sosi B/w is by far the most common type from the Tusayan Series. There was no importation of Tusayan White Ware after the Primary occupation, judging from the absence of later types of that series, as well as the stratigraphic placement of Tusayan pottery at Salmon. This series, too, ceased to be imported coincident with the end of the Chacoan occupation.

Both Chuska and Tusayan White Ware Series show their strongest associations with Primary types in factor analysis. Unfortunately, the sample sizes for these were so small that the analytical unit for the analysis had to be the whole series. It may be seen from the correlation matrix that the highest correlation of the Chuska Series White Ware is with Primary occupation types, and that its highest degree of association is with Chaco-McElmo B/w and Tusayan White Ware. Similarly, Tusayan White Ware shows high positive correlations only with the Primary types, particularly with Chaco-McElmo B/w and Chuska White Ware. The factor analysis indicates high loadings for Chuska and Tusayan White Ware together in one factor (Factor 1) in which the Primary types of Mancos and Chaco-McElmo B/w are also strong. Thus, both series are associated with Primary types in general, and are also highly associated with each other, presumably due to similar conditions of importation or usage at Salmon Ruin.

The imported Smudged Red Ware from the northern Mogollon is undoubtedly Primary also, and very possibly early in the Primary occupation in temporal affiliation. Smudged Red is found in conjunction with the early Cibola group and with other Primary types (see Table 23.11, Factor 3). In fact, the highest correlation of Smudged Red is with the early Cibola B/w group.

San Juan Red Ware consists only of La Plata and Deadmans B/r, both quite rare at Salmon, due to the fact that Salmon is spatially removed and temporally too late to receive any quantity of San Juan Red Ware ceramics. There is no evidence that this series was manufactured in the Salmon vicinity. It most likely arrived in the Salmon area from the Four Corners area or centers of production in the northern part of the San Juan Anasazi range. Given the time spans of these b/r types, it is surprising that any appear at Salmon at all. These types apparently ended at about AD 1000, but they appear in very small amounts in the Primary occupation at Salmon at AD 1088. Perhaps this is indicative of the temporal lag for some intrusives, or simpy the use of heirloom pieces.

Tsegi Orange Ware is also predominantly Primary in assignment. The highest correlation of Tsegi Orange Ware as a series is with Primary types, especially with Mancos B/w; there is no doubt that the Tsegi Orange Ware was imported from the very beginning of Salmon's Chacoan occupation. And, like many other intrusive series, the importation of this series virtually ceased at the end of the Primary occupation. As with Chuska White Ware, the individual types produced sample sizes too small for statistical treatment. Treated as a whole, the Tsegi Series shows its highest associations in factor analysis with Primary occupation types (see Factors 2 and 3). There is also evidence that the b/r types (Medicine and Tusayan B/r) preceded the appearance of the polychromes (Citadel and Cameron) from northern Arizona. In this series, about 70 percent of the sherds present at Salmon are b/r, mostly Tusayan. These b/r types are of undoubted Primary affiliation at Salmon.

Some time during the latter part of the Primary occupation, Citadel Polychrome was added to the b/r types appearing from the Tsegi Series. This was probably after AD 1100, which would agree with the beginning date for Citadel Polychrome given by Colton and Hargrave (1937). The import of Citadel Polychrome may have continued slightly after the end of the Primary at AD 1130, since it is found in some Intermediate strata between AD 1130 and 1200. Citadel Polychrome also has a relatively high correlation with McElmo B/w, the predominant b/w type of the Intermediate period. Although Colton and Hargrave (1937) give an end date of AD 1150 for Citadel, Breternitz (1966) indicated that it continued in production until AD 1200. In any event, the minor amounts of Citadel Polychrome in the Intermediate ceased entirely prior to AD 1200, and there is no Tsegi Orange Ware in the Secondary assemblage. (A very few early Tusayan Polychrome sherds dating to the thirteenth century have been found at Salmon, contemporary with Mesa Verde B/w.) Judging from the predominance of the b/r group of Tsegi Orange Ware at Salmon, the vast majority of this pottery was imported during the Primary occupation. Although a small amount of Citadel Polychrome is dated to the Intermediate (or was still in use from earlier times), import of Tsegi Orange Ware dropped sharply with the close of the Primary occupation. Ceramic contacts with northern Arizona (both Tusayan White Ware and Tsegi Orange Ware) had probably ceased by AD 1150, and was never renewed during the Secondary occupation. This left the White Mountain Red Ware as the only major intrusive series present during the Secondary occupation.

White Mountain Red Ware was imported to Salmon during all phases of its occupation. Judging from the time spans assigned to these types by Carlson (1970) and Breternitz (1966), the b/r types of Puerco and Wingate should be associated with the Primary period. The Intermediate should include both Wingate B/r and Wingate Polychrome, and the Secondary should be mostly St. Johns Polychrome. This sequence is supported by both stratigraphic and associational data at Salmon. Examination of the factor analysis (see Table 23.11) as well as the fine-grained image factor analysis reveals a number of salient points about the long sequence of White Mountain Red Ware traded into the Salmon community:

1. Puerco and Wingate B/r are definitely Primary in their temporal association, as are the black-on-reds of the Tsegi Orange Ware.

2. Between the two b/r types, Puerco has slightly earlier associations than Wingate. The highest correlation of Puerco B/r is with Mancos B/w; it also associates with the early Cibola B/w group. The highest correlation of Wingate B/r is with McElmo B/w, which is both contemporary with and later than Mancos B/w (i.e., in the Intermediate). Nor do the two b/r types of the series have a high mutual correlation between them (0.06), which would be expected with slightly different but overlapping time spans. Puerco B/r is confined to the early Primary

occupation, whereas the import of Wingate B/r spanned the Primary and Intermediate periods until about AD 1175.

3. There is strong evidence that the polychromes of the White Mountain Red Ware, like those of the Tsegi Orange Ware, were later in appearance at Salmon than the corresponding b/r types of these series. None are associated with the Primary. Wingate Polychrome appears in the Intermediate between AD 1150 and 1200, and St. Johns Polychrome is the only White Mountain Red Ware type found in conjunction with the Mesa Verde B/w of the Secondary.

The temporal position of Wingate Polychrome (Houck and Querino Polychromes) is difficult to establish because it was not extensively imported to Salmon compared to the succeeding St. Johns Polychrome. A slight temporal priority for Wingate vis-à-vis St. Johns Polychrome is indicated by the fine-grained factor matrix; Factor 1 shows that Wingate Polychrome and St. Johns Polychrome have different loadings, with St. Johns associated with Mesa Verde B/w but not so with Wingate Polychrome. In Factor 4, Wingate Polychrome is associated with banded McElmo and to some extent with Mesa Verde B/w. On the other hand, the type appears to be found in the Intermediate period as well. Wingate Polychrome thus spans the transition between the Intermediate and Secondary periods, and was probably imported between AD 1150 and 1200, when it was supplanted by the more popular St. Johns Polychrome. Its negative correlation with Mesa Verde B/w indicates that its import did not last long into the AD 1200s.

4. The appearance of St. Johns Polychrome in consistent high association with Mesa Verde B/w marks the Secondary assemblage in every factor analysis program. In the correlations (see Table 23.10), St. Johns Polychrome is negatively related to every decorated type except Mesa Verde B/w. Mesa Verde B/w and St. Johns Polychrome are shown to have a close relationship temporally in the first factors of every factor analysis run, and with every method of rotation. St. Johns Polychrome is, then, the only major intrusive type present in the Secondary occupation.

Although a few sherds of what may be late St. Johns Polychrome or Pinedale Polychrome are present at Salmon, there is no ceramic evidence of continued contact with the White Mountain Red Ware Series beyond about AD 1275. If the Secondary had continued to AD 1300, increased amounts of Pinedale and Springerville Polychromes would be evident, and they are in fact lacking. The latest absolute dates are from the reroofing of the Great Kiva in AD 1263–1264. How long the Secondary occupation people remained at Salmon after their last construction effort is unclear; ceramic evidence (especially the White Mountain Red Ware Series) suggests that the site was abandoned before AD 1300.

In sum, the associations of White Mountain Red Ware types, together with stratigraphic evidence, confirm that the sequence of the first appearance of types of this ware at Salmon substantiates the time spans given by Carlson (1970) in the order of Puerco B/r, Wingate B/r, Wingate Polychrome (Houck and Querino Polychromes), and St. Johns Polychrome. There is no evidence of these types as intrusives on the San Juan significantly later than their estimated date of manufacture in the Little Colorado River area. The occupation period association of these red ware types at Salmon is as follows: Secondary Period (AD 1200–1275?) St. Johns Polychrome, St. Johns B/r; Intermediate Period (AD 1130–1120) Wingate Polychrome, Wingate B/r; Primary Period (AD 1088–1130) Wingate B/r, Puerco B/r.

Finally, the temporal significance of utility ware changes is not as great as in the decorated ceramics. Not only did utility ware change at a slower rate, but the changes were more minor and not easily monitored on a typological level. However, even using rough-sort data, certain trends are apparent in the utility wares:

1. Intrusive utility ware pottery (mostly trachyte-basalt tempered corrugated from the Chuska Valley) is by far more common in the Primary occupation than in later occupations. Intrusive corrugated ware from the Chaco-Cibola area has also been identified in small quantities, and is also confined to the Primary occupation. Thus, the situation mirrors that of the decorated wares—the majority of ceramic contact with other regions occurred in the Primary occupation. Thereafter, utility ware ceramics become almost totally locally made as shown by the nearly universal use of crushed rock temper and local clays in the Secondary occupation.

2. Although the San Juan utility ware of the site consists of both corrugated and plain gray utility (Mummy Lake Gray?; Breternitz et al. 1974:13), the latter is confined to the earlier portion of the occupation. Plain gray utility (uncorrugated exterior) is always numerically less than corrugated, and occurs in conjunction with corrugated only in the Primary and Intermediate periods. The Secondary contains only corrugated utility ware. This is reflected in the associational data, wherein plain gray is associated with Primary and Intermediate types, while corru-

gated is associated with the Secondary types Mesa Verde B/w and St. Johns Polychrome. In part, this also reflects a general increase in corrugated to decorated ratios through time; more utility ware relative to decorated pottery was produced and used in the Secondary than in the Primary occupation. Although San Juan corrugated pottery was being produced and used at the site from the beginning, the relative increase in corrugated utility ware results in a strong correlation of corrugated pottery with Mesa Verde B/w.

3. Within the corrugated group, there is evidence of a gradual shift through time in vessel form and style of corrugation. Following the description of corrugated ceramic shifts from Mancos Corrugated to Mesa Verde Corrugated (Breternitz et al. 1974:17–23; see also Rohn 1971), two classes of San Juan Corrugated were defined at Salmon. These were termed Pueblo II style and Pueblo III style, with the Pueblo II style having wider, less obliterated, and more deeply indented coils than the Pueblo III style. The rim eversion also increased and the vessels became more egg-shaped and less globular through time. Two extremes are apparent, corresponding to Mancos and Mesa Verde Corrugated, with a complete continuum between the two. The classes of Pueblo II and III corrugated were used as sorting categories on the rough-sort form at Salmon for a time, but the distinction was eventually dropped due to the complete continuum between the two, and hence the difficulty of assigning particular specimens. For the several rooms on which the Pueblo II and III styles were separated during rough sort, there does appear to be stratigraphic evidence of a trend from a mixture of Pueblo II and III styles in the Primary strata to exclusive use of the Pueblo III style in the Secondary strata. In sum, utility wares also exhibited temporal trends in terms of the amounts of intrusive utility pottery, the ratio of plain gray to corrugated San Juan Gray Ware, the ratio of utility to decorated ceramics, and a change in texturing style and vessel shape from Pueblo II to III times. A more detailed study of temporal changes in corrugated attributes might allow greater temporal differentiation. At the typological level of analysis, general trends could be determined, but they did not produce the temporal distinctions available from the decorated ceramic types.

Chapter 24

CERAMIC CHRONOLOGY AND TEMPORAL CHANGE AT SALMON

by Hayward Franklin

Salmon Pueblo's long time span, including the latter part of Pueblo II and most of Pueblo III, offers a good opportunity to study diachronic culture change. To evaluate temporal change at Salmon Ruin, we used ceramic cross-dating, absolute dates associated with ceramics, stratigraphic evidence, factor analysis, discriminant analysis, and analysis of variance—all applied to the ceramic type data collected on some 250,000 sherds. These were recorded on the rough-sort and limited-attribute forms. The former was used on approximately 90 percent of the ceramics recovered from Salmon; the latter was used mostly on Primary strata ceramics.

We knew from the beginning of the project that Salmon Ruin contained two basic components: an early one of Chacoan affiliation (termed Chacoan or Primary), followed by an occupation of the site by Middle San Juan groups from the mid-1100s through the late 1280s (termed the Secondary occupation). As work proceeded, however, two unanticipated discoveries were made: (1) the pueblo was never completely abandoned during the hiatus between the major Primary and Secondary occupations (hence the addition of a tentative Intermediate phase); and (2) San Juan White Ware ceramics were predominant at all times, even during the Primary occupation. Although the Primary occupation was of Chacoan affiliation in architecture, numerous San Juan ceramics were present, most notably Mancos and McElmo B/w of the Primary period. The nature of this mixed San Juan and Chacoan intrusive ceramic assemblage is discussed in another chapter.

CROSS-DATING

Ceramic types in the Salmon Ruin area have been defined (and redefined) in prior archaeological investigations, and their temporal spans have in many cases been worked out fairly accurately by means of dendrochronological associations. This is one reason for the use of the type-variety system in Salmon ceramic analysis. Despite its disadvantages, the typological system automatically yields cultural and temporal information via comparison to ceramics recovered in dated contexts by previous investigators in the region.

The presence of ceramics types identified and dated at sites outside Salmon allows an estimate of the occupational dates of Salmon, as well as of associated ceramic assemblages within each depositional period. Figure 24.1 provides the temporal spans of the major types recovered at Salmon. The rarest types are excluded because they are of limited utility in dating strata; small samples are subject to considerable analytical bias. Nothing quantitative is implied by this figure; the relative quantities of each of these types may be found in the sherd counts presented below. For example, Crumbled House B/w is represented at the site by only a few sherds, whereas Chuska and Toadlena B/w of the same series are more abundant.

The major sources for the ceramic time spans given in Figure 24.1 are Breternitz (1966) and Colton and Hargrave (1937). Although these spans were derived from recognized sources, it must also be recognized that authors vary somewhat in their estimates of the beginning and end points of these types, and continuing research continues to produce revisions. The temporal spans provided here are nevertheless generally supported by other evidence at Salmon. The results from cross-dating suggest some general conclusions.

First, the early ceramic complexes at Salmon should be varied, later becoming more homogeneous, after about AD 1130. Many of the exotic ceramic types that arrived at Salmon via exchange from other Puebloan areas have terminal dates of about AD 1100 to 1130. In fact, the only intrusive series present in abundant quantities in the Salmon assemblage from after AD 1130 is White Mountain Red Ware. After AD 1200 there is only Mesa Verde B/w, St. Johns Polychrome, and small amounts of pottery from the Chuska Valley. The early heterogeneity thus gave way to a much smaller, less varied group of types after AD 1200.

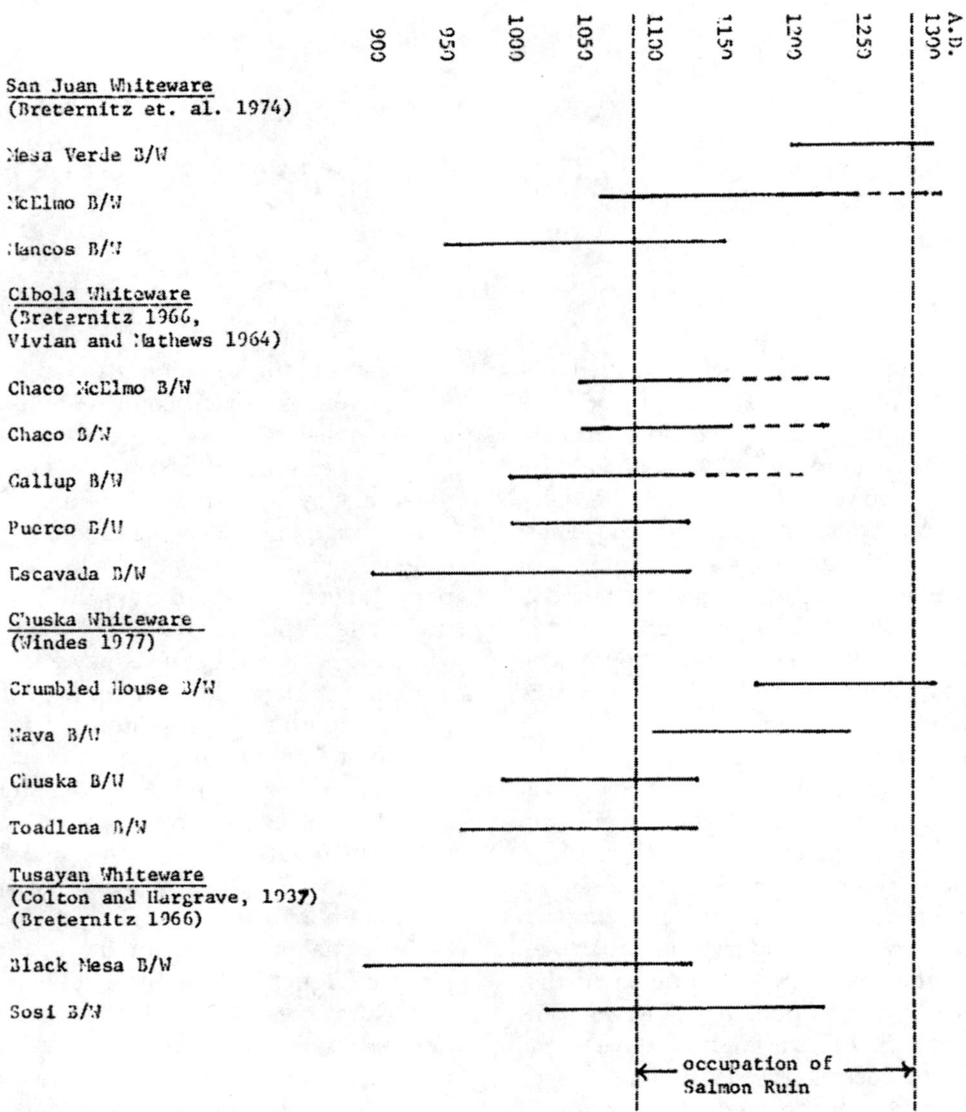

Figure 24.1. Time spans for important ceramic types at Salmon (see also next page).

Second, the Primary occupation assemblage (AD 1090–1120/1130) should contain types from a wide variety of sources, such as San Juan White Ware, Cibola White Ware, Chuska White Ware, Tusayan White Ware, San Juan Red Ware, White Mountain Red Ware, Tsegi Orange Ware, and Mogollon Red Ware. Given these time spans, some types should be evident only in the earliest part of the Primary, because these types were declining in popularity if not discontinued by the AD 1090 construction of Salmon. These include Puerco B/r, Puerco, Escavada, Red Mesa, and Cortez B/w, Forestdale Smudged, and San Juan Red Ware. On the other hand, types such as Chaco and Mancos B/w should be found through the entire Primary period, to about AD 1130.

Third, the only types that ought to appear in the Intermediate period assemblage are McElmo B/w, Wingate B/r, Wingate Polychrome, and perhaps Nava B/w. Representation of other intrusive series should be gone by AD 1130. Finally, the assemblage from the Secondary occupation after AD 1200 should logically consist of associated Mesa Verde B/w, some McElmo B/w, and St. Johns Polychrome. The only representation of other series might be in the form of small amounts of ceramics from the Chuska Valley.

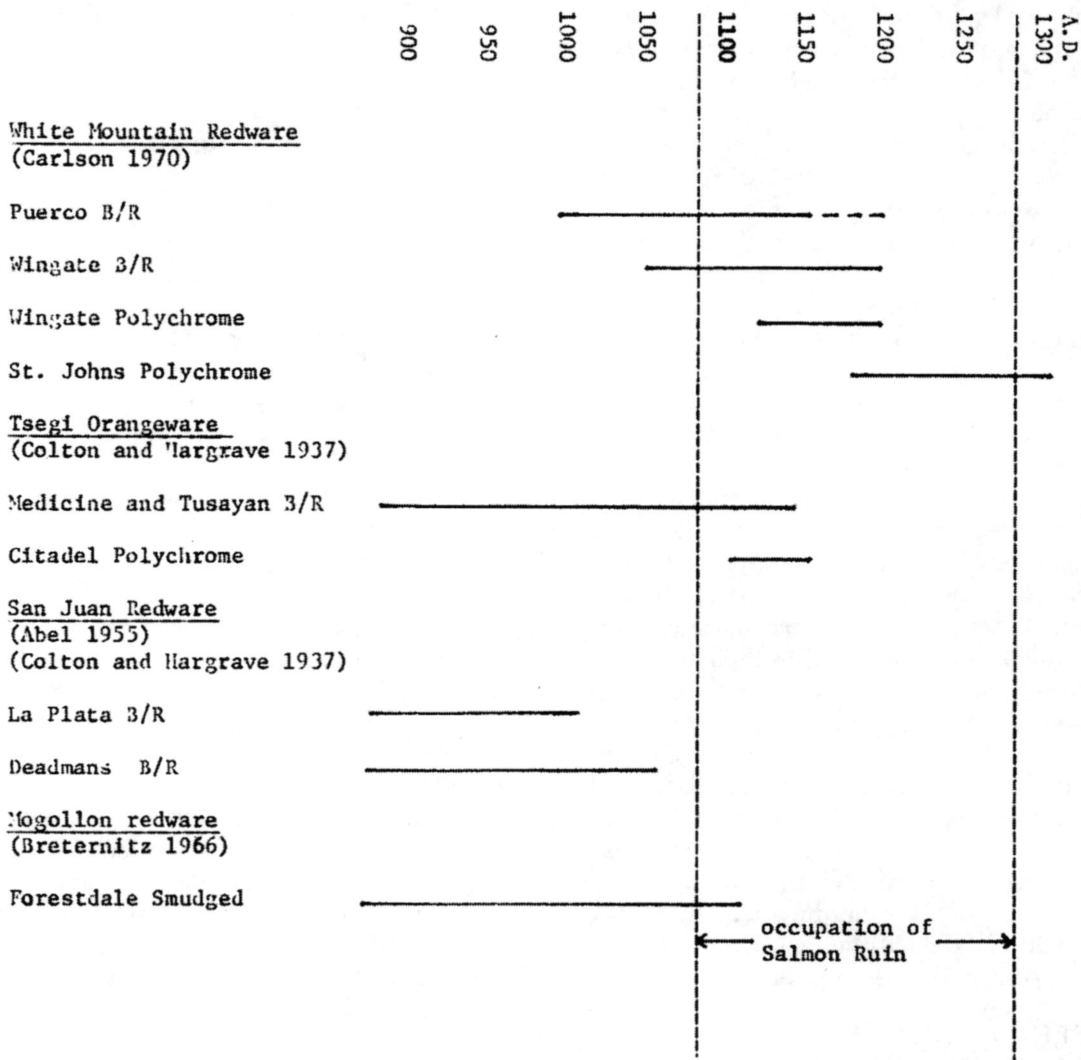

As mentioned, other lines of evidence largely support the time spans for these types, as suggested by the literature. However, the Salmon data suggest discrepancies with some of the dates determined elsewhere. Despite a period of temporal overlap in the early AD 1200s, McElmo B/w does not completely coexist with Mesa Verde B/w throughout the Secondary occupation at Salmon; later strata are almost exclusively Mesa Verde B/w. Further, in spite of recent evidence from Chaco Canyon indicating the persistence of Chaco B/w into the 1200s, there is no evidence of the importation of Cibola White Ware types at Salmon after 1130; there was a sharp decline in their appearance north of the San Juan River. Chuska and Tsegi pottery underwent a similar sharp drop in frequency at the same time (ca. 1130), although there is no disagreement with the total spans of the succeeding types as listed in Figure 24.1. The Pueblo III types of these series (Crumbled House B/w, Tusayan Polychrome) are rare to nonexistent in Secondary strata. There is no evidence of continued importation of Tusayan White Ware types after the same date, although Sosi B/w is listed as lasting until 1200. Puerco B/r was likewise not brought in after about 1130, and in fact it declined in the early Primary (early 1100s), although Carlson (1970) has stated that the type possibly persisted until 1200. Finally, San Juan Red Ware types theoretically ceased prior to the building of Salmon Ruin at 1090. However, they were occasionally present in the earliest Primary strata. This may reflect prolonged use of vessels after manufacture or trade-lag, as there is no evidence that these types were manufactured at Salmon Ruin or in its vicinity.

Such discrepancies do not necessarily indicate that the temporal spans are incorrect in other areas; areal differences are to be expected. Further, most of these involve intrusive types that were made elsewhere, and dates on intrusive types may not reflect the entire temporal span of manufacture in their homeland areas. Source area analysis at Salmon suggests that much of the San Juan White Ware present was of local manufacture, whereas all other series were imported. Hence, time spans for San Juan types identified at Salmon do represent manufacture dates, whereas all other series and types are intrusives and are thus subject to the vagaries of ceramic exchange. At Salmon, the most important factor in the diminution of intrusive series and types (aside from White Mountain Red Ware) at about AD 1130 seems to have been the truncation of trading contacts with other regions, which resulted in the attenuation or complete absence of most intrusive ceramic series at Salmon after the end of the Primary occupation despite the fact that those types, as well as succeeding types, continued to be produced in their homeland areas. The diminution of intrusive ceramics after AD 1125–1130 was evidently quite abrupt, and was probably due to the end of the Chacoan occupation and the collapse of the widespread Chacoan trade network of which the Salmon outlier was a part.

Cross-dated ceramics can thus be used as a guideline to determine the expected ceramic sequence for the site, while other independent lines of evidence relying on data within Salmon itself can be examined for comparison to cross-dating results.

CERAMIC TRENDS IN SALMON STRATIGRAPHIC SEQUENCES

The major test of the hypothesized ceramic progression of types, as well as the sequence of occupation phases, lies in the analysis of stratigraphic changes. Stratigraphy can be used as a means of relative dating in every locus within the excavated portions of Salmon Ruin, but absolute dates, via dendrochronology, ^{14}C, or archaeomagnetic dating are not available for every level. Despite the importance of stratigraphy and its ubiquitous availability as a tool for temporal assessment, the use of stratigraphy at Salmon was plagued with problems. A few are mentioned here, but the details of stratigraphic and contextual problems are discussed by R. Adams in Chapter 6 of this report.

One difficulty with interpretation of Salmon's stratigraphy involves the absence of a single, extramural trash mound. If such a midden or trash mound did exist outside the main structure of Salmon Ruin, it has been removed by cycles of erosion and deposition of the San Juan River or modern agricultural disturbance in the vicinity. It seems likely that trash dumped over the edge of the terrace on the riverside would have been removed by periodic flooding of the river.

A second obstacle to understanding Salmon's stratigraphy is the extensive reoccupation, remodeling, and reuse of the pueblo by the Secondary occupants. These later occupants completely removed materials from the Chacoan occupation in many rooms. In such instances, they reused rooms down to the original Primary occupation floors, leaving essentially nothing of the material culture of the earlier people. In other cases, Secondary intrusion extended only partway down into the rooms, leaving Primary materials in situ below; this is particularly true of the reoccupation of the multistoried portions of the pueblo. Although Primary materials may be left below the reused Secondary portions of these rooms, they are not necessarily unaffected by the reuse above. Mixture of Primary and Secondary materials occurred during construction activities such as the addition of partition walls and the insertion of kivas into rectangular or square rooms, through trash disposal down from the second story into the abandoned first story, and through the placement of Secondary burials down into the Primary materials remaining in the lower part of the first story. Where rooms were cleaned out by the Secondary occupants, parts or all of the previous strata relating to the Intermediate and Primary periods were removed. This material was either transported out of the community altogether and deposited elsewhere, or thrown into a nearby room not desired for rehabitation, thus forming a layer or layers of redeposited or mixed Primary-Secondary levels. These processes result in poor samples for the Primary occupation in general, removal of the Primary occupation material entirely from many rooms, contamination or mixture of Primary and Secondary in other cases, and redeposition of Primary artifacts into stratigraphic contexts that do not reflect the original context of use of these materials.

Moreover, the small population that continued to occupy the site after the end of the Primary and before the Secondary (between ca. AD 1130 and 1200) was not widespread. The paucity of strata assignable to the Intermediate period is ascribable to a relatively small population at this time in conjunction with the probable removal of evidence of this period in the massive architectural remodeling of the AD 1200s.

Consequently, it is difficult to find at Salmon a complete and undisturbed in situ stratigraphic sequence representing all the major occupation periods. Fortunately, a number of rooms were abandoned during the Primary, and were then filled with a sequence of Primary and Intermediate trash that was never removed by Secondary occupants. Even here, however, intrusive Secondary burials in the earlier trash strata and evidence of redeposition of Primary materials in the upper strata is often evident. The rooms considered the most desirable for stratigraphic evidence with a long sequence of deposition are 31A, 31B, 31W; 33C, 33W; 81W; 82W; 93W; 102A, 102W; 100W; and 129W. In places, the deeper portions of the plaza also contain stratified deposits that accumulated over a period of more than one occupation. Other rooms such as 62W and 91W produce long sequences, but with substantial redeposition and a complex history involving multiple mounds and lenses of trash with less than clear sequences of deposition. Rooms in both wing areas of the site were of only one story. Consequently, these were more severely affected by the Secondary reuse problem than the multiple-storied sections of the back part of the pueblo. In the wings, where there was some remnant of Primary activity, it was in thin deposits sealed beneath Secondary floors. In Rooms 6 and 124, for example, large square rooms of the Primary were converted into circular kivas in the Secondary. In doing so, Primary and any Intermediate strata were removed down to the level of the kiva floors. Fortunately, the kiva floors lie slightly higher than the floors of the original Primary square rooms, within which artifactual remnants of the Primary usage of the square rooms remain. In fact the best contrast between unmixed Primary and Secondary ceramic complexes is seen in such cases, due to the sealing of in situ Primary deposits by a Secondary floor. Although in such instances the Primary to Secondary contrast may be easily seen, none of the rooms in the wings contains the desired long stratigraphic sequence of Primary and Intermediate trash that is seen in some rooms in the more central part of the pueblo. If complete sequences of early periods were present in these situations, they were largely removed during the Secondary reuse.

A number of the most promising rooms were examined for stratigraphic relations and ceramic changes. The first of these was Room 93W, examined intensively in 1974, followed by Room 31W and Room 6W. As additional rooms were completed, several more were chosen for similar examination. In the end, the following rooms were examined for their ceramic sequences: 93W, 31W, 33W, 82W, 102A and W, 100W, 91W, 129W, and Plaza Trench 13P. Preliminary reports were prepared on the ceramic sequences of several of these rooms. In the end, the stratigraphy of every excavated room was examined for ceramic changes.

The technique of factor scoring all strata facilitated assessment of ceramic-stratigraphic changes in many rooms without having to tediously compile types by strata tables. Because factor scores yielded a convenient approximation of the ceramic contents of each stratum, it could easily be determined which rooms contained long uninterrupted sequences as opposed to rooms with extensive reuse, mixture, or redeposition problems. Factor score codes equate with ceramics in a level as follows: intrusive dominant Primary – 1 or A; San Juan White Ware, Mancos-McElmo B/w dominant Primary – 2 or B; McElmo B/w dominant strata – 3 or C; Mesa Verde B/w dominant Secondary strata – 4, 5, and 6 or D and E.

METHODS

The methods for examining stratigraphic sequences were as follows:

1. All ceramics were rough sorted (according to type and variety). All Primary strata were also analyzed on the limited-attribute form.

2. Rooms with obvious potential for a long sequence on the basis of field observation, R. Adams's recommendations, and factor-scored strata were then examined more closely.

3. The actual sequence of deposited layers in these rooms was taken from field notes. Consultation with Rex Adams saved considerable time in this regard, and the compilation of the Salmon codex greatly simplified the time-consuming task of sorting through the strata designations and contextual relationships of individual strata. Nevertheless, considerable time was spent determining stratigraphic sequences from profiles and field notes. The complexity of Salmon room strata, with as many as 150 strata identified in some rooms, and the fact that excavation was spread over several years under different personnel, contributed to the difficulty of stratigraphic assessment.

4. Frequency tables were compiled and percentages were calculated for each ceramic type in each stratum. Here, the cross-tab format of the SPSS program package was found to be convenient, because it is used to plot two variables against each other (here, stratum vs. type) and automatically prints vertical and horizontal percentages. Because the frequency, the percentage of the total for the type, and the percentage of the total ceramics in the stratum are provided in the printout, considerable hand calculation is avoided. In addition, the percentages of each stratum/type cell can be compared to the marginal

percentages vertically and horizontally to determine if the cell's frequency is above or below the expected frequency for the room as a whole.

5. Finally, tabular data were used to graph ceramic changes in series, wares, or types within the room to illustrate general trends.

Completion of this process on a number of rooms with relatively long sequences revealed a close correspondence in ceramic trends. The strata in each room were not identical in detail, but substantial agreement was evident in the overall patterns of ceramic change. In rooms with sufficiently long and undisturbed sequences, the Primary, Intermediate, and Secondary ceramic complexes could always be seen superimposed. It was then apparent that other rooms contained truncated portions of the entire sequence revealed in the trash-filled rooms. By comparison to the rooms with complete sequences, the problems of reuse of Primary levels, mixture, and redeposition could be monitored ceramically in the fill of the remaining rooms.

It is clearly impossible to present the sequence of types and varieties in all excavated Salmon rooms. Because of substantial agreement between the best trash-filled rooms in terms of ceramic trends, however, a small sample of rooms in different areas of the pueblo as well as a plaza trench were selected to illustrate the major ceramic trends.

Room 82W

Centrally located in the pueblo, Room 82W is situated immediately east of the Tower Kiva. It appears to have also been central in its function during Primary times. As one of a number of rooms surrounding the Tower Kiva, Room 82W was in a position to have functioned as a special room associated with ceremonial residence and/or observances. Early in the Primary occupation, this room contained an "altar," a partition wall, and a "platform," along with a ceramic assemblage high in exotic intrusive ceramics. After its use as a ceremonial room, 82W was slowly filled with later Primary trash (C-9-21 and C-10-22) that contained increasing amounts of San Juan White Ware ceramics as time went on. The next trash layer deposited (C-7-19) contained mostly McElmo B/w, and may be assigned to the Intermediate period. F-2-17 (and its subdivisions) refers to several strata connected with the wooden remains of a platform and the upper parts of a jacal wall in the room. These had been used during the Primary occupation of the room, but are situated stratigraphically higher than the trash layers C-7-19 and C-9-21, which accumulated prior to the collapse of F-2-17. Following this, additional trash deposits continued to accumulate within the structure (C-6-16 through M-3-13.5), in which McElmo B/w was replaced by Mesa Verde B/w as the dominant type, and intrusive ceramics declined in frequency. Finally, an artificial fill layer was placed in the room (D-1-09) to prepare the surface for the Secondary floor (H-1-06, I-1-08). On it was a hearth (l-1-07), and superimposed above the Secondary floor were several layers of Secondary trash (C-1-04 through B-2-05), followed by the Secondary roof (F-1-03). Thereafter, only postoccupational fill (B-1-02) was encountered up to the present surface.

Room 82W illustrates an interesting phenomenon common at Salmon Ruin: the roofs (and platforms) were often still intact for some time after the surfaces under them (i.e., floors) were no longer in use. This allowed fill (usually trash) to accumulate between the roof and corresponding floor. When the roof did collapse, it then came to lie stratigraphically above strata that are somewhat later in time. This process accounts for stratigraphic reversals in ceramic types and factor scores relative to the strata immediately below them. It should be remembered that the actual construction and initial usage of roof features was with the floors below them, thus accounting for reversals of the sequence in these cases.

Another process that complicated a number of rooms was the reoccupation of Primary roofs by Secondary people. In the case of two-story rooms, the Secondary people penetrated no further than the surface of the first-story roof (i.e., floors of the second story). Reuse of these surfaces usually produced a mixed Primary-Secondary assemblage. In cases of extensive reuse, the Primary ceramics were removed entirely so that the surface contained only Secondary artifact assemblages, although tree-ring dates on the beams may indicate Primary construction dates in the late AD 1000s and early 1100s.

Analytical stratigraphic confusion also resulted from Secondary occupants placing burials beneath these first-story roofs atop or into trash deriving from Intermediate or Primary times. Two such instances occur in 82W. Burials in pits L-3-12 and L-4-15.5 are Secondary in temporal assignment as judged by the ceramic accompaniments, but they occur stratigraphically below the occupational surface used in Secondary times (H-1-06). The lower burial contained a Mesa Verde B/w bowl, but it intruded into Intermediate trash below the Secondary living surface. For this reason, burial pit ceramics are not included in stratigraphic assessments.

In 82W the adobe and wood platforms (F-2-17 and its subdivisions) illustrate the operation of these factors. Originally constructed and used by Primary occupants, they fell only after later trash had accumulated. Further, they were later contaminated ceramically via reuse or placement of burials by Secondary inhabitants (hence the factor score of D for this stratum, instead of the logical A).

The graphic illustration of ceramic trends deserves some commentary. Small fluctuations are of little consequence in these graphs; the larger trends are all that are intended for illustration. Small reversals of the major trends are accounted for by differing sample sizes which affect the percentages of types, as well as the processes mentioned above, which can interfere with the stratigraphic sequence. The decorated sherds do not reflect the absolute decorated totals for the strata; plain portions of decorated vessels were not included, nor were sherds unidentified to series and type. Mixed strata, except for mixtures between adjacent strata, were deemed a source of possible confusion and were eliminated. All graphs used here are based on percentages (mostly percentages of total decorated) within each stratum. In this way there is some standardization and control for differing ceramic sample sizes within strata; however, actual numbers of given types may be quite small in some strata, causing percentages to vary on the basis of minute (and culturally inconsequential) sample size differences. The counts do represent analysis of a complete sample of all pottery available from each stratum; the decorated sherd count is well above 100 sherds for the major trash strata, whereas behavioral surfaces may have smaller sample sizes. Despite sample size and stratigraphic problems, major trends do appear from percentage tabulations of ceramic types by stratigraphic placement.

The stratigraphic sequence of ceramics in 82W is one of the more complete and continuous at Salmon, with a stacked sequence of factor scores from A to E (Table 24.1). Figure 24.2, based on ceramic series only, illustrates the predominance of the San Juan White Ware in all strata, although the percentage of decorated sherds accounted for by San Juan White Ware diminishes in earlier strata, and drops to about half of the decorated ceramics on the Primary floor.

Intrusive ceramics (all decorated series) in the assemblage rise as San Juan ceramics decline in frequency in earlier strata. This is especially notable for Cibola White Ware, which increases dramatically as the Primary floor is approached. Less suddenly, the Chuska, Tusayan, and Tsegi Series ceramics also reach peaks on or near the Primary floor. Although they reach a peak of frequency in the Chacoan occupation, the intrusive ceramics from the Chuska and Tsegi Series are also present in late Primary and Intermediate strata (but are inconsequential in Secondary ones). This indicates that small quantities of ceramics of these series continued to be imported in the middle AD 1100s, or perhaps there was continued use of previously imported vessels after the end of the Primary occupation.

Smudged Red Ware is strongly associated with the earliest Primary assemblages in 82W (as elsewhere in the pueblo); 11 of 13 sherds occurred in association with the Primary floor. The only sherd of San Juan Red Ware in the room (La Plata B/r) also was located on the floor. The White Mountain Red Ware Series, however, was present for a much longer period, although it also reached a percentage peak in the Primary. Its persistence through Primary, Intermediate, and into Secondary strata reflects the continued import of ceramics of this series after the end of the Primary period; this has been noted in every room with a long sequence. The continued import of White Mountain Red Ware ceramics despite the decrease of every other intrusive series after the Primary period at Salmon is an interesting phenomenon.

Figure 24.3 illustrates the fact that despite some temporal overlap, the peaks of popularity for Mesa Verde, McElmo, and Mancos B/w are quite distinct, and occur in successively lower strata. Mesa Verde B/w declines nearly continuously in earlier strata; the slight rises in C-5-15 and F-2-17 are caused by intrusive Mesa Verde ceramics below the Secondary floor. McElmo B/w reaches a peak in C-8-20, and then begins to decline. Although present in both Primary and Secondary strata, its relative frequency is much lower both before and after the Intermediate strata of C-7-19 and C-8-20. Mancos B/w displays a sharp increase in Primary strata beginning with C-9-21, becoming even more common than McElmo in lower Primary strata.

Within the intrusive Cibola Series assemblage, there is little indication of temporal priority of one type over another. Seventy-four percent of all the Cibola Series ceramics in 82W occurred on the floor unit, including all major types (Puerco-Escavada, Gallup, Chaco, and Chaco-McElmo B/w). The small amounts of Cibola ceramics found in higher strata (e.g., M-3-13.5) are undoubtedly from redeposited or reused vessels.

All Chuska Series ceramics are from Primary occupation strata (C-9-21 and below). As is usual at Salmon, the majority of these are Chuska and Toadlena B/w. Mineral-painted Chuska types are very rare at Salmon; only one sherd was found in the Primary strata of Room 82W. No temporal sequence of Chuska Series types can be demonstrated in this room but all are associated with Primary strata.

Table 24.1. Ceramic counts and percentages (in parentheses) by stratum for Room 82W.

Stratum	Factor Score	Mesa Verde	McElmo	Wetherill	Mancos	Cibola Series	Chuska-Tusayan Series	White Mtn Red	Tsegi Orange	Smudged Red	San Juan Red	Total
F-1-3	E	65	1	–	4	1	–	–	–	–	–	71
		(91.5)	(1.4)	–	(5.6)	(1.4)	–	–	–	–	–	
C-1-4	E	34	10	–	–	–	–	–	–	–	–	44
		(77.3)	(22.7)	–	–	–	–	–	–	–	–	
H-1-6, O-1, L1	E	22	3	–	–	–	–	–	–	–	–	25
		(88)	(12)	–	–	–	–	–	–	–	–	
D-1-9	E	63	19	1	3	–	–	3	–	–	–	89
		(70.8)	(21.3)	(1.1)	(3.4)	–	–	(3.4)	–	–	–	
M-3-13.5	D	166	99	4	8	6	–	17	–	1	–	301
		(55.1)	(32.9)	(1.3)	(2.7)	(2)	–	(5.6)	–	(0.3)	–	
C-5-15	E	137	47	1	3	2	–	5	–	–	–	195
		(70.3)	(24.1)	(0.5)	(1.5)	(1)	–	(2.6)	–	–	–	
C-6-16	C	3	7	2	1	–	–	–	–	–	–	13
		(23.1)	(53.8)	(15.4)	(7.7)	–	–	–	–	–	–	
F-2-17 and subdivisions	D	14	20	–	1	–	–	8	–	–	–	43
		(32.6)	(46.5)	–	(2.3)	–	–	(18.6)	–	–	–	
C-7-19	C	7	75	–	5	1	–	7	1	1	–	97
		(7.2)	(77.3)	–	(5.2)	(1)	–	(7.2)	(1)	(1)	–	
C-8-20 and C-8.5-20.5	F	–	59	–	2	2	–	1	1	–	–	65
		–	(90.8)	–	(3.1)	(3.1)	–	(1.5)	(1.5)	–	–	
C-9-21	B	1	19	–	9	1	6	1	–	–	–	37
		(2.7)	(51.4)	–	(24.3)	(2.7)	(16.2)	(2.7)	–	–	–	
C-10-22	B	–	22	–	10	2	7	–	1	–	–	42
		–	(52.4)	–	(23.8)	(4.8)	(16.7)	–	(2.4)	–	–	
H-1, H-2, Flr Unit W/G, I, L	A	1	51	–	80	55	18	24	13	11	1	253
		(0.4)	(20.2)	–	(31.6)	(21.7)	(7.1)	(9.5)	(5.1)	(4.3)	(0.4)	
Subfloor T & D Strata	A	–	1	–	4	4	2	–	1	–	–	12
		–	(8.3)	–	(33.3)	(33.3)	(16.7)	–	(8.3)	–	–	

Note: Percentages are of total decorated; includes mixed strata but no pits unless with room floors. Floor-related strata are groups in G, H, I and L associations. Data are from rough-sort file down through C-8-20; lower strata taken from limited-attribute data available for the Primary strata only. No plain white sherds included, no sherds unidentified to type.

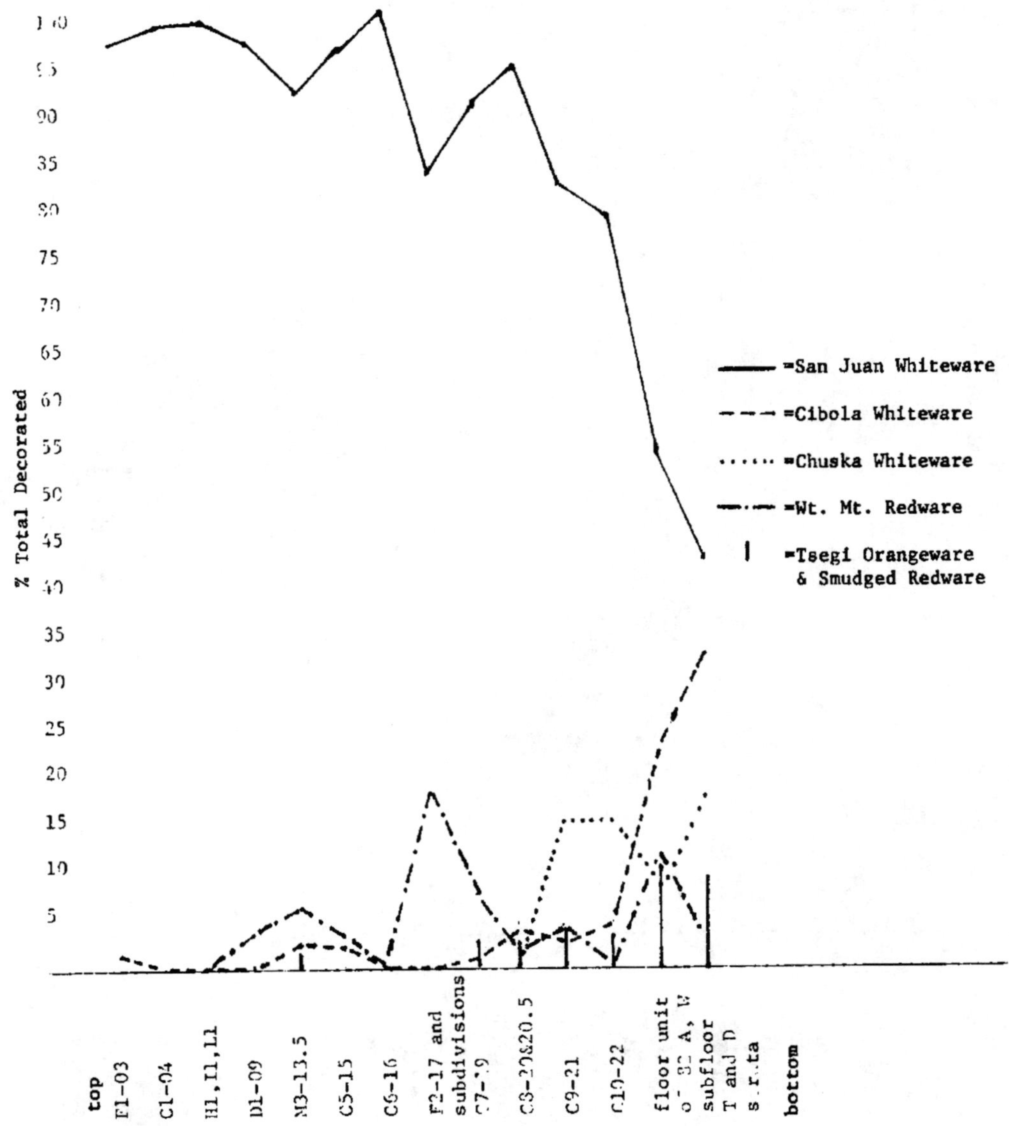

Figure 24.2. Stratigraphic series of decorated, typed sherds in Room 82W at Salmon; floor units (G, H, I, and L) are grouped together.

In the White Mountain Red Ware, there is evidence that the Puerco and Wingate B/r types are earlier in appearance than the polychromes. St. Johns B/r and Wingate Polychrome do not appear in any quantity in the assemblage until M-3-13.5. No St. Johns Polychrome was recovered from 82W. Black-on-red types, however, are found from the Primary floor up through the end of the Intermediate at D-1-09, immediately below the Secondary floor. Further, all sherds of Puerco B/r are associated with the Primary floor; Wingate B/r sherds were present on the floor but continue through later Primary and Intermediate strata. Thus, the room supports the sequence of Puerco B/r, Wingate B/r, and Wingate Polychrome. Tsegi Orange Ware is represented by only 17 sherds in 82W, but 13 of these occurred on the Primary floor.

Ceramics found below the lowest floor do not differ drastically from those of the Primary floor unit itself. Pre-Primary assemblages are always subject to some degree of sample error, because they are always few in number. The 12 decorated sherds recov-

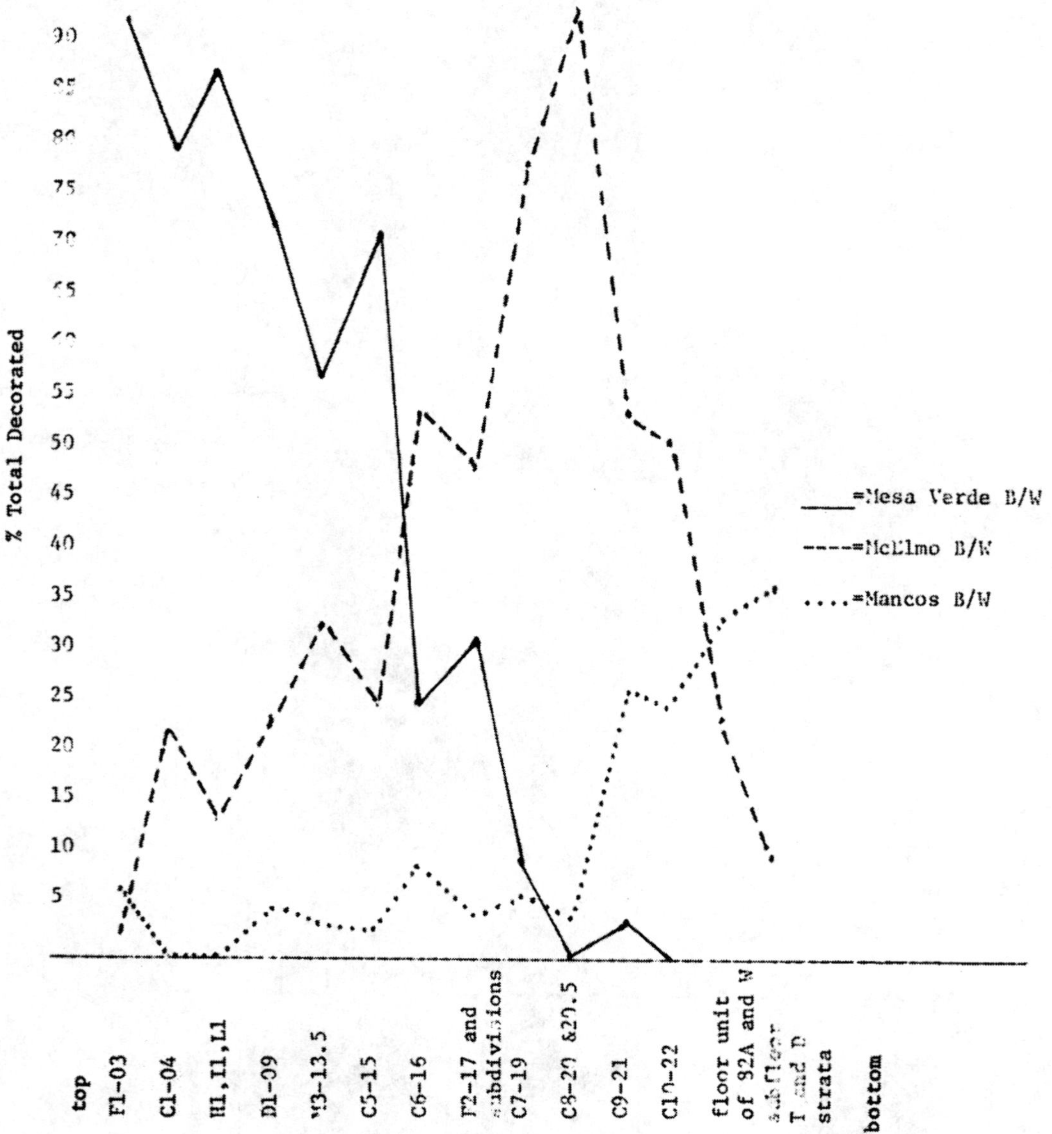

Figure 24.3. Stratigraphic series of San Juan White Ware types in Room 82W at Salmon; floor units (G, H, I, and L) are grouped together.

ered from subfloor strata in 82W are assignable to the same ceramic types as identified on the Primary occupational surface itself.

Room 33C, W

33W is a two-story room situated in the next-to-back-wall position in the west arm of the site. As in 82W, there is a long sequence involving multiple trash strata that span the three major occupations. The floor-related ceramics, as in 82W, are strongly intrusive Primary, and the room may also have had a platform or shelf similar to that in 82W. The stratigraphic sequence again involves a Primary floor unit (G, H, K, and L strata) followed by several other Primary strata. Although two of these (F-3-13 and F-4-15) were originally classed as roofs in the field, R. Adams believes that these represent debris from roof repair or activity areas within the trash. Between these are the G-1.5 and S-1 surfaces, which are not true floors (structurally speaking) but may have been activity areas in the accumulating Primary trash. Late Primary trash above this consists of levels C-2-10, M-1-11, and C-3-13. The actual Primary roof is F-2-09. Originally constructed during Primary times as the first-story roof (second-story floor), F-2-09 may have been used continuously into the Intermediate,

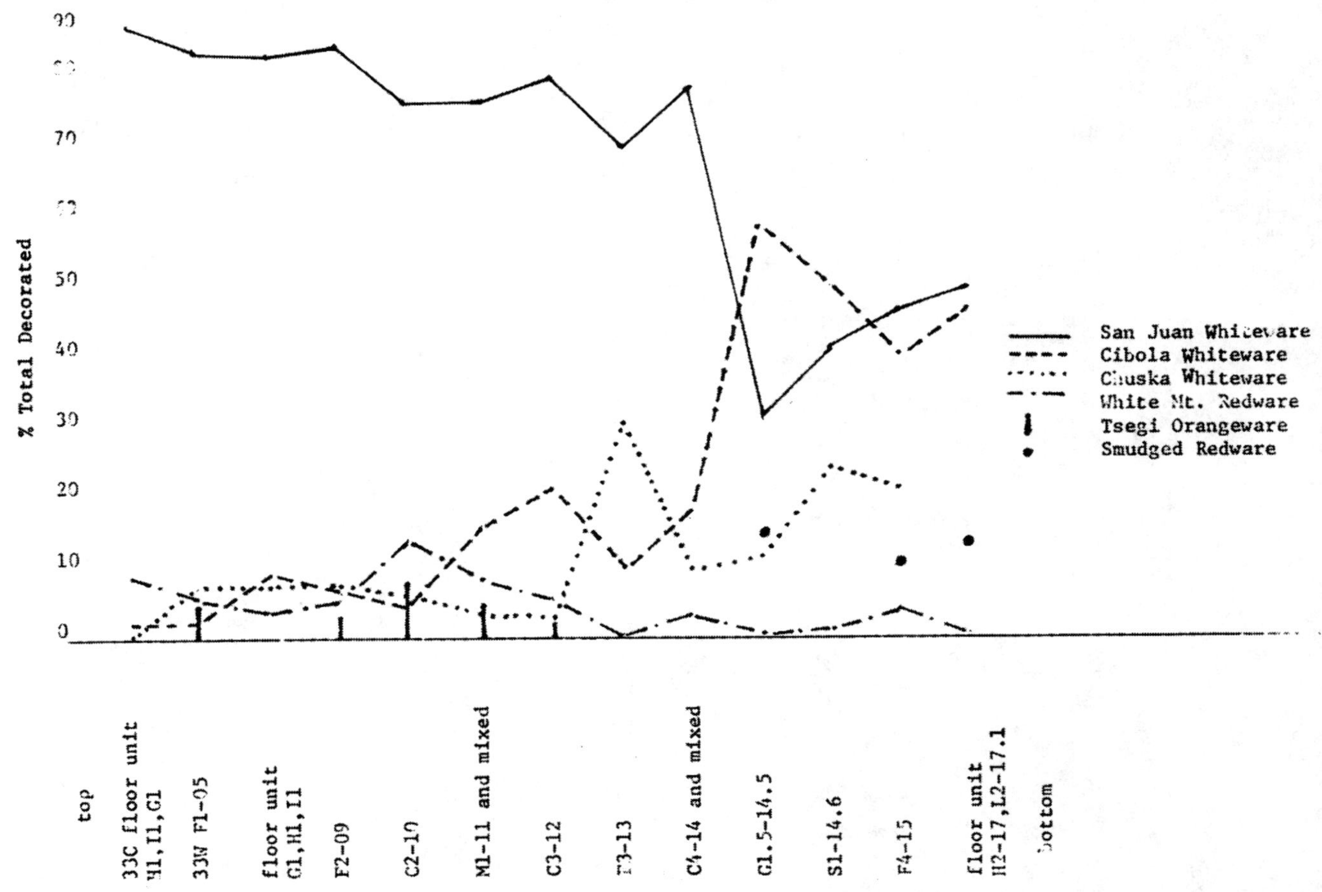

Figure 24.4. Stratigraphic sequence of six ceramic series from Room 33W.

as seen from the high amounts of McElmo B/w and a few of the intrusive series so evident on the floor below. A floor placed over this roof (G-1, H-1, and I-1) relates to an Intermediate or very early Secondary floor placed in the room. It is one of the few places at the site where an Intermediate or early Secondary floor surface has been identified. The fallen roof to this floor is F-1-05, which rests on the floor itself. Thereafter, the room was remodeled by Secondary occupation people, with a small circular kiva placed into the upper part of the room. The kiva floor unit, Room 33C (H-1, I-1, and G-1), contains abundant Mesa Verde B/w. Above this is a Secondary roof (F-1-3) to the kiva, followed by postoccupational fill.

The long sequence of 33W is reflected (as in 82W) by a stacked sequence of factor-scored strata (Table 24.2). As in 82W, the early intrusive dominated Primary is succeeded by more San Juan White Ware dominated Primary, then by Intermediate (F-2-9, G-1, H-1, and I-1), and later by Secondary construction in the form of Kiva 33C, containing its own strata. The trends of ceramic series in the assemblage are similar to those in 82W in many ways (see Figures 24.4 and 24.5). First, San Juan Series White Ware drops drastically in the Primary strata, and is exceeded by intrusive series in some, especially by the Cibola Series. As in 82W, San Juan ceramics amount to approximately 30–50 percent of the total decorated assemblage in Primary strata.

Cibola Series ceramics increase markedly relative to San Juan ceramics in the Primary strata. In the G-1.5–14.5 assemblage they exceed 50 percent of the decorated sherds. As usual, Cibola ceramics are the most frequent of all intrusive ceramics encountered in the Primary occupation.

Chuska White Ware and Tsegi Orange Ware, common in early Primary strata, also continue into the late Primary and Intermediate strata, but become

Table 24.2. Ceramic counts and percentages (in parentheses) by stratum for Room 33C/33W.

Stratum	Factor Score	Mesa Verde	McElmo	Mancos	Cortez	Cibola Series	Chuska-Tusayan Series	White Mtn. Red	Tsegi Orange	Smudged Red	Total
33C kiva floor H-1-5, I-1-6, G-1-6	E	44 (71)	8 (12.9)	3 (4.8)	--	1 (1.6)	--	5 (8.1)	1 (1.6)	--	62
33C F-1-5	B	22 (12.5)	94 (53.4)	26 (14.8)	3 (1.7)	3 (1.7)	11 (6.3)	10 (5.7)	6 (3.4)	1 (0.6)	176
Floor G-1, H-1, I-1	B/C	11 (22.4)	22 (44.9)	8 (16.3)	--	4 (8.2)	3 (6.1)	1 (2)	--	--	49
Room 33W F-2-9	C	22 (8.2)	143 (53.2)	58 (21.6)	--	18 (6.7)	12 (4.5)	14 (5.2)	2 (0.7)	--	269
C-2-10	B	2 (3.7)	22 (40.7)	16 (29.6)	--	2 (3.7)	2 (3.7)	6 (11.1)	4 (7.4)	--	54
M-1-11 (mixed)	B	4 (2.3)	47 (27.3)	71 (41.3)	8 (4.7)	23 (13.4)	2 (1.2)	11 (6.4)	4 (2.3)	2 (1.2)	172
C-3-12	B	--	48 (25.1)	91 (47.6)	8 (4.2)	35 (18.3)	3 (1.6)	4 (2.1)	1 (0.5)	1 (0.5)	191
F-3-13	A	1 (2.5)	2 (5)	23 (57.5)	--	2 (5)	11 (27.5)	--	--	1 (2.5)	40
C-4-14 (mixed)	A	--	14 (29.2)	21 (43.8)	1 (2.1)	8 (16.7)	3 (6.3)	1 (2.1)	--	--	48
G-1.5-14.5	A	--	2 (3)	16 (23.9)	--	35 (52.2)	5 (7.5)	--	--	9 (13.4)	67
S-1-14.6	A	--	--	2 (40)	--	2 (40)	1 (20)	--	--	--	5
F-4-15	A	3 (4.9)	8 (13.1)	18 (29.5)	--	17 (27.9)	9 (14.8)	1 (1.6)	--	5 (8.2)	61
C-5-16	A	--	--	1	--	--	--	--	--	--	1
Lower Floor H-2-17, L-2-17.1	A	--	--	5 (50)	--	4 (40)	--	--	--	1 (10)	10

Note: Data derived from rough-sort and limited attribute analyses; no plain white sherds included. Percentages are of total decorated.

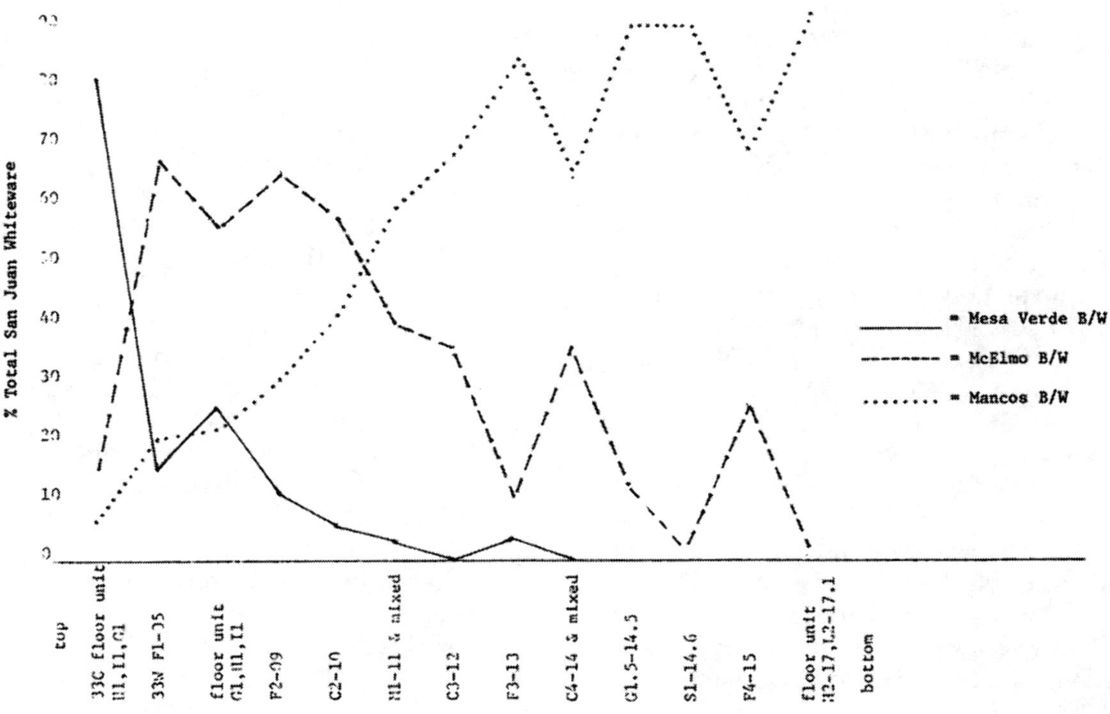

Figure 24.5. Stratigraphic sequence of San Juan White Ware types from Room 33W.

nonexistent by Secondary times in the kiva in 33C. As in 82W, this may indicate somewhat greater temporal persistence for the Tsegi and Chuska Series than for the Cibola White Ware.

Smudged Red Ware is again associated with the intrusive-dominant Primary strata. The majority was found from G-1.5 down to the Primary floor. The presence of sizable quantities of White Mountain Red Ware marks a departure from the usual decline in intrusive frequencies after Primary occupation strata. Here, White Mountain Red Ware has a fairly constant representation in all strata. Although present in all time periods, the types of this series are relatively (and absolutely) more common in Intermediate strata. Again, a long and uninterrupted importation of White Mountain Red Ware spanning the entire Salmon sequence is indicated.

Several observations can be made about specific types in the Room 33 sequence. First, in Cibola White Ware, Puerco-Escavada B/w begins early in the sequence (three or four sherds on the Primary floor are of these types). Chaco and Gallup B/w were found throughout the Primary strata, with Chaco B/w the most common Cibola White Ware type, as is typical. Chaco-McElmo B/w was found in most of the Primary strata, but was higher in Primary trash than the Puerco-Escavada B/w. Chaco-McElmo does not outlast Chaco or Gallup in the Primary sequence in 33W, or in any other room. Evidence is slim and subject to sample error, but Puerco-Escavada seems to appear earlier in the Primary strata of this room than does Chaco-McElmo.

San Juan White Ware types again show distinct peaks in the assemblage for the three sequential types (Figure 24.5). Mesa Verde B/w drops quickly from 80 percent of the decorated ceramics on the kiva floor of 33C to 15 percent in F-1-05. In the upper portion of 33W, in Intermediate strata, McElmo B/w accounts for 60–70 percent of the San Juan White Ware assemblage. At M-1-11, Mancos B/w becomes the dominant San Juan White Ware type and increases from there with increased depth as the percentage of McElmo B/w declines in earlier Primary strata. At the Primary floor, Mancos B/w constitutes more than 90 percent of the San Juan White Ware assemblage.

Chuska White Ware is present in all Primary and Intermediate strata up through F-1-05; it is relatively more frequent in Primary strata from C-3-12 downward. There is no strong evidence for temporal priority of one Chuska Series type over another; the assemblage is dominated by Toadlena and Chuska B/w, as is usually the case. Nava B/w (McElmo style) seems to be present as early as Chuska and

Toadlena B/w, but this type does not outlast Chuska and Toadlena in the 33W sequence. The only sherd of Crumbled House B/w does occur relatively late, in F-1-05 just below the Secondary kiva floor.

In White Mountain Red Ware, there is again evidence for temporal priority of the black-on-red types over the polychromes in stratum of first appearance. Puerco and Wingate B/r are present in three lower Primary strata wherein no polychromes of the series appear. Wingate Polychrome appears in the sequence first in F-2-09, and St. Johns Polychrome makes its first appearance higher up, in F-1-05 (early Secondary). However, Wingate B/r persists through all Primary and Intermediate strata; this most popular of the White Mountain Red Ware types at Salmon was not supplanted by the polychromes in the sequence until nearly Secondary times (ca. AD 1200). The 33W sequence provides no strong evidence of a similar sequence in the Tsegi Orange Ware, although there is evidence elsewhere in the site that the black-on-reds of this series did appear earlier. There is slight evidence that Citadel Polychrome persisted later than Tusayan or Medicine B/r, because it is found as high as F-1-06, unlike the black-on-reds. There is no evidence here, or anyplace else at Salmon, that Tsegi Orange Ware was imported during the Secondary period.

Room 100W

Room 100W is a Type 1 Salmon room (large and square, and single story) in the east arm of the pueblo. Like 82W and 33W, it was used for trash deposition over a long period of Salmon's history, starting during the Primary and continuing through the Secondary period. Stratigraphically, the Primary floor (H-1-19) is overlain by two mounds of trash that represent a series of strata deposited during Primary and Intermediate times (Figure 24.6). The south mound consists of four strata (C-10-15 through C-13-18). The north mound is composed of C-7-12 down through C-9-14. The south mound is believed to be the earlier of the two, although the field notes are not clear on this point. This temporal reconstruction reflects the original belief of the room's excavators, with strata sequence numbers that go down through the north mound and then transfer to the top of the south mound. Also, the profiles indicate that the north mound strata overlap those of the south mound, and this reconstruction produces a stratigraphic sequence of ceramics that agrees with that of other trash-filled rooms; otherwise there would be reversals in ceramic trends. Factor scores of these strata (Table 24.3) also indicate that at least most of the south mound strata contain earlier ceramics than those in the north mound. However, the basal strata of both mounds rest on the floor, and may therefore be slightly mixed with floor-related materials.

Overlying the two mounds was a series of covering strata (C-1-04, C-2-05.2, C-2-05.3, and C-3-06) that contained large amounts of Mesa Verde B/w along with a mixture of Primary and Intermediate redeposited sherds. Finally, the Primary roof collapsed on top of the refuse below, effectively ending further disturbance. The Secondary occupants never reoccu-

Table 24.3. Ceramic factor scores by strata for Room 100W.

Stratum	Type	Old Factor Score	New Factor Score
B-1-02	Postoccupation fill	–	E
N-1-03	Primary roof	4	E
C-1-04	Trash	3	D
C-2-05 and C-2-.05.3	Trash	3	C/D
C-3-06	Trash	9 (mixed)	B/C
North Mound			
C-7-12	Trash	3	C
C-8-13	Trash	3	C
C-9-14	Trash	3	B
South Mound			
C-10-15	Trash	2	B
C-11-16	Trash	2	B
C-12-17	Trash	1	B
C-13-18	Trash	1	B
H-1-190	Primary floor	1	B

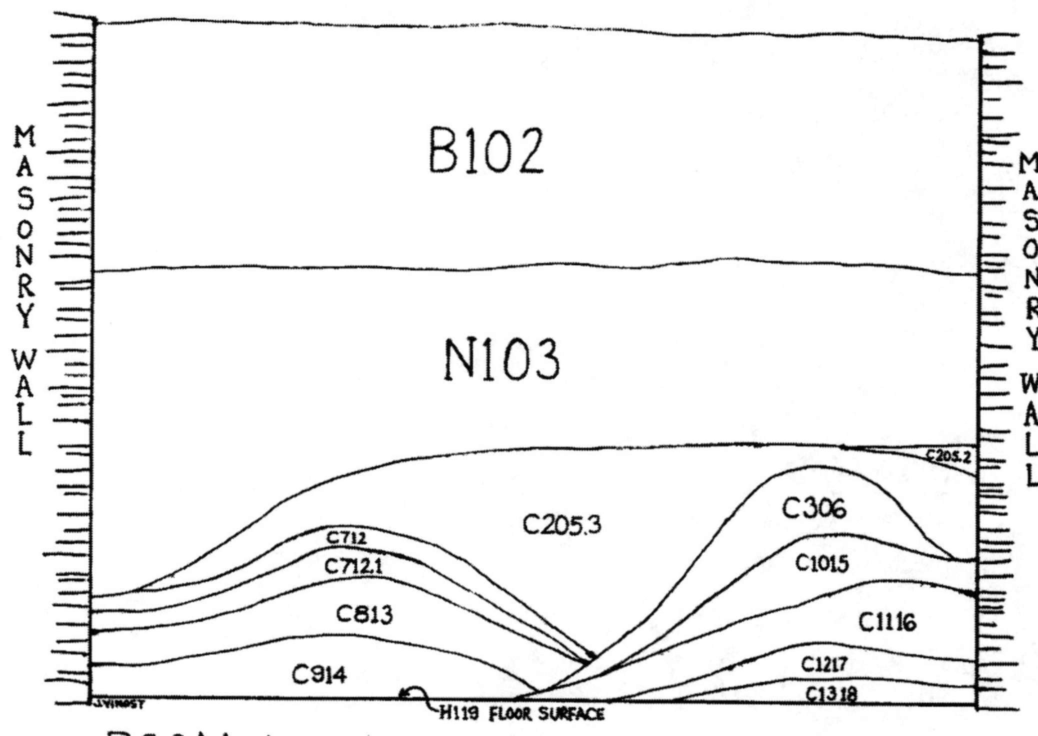

Figure 24.6. Schematic profile of east wall of test trench in Room 100W.

pied the room, but instead deposited trash there, including Primary materials cleaned out of nearby rooms that they reused as habitations.

The ceramics in Room 100W were completely rough sorted twice, first in 1977. These ceramics were later rough sorted again to make sure that the recordings of San Juan White Ware varieties and types were compatible from top to bottom. The two ceramic profiles thus obtained were compared, with quite similar results. Figure 24.7 illustrates the ceramic trends of the three major San Juan types as well as Chaco B/w. Other intrusive ceramics were not graphed because they are rare in the 100W strata assemblage, and because they largely follow the pattern given for Chaco B/w. This graph plots midpoints of curves in an earlier graph in order to deemphasize short-term fluctuations and reveal the more general trends. The trends of the four types graphed in Figure 24.7 illustrate the familiar patterns seen in other trash-filled rooms. Mesa Verde B/w displays a sharp decline as McElmo B/w rises to 60 percent of the decorated assemblage in the middle strata. In earlier strata, Mancos and McElmo B/w coexist, although the former is more numerous. The curve for Chaco B/w is similar in trend to that for Mancos B/w; these are contemporaneous Primary occupation types. Both Mancos and Chaco B/w rise in popularity in earlier strata, but Chaco B/w never exceeds the locally available Mancos B/w.

This sequence may be divided into three main groups in terms of stratigraphy and ceramic assemblages. First is the upper group of strata down through C-2-05.3 (and perhaps C-3-06), which consists of covering fill over the earlier mounds and is of Secondary origin. Mesa Verde B/w constitutes 50–70 percent of the decorated pottery in these strata. There is also abundant mixture of earlier materials in these levels, however, most likely as a result of the cleaning of neighboring rooms by the Secondary occupation people.

Second is the north mound group of strata (C-8-13, C-9-14, and C-10-15), in which Mesa Verde B/w drops to low percentages. The existence of this type here is perhaps due to downward mixture from the overlying Secondary strata. McElmo B/w climbs to 50–60 percent of the decorated pottery, with Mancos B/w totaling about 20 percent. Intrusive ceramics are generally less than 5 percent of the decorated assemblage.

Finally, the last group includes the south mound strata C-11-16, C-12-17 and C-13-18, as well as the floor surface H-1-19 and subfloor materials. In these

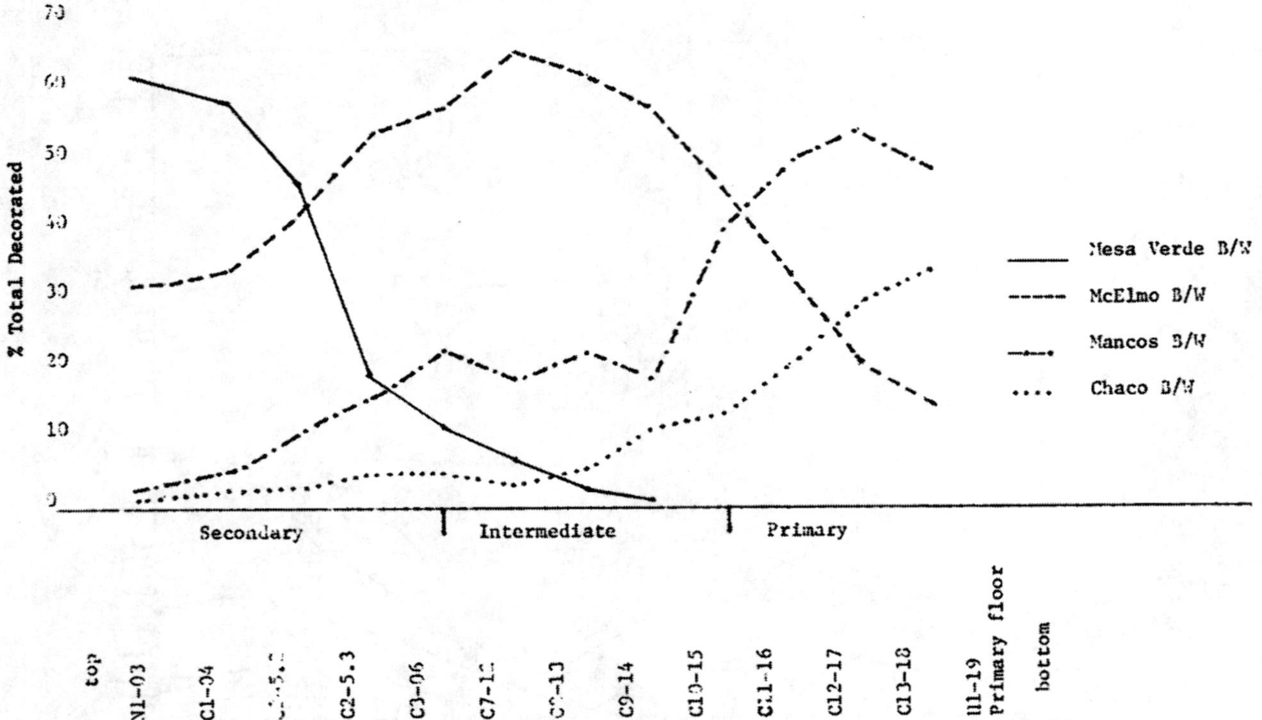

Figure 24.7. Stratigraphic trends of four ceramic types in Room 100W.

strata, Mesa Verde B/w is nearly absent and McElmo B/w has dropped to 20 percent or less of the decorated assemblage. Mancos B/w is the dominant type, comprising 40–60 percent of the decorated ceramics. Although some Cibola Series B/w were scattered throughout the upper levels due to redeposition, they were found in situ in these Primary strata, amounting to between 20 and 30 percent of the decorated sherds.

In sum, there is both stratigraphic and ceramic evidence of three major time units represented in the strata of 100W (Figure 24.7). Although the ceramic frequency trends are in a sense continuous, the rather drastic changes in amounts of Mesa Verde relative to McElmo B/w mark the Secondary-Intermediate transition, whereas the sudden increase of Mancos B/w accompanied by the intrusive decorated types is an objective measure of the Primary period layers.

Factor scores on these strata based on two separate sortings of the same pottery also support these conclusions. Table 24.3 shows that all strata assigned to the Primary scored B, 1, or 2 (i.e., Mancos dominant or intrusive dominant Primary). All the strata in the north mound scored C or 3 (McElmo dominant) except for C-9-14 which rests on the Primary floor and may have been mixed with its materials. The covering strata above the mounds all have later factor scores of D or E, despite the admixture of redeposited Primary ceramics in these levels noted above. Finally, the Primary roof scored E (Mesa Verde B/w dominant) because Secondary ceramics were associated with the roof, which was originally of Primary construction and which presumably originally contained a Primary ceramic assemblage.

A chi-square test on the ceramic contents of the combined Primary strata (116 sherds) versus the combined Intermediate strata (309 sherds) showed significance at the .001 level. The major variable accounting for the difference was the amount of Mancos versus McElmo B/w in the two periods. For Primary strata, Mancos B/w and Cibola White Ware exceeded the expected values; in the Intermediate strata, by contrast, McElmo B/w exceeded the expected value. Therefore, the major difference between Primary and Intermediate strata lies in the shift in dominance from the ceramic complex of Mancos B/w plus intrusive ceramics, to a later dominance by McElmo B/w with a decline in the quantities of Cibola and other intrusive ceramics.

A hint of microtemporal change within the Primary strata can be discerned in 100W, as well as in the Primary strata of 82W and 33W. In the 100W assemblage, the floor and the earliest trash level (C-13-18) contain higher intrusive counts than the superimposed Primary levels of C-11-16 and C-12-17. Figure 24.7 likewise shows that Mancos B/w reaches a peak of popularity above the actual floor, whereas Chaco B/w increases to a peak on the floor itself. This trend is similarly seen in the factor scores of the Primary strata, in which the lowest trash deposits as well as the floor scored 1 (high intrusive Primary), changing to 2 (Mancos B/w dominant) in succeeding Primary strata. The microtemporal trend is not as obvious in 100W as it is in 82W and 33W due to the fact that intrusive sherds were never as common in the Primary of 100W as in the other two rooms, so the change from intrusive to San Juan Primary is less visible. This phenomenon is related to spatial differences in the frequency of intrusive ceramic usage across the pueblo during the Primary.

Plaza Trench 13P

Trash deposits in the plaza area also offer the potential for viewing ceramic changes stratigraphically. Unfortunately, most plaza test trenches revealed few suitable loci due to shallow deposition, mixture of deposits, and incomplete sequences. For instance, the test trench line 13P, which extended east to west across the plaza along the 36-37S line, was excavated in several sections as blocks. Although five tests along this line removed material down to sterile soil, only one section, just west of the Great Kiva, proved to have sufficient depth with both Primary and Secondary materials in a stratified sequence; this group of meter-square units (36-37S by 10-12W) was thus chosen for complete analysis on the rough-sort form.

This section of 13P was excavated in 1974, revealing a series of refuse levels and a use surface. The total depth of the deposits was about 2 m below the present surface. The stratigraphic sequence at this location is as follows: A-1-01 – surfaces; M-1-02 – unstructured trash; C-1-03 – structured trash; Q-1-04 – plaza surface (Secondary period); C-2-06 – structured trash; C-3-06 – structured trash; L-1-07 – pit fill; B-1-08 – nonoccupational fill; and J-1-09 – preoccupational fill.

In total, 3920 sherds were analyzed from the trench, a complete sample. Most were from the structured and unstructured trash (C and M) strata. The more extensive trash accumulation in this spot is probably due to it being one of the topographically lowest spots in the plaza area. In fact, the trash levels account for about 85 percent of the total sherds. Sample sizes are about 200 sherds each for all strata except the use surface Q-1-04 (22 sherds) and J-1-09 (three sherds). The sequence of types in the plaza largely reflects the trends seen in the rooms, although not as distinctly. The reason for the lack of detail in the plaza sequence may be the fact that the entire sequence is represented by only 2 m of fill, whereas the strata in rooms covering the same time span are 6–8 m deep. There was also the presence of rodent burrows (mentioned in the field notes), which would tend to obscure the original relationships by mixing materials between strata.

Examination of the sequence (Table 24.4 and Figures 24.8 and 24.9) reveals the following trends. First, the upper levels down to the plaza surface (Q-1-04)

Table 24.4. Ceramic counts and percentages (in parentheses) by stratum for plaza trench 13P.

Stratum	Mesa Verde	McElmo	Mancos	Wetherill	Cibola Series	White Mtn Red Ware	Tsegi Orange	Smudged Red	Total
M-1-2	107 (55.4)	55 (28.5)	1 (0.5)	–	6 (3.1)	14 (7.3)	3 (1.6)	7 (3.6)	193
C-1-3	95 (84.8)	11 (9.8)	–	–	1 (0.9)	5 (4.5)	–	–	112
Q-1-4	5 (62.5)	1 (12.5)	1 (12.5)	–	–	1 (12.5)	–	–	8
C-2-6	250 (57.7)	113 (26.1)	12 (2.8)	2 (0.5)	16 (3.7)	39 (9.0)	1 (0.2)	–	433
C-3-6	75 (44.9)	64 (38.3)	9 (5.4)	–	12 (7.2)	7 (4.2)	–	–	167
L-1-7	36 (36.0)	43 (42.4)	5 (5.0)	–	6 (6.0)	10 (10.0)	–	–	100
B-1-8	9 (15.3)	25 (42.4)	8 (13.6)	1 (1.7)	8 (13.6)	4 (6.8)	–	4 (6.8)	59
J-1-9	–	2 (66.6)	1 (33.3)	–	–	–	–	–	3

Derived from rough-sort data. No plain white sherds included. Percentages are total decorated. No Chuska Series ceramics from 13P.

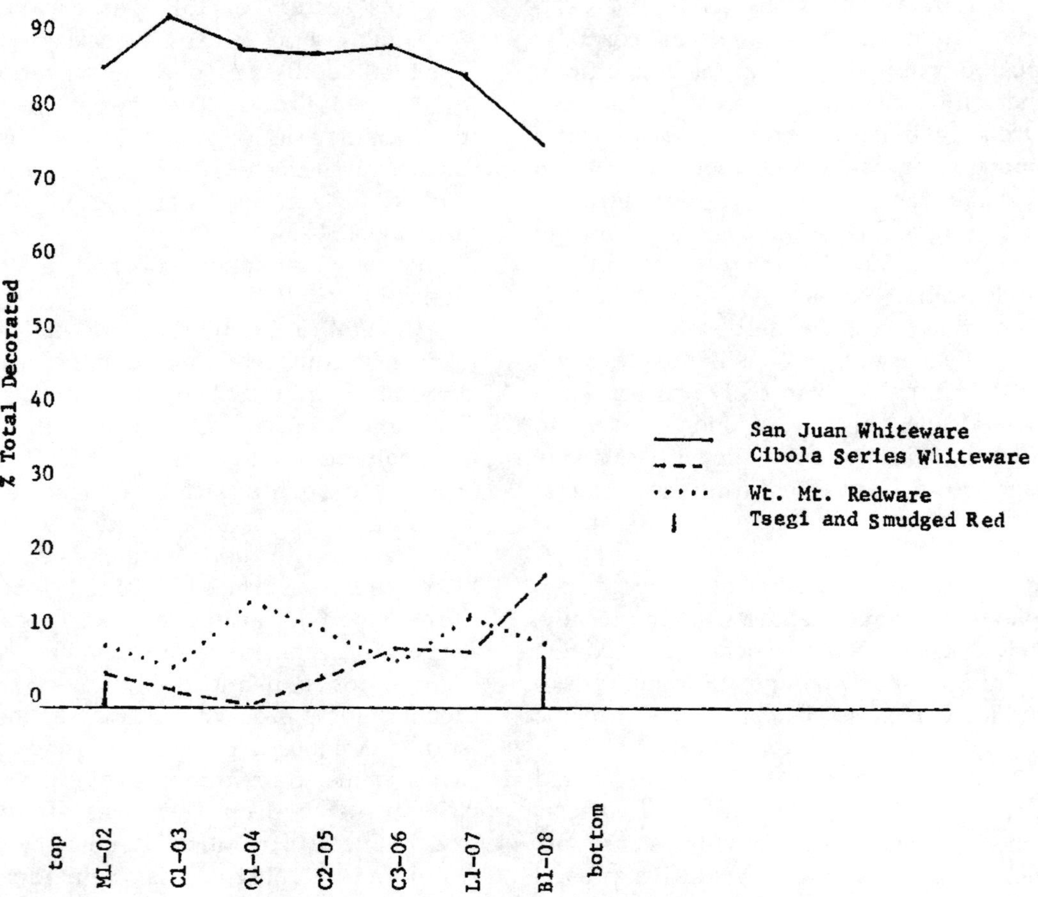

Figure 24.8. Four ceramic series plotted by stratum in Plaza Unit 13P.

and the trash immediately below (C-2-05) belong to the Secondary occupation. Mesa Verde B/w is more than 50 percent of the decorated assemblage in all these strata, and intrusive ceramics are rare. Some amounts of Primary intrusive ceramics are found in a redeposited condition in the M-1-02 assemblage, along with Mesa Verde B/w near the present surface. The prevalence of Mesa Verde B/w in the trash strata just below the plaza surface (C-2-05) indicates that this surface was formed during the Secondary occupation, because there is some early Mesa Verde pottery under it. Perhaps it marks the distinction between two phases of the Secondary occupation, as seen in several other places at the site.

Below this, C-3-06 and L-1-07 are probably Intermediate in time, although Mesa Verde B/w is still present; approximately equal amounts of Mesa Verde and McElmo B/w are present at these levels. There are no really "pure" Intermediate strata (i.e., with McElmo B/w comprising more than 60 percent of the decorated ceramics), compared to the much deeper stratigraphic profiles in Rooms 82W, 33W, and 100W.

The lowest strata (B-1-08 and J-1-09) are probably Primary in time. Here, McElmo B/w is the dominant San Juan White Ware, although there is a small quantity of Mesa Verde B/w due to the mixture problem. The quantity of intrusive ceramics increases relative to local San Juan Mancos and McElmo B/w.

San Juan White Ware ceramics, always the most prevalent in all strata, display the typical decrease relative to intrusive ceramics in earlier strata. The Primary level assemblage from B-1-08 contains 72.8 percent San Juan White Ware (mostly Mancos and McElmo B/w) compared to 84 percent in the stratum immediately above it. Higher San Juan percentages are seen in increasingly higher strata. The slight reversal in M-1-02 is due to the presence of redeposited intrusive ceramics, as noted above.

The three San Juan types again demonstrate distinct temporal peaks of popularity. Mesa Verde

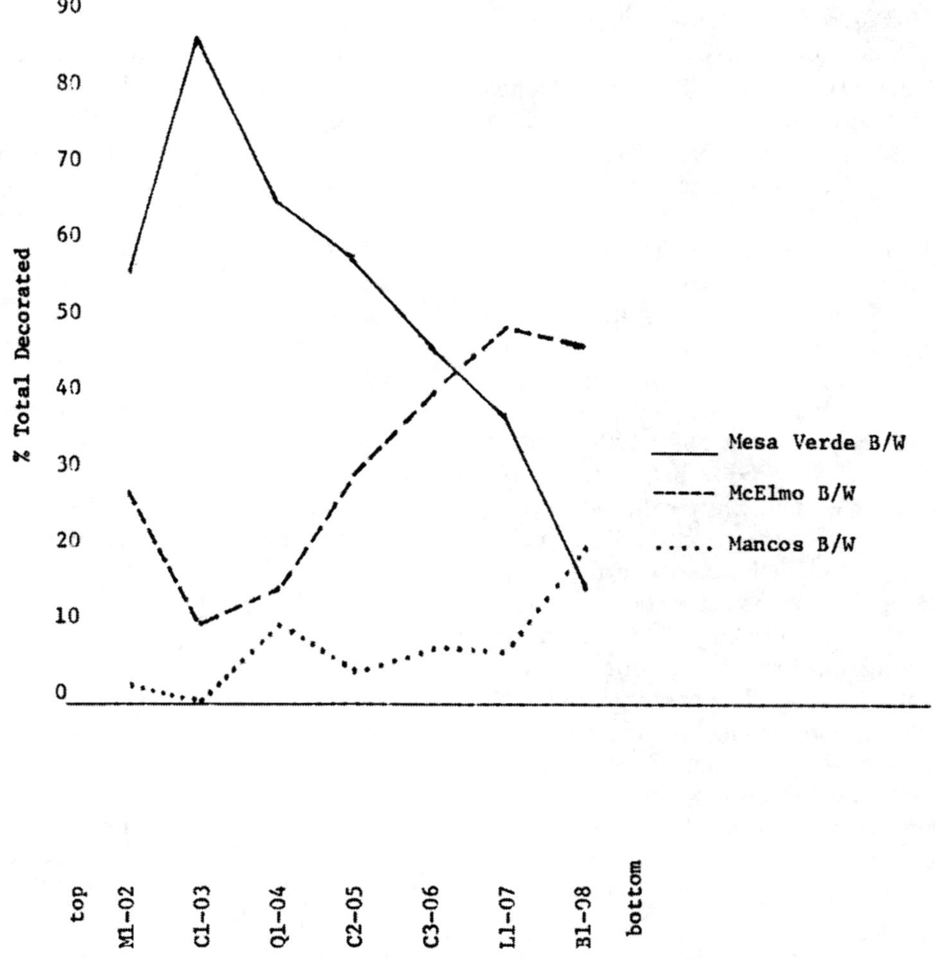

Figure 24.9. San Juan White Ware types by stratum in Plaza Unit 13P.

B/w falls in quantity below the Secondary plaza surface (Q-1-04). McElmo B/w increases with depth, reaching a peak before the lowermost strata. Mancos B/w is minor through most of the strata, becoming more common in Primary stratum B-1-08 at the bottom of the profile. The small amount of Wetherill B/w identified was found scattered throughout the Primary and Intermediate strata and displays no coherent stratigraphic or temporal position.

Cibola Series ceramics are relatively more numerous in the basal stratum B-1-08, as might be expected. Nearly all Cibola White Ware sherds appear below the plaza level; of 30 Cibola sherds, only 5 appear above the plaza level, and these are redeposited in M-1-02. There is little evidence for temporal trends within the Cibola Series. On the basis of small sample sizes it may be mentioned only that the highest percentage for Puerco-Escavada B/w is at the bottom (B-1-08), whereas that for Chaco-McElmo B/w is stratigraphically higher. Chaco and Gallup B/w show no temporal differences between them.

White Mountain Red Ware types are found throughout the sequence in about equal percentages. Puerco and Wingate B/r are the only types represented in the Primary B-1-08; Wingate and St. Johns Polychromes are not present in appreciable amounts until higher in the sequence (C-2-05).

Tsegi Orange Ware and Smudged Red Ware are poorly represented, and were found in a redeposited condition in M-1-02, at the top of the sequence. However, there were also four Smudged Red Ware sherds in situ in the Primary stratum B-108, confirming the Primary assignment of this type. Thus despite a relatively shallow deposition with evidence of mixture and redeposition of some Primary materials, the 13P sequence nevertheless confirms the major trends visible in the room profiles.

SUMMARY OF STRATIGRAPHIC-CERAMIC TRENDS

There is substantial agreement in ceramic trends between the three rooms and one plaza test used for illustration here. Several other rooms with long continuous histories of deposition reflect similar ceramic trends. Despite the contextual and reoccupational problems noted above, these trends are quite consistent in the longer and most complete sequences.

One additional factor obscuring our view of ceramic change is usually referred to as "heirloom" usage—the persistent use of tools after the period of their manufacture. It is usually assumed that the rise and fall of popularity of a ceramic type reflects trends both in manufacture and in use. This is probably true to a great extent. However, periods of manufacture and usage do not necessarily coincide exactly. Depending on their longevity, articles may continue to function for years after their manufacture, as the collection of antiques in our own culture illustrates. Although prehistoric ceramics are also subject to the same potential discrepancy between manufacture spans and use spans, the relatively high breakage rate of vessels as opposed to other artifact categories tends to limit the quantities of heirloom ceramic vessels in use long after their production. But because this factor undoubtedly does play a role, some of the overlap between ceramic types is probably due to the continued use of older vessels. The initial appearance of types and varieties thus provides a better indicator of trends, and is probably more accurate, than end dates.

San Juan White Ware accounts for the vast majority of the decorated assemblages at all times, especially in the Secondary and Intermediate time periods, and to a somewhat lesser degree in the Primary. There is considerable variation in the relative frequency of San Juan ceramics across Primary strata, due to synchronic variables, but types of this series still predominate. San Juan decorated sherds are about 90 percent in Secondary strata, falling to an average of about 70 percent in Primary strata as a whole.

Peak frequencies of the Mesa Verde, McElmo, and Mancos B/w types occur in that order proceeding downward through the sequence. In every room with a continuous sequence, Mesa Verde B/w marks the Secondary strata, often occurring with architectural evidence of reuse and rebuilding as well. B/w, although present for a considerable time, reaches a peak in the Intermediate strata between AD 1130 and 1200. Here, strata are often 70–80 percent McElmo B/w, with small amounts of Mesa Verde and Mancos B/w. McElmo B/w is present in smaller quantities in the Primary, in fact from the very beginning of the Salmon sequence. During the Primary it is associated with the mineral-painted Mancos B/w. Carbon painting thus extends back to at least AD 1090 in the Salmon area, with an overlap of 50–60 years between carbon (McElmo B/w) and mineral (Mancos B/w) painting on San Juan White Ware. McElmo B/w also persisted (in use if not manufacture) into Mesa Verde B/w times. However, Salmon strata suggest that McElmo did not persist as a style completely through the period of Mesa Verde B/w in the AD 1200s. Late Secondary strata (after ca. AD 1240) contain little McElmo B/w associated with the Mesa Verde B/w, a subject of some dispute, was probably only between AD 1200 and 1250 (at the most), judging from Salmon strata.

Mancos B/w is found in appreciable quantities only in the Primary occupation strata. Typically, Mancos and McElmo B/w together account for the San Juan Series representation in Primary strata. There is no evidence that Mancos B/w persisted into contemporaneity with Mesa Verde B/w, and in fact it was probably not made after AD 1130.

Wetherill B/w (as a carbon-painted Mancos B/w) was used as a sorting category but was not found to have stratigraphic integrity. The small amounts of this variety seemed to occur at random through Primary and Intermediate strata with the major types of Mancos and McElmo B/w. Thus, it does not have a distinct temporal position independent of its two close relatives in the San Juan Series at Salmon.

SEQUENCE OF STYLISTIC VARIETIES IN SAN JUAN WHITE WARE CERAMICS

Rooms with long stratigraphic sequences also provided some insight into the sequence of stylistic varieties within the San Juan types. This sequence, as recorded on the rough-sort forms, was studied in Rooms 100W, 102A, 102C, and to a lesser extent 33W. Room 102A and C was especially suitable for temporal assessment of San Juan varieties, having an especially strong San Juan White Ware assemblage and an abundance of stratigraphic distinctions spanning the Primary-Intermediate and early Secondary periods (Figure 24.10). A separate sorting was made of the San Juan White Ware ceramics of this room, especially for the purpose of tracing stylistic change. Naturally, numerous attributes (e.g. temper, paste, vessel form) experienced temporal changes, but changes in decorative style were easily monitored over a wide spectrum of rooms and strata because they were recorded as part of the rough-sorting

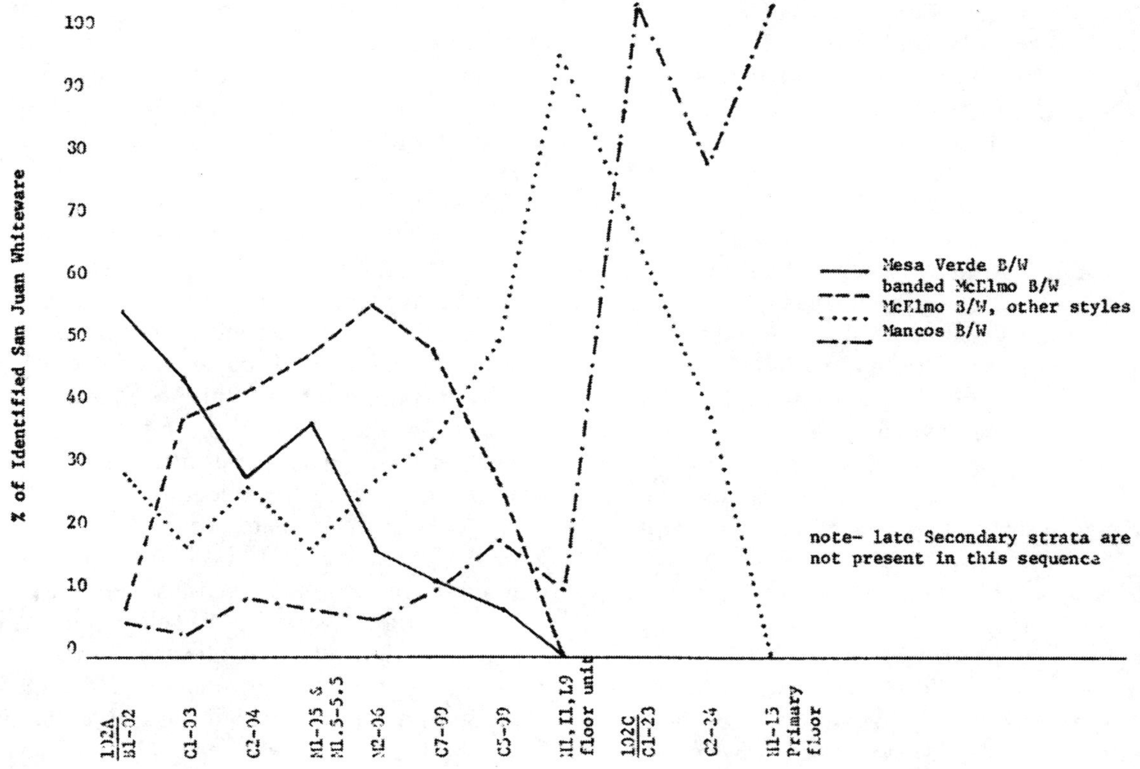

Figure 24.10. San Juan White Ware types by stratum in Rooms 102A and 102C; banded McElmo B/w is shown as separate variety.

procedure. The sequence of stylistic varieties as recognized on sorting forms from these three rooms revealed the following trends.

Mancos B/w stylistic varieties are completely contemporaneous. The type is easily separated into stylistic varieties because they are quite distinct within the type, and do not occur on the same vessels. In spite of the multitude of designs used on Mancos B/w (hatched panels, wide-line, Sosi style, dots, triangles), there is no evident difference in the temporal spans of any of these at Salmon Ruin. All are apparent in the earliest Primary strata, and all were in use until Mancos B/w as a whole died out at the end of the Primary occupation, or no later than AD 1130. The important variations in the distribution of Mancos B/w are spatial (social and functional in cause) and not temporal, at least for the 60 or so years of late Mancos B/w represented here.

McElmo B/w stylistic varieties include most of the same varieties as Mancos B/w, with the addition of the banded style. The hatched, wide-line, and triangle motifs are the decorative equivalent of the same styles on Mancos B/w, and often occur in the same Primary strata with the Mancos varieties. Wide-line and hatched McElmo B/w also persisted into the Intermediate strata wherein mineral-painted San Juan pottery was absent or declining. All McElmo styles except banded are contemporary, and were present in Primary and Intermediate strata. During the Primary, they were contemporary with the same styles of Mancos B/w.

The banded variety of McElmo B/w is of special interest because it apparently marks a stylistic decorative transition into classic Mesa Verde B/w banded designs. These banded McElmo or proto-Mesa Verde B/w examples should thus be found in stratigraphic positions just below Secondary strata with fully developed Mesa Verde B/w, and this was in fact the case in the three rooms where this sequence was studied in detail. Banded McElmo B/w entered the stratigraphic picture considerably later than the Sosi (wide-line), Dogoszhi (hatched), or other varieties of style. It first appeared in assemblages from strata that scored 3 or 4 (C or D) in factor analysis (i.e., McElmo B/w dominant assemblages), and in strata that are Intermediate in position between the end of the Primary and the start of the Secondary. Banded McElmo B/w was produced only in the Intermediate (ca. AD 1130–1200), but it never completely replaced use of the older wide-line and hatched panel styles of the Primary period. For example, the ratio of banded to nonbanded McElmo in Room 100W ranges from 1:6 in the earliest Intermediate stratum to 1:2 in the upper Intermediate or early Secondary stratum in which Mesa Verde B/w makes its first appearance. In Room 102A, there are Intermediate strata where banded McElmo is the most frequent type encountered. Even here, however, banded McElmo is accompanied by other McElmo styles until the appearance of classic Mesa Verde B/w bands in Secondary strata. Table 24.5 presents the stratigraphic changes in San Juan varieties. All Mancos varieties are combined here, because there is no temporal difference between them.

The temporal position of banded McElmo B/w in Room 102A was also evaluated with a Spearman's rank correlation statistic, comparing stratigraphic position to frequencies of banded McElmo B/w, Mesa Verde B/w, and Mancos B/w. The correlation for banded McElmo to Mesa Verde B/w is +.58, whereas the correlation of banded McElmo with Mancos B/w is only +.29. Hence, banded McElmo overlaps temporally with Mesa Verde B/w to a greater extent than it does with Mancos B/w. Other McElmo styles began earlier, as is shown by a +.52 correlation of these styles of McElmo with Mancos B/w.

The transition from banded McElmo (without band-framing lines) to the addition of single wide-line framers, and finally to classic Mesa Verde B/w band designs with multiple thin and thick framers is demonstrated in the upper strata in 102A to be a complete continuum of stylistic development. There can be no doubt that classic Mesa Verde B/w banded designs were a direct outgrowth of banded McElmo of the Intermediate period, going back perhaps to AD 1130. There is even a small quantity of mineral-painted, banded Mancos B/w. Banded classic Mesa Verde B/w, therefore, had stylistic ancestors in earlier types at Salmon.

The other major style in Mesa Verde B/w, however, does not seem to have earlier precursors within this series. The all-over group of styles is not only conceptually quite unique, but stratigraphically they appear suddenly in the sequences. I have previously suggested that some of these all-over designs were copies of contemporary White Mountain Red Ware designs (Franklin 1980b). In any event, the classic Mesa Verde B/w band designs are fully contemporary with the all-over decorations after about AD 1200. All-over designs are not found on the McElmo B/w of the intermediate period at Salmon. Hence, banded decoration of classic Mesa Verde B/w can be traced through a period of development in the pre-AD 1200 period, whereas all-over designs on Mesa Verde appear as a fully developed design variant contemporary only with the classic banded designs. When both classic banded and all-over Mesa Verde styles are present in the stratigraphy, the banded always dominates the assemblage. Banded Mesa Verde B/w amounts to 85–90 percent of the type as a whole in Secondary strata. As with Mancos B/w, the stylistic varieties of which are synchronous, the implications lie in synchronic, spatial distribution related to social-functional causes, rather than to temporal variables. There is no evidence that the ratio of banded to all-over Mesa Verde designs changed appreciably during the time span of classic Mesa Verde B/w at Salmon, but more detailed analysis of microtemporal change in Secondary strata would be necessary for verification.

Table 24.5. Factor scores for strata in Room 102A and C.

Stratum	Old Factor Score	New Factor Score
Room 102A		
B-1-02	6	F
C-1-03	4	D
C-2-04	4	C
M-1-05 and M-1.5-05.5	4	C/D
M-2-06	3	C
C-7-09	3	C
C-5-09	3	C
H-1-13	2	B
I-1-22	2	A
L-9-20	3	C
L-10-21	2	A
Room 102C		
C-1-23	1	A
C-2-24	1	A
H-1-25	1	–

CONCLUSIONS

In all, the strata of rooms with continuous series of stratigraphic deposition demonstrate the uninterrupted continuum of stylistic development in San Juan White Ware spanning the period from AD 1090 through ca. AD 1275. Gradual and continuous change is seen in the stratified sequence of the three varieties, and the lack of any large gaps in the stylistic or stratigraphic sequence of San Juan White Ware also implies, of course, that the ruin was never completely abandoned during the period of AD 1090–1275. Populations certainly changed in identity—the Chacoan Primary is very different from the Secondary occupation—but San Juan White Ware was manufactured and/or used and deposited in trash for the entire time span of the three major periods at

Salmon. Of course, the small number of strata and the relative paucity of ceramic samples assigned to the Intermediate strata suggest that it was a smaller population that resided in the pueblo after the end of the Primary and before the advent of the Secondary occupation. The presence of McElmo dominant strata in all room sequences with complete and undisturbed deposition illustrates that a small San Juan Puebloan population must have continued to reside in the pueblo in the AD 1130–1200 period.

Cibola Series types are confined to the Primary strata at the bottom of the sequences, except for redeposited sherds in Secondary strata, a condition seen in some of the rooms used for illustration here. All Cibola types from Puerco-Escavada B/w through Chaco-McElmo B/w are typically associated in Primary levels, and there is no indication that any of these types continued beyond the end of the Primary occupation. Between the early Cibola types of Puerco and Escavada B/w, and the late Chaco-McElmo B/w, there is some stratigraphic evidence (admittedly scanty) that does not appear in every room for the temporal priority of the early group. Based on inevitable small sample sizes, it appears that Puerco, Escavada, and the minuscule Red Mesa B/w group of types is most frequent on Primary floors and subfloor levels, whereas Chaco-McElmo B/w is present throughout the Primary strata. There is no evidence of temporal separation of the time spans of Chaco and Gallup B/w, which are in evidence throughout Primary strata.

All other intrusive series are less frequent than Cibola White Ware, and trends are difficult to observe due to small sample sizes and sample error in given room sequences. Stratigraphically, however, most Chuska White Ware and Tsegi Orange Ware appears correlated with Primary strata, along with the Cibola ceramics. There is no doubt that the majority of contact with other Puebloan areas was during the Chacoan occupation. However, in some sequences it appears that importation (or use) of some Chuska and Tsegi types persisted slightly longer than the Cibola Series ceramics; frequency curves do not show as drastic a decline for these intrusive ceramics after the Primary as with Cibola pottery. Whether this is due to continued import of ceramics on a reduced scale from the Chuska and northern Arizona areas or simply to a continuous use of vessels within the site for a period of time after the close of the Primary is not known. However, the lack of Pueblo III types from either of these two series, as well as the frequency curves of these series, indicates that they were essentially absent by Secondary times. There is very little evidence of a temporal sequence between the individual Chuska types; Chuska and Toadlena B/w are the dominant types present wherever types of this series are located. Among Tsegi Orange Ware, the evidence indicates that Tusayan and Medicine B/r were present in Primary strata. Citadel Polychrome (the only other major Tsegi type found at Salmon) appeared later, in late Primary and Intermediate strata.

The Smudged Red Ware from northern Mogollon (Forestdale Red?) is a consistent accompaniment of other intrusive types in Primary strata. Its appearance is evidently brief in the Salmon sequence, declining in frequency even during the Primary strata, and absent altogether after that. The remaining intrusive series, White Mountain Red Ware, displays a very different stratigraphic pattern from other intrusives. The several types of this series appeared at Salmon in an unbroken progression through Primary, Intermediate, and Secondary strata. There is no diminution at the close of the Primary as noted for other intrusive series. There is considerable stratigraphic evidence for the first appearance of types in this series in the expected order of Puerco B/w, Wingate B/r, Wingate Polychrome, and St. Johns Polychrome, allowing, of course, for expected overlap in the spans of each type. Primary levels produce only the black-on-red types, Intermediate strata produce both Wingate B/r and early polychrome, and by Secondary times, only polychrome pottery is in evidence. Therefore, the sequence of these types at Salmon tends to support the time spans originally assigned by Carlson (1970). The persistent importation of White Mountain Red Ware to all components at Salmon is an interesting phenomenon, marking a departure from the patterns exhibited by all other intrusive series.

In essence, stratigraphic evidence at Salmon from a number of key sequences supports the ceramic sequence as originally estimated from cross-dating. There is no reason to believe that either local (San Juan) or intrusive series types deviate appreciably in date from the temporal spans assigned to them by other investigators. The relatively long sequence from AD 1090 to about AD 1274 at Salmon, however, has allowed a more detailed examination of the evolution of San Juan White Ware than at the shorter occupation sites excavated to date. This has resulted in the verification of the stratigraphic validity of a McElmo phase (here called the Intermediate) prior to the phase marked by Mesa Verde B/w. It has further permitted a view of the stylistic evolution of the three major types, which form an unbroken continuum of development across the three temporal periods of Salmon Ruin's occupation.

Chapter 25

DIACHRONIC VARIATION IN SAN JUAN WHITE WARE FROM SALMON

by Hayward Franklin

With the Salmon rough sort finished by November 1978, and after analysis of the basic chronological information derived from correlations and factor analysis of the best-sampled ceramic types, a new correlation matrix could be developed that included a fine-grained differentiation of the San Juan types by specific stylistic variety. This new matrix also separated the White Mountain Red Ware types that had formerly been lumped together.

Beginning in 1976, San Juan White Ware types were divided during rough sort into several varieties based on stylistic attributes. The-best defined styles within each type were classed separately, but due to time constraints, the rest were combined into a general or undifferentiated category. We were thus able to monitor the most obvious and prevalent stylistic distinctions within the major San Juan types at Salmon, as follows:

- Mancos Black-on-white—wide-line (Sosi style), hatched panels (Dogoszhi style), "Aztec style" (fine-line hatched panels as in Chaco B/w), and a general or undifferentiated category including triangle, dot, checkerboard, and other elements.
- McElmo Black-on-white—the same categories of wide-line, hatched panels, and undifferentiated, plus a banded category with designs not bounded by formal band framers as in Mesa Verde B/w.
- Wetherill Black-on-white—essentially a carbon-painted version of Mancos B/w, consisting mainly of the special styles within Mancos B/w; that is, triangles, dots, or checkerboard, but never fine hatching as in the Aztec variety of mineral-painted Mancos.
- Mesa Verde Black-on-white—subdivided into banded (having multiple band framers above and below the band of design) and all-over (with two, three, or four part design divisions involving a combination of solid and hatching line work).

As before, the matrix was examined to obtain a preliminary idea of the correlations (i.e., degree of association) of each of these named styles with other styles and with types outside the San Juan White Ware Series. Partial correlation was used in three ways: zero order partial correlations, control for total sherd count, and control for total decorated sherd count. Partial correlations, uncorrected for totals, were all positive, because in a general sense, all types and varieties are associated with each other often enough to produce no negative correlation. Negative correlations did appear, though, between types and varieties not strongly associated in time—in the correlation matrix controlled for total sherds and the one controlled for total decorated sherds. For example, correlations in the uncorrected matrix ranged from approximately .00 to .85. In the matrix corrected for the total decorated assemblage, the range of maximum negative to maximum positive correlation was –.36 to .47. The total range of variation in correlations remained the same (about .85), but it moved from positive to negative when the correction factor was introduced.

The general or undifferentiated categories of the San Juan varieties correlated somewhat differently from the named varieties because the general categories form a larger miscellaneous group and a larger sample size than the named varieties. Also, because the general categories consist of a number of undifferentiated styles, they could not be expected to show the spatial or temporal differentiation of the more specific, named style varieties.

HYPOTHESES IN RELATION TO SAN JUAN VARIETIES

Prior knowledge of the stratigraphic arrangements in several rooms with good sequences and the logical sequence of stylistic evolution in San Juan White Ware produced several ideas regarding the relationship of stylistic varieties of the San Juan Series. (1) Mancos B/w Aztec style and perhaps some Dogoszhi-like hatched panels should associate more with Cibola White Ware than do the other varieties of Mancos B/w. (2) The wide-line, hatched, and miscellaneous varieties of both Mancos and

McElmo B/w should be strongly associated because they are believed to be from contemporaneous stratigraphy. (3) Banded McElmo B/w ought to have a lower correlation with Primary occupation types than other McElmo B/w varieties do because banded McElmo is thought (from style development and stratigraphy) to have evolved later than the other McElmo varieties. It is stylistically transitional into Mesa Verde B/w banded designs and should logically be temporally transitional as well. (4) The varieties within Mesa Verde B/w should show similar low correlations with other types of earlier time periods because these Mesa Verde varieties are apparently synchronic. However, between them, they should not necessarily show a high degree of association because they may have operated in different ways in the Secondary occupation.

Correlation Results

In examining the fine-grained correlations, substantial support was found for all of these hypotheses. Because the major results regarding types are largely repetitive of the factor analyses based on the correlation matrix, they are not elucidated here. The main determinant of variation in the sample was temporal, as in the previous gross correlations, but the relationship between the styles of San Juan types also became more clear. High positive correlation (association) indicates not only contemporaneity between types, but probably a functional (use) similarity as well. Conversely, absence of positive correlation or negative correlation indicates either noncontemporaneity or, to a lesser extent, spatial (use) differences for types that are known contemporaries of each other based on other information.

Factor Analysis

Factor analysis of the fine-grained correlation matrix, corrected for the total decorated sherd count and using the varimax rotation (Table 25.1), produced eight factors. The last four factors had eigenvalues of less than 1.0 and were therefore not considered because of their low variance. The first four factors reflect the same Primary-Intermediate-Secondary trichotomy revealed in the more general coarse-grained factor analysis, but the focus of attention here is the finer variability of the stylistic varieties.

The fine-grained correlation matrix was also rotated using the image method, which produces a larger number of factors and spreads the variation across them more evenly; image factoring produced 13 such factors. Although the same temporal relationships still account for most of the variation, image factoring illustrates the finer variation within each of the three major time blocks. In image factoring, the general or undifferentiated varieties were excluded to reduce the problem of large sample size and the inherent positive correlation of these with all other ceramics of the same period. Image factoring was the most successful in revealing the ceramic associations of the stylistic varieties of San Juan types as well as those of the individual White Mountain Red Ware types, which were formerly grouped into black-on-red versus polychrome. Table 25.2 gives the first 5 of the 13 factors produced by image factoring.

Chronological Interpretation

The correlation and factor results largely confirmed and substantiated information derived from cross-dating, stratigraphically visible stylistic evolutions within the San Juan White Ware, and the logical seriation of these varieties. These lines of evidence suggest the following conclusions regarding their temporal relationships.

1. The relatively high degree of intercorrelation between varieties within each San Juan Series type indicates that such varieties are more or less synchronous within types themselves. The slight exception to this is banded McElmo B/w, but even its highest correlation is with other McElmo varieties.

2. There is an opposition between Mancos B/w and McElmo B/w dominant San Juan Primary occupation types on the one hand and the Cibola Primary occupation types on the other (see Table 25.2, Factor 1). This difference is due to social and functional parameters within the Primary occupation. San Juan and intrusive types were in use concurrently in the Primary occupation, and their lack of association in some factors is not due to temporal differences.

3. Wide-line and hatched varieties of Mancos and McElmo B/w are strongly associated. The two styles in carbon and mineral paint are not only contemporary in the Primary occupation but probably functioned in similar ways as well. In this sense, it may have made little difference, culturally, whether wide-line or hatched San Juan pottery was produced in mineral or carbon paint. In fact, the same styles were produced using both paints (i.e., Mancos B/w and McElmo B/w) throughout the Primary period of AD 1090 to ca. AD 1130. The co-occurrence of the mineral and carbon painted types may even predate Salmon evidence (because AD 1090 is the earliest construction date). But at least there was a period of approximately 40–50 years during which the San Juan White Ware at Salmon had a wide range of

Table 25.1. First four factors of the fine-grained analysis of varieties using the varimax rotation.

Type	Factor 1	Factor 2	Factor 3	Factor 4
Early Cibola	–.11	.19	.38	.05
Gallup B/w	.31	–.19	.45	–.15
Chaco B/w	.03	–.02	.73	–.22
Chaco-McElmo B/w	.35	–.02	.02	–.01
Mancos B/w (hatched)	–.05	.44	.48	–.06
Mancos B/w (wide-line)	.01	.40	.35	.09
Mancos B/w (Aztec-variety)	–.05	.11	.40	–.14
Mancos B/w	.26	.19	.44	–.20
Wetherill B/w	.19	.48	.13	–.08
McElmo B/w (banded)	.04	.64	–.19	.28
McElmo B/w (wide-line)	–.14	.74	.14	.15
McElmo B/w (hatched)	–.01	.83	.11	–.12
McElmo B/w	.02	.11	–.06	–.02
Mesa Verde B/w (banded)	–.96	.01	–.10	.09
Mesa Verde B/w (all-over)	–.59	.00	–.11	.41
Mesa Verde B/w	.54	–.62	–.24	.05
Puerco B/r	.02	.05	.10	.00
Wingate B/r	.32	.08	–.09	.00
St. Johns B/r	–.20	.12	–.12	.74
Wingate Polychrome	.04	–.07	–.03	.05
St. Johns Polychrome	–.14	–.08	–.12	.28
Chuska Series White Ware	–.03	.07	.14	–.01
Tsegi Orange Ware	.10	.46	.16	–.20
Smudged Red Ware	–.04	.19	.41	.09

Includes general varieties; utility ware deleted.

Table 25.2. First five factors of the fine-grained analysis of varieties using the image factoring method.

Type	Factor 1	Factor 2	Factor 3	Factor 4	Factor 5
Early Cibola	–.10	.05	.13	.29	.15
Gallup B/w	–.12	–.30	–.11	.06	.50
Chaco B/w	–.03	–.19	.11	.09	.49
Chaco-McElmo B/w	.53	.19	.09	.08	.15
Mancos B/w hatched	.29	–.07	.06	.20	.14
Mancos B/w wide-line	.30	–.02	–.02	.31	.06
Mancos B/w (Aztec variety)	.04	–.07	.11	.12	.21
Wetherill B/w	.41	–.21	–.18	.19	.01
McElmo B/w banded	.66	.13	–.35	–.07	–.31
McElmo B/w wide-line	.66	.15	–.15	.03	–.19
McElmo B/w hatched	.72	–.08	–.24	.08	–.15
Mesa Verde B/w banded	–.08	.64	.52	–.26	–.31
Mesa Verde B/w all-over	–.01	.69	.33	–.17	–.32
Puerco B/r	.07	–.03	–.09	.08	.06
Wingate B/r	.15	–.19	–.36	.05	.01
St. Johns B/r	.14	.50	.04	–.03	–.28
Wingate Polychrome	–.05	–.01	–.02	.06	–.02
St. Johns Polychrome	–.11	.20	.14	–.01	–.14
Chuska Series White	.08	–.04	–.02	.49	.06
Tsegi Orange	.31	–.21	–.07	.31	.01
Smudged Red	.15	.05	.07	.09	.19

Analysis does not include undifferentiated varieties; first 5 of 13 factors.

definable styles, including wide-line and hatched panels, and was apparently made with various combinations of mineral and carbon pigments.

4. The Aztec (or Chaco-like) variety of Mancos B/w is a synchronic variant of Mancos B/w. It has somewhat different associated pottery than the other Mancos B/w varieties, although it was contemporary with them in the Primary period. Its highest correlations are with Cibola types, and its highest factor loadings are with Chaco B/w, aside from the expected interassociation with other Mancos varieties. The fact that the highest correlation of this variety (aside from other Mancos varieties) is with Chaco B/w leads to two possible conclusions: either Chaco B/w is misidentified as Aztec variety or the San Juan look-alike of Chaco B/w was being used (functionally) in the same way as the Cibola type. Although misidentification between similar types in different series can never be completely ruled out, there is a body of Mancos B/w (i.e., with San Juan pastes and slips) that resembles Chaco and Gallup B/w stylistically. The use of hatched panels or frets in the hatched and Aztec styles resembles the design treatment of Gallup and Chaco B/w respectively. Although a number of other Mancos B/w attributes demonstrate a close relationship to the contemporary Cibola ceramics (e.g., thin walls, sherd and/or sandstone temper, slips, and certain vessel forms), the design resemblances are the most obvious.

The concept of the manufacture of imitation Chaco and Gallup B/w by San Juan potters is supported by the evident direction of cultural influence, which was mainly, and in many respects, from Chaco to the San Juan area and was undoubtedly given impetus and augmented by the construction of actual outposts of Chacoan culture in the region north of the San Juan River. Further, the Chacoan inhabitants were somewhat removed from the source of their accustomed ceramics and could obtain them only via the north road route or other Chacoan outposts. There is no evidence that Cibola White Ware was produced at Salmon. The relative rarity of intrusive ceramics including Cibola White Ware is evident from the Primary occupation sherd counts. The gap between supply and demand for Cibola ceramics by the Chacoan population was presumably filled by other ceramics, especially the available San Juan White Ware. Although the majority of the San Juan pottery incorporated into the Salmon Primary occupation assemblage bears little resemblance to Chacoan types, there is within Mancos (not McElmo) a body of pottery similar to and, in some cases, mimicking the types of Gallup and Chaco B/w. Some designs of Cortez B/w are also similar to the Cibola counterpart Red Mesa B/w, but the construction of Salmon occurred too late to reveal these earlier types in any great quantity. The stylistic resemblance of hatched Mancos B/w and the refined Aztec variety to Gallup and Chaco B/w is supported by evidence from associational (correlation) studies suggesting that the use of a Mancos Aztec variety, and to a lesser extent the Gallup-like hatched style, was also similar. A resemblance of function as well as of technology and design style reinforces the conclusions that some products of Mancos potters were intended to replicate, for all intents and purposes, their Cibola White Ware counterparts.

5. Wetherill B/w associations are much the same as those of Mancos and McElmo B/w. In some factors its loadings are more like Mancos B/w and in others more like McElmo B/w. Wetherill B/w is intermediate between Mancos and McElmo B/w in associations, styles of decoration, and paint type. The type has little heuristic value due to its lack of differentiation from Mancos and McElmo B/w typologically, temporally, stratigraphically, or associationally. Although Wetherill B/w theoretically represents a transition from mineral to carbon painting (Hayes 1964), there is at least a 40-year overlap between fully developed McElmo B/w and mineral-painted Mancos B/w, so Wetherill B/w has not been shown to have a transitional, temporal placement between the better defined Mancos and McElmo B/w types at Salmon.

6. McElmo B/w varieties are largely contemporary with their Mancos counterparts, as shown by high intercorrelations between corresponding varieties. It is equally apparent, however, from the associations with Mesa Verde B/w and with dated intrusive ceramics that McElmo B/w outlasted Mancos B/w (all varieties). The existence of Intermediate strata containing mainly San Juan McElmo B/w with little Mancos or Mesa Verde B/w is reflected in the factor analysis. In factors with strong loadings for Mancos B/w, McElmo varieties are also strong. On the other hand, there are factors with high loadings for McElmo B/w and not Mancos B/w, which illustrates the temporal persistence of carbon-painted McElmo B/w, despite the earlier coexistence of the two paint types in the Primary occupation.

7. Banded McElmo B/w, stylistically transitional into Mesa Verde B/w, is also transitional in its associations with other types. In image factoring, banded McElmo differs substantially from the pattern of other McElmo B/w varieties in four factors; specifically, banded McElmo had a lower loading in Primary factors than did the other varieties of McElmo

B/w. Although its association with Mesa Verde B/w is not a strong one (true of all McElmo B/w), it is somewhat more highly associated with Mesa Verde B/w than are the wide-line or hatched McElmo B/w varieties. The strongest correlation of banded McElmo is, nevertheless, with other varieties of McElmo B/w. The associations of banded McElmo support its temporal placement as later than wide-line and hatched McElmo B/w styles and earlier than true Mesa Verde B/w bands (with multiple band framer lines).

8. There is no evidence that either banded or all-over varieties of Mesa Verde B/w had temporal priority; both scored about the same against factors with high Primary and Intermediate types. Therefore, differences in association between the two major Mesa Verde B/w stylistic varieties must be due to spatial (social-functional) causes rather than temporal ones. Both Mesa Verde B/w varieties have an inverse relationship with McElmo B/w, as seen before, indicating that the period of overlap between McElmo and Mesa Verde B/w could not have been very long. In factors accounting for the higher amounts of variance, Mesa Verde and McElmo B/w are always opposed in factor loadings regardless of the method of rotation, although less so for banded McElmo than for other McElmo B/w varieties. Despite the excellent evidence of a stylistic evolution from McElmo (wide-line and hatched) to McElmo banded into Mesa Verde B/w, the overlap period between the McElmo and Mesa Verde portions of the continuum must have been brief to account for the low degrees of association. This, in turn, tends to validate the distinctive temporal and typological identity of McElmo and Mesa Verde B/w.

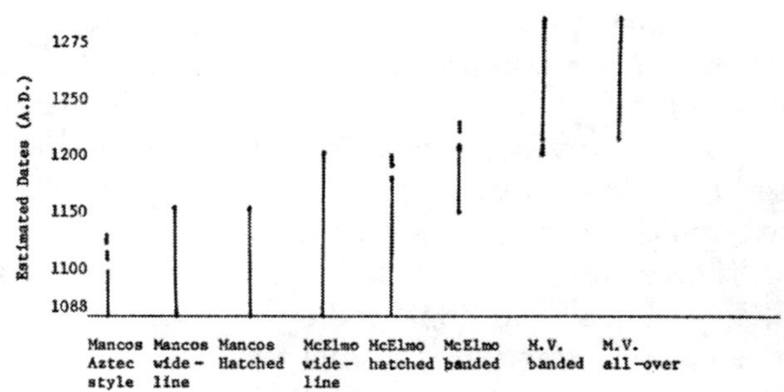

Figure 25.1. Estimated dates of occurrence for San Juan Series types at Salmon Ruins.

Figure 25.1 illustrates the temporal relationships between San Juan varieties and their estimated dates. It is shown that Mancos and McElmo B/w were largely contemporaneous during the AD 1090–1160 period (especially the wide-line and hatched styles) and that varieties of Mancos B/w were all contemporaneous in the Primary occupation. McElmo B/w slowly replaced Mancos B/w in the period from about AD 1130 to the advent of Mesa Verde B/w at about AD 1200. The varieties of McElmo B/w were largely contemporary, with the exception that banded McElmo strata were later (ca. AD 1130) than the wide-line and hatched varieties, which were present during the building of the site in AD 1090.

Mesa Verde B/w replaced McElmo B/w between AD 1190 and ca. AD 1225. Banded McElmo (especially) may have coexisted with the developing Mesa Verde B/w for a time but not throughout the span of Mesa Verde B/w. Many Secondary occupation strata contain little or no McElmo B/w in association with the abundant Mesa Verde B/w. Replacement of the formerly distinct wide-line and hatched styles of McElmo B/w was probably complete by AD 1200.

There is no evidence for temporal priority of Mesa Verde banded versus all-over styles, although the banded Mesa Verde B/w was derived from banded McElmo B/w. The all-over style seems to have been a novel development owing little to previous styles within the San Juan Series. Its most striking design resemblances are to White Mountain Red Ware (Franklin 1980b). The relative paucity of the allover style (15% of all Mesa Verde B/w) and its difference in distribution from banded Mesa Verde B/w in the Secondary occupation at Salmon suggest differential usage of the two styles.

OTHER RESEARCH REGARDING SALMON INTRASITE CERAMIC VARIABILITY

Two other reports have dealt with intrasite distributions of decorated ceramics; both are Master's theses. One is by Jim Priesnitz, "A Preliminary Investigation of Organizational Loci at Salmon Ruin, a Chacoan Outlier in Northwestern New Mexico," completed in 1979 at Eastern New Mexico University in Portales, and the other was completed in the same year by Suzanne Bradley at the University of Denver, "Salmon Ruin: West End Ceramics."

James Priesnitz's Thesis

In an excellent pilot study of the Primary occupation ceramics and their distributions, Jim Priesnitz laid the groundwork for the present study—but on a more limited spatial basis. Many of the conclusions reached in the smaller sample of his study have been corroborated in the present work. A review of the methodology and essential conclusions of Priesnitz's thesis is therefore given here.

The basic premises and assumptions made by Priesnitz in his thesis are identical to those used here, including the assumption that exotic ceramic items were inherently more valuable and, hence, were used either by a restricted (high-status) portion of the population or for certain restricted functions.

The proveniences used in the testing included behavioral (roof and floor) and refuse strata from 18 rooms from the initial AD 1090 building period of Salmon Ruin, thereby avoiding the complications of microtemporal change, which had not been studied at that time. Rooms in the east and west arms and the Tower Kiva area (62W, 81W, and 82W) were included. No rooms from the East or West Wings, the 119W–129W block, or the 93W–102C block were included, nor was the Great Kiva.

Both studies used data from the same seven decorated ceramic series used here (i.e., all ceramic series present in the Primary occupation except for the poorly sampled San Juan Red Ware), including plain white and plain red sherds identified to series. Both studies recognized that this approach would mask the variation on a type and variety level of analysis but that samples for particular types were so low in given cases that sample error would play havoc with any attempt at distributional analysis at that level (Priesnitz 1979:64). Data for distributional analysis consisted of percentages of the seven ceramic series for each of the stratigraphic analytical units. Data were taken from limited-attribute analysis of Primary strata conducted by laboratory members, and sherd counts were reduced slightly by using marginal notations made by analysts on the CLAP forms to eliminate some redundancy for duplicate sherds to the same vessels.

The sets of data (from behavioral and trash units) were considered separately in the assessment of distributions of ceramic series. Floor units consisted of a combination of G, H, I, and L strata, as in this report; the counts were combined from these floor-related strata types. The trash strata consisted of C strata; small samples from contiguous trash levels were sometimes combined.

The major statistical technique used on the ceramic stratigraphic data was multidimensional scaling (Kruskal and Wish 1978). The KYST program was used to produce a spatial plot of the provenience units in terms of their similarities or differences in percentages of ceramic series. Then, a cluster analysis program (HCLUS of Wood 1974) was used to visually delineate the spatial relationships of the multidimensional scaling results by applying cluster analysis to the Euclidean distances on the MDS scatterplot (Priesnitz 1979:77).

Results

The results of the statistical techniques were applied to several analytical hypotheses. The conclusions derived may be summarized as follows (see also Priesnitz 1979:134–147).

1. Problems of small sample sizes, mixing, and the reliability of behavioral units (floors and roofs) allowed only general conclusions.

2. Although San Juan ceramics were dominant in the Primary occupation as a whole, and there was not a mutually exclusive distribution of local (San Juan) versus intrusive ceramic series, there was nevertheless considerable spatial variation in the relative amounts of these ceramic classes, both in trash and in behavioral strata.

3. The nonrandom distribution of ceramic series displayed a correlation between room placement in space and the ceramic dimension of local versus intrusive.

4. Specifically, rooms around the Tower Kiva (62W, 81W, and 82W) and those in the west arm (31W, 33W, and 43W) were similar in containing higher percentages of intrusive pottery than most rooms in the east arm. The exception to this division was the high intrusive percentages of Rooms 83W and 84W in the east arm.

5. At least two residential units in the west arm, and 83W and 84W in the east arm, contained high counts of Cibola Series pottery. One in the east arm (97W, 100W, and 101W) contained relatively more San Juan pottery. Therefore, a hypothesis of differential patterning by residential suites was supported by the data from at least three residential suites.

6. The hypothesis of a dual division above the level of the kin-based residential unit was partially supported because the Tower Kiva area and the west arm were similar in containing abundant intrusive ceramics. All the low intrusive rooms in the sample occurred east of the Tower Kiva area. However, the high amounts of intrusive ceramics in Rooms 83W and 84W departed from this generalization.

7. There tended to be a high degree of association between Cibola and other intrusive series. Because all intrusive decorated pottery tended to be associated, there was validity in generalizing to a basic local versus intrusive division in decorated ceramic distributions.

8. Distributions of ceramic series in trash produced similar patterns to the distributions for behavioral strata, with the exceptions of 82W and 84W where the floors and trash above them were quite different in ceramic composition.

9. There was some suggestion of an association of specialized activities with high intrusive Rooms 84W and 43W and with ceremonialism in the Tower Kiva area.

10. The hypothesis of a resident local San Juan population in the Primary occupation along with the Chacoan population was tentatively accepted on the basis of the contrast between two high intrusive residential suites and one low intrusive suite. However, the differences observed could have been the result of differential use of local versus nonlocal ceramics by the Chacoan population alone.

11. Further corroborative evidence is needed, in terms of both a broader spatial sample for examination and the need to integrate other data classes more fully with the ceramic and architectural data. In particular, lithic, botanical, and ornament data need to be incorporated for a more thorough understanding of the function of rooms.

Comparison to the Salmon Ceramic Study

The results reported here agree in large part with those of Priesnitz. The present work can actually be seen as an extension of the pilot study (but including a much larger sample of rooms), an assessment of microtemporal change in the Primary period, and an attempt to further integrate other data classes toward a synthetic approach to room function. The newer data do not disagree with the earlier patterning achieved by Priesnitz, but rather they confirm and augment it.

Methodologically, the two tests were practically identical. Basic temporal control, ceramic data classes, and the use of stratigraphic levels assigned to the trash and floor units are very similar. Slight differences in approach may be enumerated:

1. Priesnitz used plain white and red sherds identified to a ceramic series but lacking painted decoration. These were excluded from the counts here.

2. Priesnitz reduced sherd counts somewhat via marginal notation made on the forms during analysis. This study used raw counts alone, partly because marginal notations and even intensive efforts at reconstruction failed to alter the numerical relationships between decorated series in most cases. Tests by Priesnitz (1979:60) also showed a high correlation between raw sherd count, counts reduced through marginal notations, and intensive reconstruction.

3. Analysis here split roofs and floor units in distributional analysis, whereas these were combined as "behavioral" by Priesnitz. The division of roofs from floors in the cluster analysis here was done to eliminate the variable of possible differential use of roofs and floors, plus the realization of the inadequate and variable nature of the Primary occupation roof sample.

4. Microtemporal change, controlled by Priesnitz by using only the rooms constructed first, has now been examined in greater detail, and distributional mapping can be interpreted more satisfactorily with this in mind.

5. Statistical treatments differed, although the main results are largely corroborative. Multidimensional scaling and cluster analysis based on the MDS distances were used by Priesnitz, whereas in this study the cluster analysis (HCLUS) program was applied directly to the ceramic series percentage data without MDS. This decision was based on a preliminary test of a comparison of the results of cluster analysis based on MDS distances and a direct application of cluster analysis to the raw percentage data. The two methods produced essentially the same results. Moreover, because distributional assessment was required for a large number of proveniences and by additional ceramic classes including the utility ceramics, the ease of application of the HCLUS program directly to the relative frequencies facilitated computer operations.

The net results of the study by Priesnitz and this one are largely mutually supportive. There is basic agreement on all the points mentioned above, including the realization of the limitations of ceramic samples, spatial variability, assumptions of reliability of floor units, and the level of analysis (ceramic series) used in both cases. The cautionary notes of Priesnitz are well taken, as is the suggestion that a larger spatial ceramic sample as well as additional data classes are necessary for a full appreciation of the variability between loci.

The major conclusion reached in both studies is that variability in ceramic series tends to be organized by room blocks and suites. Units found to be high intrusive in the earlier study have also been found to be so with more recent work.

The only point of possible discrepancy is in regard to a hypothesized east-west division in series distributions. Although Priesnitz's patterns appeared to suggest that intrusive ceramics were greater in the west arm and in the Tower Kiva areas than in the east arm, there was already the discrepancy of Rooms 83A and 84W in the east arm, which were high in intrusive ceramics in the initial sample. By using a much larger sample of rooms and including the wings, it appears that there is little support for a spatial dichotomy. There is definitely a strong tendency for ceramic series to accord with groups of contiguous rooms, but the spatial positions of these blocks and suite groups do not conform to a strict east-west division. The high intrusive blocks of 93W–102C, 83W–84W, and 119W–129W, as well as the excavationally isolated Rooms 56W and 98W east of the Tower Kiva are at variance with the hypothesis that this entire area should be highly San Juan in nature. The reverse is true on the other side of the pueblo. Whereas the west arm rooms are highly intrusive in general, Room 30W is less so than other rooms in that block. Further, the West Wing rooms tend to be San Juan dominant, at least in the later Primary floor strata. Finally, the site is excavationally biased toward the eastern part of the site. Only nine rooms have been excavated to Primary occupation levels west of the Tower Kiva area, whereas 20 rooms have been excavated to this extent east of the Tower Kiva area. In this perspective, there appears to be little support for a true east-west division in decorated ceramic series distributions, but this cannot be thoroughly examined without additional excavation.

Suzanne Bradley's Thesis

Suzanne Bradley's thesis (1979) concerned the West Wing of the pueblo only (Rooms 1W–7W). The purpose was to explore the chronological and spatial (social-functional) parameters of ceramic types and attributes. As such, this study was limited in area and dealt with both the Primary and Secondary occupations of the West Wing rooms.

Cluster analysis was conducted using typological data on decorated types derived from the rough-sort file. The cluster analysis was run on a typological database, including both Primary and Secondary component proveniences. The resultant patterns strongly suggested that there were two temporal components in the West Wing corresponding to the Primary and Secondary time periods. The cluster results were due to a combination of social and functional variables, of which the dominant variable appeared to be temporal, although spatial patterning was also evident. The closeness of joins for the two Secondary kivas (6A and 5A) was related to their obvious architectural and functional differences from the rooms behind them (Bradley 1979:75). There were also some hints that the two suites of rooms present in the West Wing had ceramic identity in both the Primary and Secondary occupation. Because the nonrandom distributions were attributable to a combination of three variables, however, the results were difficult to interpret in terms of synchronic patterns. Two suites of rooms, then, could be identified architecturally and also held some validity ceramically. Since the front square rooms had hearths (Rooms 5W and 6W), the lack of hearths in Rooms 4W and 3W/7W "suggests that they may have functioned as store rooms rather than actual living rooms" (Bradley 1979:19). Similar patterns of room sizes, internal features, and inferred functions are evident for many suites across the pueblo in Primary times.

Bradley used discriminant analysis to evaluate the temporal discriminatory power of a large number of ceramic attributes recorded during attribute analysis of West Wing rooms. Discriminant analysis resulted in substantial agreement of the best discriminating variables with the Primary and Secondary occupational sequences in West Wing rooms. Temporal distinctions in ceramic attributes accorded well with the sequence of occupation of these rooms, as well as with the defining characteristics of types belonging to the Primary and Secondary periods.

As a test of spatial variation for the reconstruction of social-functional parameters, the thesis reached few specific conclusions. Nonrandomness of distribution was demonstrated, and the strong effects of temporal change were made apparent. Other patterns seemed to be related to a combination of social and functional causes that could not be interpreted without additional data.

As a test of statistical techniques, Bradley's work is notable for applying cluster and discriminant analysis for the first time to Salmon ceramic data and gaining useful results. Method 2 (furthest neighbor) and Method 7 (flexible method) proved the most understandable, with less "chaining" effect, which accords with similar conclusions made about the use of cluster analysis in this report. Also, Bradley incorporated lithic and botanical data with the ceramic data on the same set of rooms for the first time at Salmon.

There were several differences in approach between the studies. Bradley's cluster analysis data consisted of rough-sort data, not limited-attribute data, and the type, not the series, was the analytical unit used as input to the computer program. Cluster analysis was run on both Primary and Secondary occupational strata together because time was one variable to be tested. In the studies by Priesnitz and in this report, the temporal variable was controlled (grossly) to the Primary occupation prior to clustering. This reduced the variables to synchronic causes with minimal interference from temporal change, except that which occurred within the 40 or so years of the Primary occupation. Thus, the distributional aspects of the ceramic data were somewhat clearer and easier to interpret.

Although Bradley's study did not draw specific social-functional reconstructions for either occupation, the patterning of decorated ceramics observed is not at variance with either the temporal or spatial patterns (in the Primary occupation) identified for the site as a whole.

The two theses summarized here thus proved to be ground-breaking experiments both in the use of statistical techniques and in the delineation of ceramic patterning by rooms and groups of rooms, particularly in two spatially limited areas of the site. The conclusions have been mostly supported by subsequent work on larger samples from across the pueblo.

Chapter 26

TEMPERING MATERIALS IN SAN JUAN CERAMICS FROM SALMON

by Hayward Franklin

Most of the San Juan Series decorated and utility ceramics at Salmon Ruin appear to have been tempered with various lithic materials, which are referred to here as San Juan crushed igneous rock. Although sand or sandstones as well as crushed sherds have also been identified as tempering materials (especially in Mancos B/w), the great majority of the carbon-painted McElmo and Mesa Verde Black-on-white, and almost all of the corrugated pottery, has been tempered with lithic fragments.

Table 26.1 shows that the utility sherds are tempered almost exclusively with crushed rock, as is most of the white ware. There was an increase in the use of crushed rock temper through time from Mancos Black-on-white through McElmo to Mesa Verde B/w. In Mancos, which had the most variable type, the crushed rock was often used in combination with other materials, but less so in the later types. There was a corresponding decrease in the use of sherd and sand or sandstone for temper through time, until in Mesa Verde B/w these became rare temper types. In the assemblages from all phases, however, crushed rock is the most frequent kind of inclusion in both gray and white ceramics of the San Juan Series. Similar high amounts of crushed rock tempers have been identified elsewhere north of the San Juan River; most of the temper in these wares from Aztec Ruin and along the La Plata seems to consist of similar materials. At ENM 5108 near Salmon, "32 percent contained local igneous rock from the San Juan Valley" (Warren 1975a).

IDENTIFICATION OF CRUSHED ROCK TEMPER

Identification of the mineral constituents of the crushed rock temper at Salmon was undertaken by A. Helene Warren. Although her analysis was never completed, she examined many sherds with a binocular microscope, and some by means of petrographic analysis as well. For a sample of 114 sherds (carbon painted) from the upper levels of Room 93, she stated that most "contained intermediate igneous rock or sandstone temper" (1974:3). In working with sherds from Room 100, she stated: "The predominant temper type found in the sherds from Room 100 is a crushed igneous rock with an abundance of biotite, or gold colored mica. It occurs in both corrugated and San Juan White Ware sherds. Crushed sandstone also appears as a temper type in small quantities, in carbon-painted ceramics and in Chaco B/w" (Warren 1975b:3). The most commonly recorded temper type in this class of pottery is an igneous rock of intermediate composition "having icy white feldspar, quartz, green to black hornblende prisms, mica, trace of green pyroxene, and magnetite" (Warren 1975b:4). Dr. Leroy Corbitt, ENMU geologist, also examined specimens of crushed rock temper in sherds with a binocular microscope, and the minerals he was able to identify were large amounts of feldspars (mostly albite or oligoclase but little or no orthoclase feldspar), quartz in small quantities (5%?), and hornblende and biotite as common accessory minerals (personal communication, 6 October 1977). Additional work by Phil Shelley (Salmon lithics laboratory) and this author using binocular microscopes at 30–60x confirmed the analyses by both Warren and Corbitt.

SOURCE IDENTIFICATION

Three major sources of rock materials were available to potters at Salmon: riverine sand along the banks of the San Juan and tributary washes, outcrops of Nacimiento sandstone in the terraces to the north of the site, and Pleistocene gravels containing abundant igneous cobbles on the current terrace surfaces. All of these materials were probably included at one time or another, intentionally or unintentionally, in pottery made in the Salmon vicinity. The problem is to distinguish between them and to determine which source materials match the pottery tempers.

Crushed Igneous Rock

Ever since Anna Shepard analyzed tempers of San Juan pottery along the La Plata River (1939), it has been known that prehistoric people north of the

Table 26.1. Percentage of temper types in San Juan decorated and utility ceramics from Salmon.

Type	Crushed Large Rock	Sandstone	Sherd	Sherd & Sandstone	Sherd & Crushed Rock	Other	Total Sample
San Juan Corrugated	93.7	1.1	0.3	0.3	2.8	1.8	3589
San Juan plain gray	93.1	1.9	1.1	0.1	3.3	0.5	943
Mancos Black-on-white	31.2	5.9	17.6	10.6	32.2	2.5	1008
McElmo Black-on-white	63.0	3.6	13.2	1.5	17.8	0.9	1227
Mesa Verde Black-on-white	77.9	2.9	3.8	0.0	14.4	1.0	104

Table 26.2. Particle sizes (in millimeters) of crushed rock temper and comparative rock sources near Salmon (quartz and feldspars only).

Sample Type	Range of Means	Range of SDs	Average of SDs	Mean of Means	SD of Means
Crushed rock temper in 50 San Juan Corrugated sherds (5 readings per sherd)	0.4–1.2	0.2–0.4	0.3	0.7	0.2
Igneous rock (6 samples) matching composition of temper (10 readings per sample)	1.0–4.8	0.3–2.8	1.0	2.1	1.5
Nacimiento sandstone (4 samples; 10 readings per sample)	0.3–0.5	0.1–0.2	0.15	0.4	0.1

SD = standard deviation.

San Juan River frequently used lithic materials as tempering agents in ceramics. It was her belief that the andesitic temper she observed in many of the sherds from that district was obtained from andesites and diorites found in cobble form on the riverine terraces near archaeological sites. Helene Warren's opinion has also been that a similar situation existed at Salmon Ruin, where cobbles of igneous rocks are abundant on the sandstone terraces of the immediate vicinity (Warren 1974). The mineral suite in the majority of San Juan utility and white ware sherds certainly suggests an igneous rock composition; this mineral group would typically include andesites, diorites, granodiorites, or even monzonites. The range of minerals would probably not include very mafic rocks (basalts, gabbros) or acidic rocks (granites or rhyolites).

The currently available cobble aggregate of Pleistocene deposition represents a lithologically complex assortment brought down from the mountainous areas of Colorado. Igneous plutonic and extrusive rocks are fairly abundant; others show evidence of metamorphism, and the cobbles range in composition all the way from basalts to granites and quartzites. Salmon lithics laboratory personnel (directed by Phil Shelley) made several transect collections that yielded a random sample of surface cobbles on the San Juan, Animas, and La Plata Rivers. The results, in graph form, show that in the San Juan area, andesites and diorites are indeed fairly common (about 15%; n = 597). However, the most common material is quartzite, comprising about 47% of the sample. Also occurring are basalts (about 12%), granites (about 10%), and smaller amounts of metamorphic rocks (schist) and sandstone fragments (Shelley, Chapter 47). The crushed rock temper with minerals in the range of andesite-diorite-granodiorite would correlate with the andesites and diorites of the modern terraces (Hurlburt and Klein 1977). Apparently the ancient potters were not using the currently abundant quartzites, or the basalts; that is, there was a selection for certain rock types. The present lithic cobble assemblages in the vicinity of the site are perhaps relatively low in andesitic-dioritic rocks because of depletion by prehistoric collection.

A small collection of cobbles from the terrace gravels near Salmon was also made specifically for comparison to pottery temper. Included in this batch are andesites, diorites, granodiorites, and basalts (identification by Corbitt, Shelley, and this author). Of these, the rocks that compare most favorably to the pottery temper are in the range from andesite to granodiorite in composition. Specifically, such rocks contain the same suite of minerals seen in the temper: plagioclase feldspars (mainly oligoclase or andesite; over 60%), some quartz (10%), ferromagnesian minerals including abundant hornblende (about 10%), and biotite (about 10%), with rare pyroxenes and small amounts of magnetite. Corbitt's selection of the hand specimens that correlated best with the pottery temper was identified as a diorite or granodiorite (personal communication, 6 October 1977). Indeed, the pottery temper shows little in the way of fragments of groundmass or flow structure characteristic of an extrusive rock such as an andesite; all fragments show well-developed crystalline structure. Further, the lack of abundant darker plagioclase feldspars (andesite to labradorite), the rarity of pyroxenes, and the fairly frequent quartz grains all imply that the rock source is closer to a granodiorite in composition than to a true andesite. The rock source must have had observable quartz and a lack of many of the mafic minerals. (At least some quartz was seen in all hand specimens examined except basalts, and hornblende and biotite were major ingredients.) The range of variability in the temper is difficult to measure, but it is possible that everything from an andesite to a granodiorite was used as temper from time to time.

These specimens also exhibit an interesting range of weathering. Of nine rocks with a composition similar to the pottery temper, three or four were friable enough to crush on a mano and metate without difficulty. In fact, a series of diorites illustrated the probable decomposition sequence from rounded cobble to fractured and decomposed. If the cobbles of the terraces were in fact the source of such temper, potters would likely have selected the more weathered, friable rocks because it would have been impossible to disintegrate an unweathered igneous cobble using grinding equipment made for the most part from sandstone (or even quartzite). Despite the apparent difficulties in using crushed rock as a tempering agent rather than potsherds or other more easily worked temper sources, there is evidence of a long tradition of using lithic tempers among the northern Puebloans, and even in areas such as the Chuska Valley (sanidine basalt), south of the San Juan River. Surely potters would at least have chosen the most easily crushed specimens of this class to work with.

The temper was also analyzed for degree of angularity and size of fragments. Both the crushed rock temper and the minerals of the igneous cobbles displayed a high degree of angularity, suggesting that crushed rock rather than a sand or sandstone was used. Certain rounded or subangular fragments mixed with the crushed rock in temper are probably sand or sandstone inclusions that found their way inadvertently into the clay body, and were not intentionally added.

We measured the size of crushed rock temper in 50 sherds of San Juan corrugated selected from a variety of proveniences and phases within the site. Corrugated was chosen because crushed rock is most common in this class, and because refiring tests have established that the utility pottery of the San Juan Series was likely of local manufacture. As far as could be determined, sherds were from different vessels. Five particles in each sherd were measured using a binocular microscope with a micrometer reticle graduated to tenths of a millimeter. The five measurements were then averaged for each sherd. The mean particle size is 0.7 mm for the entire sample (Table 26.2), and the standard deviation between sherds is 0.17 mm. In fact, the range within each sherd appears to be greater than that between the sherds. The five readings per sherd usually ranged from about 0.3–1.1 mm. The average standard deviation of particles within sherds is 0.26 mm, whereas the standard deviation between sherds is only 0.18 mm. This suggests that a large range of particle sizes is typical of most of the corrugated vessels with crushed rock temper. A wide range of sizes in a single sherd also indicates a crushed rock source rather than a better-sorted sand or sandstone. There is no evidence that San Juan corrugated from Primary or Secondary horizons is different in mineral content of crushed rock, in particle size, or between loci across the site, although a larger sample from each provenience would be needed for an accurate test.

By comparison, the mean particle size for six specimens of igneous rock containing minerals typical of the pottery temper is 2.1 mm, with a range of 1 mm to 4.8 mm between sample averages (see Table 26.2). This suggests that if such rocks were being ground for temper, then many of the minerals were fragmented in the process, because the mean size in pottery temper is 0.7 mm. The largest fragments of pottery temper measure about 1.0 to 1.4 mm in diameter, still smaller than the average size of particles in the rock specimens examined.

Sandstone

Some of the San Juan ceramics at Salmon were tempered with sand or sandstone; this distinction is not always clear when the sandstone matrix is not visible. Of all San Juan types at Salmon, Mancos Black-on-white seems to contain the most sand. Warren stated that "sandstone temper in the Salmon pottery is not common" (1975b:11). She identified sandstone as a temper type in some of the carbon-painted material, and allowed for the possibility that Nacimiento sandstone (locally available) was used at times (Warren, personal communication, 15 December 1974; Warren 1975b:4–5). Table 26.1 gives the amounts of identifiable sandstone temper in the San Juan ceramics. Obviously, the accuracy of determination rests on the ability to distinguish local sandstones from actual crushed rock in temper form. A sandstone composed of only well-rounded quartz grains should not be difficult to identify, but sandstone composition may include a variety of constituent particles reminiscent of an igneous rock. Warren (personal communication, 15 December 1974) has pointed out the difficulty of distinguishing some sandstones from an igneous rock of similar composition: "In an area where sandstone with both quartz and volcanic or igneous rock are major constituents, it would not be unlikely to find a confusing aggregate or rock fragments in the sherds" (Warren 1975b: 5).

The sandstone most accessible to the Salmon potters is from the Nacimiento Formation of Paleocene age (Fassett and Hinds 1971; Baltz et al. 1966). Downstream on the San Juan, the older Oho Alamo Formation is exposed, with the closest exposure being about 5 miles from Salmon (see map in Fassett and Hinds 1971). According to Baltz (1967:39), the uppermost section of the Nacimiento Formation consists of "several beds of . . . conglomeritic coarse-grained arkosic sandstone interbedded with dark-gray and olive green shales and shaley sandstones." There is evidently a good deal of variation in the composition of the Nacimiento as seen in different exposures. In the area of the Hogback, for example, it contains "much fresh angular orthoclase feldspar and other detritus" (Baltz 1967:40). The Nacimiento may also be conglomeritic and manganitic in places (Reeside 1924). The amount of quartz and ferromagnesian minerals and their grain sizes are all variable across its extent (Baltz 1967). In color, the Nacimiento may range from light tan to brown or olive green in different members.

The sandstone from the Ojo Alamo Formation is apparently even more variable in composition than the Nacimiento. It is characterized as a coarse sandstone containing siliceous pebbles and lenses of shale. It is likewise conglomeritic, and arkosic (over 25% feldspars), containing silicified wood, jaspers, and quartz. Significantly, it also contains rock fragments including "rhyolite, andesite, and other porphyries, and rarely granite, gneiss and schist" (Reeside 1924:29). Further, the unconformable contact between the Ojo Alamo and Nacimiento Formations noted by Baltz (1967:41), due to the intertonguing of the two formations, would make identification difficult in some circumstances. The variability of lithic inclusions in these sandstones relates to the variability in parent rock composition and transportation. They are "all part of a huge apron of volcanic and organic debris that was derived from the rising highlands lying north and northeast of the San Juan Basin and was spread to the southwest into the basin" (Baltz 1967:41).

The wide variety of materials potentially present in the sandstone formations of the Salmon vicinity supports the contention that identification of this material as separate from a crushed igneous rock might well be difficult. Considerations of least effort would make the crushing of a sandstone rather than an igneous rock more appealing. Whether or not the crushed rock in pottery temper could have come from a sandstone of variable composition instead of terrace cobbles is a moot question (Fred Nials, personal communication 1979).

To examine the nature of the Nacimiento in the immediate vicinity, four samples of the sandstone from the terraces immediately behind Salmon Ruin were examined. Three of the four samples are light tan in color and the fourth is dark brown to green. The predominant mineral is quartz in all four samples, followed by frequent biotite, often in massed sheets, either black or gold in color. Some feldspars are present, but their exact percentage could not be determined macroscopically. The quartz constitutes well over 50% of the grains in the samples studied, and there appears to be no major constituent other than quartz, feldspar, and biotite. No fragments of igneous rock or conglomerates were noted, nor were hornblende or pyroxenes visible. Most particles are subangular, not rounded. All samples effervesced in acid (5% solution) and are quite friable. The darker sample also contains fine dark granular particles that are probably manganitic or ferruginous compounds; other than this, the composition appeared the same as the light tan examples.

Ten measurements from each of the four specimens were taken to determine particle size (see Table 26.2). The mean particle size for the four samples combined is 0.4 mm; the range of means between samples is 0.3 to 0.5 mm. The standard deviation within samples ranged from 0.10 to 0.22 mm, with an average of 0.15 mm. There does not appear to be a great amount of size variation either within or between sandstone samples.

The absence of extreme variability in mineral content, particle size, or shape among the samples examined implies that the Nacimiento Formation in this locality is fairly consistent internally. It differed from the igneous rocks examined in that the sandstone seems to lack hornblende or pyroxenes but does (like most of the igneous rocks) contain abundant biotite, it has a much higher percentage of quartz, it has subangular grains as opposed to angular ones, and it has a smaller average grain size and a more internally consistent grain size than the igneous rocks. Of course, this may not hold true in other areas of Nacimiento exposure, considering the potential variability noted in the literature.

Riverine Sand

Sand from the San Juan River near the site proved to be fine-grained (average about 0.2 mm in diameter, with no particles larger than 0.7 mm) and mostly rounded quartz. It does not seem to have been used as tempering material in any significant amount of the San Juan ceramics at the site, although it may have been included with the alluvial clay from the San Juan banks, which was apparently used for some of the San Juan pottery.

USE OF SANDSTONE VS. IGNEOUS ROCK

It seems that the majority of the temper classified as crushed igneous rock temper does in fact come from that source. The crushed rock temper matches disintegrated andesites, diorites, and granodiorites more closely than the sandstone in the following respects:

1. The same minerals in about the same frequency are found in both igneous rock and pottery temper classed as such. The tested sandstone lacked some of the ferromagnesian minerals of the pottery temper and contained much more quartz.

2. Both cobbles and temper showed high degrees of angularity; sandstone here appears to be subangular.

3. The mean particle size of the crushed rock temper lies between that of the sampled rock and sandstone. This is explicable, however, as the result of fragmentation of rock particles during crushing. Perhaps more significant is the greater range of particle sizes found in igneous rocks and in the crushed rock temper. On the other hand, the sandstone particles displayed a smaller average and range of sizes. The standard deviation (average) within sherds with crushed rock temper is 0.3 mm, whereas for sandstone it is only 0.15 mm. Most sherds with crushed rock temper contained a range of sizes greater than the size variation seen in sandstone.

It does not seem possible, then, that the often identified crushed rock temper seen at Salmon could have been derived from the sandstone in the immediate vicinity. As an experiment, samples of sandstone and igneous rock were crushed on a mano and metate and mixed with local clay. After firing, analysis could still reveal the identity of the two temper types.

CONCLUSIONS

Crushed igneous rocks of intermediate composition and, less commonly, sandstones were used as temper in the San Juan pottery of the site. Igneous rock cobbles and sandstone from the Nacimiento Formation were probably the sources of these materials. Although the two sources may be confused, samples were distinguishable on the basis of mineral content, size, and angularity of particles. The igneous rocks used for temper approximate andesite, diorite, or granodiorite in composition, angularity, and variation of particle size. Weathered rocks would have been easier to grind.

Most of the pottery identified as containing crushed rock does apparently contain igneous rock rather than sandstone. The temper is closer to actual igneous rocks in terms of its mineral suite, particle size, and angularity. Igneous rock and local sandstone could be distinguished in test briquettes.

The actual use of sandstone therefore appears to have been minor in the San Juan ceramics, although the two sources may appear similar enough in some cases to have affected the accuracy of identification during routine sorting. In the 50 sherds examined for this test, only 2 appeared to have sandstone temper; the rest had crushed rock. The precise frequency of sandstone versus crushed rock could be determined only with additional technical testing.

Although it may seem illogical from an economic standpoint to crush a hard igneous rock for temper, this appears to have been a major tempering tradition in San Juan pottery from the beginning of the site until its end, a span of nearly 200 years. The processes involved in temper preparation may have contributed to a mixture of crushed rock and sands or sandstones in the final clay (Shelley, personal communication). Certainly some sherds display nonplastic inclusions resembling both a crushed rock and a sand or sandstone. In a hypothetical example, a weathered igneous rock may have been disintegrated on a sandstone metate, resulting in particles of both in the temper. If this mixture were then introduced into a clay body derived from the San Juan alluvium, where admixture with riverine sand is common, the resultant temper would be an amalgam of sand, sandstone, and igneous rock. Even when sandstone was a consciously selected tempering material, we cannot be sure that it was treated conceptually differently than an igneous rock. Both forms of temper are crushed rock in a general sense.

Chapter 27

REFIRING ANALYSIS OF SAN JUAN CERAMICS FROM SALMON RUINS

by C. Dean Wilson

Ceramic types can often be traced to specific areas of origin; the basic areas of origin for most of the intrusive ceramic types found at Salmon have in fact been identified. This information has been helpful in determining the nature and extent of prehistoric interaction between various localities, including Salmon Ruin.

San Juan types are the most common ceramics from all occupations at Salmon Ruin, so it is logical to assume that they represent the local pottery tradition. However, San Juan ceramics were also made over a very large geographic area north of Salmon Ruin (Breternitz et al. 1974), and using the current typology it is impossible to distinguish San Juan types that were made locally from those that were intrusive into the site. Very little information concerning the specific area of origin for San Juan ceramics is actually available. This causes difficulty in trying to interpret the overall prehistoric system of interaction.

It is thus desirable to determine whether the San Juan ceramics found at Salmon Ruin were in fact local products, and if they were manufactured in more than one location, we need a method to distinguish the locally made from the intrusive products. Locally made San Juan ceramics includes pottery made at Salmon and at other nearby localities along the San Juan River. Intrusive San Juan ceramics were made much farther away in regions such as the Mesa Verde and La Plata areas to the north.

Attributes such as temper and style have been used (Franklin this volume; Washburn 1977) in an attempt to distinguish locally made from intrusive San Juan ceramics, but although these approaches have met with some success, they also have definite limitations. Design styles are easily borrowed by potters from different communities (Bunzel 1929), and it would be very difficult to determine the place of origin for types as widespread as those of the San Juan White Ware. Crushed igneous rock from similar formations appears to have been used by San Juan potters over a very wide geographic area (Shepard 1939; Abel 1955), so it would also be difficult to determine the area of origin by type of temper. Some other attribute that is more sensitive to the area of origin for the San Juan ceramics is needed. One possibility is to identify the origin of the clay through refiring analysis.

Refiring analysis, which has been used previously in the Southwest (Shepard 1939; Vivian and Mathews 1964; Windes 1977; Franklin 1979a, 1979d), offers a quick, easy, and inexpensive way to distinguish and compare clay and ceramic samples. Clay and ceramic samples are fired in a standard atmosphere to a standard temperature so that the variability in the results refers as much as possible to the nature of the samples themselves.

All samples in this study were therefore refired under identical circumstances to 910° C, and then were allowed to cool slowly to room temperature. The only major variable affecting the resultant color of clay and ceramic samples should thus be the amount of mineral impurities, particularly iron oxides, present in the clay. Clay from the same source area (presumably containing the same amounts of mineral impurities) should fire to the same color, as determined using Munsell colors. The Munsell colors of sherd samples, environmental clays, and raw potter's clay found in an archaeological context at Salmon were grouped into named categories by hue: red (2.5 YR and 10R), yellowish red (5YR and 7.5YR), and buff (10YR, 2.6Y, and 5Y). Use of this methodology requires great care, however, because different clay sources may fire to the same color, or a specific clay formation may occur over a very wide geographic area. If a locally available clay fires to the

---

This chapter was written prior to completion of Dean Wilson's thesis in 1985.

same color as local ceramics, it is likely that the clay was used to make the local pottery, but it is not a certainty. If the samples fire to a very wide range of colors, several clay sources may be assumed to be represented. If some of the samples fire to colors that do not appear in raw materials available near the site, these likely were made using clay from more distant localities, and thus are intrusive to Salmon Ruin.

THE PROPOSITIONS

Clay refiring analyses can be used to help identify San Juan pottery from Salmon Ruin. Several propositions involving the nature of San Juan ceramics from Salmon Ruin that can be tested using clay refiring are listed below.

Proposition 1 (behavioral)—San Juan potters who used particular types of temper and made particular forms of pottery also used particular clay sources. This should be true of San Juan potters at Salmon, who, at any given time, would have used clays from limited specific source areas.

Test implications: A statistically significant correlation should be evident between refired color and the other clay attributes recorded. Because this proposition tests whether refired color is in fact related to other attributes, and thus culturally significant, the following propositions may be tested only if Proposition 1 proves to be true.

Proposition 2 (temporal)—The clay used to make San Juan pottery found at Salmon Ruin changed through time. This could involve either changes in the local clays used by San Juan potters at Salmon Ruin, or changes in the amount of intrusive pottery brought into Salmon Ruin.

Test implications: The refire color of San Juan ceramics should vary through different time periods at Salmon because changes may have occurred over time in the local clays used by potters at the site. A decrease in the amount of San Juan ceramics containing nonlocal clays at the site may also be expected to occur through time with a concomitant increase in the amount of San Juan ceramics made from locally available clays.

Proposition 3 (spatial-regional for the Primary period)—There is evidence in the San Juan ceramics from the Primary occupation of a large Chacoan interregional exchange system. This exchange system involved interaction with groups to the south and west whose ceramics can be easily distinguished from those made at Salmon Ruin, as well as interaction with other groups making San Juan ceramics. This implies that the overall Chacoan redistributive system was very extensive.

Test implications: A fairly high amount of the San Juan ceramics from the Primary occupation strata of Salmon should be intrusive from regions to the north. A fairly high amount of the tested pottery should contain paste and slips that fire to colors not locally available to Salmon Ruin, but available in other regions where San Juan ceramics were made.

Proposition 4 (spatial-intrasite for the Primary)—During the Primary occupation, the interregional trade between Salmon and other regions producing San Juan pottery was directly attributable to the Chacoan presence at the site. Intrusive San Juan ceramics are viewed as having the same function as other intrusive ceramics at the site, and should therefore be found in association with them.

Test implications: Intrusive San Juan ceramics at Salmon should be associated with the same rooms, room blocks, and stratigraphic units as other intrusive ceramic types, particularly those associated with the Chacoan presence. Therefore, a significant amount of San Juan ceramics would be expected to fire to colors not available in clays from the vicinity of Salmon Ruin, but available in other regions where San Juan ceramics were made. San Juan ceramics from sites in these other regions should contain ceramics that do fire to these colors.

Proposition 5 (spatial-regional for the Secondary occupation)—At Salmon Ruin during the Secondary occupation, very little trade occurred with other regions. Specifically, this trade involved very little interaction with other regions where San Juan ceramics were made, and the great majority of the San Juan ceramics from Salmon Ruin's Secondary occupation were local products.

Test implications: There should be very few San Juan ceramics from the Secondary occupation that may be identified as intrusive from regions north of Salmon Ruin. The tested San Juan pottery should have a relatively limited number of attributes, indicative of production in a limited area. Very few should have paste and slips firing to colors not locally available to Salmon Ruin.

REFIRING THE RAW CLAY

Clays from the vicinity of Salmon, as well as samples of raw potter's clay found in the excavations, were refired and analyzed to determine which refired paste and slip colors may indicate locally made ceramics. Clays and San Juan ceramics from other regions were also tested; 38 samples of possible potter's clay were collected along the San Juan River from Largo Canyon downstream to Farmington, New Mexico. Tributaries flowing into the San Juan River in that stretch were also sampled.

Ethnographic sources indicate that modern pueblo potters use locally available and specific clay sources; they seldom go more than a few miles to obtain clay. There was thus probably a similar local clay catchment area for Salmon Ruin and other sites along the San Juan River. We used the largest sample we could find in the vicinity of Salmon Ruin to obtain a thoroughly representative sample of suitable potter's clays, in order to determine the colors to which prehistoric potter's clay might have fired. The sample included clays from as many shale formations and alluvial drainages as possible.

Almost all of the clays from the vicinity of Salmon Ruin fired to red (2.5YR) or yellowish red (5YR or 7.5YR). Only 1 of the 38 samples collected fired to buff (10YR). We also used a sample of 98 worked and unworked clays found during the excavations of Salmon Ruin; only raw clays suitable for pottery were tested. Almost all of these clays also fired to red or yellowish red, and only one fired to buff (10YR).

The clays available in the vicinity of Salmon and those actually found in cultural context during the excavation of Salmon Ruin therefore appear to be very similar. Most clays in both groups fired to a 5 YR hue, with other hues in the red and yellowish red categories also represented in significant amounts. Clays firing to these colors, then, might have been used to manufacture local San Juan pottery. The presence of a single buff (10YR) clay in both groups indicates that a buff-firing clay source was also available at Salmon Ruin, but it was not used as much as the red or yellowish red firing clays. Because buff-firing clays would probably have been desirable as slip, these samples may represent materials that were brought into Salmon Ruin for such a purpose. If this is true, locally made ceramics should contain a red or yellowish red firing paste and a buff-firing slip that is 10YR in hue. This paste-slip combination, then, may be expected to be found in ceramics that were made at or in the area of Salmon Ruin.

CLAY FROM SURROUNDING LOCALES

To identify intrusive San Juan ceramics, it is necessary to determine the firing color of clays found in ceramics from other regions. For example, a sample of clay from the Hogback west of Salmon Ruin fired to whitish buff (2.5Y); San Juan ceramics from areas where Hogback clay is available may thus be expected to contain clays that fire to a whitish buff.

Clay and ceramics from the Mesa Verde and La Plata regions were also tested (see Shepard 1939; Franklin 1979e). Most fired to buff, although a few fired to yellowish red. The single clay sample from Mesa Verde National Park fired to a light yellowish red color; more clay samples from that area need to be tested before a representative sample is obtained. The vast majority of San Juan ceramics from the Mesa Verde region also fired to buff (Windes 1977; Wilson 1985).

The clays used by potters at or near Salmon Ruin, then, appear to fire to a different range of colors than the clays available to San Juan potters in other regions to the north. San Juan ceramics that fire to whitish buff colors (2.5Y, 5Y) at Salmon Ruin may be particularly useful in identifying San Juan pottery that is intrusive, because clays firing to these colors do not appear to have been utilized by potters at Salmon Ruin. Whitish buff firing clays were used by potters in other regions where San Juan ceramics were made, but may occur at Salmon Ruin if trade with these regions took place. Therefore, the color of refired San Juan ceramics may be used at least to some extent to distinguish locally made from intrusive San Juan ceramics at Salmon Ruin.

COMPARISON OF ATTRIBUTES

In total, 1038 San Juan sherds from Salmon Ruin were refired and analyzed for this study. Attributes recorded for these ceramics include provenience, type, style, and temper, as well as the firing color of the clay present. A combination of different attributes should provide information that is culturally significant, and thus add to the understanding of the different occupations at Salmon Ruin.

Ethnographic sources indicate that communities of potters consistently use distinct and relatively uniform combinations of raw materials. This results in specific paste, slip, and temper combinations in ceramics made in a specific community, which would differ from that found in the ceramics made in another community. Different combinations of such attributes may thus be used to better identify pottery made at different localities.

The sample tested may be initially divided into two basic categories—corrugated and decorated black-on-white. Only corrugated sherds containing crushed igneous temper were tested because the present study is limited to types belonging to the San Juan tradition, and crushed igneous temper is a distinguishing characteristic of San Juan corrugated ceramics. In total, 195 corrugated sherds were tested, including 65 from each of the three major occupations. The great majority of the corrugated samples fired to red (10R or 2.5YR) or yellowish red (5YR or 7.5YR). Only a very few of the corrugated samples fired to yellowish red–buff (10YR), and none fired to whitish buff (2.5Y or 5Y). Similar results were obtained by Franklin (1979d).

We also tested 853 decorated black-on-white sherds, with about equal amounts from each major occupation. Significant amounts of the paste clays fired to yellowish red, yellowish red–buff, and whitish buff colors. Therefore, the paste color of decorated black-on-white is quite variable.

Corrugated ware from the site contains a higher amount of red and yellowish red firing pastes compared to the decorated black-on-white. A significant amount of the decorated black-on-white pottery also contains a high amount of whitish buff firing pastes, which are never present in the corrugated samples. A chi-square test comparing the two types of ware was statistically significant at greater than the .001 level.

The exact cause of the differences in color is unknown. Because there are fairly equal amounts of corrugated and decorated black-on-white ceramics from each major occupation, temporal differences between the two samples cannot be the cause. One possibility could be that corrugated pottery may have been traded less than decorated because the two wares may have served different functions. Another possible cause for these color differences could be that the corrugated sample was carefully selected so that only sherds containing locally available crushed igneous temper were tested. On the other hand, decorated San Juan ceramics containing a variety of tempers were tested, because they can be identified in other ways. This could increase the representation of intrusive San Juan ceramics in the decorated b/w samples, if potters in other areas used tempers other than the locally available crushed igneous rock.

A separate slip clay was also usually applied over the paste in most of the tested San Juan decorated pottery. Definite paste-slip combinations appear to exist in the entire sample. Red and yellowish red firing pastes for example are usually associated with yellowish red–buff firing slips. This represents a combination of two clay resources available in the vicinity of Salmon Ruin, indicating that ceramics firing to this combination were probably locally made. The fact that whitish buff firing slips are usually not associated with red or yellowish red pastes indicates that clays firing to this color were probably not available to local potters. Yellowish red–buff and whitish buff pastes are usually associated with slips firing to the same color as the paste, indicating that when buff firing pastes were used it was not necessary to use a different clay for the slip. These apparent paste-slip combinations can help distinguish between San Juan ceramics produced in different areas.

The sample of San Juan B/w types was also separated according to whether mineral or carbon paints were applied. Mineral-painted types contain a significant amount of yellowish red–buff and whitish buff firing pastes (10YR or yellower), whereas carbon-painted types contain a significant amount of yellowish red and yellowish red–buff firing pastes. A chi-square test comparing the paste colors between samples with the different types of paint was statistically significant beyond the .001 level.

A similar relationship between the paste firing color in ceramics with mineral and carbon paint has previously been noted for San Juan decorated black-on-white types from other areas (Windes 1977; Shepard 1939). It has been postulated that the difference could be due to the ability of reddish firing clay to absorb carbon paint, but observations of the tested paste and slip of San Juan ceramics make this seem unlikely—no differences were observed in the clarity of the carbon paint between samples with buff or reddish firing pastes. It is also interesting to note that the majority of red and yellowish red firing pastes occur with a yellowish red–buff slip, which usually represents the painted surface. These slips are usually quite thick, and the carbon paint seldom seems to have been absorbed into the separate red or yellowish red pastes. If reddish firing pastes were used because of their ability to absorb and hold carbon paint, it seems very odd that thick buff firing slips were applied over these pastes. It seems more likely that the relationship between paint type and firing paste color was caused by a combination of temporal, spatial, and cultural factors.

Crushed igneous rock appears to have been the principal temper in the locally made San Juan ceramics (Franklin, Chapter 26), but crushed igneous rock was also used for temper over a very wide geographic area of San Juan ceramics production. The presence of specific temper and paste combinations, however, may help to better distinguish locally made from intrusive San Juan ceramics. Paste firing color and basic temper types were therefore compared for all San Juan decorated black-on-white types tested. Samples containing crushed igneous temper more often contain red and yellowish red firing pastes than do samples containing other types of temper. Samples containing temper other than crushed igneous rock (e.g., sherd or sand tempers) more often contain yellowish red–buff and whitish buff firing pastes. A chi-square test shows that these differences are statistically significant at greater than the .001 level.

Certain paste and temper combinations do in fact occur. The association between crushed igneous temper and red or yellowish red pastes represents a locally available combination of temper and clay sources. Yellowish red–buff and whitish buff firing pastes with tempers other than crushed igneous rock may have been used in other regions, and thus are intrusive to Salmon Ruin.

Temper that contains sherd fragments may also be used to better determine whether or not pastes firing to certain color(s) relate to the distinction between local and intrusive San Juan ceramics. Sherds from Salmon Ruin fire to a wide variety of colors; the sherd fragments used as temper in locally made ceramics should thus also fire to a wide range of colors. The sherd fragments found in the paste were divided into two very basic color categories: one is reddish, which includes sherd temper fragments firing to the yellowish red–buff colors locally available at Salmon Ruin, and the other is whitish buff. Most tested sherd-tempered ceramics with pastes that fired to red, yellowish red, and yellowish red–buff contained sherd temper fragments of both basic color categories. This may further indicate a local origin for reddish firing pastes, because sherds firing to a wide range of colors were available at Salmon Ruin for use as temper. Most of the samples containing whitish buff (2.5Y, 5Y) firing pastes have only whitish buff firing sherd fragments as temper. San Juan ceramics firing to whitish buff pastes were thus not local products of Salmon Ruin.

The comparison of different material attributes found in San Juan ceramics indicates that certain combinations of material types do occur in the San Juan ceramics from Salmon Ruin. For example, a combination of a reddish firing paste, yellowish red firing slip, carbon paint, and crushed igneous rock temper all seem to indicate a combination of material resources used by prehistoric potters at or near Salmon Ruin. Other combinations may indicate San Juan ceramics that were made at other regions and brought into Salmon Ruin. Stylistic attributes were also compared to paste firing colors, but were not found to be statistically significant.

The most sensitive and reliable attribute indicating the area of origin for the San Juan ceramics tested is probably the firing color of the paste clays. From the combination of the data described, it appears that locally made and intrusive San Juan ceramics can in fact be identified as follows: Pastes that fire to red and yellowish red colors appear to represent locally manufactured ceramics, whereas yellowish red–buff firing paste represents a combination of local and intrusive ceramics, and whitish buff firing pastes represent intrusive San Juan ceramics.

CHANGES IN REFIRED PASTE COLOR THROUGH TIME

Because the firing color of paste appears to be a good indicator of local versus nonlocal manufacture of San Juan ceramics, it may also be used to determine changes in the amount of locally made and intrusive San Juan pottery through the different occupations at Salmon Ruin. This information can be used to test Proposition 2, involving temporal changes in clay use, and Propositions 3 and 5, which relate to different specific occupations.

The basic time period represented by the ceramics tested may be determined typologically and also according to the different types represented in excavated strata. Roughly, where a majority of the assemblage is Mancos B/w the Primary occupation is represented; similarly, McElmo B/w may represent any of the occupations, but for the most part it represents the Intermediate occupation, and Mesa Verde B/w represents the Secondary occupation. The basic time units represented can also be determined by the stratigraphic unit from which the ceramics were excavated, when specific stratigraphic units are known to represent certain occupations.

The sample of the different types tested included 253 Mancos B/w, 345 McElmo B/w, and 241 Mesa Verde B/w sherds. The Mancos B/w sample contained a fairly high amount of yellowish red–buff and whitish buff firing pastes, and a smaller but still significant amount of yellowish red firing pastes. The McElmo B/w sample contained a fairly high amount of yellowish red and yellowish red–buff firing pastes, and a much smaller but still significant amount of whitish buff firing pastes. The majority of the Mesa Verde B/w sample contained yellowish red firing pastes, whereas a smaller but significant amount of yellowish red–buff, whitish buff, and red firing pastes are also represented.

The paste firing colors of the three different types reveal the following differences between types: Mancos B/w has a greater amount of whitish buff and yellowish red–buff firing pastes than does Mesa Verde B/w. Mesa Verde B/w, however, has a greater amount of yellowish red and red firing pastes. For all paste colors observed, the amount of McElmo B/w representing a specific color always falls between that of Mancos B/w and Mesa Verde B/w. Therefore, the changes in paste firing color through time appear to represent a gradual trend. A chi-square test that compared the paste color differences between types found these differences to be statistically significant at greater than the .001 level; the three sequential types thus tend to have different refired colors, in general.

The trend in paste firing color for San Juan ceramics from stratigraphic units representing the Primary to Intermediate to Secondary occupations is very similar to the color changes noted in Mancos B/w to McElmo B/w to Mesa Verde B/w types. A chi-square test comparing ceramics found in stratigraphic units representing the three occupations was statistically significant at greater than the .001 level.

Changes in paste firing color for crushed rock tempered corrugated pottery through time were also determined. Most of the corrugated pottery from the Primary occupation fired to reddish yellow, with a smaller but significant amount of yellowish red–buff firing sherds also present. Most of the corrugated from the Intermediate occupation fired to a reddish color, with a smaller but significant amount of red and yellowish red–buff firing sherds also present. The corrugated from the Secondary occupation also fired mostly to red, with a smaller but significant amount of yellowish red firing sherds also present.

Thus, a gradual increase in red firing sherds and a decrease in yellowish red and yellowish red–buff firing sherds occurred through time. A chi-square test comparing the differences in firing color of corrugated ware to occupational period showed significance at greater than the .001 level.

Samples of Mancos B/w sherds from the Primary and Intermediate occupations fired to the same basic color, as did the overall Mancos B/w sample. A chi-square test comparing the differences between Mancos B/w from different occupations was significant at the .001 level.

The paste firing colors for McElmo B/w from each major occupation were very similar to the overall McElmo sample tested. A gradual trend, however, may be observed that involves a gradual increase of yellowish red firing pastes and a decrease in yellowish red–buff and whitish buff firing pastes through time within McElmo B/w. A chi-square test indicates that differences observed were significant at the .250 level, and thus may be considered only slightly significant.

The Mesa Verde B/w sherds from the early Secondary period contain a high amount of yellowish red firing pastes and a low but significant amount of yellowish red–buff and whitish buff firing pastes. Most of the Mesa Verde B/w representing the late Secondary period contain yellowish red firing pastes, along with a lower but significant amount of red firing pastes. Therefore, an increase in the amount of Mesa Verde containing red and yellowish red firing pastes and a decrease in yellowish red–buff and whitish buff firing pastes occurred through time. A chi-square test indicates that these differences are significant at the .001 level.

The combination of the data presented appears to indicate several definite trends through time involving the clays used to make the San Juan ceramics found at Salmon Ruin. Local potters at Salmon Ruin apparently used lighter yellowish red firing clays for corrugated pottery during the earliest occupation, and then adopted darker yellowish red and red firing clays in the later occupations. There was also a gradual decrease in the amount of intrusive ceramics brought into Salmon Ruin. Therefore, Proposition 2 appears to be correct.

The Chacoan presence at Salmon Ruin during the Primary occupation appears to have resulted, directly or indirectly, in a higher amount of intrusive San Juan ceramics being brought into Salmon Ruin. Therefore, Proposition 3 appears to be supported.

After the Chacoan abandonment of Salmon Ruin at about AD 1130, the amount of intrusive San Juan ceramics brought into the site gradually decreased. This would be expected if the Chacoan presence at Salmon Ruin was indeed responsible for the high amount of intrusive San Juan ceramics in the preceding occupation.

This trend involving the gradual decrease in the amount of intrusive San Juan ceramics appears to have been consistent and continual except for the fact that Mesa Verde B/w, representing the early Secondary occupation, contains a fairly high amount of pastes firing to colors that appear to represent intrusive San Juan ceramics. This amount of intrusive ceramics, however, is not as high as for the San Juan ceramics represented in the Primary occupation. The beginning of the Secondary occupation may have been the result of a migration from regions to the north into Salmon Ruin, which could account for the amount of intrusive Mesa Verde B/w during the early part of the Secondary occupation. The influx of Mesa Verde B/w from these regions to the north and west of Salmon Ruin, however, does not appear to have continued after this initial migration. Almost all of the Mesa Verde B/w from the late part of the Secondary occupation appears to be of local manufacture. Much of the Secondary occupation, then, may be viewed as a period in which very little exchange of any ceramics between Salmon Ruin and other regions occurred. Therefore, Proposition 5 also appears to be correct.

INTRASITE VARIATION IN PASTE COLOR

It is difficult to determine whether the high amount of intrusive San Juan pottery present during the Primary occupation related only generally to the Chacoan influence, or whether it was directly caused by the Chacoan presence at Salmon Ruin. Rooms, room blocks, and stratigraphic units containing various amounts of intrusive types associated with the Chacoan occupation were compared with the amount of intrusive San Juan ceramics. A chi-square test comparing the relationship between the two different groups of intrusive ceramics, for several different types of association, was not found to be statistically significant. Therefore, intrusive San Juan ceramics and intrusive ceramics associated with the Chacoan ceramics are not significantly associated. Proposition 4 is therefore not supported by the evidence.

SUMMARY

Paste firing color does, in fact, appear to represent a significant attribute for determining the presence of locally made versus intrusive San Juan ceramics at Salmon Ruin. Refiring has been useful in looking at the behavioral, temporal, and spatial variation involving San Juan ceramics. This information may later be combined with the other ceramic data from Salmon Ruin to further establish overall relationships.

Chapter 28

1980 CONCLUSIONS FROM THE SALMON CERAMIC ANALYSIS

by Hayward Franklin

Ultimately, the distribution of all artifact categories should be assessed prior to reaching final conclusions. Earl Morris (1928:417) put it succinctly: "generalizations upon the basis of incomplete data are a task that offers no marked appeal." A complete analysis of the hypotheses concerning the Primary occupation cultural assemblage, therefore, cannot be made at present. However, several hypotheses developed by Irwin-Williams for the Salmon Project can be explored by evaluating the distribution of regional ceramic series and vessel form and ware combinations from the Salmon assemblage.

Although spatial aspects of social organization are the focus of this study, there was no attempt to reconstruct the social organization in its entirety. Such inferences could only be made using locally produced ceramics, and at a much finer level of analysis. In any case, inferences regarding specific details of organizational systems are fraught with possibilities for error, and require the kinds of assumptions that could not be made here. Allen and Richardson (1971) went so far as to suggest that the study of kinship systems should be left to ethnologists. These authors did suggest, however, that examination of other, more general dimensions of societal organization could be more profitably pursued with archaeological data, including analysis of levels of political organization, religion, settlement pattern, household organization, and economic relations and exchange within and between communities (Allen and Richardson 1971).

Dozier (1965) also suggested some other parameters of modern pueblo societies that are amenable to archaeological testing. It is only at this more general level that conclusions about Chacoan society can currently be offered. The specifics of residence and descent groups cannot be approached satisfactorily at Salmon without examining the broader and more general questions of the culture contact relationship between Chacoan and local San Juan populations, identification of the residential loci, and the functional specificity of loci.

ORIGINAL HYPOTHESES

Returning to the original hypotheses, and the model from which they were derived, we can now evaluate the propositions in light of the evident patterns of ceramic, nonceramic, and architectural data.

1. Chacoan society provided access to a variety of nonlocally available exotic and luxury items by virtue of centralized authority and integration into the widespread Chacoan trade network.

There is considerable support for this hypothesis. Most of the ceramic types and series from the Primary occupation are from sources elsewhere in the region. Moreover, the appearance of exotic lithic materials, some of which came from the same general areas as the intrusive ceramics, provides credence to this hypothesis.

The most intrinsically valuable class of items is probably ornaments. A distributional study of ornaments at Salmon would help to evaluate this hypothesis. In a master's thesis (McNeil 1986) that addressed the distribution of ornaments at Salmon, one conclusion made was that the Tower Kiva area rooms and the Great Kiva contain an abundance of ornaments, suggesting that valuable items such as ornament forms were concentrated in and around socioreligious structures. Unfortunately, the great likelihood that ornaments were carried away by departing Chacoans or reused by Secondary occupation people, plus the relatively small sample sizes compared to ceramic or lithic classes, makes distributional analysis for Primary ornament forms very difficult.

Intrusive ceramics at Salmon have been identified as such by various means, including paste and temper analyses, petrographic research, and refiring tests. There is no doubt that Salmon received considerable ceramics from other regions. Because they are less common than locally produced items and because the most common intrusive series present is Cibola-Chaco, intrusive ceramics are assumed to have been of considerable value to the Chacoans.

There is every reason to suppose that the Chacoan trading network was the means by which foreign items reached Salmon, either directly via Chacoan population centers in Chaco Canyon or indirectly by way of other Chacoan outlying settlements. The study by Whalley (1980) confirmed these strong contacts with other sites in the area. Not only did the heaviest use of the Chacoan North Road coincide with the Primary occupation at Salmon (Morenon 1975, 1977), but pottery from the surface along the North Road reflects the same intrusive ceramic types known for the Chacoan occupation at Salmon Ruins (Franklin 1975a, 1975b).

2. Uneven access to or use of exotic or rare ceramic vessels, as with other luxury goods, was concomitant with concentrated socioreligious activity in the hands of a theocratic minority. Such activities were restricted to certain loci.

This hypotheses was confirmed by two test implications. Intrusive ceramics are concentrated in assemblages from rooms of inferred socioreligious function, particularly in the Tower Kiva area. Rooms 82A, 82W, and 62W contain high amounts of intrusive ceramics in general, with high counts of special white ware forms in 62W, red ware in 82A, and Chuska pottery in 81W. Although intrusive ceramics are not confined to these rooms, they are present in high proportions in the Tower Kiva block. Moreover, these are also among the few rooms with relatively high frequencies of the intrusive Washington Pass chert. In addition to the evident socioreligious function of these rooms is the abundance of intrusive and special forms of pottery that indicate intensive Chacoan and perhaps elite Chacoan activity.

3. One higher level integrative mechanism may have been a dual organization (moiety) dividing the pueblo spatially into two equal parts with the dividing line at the Tower Kiva.

There is little support for this hypothesis. Although a suggestion of such a trend was evident in earlier preliminary testing, the pattern does not hold up under a larger sample from across all Primary rooms. In any event, the excavational sample is too biased toward the eastern part of the site for a fair judgment. The concept that the western part of the site should be heavily intrusive whereas the eastern half should produce greater San Juan frequencies is not borne out; there are contradictory proveniences in both halves of the pueblo. It is unlikely that a moiety, at least as presently found among the modern Eastern Pueblos, would either be localized spatially in the pueblo or have differential ceramic accompaniments as tangible evidence of its existence.

4. Residence or kin-based groups will continue to exist despite the overlay of higher level integrating mechanisms.

The analysis of the room suites (P. Reed 2005b) provides considerable support for this hypothesis. Suites consist of front-to-back alignments of rooms united internally through connecting doorways, but with little or no access to adjoining rooms. Each suite has up to four rooms on the ground floor (and probably other rooms on upper floors), with a single-story, spacious square room in front. Hearths are present in all large square rooms, but are absent or rare in the narrower multistory rooms to the back. From the situation and size of such suites of rooms alone, it would seem that they should form the loci for a number of comparable societal units. Similarities to household units as defined by Rohn (1965) lend support to the idea that these suites were the residential basis of the Primary occupation community. By extension, it is tempting to think of them as being occupied by a kin-based residential social group, such as an extended family.

In terms of ceramic series, the suites of rooms (inferred to relate to residential groups) are more consistent internally than between suites. This implies that the inhabitants of particular suites used particular ceramic types more extensively than did members of other suites. Under this model, this finding is a reflection of the cultural affiliation and perhaps the status of individuals and families, but does not necessarily relate to residential patterns of descent groups.

The ceramic variables of vessel form and ware, presumably reflecting function, cut across residential units. Large square rooms in different suites were grouped together in cluster analysis, as were rooms at the back of the pueblo. Function tends to be organized by row (laterally) across the site, whereas suites were arranged front to back. Each suite apparently contains a number of rooms of fairly distinct functions, equivalent to the same ranges of functions present in other similar suite groupings. Front row square rooms are inferred to have multiple usage as living rooms, whereas rooms toward the back show evidence of storage, and later trash disposal, especially on the ground story. Certainly the ground story rooms toward the back of the pueblo would not have been desirable as living quarters because they were small, dark, and difficult to access. In fact, the ceramic evidence suggests that at least one function for them was storage.

5. Under the general model, residence units should reflect the differential status of their occupants within

the Primary occupation community, either in differential access to rare items among Chacoans themselves or in the incorporation of non-Chacoan Middle San Juan population groups into the community. The latter group would presumably have relied to a greater extent on locally produced San Juan pottery.

This question is perhaps the most difficult to answer satisfactorily. The seeming incongruity (architecturally) of the Chacoan pueblo containing an abundance of non-Chacoan local ceramics requires an explanation. Although the number of types and series of intrusive pottery exceeds the number of local types, quantitatively, San Juan series Mancos and McElmo Black-on-white types together comprise 72 percent of the decorated assemblage. San Juan Gray Ware, the utility ware inferred to be of local manufacture, occurs in similarly high proportions. Although refiring evidence suggests that some proportion of San Juan decorated ceramics was made north of the San Juan River (Wilson 1985; Chapter 28), most of the decorated and utility ceramics from the Primary occupation were probably manufactured at Salmon or in the immediate vicinity. There are two probable explanations for this finding: (1) the Chacoan population relied to a great extent on locally produced pottery to make up for a deficit of Chacoan or other intrusive ceramics, which were preferred and perhaps reserved for certain purposes; or (2) Salmon Pueblo was inhabited by a multicultural population that included Chacoan people and local Middle San Juan groups. Choosing one of these alternatives is difficult using only ceramic data, although the differential distribution of intrusive compared to local ceramics sheds some light on the matter. For example, in a study of the distribution of ceramic series at Salmon, Priesnitz (1979:142) concluded that there was some evidence for the presence of Middle San Juan groups.

The assemblages from residential suites vary significantly in their composition of local and intrusive ceramics. There tends to be less variation within their constituent rooms than between suites in terms of floor context materials and those found in the lower trash levels. If these arrangements did constitute residential social groups, then it is evident that some groups utilized imported ceramics more than others did. Three suites or partially excavated suites exhibit relatively high intrusive ceramics, whereas three are dominated by San Juan Series decorated types.

The fact that certain residential suites were high in intrusive pottery whereas others contained nearly 100 percent San Juan decorated ceramics suggests that residence was the major spatial and organizational variable determining the differential usage of local and intrusive decorated ceramics. Intrusive suites are spread widely across the site, as are local suites. The most obvious contrast is in the east arm of the site, where the most highly San Juan block of rooms (90W, 91W, and 92W) is situated adjacent to the highly intrusive suite portion of Rooms 83W and 84W. Following this suite to the east, the block of Rooms 97W, 100W, and 101W is again San Juan dominant. Thus, high versus low intrusive suites may be found immediately adjacent to each other.

Moreover, specialized loci (outside of residential suites) are dominated by intrusive ceramics, with Chacoan ceramics most prevalent. Rooms with inferred socioreligious functions and specialized milling and food preparation loci contain above-average amounts of intrusive ceramics. San Juan dominant rooms are exclusively residential suites. Specialized activities, as they can be inferred at present, seem to have been largely Chacoan in nature. The Great Kiva complex is a possible exception, in that its assemblage appears to be quite average in ceramic composition, in line with its possible integrative function.

In general, then, residential suites may be either relatively intrusive or San Juan in ceramic series, whereas all specialized rooms and blocks are intrusive in nature. This distribution of the intrusive-local dichotomy in decorated pottery lends support to the view that a nonlocal population was present in the Primary, but that these folks did not participate extensively in specialized (especially ritual-ceremonial) activities in the Tower Kiva block. Pushing the logic a step further into the realm of speculation, if the social control mechanisms were socioreligious in nature, and if loci with evidence of socioreligious activity were Chacoan in affiliation, then the Chacoans' dominance of the higher level social control mechanisms, at least, may be inferred. Such organizational control at the higher, more inclusive levels probably provided the oversight necessary to plan and build the pueblo, as well as regulating spatial usage within the pueblo. This leadership presumably administered exchange and long-range contacts with other areas, particularly great houses in Chaco Canyon.

Aside from the localization of relatively high amounts of San Juan pottery in some residential suites, there is some additional evidence for the manufacture of San Juan White Ware and Gray Ware at Salmon. The testing of clays of local availability in the Salmon area by Wilson and this author suggested that considerable amounts of San Juan White Ware and utility ware could have been produced from them. Moreover, 29 usable potter's clay samples were found in Primary archaeological contexts in

Salmon Ruin, and some had actually been worked. All could have been obtained in the Salmon catchment area, judging from refired colors compared to clays obtained from the local environment (Wilson 1985). The majority of San Juan White Ware and utility ceramics produced refired colors that matched the range of raw clays found in Primary strata, and in turn accorded well with those obtainable from the San Juan drainage near Salmon Ruin. The distribution of these raw and worked clay samples suitable for ceramic manufacture within the site revealed a high degree of correspondence with rooms known to be high in San Juan decorated pottery.

In addition, the Primary assemblage contains evidence for the presence of tools used in ceramic manufacture. Both polishing stones and hematite pigment are present in Primary strata, and although these items are undoubtedly multifunctional, one likely use was polishing and decorating vessels. In total, 90 polishing stones and 19 hematite pieces were located in Primary strata; these items occur both separately and together. Where they occur together, there is a uniform ratio of two polishing stones to one piece of hematite pigment. Further, in all instances where both are found in the same strata, they come from either the same meter grid or adjacent grids. These may possibly reflect tool kits or partial tool kits of potters. Finally, in the cases where these items are associated with each other, the strata in which they are found are all San Juan dominant (factor scores of B or C), except for one instance. So when these items occur together, as they should if they relate to ceramic manufacture as opposed to some other function, they tend to be found in strata dominated by San Juan ceramics.

Evidence for ceramic manufacture in the Primary is uniquely associated with San Juan ware; no other ceramics series or ware, based on refiring analysis, was made locally. Furthermore, the association of raw clays and nonceramic items such as polishing stones and hematite in San Juan dominant strata also supports this finding. This production evidence, in turn, can be used to explore the hypothesis of a resident San Juan population within the Chacoan pueblo at Salmon.

In sum, the correlation of San Juan ceramics with residential suites, combined with evidence of San Juan White Ware and Gray Ware manufacture within the pueblo during the Primary occupation, could support the alternative of a resident San Juan population. A full test of this hypothesis, however, can only be made using a much larger sample of rooms and incorporating nonceramic artifactual data. Is there evidence of a whole complex of northern San Juan Puebloan affiliated cultural items, and do these all cluster together in room suites having an abundance of San Juan ceramics? Can a site-unit intrusion be inferred for the loci in the pueblo wherein a Middle San Juan complex occurs? Of course, if San Juan people were integrated into the pueblo but did not retain their accustomed material culture, or if the San Juan population did not reside in or utilize restricted portions of the pueblo, then there would remain little or no direct evidence of their presence in the archaeological record.

6. Functional differentiation, implied by the model, could include several aspects: functional specialization of loci, manufacture of tool kits or craft arts, and potentially the presence of specialists in terms of personnel. Functional specialization in any of these respects, either of loci or of personnel, could have been part time or full time.

The tests here are restricted to the more accessible aspect of locus or room function differentiation, and not the potentially specialized production of material culture classes or of the people who made them. It is possible, of course, that loci may be functionally specialized without the personnel who used them being specialists themselves; the functional specialization of rooms in modern houses may provide an accurate analogy.

The term "function" is used broadly, overlapping with evidence of residence and socio-political organization. However, the ceramic attributes of vessel form and ware are likely sensitive to certain functional parameters, rather than to cultural affiliation, status, or residence. Indeed, the function of rooms should cut across the dimension of ceramic series, and also the spatial dimension of residential suites. Five vessel form–ware combinations were involved in spatial assessment: white ware bowls, white ware jars, all other white ware including special forms, red ware (almost totally bowls), and the utility ceramics (all jars). Cluster analysis of these five ceramic classes revealed the following trends:

1. Vessel forms and wares, as well as lithic flaked and ground stone classes, do cut across room organization by suites, suggesting that each suite contained a series of rooms devoted to different functions. The hypothesis that room function should cut across the dimension of residence was confirmed.

2. Rooms with high amounts of intrusive pottery tended to have low utility ware frequencies except for specialized cooking and food preparation loci.

3. Ceremonial loci (around the Tower Kiva and the Great Kiva) likewise have lower than average utility ware percentages. This is perhaps expectable for areas of ceremonial activity.

4. In residential suites, the large square rooms in front toward the plaza all have higher than average amounts of utility ceramics. All of these rooms have hearths, so the use of utility ceramics may have been related to domestic cooking. The spacious single-storied nature of these rooms as well as their internal features suggests multi-functional usage typical of a residential living room. Decorated bowls (for serving?) are common.

5. Rooms toward the back of the pueblo away from the plaza, on the other hand, contain more jars than bowls. Both utility and white ware jars are relatively abundant compared to large square rooms. The inaccessibility of ground floor rooms toward the rear of the pueblo, their small size, the lack of other evidence for domestic activity, and these ceramic trends together argue for storage and/or sleeping quarters. Utility and white ware jars would have been used in such places for storage, presumably of food.

6. Rooms with evidence of milling activity (rows of metate troughs) or specialized cooking and food preparation rooms in the gallery at the front of the pueblo contain the highest percentages of utility ceramics and/or white ware jars. Jars always exceed bowls in these rooms. Decorated or utility jars were presumably used to store food before and after processing, and to transport such food to other areas for consumption (large square rooms?) or storage (back wall rooms?).

7. Specialized rooms devoted to ceremonialism or milling and food preparation all contained above-normal amounts of intrusive decorated ceramics. The utility ceramics in such areas also tended to be intrusive, especially from the Cibola or Chuska Series. The association of specialization as determined from vessel form–ware distributions (and nonceramic data) with intrusive decorated series suggests that these were areas of intensive Chacoan activity.

SUMMARY

The Salmon Primary occupation was structured spatially into a number of generalized residential suites (either high or low for intrusive ceramics internally), as well as several areas of specialized rooms or room blocks. Among the latter were rooms used for ritual-political activities (Rooms 81W, 82W and A, and 62W) and milling-food preparation (Rooms 82W, 93W, 102C, 97W, 129W, and 119W). Whereas residential suites were abundant in either exotic ceramics or locally produced ceramics, all the rooms evidencing special functions had above-average amounts of intrusive decorated and utility series. The use of space was structured and organized, as was the layout and construction of the pueblo. All current evidence points toward the conclusion that the Chacoans planned, built, and occupied the community with forethought and organizational direction. The congruence of many lines of evidence supports the view that room utilization was diverse, and in some cases highly specific to certain cultural activities. The organizational abilities of the Chacoans are apparent in the planning and construction of the pueblo as well as in the allocation of space to the diverse functions that took place within residential suites, or in functionally more specific rooms and blocks of rooms.

The diversity of room functions, their spatial arrangement, and the localization of at least two broad specialty categories of cultural life within the pueblo that are associated with high amounts of intrusive ceramics also attest to societal control and organization on the part of the Chacoan population, and perhaps only a small element of that population. Whether the evident centralized organizational direction involved a strict distinction on the basis of kinship, rank, or cultural affiliation, or along other lines, cannot be determined at present. Similarly, evidence for a strict division of labor or specialization for the population in the areas of economic activities or craft arts is likewise problematic. At least, it is evident that some areas were definitely devoted (at least predominantly) to specific functions. Socioreligious control by a group with Chacoan affiliation may be inferred from the Tower Kiva area rooms and the Chacoan nature of all rooms wherein specialization of function has been derived from the archaeological evidence. A more complete integration of associated ceramic, lithic, botanic, ornamental, and osteological data sets is necessary for a better evaluation of room function, residence, and sociopolitical organization.

The ceramic data appear to support, at least partially, all but one of the initial hypotheses. Regardless of the interpretations offered here, at least there is no doubt that there was patterning in the Primary occupation, not only ceramically, but in other research areas as well. Some major areas of social interaction have been illustrated, if not the precise social groups responsible for them. As Binford (1972: 136) stated: "We may not always be able to state or determine what specific activities resulted in observed differential distributions, but we can recognize that activities were differentiated and determine the formal nature of the observed variability."

Chapter 29

A SYMMETRY ANALYSIS OF THE DECORATED CERAMICS FROM SALMON PUEBLO

Dorothy K. Washburn

Typological analysis of the ceramics from Salmon Pueblo indicated that there were three occupational periods: Primary, Intermediate, and Secondary, partially characterized by Cibola, McElmo, and Mesa Verde ceramics, respectively (see Franklin, Chapters 19–28). This study explores how focusing on one feature of the ceramics—the consistencies and changes in the structure of design as measured by plane pattern symmetry classes that have been found to metaphorically reflect cultural principles and practices—can further illuminate the nature of the society at Salmon between the late eleventh and early thirteenth centuries. A full treatment of the theory and method for this approach can be found in Washburn and Crowe (1988), and a number of examples using this analytical tool can be found in Washburn and Crowe (2004) and Washburn (2004).

THEORY OF SYMMETRY ANALYSIS

Justification for the application of symmetry analysis to design is predicated on the hypothesis (Washburn 1988, 2002, 2004) that design structure metaphorically reflects cosmological and social relationships (Washburn 1999). Previous research has shown that a community's institutionalized beliefs and practices, which perpetuate their world view and lifeway, are metaphorically embedded in image and design (Sekaquaptewa and Washburn 2004). Some of these cultural metaphors appear in representational mode, as can be seen in the murals from the Hopi sites of Awa'tovi and Kawaika'a (Sekaquaptewa and Washburn 2003), whereas others are conveyed in abstract geometric designs that are found on ceramics, tile, wood, textiles, or basketry. The metaphors are embedded in the specific ways that the elements and motifs in the design are arranged in a pattern. Such arrangements can be systematically described by the geometric symmetries that organize the designs as they are repeated in the plane. In this way the consistencies and changes in design structure reveal and describe the crucial cosmological and institutional relationships that knit a community together. By directly tapping into the fundamental beliefs, social relationships, and practices of the people who made and used the decorated items, we can better characterize the way they organized themselves to interface with their natural environment as well as interacting with other communities.

Ethnographic and archaeological studies of how design structure persists or changes relative to other cultural factors (Washburn 1977, 1983, 1986, 1987, 1990, 1991, 2001; Washburn and Humphrey 2001; Washburn and Matson 1985) underpin the general model (Washburn 1999, 2002) that relates consistencies and changes in patterned design to structural features in different social institutions and cosmological orientations. I summarize here the correlations between design and cultural activities that relate specifically to the Southwest Anasazi situation. Briefly, a site with ceramics that show a homogeneous design structure system represents an integrated community whose populace shares a cosmology and associated institutionalized social, economic, and political practices. Conversely, the presence of mixed design structure systems at a site suggests that other factors are in play, such as in-migration or occupation or control by different cultural or political groups. Also, a site whose ceramic sequence displays a marked shift from one design system to another suggests that social discord and disintegration have upset the extant structural relationships of the people, whether due to the onset of externally induced perturbations, such as environmental shifts, internal strife, or external incursions that have forced a redefinition and restructuring of the fundamental nature of the society.

My study was completed prior to P. Reed's chronological revision, which no longer uses the original Primary, Intermediate, and Secondary divisions. See Reed, Chapter 12, for equivalence between the old and new periods.

In the Puebloan world of the eighth through thirteenth centuries, bifold rotation symmetry, coded as p112, structured most of the ceramic designs decorating the everyday serving and storage vessels used by families in the small farming communities along the San Juan in the greater area around Salmon. As well, this symmetry prevailed on ceramics made by farming communities in the greater Four Corners area west and south into Arizona, north into southern Colorado and Utah, and east and south into New Mexico. This symmetry structure describes a design in which the two parts of each repeated motif require two 180° rotations for them to return to their original positions (Figure 29.1). In many patterns, as in the ubiquitous series of right triangular units, the motif unit hook ends are actually interlocked in this two-fold arrangement. In others, as in the stepped units, they are visually but not literally interlocked. In all of these two-fold arrangements, this positioning metaphorically represents the reciprocal and complementary nature of relationships and the institutions and practices that support these relationships in these societies.

I have shown in an earlier publication (Washburn 1999) how this bifold rotational structure was metaphorical for the Hopi farming lifeway as it is sustained by cosmological principles and social institutions and practices that involve interlocking reciprocities and obligations between individuals as members of religious and social institutions and between the community and its relationship with the environment. From the practice of interlocking a man and woman's hair, which is considered the real moment of marriage, to the interfacing of clan and religious society obligations, to a communities' need to communally observe these practices—every level of Hopi society is related in interlocking roles and obligations. Through adherence to these complementary duties and responsibilities, the members of small farming communities are bound together in ways that regulate and ensure the performance of social and economic practices that lead to survival of the whole community.

Archaeologically, this type of community organization is metaphorically represented in a design system that structures banded designs with p112 symmetry. Although these designs appear as infinitely varied combinations of dots, triangles, stepped units, and lines made in communities throughout the Four Corners regions, they are predominantly structured by the p112 system. At Salmon Ruin this design system structures band patterns on the simple designs made on early types such as Mancos, Cortez,

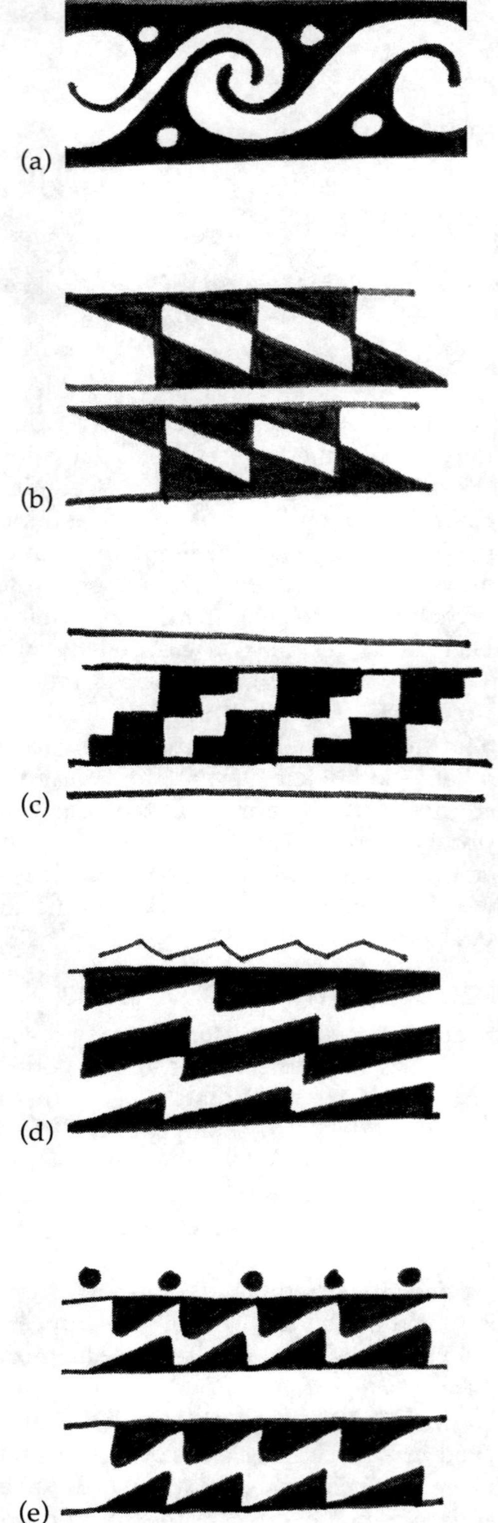

Figure 29.1. Examples of Primary period designs produced by the local San Juan population at Salmon characterized by p112 bands of design: (a) 325058; (b) 327203; (c) 52545; (d) 78161; (e) 79512.

and Red Mesa Black-on-white during the Primary occupation through the latest bands of design on Mesa Verde Black-on-white that are sandwiched between line series on highly polished vessels topped with neatly ticked rims made during the Secondary occupation.

UNDERSTANDING SALMON RUINS USING SYMMETRY ANALYSIS

From the perspective of the symmetry system that characterizes designs on Salmon ceramics, the data suggest the following scenario: A local San Juan farming population lived in the area throughout the Primary and Secondary occupations. They consistently organized the designs on their ceramics using bifold rotation. However, during the Primary occupation the small village lifeway was interrupted by the incursion of a group of great house administrators who brought specialists to direct the local farmers to build the pueblo and who organized the farmers to produce food to sustain the occupants (with specialized milling facilities; see Shelley, Chapter 48), as well as to supply food to Chaco Canyon (see Irwin-Williams, Chapter 16, for discussion of specialization).

Chacoan outliers, such as Salmon and Aztec, appear from a symmetry perspective to have been administratively tied to the great house complex in Chaco Canyon. Specifically, symmetry analysis has revealed two different design structure systems: (1) a local San Juan Basin one-dimensional system dominated by symmetry class p112, emblematic of the organization of small farming communities, and (2) a two-dimensional system identical to that in Chaco Canyon. The local design system consists of countless element and motif variations structured by p112 (typologically known as Red Mesa, Cortez, Mancos, etc.). This design system was likely the product of many potters' creative efforts to portray their conceptualizations of the cosmo-social principles and relationships that bound the members of these small farming villages into cohesive and ongoing communities. In contrast, the Chacoan system at Salmon consisted of a limited pattern repertoire, used repeatedly, that was identical in symmetry and pattern to that found on identical vessel forms at Chaco Canyon great house sites, especially Pueblo Bonito. This two-dimensional system of hatched patterns structured by p2, as well as p1, pgg, and pmg, many of which were constructed by a continuous line layout system, suggests a high degree of sophistication in design formation and specialization in execution that was not previously evident on the ceramics made in any of the local Four Corners farming communities.

With this approach, symmetry analysis enables us not only to describe the character of the local San Juan occupation, but also to detect the appearance of populations moving in from other areas. During the Primary occupation, populations from Chaco who arrived to direct the construction of a great house used a different ceramic design system. During the Secondary occupation, the local San Juan p112 symmetry system again became dominant, but the additional appearance of finite symmetries on some McElmo B/w and Mesa Verde B/w vessels and the glide reflection symmetry, p1a1, on some Mesa Verde B/w ceramics appear to represent other social practices and cosmological principles and rituals that were brought by other groups moving into the area.

THE SAMPLE

The sample analyzed includes 842 designs from 571 decorated whole and partial vessels and rim sherds from 52 rooms representing all areas and all periods of the site. Most vessels are listed by their 6-digit Pottery Order (PO) number; some are listed by their 5-digit Record Key (RK) number.[1] Typological assignments made for each vessel are for general orientation only. My work shows no correspondence between symmetry class and ceramic type. In fact, I argue that the plethora of different ceramic types assigned to contemporaneous decorated ceramics has obscured our understanding of the nature and extent of Anasazi culture in the San Juan Basin. It should be noted that symmetry analysis normally requires whole vessels that display the entire design. However, some narrow banded designs that encircle the vessel wall just below the rim, especially on the interiors and exteriors of bowls or on jar shoulders and necks, can be classified using large rim sherds. Thus, the overall two-dimensional patterns on Chaco B/w from the Primary occupation must be viewed in their entirety for classification, whereas the narrow banded designs from the Mesa Verde area can be classified from rim sherds. This layout feature greatly increased the size of the Secondary sample. In fact, 82 percent of the Mesa Verde banded designs from the Secondary occupation were classified from rim sherds. This analysis approach weighted the sample so that it overwhelmingly represents the Secondary occupation (more than 700 designs) with some "Intermediate" designs studied; 99 designs from the Primary occupation were analyzed. However, this weighted representation of the later occupants fairly characterizes the relative proportion of artifacts

[1]The symmetry data generated in this study are available at Salmon Ruins Museum.

recovered from the site. Due to the fact that Primary occupation trash may well have been removed by the meandering San Juan River as well as during the clearing and remodeling efforts of the Secondary occupants, we have relatively little Primary artifactual debris.

Franklin's analysis (Chapter 25) of the stylistic variation in the San Juan white ware from stratified samples from Rooms 33, 100, and 102 revealed no temporally measured stylistic variation in Mancos B/w, but an increase in banding in McElmo B/w over time. The fact that this increase appeared to precede the appearance of the classic banded Mesa Verde B/w led him to define an Intermediate occupation characterized by McElmo B/w ceramics. However, I have combined the Intermediate material with the Secondary occupation ceramics because, by symmetry analysis, they shared the same San Juan p112 cosmological and social orientation. (This approach meshed well with the revised chronology for Salmon, which also combines the Intermediate and Secondary periods; see P. Reed, Chapter 12.) Thus, symmetry analysis enables us not only to describe the character of the San Juan occupation, but also to detect the appearance of new groups. For example, the finite symmetries on some McElmo and Mesa Verde B/w and the glide reflection symmetry, p1a1, on some Mesa Verde B/w appear to represent new social practices and cosmological principles and rituals brought by groups moving into the area.

The assignment of each vessel to the Primary or Secondary occupation was determined from the stratigraphic sequence during the original project (see R. Adams 1980) and via consultation with Paul Reed (working through and modifying the original stratigraphic data based on a reassessment of the data). In cases where the Primary material came from a Secondary stratum, it was found to be either intrusive as trash that had been moved from another location at the site or clearly of Primary affiliation because of vessel shape, design, or other association. That is, Primary material was found in Secondary B strata, which were composed of wall-fall or post-occupational rubble, C strata (structured trash) that were mixed as a result of the Secondary residents clearing and remodeling rooms, or M strata of unstructured trash. The presence of Primary material in roof strata is interesting as it suggests that the later occupants continued to use whole vessels, whatever their origin.

OVERVIEW OF SALMON

To clarify the nature of Salmon and its relationship to similar great house communities in Chaco Canyon, to nearby Aztec Ruins along the Animas River, and to other large and small neighboring sites in the Middle San Juan region, Irwin-Williams developed the Salmon excavation plan around an adaptive systems view of prehistory. In her model, occupation began along the San Juan in the AD 700–800s with small Prudden-unit type horticultural villages composed of localized extended lineage groups dispersed over the landscape in areas favorable to agriculture. Between 800 and 1100 rainfall fluctuations in the greater San Juan Basin forced farmers to choose among several possible strategies for survival: move into and exploit new eco-zones, disperse or migrate to other areas, or aggregate into larger communities and develop new water-control technologies. Irwin-Williams believed that the large sites at Chaco, as well as the outliers like Aztec and Salmon in both their Primary and Secondary occupational stages, represented examples of a nucleated strategy that was similarly followed at sites like Grasshopper in the central Arizona highlands, Mug House on the Mesa Verde, and Arroyo Hondo in the upper Rio Grande valley. Ultimately, however, she concluded that these nucleated centers collapsed from subsistence stress because they were less flexible than the small dispersed hamlets from which they evolved (see Irwin-Williams, Chapter 16).

Irwin-Williams designed her sampling strategy to recover information about a number of different kinds of activities and architectural units in the Primary occupation. Linear transects of rooms (e.g., Rooms 83–86) were excavated to explore internal pueblo connections among rooms in the front-to-back suites characteristic of the Chacoan building plan. Rooms along the back wall in the northwest sector (Rooms 30, 31, 33, 37, and 43) were excavated to determine the nature of the rear storage rooms associated with the front living rooms of the room suites. The Great Kiva (Room 130) was excavated to determine its similarity to similar kivas at Aztec and other Chacoan sites. The plaza was trenched and tested to determine the nature of activities in this open area, and rooms that faced the plaza during the Primary Chacoan occupation (Room 93, 102) were excavated. The Tower Kiva (Room 64) and the surrounding rooms (51, 53, 57–59, 67, 81, 82) were intensively excavated to determine the nature of this kiva and the activities in the presumably associated rooms.

Irwin-Williams viewed the Chacoan occupation at Salmon as a nucleated form of Puebloan society but believed that the Secondary occupation represented the phenomenon of population aggregation (see Chapters 2 and 16). During the Secondary occupation, many rooms in the pueblo were remodeled by family units. Adjoining rooms in the northeast corner and in the Southeast Wing were excavated (Rooms 118, 199, 121, 123, 124, 127–129) to determine the nature of the modifications that were superimposed on Primary rooms by the Secondary occupants, and some rooms were excavated to explore unique materials or features.

More than 30 percent of the site was excavated, producing a remarkably detailed picture of a three-story pueblo with perhaps 300 rooms. A series of tree-ring dates indicates that the main pueblo was constructed in phases between AD 1090 and 1105. Then building activity slowed, and the last repairs were made in 1116–1118 (Reed, Chapter 12). Some time before the Primary occupation ended at 1125–1130, a number of the doors connecting the back-to-front suites of rooms were sealed. McElmo B/w ceramics and other signs of activity in the pueblo (trash accumulating in rooms) represent a continuing Intermediate (or early San Juan) population from the 1120s into the late 1100s. By 1190 or 1200, a renewed occupation was underway at Salmon; this would last until the 1280s. Architecture reveals a clear contrast between the large square plaza-facing rooms with cobble and adobe foundations and T-shaped doorways and two large kivas built during the Primary occupation and the subdivided and remodeled habitation rooms and the many small kivas built by the Secondary occupants. This contrast is supported by symmetry analysis, which reveals the presence of two distinct populations: the Chacoans and a local San Juan group.

I elaborate on this generalized reconstruction from the perspective of design structure as social metaphor by analyzing, where possible, the character of ceramic assemblages from the same kinds of room associations examined during the original Salmon Project. The results reported here revise Irwin-Williams's explanation of the Primary occupation but reconfirm and refine her reconstruction of the Secondary occupation. Working from the general premise that an assemblage of designs characterized by a prevailing structure is indicative of a homogeneous community, the results reported here do not support Irwin-Williams's conclusion that the Primary occupation represents an agricultural community that "budded off" from an existing Chaco town and moved to the San Juan. Rather analysis of design structure indicates that the Primary occupation ceramics display two distinct structural systems—an existing local San Juan structure system and a foreign structure system imposed from Chaco.

Although Irwin-Williams's reconstruction recognized that the Salmon Primary occupation was a town created by people from Chaco who somehow shared residence with local inhabitants, her adaptive model implies that these Chacoan immigrants were agriculturalists who moved to the San Juan to take advantage of its perennial water. Symmetry analysis suggests, however, that the Chacoan population was small and lived in a few large plaza-facing rooms. The fact that the vessels on which this foreign design system appear are not everyday wares but are specialized forms, most of which appear unused, suggests that they were made as symbols of authority or were used for special ritual purposes by a small group of individuals whose roles were to oversee the construction of the site and organize and direct food production and other resource procuring activities that may have been stored in the back rooms. Indeed, symmetry analysis demonstrates that for a relatively short time during the late eleventh and early twelfth centuries (1090–1130), Salmon was closely tied to the Chaco Canyon sites, as indicated by identity in design structure and pattern on a small number of specific vessel forms that were probably administrative or religious rather than everyday in nature. Furthermore, the identity in two-dimensional pattern and symmetry apparently existed only on the ceramics used at the administrative level; local hatched copies were produced within the local one-dimensional system. Throughout the presence of the Chacoans, the local San Juan populations continued their communal agricultural lifeway, as exhibited by the prevailing p112 design structure on the locally made ceramics at Salmon and other neighboring sites.

Unfortunately, the 1980 Salmon report did not address the Secondary deposits or occupation in any detail. However, symmetry analysis of the Secondary ceramics suggests that this period represents more than a continual aggregation of local people. The high degree of consistency in pattern, which contrasts with greater variability in the local San Juan wares during the Primary occupation, as well as the presence of new symmetries, suggests instead that the people who remodeled Salmon moved into the area bringing with them ceramics similar to those made at contemporary sites in the Mesa Verde region. The distinctive nature of several subsets of designs and design structures indicates not only the presence of more than one in-migrating group, but also the presence of certain individuals who may have specialized in producing and decorating vessels, although probably not in the same capacity as the specialists who may well have been directed to produce the hatched two-dimensional patterns on the special vessels during the Chacoan hegemony.

In fact, some of the ancillary studies also imply the presence of new populations in the area during this final phase of site occupation. Flint corn is associated with the Chacoan deposits, whereas flour corn varieties seem to dominate the Secondary deposits (see Chapters 35 and 47). It has also been suggested that the Secondary occupation at Salmon sheltered people with more diverse rituals, as evidenced by the presence of the many small Mesa Verde style kivas. Irwin-Williams (Chapter 16) observed that this virtual explosion of small kivas in the Secondary period supports the overall view of the society as less ideologically integrated and centralized than the Chacoans.

Salmon's Primary Occupation

Prior to 1974, ceramics from Salmon were subjected to an exhaustive, highly detailed attribute analysis (Bennett 1974), but this approach succeeded in analyzing only several hundred sherds in 3 years of work. Thus, the Salmon Ceramic Laboratory under Hayward Franklin switched to less detailed rough-sort and limited attribute typological analyses. From the stratigraphic profiles in a number of rooms (31, 33, 82, 91, 93, 100, 102, 129, and plaza trench 13P) Franklin found a close correspondence in the type sequences in all these areas of the site. Unfortunately, of the room profiles examined, most do not overlap with the sample analyzed in this study because the Salmon ceramic laboratory studied sherds and my work focused on design symmetry on whole or partial Chacoan vessels. For example, it would have been optimum to study Primary vessels from Room 82W, a special room with an archaeo-astronomical feature and a platform (see Baker 2005). I was able to record only five Mancos and McElmo bowls from that room in C strata trash contexts. Room 33W also had a long stratigraphic sequence analyzed by Franklin that was slightly larger in my symmetry sample. However, although it included 6 vessels from the Primary occupation and 16 vessels from the Secondary occupation, all represented local San Juan wares rather than Chacoan or related wares. Red ware and polychrome vessels are not well represented in my sample. Only two Wingate B/r vessels were recorded, one from a mixed Primary and Secondary stratum in Room 129W and one from a Secondary stratum in Room 93W. Only four St. Johns Polychrome vessels were recorded—all from Secondary and post-Secondary strata in Rooms 33, 37, 58, and 91.

Franklin concluded that Salmon had an Intermediate occupation marked particularly by McElmo B/w, a type that included both Sosi style wide lined designs and Dogoszhi hatched elements that linked the San Juan inhabitants of the area from the Primary and Secondary occupations. This typological perspective has promoted the view that Salmon hosted a long uninterrupted local San Juan white ware sequence from the Primary occupation represented by Mancos B/w through the Intermediate occupation represented by McElmo B/w to the Secondary occupation represented by Mesa Verde B/w. From typological and stylistic considerations, Franklin (Chapter 22) believed that the Primary population consisted of local people who made carbon-painted Wetherill and McElmo and mineral-painted Mancos, and Chacoans who brought in intrusive Cibola style ceramics (Chaco B/w, Gallup B/w, Chaco McElmo).

Surveys in the Middle San Juan region (cf. Marshall et al. 1979; Powers et al. 1983; Stein and McKenna 1988) have documented the presence of many small farming communities in the area before, during, and after the Chacoan presence. More important is that this work has suggested not only that Aztec and Salmon were just two of many great house sites along the San Juan River, but also that these sites followed the typical pattern of being built by Chacoans and reoccupied by Mesa Verdeans. Ceramics from Bice's (1983) excavations at the Sterling Site, a small great house site on the south side of the San Juan near Farmington, in the immediate area of Salmon, revealed the typical presence of what has been called the Cibola-Chaco, Chuska, and Mesa Verde traditions (Franklin and McKenna 2004). Likewise, Wheelbarger's survey and excavations at sites on the B-Square Ranch (which borders the San Juan for 5 miles from its junction with the Animas River) has identified many Chacoan site intrusions (Wheelbarger 2005). For example, at the Point site, a great house with an unexcavated large (perhaps great) kiva, three of the four whole vessels taken from the unexcavated site by the owner are surely of Chacoan affiliation, displaying hatched patterns composed of solid tipped triangle motifs with heavy outlined borders that are identical to those on vessels from Pueblo Bonito and other Chacoan sites.

At Salmon and neighboring sites, then, ceramic typology describes the first occupation at these great houses as represented by locally made San Juan wares and intrusive Chaco and Chuskan wares. But although typology distinguishes these two groups, it does not clarify the differences in the nature of the two populations who made and used these wares, which can lead us to better understand the nature of the Chacoan presence in the Four Corners area. Irwin-Williams had suggested that although they made a different type of ceramics, the Chacoans represented another farming population who built a large site to accommodate the increasing numbers of people seeking well-watered living areas. Symmetry analysis, however, suggests a far different scenario. Classification of the designs on their vessels by their symmetries reveals a clear distinction between the use of the two-dimensional symmetries, especially p2 and pgg, to structure hatched designs on the Chaco B/w and Chuska B/w special vessel forms, and the one-dimensional symmetries, especially p112, on the local San Juan Mancos–McElmo B/w everyday wares as well as the local hatched copies of the Chacoan wares.

I analyzed 99 designs from the Primary occupation on the basis of their stratigraphic position. This assemblage includes vessels and large sherds that were clearly Chacoan in nature (including Chuskan copies) if not origin (e.g., the one Mesa Verde B/w sherd with a Chacoan-style design) and the ceramics produced by the local populace (see Figure 29.1), who lived in the area before the Chacoans arrived and who probably provided the work force to build the great house pueblo (Table 29.1). Unfortunately, no specific burial, roof, or floor assemblages offered large enough samples to characterize the nature of the Primary Chacoan occupation. Although Room 129 produced a large sample (21 designs) from Primary strata, these were largely of local San Juan rather than Chacoan affiliation and they were from the trash. Nevertheless, as predicted, p112 was the preferred symmetry, structuring 65 percent of these designs. This same local San Juan p112 symmetry system prevailed at neighboring unit pueblo or farming villages (Wheelbarger 2005). Overall at Salmon, 56 percent of the San Juan designs were structured by this symmetry, whereas 50 percent of these designs at the nearby Mine Canyon site and 46 percent of these designs at the Tommy site were structured by p112.

In contrast, the Chacoan ceramics are characterized by a number of distinctive features that differ markedly from those that typify the local San Juan ceramic system. Chacoan patterns are predominantly two-dimensional rather than one-dimensional in layout. The most common two-dimensional symmetry in the Salmon assemblage, p2, contrasts with the prevailing use of the one-dimensional p112 symmetry on the local San Juan ceramics. These p2 patterns, as well as other two-dimensional patterns, appear on distinctive nonlocal vessel forms—cylinder jars, small shallow dishes, and sharp, narrow-shouldered pitchers (Figure 29.2). The patterns are typically arranged to cover the entire design surface of these vessels rather than being confined to a narrow band below the rim. Often the patterns are placed at an angle to the vessel rim line; in this position they appear to be abruptly truncated by the rim line rather than being parallel to the rim, like designs in the local San Juan design system. Finally, in contrast to the apparently endless variation in element elaboration on the designs made within the local p112 system, the repertoire of Chacoan patterns is very limited. Many patterns are not only produced repeatedly but also are identical to those found on the same vessel forms at other great house outliers and great house sites in Chaco Canyon.

These symmetry and pattern differences give a distinctive cast to ceramics typed as Chaco B/w and to the related hatched versions that were rendered in both carbon and mineral paint in one and two dimensions: Dogoszhi style in Arizona, Chuska types with trachyte temper from sites along the Chuska Mountains in northwestern New Mexico, and local Cibola types, such as Gallup B/w, in the Chaco Canyon area and north to sites along the San Juan. Franklin (Chapter 22) viewed many of these "intrusive" types as the result of trading contacts that decreased dramatically at the end of the Primary occupation and the collapse of the widespread Chacoan trading network of which the Salmon outlier was evidently a part. However, I believe that trade is too often used to explain the extralocal appearance of a type. Symmetry analysis suggests, alternatively, that these hatched Dogoszhi, Chuska, and other Cibola types were not trade wares, but rather represent vessels that were made specifically to be used by individuals in certain administrative positions and/or for certain special purposes at these great house outliers. Archaeologists have given them different type names according to their locale, paint, and temper characteristics, but the patterns and their symmetries among all these types are identical. This identity is emblematic of their role as visual markers of their owner's status and ties to the central Chacoan enterprise.

From a symmetry perspective, some vessels certainly were either brought from Chaco Canyon for the use of the Chacoan administrators living at Salmon, or locally made copies of patterns emblematic of the Chaco symmetry system. Paste analysis of one of these Chacoan vessels (140940; Lori Reed, personal communication) revealed sand temper, strongly suggesting that this two-dimensional patterned vessel was made in Chaco Canyon and brought to Salmon.

(a)

(b)

Figure 29.2. Examples of Chacoan p2 patterns from Pueblo Bonito: (a) a p2 pattern on cylinder jars 3229; (b) a p2 pattern on a cylinder jar 5437; (c) a p2 pattern on shallow bowl 5534.

Table 29.1 lists and Figure 29.3 illustrates the hatched designs that are clearly Chacoan in source or derivation (design 305229 is a solid copy of a hatched pgg design). Six of these designs were found in Primary or Intermediate stratigraphic contexts in storerooms (Room 31) along the original east-west axis of the pueblo, in rooms associated with the Tower Kiva (Room 81) and in plaza-facing large rooms (Rooms 102, 129). The other nine designs found in Secondary or unknown strata were assigned to the Chacoan occupation after considering their pattern symmetry, vessel form and design, and specific strata affiliation. For example, 306793, found in a questionable Secondary stratum, has a pattern that is not only organized by a Chacoan symmetry (pgg) but is also identical to the pattern on 75415, which was found in a Primary stratigraphic context. The difference between the two patterns lies only in the number of hatched triangles at the end of the motif units. It is significant that this pgg pattern is identical to the designs found on Pueblo Bonito vessels 336123 from Room 225, 336169 and 336178 from Room 266, 336208 from Room 309, and cylinder jar 336496 from Room 329. The same pattern was also found on vessel 334614 from Room 15 at Pueblo Del Arroyo and on vessel 810 from Aztec Ruins. According to symmetry analysis, therefore, certain vessels found in Secondary strata can be assigned to the Chaco design system because their designs are structured by the same nonlocal symmetries and placed on the same nonlocal vessel forms as those from Primary strata that are found on the same vessel forms with the same patterns and symmetries that were found in sites from Chaco Canyon. It is interesting that these same motifs are frequently rearranged into p2 structured patterns, as on vessels 3392 from Room 28, 4981 from Room 62, and 5534 from Room 45—all special rooms in Bonito.

The hatched pgg pattern on 306793 has been copied in a solid version on vessel 305229 from Room 102. At nearby Aztec Ruins, vessels 2320 and 6984 display the same solid version of this pattern, although the latter copy is irregular. Sloppy execution, mistakes in copying the symmetry, and variations in motif shape are characteristic of copies. For example, the p2 pattern found on vessel 74196,

Table 29.1. Chacoan ceramics from Salmon.

Room	Catalog	Ceramic Type	Form	Symmetry	Stratum	Affiliation
4A or 4B	PO 441255	Chuska or Chaco McElmo B/w	Bowl	P112	B-1-2	Post-Secondary
31W	PO 140940	Chaco B/w	Bowl	P2	L-2-10	Primary
37W	PO 318746	Chaco B/w	Bowl	Pmm2	C-2-8	Secondary
43W	PO 426982	Chuska B/w	Bowl	Pmm2	S-2-6.6	Secondary
81W	RK 74196	Chuska B/w	Canteen	P2	C-6-11	Primary
81W	RK 75415	Chuska B/w	Pitcher	Pgg	F-2-13	Primary
93W	PO 308929	Chuska B/w	Bowl	P112	F-1-10	Secondary
97W	PO 306793	Chuska B/w	Bowl	Pgg	N-1-3	Mixed Primary and Secondary?
98W	PO 143274	Chaco B/w	Pitcher	P111	B-1-2, E-1-3	Secondary
102A	PO 305229	Mesa Verde? B/w	Bowl	Pgg	C-2-4	Secondary
102B	PO 401557	Chaco B/w	Bowl	P2	B-1-2, C-1-3	Secondary
102C	RK 73734	Chaco B/w	Bowl	P111	C-2-24	Primary
129W	RK 78185	McElmo B/w	Jar	Pm11	C-88-99	Primary

typed as Chuska B/w and painted in carbon paint, appears to be a sloppy version of the very neatly drawn, mineral-painted, and heavily outlined patterns on vessels from Salmon typed as Chaco B/w (see Figures 5.3–5.5 in the 1980 report, volume II). Indeed, the fact that the hooked units on 74196 vary in the number of turns suggests that these carbon-painted versions may be local efforts to copy the nonlocal Chacoan design system.

The p2 pattern found on vessel 140940, which has nonlocal sand temper, is a very typical Chacoan system pattern not only in its two-dimensional symmetry but also in its overall layout, which is truncated by the vessel rim edge. The entire interior of this small shallow bowl is covered with the pattern; no banding line contains the pattern within a design field. Again, this identical pattern is found on vessels from special rooms in Pueblo Bonito: 336496 from Room 329, 336499 from Room 330, and cylinder jars 3414, 3263, and 3229 from Room 28. Similarly truncated patterns are found on identically shaped small shallow bowls from Rooms 28, 62, 266, 320, 326, and 330 in Pueblo Bonito.

It is important to emphasize the fact that it is not the hatching per se that marks them as nonlocal designs because there are many hatched designs on the earlier local types, such as Mancos B/w to the Gallup B/w and Dogoszhi B/w types that were contemporaneous with Chaco B/w. The critical difference here is that the hatched designs made and used by the local San Juan populations, whatever their type designation, are efforts to copy patterns in the Chacoan system, except that they are structured by symmetries from the local design system. That is, they are one-dimensional versions of patterns structured by two-dimensional symmetries. Thus, a p2 pattern characteristic of the Chacoan system is rendered by local potters in its one-dimensional version as a p112 band design. To illustrate this process, examine the three two-dimensional patterns structured by the typical Chacoan symmetry p2 as seen on 140940, 74196, and 401557 in Figure 29.3. Although according to motif they are three different designs, they are all structured by p2 symmetry. Two of these two-dimensional designs (74196, 401557) are constructed of multiple one-dimensional bands—in this case two horizontal rows of interlocking units—that can be separated to create two one-dimensional p112 bands.

Unfortunately, the small sample from Salmon does not include examples of how the Chacoan two-dimensional patterns were copied by local potters as one-dimensional versions. The sample does include, however, an example of a different one-dimensional hatched p112 design, a typical Dogoszhi style running curvilinear design on a bowl rim sherd (308929) found on a Secondary roof from Room 93. The fact that the design was painted with carbon-based paint suggests that it was a local product of San Juan or Chuska potters, since it is a copy of identical mineral-painted designs found in Room 323 (336255) and Room 312 (336400) at Pueblo Bonito. This same recasting of the Chacoan two-dimensional symmetries into one-dimensional band designs that conform to the local system is also found in the ceramic assemblages at the small unit pueblo sites known as

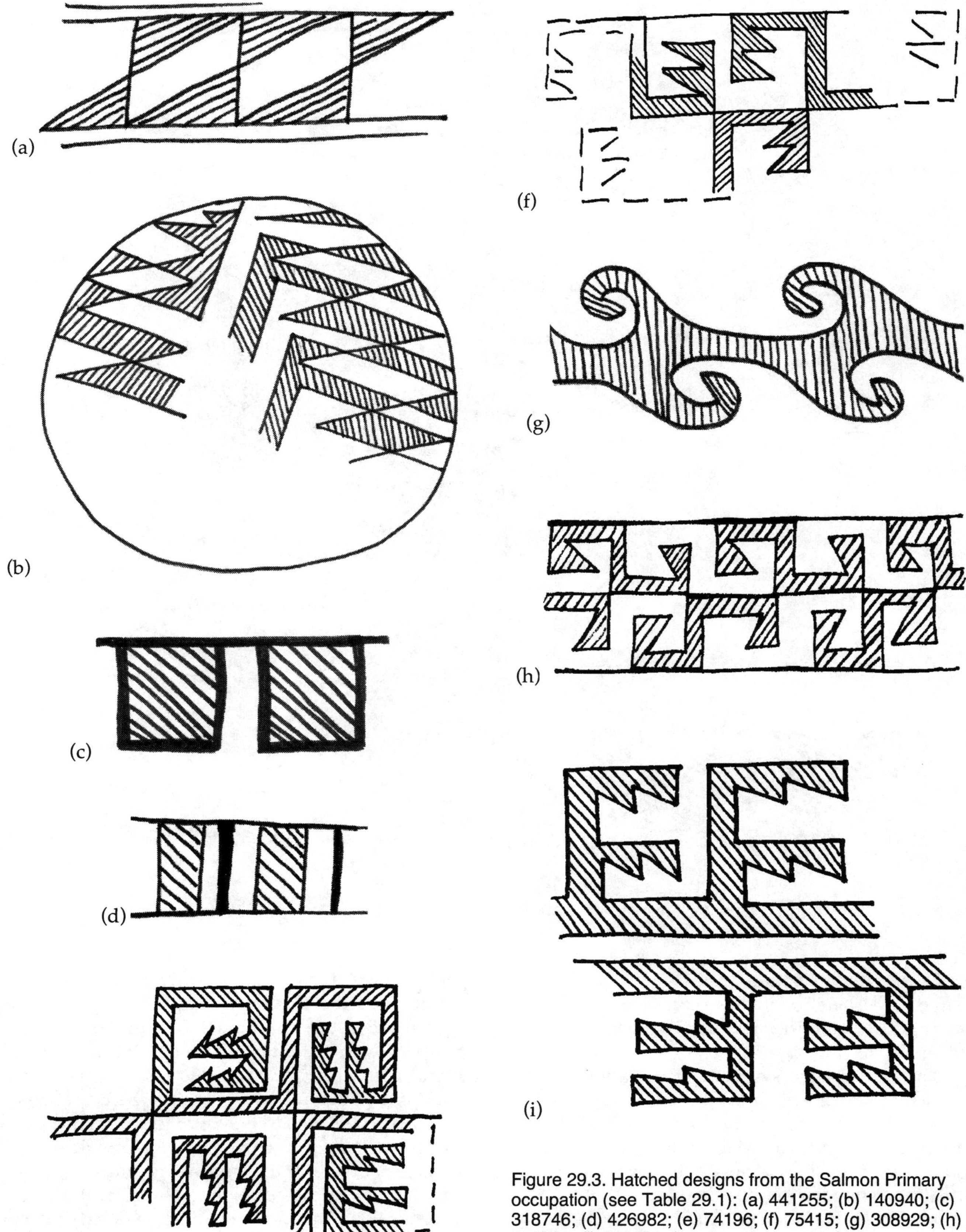

Figure 29.3. Hatched designs from the Salmon Primary occupation (see Table 29.1): (a) 441255; (b) 140940; (c) 318746; (d) 426982; (e) 74196; (f) 75415; (g) 308929; (h) 306793; (i) 143274 (continued next page)

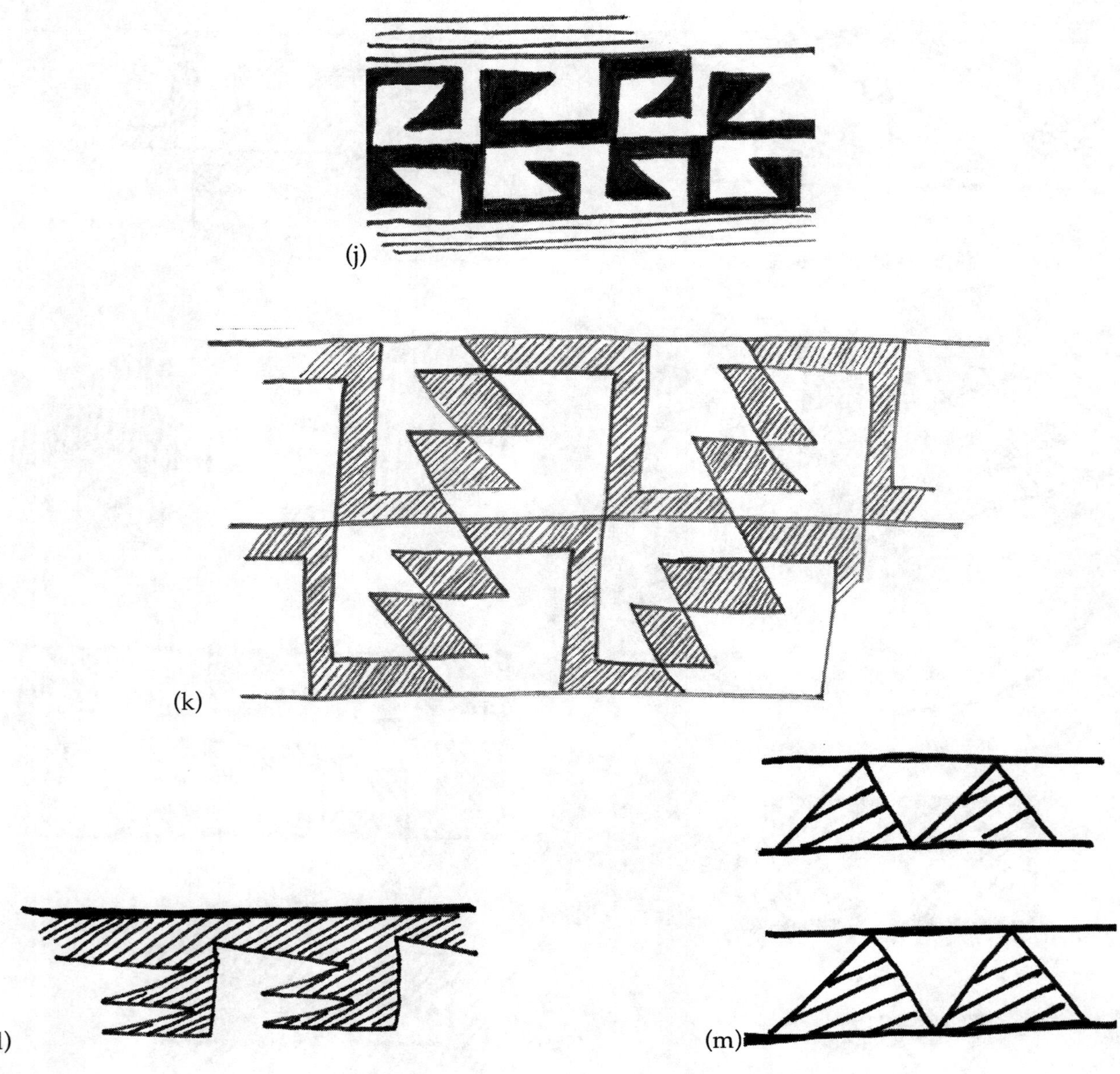

Figure 29.3 (continued): (j) 305229; (k) 401557; (l) 73724; (m) 781185

the BC sites on the south side of the wash in Chaco Canyon. It also undoubtedly occurs at all other great house outliers and the surrounding contemporaneous small sites.

The very limited symmetry and pattern repertoire that characterizes the Chacoan ceramics suggests that they were produced by "specialists" in Chaco, or at least by a group of potters assigned to produce specific kinds of vessels for specialized uses by a limited number of individuals. Costin (1991) has compiled a useful list of criteria that describe motor patterns of line work, technical aspects, and raw material similarities that mark the work of craft specialists. Although these criteria could well be studied for the Chacoan vessels, I suggest that specialization can also be detected in the recurrent production of identical patterns with identical symmetries on identical vessel forms. Costin cites the Inka style pottery as one example where specialists attached to the royal house produced highly standardized ceramics for the ruling class. Likewise, I suggest that the application of a limited pattern repertoire to special vessel forms—e.g., cylinder jars, small shallow dishes, and sharp-shouldered pitchers that were used at the Chacoan great houses—is a similar situation.

In addition to this distinction between the two-dimensional Chacoan design system with symmetries such as pgg, pmg, p2, and p1, and the local one-dimensional counterparts, i.e., with symmetries p1a1, pma2, p112, and p111, the Chacoan design system is also characterized by many hatched designs that, when reduced to a band design, can only be repeated by translation. For example, the two translated hatched design bands on a neck fragment from the sharp-shouldered pitcher (143274) are repeated by translation, rather than being related in bifold rotation, because they are not the same size nor are they positioned equally beneath one another, there being more repeats of band B than band A. The pattern on bowl 73734, found in a Primary stratum in Room 102, has hatched triangles hanging from a rim in translation. Finally, there are designs composed of vertically oriented hatched panels, as exemplified by vessels 318746 and 426982. Although these examples were found in Secondary strata, they are identical to designs found on special vessel forms at Chaco, such as on the cylinder jar 5-2049 and on the sharp-shouldered pitcher 5-3022, both from Room 33, Pueblo Bonito, as well as on the cylinder jar (334575) from Pueblo Del Arroyo.

In sum, symmetry analysis has revealed the presence of a ceramic design system during the Primary occupation at Salmon whose distinctive structuring of hatched designs on nonlocal vessel forms is identical to that in Chaco Canyon. Although the sample of Chacoan assemblage vessels from Salmon is very small, there are sufficient examples with patterns and symmetries identical to those on ceramics from Chaco to argue for a direct tie between outlier sites such as Salmon and the main sites in Chaco Canyon, especially Pueblo Bonito. Although no cylinder vessels have been found at Salmon, the absence of this form should not be used as evidence that cylinder jars were not used. There is evidence at Salmon for the other special Chacoan vessel forms—sharp-shouldered pitchers (143274) and the small shallow bowls (140940).

It could be argued from typological differences or by simply separating the solid from the hatched designs that there were both local and foreign populations at Salmon. However, such analyses do not account for the fact that the local one-dimensional hatched copies were derived from the imported two-dimensional originals. This distinction suggests that the special vessel forms with two-dimensional patterns were used by individuals to mark their status or role as administrators and their authority to exert some kind of control over the local population. The local potters, who may have been directed to make these special forms, also made and used hatched copies in the local one-dimensional format. This appears to have been the case at other great house outliers as well, suggesting a distinctive, well-defined ceramic design system peculiar to the great house community in Chaco Canyon that was replicated at outlying communities for the use of a small resident population of individuals sent from Chaco as administrators who were directing or controlling local activities.

In short, highlighting the contrast between the core Chaco system (characterized by a specific and limited repertoire of two-dimensional patterns) and the local San Juan system (characterized by highly varied one-dimensional designs) sharpens our understanding of the nature of the Chacoan presence. That is, the appearance of identical designs on identical vessel forms at both the Chaco great houses and great house outliers indicates a direct link between the great house outliers and the great houses in Chaco Canyon as well as the use of these distinctive forms by special individuals in some functional capacity other than everyday eating and storage. It suggests that local San Juan settlements all around the San Juan Basin were dominated for a time by a group from Chaco Canyon who directed the building of great houses, each of which housed administrators whose positions were marked by ceramics identical in vessel form, symmetry, and pattern to those in Chaco Canyon, especially at Pueblo Bonito. I believe that these two-dimensional design symmetries and the unusual vessel shapes on which they are found—shallow bowls, cylinder jars, and other effigy forms—mark a deliberate incursion of people from the south.

This phenomenon of populations moving north was not limited to their presence in Chaco Canyon. Indeed they appeared much earlier along the Gila and Salt Rivers in southern Arizona, where they crystallized into a population with an irrigation tradition that archaeologists have labeled Hohokam. Pulses of northward movements occurred again in Pueblo IV times, as populations with distinctive religious imagery and practices moved north along the Rio Grande, establishing settlements at Kuaua and Pottery Mound, before they moved west to establish settlements at Hawikuh, Kechipauan, and other sites along the Zuni River, and still farther west on the Hopi mesas at Awa'tovi, Sikyatki, Kawaika'a, and other sites.

The phenomenon of migration has occurred throughout the long trajectory of Southwestern prehistory as community segments or family groups budded off from communities with insufficient land to support growing populations. However, it appears from the distinctive differences in design structure systems that the Chacoan phenomenon does not represent a simple process of segmentation. Rather, it appears to represent an incursion of groups with a different culture bearing a different political and economic agenda. The Chacoan ceramics are a highly homogeneous assemblage with a very restricted pattern and symmetry repertoire applied to a limited number of vessel forms that are not everyday eating and storage containers. The marked difference in this assemblage from that in use by local San Juan residents leads me to reject the explanation that the "Chaco phenomenon" simply represents a movement and aggregation of agricultural peoples from Chaco to the San Juan. The architecture and the artifact assemblage differ markedly from situations where family groups of migrants bud off and move into another area to settle and ultimately blend into the existing population, as is the pattern recorded in Hopi oral tradition.

In fact, the period 1000–1150, which witnessed the construction of the extensive system of Chacoan great houses, was a time of favorable conditions for settlement expansion: aggrading floodplains, rising water tables, and sufficient precipitation for dry farming would have created the conditions not only for the expansion of local San Juan farming communities but also for any extraregional exploratory or expansionary movements. By correlating evidence from hydrology, palynology, geology, and dendrochronology, Dean (1988:31) and Van West and Dean (2000:35–37) found that the long-term environmental changes that required major adaptive response from human populations—i.e., migration out of such regions—did not begin before the onset of the 50-year drought at 1130–1180, that is, after most of the great houses were built.

There is evidence of prevailing aridity over the West between 900 and 1300 (Cook et al. 2004), but these conditions may have only been local and short term (cf. Dean 1988), and populations could have responded with expanded wild food gathering or increased diversification by farming in different microzones. It appears that the grand plans of the Chacoans were fatally truncated by the classic lag in human perception of and response to conditions of increasing aridity because the conditions must have varied enough from year to year to allow populations to "hang on" until the persistent drought conditions beginning c. 1130 made it clear that dry farming was doomed. In this way, the Chacoans who began building Salmon in AD 1088 or other outliers for that matter (cf. the great houses along the La Plata; Dykeman and Langenfeld 1987) were only able to establish the infrastructure when the drought intensified and curtailed whatever exploitative or extractive activities they may have planned. Although some researchers have suggested that the Chacoans did respond by moving their system to Aztec, near a permanently flowing stream, this large complex too was ultimately defeated by environmental degradation.

Archaeologists can chart the human response to this adverse mid-twelfth-century climatic shift with the cessation of building by AD 1150 in Chaco Canyon followed by site abandonment in the surrounding regions. Indeed within only a few decades, the vast network of administrative outposts that were built around the San Juan Basin in the late eleventh century, which appear to have followed the establishment of the center in Chaco Canyon, slowly had their activities curtailed, as evidenced by sealed doorways and trash-filled rooms, until they eventually were abandoned.

At Salmon, a number of Primary rooms (81, 83, 84, 91, and 129) that were excavated to floors were apparently abandoned during the period of the Primary occupation, suggesting that activities at the site were being curtailed prior to abandonment. For example, Room 129,which had a T-door and large fire pits and was actively used for a number of Chacoan living activities, was abandoned and filled with trash before the end of the Primary occupation. In addition, many of the doors in two-story storage rooms were sealed as they were abandoned and filled with trash during the Primary occupation, indicating a restricting of access and/or closure of sections of the pueblo as the Chacoan operation was scaled down in the face of adverse conditions.

The ultimate purpose of Chaco and these outliers is unclear; many have never been investigated beyond surveys and surface collections, which link them to the road system and ultimately to Chaco Canyon itself. Some evidence that the storerooms (cf. Room 30W; Doebley and Bohrer 1980; K. Adams 2005) at Salmon may have been built to store quantities of corn for later shipment to Chaco Canyon suggests that outliers along well-watered floodplains were built to produce food for the administrative center in Chaco Canyon. In fact, the corn found stored in these rooms is a hard flint variety that would have been best processed on trough metates, such as those found in the multiple bins in Rooms 82, 93, 97, and 129, which could have served work groups. The Hopi today store corn on the cob stacked against the walls in rooms and grind it only when needed for food or ceremonial use; it may be that, for reasons of transport efficiency, corn was ground to meal before it was transported the c. 50 miles south to Chaco Canyon. Notably, trough metates were typical of the Hohokam, whereas slab metates prevailed among the San Juan Anasazi; this evidence parallels the similarity of the Chaco and Hohokam two-dimensional p2 and pgg design structure system.

Paul Reed (2004, 2005) has suggested that at Salmon the presence of grinding bins, hearths, and storage pits indicates that people lived in these large rooms, a conclusion contrary to that of other archaeologists who see little evidence of habitation refuse or features in many Chaco great house sites. But this view of Chacoan sites as periodic ceremonial centers may be a factor of site size and may pertain only to the sites in Chaco Canyon proper. Small outliers such as Guadalupe may have functioned as lower level guard outposts that were not designed for occupation, whereas larger outposts such as Salmon may have been inhabited by individuals from Chaco Canyon who were sent to organize the building of the site and then oversee the regional activities under its control. After all, *someone* had to be on-site directing this massive preplanned building program given that there is no precedent at local sites for this kind of cored masonry engineering and architectural layout of plaza-facing T-door rooms backed by connected suites of smaller rooms. In short, archaeologists are left with a degree of identity in architecture and specialized artifactual evidence that indicates that these Chaco-affiliated sites represent some kind of planned and centrally directed politically and/or economically motivated activities. The symmetry analysis presented in this paper indicates that the Chacoan footprint differs markedly from the population aggregation and site enlargement activities that occurred in other areas of the Southwest in response to changing environmental conditions.

A model for such center/outpost hegemonic activity can be found in the relationship between the Incan rulers in their capital at Cuzco and the outposts they established in each of their conquered territories. The outposts included specially constructed architectural complexes built for the administrators who directed the activities in each conquered state. Ceramics used by the rulers at the capital in Cuzco as well as by the administrators of the outposts throughout the empire were unique vessel forms with standardized decorative patterns that were distinctively different from any local wares. They visually marked the presence of the ruler and the authority of his rule throughout the empire in the guise of local Incan administrators. Schreiber (1987) has noted how the grafting of these Incan administrators onto existing local valley systems enabled Cuzco to exert control over vast and distant regions.

A symmetry analysis of the ceramic designs produced before, during, and after the Inca occupation from one of these conquered states, the Ica Valley, revealed that Cuzco ceramics and their copies, found only in the administrative buildings in these outlying posts, were distinctively different from the local design system that existed prior to Inca control and that was reactivated after the disintegration of the Empire. The rest of the site was dominated by ceramics made by the local populace in their local tradition for their own use (Washburn 2004). That is, although the Inca physically occupied and politically controlled many aspects of life in the Ica valley by extracting tribute in the form of textiles (Morris 1982:167) and *mit'a* labor from the local populations, the local culture, as marked by the continuity in the pattern symmetries on the local ceramics, continued unchanged. This superficial political and economic control allowed continuity in the local design system, which has also been observed in studies of other kinds of artifactual evidence (Conrad 1977; Morris and Thompson 1985).

Indeed, this model of superficial control and economic exploitation might be worthy of further examination as we attempt to understand the Chaco phenomenon. Notable is the extensive Inca road network (Hyslop 1984) that was used to unite the empire, along which are not only major centers but also *tampu*, places of local administration as well as lodgings and storage facilities for travelers and laborers built a day's walk apart. Perhaps some of the Chacoan outliers and other smaller sites with distinctly Chacoan architecture were part of such a network.

Salmon's Secondary Occupation

Symmetry analysis indicates that what has been labeled the Secondary occupation—thirteenth-century remodeling and building activities of people using ceramics typical of the Mesa Verde area—represents, for the most part, a continuation of the same kinds of village organization and farming activities by the local San Juan farmers that occurred during the Primary period, although perhaps in larger communities. For this reason I have combined the ceramics from the purported Intermediate period that was said to represent continued occupation of the site between the Primary and Secondary occupations with the ceramics made by the later populations moving in from the Mesa Verde area. It should be noted, however, that because I assigned the ceramics to occupation periods based on their stratigraphic provenience, ceramics typed as McElmo B/w are found in both the Primary and Secondary occupations.

Although the Intermediate and Secondary ceramics display the same prevailing symmetry, and by inference, cultural orientation, at the same time, symmetry analysis of this body of design has revealed new symmetries presumably carried by the in-migration of new groups. The Hopi model of migration and settlement is a useful and probably accurate guide to understanding the presence of different symmetries. Hopi oral tradition records many movements and temporary settlements from many different directions of small groups as they made their way to join the villages on the Hopi mesas. The first groups to arrive farmed the best lands and set up a calendar of rituals that supported a life of hand-cultivated corn agriculture as offered by Maasaw. Later arriving groups who requested acceptance into these original villages were required to contribute an efficacious ceremony to gain admittance. Groups that were rejected often established temporary villages on the outskirts, hoping their petition to join the village would eventually be accepted.

This pattern is marked archaeologically by a number of sites in the area around an established community. Their ceramic assemblages often differ from those of the village they wished to join as each encapsulated the different ritual content that was being proffered. As new societies and the ceremonies they owned were accepted into the community, new kivas were built to accommodate their ritual activities. From this perspective one possible explanation for the more than 20 small Mesa Verde "keyhole" kivas that were built during the Secondary occupation at Salmon is that each represents the presence of different societies and/or in-migrating groups. Because we have learned much about ritual beliefs and practices from examining the elaborate murals at the Hopi sites of Awa'tovi and Kawaika'a (Sekaquaptewa and Washburn 2004), the content of the mural designs on the walls of kivas in Rooms 121 and 124 should be further explored to determine the nature of the ideologies represented at Salmon.

There may be some merit to separating the ceramics of the local San Juan populations who lived at and around Salmon throughout the earlier occupation of the site from the later San Juan populations who apparently came from Mesa Verde. In doing so we can more clearly define, by the appearance of new symmetries, the arrival of new groups with new cosmologies and associated rituals and ceremonies. Thus, although the majority (51%) of the classic banded designs with the series of thick and thin framing lines that characterize Mesa Verde B/w ceramics from the Secondary occupation display the p112 symmetry that characterizes the general San Juan area lifeway (Figure 29.4), the appearance of several other new symmetries suggests that other groups were continuing to move into the area during this final occupation period.

In his study of San Juan white ware, Franklin (Chapter 25) noted the presence of a new design layout—what he called "allover" designs—that corresponded to the "other major style in Mesa Verde B/w." He did not, however, see a precursor for this design system in earlier San Juan types. Presumably, this layout corresponds to the finite C1, C2, and C4 spirals and D1, D2, and D4 reflected motifs that cover the center bottoms of bowl interiors that did, in fact, appear only in the later Secondary context (Figure 29.5). Symmetry analysis suggests that the "sudden" appearance of this new "style" may be indicative of the arrival of new beliefs and accompanying social institutions that came with in-migrating groups, or at least the arrival of people with a different way of representing concepts. The cyclic interlocking layout is substantially different in its metaphorical implications from the dihedral dualistic layout and these, in turn, are different from the one-dimensional band layout of the local San Juan system.

The new pattern system introduced during this later occupation appears in a banded format as the symmetry p1a1. Prior to this time, this symmetry structured only 1.2 percent of the local San Juan designs, specifically one composed of a banded pma2 zigzag structure filled with series of alternating lines (Figure 29.6a). However, during the Secondary occupation, the use of this structure increased dramatically to 12 percent of all designs and specifically to 15 percent of the designs on the late ceramics framed by distinctive series of banding lines typed as Mesa Verde B/w. Moreover, one motif combination in particular, bifold opposed stepped units (Figure 29.6b), appears on 65.5 percent of these p1a1 designs. The next most frequent p1a1 motif configuration is one of dotted triangles (Figure 29.6c). The repetitive use of this pattern recalls the same situation found on Chacoan system ceramics. Given that these late Secondary sites were larger than the earlier unit pueblo communities, this standardization of pattern suggests an accompanying shift in work roles toward, at the least, a production situation in which the most accomplished potters and painters were making most of the wares. However, since they were

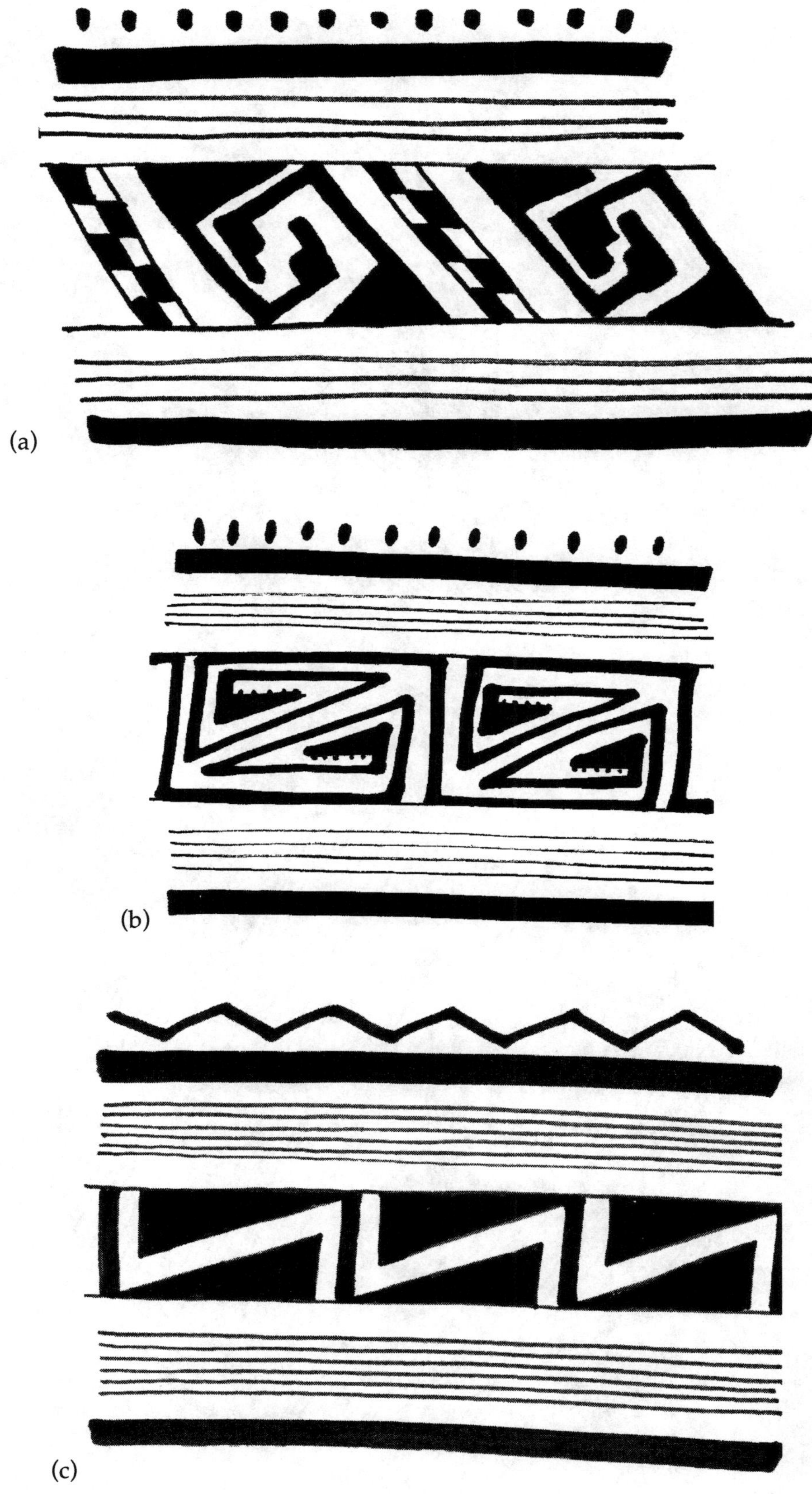

Figure 29.4. Examples of Mesa Verde B/w designs structured by p112: 132758, 218892, and 236461.

(a)

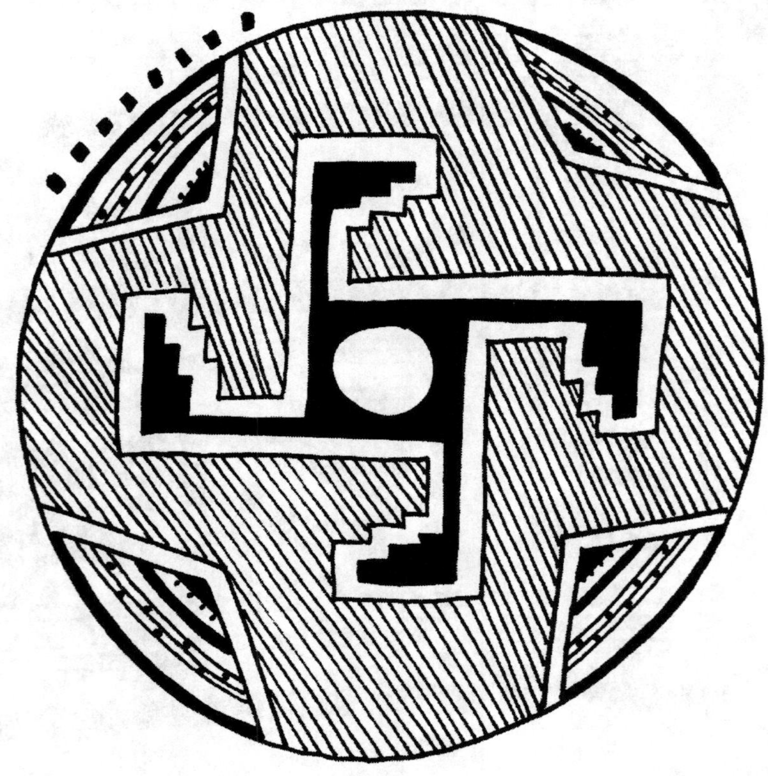

(b)

Figure 29.5. Examples of finite designs introduced during the Secondary occupation: (a) C2 on 229074; (b) C4 on 313500.

(a)

(b)

(c)

Figure 29.6. Examples of p1a1 designs: (a) 408980, (b) 113584, (c) 122121.

found on everyday wares, not on special vessel forms as they were at Chaco, they probably were not special purpose wares made for a limited audience.

The important fact is that p1a1, glide reflection, is a distinctively non-Anasazi design structure that, in this one-dimensional format, as in the two-dimensional pgg format, was used to structure patterns on many earlier Chacoan special vessel forms as well as on earlier Hohokam vessels. I have long suggested that the Chacoan system as evidenced by the two-dimensional design symmetries on the cylinder jars was influenced by Mesoamerican activity (Washburn 1980). Zaslow has clearly demonstrated this link, showing how this glide reflection layout describes one and two-dimensional designs on Oaxacan, Hohokam, and Upper Gila ceramics (1977, 1981). Figure 29.7 shows how a typical Hohokam pgg pattern layout became truncated in the San Juan Basin to produce p1a1 designs that are placed within banding lines. Supporting this Hohokam source and thus the southwest to northeast direction of movement is the falloff in frequency of its appearance at sites with increasing distance from its source. For example, it structures 17 percent of the designs at Aztec and 11 percent at Salmon along the San Juan, but only 6 percent of the designs at Mug House and 4 percent of the designs from Long House farther to the north and east on the Mesa Verde.

Changes in use of certain symmetries can be useful indicators of changing importance for the ideas they metaphorically represent. This is the case with the pma2 symmetry (Figure 29.8), which describes the structuring of interlocking rows of triangles or, in the negative space between, a zigzag. Rows of pendant triangles and the zigzag, found on the earliest Anasazi ceramics designs, are ancient image metaphors for rain and lightning, which were the lifeline for these small agricultural communities. At Salmon this structure increased from 3.5 percent during the Primary occupation to 11 percent during the Secondary occupation, a sign that increasing concerns with rain prompted increased depiction of these concerns on their ceramics.

With the exception of the incursion of the Chacoan system during the Primary period of occupation at Salmon, symmetry analysis indicates that the small-scale dry farming unit pueblo community model encapsulated by the p112 design structure prevailed over much of the San Juan Basin into the thirteenth century, when the cumulative effects of drought and resource stress led to widespread abandonment of the region. Even as more people were moving to permanent water courses, such as along the San Juan River, the inhabitants at Salmon apparently continued to pursue the existing subsistence strategy, as suggested by continuity in the prevalence of the p112 design system during this "Secondary" occupation period, even as the evidence of an increase in the use of wild plants and animals during this later period suggests that the population was beginning to take steps to supplement their corn-based lifeway (K. Adams 2005; Durand and Durand 2005). Indeed, this move to a more diversified subsistence base was similar to the Hopi strategy in which various food sources and mini environments were exploited in an effort to maintain their dry farming corn agriculture lifeway and supporting belief rituals.

If this reconstruction describes the situation during the late Secondary period, then we should see a continuation of the prevailing p112 patterns and the principal organizing principles they metaphorically represent with the addition of new symmetries, such as p1a1, that mark new rituals and ideas brought by other groups moving into the area. Again, Hopi oral tradition offers some guidance. The present-day Hopi village composition is a snapshot of the slow process of aggregation that occurred over centuries as groups, desiring to move to the area, petitioned to join a village. The diversity of practices depicted in Pueblo IV kiva murals and ceramic designs during the fourteenth to sixteenth centuries suggests that a number of different ritual societies moved to the Hopi mesas. The fact that Hopis today have difficulty "reading" some of the murals suggests that some of these practices and rituals are no longer practiced.

INTRASITE ARCHITECTURAL AND ACTIVITY ASSEMBLAGE

One of the benefits of a large sample is the opportunity it gives to examine specific intrasite assemblages, such as those from floors, roofs, and burials, as well as from special types of rooms, such as room suites, storage rooms, and special purpose rooms such as those associated with the Tower Kiva. If prevalence in design structure on ceramics from a given site is indicative of a community unified in worldview and social practices, then we can postulate that a prevailing ceramic symmetry at Salmon during the Secondary occupation suggests the sharing of beliefs and practices by all community members. Specifically if we find that the p112 system prevailed at Salmon during the Secondary period, we should not expect to find any intrasite dichotomies or differences in functional assemblages. To test this proposition, I examined assemblages from roofs

Figure 29.7. Two-dimensional pgg pattern, (a) truncated to become a one-dimensional p1a1 design and (b) after Zaslow (1977: Figure 4a, b).

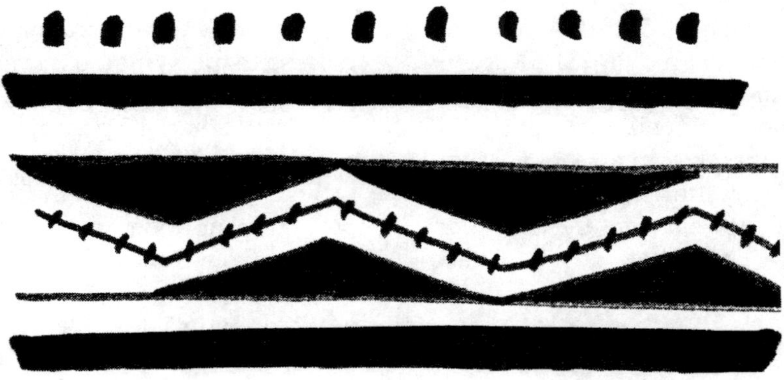

Figure 29.8. Pma2 symmetry as a metaphor of lightning and rain on Salmon vessel 221288.

and burials (floor assemblages in my sample were too small) as well as material from the plaza area, and from storage rooms along the back wall, rooms associated with the Tower Kiva, and kivas and rooms in the East Wing.

It should be noted that although the roof and burial associations are arguably reliable indicators of actual past activity associations, materials found in B and C trash strata, even those carefully excavated as separate episodes of discard, represent materials from unknown original locations and associations. In fact, the stratified trash excavated in Primary rooms from different areas and functional room types (i.e., Southeast Wing rooms, plaza tests, back storage rooms, and Tower Kiva associated rooms) contained Secondary trash. Thus, although this trash does not shed light on Primary activities in those rooms, the stratified sequences did reconfirm that there was no significant difference in use of the p112 symmetry throughout the site ($\chi^2 = 9.76$ with 10df).

Habitation Room Associations

The only room associations for the Primary period that could be examined by symmetry analysis were from the two front gallery rooms, 93 and 102 (originally one long room, but subsequently subdivided c. AD 1116). They appear to have been living rooms. Room 93 had hearths on every floor, with multiple hearths in the lower Primary floors and an especially large hearth on the lowest Primary floor. Both rooms yielded high percentages of corrugated cooking ware and Cibola pottery. The symmetry sample from the Primary period is represented by a hatched Chuska B/w bowl from Room 93 and two Chaco B/w bowls and one solid motif two-dimensional pgg patterned bowl from Room 102. Although they were found on a roof, in trash, and in a mixed stratum, I think they represent the vessels used by the Chacoan occupants. The rooms with trough milling stones, Rooms 82, 93, 97, and 129, likewise produced a high percentage of Cibola white ware intrusive sherds, according to Franklin. The Room 97 assemblage has a pgg patterned Chuska B/w bowl and Room 129 has a Chuska B/w jar with two pm11 bands of design—a symmetry that is never very frequent on San Juan wares. In short, a symmetry analysis of even the few vessels from these Primary rooms supports the presence of activity by Chaco-affiliated individuals.

Burial Associations

Seven burials, one with vessels displaying more than 13 designs, were analyzed for symmetry. In Room 33B, a multiple burial (Feature 33B-1) with three juveniles contained vessels and designs from the later phases of the San Juan tradition. The designs are painted in carbon paint and the rims, even on the St. Johns Polychrome bowl, are ticked. Two of the bowls have stepped units arranged in the Hohokam-like p1a1 symmetry; 101316 has this design on both the interior and exterior of the bowl. The same symmetry is present in the design on the exterior of bowl 101318, the interior of which has a p112 design, but it is irregularly executed as if the painter was not certain how to combine the motifs to render this symmetry. The ladle has a poorly executed p112 design on the interior, but six carefully drawn birds or animals around the exterior below the rim. The mug is a classic Mesa Verde mug in shape and displays a common checkerboard pattern.

The richest burial, with 13 designs on 9 vessels, was found in Room 127. Again, all were in the San Juan tradition found in a Secondary context. The nonindigenous p1a1 symmetry was used to structure the designs on three bowls. On one bowl this symmetry structured both the interior and exterior design; on another the exterior design was a series of three birds; and on the third a series of zigzags, classic signs of lightning, encircled the exterior of the bowl. Another bowl had a checkerboard pattern, a mug had a hatched and solid p112 pattern, and a ladle had a C4 pattern in the center. A pitcher, a canteen with hanging loops, and a bowl completed the ensemble, each displaying p112 structured patterns. Although the vessels in these two burials displayed a variety of design structures (cf. p1a1 and C4), ethnographic accounts of burials suggest that individuals are buried promptly with whatever vessels are at hand so that the assemblage of locally made vessels might reasonably be augmented, if necessary, by imports, trade wares, or heirlooms.

Roof Associations

Twelve roof assemblages were analyzed to determine whether such small assemblages could represent the symmetry system that characterized the entire site during the Secondary occupation. Taken together, 47 percent of the designs from all roof-associated vessels were structured by p112; this includes 47.5 percent of the vessels from Room 37, 59 percent from Room 98, 37 percent from Room 67, 50 percent from Room 127, and 59 percent from Room 129. It should be noted that a Primary Chacoan roof on Room 98 was used by the Secondary occupants, as evidenced by a group of 19 mugs, 2 pitchers, and 1 bowl. The designs on these vessels were structured by seven different symmetries, although p112 predominated at 59 percent. Clearly the symmetry frequencies in these groups of vessels mirror the popularity of p112, which characterizes the San Juan occupation throughout the entire site. Chi square analysis (2.98 at 11df, significant at the .99 level) confirms that there was no significant difference among the different roof assemblages in preference for the prevailing use of p112 symmetry on the roofs of these rooms from all areas of the site.

Plaza Associations

While searching for an undisturbed trash midden that would yield a chronological sequence for the site, Franklin studied ceramic profiles from a number of test trenches in the plaza. No undisturbed middens were located, but from a study of 3920 sherds from 2 m of trash in trench 13P he was able to confirm the general Cibola to San Juan sequence observed in other areas of the site. In the Salmon symmetry database 83 designs were recorded from 9 localities in the plaza—all designs were from Secondary strata. Most of the samples were too small for analysis, undoubtedly because material discarded on the plaza would have subsequently been broken by everyday activity into fragments too small for symmetry analysis. The largest sample, from Test P16 (34 designs), revealed a lower than expected frequency for the prevailing p112 symmetry of only 35 percent. Indeed p112 was present in only 39 percent of the sample from all nine plaza localities combined. The other symmetry, p1a1, occurred in 12 percent frequency from all nine sample localities combined, which mirrors its 12 percent appearance overall in the Secondary occupation at Salmon. The low frequency for p112 in the plaza area may be a factor of sample size. When larger samples were examined from the stratified sequences in other localities, for example from storage Room 37, or from the rooms in the Southeast Wing or the Tower Kiva associated rooms, the frequencies of p112 rose to the typical 40–50 percent range.

CONCLUSION

During the Primary period, the local San Juan people decorated their ceramics 54 percent of the time with p112-structured designs. The preference for this symmetry continued into the Intermediate and Secondary periods, with p112 being used on 42 percent of the designs. Even with a 12 percent drop in use frequency during the Secondary period, no other symmetry comes close. This symmetry characterizes the reciprocal relationships that structure the activities of members of small communities. In contrast, the Chacoan hatched designs on the special vessel forms were predominantly structured by two-dimensional p2 and pgg symmetries. The locally produced hatched attempts to copy this intrusive design system were one-dimensional versions (p112 and p1a1 respectively) of these two-dimensional layouts.

A symmetry analysis of decorated ceramics from the Salmon site was able to clarify the distinction between the two-dimensional patterns on special vessel forms found exclusively in planned multistory great house complexes and the local one-dimensional design system found on everyday pottery found at the small unit pueblo farming villages. By documenting the nature and extent of the Chacoan phenomenon as a foreign design system, we are now able to determine more specifically the relationship of Salmon to other Chacoan outliers and to the main complex in Chaco Canyon.

The identical nature of the patterns and their symmetries on identical vessel forms found at the great house sites in Chaco and at Chacoan outliers such as Salmon and Aztec (see Washburn 2005) suggests that these special vessel forms with their limited pattern repertoires were being produced for a few individuals who held administrative positions linking the outliers to the operation center in Chaco Canyon. An extensive paste and temper analysis of these special vessels will be necessary to determine whether they were being made in Chaco Canyon and then taken to the outliers by the administrators, perhaps as visible markers of their posts, or made locally at the outliers by potters copying the few examples brought with the individuals who were sent to administer the outposts.

The identity between the vessel forms and designs from great houses in Chaco Canyon and Chacoan outliers suggests the operation of a closely linked network. Apparently these outliers were inhabited by a small group of administrators who oversaw the production of food and the procurement of other resources that were subsequently directed along the road network to the center in Chaco Canyon. By adding the new findings from this symmetry analysis of the ceramics to the well-known architectural evidence of E or D-shaped great house sites with large high-ceiling rooms, T-shaped doors, connected room suites, in-room platforms, wall niches, and association with a great kiva, we can begin to model in greater detail the nature of the linkages between Chacoan outliers and the main sites in Chaco Canyon and thus move toward an explanation of the entire Chacoan phenomenon that Cynthia recognized so long ago.

Throughout the Intermediate-Secondary period at Salmon, the design structure system was characterized by a consistent use of the same p112 symmetry that was used to decorate the local San Juan sites during the Primary occupation period. The architectural remodeling of the large Chacoan rooms into smaller specific-purpose living and activity rooms, and the addition of a number of small kivas within the main room block presumably for the use of different religious societies, suggests a marked shift in social and ritual organization. Whereas the early great kivas may have served the ritual needs of the entire community with all-inclusive ceremonies, the later building of many separate, small kivas suggests a community that developed from the joining together of many different groups who moved to the villages at different times, each bringing their own rituals. Today a network of reciprocities and obligations between different social and religious institutions operates at Hopi to knit these different groups together into a cohesive communal whole.

Symmetry analysis of the Secondary period ceramic designs reveals a steadfast adherence to a set of social and cosmological community principles that began along the San Juan before the Chacoan intrusion. Symmetry analyses of roof assemblages as well as stratified trash indicate a prevailing use of the reciprocal organizing principles. This same symmetry prevails at similar neighboring sites. Fifty percent of the designs at the Mine Canyon and Lone Kiva sites and 46 percent of the designs at the Tommy site are organized by p112. At the same time, symmetry analysis reveals the addition of new people and ideas at Salmon, exemplified by the notable increase in ceramic designs structured by p1a1. This influx of new ideas and rituals is well documented in Hopi oral tradition describing the founding and growth of the Hopi villages, whose inhabitants are thought to have descended from the Anasazi, some of whom were resident at Salmon.

Chapter 30

SALMON RESEARCH INITIATIVE: CERAMIC RESEARCH INTRODUCTION AND METHODOLOGY

by Tori L. Myers and Lori Stephens Reed

Excavations at Salmon Ruins in the 1970s produced one of the largest ceramic assemblages in the Four Corners region. Hayward Franklin directed the Salmon Ceramic Laboratory and wrote most of the final ceramic volume for the 1980 Salmon report (Franklin 1980a). Much of the original work is presented in this new report (see Chapters 18–28). For its time, the Salmon analysis was innovative, with a computerized system of data analysis, a focus on ceramic resource procurement, a method for ceramic dating of proveniences, and examination of design styles within larger typological categories (e.g., definition of subtypes of Mancos B/w).

In June 2003, a sample of 14,213 ceramics from six rooms and kivas—30, 64 (the Tower Kiva), 90, 100, 123, and 127—was selected for reanalysis as part of the new Salmon Research Initiative (Table 30.1; see P. Reed, Chapter 1). Figure 30.1 shows the distribution of these rooms across Salmon Pueblo. Room 100W, which yielded the largest sample of sherds, was a primary focus of the study, given the extent of its Chacoan occupation. Franklin and his colleagues analyzed a very large sample (ca. 250,000 sherds rough sorted) during the original project. We did not intend to reanalyze a similarly large sample of Salmon sherds. Instead, we targeted a much smaller portion of the dataset. The original concept for reanalyzing a sample of the assemblage came about as we recognized the lack of correlation between the ceramic database and the artifacts themselves. In other words, there was no physical way to track a sherd to the data or vice versa. This was true even though the original Salmon laboratory had assigned discrete numbers to almost every ceramic artifact. These Pottery Order (PO) numbers would have allowed the physical sherds to be matched with individual lines of data but the PO numbers were never put into a database. The original Salmon ceramic data, which are available in two discrete databases, thus lack the tracking features necessary to examine the ceramics from the database.

In addition to providing an analytical data set in which ceramics and data could be united, our research initiative also posed a series of ceramic-based research questions requiring several criteria. First, since the 1970s, ceramic typology and its associated chronology have gone through some changes that required reevaluation of the typeable ceramics from the site. For example, L. Reed and Goff (2003) have revised the chronological sequence for the Chuska series, moving many of the date ranges for the Chuska types later in time than had been previously proposed. Further, we wanted to identify stylistic changes in Mancos Black-on-white and the transition from Mancos to McElmo Black-on-white that might have temporal significance. With a research emphasis focused on exploring Chacoan deposits, it was important to track white ware transitions as closely as possible.

A second area of research interest was the identification of local production, particularly given the evidence for local manufacture of Cibola ceramics at the Tommy site (L. Reed 2005), a small Pueblo II–III habitation located down the San Juan River from Salmon. To accomplish this task, we needed a detailed analysis of ceramic paste and temper to compare with nonlocal Cibola ceramics. We also needed to compare crushed rock–tempered ceramics with the same local paste characteristics with nonlocal Northern San Juan ceramics. We therefore chose a sample for oxidation (refire) analysis and a smaller subsample for subsequent petrography and inductively coupled plasma arc spectrometry (ICP).

The Salmon whole vessel study and the sourcing study (oxidation, petrographic, and geochemical analyses) are ongoing research endeavors that began with this first phase of analysis involving five rooms and the Tower Kiva. The second phase of the Salmon ceramic project continues with a 2005 National Science Foundation (NSF) grant for which analysis and research have just begun, so the whole vessel and sourcing studies are not reported in this volume.

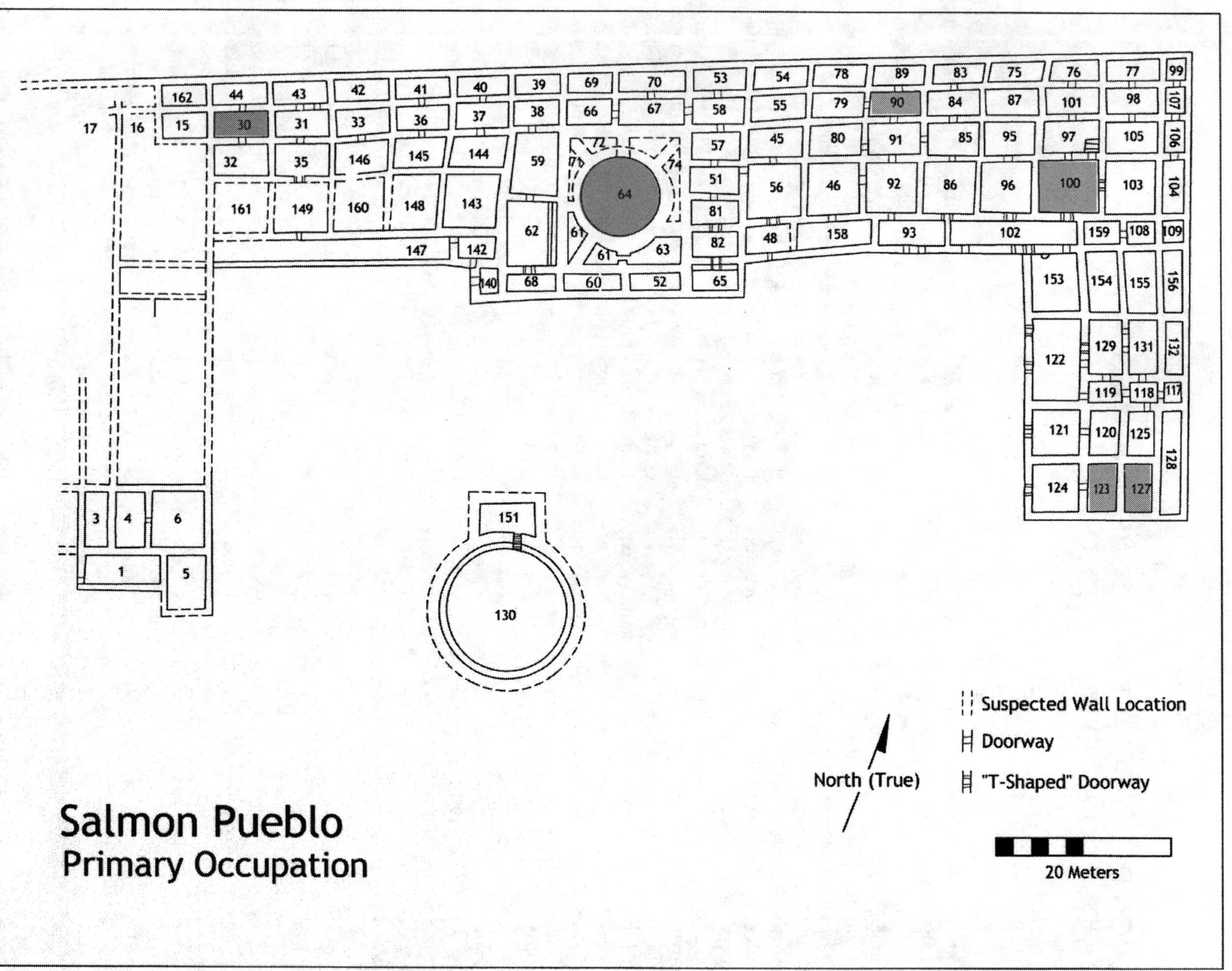

Figure 30.1. Map showing distribution of rooms sampled during new ceramic research at Salmon Pueblo.

Table 30.1. Frequencies of analyzed ceramics from Salmon rooms.

Room	Sherd Count	Percent
030A	908	6.4
030B	998	7.0
030W	1,180	8.3
064W (Tower Kiva)	431	3.0
090W	448	3.2
100W	7,161	50.4
123A	8	0.1
123B	157	1.1
123W	146	1.0
127W	2,776	19.5
Total	14,213	100.0

Completion of these reports will occur with the end of the NSF phase of the project in 2008.

Throughout this chapter and the next three (Chapters 31–33), we use several terms that need clear definition: Animas Variety, Northern San Juan Animas Variety, and Cibola Animas Variety. The macro- and microscopic attributes of local production and the need for terminology to identify these ceramics beyond broad tradition designations became clear during analysis of pottery from Salmon, Aztec (L. Reed and Myers 2006; P. Reed et al. 2005), and the Tommy Site (L. Reed 2005). Thus, Animas Variety was chosen as the variety name for ceramics produced in the Middle San Juan region, using local clays and temper resources but maintaining some attributes of the broad traditions within which the variety name is placed (e.g., Northern San Juan and Cibola). We should also note that the term Northern San Juan is interchangeable with the older typological term Mesa Verde tradition.

SAMPLING METHODOLOGY

Before beginning the analysis, a sampling methodology was designed through which ceramics from floor surfaces, deposits just above the floors, and roof-fall would be fully analyzed. In addition, trash fill and other fill deposits of interest would be sampled by analyzing only the typeable ceramics. These two approaches were used to capture the available data from Chacoan and San Juan floor assemblages and ceramics that may have been stored in roof contexts, as well as in obtaining the best assemblage from trash fill without analyzing all of the ceramics. The trash fill had been analyzed during the original project, but we were primarily interested in what the typeable ceramics therein could reveal about chronology and local versus nonlocal production. The particular strata selected for each room are presented in Chapter 32, along with ceramic assemblage discussions for each room.

Provenience and Ceramic Attribute Data

During the original Salmon excavations, Record Key (RK) numbers were assigned to individual 1 x 1 m units, feature areas, and other provenience units. These numbers were computerized and designed to track work completed at the site. RK numbers were used in many of the individual analytic databases created during the original Salmon Project. Unfortunately, a master computer index file with all the RK numbers was apparently never created. As a result, a complete RK database does not exist, severely limiting the utility of RK numbers as a tracking method.

To provide a tracking and inventory system for the Salmon Collection, Field Specimen (FS) numbers were assigned to ceramics and other artifacts from Salmon as materials were repackaged and curated (see P. Reed, Chapter 1). The FS number links each bag of ceramics from the ceramic database to the artifact catalogue and provenience database. Ceramics from each bag (FS) were sorted into lots based on individual grouping of analytical attributes (described below). The data from each lot were entered into an Access data table. Ceramic(s) representing a single lot were placed into their own 2-mil ziplock bag with an analysis tag indicating FS, Lot, and Ceramic Type. If a sherd was selected for oxidation analysis or other special analysis, the sherd was assigned a Cat (Catalogue) number in the database and on the analysis tag. A fragment was then taken from the sherd for special analysis and placed in its own bag with an identifying tag. When all sherds from an FS bag had been analyzed, all of the lot bags (except the special analysis Cat bags) were placed back in the larger FS bag. Special analysis samples identified by Cat numbers were placed in a separate box for later analysis.

Vessel Form and Morphological Data

A series of attributes were recorded to describe and classify ceramics in relation to vessel shape, size, and potential function. These attributes are standard data collected for most ceramic analyses; they include vessel form, vessel part, wall thickness (white ware bowls), rim radius, rim arc, rim eversion (gray ware rims), and vessel appendage.

Vessel Form

Vessel form describes the general shape of a vessel based in many cases on known ethnographic data. Nineteen categories of vessel form were identified in the Salmon assemblage, including some classifications outside standard vessel definitions, such as fired raw clay and raw clay samples. Bowls were identified based on the presence of interior surface treatment, such as polishing, slipping, or painting; bowls were one of the more common vessel forms at Salmon. Jars were the most common form because of the large number of gray ware body sherds classified under the general jar form. Jar body fragments were identified based on the lack of surface manipulation on the interior surface, such as polishing, slipping, or painting. Jar rims were identified primarily on the same basis; however, white ware jars occasionally had slip running over the edge into the interior. Ollas are jar forms that have a long restricted neck, in contrast to wide-mouthed jars that have no neck or shoulder and are completely open and deep.

Much of the variation in the Salmon gray ware rim assemblage was subsumed under the general category of jar. Seed jars are neckless and have a globular or spherical shape with a narrow opening at the top of the sphere. The seed jar was one of the earliest vessel forms made in the Southwest due to its basic shape, which provides for a sturdy vessel (Skibo and Blinman 1999; L. Reed et al. 2000). Kiva jars are a modification of the seed jar shape with an added interior lip that holds a lid. A pitcher is essentially the same shape as its modern counterpart; it is generally a small, necked jar with a handle attached from the rim to the lower body. Canteens come in various shapes, but they must have a small orifice similar to a seed jar and lugs on either side for stringing a handle or strap.

Mugs are known primarily from Pueblo III contexts and as Mesa Verde style black-on-white forms, although Salmon produced a number of McElmo Black-on-white mugs as well. They closely resemble mugs of their modern counterparts, with a flat base, similar size, and comfortable handle. Ladles have small bowls with handle attachments that may be either an extension of the bowl shape (gourd shape) or a hollow or solid coil attachment from the side of the ladle. Pipes are of various forms, including stemmed forms with a bowl attached to the end (similar to modern pipes) and cloud blowers produced from a single coil of clay. The only pipe identified in the Salmon sample was a stem fragment.

Miniature vessels were made by coiling, as opposed to pinching, and are tiny versions of bowls, jars, or other common forms. Effigy and figurine vessels come in various sizes, representing human and animal forms, and were produced in various wares. Flutes, consisting of long, cylindrical forms with small holes set closely together, are rare in the analyzed assemblage; one probable flute was identified in Room 100W. Pinch pots are generally small bowls or jars that were produced by pinching a ball of clay into the shape of a vessel. They may be highly polished or left plain and are frequently found as unfired vessels. Finally, sherds that could not be identified to vessel form were placed in an indeterminate category.

Vessel Part

Vessel part typically describes the area of a vessel from which a sherd originated, but it also relates to the total amount of vessel present for use in cases of whole or partial vessels. Rim refers to the finished edge around the opening of the vessel. The presence of a rim sherd requires additional information and measurements to be recorded in the database, and is often essential for correctly assigning a typological classification. Neck refers to the area between the finished edge (rim) and the sloping face (shoulder) of a jar, olla, canteen, or necked seed jar. Shoulder is the angled upper portion of a jar (or similar vessel form) leading to the widest point of the diameter of the vessel. Neck-body join indicates that the sherd comprises only the angle created where the neck meets the shoulder, and does not include any significant amount of the flat, sloping area that makes up the shoulder. Body refers to the entire area between the widest point of the diameter and the base of the vessel. In many cases, it was not possible to identify exactly where a sherd originated on a large jar form, so body sherds can include the upper portion as well as the lower portion. The base is the bottom part of the vessel, which holds the entire weight of the vessel and its contents, and most commonly encounters surfaces such as floors or storage areas. Handles are most frequently associated with ladles, canteens, pitchers, and mugs, but can also be found on jars, ollas, and bowls. A handle is modeled into or appended onto a vessel to facilitate use, transportation, and/or storage.

In some cases, enough pieces of a vessel were present that more than one vessel part was represented by the sherd or group of sherds. Vessel part includes choices that reflect multiple parts of a vessel for just such a situation. A whole vessel was recorded as "complete" and a partial vessel was recorded as "partial"; certain measurements and information were recorded in the database in association with various parts of the vessel. When a number of pieces from the same vessel were present within the same FS, the vessel was recorded as "reconstructible" and as many measurements as possible were taken on various areas. Reconstructible vessels were not reconstructed during the project due to the amount of space needed to curate whole and reconstructed vessels compared to the space required to store the sherds in a bag.

Vessel Appendage

Handles, partial handles, or evidence that a handle was attached to a location in the past were further described in the vessel appendage category. Handles were often decorated to match the vessel decoration. An indeterminate handle stub is an area on a vessel where the handle has been completely broken off, leaving a roughened spot, hole, or indentation. A gourd handle, found on some ladles, is semicircular in cross-section and attached to the bowl of the ladle in a way that makes the whole item look like a gourd split in half. A hollow handle is also usually found on ladles, and is attached to one side of the ladle bowl as an entirely separate piece. The handle is hollow to prevent it from exploding during drying or firing. A slab handle is sometimes found on ladles as a straight, flat extension from the rim of the ladle bowl. It is also sometimes found on mugs as a wide handle reaching from rim to base. More common on mugs are strap handles, a thicker and narrower band that is often decorated. Strap handles are also found on ollas, pitchers, jars, and even bowls.

A single coil handle is simply a coil of clay that has been attached to the vessel in the shape and location of a handle. These are most common on pitchers, but also occur on jars and ladles. A multiple coil handle is made of two or more coils placed together to make a handle. The individual coils must be visible for this classification to apply, but decorative variations are common where the coils are integrated into the decoration. Multiple coil handles are often found on pitchers. A pinch handle is modeled rather than attached as a separate piece of clay, and has an unfinished appearance much like a pinch pot.

Lugs are also modeled rather than attached to the vessel, but are smoothed and rounded to match the surface decoration of the rest of the vessel. They can be pierced while the clay is still wet, creating small holes through which string can be passed for carrying or hanging the vessel. Lugs are common handles on bowls, jars, and ollas. A similar treatment for making a handle out of perishable material is simply to pierce the wet clay near the rim, leaving pierced holes. This handle modification is often seen on seed jars, in particular. Finally, an appliqué is a decorative element usually placed on the exterior surface of a vessel near the rim, much like a lug. Appliqué elements are seen on bowls and canteens, but are most common on corrugated gray jars as decorative accents.

Wall Thickness

White ware bowls were measured to explore wall thickness. The thickness of bowl wall reflects manufacturing constraints, as well as the period of production. Due to their size and restricted openings, jars are more likely to have varying wall thickness, as it is not always possible for the potter to scrape the coils evenly. Bowls are easier for the potter to manipulate and are thus expected to have a mostly uniform wall thickness. The wall thickness of locally produced white ware vessels can be compared to white ware vessels that have been imported to compare manufacturing techniques. Also, the wall thickness of Pueblo I and Pueblo II bowls is often much thinner than that of Pueblo III bowls, giving wall thickness a temporal application as well.

Rim Dimensions

Rim dimension measurements include radius, arc, and eversion. All rim sherds of sufficient size were matched to a chart divided into half-centimeter increments and measured for rim radius. This chart, based on Rice (1987:223), also gives the measurement of arc, or degrees of a full circle represented by the rim fragment. If a sherd was so small that the number of degrees measured for the arc is less than twice the number measured for the radius, the sherd was considered too small to give a reliable measurement of radius. Thus, a bowl rim with a 13 cm radius would ideally also have at least 26 degrees of arc. The total rim diameter from a vessel rim fragment can be estimated by doubling the radius measurement. The rim arc measurement provides a means of evaluating how much of the rim fragment represents the entire orifice of the vessel. For example, a bowl rim with a 13 cm radius provides an estimated orifice diameter of 26 cm for the bowl, and a corresponding rim arc of 26 degrees indicates that the rim represents 7 percent (26/360 degrees of the orifice circumference) of the actual orifice. Thus, the rim arc provides an evaluation of the diameter measurement.

In addition to these measurements, all gray ware rims of sufficient size to include the entire neck curve were measured for rim eversion, or the number of degrees from 90 that the rim curves toward the exterior of the vessel. This measurement was taken by orienting the rim sherd such that it is in the position it would be on a whole vessel against the vertical axis of the radius chart. The curvature was then measured in degrees from the vertical axis.

Among Cibola and Northern San Juan gray wares (Blinman and Wilson 1989; Breternitz et al. 1974; Toll and McKenna 1997), the measure of eversion allows the analyst to discriminate between Pueblo II and Pueblo III vessels. Even lacking a sufficient amount of vessel to assign a ceramic type based on the combination of corrugated styles present (e.g., patterned or zoned corrugated), the eversion measurement would be sufficient to assign the vessel to either Pueblo II or III. Unfortunately, among the Middle San Juan gray wares, rim eversion may not be an accurate temporal marker for the Pueblo II through Pueblo III periods. It is possible that Mesa Verde style rims (with rim eversion between 61 and 90 degrees) did not occur in the Middle San Juan until the late decades of the 1200s, and the two earlier rim eversion groups—0–30 degrees (Mancos style) and 31–60 degrees (Dolores style)—were produced throughout the Pueblo II and Pueblo III periods. As discussed in the following chapters, a larger sample of rims and vessels from well-dated strata are required before a confident temporal assessment can be provided.

Vessel and Sherd Function

Two attributes—use-wear and modification—fall within the larger category of specific vessel function and postbreakage sherd function. Use-wear primarily relates to food and beverage preparation, cooking use, and serving. Observed traits included sooting, abrasion, chipping, and unidentifiable deposits. The remains of fugitive red pigments were also present on some sherds as evidence of possible ceremonial activities. Abrasion and pitting on the exteriors and bases of sherds or vessels suggest that they were moved frequently during use and rubbed against other items with rough surfaces. Sooting is often indicative of direct cooking over a fire; however, at Salmon, many rooms experienced fires or were filled with trash deposits that could account for the presence of soot and ash on sherds. The most confident evaluation of soot comes from whole or reconstructible vessels from which the patterning of soot and oxidation can be fully evaluated. Numerous types of soot result from cooking use, including encrusted soot, greasy soot, and soaked in soot (Skibo 1992). Much of the ashy type of soot seen on sherds, particularly as it occurs on both surfaces, is most often from postdepositional deposits or room burning. Thus, vessel function evaluation of soot from individual sherds is difficult and often inaccurate.

Large broken sherds and ladles often exhibit scoop use, or angled grinding along the rim or edge where the edge grazed the inside of a storage or cooking vessel during stirring or scooping. Rim chipping on jars or vessels with cooking soot is common use-wear created by stirring the contents. Rim abrasion can also be related to stirring or can come from reuse of a sherd or partial vessel. Interior pitting and abrasion is usually related to stirring or scooping of the contents, either in storage or during cooking, but can also be related to long-term storage of acidic liquids such as alcohol, or medicines with high tannin content.

Cleaning vessels with sand may also have created some of the interior abrasion noted; patterned abrasion on some bowls with slips worn in a circular pattern may have been the result of repeated washing with sand. Spalling is usually related to sudden temperature changes, such as adding very hot or very cold material to a vessel at the opposite temperature. Spalling, especially on the exterior, can also occur due to air pockets during firing, or from banging the vessel against a hard surface. Vessel deposits sometimes include pigments, which may be related to ceremonial activities, or the result of cooking or storing certain food items that react with the interior of the vessel.

Modification of sherds or partial vessels, especially after breakage, was common at Salmon, often involving the manufacture of ground and flaked items such as discs or other shapes. Drill holes were also common, indicating attempts to repair vessels. Drill holes near the rim can also be for suspension of the vessel or to facilitate adding a handle made from a perishable material. Incising of designs into a vessel that had already been fired was rare at Salmon. Rims were often reshaped, and there is at least one example of a possible spoke shave tool.

Technology

Because of our interest in identifying local production and further defining locally made Cibola pottery, the most important attributes were those related to technology. Technological attributes consisted of paint, surface treatment, slip application, paste characteristics, temper, and ware identification. The two most difficult to classify and the most subjective in many aspects were slip application and paste characteristics. The Animas Variety paste characteristics became clear, however, with training and by comparison to Cibola and Northern San Juan pastes.

Paint

The type of paint used to decorate a vessel can be an important indicator of time period and ceramic type within certain ceramic manufacturing traditions. Mineral paint is characterized by a black to rust color (misfired by the addition of too much oxygen). It sits on top of the painted surface in a distinctly separate level that is visible under the binocular microscope and can often be felt with the fingertips. Mineral paint is made by finely crushing iron, manganese, and other dark minerals.

Organic or carbon paint is characterized by an inky black color that can wane to brown if badly misfired. During firing, organic paint soaks into the ceramic surface and melds with it, leaving bleeding edges along the design edge that can often be seen with the naked eye. Organic paint is made by cooking down plant matter to a thickened, glue-like consistency that is thinned with water before application. Mineral paints are often combined with organic paints as a binder, resulting in bleeding edges or a ghost image of the design beneath the raised mineral paint lines.

Clay paint was used on White Mountain Polychromes, on which the exterior of a bowl or parts of a vessel design are executed in white slip clay over the solid red slip background (St. John's Polychrome) or in red slip clay over the solid plain or white slip background (Wingate Polychrome).

Subglaze refers to a condition where the vessel has been fired so hot that the paint vitrifies on the surface of the vessel and has a shiny, reflective appearance when viewed with binocular magnification. The presence of paint does not necessarily mean that the vessel has been slipped. Among Animas Variety vessels, polished unslipped surfaces are often painted.

Cibola tradition ceramics were painted exclusively with mineral paints until Pueblo III, when the only organic-painted ceramic type manufactured was Chaco-McElmo Black-on-white (Toll and McKenna 1997). This signifies a major difference from the Animas Variety Cibola vessels, as organic or mineral-organic paints were sometimes used to decorate Pueblo II period ceramics. In the Northern San Juan tradition, the use of organic paint occurred only in the Pueblo III period, although several ceramic types were manufactured throughout this time. Again, the Animas Variety of Northern San Juan vessels were often painted with organic paint or a combination, rather than just mineral paint, throughout Pueblo II. The Animas Variety of both Cibola and Northern San Juan traditions thus resembles the Chuska tradition, where organic-painted ceramics were produced throughout the entire sequence of ceramic manufacture alongside mineral-painted ceramics (see Peckham and Wilson 1967; L. Reed and Goff 2003).

Surfaces

Exterior surfaces often exhibit treatments different from interior surfaces. Plain gray surfaces are scraped or smoothed, but not embellished in any way. Plain with finger drags is a surface where wide vertical lines are scratched into the clay using the fingers as a tool. Plain with incised designs has simple designs etched into the wet clay with a sharp-pointed tool. Plain with incised coil junctions is a type of zoned surface treatment where plain surface areas alternate with areas of visible, horizontally placed coils that have been etched along the crease where two coils connect. Rubbing a smooth stone over a ceramic surface produces various degrees of polish.

Neckbanding is a gray ware surface style for which the flattened bands (coils) around the neck portion of the vessel are left unobliterated. Wide neckbands (> 10 mm wide) are indicative of middle to late Pueblo I assemblages (e.g., Moccasin Gray, Tohatchi Banded); these types were not identified in the Salmon collection. Narrow neckbands (< 10 mm wide) are common in assemblages dating to the late Pueblo I through middle Pueblo II periods and narrow bands are often part of zoned or patterned corrugation designs.

Corrugated surfaces are created using a number of techniques; corrugation styles are often combined to form elaborate zoned or patterned corrugated surfaces. Plain corrugated indicates that the coils have been laid horizontally on top of one another but have not been embellished with indentation, or incising. Clapboard corrugated has the appearance of an old-fashioned washboard, where the bottom of each coil overhangs the next lower coil with a sharp angle. Indented corrugated is a surface treatment whereby each coil that is applied horizontally to a vessel is pressed down at regular intervals with the potter's finger. This surface treatment is especially useful on gray ware cooking vessels because it adds strength to the coils as well as surface area to distribute heat through the vessel more evenly. Indented corrugated can be further decorated with finger drags over the indentations, incised designs over the indentations, punctate designs built into the indentations, the addition of appliqué elements, or smeared segments made with a flat tool. Corrugation can also be partly to mostly obliterated by smearing or polishing.

The rim of a gray ware vessel is described as a fillet, or a wide flattened coil at the top, with the same variations in corrugation or surface treatments described above. By the late Pueblo II and Pueblo III periods, zoned corrugated and patterned corrugated styles had developed wherein one or more corrugation patterns (e.g., clapboard, plain, indented) and occasionally narrow bands were applied in zones (rows) or patterns (small isolated sections) on the same vessel.

Exterior surfaces on brown ware—ceramics imported from the Mogollon region—include plain, plain and painted, polished, polished with incised designs, slipped, indented corrugated with slip applied over the corrugations, and pattern corrugated. Exterior surfaces on red ware—ceramics imported from the White Mountain, Kayenta, and Northern San Juan regions—include plain, plain and painted, polished, polished and painted, slipped, and slipped and painted.

Exterior surfaces on white wares (local and imported) were most commonly slipped or slipped and painted in the Pueblo II and III periods. Incised designs over a slipped surface are very rare but do occur. As mentioned above, Animas Variety vessels are sometimes painted but not slipped, with the paint applied over either a plain or a polished surface. Exteriors of bowls, in particular, are often plain or polished, especially those imported from the Cibola and Northern San Juan regions. Sometimes bowls with interior decoration have corrugated rather than smoothed exteriors; variations include zoned and indented corrugated, zoned plain corrugated and plain gray, fillet with indented corrugations, and obliterated corrugation, although the latter may be more a result of excess handling of the vessel to smooth or polish the interior than it is an intentional obliteration of the indentations.

Interior surfaces on gray wares are often scraped smooth, providing a surface conducive to cooking, storage, and cleaning. Interior surfaces of gray ware may have light polishing and occasional unobliterated coils—that is, the coils are not smoothed over, usually because the vessel opening is too small to provide access for the potter's hand. Interior surfaces on brown wares include plain, polished, polished and painted, and polished smudged. Smudging is a technique used mainly among Mogollon potters and those farther to the south to apply a lustrous black color to a vessel. Smudging is accomplished by smothering a reduced kiln fire toward the end of the firing, causing the remaining organic elements of the fire to blacken the exposed surface(s) of the vessel. Interior surfaces on red wares include plain, plain and painted, polished and painted, slipped, and slipped and painted. Most White Mountain and Tusayan Red Ware ceramics from Salmon are bowls, whereas red wares from the Northern San Juan region include various jar forms. Interior surfaces on white wares include plain, plain and painted, polished, polished and painted, slipped, slipped and painted, and on one occasion slipped with an incised design.

Slip

Slip characteristics ascribed to Animas Variety ceramics clearly delineate the variability in slip recipe and application. This attribute became one of the primary means of identifying the Cibola Animas Variety, in addition to paste and temper. Our slip codes included washy (Cibola-like), thin, thick chalky, thick crackly, none, and indeterminate. To identify a slip as washy, the surface of the vessel must be completely visible through the slip in more than one area and the strokes of the slip application tool must be visible as well. The term chalky was used to describe a class of Animas Variety slips. In most cases, the chalky appearance derives from the clay used, but when the slip is applied thickly, the chalky texture is most noticeable. Animas Variety slips are most similar to Chuska slips, with a dull, almost nonreflective appearance even when they have been well polished. The high silt content of the Animas Variety slips seems to provide the dull, chalky character. Under binocular magnification, Animas Variety slips exhibit natural sand and mineral inclusions that, although small enough to allow the slip to be polished if desired, cause small cracks to radiate outward. If exposed to the elements, these slips wear unevenly as the cracks allow large flakes to fall off. In contrast, Northern San Juan slips are not only brighter white in color, but also lack individual grains or inclusions in the clay comprising the slip, despite their comparable thickness on Pueblo III vessels. Although it is common for Northern San Juan slips to have cracks, these are due to the high polish applied to them, and for the most part the cracks do not cause the slip to be unstable as it ages.

Paste

Paste was a distinction added to the Salmon analysis to differentiate characteristics of locally produced versus imported ceramics. Choices included indeterminate, not analyzed, and local. Not analyzed is used for all ceramic types and traditions that do not have an Animas Variety, such as Chuska, Kayenta, all red wares, and brown wares. Local paste is characterized by several observable traits that are often visible to the naked eye. One of these is a color difference. It is well known and understood that color itself is a highly subjective measure because each person sees and translates color differently; this difference is thus defined less by color and more by value. In cross-section, the paste found in a Northern San Juan or Cibola tradition sherd is nearly always stark white, or in noncolor terms, light. The cross-section of many Animas Variety pastes ranges in color from yellow to tan to brown, or in noncolor terms, dark. Similarly, this value difference is apparent when comparing most Chuska cross-sections to either a Northern San Juan or Cibola cross-section of paste. Typical Chuska paste can be described as having a brown to violet color, or very simply it is much darker in appearance than the other traditions. So the color difference noticed in Animas Variety paste is most easily described in terms of hue, but it can be reduced to value and the difference among the traditions is still apparent.

Another difference between the Animas Variety pastes and those of imported ceramics is the degree of siltiness. Silt content in paste can be evaluated objectively through petrography, but it is also observable subjectively through the binocular microscope. Many Animas Variety pastes have such high silt content that it seems unlikely the vessel was able to dry without cracking and falling to dust. Although this content may be only 10–15 percent, the balance between silt, clay, and temper or natural inclusions is vastly important in ceramic manufacture. Tempering materials often must compensate for too much silt or too much clay for vessels to be functional. Under the binocular microscope, silt is visible as graininess within the paste, which prevents the paste from adhering to itself completely. This grainy appearance is rarely associated with Cibola or Northern San Juan pastes. At some sites in the Middle San Juan region, such as the Tommy site (L. Reed 2005), the color (value) difference in local pastes is not as common as it is at sites such as Salmon and Aztec. Despite the lack of the color clue, however, local pastes can still be easily differentiated from imported ceramics by the silt content observable microscopically.

Temper

Although many temper types were identified at Salmon, all can be reduced to various combinations of sand, sherd, and crushed rock. Certain tempers are specific to certain ceramic traditions. Sand and shale are both common in Animas Variety pastes, and they may not be temper at all but simply natural inclusions. Shale pellets are usually gray and oval shaped, and may suggest that at least some clay sources were geologic and not alluvial.

Sand was described under various categories, including angular quartz sand and granitic sand, which are apparently derived from decomposing sandstone. Coarse quartz sand is large grained and mostly rounded, and may also derive from local decomposing sandstone. Medium quartz sand is finer grained and primarily composed of quartz grains. Fine quartz sand consists of extremely small grains of well-sorted, rounded quartz, as in typical Kayenta White Ware (Colton 1956). Multilithic sand is characterized by many shapes and colors of sand grains due to its derivation from different parent rocks. Kayenta and Cibola sand tempers are usually some form of quartz sand, although sandstone is common in Cibola temper, as is multilithic sand, which was probably gathered from washes. Cibola temper also usually includes crushed sherd with the sand or sandstone along with occasional fragments of trachyte derived from crushing trachyte-tempered sherds. Tempers found in Animas Variety Cibola sherds include sand and undissolved clay pellets, sand and sherd, sand and shale, sand and mica, sand, sherd and shale, or silt and sand. Silt and sand was identified as temper in Animas Variety pastes containing no other tempering material and for which the silt appeared to overwhelm the clay particles; both materials were probably natural inclusions in the clay.

Northern San Juan temper was derived from crushed igneous rock types. The traditional Northern San Juan rock is diorite porphyry (also known as andesite/diorite), a white or sometimes blue-gray rock with black minerals. Although this returns us to the color problem again, this rock can be identified by its texture rather than its color if necessary. Diorite porphyry is a fine-grained diorite. The individual crystals that make up the rock groundmass are not visible under the binocular microscope, although the dark flecks against the lighter rock mass are easily seen. Diorite porphyry is found in combination with sherd, sand, and other crushed rocks that are not as distinctly identifiable.

Temper in the Animas Variety of Northern San Juan sherds is also a crushed rock, but a different type known as augite diorite. Augite diorite is a coarser-grained diorite with individual crystals (abundant quartz and feldspar) that are visible under magnification. It is clear to whitish, with areas of dark mineral conglomerations as well as scattered crystals of olivine, a yellowish green mineral. Augite diorite is typically found in combination with one or more of the following: sand, sandstone, shale, sherd, other crushed granitic rocks, and sometimes diorite porphyry. This combination in particular is seen mostly in locally produced ceramics that have silty but not discolored pastes. Another significant characteristic of the local Animas Variety is the coarsely crushed, large size of the igneous material and the less common use of crushed sherd compared to the imported Northern San Juan ceramics.

Another rock type typically found in Animas Variety pottery is coarse angular granite, a crushed rock that is clear to whitish and has sharp edges and angles. It contains a high percentage of quartz and feldspar, but lacks dark minerals, with the exception of occasional loose biotite mica fragments. When this temper is used, the percentage of tempering material compared to the paste is much higher than with other Animas Variety tempers. Coarse angular granite is usually present by itself, but it also occurs in combination with mica or sand. Fine angular granite and crushed quartzite are minor temper types. Crushed unidentified granites and igneous rocks were also used for temper in the Animas Variety ceramics, although they are not as common as augite diorite. These were referred to as crushed igneous rock or crushed rock (non-A/D), and are found in combination with sand and/or sherd.

Chuskan temper is primarily trachyte, another igneous rock that has a distinctly granular and greenish appearance (Carpenter 2005; Shepard 1939). It is unmistakable from most other rocks, although the white trachyte form is similar in appearance to augite diorite and can be misidentified. Trachyte has been observed in Chuska tradition ceramics in combination with mica, sand, sandstone, sherd, and other crushed rock. Trachyte also occurs with red minerals that make up the cementum between individual crystals.

Ware

Ware categories include white, gray, brown, and red. White wares are either white-slipped, painted, or both. A vessel that is unslipped but fired in a reduced atmosphere with a black paint design is considered a white ware, despite its lack of white slip. Gray wares are unpainted, but often decorated with a variety of surface treatments. Brown ware describes a specific group of ceramics manufactured in the Mogollon or other southern cultural areas. Early, undecorated Upper San Juan ceramics are also sometimes referred to as brown ware. For these earlier ceramics, brown-reducing rather than gray-reducing clays were used. In the Middle San Juan, the local brown ware tradition did not extend into the Pueblo I period. Although Animas Variety clays are largely brown reducing, we refer to them as white wares to dispel confusion and to maintain the typological distinctions used to identify them. Red wares are either slipped with clay that turns orange to red when fired in an oxidizing atmosphere or made from unslipped clay that turns orange to red when fired similarly. Misfired white wares or gray wares are not considered red wares, as each cultural region that exports red wares has specific characteristics that are not seen on misfired wares of other types.

Summary

The methodology and analytical attributes presented in this chapter comprise the analysis format used during the Salmon Research Initiative for the ceramic artifacts. This methodology was employed to address the primary research questions of local production, possible presence of Cibola potters or replication of Cibola pottery at Salmon, vessel use and subsequently room function, and ceramic exchange.

Acknowledgments

During the course of the project, many individuals assisted us along the way and without their help, the ceramic project would have been deficient. First, we would like to thank Bill Doelle and Paul Reed with the Center for Desert Archaeology for the opportunity to analyze such an amazing assemblage of ceramics. Second, we would like to thank the late Cynthia Irwin-Williams for her lifetime of dedication to Salmon. It is our hope that she would be pleased by work and interpretations. Larry Baker, Salmon's director, has devoted much of his life to Salmon and gave us great support along the way. We especially want to thank Linda Cordell for her support and advice as we agonized over the typological issues for Middle San Juan ceramics and deciding on an Animas Variety. Dean Wilson has also been a great friend and mentor and we owe him many thanks. Over the course of the project, we were fortunate to have the assistance of interns from the University of Colorado, Boulder. We would like to thank Bonnie Gibson and Sheila Goff for all of their hard work on the Salmon analysis; we enjoyed working with them immensely. Kathy Niles Hensler has worked with Animas Ceramic Consulting for many years and her knowledge and advisement in working with the technological data, particularly geochemical analyses, has been invaluable; a thank you is not enough. Also, we are grateful to a number of colleagues who have offered advice, consultation, and great debate over the last few years concerning Salmon, ceramics, and regional patterns in general: Doug Dykeman, Kris Langenfeld, Gary Brown, Laurie Webster, Joell Goff, Scott Ortman, Jonathan Till, Donna Glowacki, Nancy Espinosa, Linda Wheelbarger, and Ben Bellorado. Thank you all.

Chapter 31

A MIDDLE SAN JUAN TYPOLOGICAL AND CHRONOLOGICAL PERSPECTIVE

Lori Stephens Reed

Since the excavation of Aztec Ruins by Earl Morris (1924, 1928), the ceramics of the Middle San Juan region have been studied and assessed by reference to known ceramic series, wares, and types from outside the region. This approach allows newly excavated ceramic assemblages to be brought into perspective. Morris, however, did not complete an analysis of the ceramics from Aztec beyond an impressionistic evaluation of the assemblage and type assignments for limited exotic, whole vessels (1924, 1928). As a result of the Salmon excavations in the 1970s, Hayward Franklin (1980a; Chapters 18–28) and his laboratory staff analyzed thousands of sherds and whole vessels, placing them within standard ceramic typologies for Northern San Juan (Mesa Verde), Cibola, Chuska, Kayenta (Tusayan), and Mogollon pottery.

At the time, Franklin was aware that the majority of crushed rock–tempered pottery was locally produced, with a smaller percentage imported from sites in the Northern San Juan region (e.g., the Cortez, Dolores, and Mesa Verde areas). He also realized the difficulty of segregating local from nonlocal pottery in the absence of petrographic and geochemical sourcing data. Nevertheless, such methods were ultimately beyond the scope of the original Salmon project, and the Salmon ceramic laboratory was not able to separate locally produced pottery from imported Northern San Juan ceramics at a typological level.

A number of issues prompted our reconfiguration of the typology for Northern San Juan and Cibola series pottery in the Salmon assemblage. First, we identified specific paste, slip, and temper characteristics that set local Northern San Juan ceramics apart from trade ware pottery of the same series. Second, similar characteristics were identified within a subset of local pottery showing Cibola series attributes. Third, we explored aspects of the Northern San Juan series that required revision as a means of providing better chronological control (through ceramic mean dating). Fourth, stylistic and morphological changes observed in Mancos B/w ceramics prompted subdivision of this type to account for transitions sensitive to chronological and developmental changes. Last, we investigated nonlocal ceramic traditions—Cibola, Chuska, Northern San Juan, Kayenta (Tusayan), and Mogollon—identified in the reanalyzed assemblage from Salmon.

CERAMIC MEAN DATING

Mean ceramic dates and ranges were calculated using a methodology developed by P. Reed (1999) that represents a modification of the ceramic mean date formula (South 1977). Rather than producing just a mean date, which seems falsely precise, P. Reed used Excel to generate ceramic ranges for sites and features. The published date ranges and frequencies for individual ceramic types were entered into a spreadsheet by room and stratum. The type frequencies were then weighted by the total number of items per provenience. Finally, a mean date and ceramic range based on the weighted scores was produced. Two ranges were used: (1) the maximum or full ceramic range and (2) the interquartile or "best" range that includes 50 percent of the total range (on either side of the mean). For a hypothetical mean date of AD 1050, the maximum ceramic range is 950–1150, with a best range of 1000–1100.

LOCAL ANIMAS VARIETY CERAMICS

A number of characteristics set local Middle San Juan ceramics apart from those produced in the Northern San Juan region to the north and the Cibola–San Juan Basin region to the south. These characteristics are based on the local resources available to potters in the Middle San Juan—the clay resources and the materials available for use as temper. It was the combination of these resources along with paint and slip use that made locally produced Animas Variety (Northern San Juan and Cibola) ceramics distinct.

Experimentation with local clays indicates great variability in the resources available to ancient potters. San Jose and Nacimiento Formation clays near Salmon and Aztec Ruins are unpredictable in their use for making pottery. San Jose clays are often difficult to dissolve and are frequently found in limited quantities. Farther down the San Juan River, the Fruitland and Kirtland Formation clays are difficult to work with due to high silt content although some sources work well with levigation. Based on hardness testing and refiring analysis, it appears that Animas Variety pottery was low-fired compared to ceramics from other regions, probably because of the limitations of the clay resources. Our experiments with the resources of the Middle San Juan are just beginning and will continue with future research.

Animas Variety pastes tend to be very silty, with many having a crumbly texture when broken to examine temper. Their color is a dull buff, yellowish, tan, or dark brown, giving them an almost dirty appearance. These attributes are best characterized in Figure 31.1, showing a Northern San Juan Animas Variety paste cross-section from a Mesa Verde B/w sherd. The darkness of the paste and the angularity of the crushed augite diorite grains are visible in the photograph, taken through a Meiji binocular microscope with a camera mount. The large size of the temper grains and the amount of temper in the paste influenced the crumbly fracture of the sherd. The fracture is rarely clean due to a combination of high silt content, low-fired paste, and coarsely crushed temper. Even in the white ware ceramics, the temper grains tend to be coarsely crushed rather than finely crushed like most of the Northern San Juan ceramics. Cibola Animas Variety ceramics tempered with sand or sand and sherd also have large-grained sand, and the paste is generally dark brown to yellowish with a crumbly texture.

As shown in Figure 31.2, the paste of the Animas Variety Chaco-McElmo B/w sherd is lighter than the local Mesa Verde B/w example, but the texture is distinctively soft and crumbly, providing a cross-section photograph that appears highly uneven and blurry in some areas. This particular example has relatively large sand grains, crushed sherd (dark black fragments), and undissolved clay pieces (lighter, round fragments). The darker colors of the Animas Variety pastes generally contrast with Cibola and Northern San Juan ceramics, which tend to have white, light gray, or dark gray pastes.

The Northern San Juan Mancos B/w (Reserve style) example shown in Figure 31.3 demonstrates the significantly lighter paste of the imported white ware from the north, the more homogenous paste texture, and the distinctive augite diorite temper with primarily white groundmass and abundant dark minerals. Finally, Figure 31.4 shows a Cibola trade ware example of Gallup B/w with a homogenous paste texture, lighter paste color, and sand and sherd temper (crushed sherd is visible as the large dark fragment at the top of the paste).

Slip application on Animas Variety white ware is variable, but most sherds exhibit a visibly silty appearance. Most local slips have a yellowish cast and a distinctive graininess, which seems to have prevented them from holding polish. Many of the vessels have polish striations, but the expected polishing sheen is either completely absent or not prominent. These slip characteristics and lack of polish contrast with the Northern San Juan and Cibola White wares, which have much better slip texture and polishing.

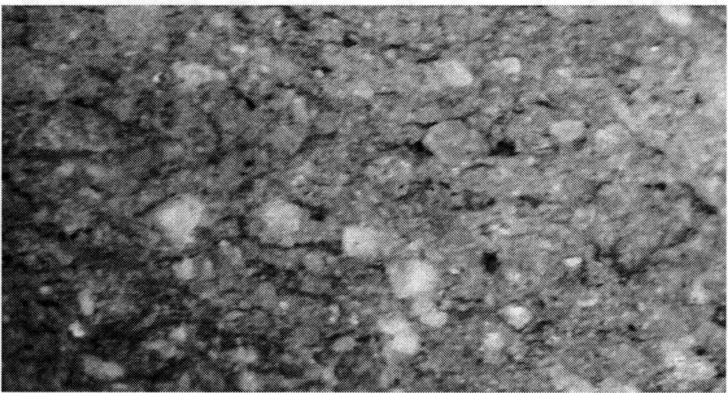

Figure 31.1. Paste cross-section of a Northern San Juan, Animas Variety Mesa Verde B/w (FS 38635) as seen through 20x magnification; tempering material is crushed augite diorite and sand.

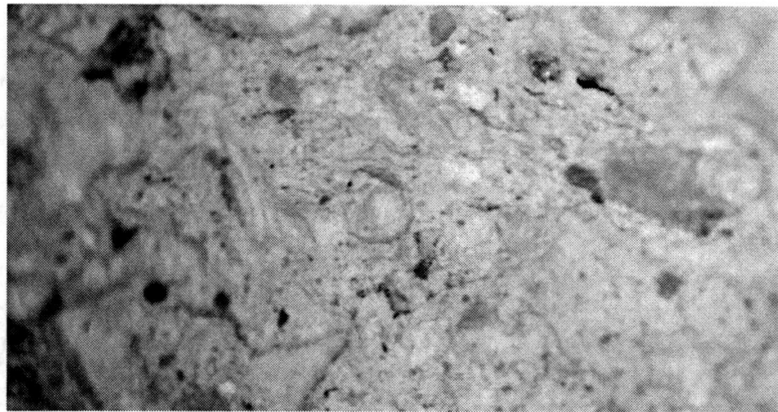

Figure 31.2. Paste cross-section of a Northern San Juan trade ware Mancos B/w (Reserve style; FS 37064) as seen through 20x magnification; tempering material is crushed diorite porphyry and sand.

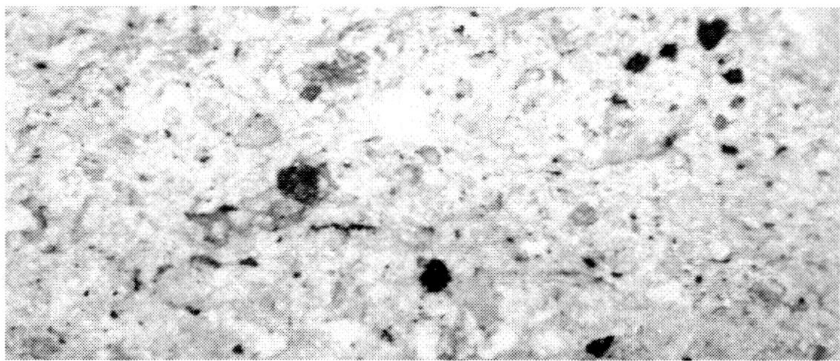

Figure 31.3. Paste cross-section of a Cibola, Animas Variety Chaco-McElmo B/w sherd (FS 37060) as seen through 20x magnification; tempering material is sand and crushed sherd.

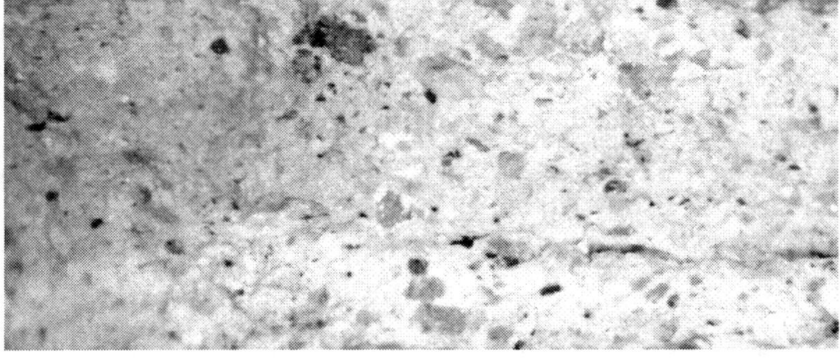

Figure 31.4. Paste cross-section of a Cibola trade ware Gallup B/w sherd (FS 30101) as seen through 20x magnification; tempering material is sand and crushed sherd.

Differentiating Middle San Juan from Northern San Juan tempering material with a binocular microscope has been challenging. To aid in this process, we worked closely with Andrea Carpenter, petrography specialist for the project. Using mineralogical criteria that could be identified with a binocular microscope, we were able to differentiate between crushed augite diorite, diorite porphyry, and granitic material within the ceramic pastes. As we continued to submit ceramic samples for petrographic analysis, the provenience of the mineralogy for these materials has become more complex (Carpenter 2005). Nevertheless, our confidence level for identifying the crushed material (with a binocular microscope) is good—roughly 85 percent.

We have identified augite diorite and diorite porphyry combinations with unclear provenience. Greater field reconnaissance for temper material is needed to resolve some of these issues; this is scheduled for the future. I can say that ceramics with augite diorite or granitic-derived temper were most likely produced in the Middle San Juan, particularly when they have the Animas Variety paste characteristics previously described. If ceramics have diorite porphyry temper and white or gray pastes, then they are nonlocal and were probably produced at sites in the Northern San Juan region. In contrast, imported Cibola ceramics have white to gray pastes, sand or sherd temper, and washy slips. The locally made Cibola-like variety ceramics have the distinctive local silty, discolored paste and discolored slips.

Northern San Juan–Animas Variety Types

The Animas Variety of the Northern San Juan (Mesa Verde) tradition includes the full range of ceramic types identified (Breternitz et al. 1974; Rohn 1977). Given the geographic location of the Middle San Juan between the greater Mesa Verde and the Chaco regions, the influence of both regions on the ceramic artifacts at Salmon and other sites in the Middle San Juan is hardly surprising. It proved difficult to apply the Northern San Juan ceramic typology to the first assemblage of Middle San Juan ceramics studied, which came from the Tommy Site (L. Reed et al. 2001b). As work proceeded on the Salmon ceramic assemblage, it became clear that the standard Northern San Juan typology did not work for Salmon either. Thus, the modified typology presented here was developed for use on all Middle San Juan assemblages (see L. Reed 2005a; Reed and Myers 2006). Type descriptions of the Northern San Juan tradition and photographs of ceramics from the Mesa Verde region were referenced extensively prior to analysis of the Salmon collections (Blinman and Wilson 1989; Breternitz et al. 1974; Rohn 1971, 1977; Stannic 1969). Collections at the Anasazi Heritage Center in Dolores, Colorado were examined for variability in design styles and temper, paste, and slip variability.

White Ware

As described above, the Animas Variety white ware is characterized by a washy to thick, chalky slip and designs painted in a variety of pigments, including mineral, organic, and a mixture of mineral and organic. The primary characteristic of the slip is the use of silty clays to create a dull surface appearance that did not hold polish as well as ceramics of the Cibola and Northern San Juan (Mesa Verde) series. Polishing striations are frequently present over the slipped surfaces, but the dull surface and lack of sheen are common traits of white ware produced at Salmon and Aztec.

Although the type descriptions presented here begin with Piedra B/w, Pueblo I sites along the Animas River valley have produced significant amounts of the locally produced earlier, Basketmaker III type Chapin B/w, as well as Piedra B/w pottery (Blinman and Wilson 1994; Horn et al. 2003; Wilshusen and Wilson 1995). Local production of these pottery types occurred simultaneously with production of Upper San Juan pottery (e.g., Rosa and Bancos B/w) at these sites, and pottery technology became a means of sharing information (L. Reed 2006).

Piedra B/w. A small number of sherds from Salmon were identified as Piedra B/w, classified according to the traditional type descriptions presented in the literature by Breternitz et al. (1974). Based on data from the Northern San Juan region, Piedra B/w dates from AD 750 to 900. Piedra surfaces are generally smoothed to well polished and designs are oriented toward the rim, in contrast to Chapin designs which are oriented to the center of the bowl. As described by Breternitz et al. (1974), Rohn (1977), and Blinman and Wilson (1989), Piedra B/w designs are executed in mineral paint. It is interesting that the four sherds identified in Room 100W at Salmon all have organic-painted designs. The use of variable pigment types on decorated pottery in the Middle San Juan is one of the hallmarks of the Animas Variety. Tempering material in the sherds from Salmon is augite diorite, sherd, and shale within a silty, brownish paste. Wall thickness varies from 4.7 to 5.3 mm.

Given the organic-painted designs on the Piedra B/w sherds from Salmon (Figure 31.5), the Piedra B/w pottery identified at Pueblo I sites in the Animas River valley is probably relevant (see L. Reed in

Figure 31.5. Piedra B/w, Animas variety.

Horn et al. 2003). Further, the variability in pigment use identified at Basketmaker III and Pueblo I sites in the La Plata valley by Shepard (1939) and Wilson (1996) has relevance to the development of later Pueblo II and III paint type distributions in the Middle San Juan region.

Cortez B/w. As discussed above, Cortez and Mancos B/w are two of the Northern San Juan types for which inconsistency in typological classification created difficulties in the Salmon analysis. A study of the Northern San Juan literature indicated that Red Mesa style designs have been classified as both Cortez and Mancos B/w throughout the years, with little stylistic consistency. Chronologically, this inconsistency would have caused mean ceramic date accuracy issues if strict stylistic guidelines had not been set forth for the Salmon analysis. Further, the influence of Cibola designs on locally produced Northern San Juan pottery was another issue that required a reexamination of the Cortez and Mancos stylistic consistency problem.

To avoid creating new types or confusing the issue further, we divided Cortez B/w into two stylistic subtypes: Kiatuthlanna style and Red Mesa style. All of the design styles that would normally be placed under Cortez or Mancos as a Red Mesa style design were classified as Cortez B/w (Red Mesa style) under the Animas Variety typology.

Cortez B/w (Kiatuthlanna style) is defined stylistically by designs following the Cibola type Kiatuthlanna B/w (Goff and Reed 1998; Windes 1977; Windes and McKenna 1989). Kiatuthlanna style has lines of fine to medium width that overlap at the junctures. Line elements repeat in a rectilinear pattern, similar to Piedra B/w designs, but the overlap at line junctures is a hallmark of Kiatuthlanna style. Solid elements consist most commonly of triangles with infrequent elaborations, such as dots or ticks. Surfaces are well polished and slips were often applied. At sites in the Cibola region, Kiatuthlanna B/w dates between AD 850 and 950–1000 (Goff and Reed 1998; Windes and McKenna 1989). We place the Kiatuthlanna style of Cortez B/w in the latter period, given the lack of associated tree dates and the small number of sites identified in the Middle San Juan yielding Cortez B/w. Congruent types of other traditions include Kiatuthlanna B/w of the Cibola tradition, Cortez B/w (unassigned style) in the Northern San Juan tradition, Kana-a B/w of the Kayenta tradition, and Tunicha B/w and Drolet B/w of the Chuska tradition.

At Salmon, one sherd from Room 90W and two sherds from Room 100W were identified as Cortez B/w (Kiatuthlanna style). All three are jar body fragments: the jar sherd from Room 90W has organic-painted designs over a polished surface and the two sherds from Room 100W have mineral-painted designs over a washy slipped surface. This variety of pigment use is expected for Animas Variety sherds. Tempering material identified in the Salmon sherds consists of augite diorite and sherd in the jar fragment from Room 90W and augite diorite and sand in the jar fragments from Room 100W. All of the Kiatuthlanna style ceramics have the typical silty, brownish paste of Animas Variety pottery.

Cortez B/w (Red Mesa style) includes all Red Mesa style designs that under the Northern San Juan (Mesa Verde) tradition would be placed in either Cortez B/w or Mancos B/w. Thus, a proposed date range for Cortez B/w (Red Mesa style) in the Middle San Juan is AD 900–1050 (Goff and Reed 1998; Toll and McKenna 1997). The influence of Pueblo I developments in the Animas and La Plata River valleys cannot be taken for granted in the dating and development of Cortez B/w in the Middle San Juan region (see my study in Horn 2003; Toll 2006; Wilshusen and Wilson 1995). The influences of local Piedra B/w and Bancos B/w of the Upper San Juan tradition in the Animas and La Plata River valleys were probably critical to the development of Cortez B/w Animas Variety; however, greater study is needed to comprehend the complexity of the Pueblo I to Pueblo II transition in the Middle San Juan region. Congruent types in other ceramic traditions include Red Mesa B/w of the Cibola tradition, Cortez B/w (unassigned style) of the Northern San Juan tradition, Kana-a B/w of the Kayenta tradition, and Naschitti and Newcomb of the Chuska tradition.

Red Mesa style was probably one of the most diverse and widespread ceramic design complexes on the Colorado Plateau. In some areas, such as the Kayenta region of northern Arizona, its simplicity remained intact with Kana-a B/w (Colton 1955), but in other areas the basic Red Mesa style became more varied with the addition of other elements. Red Mesa style emerged along with the early developments at Chaco Canyon and it is the hallmark style of the AD 900s. Given the diversity of design elements commonly associated with Red Mesa style in the San Juan Basin and Northern San Juan regions, a study of the elements and their chronological significance would be quite useful, particularly the development of hachured elements from squiggle hachure of Red Mesa style to the oblique and parallel hachure of Dogoszhi and Reserve styles. Nevertheless, Cortez B/w (Red Mesa style) includes a wide variety of design elements primarily laid out in bands around the vessel. Elements include scrolls, solid triangles (usually with dots or ticks along one side), parallel lines, and checkerboards. Parallel lines, usually wider than Kiatuthlanna style lines, often frame sets of solid elements or interlocking scrolls. Squiggle hachure elements are common and are usually thick-lined designs interpreted as the precursor to the Dogoszhi style designs of Mancos B/w of the Northern San Juan tradition.

Only nine sherds were identified as Cortez B/w (Red Mesa style) in the Salmon assemblage: three from Room 30W and six from Room 100W. None of the ceramics in the sample consisted of whole or reconstructible vessels. All of the sherds from Room 30W were bowl fragments, and those from Room 100W consisted of one jar and five bowl fragments. Paint types on the Cortez sherds were variable, including mineral, organic, mineral/organic mix, and subglaze. All sherds were slipped except the one from Room 100W that was painted over a plain surface. Slips were also variable, including washy, thin, and thick-chalky slip coverage. As discussed above, the application of washy slips on Animas Variety ceramics is suggestive of Cibola influence. Of the nine Cortez B/w (Red Mesa style) sherds, two have washy slip coverage. All of the sherds have augite diorite temper as the primary inclusions, with two examples having minor inclusions of another rock type, three with abundant sand, one with sandstone and sand, and three with sherd and sand. Paste characteristics are typical of Animas Variety ceramics with a silty, brownish to yellowish appearance.

Mancos B/w. Mancos B/w was the most problematic of the Northern San Juan ceramic types with regard to use as a chronological tool. Its history as a ceramic type in the Northern San Juan tradition has been one of conglomeration of design styles, in contrast to segregation of design styles for chronometric dating in other regions of the Colorado Plateau. As mentioned above with Cortez B/w, inconsistency in assigning Red Mesa style designs to either Cortez or Mancos B/w has resulted in confusion and an inability to use the typology to consistently identify early Pueblo I (AD 900–1000) occupations or components. Further, the plethora of design styles within Mancos B/w results in a lack of congruency with other regional typologies developed for the Colorado Plateau. Given the abundance of Chuskan and Cibola ceramics identified in the Salmon assemblage, the necessity for congruency in typological nomenclature and chronometric sequencing warranted a substyle segregation of Mancos B/w. Thus, seven substyles for Mancos B/w were developed to capture the variability in design styles and provide congruency with late Pueblo II to early Pueblo III typological nomenclature generally subsumed under the collective of Mancos B/w. These styles include Black Mesa, Mancos, Sosi, Dogoszhi, Chaco, Puerco, and Reserve. Some of these substyles are rare in the Salmon assemblage, but they may indicate stylistic influences from other regions, which are important from a sociocultural standpoint. In addition, there are temporal differences in the manufacturing ranges of some substyles that may prove useful for dating sites and excavated proveniences in the Middle San Juan.

When examined as a single ceramic type without the advantage of substyle differentiation, 324 Mancos B/w ceramics were identified in the Salmon assemblage, comprising 8 percent of all the white ware analyzed and 10.7 percent of the Animas Variety white ware. With the exclusion of Red Mesa style from Mancos B/w, the design styles included in the type represent those dating roughly between AD 1000 and 1200. Of course, all of the substyles were not produced throughout this entire temporal period, making their segregation a useful chronometric tool. The chronometry of ceramic types identified in the study and their uses in generating mean ceramic dates are discussed in the next section. Table 31.1 presents each of the substyles and their frequencies in each of the rooms studied during the Salmon Research Initiative.

Mancos B/w (Black Mesa style; AD 1000–1100) was relatively rare in the Salmon assemblage but included 14 sherds from Rooms 30A, 30W, 100W, and 127W. This substyle was defined as sherds having designs typical of Black Mesa B/w of the Kayenta (Tusayan) tradition (see Colton 1955; Hays-Gilpin and van Hartesveldt 1998). Designs in the Northern San Juan Animas Variety style are bigger

Table 31.1. Frequency of Animas Variety Mancos B/w substyles by room.

Substyle	Room	Sherd Count	Weight
Black Mesa	030A	1	6.6
	030W	4	36.7
	100W	6	81.0
	127W	3	22.4
	Subtotal	14	146.7
Mancos	030B	1	2.5
	030W	14	264.4
	064W	2	8.1
	090W	6	76.6
	100W	17	197.7
	Subtotal	40	549.3
Sosi	030A	1	8.2
	030W	29	503.1
	064W	2	10
	090W	6	85.2
	100W	74	1,637.8
	123B	3	37.3
	127W	3	38.7
	Subtotal	118	2,320.3
Dogoszhi	030A	2	25.6
	030W	20	178.8
	064W	3	20.0
	090W	3	20.4
	100W	59	1019.4
	123B	6	35.5
	123W	2	10.4
	127W	3	42.1
	Subtotal	98	1352.2
Chaco	100W	4	21.0
Puerco	030W	1	15.0
	090W	1	7.6
	100W	6	96.9
	123B	1	67.0
	123W	6	95.3
	127W	3	13.2
	Subtotal	18	295.0
Reserve	030B	1	4.5
	030W	9	82.7
	090W	1	3.4
	100W	21	419.0
	123B	2	16.3
	127W	2	34.6
	Subtotal	36	560.5
Total		328	5,245.0

and bolder, in relation to the embellishments, than in Cortez B/w styles. There are a variety of solid elements in rectilinear and curvilinear (most common) forms that have small ticks and dotted embellishments. This contrasts with the Sosi style of Mancos B/w, which lacks embellishments completely. Other solid elements include large opposed triangles, negative squares with center dots, and interlocking scrolls. The primary differences between Black Mesa style and Cortez B/w is the broad-lined elements and between Black Mesa style and Sosi style is the use of line and solid element embellishments.

Eleven of the Mancos B/w sherds were bowl fragments, and three sherds were from jars (examples in Figure 31.6). The bowl fragments came from Rooms 30A, 30W, 100W, and 127W, but the jar fragments were identified only in Rooms 100W and 127W. There were no whole or reconstructible vessels in the sample. Animas Variety ceramic paint types were typically either organic or mineral/organic mixtures. Painted surfaces were variable, including plain, polished, and slipped. Sherds with slips included six with a thick, chalky slip, one with a thick, crackly slip, three with a thin slip, and one with a washy slip. Tempering material showed some local variability, with two sherds from Room 100W having coarse angular granite, a locally available material occurring as decomposing sandstone. The remaining sherds had augite diorite as the primary tempering material, with smaller quantities of other lesser materials such as shale, sand, sherd, and other unknown igneous rock. Eleven of the sherds had the typical local paste identified as silty and discolored to brownish or yellowish, but three were vitrified.

Mancos B/w (Mancos style; AD 1000–1100) was created to capture elements and designs specific to Mancos B/w of the Northern San Juan (Mesa Verde) tradition that are not common or are completely absent from other Pueblo II traditions. I was interested in the occurrence of these elements in the Salmon assemblage, their representation in specific rooms at the site, and their association with other ceramic materials. Mancos style designs consist of small to large dots covering a portion or the entire interior of a bowl, broad lined circles as isolated elements, and ribbons, open squares, open diamonds, and other elements with dot filler. Examples of Mancos style designs are presented in Swannack (1969:89, Figure 66) and Hayes (1998:28, Figure 24c, d).

As shown in Table 31.1, 40 sherds from Rooms 30B, 30W, 64W, 90W, and 100W were identified as Mancos B/w (Mancos style). There were no whole or reconstructible vessels in the sample. Bowl sherds were found in each room assemblage, and jar sherds

Figure 31.6. Mancos B/w, Black Mesa style, Animas variety.

were present in all except Room 30B. One ladle handle was identified in Room 30W, and two ladle fragments (one bowl and one handle) were present in Room 100W. Exterior pigments were mineral (n = 3), organic (n = 8), and subglaze (n=1). Interior pigments were mineral (n = 2), organic (n = 25), and mineral/organic mix (n = 1). Plain, polished, and slipped surfaces were identified on the exteriors of the sherds, but one example had a rim fillet with indented corrugations, and a second example had plain corrugations above a plain gray surface, suggesting the original vessel was plain at the lower body and base with plain corrugations up to the rim. Both sherds with the exterior corrugations and slipped and painted interior designs were from Room 100W. Interior surfaces include the general variety of plain, polished, and slipped manipulations. Slips included the full variety of types—thick chalky (n = 20), thick crackly (n = 2), thin (n = 4), and washy (n = 3).

With the exception of two sherds having locally available crushed angular granite, all of the Mancos style ceramics had augite diorite temper as the primary material in the paste, with lesser amounts of sand, shale, sherd, sandstone, and other unidentified crushed rock appearing in various amounts and various combinations in the samples. Twenty-five sherds had the local, silty, and discolored paste typical of Animas Variety ceramics, but 15 had vitrified pastes with only remnants of discoloration or silt visible.

Mancos B/w (Sosi style; AD 1000–1125) was one of the most common Pueblo II types in the Salmon assemblage and was one of the most common design styles on the Colorado Plateau. "Sosi style" is named after the ceramic type Sosi B/w of the Kayenta tradition, which exemplifies the solid element designs of the pottery representing this style. Sosi style designs have broad-lined elements either covering the entire bowl in a quartered layout or encircling the upper body relative to the rim. Elements include broad lines oriented in rectilinear or curvilinear patterns, large solid elements (particularly triangles and checkerboards), and elements that show a lack of line elaborations. Congruent ceramic types of other traditions include Escavada B/w of the Cibola tradition, Sosi B/w of the Kayenta tradition, Mancos B/w (unassigned style) of the Northern San Juan tradition, and Toadlena and Taylor of the Chuska tradition.

Sherds identified as Mancos B/w (Sosi style) total 118; none of the ceramics in the sample were from whole or reconstructible vessels (Figure 31.7). As indicated in Table 31.1, these sherds were identified in Rooms 30A, 30W, 64W, 90W, 100W, 123B, and 127W. Vessel forms included 44 bowl fragments, 71 jar sherds, and 3 ladle fragments. Room 30A contained only one jar fragment, Room 123B contained only three bowl sherds, and Room 127W contained only three bowl fragments. The remaining rooms contained both bowls and jars, and Room 100W contained all three of the ladle rim fragments. Exterior pigments were mineral (n = 5), organic (n = 54), mineral/organic mix (n = 8), subglaze (n = 4), and none (n = 47). Interior pigments were mineral (n = 11), organic (n = 7), mineral/organic mix (n = 29), and none (n = 71). Exterior surfaces included plain,

Figure 31.7. Mancos B/w, Sosi style, Animas variety.

polished, and slipped, but four had indented corrugations and two had obliterated corrugations. Interior surfaces exhibited plain, polished, and slipped manipulations.

Slip characteristics included 62 examples with thick-chalky slips, 5 with thick crackly, 15 thin, 20 washy, and 16 with no slip. Diorite porphyry dominated the tempering material, but minor amounts of sand, sherd, shale, sandstone, and other unidentified crushed rock were identified in many of the sherds. Augite diorite and diorite porphyry were identified in the pastes of eight sherds, an indeterminate crushed rock was the dominant temper along with sand and sherd in one example, and diorite porphyry and sand were identified in one sherd with a local silty, brown paste. Of the 118 sherds, 83 had the characteristic local silty, discolored brown to yellow paste, 29 were vitrified, and 6 were not analyzed.

Mancos B/w (Dogoszhi style; AD 1040–1150) was one of the more common Mancos styles, represented by 98 sherds from most of the rooms studied (see Table 31.1). Dogoszhi style designs, which are probably the most recognizable of the late Pueblo II period styles, are considered by most researchers to be the hallmark of the late AD 1000s. Similar to all of the Dogoszhi style ceramics, Mancos B/w (Dogoszhi style) of the Middle San Juan has rectilinear and curvilinear ribbons with filler composed primarily of oblique, straight-lined hachure (Figure 31.8). With the exception of occasional solidly filled elements (e.g., triangles, scrolls, or hooks) appended to the ends of ribbon elements, Dogoszhi style designs have no other associated elements or line elaborations. Congruent ceramic types from other traditions include Gallup B/w of the Cibola tradition, Chuska and Brimhall of the Chuska tradition, Dogoszhi B/w of the Kayenta tradition, and Mancos B/w (unassigned style) of the Northern San Juan tradition.

Figure 31.8. Mancos B/w, Dogoszhi style, Animas variety.

The Salmon sample had a variety of Dogoszhi style vessel forms, including bowls, jars, ladles, and seed jars. There were no whole or reconstructible vessels in the sample. All of the rooms containing Mancos B/w (Dogoszhi style) ceramics yielded bowls and jars, but Room 123B contained one ladle fragment and one seed jar rim fragment, and Room 100W contained the second ladle fragment. Pigments used for painted designs were mineral (n = 32), organic (n = 51), and mineral/organic mix (n = 15). Exterior surfaces included a variety of treatments, such as plain, polished, and slipped, and one bowl fragment had an indeterminate band on the exterior body. Interior treatments included the same variety of plain, polished, and slipped treatments. Variability in slip applications included thick chalky (n = 49), thick crackly (n = 5), thin (n = 12), and washy (n = 19); 13 examples had no slip.

Augite diorite was the most common tempering material in the Dogoszhi style ceramics, identified in 92 of the 98 examples. Minor materials included with the augite diorite in these examples were sand, sandstone, shale, sherd, and other unknown crushed rock. One sherd had both augite diorite and diorite porphyry in the ceramic paste, which indicated mixing of rock materials from different sources. One example had locally available coarse angular granite temper. Four examples had crushed rock of indeterminate type and source along with sherd and sand. The paste of all the ceramics was silty and discolored to brown or yellow, fitting with the expected local paste signature of the Animas Variety.

Mancos B/w (Chaco style; AD 1075–1150) was identified as a specific style to capture Animas Variety ceramics with characteristics of Chaco B/w of the Cibola tradition. Given the emphasis of this and subsequent studies on the influence of Chacoan potters on local pottery and the possibility of Chacoan people residing in the Middle San Juan region, the identification of Chaco B/w style design on local ceramics was considered quite important. Chaco style designs are similar to Dogoszhi style but have ribbon lines that are thicker than the hachure lines. The hachure lines are set close together and are well executed. Both Chaco B/w of the Cibola tradition and Chaco style design on other types are relatively rare. Toll and McKenna (1997) indicated that Chaco B/w does not exceed 1 percent in any of the Chaco Canyon assemblages.

Four body fragments from a single jar of Mancos B/w (Chaco style) were identified in Room 100W, suggesting that the style is rare on locally produced crushed rock–tempered pottery. The jar design was executed in mineral paint over a washy slip. Temper was identified as augite diorite, sand, and sherd in a silty, brown to yellowish paste.

Mancos B/w (Puerco style; AD 1030–1175) was segregated as a style designation to capture the influence of Cibola and southern Cibola styles, generally classified as Puerco B/w. As described by Hays-Gilpin and van Hartesveldt (1998:77), the sets of "vertical parallel lines or checkerboards used as panel dividers to separate areas of solid elements are diagnostic." Banded design layouts are the most common presentations on jars and bowls. In the Northern San Juan (Mesa Verde) tradition, Puerco style designs occur in low frequencies within Mancos B/w, as illustrated by Swannack (1969:82, Figure 58c) on a globular, narrow-necked jar. The Chaco Center's definition of Puerco B/w within the Cibola tradition, however, is based on differences in surface treatment between Puerco and Escavada B/w. Researchers at the Chaco Center consider Puerco and Escavada B/w to be within the Sosi style and differentiate between them based on the finer surface finish of Puerco and the lack of polish on Escavada (see Toll and McKenna 1997). During the Salmon Research Initiative, however, we chose to differentiate Puerco style and Puerco B/w based on stylistic differences rather than surface manipulations (which are more sensitive to use attrition and postdepositional processes of alteration).

Eighteen Mancos B/w (Puerco style) sherds were identified; no whole or reconstructible vessels were identified (Figure 31.9). Bowl, jar, and seed jar fragments were recovered from Rooms 30W, 90W, 100W, 123B, 123W, and 127W. More than half of the Puerco style sherds were from Rooms 100W and 123W. All of the exterior pigments were identified as organic (n = 11), and the interior pigments were mineral (n = 1), organic (n = 3), and mineral/organic mix (n = 3). Exterior surfaces were slipped (n = 14), polished (n = 1), or indented corrugated (n = 3). Painted interior surfaces were all slipped. Slip coverage was predominantly thick chalky (n = 15), but one example had a thin slip and one example had a washy slip. All 18 sherds had augite diorite temper with minor amounts of sand, sherd, or shale in a local silty, discolored brown to yellow paste.

Mancos B/w (Reserve style; AD 1100–1200) follows the design characteristics of Reserve B/w of the Mogollon Rim area (see Martin and Rinaldo 1950) and Reserve B/w of the Puerco Valley as described by Hays-Gilpin and van Hardesveldt (1998). Reserve style motifs consist of opposed solid and hachured elements (e.g., Sosi and Dogoszhi style) in the same design layout (Figure 31.10). Generally, the hachured elements are larger than the solid elements. The hachure lines are oblique, not diagonal as with Tularosa B/w style designs. Some sherds could be typed as Dogoszhi style, but solid elements on Dogoszhi style ceramics only occur as appended triangles or other elements on the ends of Dogoszhi hachure.

Figure 31.9. Mancos B/w, Puerco style, Animas variety.

Thirty-six sherds from Rooms 30B, 30W, 90W, 100W, 123B, and 127W were identified as Mancos B/w (Reserve style). Jar forms were the most common, represented by 27 sherds, followed by nine bowl fragments. Although bowl fragments were few, they were identified in all rooms except 30B; jar fragments were present in all room contexts. Exterior pigments included mineral (n = 3), organic (n = 22), and mineral/organic mix (n = 2). Interior pigments on the bowls were organic (n = 8) and mineral/organic mix (n = 1). Exterior painted surfaces for jars included polished and slipped, but bowl exteriors were plain, polished, or slipped. All of the interior jar surfaces were plain, and the bowl interiors were polished or slipped under the painted designs. Slip application included thick chalky (n = 23), thick crackly (n = 1), thin (n = 7), and washy (n = 2). All of the sherds had augite diorite temper with minor inclusions of sand, shale, sherd, or sandstone. The paste was identified as a silty, discolored brown to yellow in 28 examples and vitrified in 8 examples.

Early McElmo B/w. Early in the analysis, we began to notice sherds with Pueblo II attributes that also had ticked rims or one or two thick framing

Figure 31.10. Mancos B/w, Reserve style, Animas variety.

lines below the rim, similar to McElmo B/w. Pueblo II attributes of these sherds included thin vessel walls, thin to rounded rims, and Sosi, Dogoszhi, Reserve, or Puerco style designs in a Pueblo II layout (e.g., not banded or quartered). The combination of these attributes, such as a Dogoszhi style design on a bowl with thin vessel walls, thin rounded rim, and a few dots painted on top of the rim, suggested a transition from Pueblo II designs to McElmo B/w pottery (Figure 31.11). Thus, we added the type Early McElmo B/w to identify these ceramics and to track the probable transition in design and vessel formation from Pueblo II to Pueblo III white ware. During a visit to the Crow Canyon Archaeological Center in October of 2004, Tori Myers and I mentioned this probable transition to Scott Ortman and Jonathan Till. They agreed that the same phenomenon was occurring at their sites in the Cortez area, thus supporting our supposition.

Ninety-one sherds and one partial ladle from Room 30W were identified as Early McElmo B/w (Table 31.2). Room 100W contained the majority of

Figure 31.11. Early McElmo B/w, Animas variety.

Table 31.2. Animas Variety Early McElmo B/w in Salmon rooms.

Room	Vessel Form	Sherd Count	Weight
030B	Bowl	1	14.1
030W	Bowl	4	68.5
	Ladle	3	26.6
	Subtotal	7	95.1
100W	Bowl	50	900.7
	Jar	1	23
	Ladle	15	223.3
	Subtotal	66	1147
123B	Bowl	7	124.2
	Jar	1	3.4
	Subtotal	8	127.6
123W	Bowl	5	43.6
	Ladle	1	21
	Subtotal	6	64.6
127W	Bowl	4	68.6
Total		92	1517

Early McElmo B/w sherds, which is not surprising given the known Chacoan deposits in the room. In the Northern San Juan (Mesa Verde) region, McElmo B/w has been identified at sites as early as AD 1075. Thus, our beginning date for Early McElmo B/w is AD 1050, and the ending date is AD 1100, giving the type 50 years to develop into a full McElmo style and bowl rim morphology. Without the benefit of well-dated contexts at Middle San Juan sites we have to rely on the dating of equivalent types in the Northern San Juan (Mesa Verde) region and some general contextual data to provide date ranges.

The Early McElmo B/w ceramics at Salmon included a variety of pigments. Of the eight sherds with exterior designs, seven had organic paint and one had an indeterminate pigment. All of the sherds with exterior designs also had interior designs, which is typical of some McElmo style pottery. Interior pigments consisted of mineral (n = 7), organic (n = 71), mineral/organic mix (n = 9), and subglaze (n = 3). Exterior surfaces were plain (n = 17), polished (n = 6), slipped (n = 61), slipped and painted (n = 7), and indented corrugated (n = 1). Interior surfaces were plain (n = 2), plain and painted (n = 2), polished and painted (n = 5), and slipped and painted (n = 83). Slip application included thick chalky (n = 51), thick crackly (n = 6), thin (n = 6), and washy (n = 22). Augite diorite was the predominant tempering material in 92 percent (n = 85) of the Early McElmo B/w sherds. Most of these examples had minor inclusions of sand, shale, sherd, and other crushed rock, and two examples had fragments of diorite porphyry. Five sherds had locally available granitic temper and four had unidentified crushed igneous rock that was not determined as local but was not diorite porphyry. Paste characteristics were mostly local in appearance, with 85 examples having silty, discolored brown to yellow paste and seven having a vitrified paste.

McElmo B/w. McElmo B/w pottery, as defined for the Northern San Juan region, most often occurs as bowls, but narrow-necked ollas, dippers, seed jars, and pitchers have been identified. Breternitz et al. (1974) noted that McElmo B/w includes a wider range of forms than Mesa Verde B/w, but mugs and kiva jars are more common in Mesa Verde B/w. Breternitz et al. (1974) also noted that McElmo rims include rounded and tapered forms, but in the Salmon Research Initiative, the combination of rounded and tapered forms with thin vessel walls, Pueblo II designs, and sparsely spaced rim ticking was considered an Early McElmo characteristic, transitional between Pueblo II and actual McElmo pottery. In early descriptions of the type (see Rohn 1971:168) it is identified as a variety of Mesa Verde B/w. Although Breternitz et al. (1974:42) described McElmo as transitional between Mancos B/w and Mesa Verde B/w and noted that McElmo designs are occasionally "simply crudely executed Mesa Verde patterns," our analysis of McElmo in the Salmon sample indicates that there is a distinctive patterning to McElmo designs that supports its existence as a type and not just a transitional continuum between Mancos and Mesa Verde.

In total, 986 McElmo B/w sherds were identified in the Salmon assemblage from the six rooms analyzed. Animas Variety McElmo B/w was identified based on a series of criteria, including rim morphology, vessel wall thickness, framing line pattern, exterior design pattern, interior design layout, and interior design complexity (Figure 31.12). Crudeness or sloppiness of design was not used as a criterion for classifying sherds as McElmo B/w because it was found that numerous Mesa Verde B/w sherds could also be described as crude or sloppy. Rim morphology for McElmo was primarily nontapering and flat, but rims with rounded profiles also had thick vessel walls. Mean vessel wall thickness was 6.0 mm, with a minimum of 4.0 mm and a maximum of 9.9 mm. Framing line patterns were one of the primary criteria for classifying McElmo ceramics. These patterns included no framing lines, one or more thick framing lines, and one or more thin framing lines. The most common pattern was one or two thick framing lines below the rim and the same pattern terminating the design. Exterior designs consisted solely of isolated elements occurring once or repeated several times around the bowl. Roughly 10 percent (n = 83) of the 797 McElmo B/w bowl body and rim fragments from Salmon have exterior painted designs; not all of the exterior decorations were set just below the rim. Although not part of this study, the small number of McElmo sherds with exterior designs begs the question of interior design complexity and exterior design element form. I believe that during the AD 1100s at Salmon the need for exterior bowl designs on McElmo pottery for use in feasting contexts began prior to production of Mesa Verde B/w.

Interior bowl designs below the framing lines were generally well organized on the McElmo pottery from Salmon. Although many of the elements were simple solid triangles or triangles with hachure fill, they were organized in a banded layout in an alternating pattern between a series of one or two thick framing lines. For the most part, this pattern remained relatively unchanged but did become more complex, until Mesa Verde style designs began to take their place.

All of the rooms sampled contained McElmo B/w. As shown in Table 31.3, the variety of vessel forms included bowls, jars, mugs, ladles, seed jars, and miniatures. Bowls represent the majority (81%) of vessel forms, but the number of other shapes indicates the variety of uses for McElmo B/w. Although rare, McElmo mugs were identified in Rooms 64W, 90W, 100W, and 127W. Seed jars were also identified, but the absence of McElmo kiva jars should be noted. Exterior designs were primarily executed in organic pigment (n = 217), but mineral paint (n = 1), mineral/organic mix (n = 19), and indeterminate pigment (n = 7) were also identified. Interior pigments

Figure 31.12. McElmo B/w, Animas variety.

Table 31.3. The distribution of Animas Variety McElmo B/w in Salmon rooms.

Room	Vessel Form	Sherd Count	Weight
030A	Bowl	12	160.5
	Jar	3	26.1
	Subtotal	15	186.6
030B	Bowl	20	277.1
	Jar	17	177.7
	Subtotal	37	454.8
030W	Bowl	82	1362.3
	Jar	6	95.1
	Ladle	1	9.9
	Subtotal	89	1467.3
064W	Bowl	13	175.6
	Jar	2	40.7
	Mug	1	5.5
	Subtotal	16	221.8
090W	Bowl	16	212.6
	Jar	1	4.6
	Mug	1	4.4
	Subtotal	18	221.6
100W	Bowl	573	12195.2
	Jar	109	2907.3
	Ladle	30	741
	Mug	2	58.1
	Seed jar	2	42.3
	Subtotal	716	15943.9
123B	Bowl	20	436
	Jar	1	9.2
	Seed jar	1	8.1
	Subtotal	22	453.3
123W	Bowl	18	192.2
	Jar	1	10.8
	Subtotal	19	203
127W	Bowl	43	728.6
	Jar	7	106
	Miniature	2	7.1
	Mug	1	14.4
	Seed jar	1	17.3
	Subtotal	54	873.4
Total		986	20025.7

were organic (n = 787), mineral (n = 7), mineral/organic mix (n = 24), subglaze (n = 9), and indeterminate (n = 2). Unpainted exterior surfaces were plain, polished, slipped, obliterated corrugated, and indeterminate. Painted exterior surfaces included plain, polished, and slipped; most (n = 231) were slipped. Not all of the McElmo bowl interior surfaces were slipped prior to painting; 6 were plain and painted, and 45 were polished and painted. The majority, however, were slipped and painted (n = 777).

Slip application on all vessel forms was variable, including thick chalky (n = 774), thick crackly (n = 90), thin (n = 49), and washy (n = 21). As indicated earlier, the application of washy slips is interpreted as an influence of the Chaco Cibola tradition. Augite diorite was identified in 95 percent of the McElmo B/w sherds, some of which had minor inclusions of sand, shale, sherd, sandstone, and other unidentified crushed rock. Nineteen sherds had a mixture of augite diorite and diorite porphyry, but the paste clearly fit the local pattern of high silt content and brownish discoloration. Locally available, coarse angular granite was identified in 22 examples, indeterminate igneous rock of nonlocal origin was identified in 4 sherds, and 1 sherd had completely indeterminate temper. All 27 of these sherds, however, had the characteristic local silty, discolored brown to yellow paste. Examination of the paste indicated that 859 sherds had high silt content, discolored brown to yellow appearance, 125 were vitrified, and 2 were coded as not analyzed.

McElmo–Mesa Verde B/w. Based on design characteristics of McElmo and Mesa Verde B/w, we identified a transitional type between the two as McElmo–Mesa Verde B/w. A tentative date range of AD 1175–1225 is proposed for the transitional type. Although relatively rare in the Salmon sample, we found some sherds that shared characteristics of both types and could not be easily classified as either. The sherds had either the complexity of a Mesa Verde design and a single thick framing line of McElmo B/w or a Mesa Verde design on the interior and a free-floating McElmo design on the exterior.

Seventy-eight sherds were McElmo–Mesa Verde B/w. As shown in Table 31.4, not all rooms contained the transitional type, and it occurred primarily as bowls. Designs on the exterior were executed in organic (n = 54) and mineral/organic mix (n = 2). Interior pigments were identified as organic (n = 73) and mineral/organic mix (n = 5). Exterior surfaces included 22 slipped, 1 polished and painted, and 55 slipped and painted. Interior surfaces included 77 slipped and painted, and 1 polished and painted. Slip application consisted of thick-chalky (n = 69), thick-crackly (n = 7), and thin (n = 1). All of the sherds were tempered with augite diorite, along with minor inclusions of sand, sherd, shale, and other crushed rock in most examples. Paste characteristics were local high silt, brown to yellow discoloration in 76 examples, and vitrified in 2 examples.

Mesa Verde B/w. Mesa Verde B/w, originally defined as the classic Pueblo III type for the Mesa

Table 31.4. The distribution of Animas Variety McElmo–Mesa Verde B/w from Salmon.

Room	Vessel Form	Sherd Count	Weight
030W	Bowl	4	75.6
064W	Bowl	1	7.1
100W	Bowl	49	1118.5
	Ladle	4	210
	Subtotal	53	1328.5
123A	Bowl	8	99
123B	Bowl	7	173.6
	Jar	1	21.2
	Subtotal	8	194.8
127W	Bowl	4	75.3
Total		78	1780.3

Verde region (Rohn 1971; Breternitz et al. 1974), is viewed in the Four Corners region as the epitome of ceramic development and is the hallmark of the Pueblo III period. As defined by Breternitz et al. (1974), Mesa Verde designs are well organized and symmetrical. Based on the assemblage at Salmon, they developed out of McElmo B/w through the continuum of complexity until the framing lines became more complex and banded designs lost their simplicity. Mesa Verde style framing lines have combinations of thin and thick lines or a series of thin lines with dot or tick embellishments between the lines. The most common combination of framing lines is a pattern of one or two thick lines followed by several thin lines below the rim with the same pattern terminating the design below the banded motif. The banded motif is more complex on Mesa Verde style pottery than on McElmo, with frequently interlocking elements rather than simple repeated elements (Figure 31.13). Some of the Mesa Verde bands have multiple interlocking and mirrored elements in symmetrical relationships that are extremely complex.

Most of the Mesa Verde designs are abstract and geometrical, but occasional zoomorphic figures are present either as exterior isolated elements or as isolated elements in the centers of bowls. In addition to banded design layouts, Mesa Verde bowls and jars frequently have all-over design layouts consisting of design patterns created to cover all of the open space within a bowl or on the exterior of a jar (Figure 31.14). These designs are quite complex and often include negative designs whereby the majority of the white space is covered with black paint, creating the appearance of a black background with white forming the design. Although not undertaken with the Salmon assemblage at this time, a detailed stylistic study is warranted as a means of comparing Middle San Juan and Northern San Juan (Mesa Verde) design element and layout differences from a regional perspective.

During the analysis for the 1984 Aztec Excavation Project (Reed and Myers 2006), designs reminiscent of Pueblo I Rosa style walking circles were identified on the exterior surfaces of both McElmo and Mesa Verde bowls. Further recognition of these types of elements and their frequencies in assemblages would be informative for interpreting stylistic developments and probable ancestral ties.

As shown in Table 31.5, Mesa Verde B/w was present in all rooms examined during the Salmon Research Initiative. The variety of vessel types present in the sherd assemblage included bowls, jars, ladles, and mugs. The absence of kiva jars and seed jars is noteworthy, although the next phase of analysis will include all whole vessels, which may reveal greater variety in vessel forms. Mugs were identified in Rooms 30W, 64W, and 100W. Of the 673 bowl fragments, 60 percent (n = 401) had exterior designs, suggesting the importance of exterior exposure of design symbols for feasting, serving, and other social events for which exterior designs might have been important.

Exterior pigments included organic (n = 392), mineral/organic mix (n = 36), subglaze (n = 7), and indeterminate (n = 1). Interior pigments included organic (n = 626), mineral/organic mix (n = 45), subglaze (n = 5), and indeterminate (n = 2). There was no evidence of a Mesa Verde polychrome with the use of mineral and organic on the same vessel in

Figure 31.13. Mesa Verde B/w, banded pattern sherds, Animas variety.

Figure 31.14. Mesa Verde B/w, all-over pattern sherds, Animas variety.

which an organic design was outlined in mineral or some other combination, as defined by Abel (1955). This combination of paint types is no longer recognized as a type but is often identified as a variety of Mesa Verde B/w (Breternitz et al. 1974). Given the definition of a polychrome as more than one color of pigment on a ceramic vessel, the use of two black pigments on a vessel to produce a design would not be considered a polychrome. The term "mineral/organic mix" is used here heuristically to describe the probable mixture of mineral and organic pigments or mineral pigment placed over an organic binder and not the use of the two pigments to produce a multi-paint design.

Unpainted exterior surfaces included plain (n = 1), polished (n = 16), slipped (n = 257), and indeterminate (n = 1), and painted surfaces were identified as polished (n = 3) or slipped (n = 431). Unpainted interior surfaces (primarily jar or mug forms) were either plain (n = 28) or slipped (n = 5), and painted interior surfaces were either polished (n = 8) or slipped (n = 668). Slip application was variable, similar to the other Animas Variety types, including thick-chalky (n = 624), thick-crackly (n = 50), thin (n = 26), and washy (n = 2).

Augite diorite was the predominant temper in 97 percent of the Mesa Verde B/w Animas Variety sherds (n = 688). Minor inclusions in 77 percent of the augite diorite–tempered sherds included sand, shale, sherd, sandstone, and other unidentified crushed rock. Seven sherds had both augite diorite and diorite porphyry fragments as tempering material. Five sherds had locally available coarse angular granite temper, and nine sherds had either unidentified crushed igneous rock or unidentified crushed rock and sand. Paste characteristics were primarily local high silt content and discolored to brown or yellow (n = 591), but 113 were vitrified, and 5 were coded as not analyzed.

Other White Ware Types. Sherds that could not be classified into traditional type categories were assigned to other general descriptive classes: Pueblo I–II style B/w, Pueblo II–III B/w, Pueblo III B/w, painted b/w, and slipped white. The frequencies of these descriptive classes and their distributions within the Salmon rooms are provided in Table 31.6. In total, 832 sherds were placed into one of these descriptive classes, representing 27 percent of the Northern San Juan Animas Variety White Ware. Most of these sherds were too small to identify to ceramic type but were not small enough to be excluded from the sample.

Table 31.5. The distribution of Animas Variety Mesa Verde B/w in Salmon rooms.

Room	Vessel Form	Sherd Count	Weight
030A	Bowl	30	600.5
030B	Bowl	39	765.2
	Jar	1	7.1
	Subtotal	40	772.3
030W	Bowl	29	758.9
	Jar	4	57.5
	Ladle	3	178.1
	Mug	3	85.7
	Subtotal	39	1080.2
064W	Bowl	12	178.4
	Mug	1	6.3
	Subtotal	13	184.7
090W	Bowl	81	1582.1
	Jar	11	207.8
	Mug	4	58.8
	Subtotal	96	1848.7
100W	Bowl	366	9096.7
	Jar	3	31.8
	Ladle	1	8.6
	Mug	2	45.8
	Subtotal	372	9182.9
123B	Bowl	24	408.8
	Jar	1	23.9
	Subtotal	25	432.7
123W	Bowl	5	40.2
	Ladle	1	48.9
	Subtotal	6	89.1
127W	Bowl	87	1231
	Jar	1	10.8
	Subtotal	88	1241.8
Total		709	15432.9

Table 31.6. The distribution of Northern San Juan Animas Variety untyped white ware from Salmon.

Room	Descriptive Class	Sherd Count	Weight
030A	Pueblo I–II style B/w	1	3.1
	Pueblo II–III style B/w	38	356.9
	Pueblo III style B/w	5	69
	Slipped white	15	152.5
	Subtotal	59	581.5
030B	Painted B/w	1	9.7
	Pueblo I–II style B/w	1	9.4
	Pueblo II–III style B/w	71	812.1
	Pueblo III style B/w	2	15
	Slipped white	34	341.4
	Subtotal	109	1,187.6
030W	Painted B/w	1	2.8
	Pueblo I–II style B/w	3	12.4
	Pueblo II–III style B/w	64	651.1
	Pueblo III style B/w	23	173.5
	Slipped white	14	125.8
	Subtotal	105	965.6
064W	Pueblo II–III style B/w	11	48.9
	Pueblo III style B/w	13	116.4
	Slipped white	23	319.6
	Subtotal	47	484.9
090W	Painted B/w	2	30.9
	Pueblo I–II style B/w	1	7.3
	Pueblo II–III style B/w	14	133.6
	Pueblo III style B/w	4	43.4
	Slipped white	4	61.6
	Subtotal	25	276.8
100W	Painted B/w	5	50.6
	Pueblo I–II style B/w	4	161.6
	Pueblo II–III style B/w	48	390.1
	Pueblo III style B/w	160	2,154.3
	Slipped white	96	1,398.7
	Subtotal	313	4,155.3
123B	Pueblo II–III style B/w	6	61.2
	Pueblo III style B/w	11	93.5
	Subtotal	17	154.7
123W	Pueblo II–III style B/w	11	100.3
	Pueblo III style B/w	2	11.7
	Slipped white	1	6.4
	Subtotal	14	118.4
127W	Pueblo I–II style B/w	1	4.1
	Pueblo II–III style B/w	61	501.7
	Pueblo III style B/w	2	23.9
	Slipped white	79	1,056.8
	Subtotal	143	1,586.5
Total		832	9,511.3

Gray Ware

Northern San Juan Animas Variety Gray Ware was the dominant utility ware identified in the six rooms sampled during the Salmon Research Initiative. This trend is not considered unusual, given the propensity of potters to produce their own local utility ware vessels. The exception to this trend occurred in Chaco Canyon and other sites in the San Juan Basin during the late Pueblo I and Pueblo II periods when local potters produced roughly less than half of their sand-tempered utility ware in exchange for trachyte-tempered gray ware from the Chuska Valley to the west (see Toll 2001; Toll and McKenna 1998). There has been much speculation concerning the impetus for such a high percentage of Chuskan pottery at Chacoan sites in the canyon and outliers out of the canyon, including redistribution networks, high-status elite access to goods, and ceremonial feasting.

From a pottery technology perspective, the igneous trachyte material provides superior tempering in terms of absorbing heat and preventing the ceramic material from cracking and weakening during heating and cooling. Thus, Chuskan cooking pots would have been a more desirable product in contrast to the quartz sand–tempered cooking pots of the San Juan Basin, which would have weakened more rapidly. In the same way, augite diorite–tempered cooking pots in the Middle San Juan were a superior product manufactured with locally available igneous rock materials. Ninety-two percent of the total gray ware assemblage is Animas Variety Gray Ware tempered with augite diorite, so it is clear that local potters understood the benefits of igneous temper. Given the work involved in collecting and crushing the proper river cobbles for use as temper, the benefits were worth the amount of labor involved. During our own experiments with crushing river cobbles, the key was finding the right decomposing cobble, which made crushing much easier.

It should be noted that the size of the temper grains in the Animas Variety Gray Ware is consistently large. I have speculated that the large size of the grains and the percent of temper may be the result of compensating for high-silt clays, but experimentation would be useful to test this idea. Minor inclusions identified in augite diorite–tempered gray ware included sand, shale, sherd, sandstone, and other unidentified crushed rock. The remaining 8 percent of the gray ware contained augite diorite and diorite porphyry (n = 11), coarse angular granite (locally available, n = 413), unidentified crushed igneous rock with sand or sherd (n = 13), crushed quartzite (n = 2), sand with mica inclusions (possibly granitic, n = 2), and indeterminate (n = 1). Paste characteristics were identified as local high silt content with brown to yellow discoloration in 8800 examples, vitrified in 566 examples, indeterminate in 5 examples, and coded as not analyzed in 1 example.

Vessel forms included jars (n = 9349), bowls (n = 17), ladles (n = 2), miniatures (n = 1), wide-mouthed jars (n = 2), and indeterminate (n = 1). Bowls were identified by curvature and interior surface treatment; the interiors of 14 examples were highly polished. As shown in Table 31.7, corrugated gray ware comprised the majority of the utility ware and was present in all rooms sampled during the study. Mancos Gray, a late Pueblo I to early Pueblo II type, was present only in Rooms 30W and 100W but in very low frequencies. One fragment of locally produced Fillet Rim Gray, equivalent to the Northern San Juan Mummy Lake Gray, was identified in Room 30W. Corrugated rim sherds were not assigned to the traditional type names of the Northern San Juan tradition (e.g., Mancos, Dolores, and Mesa Verde Corrugated) but were given general categories of Pueblo II, Pueblo II–III, and Pueblo III Corrugated.

The difficulties in applying these corrugated gray ware categories for dating site contexts lies in the overall morphology of the vessel from which the rim eversion measurements were taken and the possibility of functional differences as well as temporal differences in the rim eversion data. Nevertheless, Pueblo II Corrugated rims were defined by rim eversion measurements of less than 30 degrees, following the definition established by Blinman (1988) and Blinman and Wilson (1989). Pueblo II–III Corrugated rims were defined by rim eversion measurements between 31 and 60 degrees and Pueblo III Corrugated rims were between 61 and 90 degrees. Based on our rim eversion data, however, none of the rim sherds analyzed during the study fit the Pueblo III Corrugated criterion, suggesting that the Pueblo III deposits in the rooms examined may not date late enough into the AD 1200s to capture the transition into highly everted rim morphology. Further analysis of these data and associations with room stratigraphy are presented in Chapter 32.

Cibola Animas Variety Types

Cibola Animas Variety ceramics were identified in much the same way as the Northern San Juan ceramics, with high silt content paste and brown to yellow discoloration, but the tempering material was composed of various combinations of sand, sherd, shale, and sandstone. The primary criterion was paste discoloration and high silt content similar to

Table 31.7. Northern San Juan Animas Variety gray ware types from Salmon rooms.

Room	Ceramic Type	Sherd Count	Weight
030A	Corrugated gray	591	5,290.1
	Plain gray	5	29.2
	Polished gray	5	16.5
	Pueblo II corrugated	27	317
	Subtotal	628	5,652.8
030B	Corrugated gray	674	6,023.8
	Indeterminate gray	1	6.4
	Plain gray	20	151.8
	Polished gray	2	6.0
	Pueblo II corrugated	14	115
	Subtotal	711	6,303.0
030W	Banded gray	1	2.4
	Corrugated gray	469	4,809.7
	Fillet Rim Gray	1	10.2
	Indeterminate gray	6	35.5
	Mancos Gray	1	7.4
	Plain gray	84	630.9
	Polished gray	12	126.9
	Pueblo II corrugated	71	1,758.7
	Pueblo II–III corrugated	25	751.8
	Subtotal	670	8,133.5
064W	Corrugated gray	288	3,017.9
	Indeterminate gray	3	24.4
	Plain gray	10	116.3
	Polished gray	1	23.8
	Pueblo II corrugated	12	109.7
	Subtotal	314	3,292.1
090W	Corrugated gray	67	792.9
	Indeterminate gray	2	8.6
	Plain gray	29	371.0
	Polished gray	4	213.3
	Pueblo II corrugated	15	284.7
	Pueblo II–III corrugated	59	1,096.5
	Subtotal	176	2,767.0
100W	Banded gray	2	39.9
	Corrugated gray	4042	39,978.3
	Indeterminate gray	72	665.8
	Mancos Gray	3	63.4
	Plain gray	29	375.4
	Polished gray	6	55.7
	Pueblo II corrugated	144	3,580.8
	Pueblo II–III corrugated	154	5,396.4
	Subtotal	4452	50,155.7
123B	Corrugated gray	4	22.5
	Indeterminate gray	3	16.9
	Plain gray	2	11.5
	Pueblo II corrugated	24	354.3
	Pueblo II–III corrugated	6	138.8
	Subtotal	39	544.0
123W	Corrugated gray	34	291.4
	Indeterminate gray	1	9.6
	Polished gray	1	3.8
	Pueblo II corrugated	5	109.9
	Pueblo II–III corrugated	13	81.7
	Subtotal	54	496.4
127W	Corrugated gray	1932	21,506.5
	Indeterminate gray	2	33.4
	Plain gray	52	588.4
	Polished gray	3	13.6
	Pueblo II corrugated	308	3,967.0
	Pueblo II–III corrugated	31	906.8
	Subtotal	2328	27,015.7
Total		9372	104,360.2

that of the Northern San Juan Animas Variety pottery considered to have local origin; 480 sherds were identified as Cibola Animas Variety. The original conception of a local variety of Cibola pottery was from analysis of the Tommy site assemblage, a Pueblo II to early Pueblo III site located just east of the confluence of the San Juan and Animas Rivers in Farmington. Excavation of the Tommy site was conducted through a partnership of San Juan College and the Bolack Minerals Co., B-Square Ranch/Bolack Museum Foundation, during a 1999–2003 field school. During analysis of the field school assemblages we noticed large numbers of Cibola ceramics that did not fit the traditional type description but that had paste characteristics more similar to the local crushed rock–tempered pottery. In contrast to much of the Cibola ceramics from the San Juan Basin, the local Cibola ceramics produced in the Middle San Juan lacked trachyte fragments, and the sherd temper consisted of local Middle San Juan crushed sherd. This initial observation prompted our classification of sherds into a local Cibola production tract, identified as Cibola Animas Variety. All of the Cibola ceramic types are represented in the local variety in the Salmon sample (Table 31.8). Of note is the low number of gray ware ceramics in the assemblage, but given the superiority of augite diorite–tempered gray ware for cooking pots in the Middle San Juan region, the lack of sand-tempered gray ware may not be significant.

Table 31.8. Cibola Animas Variety types from Salmon.

Ceramic Type	Sherd Count	Weight
White Ware		
Kiatuthlanna B/w	2	65.2
Red Mesa B/w	12	97.4
Escavada B/w	48	557.3
Gallup B/w	62	639.6
Chaco B/w	13	73
Puerco B/w	12	159.1
Reserve B/w	15	115.4
Tularosa B/w	1	16.7
Chaco-McElmo B/w	148	1860
Pueblo I–II style B/w	15	75
Pueblo II–III style B/w	24	188.7
Pueblo III style B/w	12	121.5
Painted B/w	2	20.4
Slipped white	59	729.5
Gray Ware		
Pueblo II–III corrugated	1	48.8
Corrugated gray	20	202
Plain gray	22	150.7
Polished gray	12	133.2
Total	480	5,253.5

White Ware

Nine Cibola Animas Variety types were identified, paralleling the Cibola tradition of the San Juan Basin. They are Kiatuthlanna B/w, Red Mesa B/w, Escavada B/w, Gallup B/w, Chaco B/w, Puerco B/w, Reserve B/w, Chaco-McElmo B/w, and Tularosa B/w. All of the types have design styles typical of the Cibola tradition but have paste characteristics typical of the Middle San Juan.

Kiatuthlanna B/w (AD 850–925) has lines of fine to medium width that overlap at the junctures. Line elements repeat in a rectilinear pattern, similar to Piedra B/w or White Mound B/w designs, but the overlap at line junctures is a hallmark of Kiatuthlanna style. Solid elements are most commonly triangles with infrequent elaborations, such as dots or ticks. Surfaces are well polished, and slips were often applied. Two Kiatuthlanna B/w Animas Variety sherds were identified in the Salmon sample from Room 90W. They both had mineral-painted designs over a thinly slipped surface, and temper was identified as sand and sherd in a silty, discolored brown to yellow paste.

Red Mesa B/w (AD 900–1050) is the hallmark white ware of early Pueblo II assemblages in the San Juan Basin. Congruent ceramic types include Newcomb and Naschitti in the Chuska tradition, Cortez B/w in the Northern San Juan tradition, and Kana-a B/w in the Kayenta tradition. Elements include scrolls, solid triangles (usually with dots or ticks along one side), parallel lines, and checkerboards. Parallel lines, usually wider than Kiatuthlanna style lines, often frame sets of solid elements or interlocking scrolls. Squiggle hachure elements are common and are usually thick-lined designs interpreted as the precursor to the Dogoszhi style designs of Mancos B/w of the Northern San Juan tradition. This design style became widespread during the early developments of the Chacoan system.

Twelve Red Mesa B/w Animas Variety sherds were identified in the Salmon sample (Figure 31.15). Their distribution was rather limited, with one bowl fragment in Room 30A, one bowl fragment in Room 30B, one bowl fragment in Room 30W, one bowl and one jar fragment in Room 90W, one bowl, one ladle, and two jar fragments in Room 100W, and one bowl and two jar fragments in Room 127W. Exterior pigments included mineral (n = 4), organic (n = 2), and indeterminate (n = 1); the organic paint was identified on jar exteriors. Interior pigments were mineral (n = 3), organic (n = 3), and indeterminate (n = 1). Exterior surfaces were plain (n = 2), polished (n = 1),

Figure 31.15. Red Mesa B/w, Animas variety.

slipped (n = 2), slipped and painted (n = 6), or indeterminate (n = 1). Interior surfaces were plain (n = 5), slipped (n = 1), plain and painted (n = 1), polished and painted (n = 1), or slipped and painted (n = 4). Slip application was identified as thick-chalky (n = 2), thin (n = 4), or washy (n = 4). Tempering material was rather consistent, with sand and shale (n = 5), sand and sherd (n = 5), and sand, sherd, and shale (n = 2). Local silty, discolored brown to yellow pastes were identified in nine sherds, but three sherds had vitrified pastes retaining some of the discoloration.

Escavada B/w Animas Variety. As defined for the Salmon study, Escavada B/w consists of Sosi style designs, mostly following the style defined for the Kayenta type Sosi B/w (Colton 1955; Hays-Gilpin and van Hartesvelt 1998). Surfaces may be either highly polished or poorly polished, in contrast to the definition set forth by the Chaco Center in their differentiation of Escavada and Puerco B/w types (see Toll and McKenna 1997). Escavada designs consist of large solid elements such as parallel lines, solid triangles, scrolls, and large checkerboards without evidence of line or solid element embellishments such as the dots or ticks common to Red Mesa B/w. The primary differences between Animas Variety and Escavada of the Cibola tradition lies with the paste texture and occasionally the paint type. Escavada Animas Variety will have darker silty pastes with a brown to yellow discoloration, whereas vessels produced to the south will have cleaner, gray to buff paste with significantly less silt. In addition, Animas Variety sherds will frequently have organic paint in contrast to the mineral-painted Escavada sherds in the San Juan Basin.

Forty-eight Escavada B/w Animas Variety sherds were identified from Rooms 30W, 64W, 90W, 100W, 123B, 123W, and 127W (Table 31.9). Almost half of the Escavada sherds were from Room 100W, including an effigy/figurine base fragment and two ladle rim fragments (examples in Figure 31.16). Exterior pigments were mineral (n = 16), organic (n = 3), and mineral/organic mix (n = 2). Interior pigments were mineral (n = 19), organic (n = 5), and mineral/organic mix (n = 3). Exterior surfaces were plain (n = 8), polished (n = 2), slipped (n = 17), plain and painted (n = 1), polished and painted (n = 3), and slipped and painted (n = 17). Interior surfaces were plain (n = 21), polished and painted (n = 1), and slipped and painted (n = 26). Slip application was identified as thick-chalky (n = 1), thick-crackly (n = 5), thin (n = 4), or washy (n = 33). Washy application was the most common slip coverage identified in the Escavada B/w Animas Variety assemblage, suggesting the influence of Chaco Cibolan technology or potters at Salmon and probably the Middle San Juan region.

Table 31.9. Escavada B/w Animas Variety from Salmon rooms.

Room	Vessel Form	Sherd Count	Weight
030W	Bowl	2	49.7
	Jar	7	43.1
	Subtotal	9	92.8
064W	Bowl	1	10.7
090W	Bowl	3	42.4
	Jar	2	9.6
	Subtotal	5	52
100W	Bowl	13	136
	Effigy/figurine	1	56
	Jar	7	133.5
	Ladle	2	7
	Subtotal	23	332.5
123B	Jar	1	13.2
	Ladle	1	10.9
	Subtotal	2	24.1
123W	Bowl	3	19
	Jar	2	2.9
	Subtotal	5	21.9
127W	Bowl	2	20
	Jar	1	3.3
	Subtotal	3	23.3
Total		48	557.3

Figure 31.16. Escavada B/w, Animas variety.

Tempering material was identified as fine quartz sand (n = 2), medium quartz sand (n = 2), multilithic sand (n = 1), sand and shale (n = 4), sand and sherd (n = 17), and sand, sherd, and shale (n = 22). Identification of multilithic sand in the group of local Escavada may actually be a misidentification of a nonlocal Cibola Escavada B/w sherd, given the common use of multilithic sand in Cibola ceramics produced to the south. This particular sherd, however, did have local silty, discolored brown to yellow paste, making its provenience determination difficult without further testing with geochemical analyses. Paste characteristics for the overall Escavada Animas Variety group included 37 with high silt, discolored pastes and 11 with vitrified pastes.

Gallup B/w Animas Variety. As defined by Toll and McKenna (1992, 1997) and in other San Juan Basin literature (e.g., Goetze and Mills 1993; Goff and Reed 1998), Gallup B/w designs are characterized by the presence of hachure. Hachure designs consist of rectilinear or curvilinear ribbons filled with predominantly oblique filler lines that are wider than the ribbon lines. Through time there was a tendency for the filler lines to become finer and closer together, along with the ribbon lines becoming thicker than the filler lines. This transition in design appearance eventually moved to what we define as Chaco B/w, which was rare in all assemblages and was produced contemporaneously with Gallup B/w. This transition is apparent in the Middle San Juan, but the Animas Variety itself is rare in the Salmon assemblage and may have been produced by a small number of potters. Solid elements occur rarely on Gallup B/w as pendant triangles or curved solid elements at the end of hachure designs. Following the general definition of Animas Variety, the Gallup B/w sherds from Salmon have the characteristic high silt content paste and brown to yellow discoloration similar to the locally produced Northern San Juan ceramics.

Sixty-two Gallup B/w Animas Variety sherds were identified in the Salmon sample (examples in Figure 31.17). As shown in Table 31.10, most of these sherds are from Rooms 30W and 100W, including one ladle rim with an organic-painted design from Room 100W. Pigments identified on local Gallup B/w were varied, including mineral (n = 25), organic (n = 5), mineral/organic mix (n = 5), and subglaze (n = 1) on the exterior surfaces. Interior pigments were identified as mineral (n = 20), organic (n = 6), and mineral/organic mix (n = 1). Exterior surfaces showed variable manipulation including plain (n = 9), obliterated corrugated (n = 2), polished (n = 4), slipped (n = 12), plain and painted (n = 1), polished and painted (n = 4), and slipped and painted (n = 30). Interior surfaces were plain (n = 33), polished (n = 1), plain and painted (n = 2), polished and painted (n = 2), and slipped and painted (n = 24). Slip application was identified as thick-chalky (n = 3), thick-crackly (n = 2), thin (n = 3), or washy (n = 48).

Tempering material was identified as fine quartz sand (n = 3), medium quartz sand (n = 4), multilithic sand (n = 2), sand and shale (n = 1), sand and sherd (n = 34), sand, sherd, and shale (n = 16), and silt and sand (n = 2). The two sherds with silt and sand had so much silt and so little sand that the temper definition was modified to include silt; the clay may have been from an alluvial source that contained a small amount of sand. As mentioned above, the sherds identified as having multilithic sand may have been misidentified as Animas Variety rather than Cibola from the San Juan Basin; their pastes were vitrified. Paste characteristics for the Gallup B/w Animas Variety sherds included 44 with local high silt content and brown to yellow discoloration and 18 that were vitrified.

Chaco B/w Animas Variety. Chaco style designs are relatively rare in most assemblages, even within Chaco Canyon. Toll and McKenna (1997) indicated that Chaco B/w did not exceed 1 percent of any site

Figure 31.17. Gallup B/w, Animas variety.

Table 31.10. Gallup B/w Animas Variety from Salmon rooms.

Room	Vessel Form	Sherd Count	Weight
030A	Bowl	3	39.6
030W	Bowl	10	76
	Jar	12	165.5
	Subtotal	22	241.5
090W	Jar	3	20.3
100W	Bowl	11	173.9
	Jar	15	110.9
	Ladle	1	6
	Subtotal	27	290.8
123W	Bowl	1	23.9
127W	Bowl	2	3
	Jar	4	20.5
	Subtotal	6	23.5
Total		62	639.6

assemblage in their study of the Chaco Canyon assemblages. It is most commonly found, however, at sites in Chaco Canyon and associated great houses. Chaco style design is similar to that executed on Gallup B/w vessels, but the ribbon lines are significantly thicker than the filler lines. The filler lines are better executed than on Gallup vessels and are much thinner and set closer together, filling in more space (Figure 31.18).

Thirteen sherds were identified as a local version of Chaco B/w from Rooms 30W (n = 4), 64W (n = 1), and 100W (n = 8). Six of the sherds from Room 100W were all from the same jar and two of the sherds from Room 30W were from a single jar. All of the Chaco B/w sherds from the Salmon sample were jar fragments. Toll and McKenna (1997) indicated that Chaco B/w jars outnumbered bowls in their sample from Chaco Canyon sites. All of the Salmon sherds had mineral-painted designs over a slipped surface; the slip application for all of the local Chaco sherds was identified as washy. Tempering material was sand and shale (n = 2), sand and sherd (n = 3), or sand, sherd, and shale (n = 8). Paste characteristics were identified as high silt content and brown to yellow discoloration in 12 sherds and a vitrified paste in one sherd.

Puerco B/w Animas Variety. Puerco B/w (AD 1030–1150) is defined for this study based on stylistic criteria, rather than primarily on surface treatment as was proposed for the Chaco Project (see Toll and McKenna 1992, 1997). The Chaco Project definition was a more highly polished version of Escavada B/w, a local unpolished counterpart to Puerco B/w. As indicated by Toll and McKenna (1992:58), Puerco B/w "is the least clearly defined ceramic type of the Chaco series." I have noted this issue as well (L. Reed 1993), and I think that a stylistic solution might be more feasible and appropriate. Nevertheless, consistency in identifying Puerco B/w is the most important solution to the problem, either within a single project or among various projects.

From a stylistic perspective in the Salmon analysis, Puerco B/w Animas Variety was defined by Sosi style designs separated by sets of vertical parallel lines. With large enough sherds, the banded layout of Puerco style designs was visible. Hays-Gilpin and van Hartesveldt (1998) mentioned checkerboard elements separating space as well as vertical parallel

Figure 31.18. Chaco B/w, Animas variety.

lines, but this particular design configuration was not identified on Puerco sherds from Salmon. The most important design change from Escavada to Puerco was the use of line sets to separate solid Sosi style elements in a transition toward Pueblo III division of space within bowls and on the outside of jars, particularly in the later production of Puerco B/w ceramics (Figure 31.19).

In the Salmon assemblage, 12 sherds were identified as Puerco B/w Animas Variety from Rooms 30W (n = 2), 64W (n = 1), 100W (n = 8), and 123W (n = 1). Six are bowl fragments, five are jar sherds, and one is a seed jar fragment from Room 100W. Similar to most of the Animas Variety ceramics, paint pigments were variable, including mineral (n = 3), organic (n = 2), and mineral/organic mix (n = 1) on the exterior surfaces. Interior pigments were mineral (n = 3) and organic (n = 3). Exterior surfaces were plain (n = 1), slipped (n = 5), or slipped and painted (n = 6). Interior surfaces were plain (n = 6) or slipped and painted (n = 6).

Slip application was identified as thick-chalky (n = 1), thin (n = 1), and washy (n = 10). Similar to the other Cibola Animas Variety ceramics, temper was identified as sand and shale (n = 1), sand and sherd (n = 6), sand, sherd, and shale (n = 3), silt and sand (n = 1), and multilithic sand (n = 1). The single sherd with silt and sand had a high abundance of silt with only a few sand grains, suggesting that the clay may have been obtained from an alluvial source. Further, the single sherd with multilithic sand may have been mistyped as Animas Variety because Cibola ceramics in the San Juan Basin to the south generally have multilithic sand temper not available in the Middle San Juan. Finally, the paste of the multilithic sand–tempered sherd was vitrified, making identification difficult. Seven sherds had high silt content and brown to yellow discoloration and five sherds exhibited vitrification.

Figure 31.19. Puerco B/w, Animas variety.

Reserve B/w Animas Variety. A local version of Reserve B/w (AD 1050–1200) was identified in the Salmon assemblage based on the similarity in paste characteristics with other local ceramics and the use of primarily sand temper. Reserve B/w is generally associated with sites in the Reserve area where its primary source of production is known and where it was originally defined (see Martin and Rinaldo 1950). Based on design style, however, Reserve B/w has been identified in many areas, and production of the type is not restricted to the Reserve area of the Mogollon Rim; Hays-Gilpin and van Hardesveldt (1998) have described a Puerco Valley variety of Reserve B/w. Stylistically, the type is defined by hachured elements separated by solidly painted Sosi style elements in curvilinear or rectilinear patterns.

Fifteen Reserve B/w Animas Variety sherds were identified from Rooms 30W, 64W, 100W, 123W, and 127W (Table 31.11). This small group of sherds was evenly distributed throughout the rooms and included bowl and jar fragments (Figure 31.20). All sherds with exterior designs were executed in mineral paint over polished (n = 1) or slipped surfaces (n = 6). Interior pigments were mineral (n = 5), organic (n = 2), or mineral/organic mix (n = 2). All of the interior painted surfaces were slipped. Slip application was variable including thick-chalky (n = 1), thick-crackly (n = 2), thin (n = 4), and washy (n = 7). Tempering material was identified as sand and shale (n = 2), sand and sherd (n = 5), sand, sherd, and shale (n = 6), and silt and sand (n = 2). Regarding paste characteristics, 13 had high silt content and brown to yellow discoloration, and two were vitrified.

Tularosa B/w Animas Variety. One jar body sherd (16.7 g) from Room 30W had design characteristics on a local paste fitting the description of Tularosa B/w. As defined by Colton and Hargrave (1937), Rinaldo (1959), Rinaldo and Bluhm (1956), and Hays-Gilpin and van Hartesveldt (1998), the general design style consists of solid and hachured bands in curvilinear and rectilinear motifs over a vessel; sometimes they are in multiple banded layouts. In contrast to Reserve style designs, the hachure elements are finer lined, the hachure fill is more closely spaced, and the hachure is oblique. Hatchured elements are narrower than in Reserve style but are still noticeably larger than their opposing solid elements. Other design elements generally

Table 31.11. Reserve B/w Animas Variety from Salmon rooms.

Room	Vessel Form	Sherd Count	Weight
030W	Bowl	4	16.6
	Jar	1	16.7
	Subtotal	5	33.3
064W	Bowl	1	9.6
100W	Bowl	3	37.5
	Jar	1	5.7
	Subtotal	4	43.2
123W	Jar	2	9.6
127W	Bowl	1	6.4
	Jar	2	13.3
	Subtotal	3	19.7
Total		15	115.4

identified on Tularosa style pottery include stepped elements, barbed elements, and herringbone style line junctures. Although its most well known area of production is in the Mogollon Rim area (see Rinaldo 1959; Rinaldo and Bluhm 1956), Hays-Gilpin and Van Hardesveldt (1998) identified a probable Puerco Valley variety, although they indicated that further work is necessary to fully clarify the source location for the Tularosa B/w from the Chambers-Sanders area.

With only a single sherd identified from the Salmon assemblage it is unknown whether this represents a local variety of Tularosa B/w. The sherd had subglaze paint over a thick-chalky slipped surface. Tempering material was the typical sand, sherd, and shale identified in most of the Animas Variety Cibola ceramics with a high silt content and brown to yellow discolored paste. Without a larger sample, this identification is considered tentative at best.

Chaco-McElmo B/w Animas Variety. As described by Toll and McKenna (1997) and Windes (1985), the Cibola type Chaco-McElmo B/w began about AD 1100 and was produced in the Chaco Canyon area until approximately 1150; its production span was thus relatively short. It is the only organic-painted type in the Cibola tradition and is associated with early Pueblo III assemblages in the Chacoan region. Chaco-McElmo from the San Juan Basin has "thin, hard walls, good polish, and well-executed designs" (Toll and McKenna 1997:384). Toll and McKenna (1997) also indicated that there is affinity to Mesa Verde B/w, but the type is found in contexts devoid of Mesa Verde B/w, indicating its pre-1200s date. Chaco-McElmo slips in the San Juan Basin retain the characteristic washy appearance of the earlier Cibola types, along with the high occurrence of "slipslop" over the exteriors of bowls and interiors of jars. A high frequency of pitchers is characteristic for Chaco-McElmo pottery, but bowls, canteens, and jars are common as well. The shouldered pitchers commonly seen in Chacoan assemblages are mug-like, but true mugs are most associated with Mesa Verde B/w.

In contrast to the Chaco-McElmo from the Cibola region, Chaco-McElmo B/w Animas Variety is more variable in paint type, slip application, and vessel form (formal mugs are present; Figure 31.21). As shown in Table 31.12, 148 Chaco-McElmo B/w Animas Variety sherds were identified in all of the Salmon rooms. Bowls were the primary form in the assemblage, represented by 103 sherds. Jars were represented by 38 sherds, followed by ladle fragments (n = 2), mug fragments (n = 4), and olla fragment (n=1). Mugs were identified in Rooms 100W and 127W. Exterior pigments were identified as organic (n = 54), mineral/organic mix (n = 6), subglaze (n = 1), and indeterminate (n = 8); 79 examples had no exterior pigment. Interior pigments included mineral (n = 4), organic (n = 93), mineral/organic mix (n = 96), and indeterminate (n = 2); 43 examples had no interior pigment.

Rather than identifying Chaco-McElmo Animas Variety based on organic-painted designs, our analysis focused on design styles, allowing more probability in paint variation. The same analysis approach was undertaken for the Northern San Juan Animas Variety assemblage. Exterior surfaces included plain (n = 15), polished (n = 3), slipped (n = 65), and indented corrugated (n = 1) for the undecorated surfaces and plain (n = 1), polished (n = 5), and slipped (n = 55) for the decorated surfaces; one example was

Figure 31.20. Reserve B/w, Animas variety.

Table 31.12. Chaco-McElmo B/w Animas Variety from Salmon rooms.

Room	Vessel Form	Sherd Count	Weight
030A	Bowl	4	26.6
	Jar	8	97
	Subtotal	12	123.6
030B	Bowl	4	44.7
	Jar	1	12.1
	Subtotal	5	56.8
030W	Bowl	7	99.4
064W	Bowl	8	49.8
090W	Bowl	5	36.1
100W	Bowl	65	920.9
	Jar	19	314.5
	Ladle	2	26.6
	Mug	2	18.8
	Subtotal	88	1280.8
123B	Bowl	1	3.4
	Jar	2	17.4
	Olla	1	27.9
	Subtotal	4	48.7
123W	Bowl	4	23.3
	Jar	5	33.3
	Subtotal	9	56.6
127W	Bowl	5	46.5
	Jar	3	34.9
	Mug	2	26.8
	Subtotal	10	108.2
Total		148	1860

identified as indeterminate. Interior surfaces included plain (n = 42) and slipped (slipslop, n = 3) for the undecorated surfaces, and plain (n = 1), polished (n = 5), and slipped (n = 97) for the decorated surfaces. Slip application was variable, suggesting the merging of the Cibola type with local technology. Slips were identified as thick-chalky (n = 63), thick-crackly (n = 10), thin (n = 26), and washy (n-41); eight sherds had no slip. Tempering material was as variable as the other locally produced Cibola ceramics. Sand and sherd comprised 42 percent (n = 62) of the assemblage, followed by sand, sherd, and shale at 33 percent (n = 49). The remaining 25 percent included sand and shale (n = 10), multilithic sand (n = 9), silt and sand (n = 6), medium quartz sand (n = 5), fine quartz sand (n = 4), sand with mica (n = 1), decomposing sandstone and sand (n = 1), and angular quartz sand (n = 1). Paste characteristics were identified as high silt content and brown to yellow discoloration in 128 examples and vitrification in 20 examples. The nine sherds with multilithic sand had paste characteristics that were considered local—thus the classification as Animas Variety.

Given our differentiation of McElmo B/w into an early type based on transitional characteristics between Mancos style ceramics and true McElmo style designs and rim morphology, we decided to track the same trends in Chaco-McElmo B/w. The data were not as consistently recorded, however, and were noted as comments rather than identified as a stylistic variation in the coding of the type.

From the assemblage of 148 Chaco-McElmo B/w Animas Variety sherds, 38 were not assigned a style. Seventeen sherds were identified as Early McElmo style based on the design and rim morphology attributes described above for the Animas Variety type Early McElmo B/w, which include thin tapered or rounded rims with minimal painted dots and designs that are more Pueblo II in appearance than classic McElmo style. Other combinations of design and morphology include rims with a single framing line, thin vessel walls, and a thin-walled rim tapered to a rounded form but no rim ticking. These designs represent the transition in design, wall thickness, and rim morphology from Pueblo II to Pueblo III ceramics that occurred between AD 1050 and 1100. For the most part, many sherds fitting this description have been subsumed under Pueblo II types, with occasional mention of the presence of a few rim ticks on a thin tapered rim.

Actual McElmo style designs were identified on 68 examples, fitting well with the general definition of Chaco-McElmo B/w of the Cibola tradition and its proposed date range for the San Juan Basin of AD 1100–1150. Twenty-five examples, however, exhibited true Mesa Verde style designs with thick vessel walls, thick flattened rims, closely spaced ticking of

Figure 31.21. Chaco-McElmo B/w, Animas Variety.

various design combinations, and complex interior designs with exterior design elements as well. Thus, it is possible that an Animas Variety Chaco-McElmo variant was produced longer in the Middle San Juan region, into the AD 1200s, as populations continued to emulate Chacoan pottery or as actual Chacoan potters were residing in the region.

Other Cibola Animas Variety White Ware Types. A number of general descriptive classes were applied to identify nontypeable Cibola Animas Variety White Ware. These white ware sherds either lacked enough paint to place them into a general time period category (e.g., painted B/w and slipped white) or lacked enough design field to place them into named types (e.g., Pueblo II–III style B/w or Pueblo III B/w). Table 31.13 identifies these classes and their distributions in each of the Salmon rooms.

Table 31.13. Cibola Animas Variety white ware nontypeable ceramics from Salmon.

Room	Descriptive Class	Sherd Count	Weight
030A	Painted B/w	1	16.9
	Pueblo I–II style B/w	4	19.7
	Pueblo II–III style B/w	7	69.8
	Pueblo III style B/w	2	13.5
	Slipped white	9	79
	Subtotal	23	198.9
030B	Pueblo I–II style B/w	1	4
	Pueblo II–III style B/w	3	58.4
	Slipped white	5	66.2
	Subtotal	9	128.6
030W	Painted B/w	1	3.5
	Pueblo I–II style B/w	7	40.8
	Pueblo II–III style B/w	3	11.4
	Slipped white	3	37.1
	Subtotal	14	92.8
064W	Pueblo III style B/w	2	53.8
	Slipped white	1	5.2
	Subtotal	3	59
090W	Pueblo I–II style B/w	1	3.5
	Pueblo II–III style B/w	3	12.1
	Pueblo III style B/w	2	21.1
	Slipped white	2	29
	Subtotal	8	65.7
100W	Pueblo I–II style B/w	2	7
	Pueblo II–III style B/w	3	16.7
	Pueblo III style B/w	4	28.2
	Slipped white	20	336.6
	Subtotal	29	388.5
123B	Pueblo II–III style B/w	1	6.1
	Slipped white	1	6.7
	Subtotal	2	12.8
123W	Pueblo II–III style B/w	1	2
	Pueblo III style B/w	1	2.2
	Slipped white	4	27.7
	Subtotal	6	31.9
127W	Pueblo II–III style B/w	3	12.2
	Pueblo III style B/w	1	2.7
	Slipped white	14	142
	Subtotal	18	156.9
Total		112	1135.1

TRADE WARE FROM SALMON

Nonlocal ceramics comprised 9 percent of the total assemblage, including ceramics from the Cibola, Chuska, Northern San Juan, Kayenta, northern Mogollon, and Little Colorado regions (Table 31.14). By ware category, 43.7 percent was white ware (n = 509), 28.5 percent was red ware (n = 332), 22.1 percent was gray ware (n = 258), and 5.7 percent was brown ware (n = 66). Classification of trade ware ceramics was accomplished by consulting the typological literature from specific regions and the type collection at Animas Ceramic Consulting, Inc.

Chuska Trade Ware

Chuska Series pottery, by definition (see Peckham and Wilson 1967; Goff and Reed 2003; Windes 1977), is tempered with crushed trachyte and some combination of sherd and sand. Chuska White Ware can have a light or dark paste, but usually the paste is dark gray or purplish in color. Paint may be mineral, organic, or a mix of pigments. Most white ware types are slipped with thick, chalky, white clay slips that flake off easily. Design styles associated with other b/w ceramic series are prevalent on Chuska ceramics. Chuska Gray Ware has a dark paste and a variety of surface textures such as scraped, neck banded, neck corrugated, or corrugated. Chuska Gray Ware has long been of interest because a large proportion of the utility ware found in Chaco Canyon and other areas of the San Juan Basin was produced in the Chuska Valley (see Mill et al. 1997; L. Reed et al. 2001a). Goff and Reed (2003) have recently reevaluated the dating sequence of the Chuska typology, providing more accurate date ranges for many of the types. It should be noted that during our analysis we segregated some of the Chuska types into stylistic subtypes similar to those for Mancos B/w as a means of tracking similarities in designs. Date ranges for the Chuska types used in Salmon room mean date calculations are presented below in the section on chronology.

White Ware

Ten of the 85 Chuska White Ware sherds in the assemblage were not typeable (two painted B/w, four slipped white, one Pueblo I–II style B/w, two Pueblo II–III style B/w, and one Pueblo III style B/w). Table 31.15 gives the room associations of the

Table 31.14. Trade ware ceramics from the Salmon Pueblo reanalyzed assemblage.

Ceramic Type	Sherd Count	Weight
Chuska		
Gray		
Banded gray	1	6.8
Blue Shale Corrugated	93	750.1
Captain Tom Corrugated	2	17.1
Corrugated gray	39	372.4
Gray Hills Banded	1	6.6
Hunter Corrugated	3	129.4
Indeterminate gray	13	138.0
Newcomb Corrugated	7	147.6
Plain gray	3	34.0
Polished gray	1	8.8
Subtotal	163	1610.8
White		
Brimhall B/w	4	46.7
Burnham B/w	1	7.3
Chuska B/w	13	106.2
Crumbled House B/w	12	221.3
Nava B/w	21	379.2
Newcomb B/w	4	22.1
Painted B/w	2	8.3
Pueblo I–II style B/w	1	4.6
Pueblo II–III style B/w	2	9.8
Pueblo III style B/w	1	5.9
Slipped white	4	29.5
Taylor B/w (Puerco style)	1	13.7
Taylor B/w (Sosi style)	4	37.0
Toadlena B/w (Black Mesa style)	2	23.9
Toadlena B/w (Puerco style)	2	26.1
Toadlena B/w (Reserve style)	1	7.1
Toadlena B/w (Sosi style)	10	136.7
Subtotal	85	1085.4
Subtotal	248	2696.2
Cibola		
Gray		
Chaco Corrugated (PII-PIII)	9	199.7
Corrugated gray	1	2.6
Plain gray	6	59.5
Polished gray	3	15.1
Subtotal	19	276.9
Red		
Indeter. White Mtn. B/r	82	268.8
Indeter. White Mtn. Polychrome	4	15.2
Indeter. White Mtn. Red Ware	63	438.4
Puerco B/r	11	290.8
St. Johns B/r	60	687.5
St. Johns Polychrome	28	404.9
Wingate B/r	35	720.9
Wingate Polychrome	20	304.1
Subtotal	303	3130.6
White		
Chaco B/w	16	127.6
Chaco-McElmo B/w	57	843.8
Escavada B/w	30	397.7
Gallup B/w	61	428.9
Kiatuthlanna B/w	3	16.1

Table 31.14 (continued)

Ceramic Type	Sherd Count	Weight
(cont.)		
Pueblo I–II style B/w	7	69.5
Pueblo II–III style B/w	2	9.5
Puerco B/w	5	16.4
Red Mesa B/w	7	103.7
Reserve B/w	7	21.1
Slipped white	13	73.0
Snowflake B/w	1	8.6
Subtotal	209	2115.9
Subtotal	531	5523.4
Kayenta		
Red		
Cameron Polychrome	5	31.4
Citadel Polychrome	4	18.6
Indeterminate B/r	3	10.7
Indeterminate polychrome	2	6.1
Indeterminate red	2	9.1
Medicine B/o	2	11.1
Tusayan B/r	1	6.1
Subtotal	19	93.1
White		
Black Mesa B/w	1	2.5
Dogoszhi B/w	2	36.6
Flagstaff B/w	1	13.4
Pueblo II–III style B/w	1	5.3
Sosi B/w	4	28.8
Subtotal	9	86.6
Subtotal	28	179.7
Little Colorado		
Padre B/w	2	12.4
Mogollon Brown		
Indeterminate	1	9.6
Showlow Corrugated Smudged	1	3.2
Showlow Red	19	127.5
Showlow Smudged	21	95.1
Tularosa Pattern Corrugated (smudged interior)	2	33.4
Woodruff Brown	6	63.8
Woodruff Red	2	21.1
Woodruff Smudged	14	135.2
Subtotal	66	488.9
Northern San Juan		
Gray		
Banded gray	2	39.7
Corrugated gray	65	500.9
Indeterminate gray	7	72.6
Polished gray	2	13.8
Subtotal	76	627.0
Red		
Bluff B/r	1	8.8
Deadmans B/r	2	20.2
Indeterminate B/r	2	2.1
Indeterminate red	4	25.1
Transitional Bluff–Deadmans B/r	1	7.2
Subtotal	10	63.4

Table 31.14 (continued)

Ceramic Type	Sherd Count	Weight
White		
Cortez B/w (Kiatuthlanna style)	1	6.1
Cortez B/w (Red Mesa style)	5	60.9
Early McElmo B/w	10	191.1
Mancos B/w (Dogoszhi style)	18	233.5
Mancos B/w (Mancos style)	7	166.2
Mancos B/w (Reserve style)	6	124.4
Mancos B/w (Sosi style)	12	232.0
McElmo B/w	81	1329.0
McElmo–Mesa Verde B/w	5	180.6
Mesa Verde B/w	26	377.5
Pueblo I–II style B/w	2	13.1
Pueblo II–III style B/w	10	102.4
Pueblo III style B/w	4	73.6
Slipped white	17	144.5
Subtotal	204	3,234.9
Subtotal	290	3,925.3
Total	1,165	12,825.9

Table 31.15. The distribution of Chuska White Ware from Salmon rooms.

Room	Ceramic Type	Sherd Count	Percent
030W	Brimhall B/w	2	2.7
	Chuska B/w	3	4.0
	Crumbled House B/w	1	1.3
	Nava B/w	1	1.3
	Newcomb B/w	4	5.3
	Taylor B/w (Sosi style)	1	1.3
	Toadlena B/w (Reserve style)	1	1.3
	Subtotal	13	17.3
090W	Crumbled House B/w	10	13.3
	Nava B/w	3	4.0
	Taylor B/w (Sosi style)	2	2.7
	Toadlena B/w (Sosi style)	2	2.7
	Subtotal	17	22.7
100W	Brimhall B/w	1	1.3
	Burnham B/w	1	1.3
	Chuska B/w	8	10.7
	Crumbled House B/w	1	1.3
	Nava B/w	14	18.7
	Taylor B/w (Puerco style)	1	1.3
	Taylor B/w (Sosi style)	1	1.3
	Toadlena B/w (Black Mesa style)	2	2.7
	Toadlena B/w (Puerco style)	1	1.3
	Toadlena B/w (Sosi style)	6	8.0
	Subtotal	36	48.0
123B	Nava B/w	1	1.3
123W	Chuska B/w	1	1.3
	Nava B/w	2	2.7
	Subtotal	3	4.0
127W	Brimhall B/w	1	1.3
	Chuska B/w	1	1.3
	Toadlena B/w (Puerco style)	1	1.3
	Toadlena B/w (Sosi style)	2	2.7
	Subtotal	5	6.7
Total		75	100.0

remaining 75 sherds. Chuska White Ware was not ubiquitous in the sampled Salmon rooms. Rooms 30A, 30B, 64W, and 123A lacked Chuska White Ware completely. Room 100W contained the most Chuska White Ware, mostly Nava B/w. In fact, most of the white ware from all of the rooms was identified as Nava B/w (Figure 31.22), followed in frequency by Crumbled House B/w (Figure 31.23), Chuska B/w (Figure 31.24), and Toadlena B/w (Sosi style; Figure 31.25).

Vessel forms were primarily bowls (n = 58), followed by jars (n = 24), ladles (n = 1), ollas (n = 1), and seed jars (n = 1). Organic-painted white ware was the focus of trade with the Chuska region, with organic paint comprising 31 percent of the exterior designs and 53 percent of the interior designs. Of course, much of this higher percentage of organic-painted pottery is due to the higher frequency of Nava and Crumbled House B/w in the assemblage. Nevertheless, organic-painted types such as Newcomb, Toadlena, and Chuska B/w were similarly more common than their mineral counterparts.

Gray Ware

Chuska Gray Ware comprises less than 2 percent of the entire gray ware assemblage from the site—in stark contrast with San Juan Basin assemblages having as much as 50 percent Chuska Gray Ware. Some of this discrepancy in trade may be due to temporal factors given that Salmon was built and inhabited from the late AD 1000s and was primarily a Pueblo

Figure 31.22. Nava Black-on-white.

III great house. Thus, it was built near the end of the height of the Chacoan trade network when Chuska pottery was a focus of intensive exchange. It is also possible, however, that the Middle San Juan region, with its own available resource of igneous temper, did not import large quantities of igneous-tempered cooking pots.

Chuska Gray Ware was more evenly distributed throughout the Salmon rooms than was the white ware (Table 31.16). The only room lacking Chuska Gray Ware was Room 123A. Blue Shale Corrugated comprised the majority (57%) of the gray ware from the Chuska region. The type was identified based on rim eversion and body-sherd coil manipulation as defined by Peckham and Wilson (1967). Three Hunter Corrugated sherds (1 rim and 2 body fragments) were identified in Room 100W. Vessel forms were identified as jars and ollas.

Figure 31.23. Crumbled House Black-on-white.

Figure 31.25. Toadlena Black-on-white, Sosi style.

Figure 31.24. Chuska Black-on-white.

Cibola Trade Ware

Cibola ceramics from the San Juan Basin were identified based on descriptions provided in the Chaco Project literature (e.g., Toll and McKenna 1992, 1997) and other projects in the San Juan Basin (e.g., Mills et al. 1993; L. Reed et al. 1998; Windes 1977). Date ranges for the Cibola types used in Salmon room mean date calculations are presented below in the section on chronology. Cibola ceramics are tempered with poorly sorted sand or sand and sherd with a light gray to buff colored paste. White ware ceramics can have plain, polished, or slipped surfaces. Cibola slips are distinguished by a washy

Table 31.16. The distribution of Chuska Gray Ware from Salmon rooms.

Room	Ceramic Type	Sherd Count	Percent
030A	Blue Shale Corrugated	28	17.2
	Captain Tom Corrugated	1	0.6
	Corrugated gray	4	2.5
	Subtotal	33	20.2
030B	Blue Shale Corrugated	16	9.8
	Corrugated gray	5	3.1
	Subtotal	21	12.9
030W	Blue Shale Corrugated	4	2.5
	Captain Tom Corrugated	1	0.6
	Corrugated gray	30	18.4
	Plain gray	1	0.6
	Subtotal	36	22.1
064W	Banded gray	1	0.6
	Blue Shale Corrugated	4	2.5
	Indeterminate gray	1	0.6
	Newcomb Corrugated	1	0.6
	Subtotal	7	4.3
090W	Blue Shale Corrugated	8	4.9
100W	Blue Shale Corrugated	19	11.7
	Gray Hills Banded	1	0.6
	Hunter Corrugated	3	1.8
	Indeterminate gray	10	6.1
	Newcomb Corrugated	2	1.2
	Plain gray	1	0.6
	Polished gray	1	0.6
	Subtotal	37	22.7
123B	Newcomb Corrugated	1	0.6
123W	Blue Shale Corrugated	2	1.2
	Indeterminate gray	2	1.2
	Subtotal	4	2.5
127W	Blue Shale Corrugated	12	7.4
	Newcomb Corrugated	3	1.8
	Plain gray	1	0.6
	Subtotal	16	9.8
Total		163	100.0

Table 31.17. Cibola White Ware from Salmon rooms.

Room	Ceramic Type	Sherd Count	Percent
030A	Gallup B/w	2	1.1
030B	Gallup B/w	3	1.6
	Kiatuthlanna B/w	1	0.5
	Reserve B/w	1	0.5
	Subtotal	5	2.7
030W	Chaco B/w	2	1.1
	Chaco-McElmo B/w	2	1.1
	Escavada B/w	2	1.1
	Gallup B/w	10	5.3
	Red Mesa B/w	3	1.6
	Subtotal	19	10.2
064W	Chaco-McElmo B/w	2	1.1
090W	Chaco B/w	2	1.1
	Escavada B/w	2	1.1
	Gallup B/w	9	4.8
	Kiatuthlanna B/w	1	0.5
	Reserve B/w	1	0.5
	Subtotal	15	8.0
100W	Chaco B/w	12	6.4
	Chaco-McElmo B/w	41	21.9
	Escavada B/w	26	13.9
	Gallup B/w	29	15.5
	Kiatuthlanna B/w	1	0.5
	Puerco B/w	3	1.6
	Red Mesa B/w	3	1.6
	Reserve B/w	2	1.1
	Snowflake B/w	1	0.5
	Subtotal	118	63.1
123B	Gallup B/w	1	0.5
	Puerco B/w	1	0.5
	Subtotal	2	1.1
123W	Chaco-McElmo B/w	2	1.1
	Puerco B/w	1	0.5
	Subtotal	3	1.6
127W	Chaco-McElmo B/w	10	5.3
	Gallup B/w	7	3.7
	Red Mesa B/w	1	0.5
	Reserve B/w	3	1.6
	Subtotal	21	11.2
Total		187	100.0

appearance that does not cover the entire surface of the sherd. Designs are mostly executed in mineral paint although a single Pueblo III type (Chaco-McElmo B/w) had organic-painted designs. Cibola Gray Ware has a light gray paste and a variety of surface textures including scraped, neck banded, neck corrugated, and corrugated. Differentiation of nonlocal Cibola ceramics from the local Animas Variety described above was based on paste and temper characteristics. Animas Variety pastes have a high silt content and brown to yellow discoloration. The local temper is predominantly an angular quartz sand, sand and shale, or added sherd; the absence of trachyte fragments in any of the local Cibola ceramics is also a distinguishing characteristic.

White Ware

Cibola White Ware was identified in all rooms except 123A. Gallup, Chaco-McElmo, and Escavada B/w comprised the majority (79%) of the Cibola assemblage (Table 31.17). Gallup B/w was the most abundant; it was present in almost all the rooms sampled. The earlier types of Kiatuthlanna and Red Mesa B/w were present in Rooms 30B, 30W, 90W, 100W, and 127W but only in very small quantities. Chaco-McElmo B/w was present in Rooms 30W, 64W, 100W, and 127W, but its highest concentration was in Room 100W.

Vessel forms were highly varied including jars (n = 110), bowls (n = 71), ladles (n = 12), mugs (n = 9), ollas (n = 2), pitchers (n = 3), seed jars (n = 1), and effigy/figurines (n = 1). Table 31.18 shows the distribution of vessel forms by ceramic types. The Kiatuthlanna sherds were all from jars. Red Mesa B/w was evenly distributed between bowl and jar fragments (Figure 31.26). Escavada B/w was predominantly jar fragments, and Puerco B/w occurred mostly as bowl fragments. Gallup B/w (Figure 31.27) jar fragments

Table 31.18. The distribution of vessel forms by Cibola ceramic types.

Vessel Form	Ceramic Type	Sherd Count	Percent
Bowl	Chaco B/w	6	3.2
	Chaco-McElmo B/w	25	13.4
	Escavada B/w	7	3.7
	Gallup B/w	18	9.6
	Puerco B/w	4	2.1
	Red Mesa B/w	4	2.1
	Reserve B/w	4	2.1
	Subtotal	68	36.4
Jar	Chaco B/w	8	4.3
	Chaco-McElmo B/w	14	7.5
	Escavada B/w	20	10.7
	Gallup B/w	40	21.4
	Kiatuthlanna B/w	3	1.6
	Puerco B/w	1	0.5
	Red Mesa B/w	3	1.6
	Reserve B/w	3	1.6
	Snowflake B/w	1	0.5
	Subtotal	93	49.7
Ladle	Chaco-McElmo B/w	11	5.9
	Gallup B/w	1	0.5
	Subtotal	12	6.4
Mug	Chaco-McElmo B/w	7	3.7
	Gallup B/w	1	0.5
	Subtotal	8	4.3
Olla	Escavada B/w	1	0.5
	Gallup B/w	1	0.5
	Subtotal	2	1.1
Pitcher	Chaco B/w	1	0.5
	Escavada B/w	2	1.1
	Subtotal	3	1.6
Seed jar	Chaco B/w	1	0.5
Total		187	100.0

doubled that of bowls, but Chaco B/w (Figure 31.28) was almost evenly distributed among jars and bowls, along with a single seed jar and a pitcher. Chaco-McElmo B/w (Figure 31.29) had the most variety in vessels, with bowl, jar, ladle, mug, and pitcher fragments identified in the Salmon rooms.

Exterior pigments included mineral (n = 82), organic (n = 28), mineral/organic mix (n = 11), and subglaze (n = 4); 84 examples had no paint. Interior pigments were mineral (n = 42), organic (n = 19), mineral/organic mix (n = 12), and subglaze (n = 3); 133 examples had no paint. Washy slips were identified on 76 percent (n = 148) of the decorated surfaces, but a small number of examples had thin (n = 20), thick-crackly (n = 1), and thick-chalky (n = 26) slips. Tempering material was predominantly sand and sherd (n = 177, 85%). Other temper combinations included fine quartz sand, medium quartz sand, multilithic sand, sand and clay pellets, sand and shale, sandstone and sherd, sand, sherd, and shale, and indeterminate. Noticeably absent from the list of

Figure 31.26. Red Mesa Black-on-white.

temper was trachyte fragments, which were common in most Cibola ceramics from the San Juan Basin. It is thus not clear where these Cibola ceramics actually came from. The paste characteristics of the Cibola sherds are clearer, gray to buff colored, less silty, and harder than the Animas Variety Cibola ceramics interpreted as locally produced.

Gray Ware

Nineteen Cibola Gray Ware sherds were identified in the Salmon sample: nine Pueblo II–III Chaco Corrugated, one corrugated body sherd, six plain gray, and three polished gray. All of the corrugated sherds were indented corrugated, and two of the plain gray sherds had incised designs. The Pueblo II–

Figure 31.27. Gallup Black-on-white.

Figure 31.28. Chaco Black-on-white.

III Chaco Corrugated sherds had angular quartz sand temper, the corrugated gray body sherd had medium sand temper, and the polished gray sherd had sand and sherd temper. The plain gray sherds had fine quartz sand (n = 1), medium quartz sand (n = 3), and sand and sherd (n = 2). It is also noticeable in the assemblage of gray ware that none of the sherds have the fragments of trachyte typical of many Cibola ceramics from the San Juan Basin.

White Mountain Red Ware

Although not produced in the San Juan Basin, White Mountain Red Ware was included in the Cibola tradition during the Salmon analysis. Carlson's (1970) study of White Mountain Red Ware is the definitive work on the pottery. At its height of production, White Mountain Red Ware was one of the most highly traded ceramic types in the Southwest, with St. Johns Polychrome in particular present in sites in the Rio Grande, Jornada Mogollon, Four Corners, and southeast Arizona regions. Its production area was in east-central Arizona and western New Mexico, but its reach was far greater. Date ranges for White Mountain Red Ware types used in Salmon room mean date calculations are presented below in the section on chronology. From the rooms analyzed in the Salmon Research Initiative, 303 White Mountain Red Ware ceramics were identified, including Puerco B/r, Wingate B/r (Figure 31.30), Wingate Polychrome, St. Johns B/r, and St. Johns Polychrome (Figure 31.31).

Figure 31.29. Chaco-McElmo B/w.

As shown in Table 31.19, two rooms (64W and 123A) lacked White Mountain Red Ware, and Room 100W contained 77 percent of the red ware identified in the sample. Puerco B/r, the earliest White Mountain Red Ware (AD 1050–1175), occurred only in Rooms 90W, 100W, and 127W, whereas St. Johns Polychrome, the latest red ware (AD 1175–1300), occurred in 30W, 90W, 100W, 123B, 123W, and 127W, suggesting later occupations or mixed deposits in Rooms 90W, 100W, and 127W. Greater clarification of these deposits through ceramic mean date analysis is provided in Chapter 32, with stratigraphic evaluation.

Figure 31.30. Wingate B/w.

Classification of red ware as White Mountain series was accomplished based on the gray to buff paste, contrasting bright red to orange slip, sand and sherd temper, and distinctive design configurations. Vessel forms were variable, but bowls were the pri-

Table 31.19. The distribution of White Mountain Red Ware from Salmon rooms.

Room	Ceramic Type	Sherd Count	Percent
030A	Indeter. White Mtn. Red Ware	4	1.3
	Wingate B/r	1	0.3
	Subtotal	5	1.7
030B	Indeter. White Mtn. B/r	1	0.3
	Indeter. White Mtn. Red Ware	2	0.7
	Subtotal	3	1.0
030W	Indeter. White Mtn. B/r	1	0.3
	Indeter. White Mtn. Red Ware	4	1.3
	St. Johns B/r	1	0.3
	Wingate B/r	5	1.7
	Subtotal	11	3.6
090W	Indeterminate White Mtn. B/r	1	0.3
	Puerco B/r	1	0.3
	St. Johns B/r	7	2.3
	St. Johns Polychrome	6	2.0
	Wingate B/r	1	0.3
	Wingate Polychrome	2	0.7
	Subtotal	18	5.9
100W	Indeter. White Mtn. B/r	74	24.4
	Indeter. White Mtn. Polychr.	2	0.7
	Indeter. White Mtn. Red Ware	46	15.2
	Puerco B/r	9	3.0
	St. Johns B/r	46	15.2
	St. Johns Polychrome	15	5.0
	Wingate B/r	25	8.3
	Wingate Polychrome	17	5.6
	Subtotal	234	77.2
123B	Indeterminate White Mtn. B/r	2	0.7
	Indeter. White Mtn. Red Ware	1	0.3
	St. Johns Polychrome	3	1.0
	Subtotal	6	2.0
123W	Indeter. White Mtn. Red Ware	1	0.3
	St. Johns B/r	1	0.3
	Wingate B/r	1	0.3
	Subtotal	3	1.0
127W	Indeter. White Mtn. B/r	3	1.0
	Indeter. White Mtn. Polychr.	2	0.7
	Indeter. White Mtn. Red Ware	5	1.7
	Puerco B/r	1	0.3
	St. Johns B/r	5	1.7
	St. Johns Polychrome	4	1.3
	Wingate B/r	2	0.7
	Wingate Polychrome	1	0.3
	Subtotal	23	7.6
Total		303	100.0

mary shape, comprising 95 percent (n = 289) of the White Mountain Red Ware assemblage. Other vessel forms included 1 canteen fragment, 10 jar sherds, 1 miniature, 1 pinch pot, and 1 seed jar fragment. Tempering material in all of the examples was sand and sherd.

Kayenta (Tusayan) Trade Ware

Kayenta ceramics, which were rare in the assemblage from Salmon, included white and red ware types. Colton (1955, 1956) and Hays-Gilpin and van Hartesveldt (1998) were consulted for identification of these wares and types. Date ranges for Kayenta types used in Salmon room mean date calculations are presented below in the section on chronology. Kayenta white ware is identified by organic paint designs over a highly polished and finely slipped surface. Generally the slip is the same color as the paste, making it difficult to detect in some instances. The temper is fine, well-sorted quartz sand. Tusayan Red Ware generally has a thin, washy slip that is in many cases the same color as the paste. In contrast to White Mountain Red Ware, the slip does not contrast with the paste. Tusayan Red Ware temper is crushed sherd that characteristically is visible on the surface of the vessel as tiny white spots. With the polychrome types, there is more use of the orange paste as a means of producing one of the surface colors in the polychrome effect.

Figure 31.31. St. Johns Polychrome.

Eight Kayenta White Ware and 19 Tusayan Red Ware sherds were identified. Rooms lacking ceramics from the Kayenta region included 30A, 64W, 123A, and 127W. The lack of Kayenta sherds in Room 127W was surprising given the size of the assemblage from that room and the representation of other trade ware in the room assemblage. Room 100W contained the majority (63%) of the Kayenta trade ware (Table 31.20), including the only sherd of Flagstaff B/w.

All except two of the white ware sherds were bowls—two were Dogoszhi B/w jar sherds (Figure 31.32). All except two of the red ware sherds were

Table 31.20. Kayenta trade ware identified in Salmon rooms.

Room	Ware	Ceramic Type	Sherd Count	Percent
030B	Red	Citadel Polychrome	1	3.7
030W	Red	Medicine B/o	1	3.7
	White	Sosi B/w	1	3.7
	Subtotal		2	7.4
090W	Red	Indeterminate B/r	1	3.7
		Indeterminate red	1	3.7
	White	Black Mesa B/w	1	3.7
		Sosi B/w	2	7.4
	Subtotal		5	18.5
100W	Red	Cameron Polychrome	5	18.5
		Citadel Polychrome	2	7.4
		Indeterminate B/r	1	3.7
		Indeterminate polychrome	2	7.4
		Indeterminate red	1	3.7
		Medicine B/o	1	3.7
		Tusayan B/r	1	3.7
	White	Dogoszhi B/w	2	7.4
		Flagstaff B/w	1	3.7
		Sosi B/w	1	3.7
	Subtotal		17	63.0
123B	Red	Indeterminate B/r	1	3.7
123W	Red	Citadel Polychrome	1	3.7
Total			27	100.0

also from bowls; there was one Citadel Polychrome jar fragment and one Medicine Black-on-orange jar fragment. Examples of Cameron Polychrome and Citadel Polychrome are shown in Figures 31.33 and 31.34.

Little Colorado Trade Ware

Little Colorado ceramics, which were exceedingly rare in the Salmon sample, included only two sherds of Padre B/w identified from Room 90W. It is described and defined by Colton and Hargrave (1937), Colton (1955), and Douglass (1987). It has abundant crushed sherd temper appearing as white, gray, or tan fragments and occasionally quartz and volcanic rock fragments, especially augite. The slip is thick, chalky, and white to light gray. Painted designs are executed in organic pigment, and designs are Dogoszhi style. Individual lines are generally irregular widths, and framing lines and hachures are the same weight. The two Padre B/w sherds, in particular, stood out in the assemblage as different; they were typed as Padre B/w based on the detailed description and illustrations provided in the literature.

Mogollon Trade Ware

Trade ware from the Mogollon region was rather abundant at Salmon. There were 66 sherds, representing Showlow Red (Figure 31.35), Showlow Smudged, Showlow Corrugated Smudged, Woodruff Brown, Woodruff Red, Woodruff Smudged, and Tularosa Patterned Corrugated Smudged (Figure 31.36). The literature consulted during the analysis

Figure 31.32. Dogoszhi B/w.

Figure 31.33. Cameron Polychrome.

and classification of these ceramics included Rinaldoand Bluhm (1956), Colton and Hargrave (1937), and Hays-Gilpin and van Hartesveldt (1998). Date ranges for Mogollon types used in Salmon room mean date calculations are presented below in the section on chronology.

As indicated by Hays-Gilpin and van Hartesveldt (1998:150), there is a lot of overlap among the various brown ware types in the Northern Mogollon region that is not well understood. Hays-Gilpin and van Hartesveldt (1998:150) also indicated that "Woodruff Brown probably overlaps with that of Lupton Brown and other early brown ware types from other regions, such as Obelisk Gray, Obelisk Utility, and Sambrito Brown." L. Reed et al. (2000) have provided further clarification concerning early brown ware on the Colorado Plateau, but the continuation of brown ware technology and the variability, or lack thereof in many cases, still results in a typology problem in the Northern Mogollon region. In our analysis of Salmon, we differentiated Woodruff from Showlow based on paste characteristics and to some degree on temper, but until these types are better understood, in an assemblage such as Salmon's they would be better identified under a single type of trade ware. The actual origin of these smudged and red-slipped brown ware ceramics is unclear and segregating them into Showlow versus Woodruff provides a false sense of provenience. With the exception of Tularosa Patterned Corrugated, which has known provenience in the Reserve area, the remaining brown ware sherds could all have been easily identified as Showlow.

Figure 31.34. Citadel Polychrome.

In the Salmon assemblage, Mogollon Trade Ware was identified from Rooms 30W, 64W, 90W, 100W, 123B, 123W, and 127W (Table 31.21). Mogollon Brown Ware was lacking in Rooms 30A, 30B, and 123A. The two sherds of Tularosa Patterned Corrugated (see Figure 31.36) were from Room 100W, as were the majority (71%) of the brown ware ceramics.

Figure 31.35. Showlow Red.

Bowls comprised the majority (n = 61) of the brown ware assemblage, and the remaining sherds were identified as jars (n = 5). It should be noted, however, that bowls and jars are frequently difficult to segregate in a brown ware technology in which polishing is often applied to jar interiors as well. The jar sherds were identified as Showlow Red (n = 2), Showlow Smudged (n = 2), and indeterminate brown (n = 1).

Northern San Juan Trade Ware

Trade ware from the Northern San Juan region includes ceramics most likely produced at sites in southwest Colorado, southeast Utah, and possibly northwest Arizona with crushed rock temper. These ceramics are differentiated from the Animas Variety

Table 31.21. Mogollon trade ware from Salmon rooms.

Room	Ceramic Type	Sherd Count	Percent
030W	Showlow Red	1	1.5
	Showlow Smudged	3	4.5
	Subtotal	4	6.1
064W	Showlow Smudged	1	1.5
090W	Showlow Red	1	1.5
100W	Indeterminate	1	1.5
	Showlow Red	16	24.2
	Showlow Smudged	15	22.7
	Tularosa Pattern Corr. (smudged interior)	2	3.0
	Woodruff Brown	3	4.5
	Woodruff Red	2	3.0
	Woodruff Smudged	8	12.1
	Subtotal	47	71.2
123B	Showlow Red	1	1.5
	Woodruff Brown	2	3.0
	Woodruff Smudged	2	3.0
	Subtotal	5	7.6
123W	Woodruff Smudged	1	1.5
127W	Showlow Corr. Smudged	1	1.5
	Showlow Smudged	2	3.0
	Woodruff Brown	1	1.5
	Woodruff Smudged	3	4.5
	Subtotal	7	10.6
Total		66	100.0

of the Northern San Juan region based on the type of rock material used as temper, the paste characteristics of the ceramics, and the slip characteristics. In contrast to the predominantly augite diorite temper that is coarsely crushed, the high silt content and brown to yellow discolored paste, and the silty, yellowish discolored slip that rarely holds a good polish, the Northern San Juan trade ware has finer paste with a gray to white color, finer crushed temper with greater use of diorite porphyry as the sole igneous material and much greater use of crushed sherd, and slips of finer quality with much less silt content and higher polish. There are areas of overlap between the two because of the use of crushed rock temper, but at Middle San Juan sites the differences are relatively easy to separate. Literature resources used in the identification of Northern San Juan trade ware included Rohn (1977), Breternitz et al. (1974), and Blinman and Wilson (1989).

White Ware

Similar to the modified typology used to type the Animas Variety ceramics, we made some modifications to the typology of the Northern San Juan tradition as a means of providing congruency in the overall classification scheme. First, all Kiatuthlanna and Red Mesa style ceramics were condensed into Cortez B/w (Figure 31.37), relieving most of the confusion in deciding which early Pueblo II designs should be placed in Cortez or Mancos. Cortez B/w was then segregated into the substyles Kiatuthlanna and Red Mesa to differentiate temporal and stylistic patterning within the type. The same use of substyles was applied to Mancos B/w, a notoriously lumped ceramic type whose utility as a chronometric tool is limited—other than for identification of an assemblage or component as Pueblo II. Thus, Mancos B/w was segregated into Sosi (Figure 31.38), Mancos, Dogoszhi (Figure 31.39), Chaco, Puerco, and Reserve styles, although Chaco and Puerco styles were not present in the assemblage. The identifica-

Figure 31.36. Tularosa Patterned-Corrugated Smudged.

Figure 31.37. Cortez B/w, Red Mesa Style.

tion of transitional sherds that represent Early McElmo B/w may thus have been more clear (Figure 31.40).

In total, 204 Northern San Juan White Ware sherds were identified, including typeable and non-typeable ceramics. Rooms containing Northern San Juan White Ware are listed in Table 31.22. Rooms lacking white ware included 64W, 123A, 123B, and 123W. Following the same trend as in all the trade ware, Room 100W contained most of the Northern San Juan White Ware and all the early ceramic types Cortez B/w, Kiatuthlanna and Red Mesa styles. As discussed in Chapter 32, Room 100W produced the best assemblage and deposits of the Chacoan period occupation. Bowls comprised the majority (70%, n = 143) of the white ware assemblage, followed by jars (n = 53), ladles (n = 6), mugs (n = 1), and indeterminate form (n = 1). Bowls oc-curred in all types, and jars were well represented in Mancos B/w and McElmo B/w (Figure 31.41) but not in Mesa Verde B/w. The single mug was Mesa Verde B/w. Mesa Verde banded (Figure 31.42) and all-over designs (Figure 31.43) were also present in the Salmon assemblage.

Figure 31.38. Mancos B/w, Sosi style.

Table 31.22. Northern San Juan White Ware from Salmon rooms.

Room	Ceramic Type	Sherd Count	Percent
030A	Mesa Verde B/w	2	1.0
	Pueblo II–III style B/w	2	1.0
	Subtotal	4	2.0
030B	Mancos B/w (Dogoszhi style)	1	0.5
	Mesa Verde B/w	5	2.5
	Pueblo I–II style B/w	1	0.5
	Pueblo II–III style B/w	1	0.5
	Slipped white	9	4.4
	Subtotal	17	8.3
030W	Mancos B/w (Dogoszhi style)	1	0.5
	Mancos B/w (Mancos style)	1	0.5
	McElmo B/w	1	0.5
	Pueblo II–III style B/w	2	1.0
	Subtotal	5	2.5
090W	Mancos B/w (Dogoszhi style)	1	0.5
	Mancos B/w (Sosi style)	1	0.5
	Mesa Verde B/w	2	1.0
	Subtotal	4	2.0
100W	Cortez B/w (Kiatuthlanna)	1	0.5
	Cortez B/w (Red Mesa style)	5	2.5
	Early McElmo B/w	10	4.9
	Mancos B/w (Dogoszhi style)	15	7.4
	Mancos B/w (Mancos style)	6	2.9
	Mancos B/w (Reserve style)	6	2.9
	Mancos B/w (Sosi style)	11	5.4
	McElmo B/w	80	39.2
	McElmo–Mesa Verde B/w	5	2.5
	Mesa Verde B/w	17	8.3
	Pueblo I–II style B/w	1	0.5
	Pueblo II–III style B/w	3	1.5
	Pueblo III style B/w	4	2.0
	Slipped white	8	3.9
	Subtotal	172	84.3
127W	Pueblo II–III style B/w	2	1.0
Total		204	100.0

Gray Ware

Northern San Juan Gray Ware was identified by the presence of diorite porphyry or other crushed rock temper, temper grains that were crushed finer than the local gray ware, pastes that were grayer in color without the brown to yellow discoloration, and a harder fracture. Seventy-six gray ware sherds were identified as Northern San Juan, including rims and body fragments. Three rims were identified as Mancos Corrugated, and two were classified as Dolores Corrugated; none had the extreme rim eversion typical of Mesa Verde Corrugated. As shown in Table 31.23, the only rooms containing Northern San Juan Gray Ware were 30A, 30B, 30W, 90W, and 100W. All of the corrugated sherds were indented or clapboard corrugated with no elaboration, such as patterned or zoned corrugation.

Red Ware

San Juan Red Ware was poorly represented in the sample, probably due to the late occupation of Salmon and the discontinuation of red ware production in the San Juan region at roughly AD 1050 (Breternitz et al. 1974; Wilson and Blinman 1989). Nevertheless, 10 San Juan Red Ware sherds were identified, including 1 Bluff B/r, 1 Transitional Bluff–Deadmans B/r, and 2 Deadmans B/r. As shown in Table 31.24, all of the red ware sherds were from Room 100W. Eight were bowl fragments, one was a Deadmans B/r jar sherd, and one was an in-

Figure 31.39. Mancos B/w, Dogoszhi style.

Table 31.23. Northern San Juan Gray Ware from Salmon rooms.

Room	Ceramic Type	Sherd Count	Percent
030A	Corrugated gray	27	35.5
030B	Corrugated gray	27	35.5
	Polished gray	1	1.3
	Subtotal	28	36.8
030W	Corrugated gray	1	1.3
	Polished gray	1	1.3
	Mancos Corrugated	1	1.3
	Subtotal	3	3.9
090W	Corrugated gray	2	2.6
100W	Banded gray	2	2.6
	Corrugated gray	3	3.9
	Indeterminate gray	7	9.2
	Mancos Corrugated	2	2.6
	Dolores Corrugated	2	2.6
	Subtotal	16	21.1
Total		76	100.0

Figure 31.40. Early McElmo B/w.

Figure 31.41. McElmo B/w.

determinate red ware jar fragment. As is typical of San Juan Red Ware, all sherds were tempered with crushed rock that consisted of diorite porphyry and other types of indeterminate crushed igneous rock.

CERAMIC CHRONOLOGY AND MEAN DATE CALCULATIONS

Numerous methods have been employed for dating sites, features, and room strata in the Southwest; Franklin's (Chapter 23) factor analysis approach is thus one of many that have been applied over the years. Ceramic groups, such as those developed by Peckham and Wilson (1967) for the Chuska series and by Eddy (1966) for the Upper San Juan series, have been used to date sites based on the majority of types present and fall-off rates of types during a given time period. Several variations of South's (1977) original ceramic mean date formula have been tested in the Southwest (Christenson 1994; Gomolak 1980), whereby manufacturing date ranges for ceramic types are weighted by their counts in a site assemblage or provenience and a mean date is

Table 31.24. San Juan Red Ware from Salmon rooms.

Room	Ceramic Type	Sherd Count	Percent
100W	Bluff B/r	1	10.0
	Deadmans B/r	2	20.0
	Indeterminate B/r	2	20.0
	Indeterminate red	4	40.0
	Transitional Bluff–Deadmans B/r	1	10.0
Total		10	100.0

Figure 31.42. Mesa Verde B/w, Banded pattern sherds.

produced. For the Salmon Research Initiative, I used P. Reed's (2000) variation in methodology, which represents a modification of South's ceramic mean date formula. Rather than producing just a mean date, which seemed falsely precise, Reed's formula generates mean ceramic dates and ranges for sites and features.

The published date ranges for individual ceramic types and for more generic type and ware categories are put into a spreadsheet that also includes ware and type frequencies for a given site or provenience. When type or ware categories with date ranges greater than 300 years are eliminated (allowing use of the best-dated ceramics), the remaining type frequencies are weighted by the total number of items per provenience and a date range based on the weighted scores is produced. What Reed described as the "best range" is half the range closest to the mean; statisticians describe this as the interquartile range or midspread (Drennan 1996). Table 31.25 presents the ceramic types, manufacturing date ranges and known date ranges of presence in the Middle San Juan, and the references used to generate the date ranges.

Several ceramic types and ware categories within ceramic series were dropped from the mean date calculations during the process of assigning date ranges and evaluating the data. One of these was locally produced gray ware, which at this point in our research has questionable sensitivity to temporal change. Given that there were no Mesa Verde style, highly everted rims in the sample, there is also reason to question the temporal significance of the rim eversion chronology. All of the rooms examined had Mesa Verde components in the upper levels or mixed Mesa Verde and earlier period trash, suggesting that Mesa Verde style corrugated rims should have been present in the ceramic assemblages. At the Box B site (Mills 1991), located down the San Juan River from Salmon Pueblo, Mesa Verde style corrugated rims and vessels were identified in association with AD 1200s deposits that yielded Mesa B/w pottery. It is also possible that the Box B site dates later in the 1200s than the Mesa Verde deposits examined in the rooms during the current study at Salmon and that Mesa Verde style corrugated vessels were a late introduction to the Middle San Juan region. Until further examination of the correlation between temporal and functional differences in the absence of Mesa Verde style corrugated ceramics in the deposits at Salmon, it seems more prudent to exclude the gray ware from the mean date calculations. I have speculated that there may be functional differences between corrugated vessels with highly everted rims and those with less everted rim shapes. It does seem that the transition to vessels with rim eversions greater than 60 degrees took place quickly after the AD 1200s, but the use of vessels with eversions less than 60 degrees continued from AD 1000 without any temporal transition (see Blinman and Wilson 1989). Differences in temporal change in Middle San Juan ceramics require greater attention and research before we can confidently apply rim eversion chronology as a means of dating proveniences at Salmon.

Figure 31.43. Mesa Verde B/w, All-over pattern sherds.

Table 31.25. Ceramic traditions, types, and dates used to generate ceramic mean dates and ranges for the Salmon study.

Ceramic Type	Design Style	Date Range	References
Northern San Juan Animas Variety			
Cortez B/w	Kiatuthlanna	850–925	Breternitz et al. 1974; Rohn 1977; Windes 1977
Cortez B/w	Red Mesa	900–1050	Breternitz et al. 1974; Rohn 1977; Windes 1977; Toll & McKenna 1997
Mancos B/w	Mancos	1000–1100	Breternitz et al. 1974; Rohn 1977
Mancos B/w	Black Mesa	1000–1100	Hays-Gilpin & van Hartesveldt 1998; Colton 1956; Breternitz et al. 1974
Mancos B/w	Dogoszhi	1040–1150	Toll & McKenna 1997; Breternitz et al. 1974
Mancos B/w	Sosi	1000–1125	Breternitz et al. 1974; Rohn 1977; Colton 1956
Mancos B/w	Chaco	1075–1150	Toll & McKenna 1997; Breternitz et al. 1974
Mancos B/w	Puerco	1030–1175	Hays-Gilpin & van Hartesveldt 1998; Breternitz et al. 1974
Mancos B/w	Reserve	1050–1200	Hays-Gilpin & van Hartesveldt 1998; Breternitz et al. 1974; Rinaldo & Bluhm 1956
Early McElmo B/w	—	1050–1100	Breternitz et al. 1974
McElmo B/w	—	1075–1225	Breternitz et al. 1974; Rohn 1977
McElmo–Mesa V. B/w	—	1175–1225	—
Mesa Verde B/w	—	1180–1300	Breternitz et al. 1974; Rohn 1977
Piedra B/w	—	750–900	Breternitz et al. 1974; Rohn 1977; Eddy 1966
Pueblo I–II style B/w	—	800–1100	—
Pueblo II–III style B/w	—	1000–1200	—
Pueblo III style B/w	—	1100–1300	—
Cibola Animas Variety			
Kiatuthlanna B/w	—	850–925	Windes 1997; Reed et al. 1998
Red Mesa B/w	—	900–1050	Toll & McKenna 1992, 1997; Reed et al. 1998; Windes 1977
Escavada B/w	—	1000–1125	Toll & McKenna 1992, 1997; Reed et al. 1998
Gallup B/w	—	1000–1125	Toll & McKenna 1992, 1997; Windes 1977
Puerco B/w	—	1000–1175	Reed 1993; Hays-Gilpin & van Hartesveldt 1998
Chaco B/w	—	1075–1150	Toll & McKenna 1992, 1997; Windes 1977
Reserve B/w	—	1050–1200	Rinaldo & Bluhm 1956; Hays-Gilpin & van Hartesveldt 1998
Chaco-McElmo B/w	—	1100–1300	Toll & McKenna 1992, 1997
Tularosa B/w	—	1175–1300	Rinaldo & Bluhm 1956; Hays-Gilpin & van Hartesveldt 1998
Pueblo I–II B/w	—	800–1100	—
Pueblo II–III B/w	—	1000–1200	—
Pueblo III B/w	—	1100–1300	—
Chuska Trade Ware			
Newcomb B/w	—	875–1025	Goff & Reed 2003; Peckham & Wilson 1967
Burnham B/w	—	900–1025	Goff & Reed 2003; Peckham & Wilson 1967
Brimhall B/w	—	1000–1125	Goff & Reed 2003; Peckham & Wilson 1967
Chuska B/w	—	1000–1125	Goff & Reed 2003; Peckham & Wilson 1967
Taylor B/w	Puerco	1000–1175	Goff & Reed 2003; Peckham & Wilson 1967
Taylor B/w	Sosi	1000–1125	Goff & Reed 2003; Peckham & Wilson 1967
Toadlena B/w	Black Mesa	1000–1100	Goff & Reed 2003; Peckham & Wilson 1967
Toadlena B/w	Puerco	1000–1175	Goff & Reed 2003; Peckham & Wilson 1967
Toadlena B/w	Reserve	1100–1200	Goff & Reed 2003; Peckham & Wilson 1967
Toadlena B/w	Sosi	1000–1125	Goff & Reed 2003; Peckham & Wilson 1967
Nava B/w	—	1125–1225	Goff & Reed 2003; Peckham & Wilson 1967
Crumbled House B/w	—	1180–1300	Goff & Reed 2003; Peckham & Wilson 1967
Gray Hills Banded	—	900–1000	Goff & Reed 2003; Peckham & Wilson 1967
Captain Tom Corr.	—	950–1100	Goff & Reed 2003; Peckham & Wilson 1967
Newcomb Corr.	—	975–1025	Goff & Reed 2003; Peckham & Wilson 1967
Blue Shale Corr.	—	1000–1200	Goff & Reed 2003; Peckham & Wilson 1967
Hunter Corr.	—	1150–1300	Goff & Reed 2003; Peckham & Wilson 1967
Pueblo II–III B/w	—	1000–1200	—
Pueblo III B/w	—	1125–1300	—

Table 31.25 (continued)

Ceramic Type	Design Style	Date Range	References
Cibola Trade Ware			
Kiatuthlanna B/w	—	850–925	Windes 1997; Reed et al. 1998
Red Mesa B/w	—	900–1050	Toll & McKenna 1992, 1997; Windes 1977
Escavada B/w	—	1000–1100	Toll & McKenna 1992, 1997; Windes 1977
Gallup B/w	—	1000–1125	Toll & McKenna 1992, 1997; Windes 1977
Chaco B/w	—	1075–1150	Toll & McKenna 1992, 1997; Windes 1977
Puerco B/w	—	1030–1150	L. Reed 1993; Hays-Gilpin & van Hartesveldt 1998
Reserve B/w	—	1050–1200	Rinaldo & Bluhm 1956; Hays-Gilpin & van Hartesveldt 1998
Chaco-McElmo B/w	—	1100–1150	Toll & McKenna 1992, 1997; Windes 1977
Snowflake B/w	—	1100–1250	Hays-Gilpin & van Hartesveldt 1998
Pueblo I–II style B/w	—	800–1100	—
Pueblo II–III style B/w	—	1000–1200	—
White Mountain Red Ware			
Puerco B/r	—	1090–1175	Carlson 1970; Hays-Gilpin & van Hartesveldt 1998
Wingate B/r	—	1090–1200	Carlson 1970; Hays-Gilpin & van Hartesveldt 1998
Wingate Polychrome	—	1125–1225	Carlson 1970; Hays-Gilpin & van Hartesveldt 1998
St. Johns B/r	—	1175–1300	Carlson 1970; Hays-Gilpin & van Hartesveldt 1998
St. Johns Polychrome	—	1175–1300	Carlson 1970; Hays-Gilpin & van Hartesveldt 1998
Kayenta Trade Ware			
Black Mesa B/w	—	1000–1100	Colton 1956; Hays-Gilpin & van Hartesveldt 1998
Dogoszhi B/w	—	1040–1220	Hays-Gilpin & van Hartesveldt 1998
Sosi B/w	—	1070–1180	Colton 1955; Hays-Gilpin & van Hartesveldt 1998
Flagstaff B/w	—	1150–1220	Colton 1955; Hays-Gilpin & van Hartesveldt 1998
Medicine B/o	—	1050–1100	Colton 1956
Tusayan B/r	—	1050–1150	Colton 1956
Cameron Polychrome	—	1100–1280	Colton 1956
Citadel Polychrome	—	1125–1200	Colton 1956
Little Colorado Trade Ware			
Padre B/w	—	1100–1250	Colton 1955; Hays-Gilpin & van Hartesveldt 1998
Mogollon Trade Ware			
Showlow Corr. Smudged	—	1050–1150	Hays-Gilpin & van Hartesveldt 1998
Showlow Red	—	1000–1100	Hays-Gilpin & van Hartesveldt 1998
Showlow Smudged	—	1000–1150	Hays-Gilpin & van Hartesveldt 1998
Tularosa Pattern Corr. (smudged interior)	—	1050–1250	Oppelt 2002; Rinaldo & Bluhm 1956
Northern San Juan Trade Ware			
Cortez B/w	Kiatuthlanna	850–925	Breternitz et al. 1974; Blinman & Wilson 1989; Windes 1977; L. Reed et al. 1998
Cortez B/w	Red Mesa	900–1050	Breternitz et al. 1974; Blinman & Wilson 1989; Windes 1977; L. Reed et al. 1998
Mancos B/w	Mancos	1000–1125	Breternitz et al. 1974; Blinman & Wilson 1989
Mancos B/w	Sosi	1000–1125	Breternitz et al. 1974; Blinman & Wilson 1989; L. Reed et al. 1998
Mancos B/w	Dogoszhi	1000–1125	Breternitz et al. 1974; Blinman & Wilson 1989; L. Reed et al. 1998
Mancos B/w	Reserve	1100–1200	Breternitz et al. 1974; Blinman & Wilson 1989; Hays-Gilpin & van Hartesveldt 1998
Early McElmo B/w	—	1075–1125	Breternitz et al. 1974; Blinman & Wilson 1989
McElmo B/w	—	1100–1225	Breternitz et al. 1974; Blinman & Wilson 1989
Mesa Verde B/w	—	1180–1300	Breternitz et al. 1974; Blinman & Wilson 1989
Pueblo I–II B/w	—	800–1000	—
Pueblo II–III B/w	—	1000–1200	—
Pueblo III B/w	—	1100–1300	—
Bluff B/r	—	820–1000	Breternitz et al. 1974; Blinman & Wilson 1989
Deadmans B/r	—	880–1075	Breternitz et al. 1974; Blinman & Wilson 1989

Ceramic types of the Woodruff Brown Ware sequence were also eliminated from the mean date calculations due to uncertainties in their temporal placement and date ranges of manufacture; Hays-Gilpin and van Hartesveldt (1998:150–152) have noted the difficulties in assigning date ranges for the Woodruff series. As discussed above, identifying these sherds as trade ware in assemblages outside of the Forestdale and Woodruff areas is difficult, in contrast to Puerco Valley Red. Identifying the provenience of the material outside of the Puerco Valley and Mogollon Rim regions is difficult, and the date ranges in those areas are not currently well understood. Thus, sherds identified in this study as Woodruff Smudged, Woodruff Brown, and Woodruff Red were excluded from the mean date calculations.

The date ranges provided in Table 31.25 for each ceramic type are used in Chapter 32 to calculate mean date ranges for Salmon room strata. Although the corrugated rims were not used in the mean date analysis, their numbers were noted, along with how many rims were present and the eversion range measured for the groups of rims (e.g., 0–30 degrees, 31–60 degrees).

SUMMARY

Local ceramics produced in the Middle San Juan region, identified as Animas Variety, include varieties of both the Northern San Juan and Cibola series. During the analysis at Salmon, at the Tommy site (L. Reed 2004; L. Reed et al. 2001b), and at Aztec Ruins (L. Reed 2005a; Reed and Myers 2006), paste and slip differences in the local pottery were identified that set it apart from Northern San Juan and Cibola San Juan Basin trade ware. Animas Variety ceramics have high silt content pastes with brown to yellow discoloration, resulting from the original firing of the pottery; hardness tests conducted on Animas Variety sherds in comparison with their trade ware counterparts suggest that Animas Variety pottery may have been fired at lower temperatures. Slips on Animas Variety white ware also contain greater amounts of silt that is visible within the slip, and these ceramics were less likely to hold a polish than Northern San Juan or Cibola White Ware. Tempering materials show differences as well, including greater amounts of augite diorite in the Animas Variety ceramics, in contrast with the almost exclusive use of diorite porphyry and crushed sherd in the Northern San Juan pottery. The Cibola Animas Variety ceramics are sand and sherd tempered with greater amounts of shale, compared to the sand and sherd temper of Cibola ceramics. Of note is that the Cibola trade ware present in the Salmon sample lacked any fragments of the trachyte generally seen in Cibola ceramics in the Chaco area.

Chapter 32

NEW RESEARCH WITH CERAMIC DATA FROM SALMON PUEBLO ROOMS

by Lori Stephens Reed and Tori L. Myers

In this chapter, we examine the ceramic assemblage from each room analyzed during the Salmon Research Initiative and address several research issues: dating of room stratigraphy by ceramic mean dating, distribution of nonlocal ceramics, vessel forms, distribution of Cibola Animas Variety and Northern San Juan Animas Variety ceramics, and the distribution of slip application as it relates to identifying local production of Cibola ceramics.

The data presented here comprise the first phase of a long-term analysis of Salmon ceramics with a focus on understanding the presence of Chacoan people, technology, and artifacts at Salmon, and an exploration of subsequent San Juan period ceramic usage.

Use of ceramic mean dating for the Salmon rooms proved a useful and productive technique for aligning strata into a temporal progression and identifying mixed deposits. For each room discussed, we present a table of ceramic mean date results, along with discussion relative to the ceramics identified in each stratum.

ROOM 30W

Room 30W is part of a suite of rooms interpreted during the original Salmon excavations as Chacoan. It is located in the second tier of rooms along Salmon's north wall. The 27 stratigraphic units identified during excavation included two floor units (one each of Chacoan and San Juan age), two roof-fall deposits, and several layers of structured trash identified as stratum C, among other types of construction and wall-fall debris. As originally interpreted, most of these strata are Chacoan in age with some mixing, and the four highest, or most recent, deposits extend into the Secondary period. After an extensive fire burned much of the pueblo, including Room 30W, in the late 1100s or early 1200s, the San Juan occupants divided the room into two smaller rooms: 30A and 30B. Ceramics from these two smaller rooms are discussed individually below. In total, 1180 sherds from roof-fall, floor fill, floor, and Chacoan trash contexts were analyzed from Room 30W during the Salmon Research Initiative (Table 32.1).

Ceramic Chronology

From the typeable ceramics identified and using the methodology discussed in Chapter 31, ceramic mean dates and ranges were generated for each stratigraphic unit examined in Room 30W. Table 32.2 provides a list of all ceramics identified in the stratigraphic units and highlights those used in generating the ceramic mean dates and ranges. The stratigraphic units in Table 32.2 are listed in order of excavation from top to bottom. Ceramics identified as Animas Variety are identified in the "Variety" column, along with imported, trade ware ceramics. Thus, the table clearly indicates the Northern San Juan and Cibola ceramics classified during analysis as Animas Variety and those classified as nonlocal trade ware.

One of the initial observations from Table 32.2 is the relatively rare occurrence of Mesa Verde B/w,

Table 32.1. Room 30W stratigraphic units and ceramics analyzed.

Stratum	Description	Total
F-1-2	Secondary roof	71
G-1-3	Secondary floor fill	53
H-1-4	Secondary floor	10
I-1-5	Mixed Secondary-Chacoan floor	159
M-1-6	Mixed Secondary-Chacoan trash	18
C-1-6.5	Chacoan trash	9
C-2-8	Chacoan trash	221
C-3-9	Chacoan trash	245
C-4-10	Chacoan trash	35
F-2-11	Chacoan roof-fall	281
H-2-12	Chacoan floor	77
Unidentified	Unidentified	1
Total		1180

Table 32.2. Ceramics from Room 30W stratigraphic units.

Stratum	Tradition	Variety	Ware	Ceramic Type	Total
F-1-2	Chuska	Trade ware	Gray	Corrugated gray	1
	Cibola	Animas	Gray	Plain gray	2
				Polished gray	1
			White	Escavada B/w*	3
				Pueblo I-II style B/w*	2
				Reserve B/w*	1
	Mogollon	Trade ware	Brown	Showlow Smudged*	2
	Northern San Juan	Animas	Gray	Corrugated gray	30
				Polished gray	3
				Pueblo II corrugated	1
				Pueblo II-III corrugated	1
			White	Mancos B/w (Mancos style)*	2
				Mancos B/w (Sosi style)*	1
				McElmo B/w*	2
				McElmo/Mesa Verde B/w*	1
				Mesa Verde B/w*	10
				Pueblo I-II style B/w*	1
				Pueblo II-III style B/w*	4
				Pueblo III style B/w*	1
				Slipped white	1
		Trade ware	Gray	Corrugated gray	1
				Subtotal	71
G-1-3	Chuska	Trade ware	Gray	Corrugated gray	1
			White	Brimhall B/w*	1
				Taylor B/w (Sosi style)*	1
	Cibola	Animas	Gray	Polished gray	2
			White	Chaco-McElmo B/w*	2
				Pueblo II-III style B/w*	1
		Trade ware	White	Gallup B/w*	1
	Northern San Juan	Animas	Gray	Corrugated gray	23
				Plain gray	3
				Polished gray	1
				Pueblo II corrugated	4
			White	Early McElmo B/w*	3
				Mancos B/w (Dogoszhi style)*	1
				McElmo B/w*	1
				Mesa Verde B/w*	3
				Painted B/w	1
				Pueblo II-III style B/w*	2
				Pueblo III style B/w*	2
				Subtotal	53
H-1-4	Chuska	Trade ware	Gray	Corrugated gray	2
	Cibola	Animas	Gray	Corrugated gray	1
				Plain gray	1
				Polished gray	1
	Northern San Juan	Animas	Gray	Corrugated gray	4
			White	Slipped white	1
				Subtotal	10
I-1-5	Chuska	Trade ware	Gray	Corrugated gray	9
				Plain gray	1
			White	Brimhall B/w*	1
	Cibola	Animas	Gray	Corrugated gray	1
				Plain gray	1
				Polished gray	1
			White	Pueblo I-II style B/w*	1
		Trade ware	Gray	Corrugated gray	1
	Northern San Juan	Animas	Gray	Banded gray	1
				Corrugated gray	102
				Fillet Rim Gray	1
				Indeterminate gray	4
				Mancos Gray	1
				Plain gray	16
				Polished gray	3
				Pueblo II corrugated	1
			White	Mancos B/w (Dogoszhi style)*	1
				Mancos B/w (Reserve style)*	1

Table 32.2 (continued)

Stratum	Tradition	Variety	Ware	Ceramic Type	Total
				Mancos B/w (Sosi style)*	2
				Pueblo II-III style B/w*	2
				Pueblo III style B/w*	5
				Slipped white	3
				Subtotal	159
M-1-6	Chuska	Trade ware	Gray	Corrugated gray	1
	Cibola	Animas	Gray	Corrugated gray	2
		Trade ware	Red	Wingate B/r*	1
			White	Red Mesa B/w*	1
	Northern San Juan	Animas	Gray	Corrugated gray	3
				Plain gray	4
				Pueblo II corrugated	2
			White	Mancos B/w (Mancos style)*	1
				McElmo B/w*	1
				Pueblo II-III style B/w*	1
		Trade ware	Gray	Polished gray	1
				Subtotal	18
C-1-6.5	Cibola	Animas	White	Chaco-McElmo B/w*	1
		Trade ware	Red	Indeterminate White Mountain Red Ware	1
	Northern San Juan	Animas	Gray	Pueblo II-III corrugated	2
			White	McElmo B/w*	2
				McElmo/Mesa Verde B/w*	1
				Mesa Verde B/w*	1
				Pueblo III style B/w*	1
				Subtotal	9
C-2-8	Chuska	Trade ware	Gray	Blue Shale Corrugated*	2
			White	Crumbled House B/w*	1
				Newcomb B/w*	2
				Toadlena B/w (Reserve style)*	1
	Cibola	Animas	Gray	Plain gray	1
			White	Chaco B/w*	2
				Chaco-McElmo B/w*	1
				Escavada B/w*	1
				Gallup B/w*	9
				Pueblo I-II style B/w*	1
				Pueblo II-III style B/w*	2
				Reserve B/w*	1
		Trade ware	Red	Indeterminate White Mountain Red Ware	3
				St. Johns B/r*	1
				Wingate B/r*	2
			White	Chaco B/w*	2
				Escavada B/w*	1
				Gallup B/w*	3
				Red Mesa B/w*	2
	Indeterminate	Animas	White	McElmo style B/w*	1
	Northern San Juan	Animas	Gray	Corrugated gray	23
				Indeterminate gray	1
				Plain gray	11
				Polished gray	1
				Pueblo II corrugated	16
				Pueblo II-III corrugated	6
			White	Cortez B/w (Red Mesa style)*	2
				Early McElmo B/w*	1
				Mancos B/w (Black Mesa style)*	1
				Mancos B/w (Dogoszhi style)*	8
				Mancos B/w (Mancos style)*	6
				Mancos B/w (Reserve style)*	2
				Mancos B/w (Sosi style)*	12
				McElmo B/w*	48
				McElmo/Mesa Verde B/w*	1
				Mesa Verde B/w*	12
				Pueblo II-III style B/w*	28
				Pueblo III style B/w*	1
				Slipped white	1
		Trade ware	White	Pueblo II-III style B/w*	1
				Subtotal	221

Table 32.2 (continued)

Stratum	Tradition	Variety	Ware	Ceramic Type	Total
C-3-9	Chuska	Trade ware	Gray	Blue Shale Corrugated*	1
				Captain Tom Corrugated*	1
			White	Chuska B/w*	3
				Newcomb B/w*	2
	Cibola	Animas	Gray	Corrugated gray	1
				Plain gray	1
				Pueblo II-III corrugated	1
			White	Chaco B/w*	1
				Chaco-McElmo B/w*	2
				Escavada B/w*	1
				Gallup B/w*	7
				Puerco B/w*	2
				Red Mesa B/w*	1
				Slipped white	1
				Tularosa B/w*	1
		Trade ware	Red	Indeterminate White Mountain B/r	1
			White	Chaco-McElmo B/w*	1
				Gallup B/w*	5
				Pueblo I-II style B/w*	1
	Indeterminate	Indeterminate	White	Slipped white	1
	Kayenta	Trade ware	Red	Medicine B/o*	1
			White	Sosi B/w*	1
	Mogollon	Trade ware	Brown	Showlow Red*	1
				Showlow Smudged*	1
	Northern San Juan	Animas	Gray	Corrugated gray	83
				Plain gray	6
				Pueblo II corrugated	25
				Pueblo II-III corrugated	14
			White	Cortez B/w (Red Mesa style)*	1
				Early McElmo B/w*	3
				Mancos B/w (Black Mesa style)*	1
				Mancos B/w (Dogoszhi style)*	6
				Mancos B/w (Mancos style)*	4
				Mancos B/w (Reserve style)*	5
				Mancos B/w (Sosi style)*	10
				McElmo B/w*	19
				McElmo/Mesa Verde B/w*	1
				Mesa Verde B/w*	8
				Pueblo I-II style B/w*	1
				Pueblo II-III style B/w*	6
				Pueblo III style B/w*	11
		Trade ware	White	Mancos B/w (Mancos style)*	1
				McElmo B/w*	1
				Subtotal	245
C-4-10	Cibola	Animas	White	Escavada B/w*	3
				Gallup B/w*	1
		Trade ware	Red	Wingate B/r*	1
			White	Chaco-McElmo B/w*	1
	Northern San Juan	Animas	Gray	Corrugated gray	13
				Plain gray	3
				Polished gray	1
				Pueblo II corrugated	1
			White	Mancos B/w (Mancos style)*	1
				McElmo B/w*	5
				Pueblo II-III style B/w*	2
				Pueblo III style B/w*	1
				Slipped white	1
		Trade ware	Gray	Mancos Corrugated	1
				Subtotal	35
F-2-11	Chuska	Trade ware	Gray	Blue Shale Corrugated*	1
				Corrugated gray	14
			White	Nava B/w*	1
				Slipped white	1
	Cibola	Animas	Gray	Plain gray	3
			White	Chaco-McElmo B/w*	1
				Escavada B/w*	1

Table 32.2 (continued)

Stratum	Tradition	Variety	Ware	Ceramic Type	Total
				Gallup B/w*	5
				Pueblo I-II style B/w*	3
				Reserve B/w*	3
				Slipped white	1
		Indeterminate	White	Slipped white	1
		Trade ware	Red	Wingate B/r*	1
			White	Escavada B/w*	1
				Gallup B/w*	1
	Northern San Juan	Animas	Gray	Corrugated gray	142
				Indeterminate gray	1
				Plain gray	28
				Polished gray	3
				Pueblo II corrugated	15
				Pueblo II-III corrugated	2
			White	Mancos B/w (Dogoszhi style)*	3
				Mancos B/w (Puerco style)*	1
				Mancos B/w (Sosi style)*	3
				McElmo B/w*	11
				Mesa Verde B/w*	5
				Pueblo I-II style B/w*	1
				Pueblo II-III style B/w*	18
				Pueblo III style B/w*	1
				Slipped white	7
		Trade ware	White	Mancos B/w (Dogoszhi style)*	1
				Pueblo II-III style B/w*	1
				Subtotal	281
H-2-12	Chuska	Trade ware	Gray	Corrugated gray	2
			White	Painted B/w	1
	Cibola	Animas	Gray	Plain gray	1
			White	Chaco B/w*	1
				Painted B/w	1
				Slipped white	1
	Northern San Juan	Animas	Gray	Corrugated gray	46
				Plain gray	13
				Pueblo II corrugated	6
			White	Mancos B/w (Black Mesa style)*	2
				Mancos B/w (Dogoszhi style)*	1
				Mancos B/w (Reserve style)*	1
				Mancos B/w (Sosi style)*	1
				Subtotal	77
Indet. Strat	Northern San Juan	Animas	White	Pueblo II-III style B/w	1
				Subtotal	1
Total					1180

*Types used to generate ceramic mean dates and ranges for Room 30W.

but there was enough from the strata above the Chacoan floor (H-2-12) to indicate mixed deposits. As discussed below, however, the presence of small numbers of Mesa Verde B/w does not seem to affect the ceramic dates in any appreciable manner; the significantly larger number of Pueblo II and McElmo B/w ceramics in the various strata factors out the effects of Mesa Verde B/w. This analysis seems particularly relevant with the combined ceramic mean date and best range for the Chacoan trash fill (the C strata), for which the 21 Mesa Verde B/w and one Crumbled House B/w are overwhelmed by the large number of Pueblo II types and McElmo B/w. In addition, the absence of Mesa Verde style corrugated in these deposits also supports the mixing of some San Juan period ceramics from the occupation above the Chacoan deposits.

With the exception of stratum M-1-6, all of the mean dates and best ranges (Table 32.3) reflect a temporal stratigraphic progression from a mid-1100s occupation in the highest deposits of the room to a late-1000s occupation in the lowest Chacoan deposits. Stratum M-1-6 is out of progression probably due to the small number of sherds used to generate the ceramic dates; only five sherds from M-1-6 were typeable. Even with the 21 Mesa Verde B/w and one Crumbled House B/w from the combined C strata, the best range for the Chacoan trash fill is between 1080 and 1153, and the maximum ceramic range is 1043–1190. In one analysis of the Chacoan trash fill

Table 32.3. Room 30W ceramic mean dates and ranges by stratigraphic unit.

Stratum	Description	Ceramic Mean Date	Best Ceramic Range	Max Ceramic Range
F-1-2	Secondary roof	1160	1130-1191	1100-1221
G-1-3	Secondary floor fill	1137	1107-1166	1077-1196
H-1-4	Secondary floor	Not available	Not available	Not available
I-1-5		1120	1075-1165	1030-1210
M-1-6		1084	1049-1120	1014-1155
C-1-6.5, C-2-8, C-3-9, C-4-10	Chacoan trash	1117	1080-1153	1043-1190
F-2-11	Chacoan roof-fall	1109	1068-1151	1027-1192
H-2-12	Chacoan floor	1083	1055-1110	1027-1138

data, I ran the mean dates with the exclusion of both ceramic types, and the mean date results were only 10 years earlier (mean date at 1106 versus 1117) than when the Mesa Verde and Crumbled House sherds were in the calculation. Thus, within a trash fill dataset that large, the inclusion of later Pueblo III noise does not offset the dating significantly. In this example, however, it was clear that the late Pueblo III sherds were noise within an overwhelming late Pueblo II–early Pueblo III trash deposit.

Given the sequence of events outlined for Room 30W from excavation data in the room and across the site, the later part of the best range for stratum F-1-2 between 1160 and 1191 would coincide with the burning sequence. As described for Room 30W and much of the pueblo itself, an extensive fire burned through the site in the late 1100s or early 1200s. After the room burned, Rooms 30A and 30B were built on top of Room 30W.

Ceramic Trade Ware

Ninety-seven ceramics from Room 30W (8% of the room assemblage) were identified as trade ware or manufactured outside the Middle San Juan region. As shown in Figure 32.1, the majority of the trade ware from Room 30W had its origin in the Chuska Valley, a pattern not unexpected for deposits primarily of Chacoan age. Approximately 53 percent of the nonlocal ceramics were white and gray ware from the Chuska Valley. The gray ware ceramics include Blue Shale Corrugated and Captain Tom Corrugated, along with corrugated and plain gray body sherds. White ware includes predominantly organic-painted types—Newcomb B/w, Chuska B/w, Toadlena B/w, Nava B/w, and Crumbled House Black-white. Mineral-painted types include Brimhall B/w and Taylor B/w. The presence of organic-painted Chuska White Ware as the predominant types in Room 30W correlates with the general trend in the overall site sample analyzed from Salmon. Chuskan ceramics are present in all strata analyzed from Room 30W, with the exception of C-1-6.5 and C-4-10, two of the combined Chacoan trash strata.

Chuska sherds from floor and fill contexts represent predominantly jars (n = 41) or ollas (n = 2). None of these sherds represented reconstructible vessels, and only a handful could be refit. The olla fragments included one Blue Shale Corrugated rim and one Newcomb B/w neck. The jar sherd assemblage included a wide variety of types represented by both white and gray ware. Jar fragments included Blue Shale Corrugated, Captain Tom Corrugated, all the corrugated body fragments, Brimhall B/w, Toadlena B/w, and Crumbled House B/w.

Cibola ceramics included gray and white ware from the San Juan Basin and White Mountain Red Ware from the central New Mexico and Arizona region. As shown in Figure 32.1, the combined Cibola group represents 33 percent of the trade ware identified in Room 30W. Of the 32 sherds, 11 are White Mountain Red Ware, 20 are Cibola White Ware, and 1 is Cibola Gray Ware. The White Mountain Red Ware sherds were mostly unidentifiable, but the typeable sherds included Wingate B/r and St. Johns B/r. Two of the Wingate B/r sherds from the Chacoan trash strata (C-2-8) were the only red ware that could be refit or belonged to the same vessel. White Mountain Red Ware sherds were not present on the Chacoan floor (H-2-12) but were scattered through the Chacoan trash and into the later Secondary occupation deposits. All of the Wingate and St. Johns B/r sherds were from bowls, but the indeterminate red ware sherds included both bowls and jars.

Cibola White Ware included 20 sherds, representing Red Mesa B/w, Escavada B/w, Gallup B/w, Chaco B/w, and Chaco-McElmo B/w. Gallup B/w

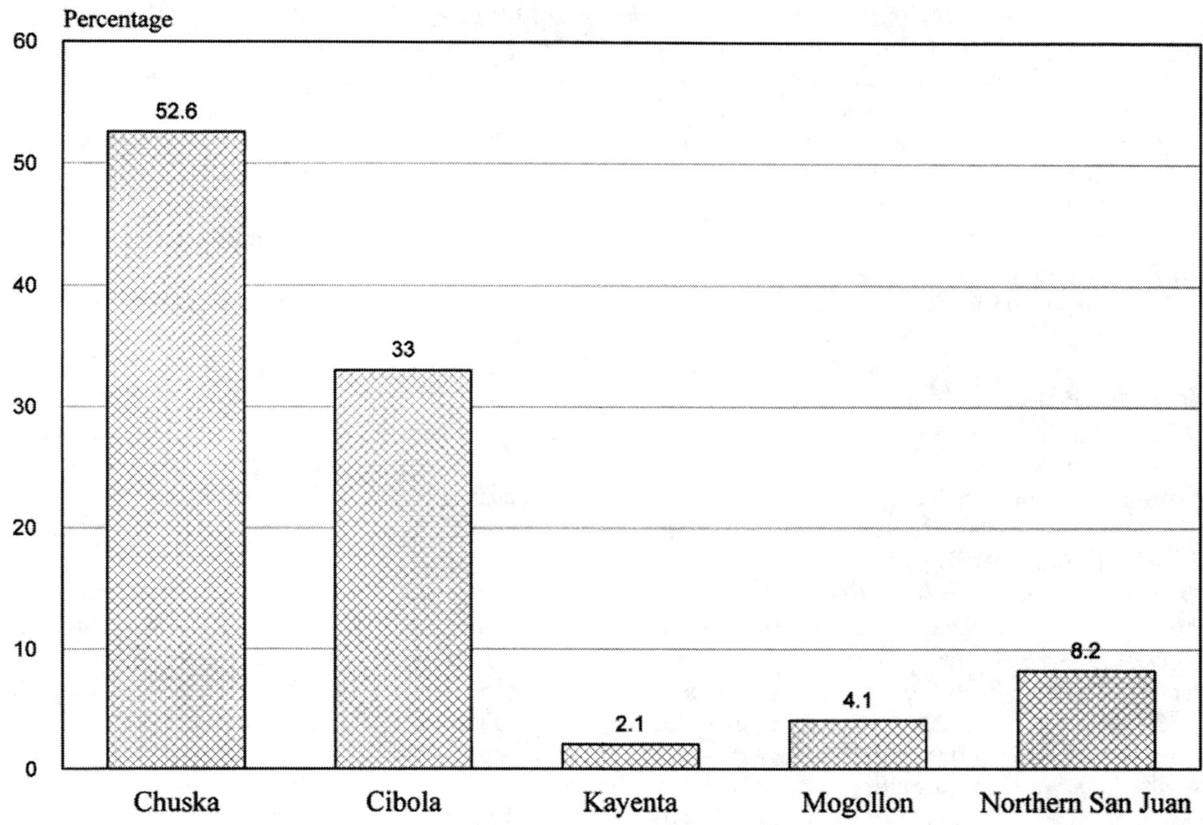

Figure 32.1. Distribution of trade ware ceramics from Room 30W.

was by far the most common Cibola trade ware in Room 30W. None of these sherds fit together or represent reconstructible vessels. One Chaco-McElmo B/w rim from stratum C-4-10, one of the combined Chacoan trash deposits, showed attributes of our designation for Early McElmo B/w, suggesting this particular sherd may represent a transition from Pueblo II design styles and layouts to early Pueblo III dotted rims and banded designs. None of the Cibola White Ware was present on either of the floor surfaces, and it seemed to be scattered throughout the room trash fill and then on the roof-fall of the Secondary occupation (see Table 32.2). Vessel forms were variable for such a small white ware assemblage, including bowls (n = 9), jars (n = 8), ollas (n = 1), pitchers (n = 1), and effigy/figurine (n = 1) fragments. As is typical of many Cibola pitchers, the neck, body, and handle had Chaco B/w designs. Finally, the single Cibola Gray Ware sherd was a corrugated body fragment.

Two sherds from the Kayenta region were identified in Room 30, including one Sosi B/w bowl fragment from stratum C-3-9, one of the Chacoan trash layers. The second sherd was a Medicine B/r jar fragment also from C-3-9.

Ceramics from the northern Mogollon region comprise 4 percent of the trade ware from Room 30W. These sherds include one Showlow Red bowl fragment and one Showlow Smudged bowl from C-3-9, and Showlow jar fragments from F-1-2.

Nonlocal Northern San Juan ceramics were few in Room 30W, totaling only eight sherds: one Mancos Corrugated rim from stratum C-4-10, one corrugated gray body fragment from F-1-2, two Mancos B/w sherds (one Dogoszhi style from F-2-11 and one Mancos style from C-3-9), one McElmo B/w from stratum C-3-9, one polished gray from M-1-6, and two Pueblo II–III style b/w from C-2-8 and F-2-11. Based on the distribution of these sherds, the Northern San Juan sample was scattered throughout the Chacoan trash and Secondary roof-fall. Thus, there is no real patterning to the distribution of these ceramics. All of the white ware sherds are from bowls, and the gray ware fragments are from jars.

In summary, trade ware ceramics are varied, occuring mostly in small numbers (except for the large sample of Chuskan pottery). There seems to be no patterning to the distribution of these ceramics within the stratigraphic units other than scattered sherds within the Chacoan trash and roof-fall units. The only pattern identified is the absence of nonlocal ceramics from the Secondary and Chacoan floors, with the exception of a few Chuska sherds.

Locally Produced Ceramics

Animas Variety ceramics, considered locally produced at Salmon or in the Middle San Juan region, were identified based on the criteria discussed in Chapter 31. These ceramics total 1080 from Room 30W. All stratigraphic units analyzed yielded Animas Variety ceramics of both the Northern San Juan and Cibola traditions. Northern San Juan Animas Variety ceramics totaled 994 sherds, including white and gray ware. From the sherd assemblage, one partial Early McElmo B/w ladle and one partial Mesa Verde B/w ladle were identified from G-1-3 in the fill above the Secondary period floor. A partial Mesa Verde B/w mug (Vessel A) was identified in F-2-11.

As shown in Table 32.2, the upper-level strata F-1-2 and G-1-3 contained a significant amount of Mesa Verde and McElmo B/w pottery, bringing the ceramic mean date and best range into the middle to late 1100s. The floor (H-1-4) of the Secondary occupation, however, contained no typeable ceramics and only one slipped white ware sherd of the Northern San Juan Animas Variety. Mancos B/w (n = 77) and McElmo B/w (n = 89) comprise the majority of the local white ware from Room 30W. Seven Early McElmo B/w sherds, bridging a transition between Mancos and McElmo were also identified. The distribution of these sherds and the nonlocal ceramics within the stratigraphic units formed the basis for the mean date, best range, and maximum ceramic range calculations given in Table 32.3. Sosi, Dogoszhi, and Mancos styles comprise the majority of the Mancos B/w ceramics identified in Room 30W. All three of these styles are predominantly late Pueblo II designs. Of the typeable Animas Variety white ware from Room 30W, 30 percent (n = 39) were Mesa Verde B/w, but the remaining 70 percent were types dating earlier than AD 1200.

Slip application, one of the attributes examined as a means of tracking Cibola influence, shows relative consistency in Room 30W with 69 percent of the Northern San Juan Animas Variety white ware having thick-chalky slips. Of the 223 sherds having slipped surfaces, the remaining 69 included 13 with thick-crackly slips, 46 with thin slips, and 10 with washy slips. It is significant that the 10 sherds with washy slips included Cortez B/w (Red Mesa style), Mancos B/w (Mancos, Dogoszhi, and Sosi styles), McElmo B/w, Mesa Verde B/w, and slipped white. When examined by stratigraphic unit, the distribution of washy slips on local Northern San Juan sherds shows no real pattern other than being scattered throughout the Chacoan trash and in the Secondary roof-fall.

Northern San Juan Animas Variety white ware ceramics included a number of different vessel forms, such as bowls (n = 243), jars (n = 64), ladles (n = 13), mugs (n = 3), and kiva jars (n = 1). Including the partial ladles identified above, Mancos B/w (Mancos style), Early McElmo B/w, McElmo B/w, and Mesa Verde B/w ladle fragments were identified. The mug fragments were from two Mesa Verde B/w mugs from stratum F-2-11. The single kiva jar rim fragment was identified as Pueblo II–III style B/w from stratum F-1-2 (Secondary occupation roof-fall).

Northern San Juan Animas Variety gray ware from Room 30W totaled 670 sherds, including two reconstructible jars (Vessels B and C) from stratum C-3-9 (a Chacoan trash layer). Vessel B was identified as Pueblo II–III corrugated, but Vessel C lacked sufficient rim fragments to classify based on rim eversion. As discussed in Chapter 31, Animas Variety gray ware has coarsely crushed igneous (augite diorite) temper with frequent inclusions of sand and shale. Sherd temper is less common than in the nonlocal Northern San Juan Gray Ware.

Cibola Animas Variety ceramics included both white ware (n = 65) and gray ware (n = 21). Both wares were identified by paste similarities with Northern San Juan Animas Variety ceramics, including high silt content and brown to yellow discoloration. Tempering material, however, consisted of various combinations of sand, shale, and sherd. Of the 21 gray ware sherds, one was identified as Pueblo II–III corrugated and the remaining fragments were corrugated, plain, or polished gray ware. Plain and polished sherds were identified as either bowl or jar fragments. Corrugated gray ware was all jar fragments. Local Cibola Gray Ware occurred throughout various strata, including Secondary roof-fall, fill, and floor deposits and Chacoan trash and floor deposits.

Cibola Animas Variety white ware included all of the typeable ceramics in the local sequence scattered throughout the Secondary and Chacoan deposits. Chaco B/w, however, was isolated in the Chacoan trash fill and on the Chacoan floor (H-2-12). As shown in Table 32.2, all of the Cibola Animas Variety ceramics were more common in the Chacoan deposits as a whole than in the Secondary deposits.

Similar to the nonlocal Cibola ceramic assemblage, Gallup B/w was the most common white ware type, comprising 34 percent (n = 22) of the local Cibola white ware assemblage. Escavada and Chaco-McElmo B/w followed in frequency at 14 percent (n = 9) and 11 percent (n = 7). All of these types were scattered throughout the Chacoan trash fill and in the Chacoan roof-fall (F-2-11).

The slip application of 71 percent (n = 35) of the Cibola Animas Variety white ware with slipped surfaces was classified as washy, corresponding with the expectation of Chacoan or Cibola influence. The remaining 29 percent included five examples with thick-chalky slips, two with thick-crackly slips, and seven with thin slips. The occurrence of ceramics with washy slips is scattered throughout the room strata, but concentrations occur in two Chacoan trash fill strata (C-2-8 and C-3-9), which contained 38 percent of the local Cibola white ware with washy slips. A second smaller concentration occurs in the Chacoan roof-fall (F-2-11), with 16 percent of the washy slipped ceramics. By ceramic type, all of the local Gallup B/w and Chaco B/w sherds from Room 30W had washy slips. Escavada B/w sherds had either washy or thin slips. Chaco-McElmo B/w had the most variability, with washy, thin, or thick-chalky slip examples.

In contrast to the nonlocal Cibola ceramics, vessel forms for the local pottery in Room 30W are more limited, with almost equal numbers of bowl (n = 31) and jar (n = 34) fragments. Gallup B/w was almost evenly divided between bowl (n = 10) and jar (n = 12) sherds. Chaco B/w included all jar fragments, whereas Chaco-McElmo B/w included all bowl fragments. Bowl and jar sherds appear scattered throughout the Room 30W strata, but a noticeable concentration of 10 bowl fragments was identified in the Chacoan roof-fall (F-2-11). This small concentration of bowl sherds consists of one Chaco-McElmo B/w, four Gallup B/w, three Reserve B/w, and two Pueblo I–II style B/w.

Summary

From the sample of ceramics analyzed from Room 30W, the assemblage is overwhelmingly local, with the combined trade ware assemblage comprising only 8 percent of the ceramics. Both Animas Variety Cibola and Northern San Juan pottery were identified, but the crushed rock–tempered ceramics comprised 98 percent of the locally produced wares. It may be that the occupants of Room 30W and nearby occupants using the room as a trash repository were producing local pottery but were using crushed igneous materials and were occasionally acquiring local Cibola pottery from other potters. It is unclear at this point in the Salmon research exactly how common Cibola Animas Variety was or what the contexts of production were (e.g., emulation of Chacoan style/technology or Chacoan potters producing the vessels). Nonetheless, the Room 30W assemblage was more Northern San Juan in technology and appearance than Cibola. Based on ceramic mean date and range calculations and tree-ring dates, Room 30W was in use (prior to division into Rooms 30A and B) between AD 1090 and about 1190.

ROOM 30A

Room 30A is one of two rooms (30A and 30B) that resulted from dividing 30W after a widespread fire swept through the pueblo sometime in the late 1100s or early 1200s. Room 30A, which is the eastern division of Room 30W, had five strata, including a floor unit, roof-fall, and postoccupational fill. Based on the abundance of burned corn and the presence of one milling bin and a storage bin, this room apparently functioned as the milling half of an integrated corn processing facility, with Room 30B (discussed below) as the storage half. In total, 853 sherds were analyzed from Room 30A during the Salmon Research Initiative (Table 32.4). These ceramics were selected from postoccupational fill (B-1-2), roof-fall (F-1-3), and floor deposits (H-1-4).

Ceramic Chronology

From the typeable ceramics identified and using the methodology discussed in Chapter 31, mean ceramic dates, best ranges, and maximum ceramic ranges were generated for each stratigraphic unit examined from Room 30A. Table 32.4 provides a list of all ceramics identified during the analysis and highlights ceramic types used in generating the ceramic chronometric data. The stratigraphic units are listed in order of excavation from the top stratum down to the lowest stratum at the floor.

Although the assemblage from stratum B-1-2, postoccupational fill above the roof-fall, is small, the typeable ceramics consist of local McElmo B/w and Mesa Verde B/w. As indicated in Table 32.5, this stratum has a mean ceramic date of 1183 and a best range from 1146 to 1219, which are within the Early San Juan to Late San Juan periods. We should note that these ceramic dates for B-1-2 are based on only four sherds.

The roof-fall strata (F-1-3) below B-1-2 contained the majority (98%, n = 842) of the ceramics analyzed. As indicated in Table 32.4, this stratum includes a variety of ceramic types and represents a mixed assemblage of earlier Chacoan and later San Juan fill.

Table 32.4. Ceramics from Room 30A stratigraphic units.

Stratum	Tradition	Variety	Ware	Ceramic Type	Total
B-1-2	Northern San Juan	Animas	Gray	Corrugated gray	2
			White	McElmo B/w*	1
				Mesa Verde B/w*	2
				Pueblo II-III style B/w	1
		Trade ware	Gray	Corrugated gray	1
				Subtotal	7
F-1-3	Chuska	Trade ware	Gray	Blue Shale Corrugated*	28
				Captain Tom Corrugated*	1
				Corrugated gray	4
	Cibola	Animas	Gray	Corrugated gray	7
				Plain gray	1
				Polished gray	2
			White	Chaco-McElmo B/w*	12
				Gallup B/w*	3
				Painted B/w	1
				Pueblo I-II style B/w*	4
				Pueblo II-III style B/w*	7
				Pueblo III style B/w*	2
				Red Mesa B/w*	1
				Slipped white	7
		Trade ware	Gray	Plain gray	1
				Polished gray	1
			Red	Indeterminate White Mountain Red Ware	4
				Wingate B/r*	1
			White	Gallup B/w*	2
				Slipped white	4
	Northern San Juan	Animas	Gray	Corrugated gray	580
				Plain gray	5
				Polished gray	5
				Pueblo II corrugated	27
			White	Mancos B/w (Black Mesa style)*	1
				Mancos B/w (Dogoszhi style)*	1
				Mancos B/w (Sosi style)*	1
				McElmo B/w*	14
				Mesa Verde B/w*	27
				Pueblo I-II style B/w*	1
				Pueblo II-III style B/w*	37
				Pueblo III style B/w*	5
				Slipped white	14
		Indeterminate	Gray	Corrugated gray	1
		Trade ware	Gray	Corrugated gray	26
			White	Mesa Verde B/w*	2
				Pueblo II-III style B/w*	2
				Subtotal	842
H-1-4	Cibola	Animas	White	Slipped white	1
	Northern San Juan	Animas	Gray	Corrugated gray	5
			White	Mancos B/w (Dogoszhi style)*	1
				Mesa Verde B/w*	1
				Slipped white	1
				Subtotal	9
Total					853

* Types used to generate ceramic mean dates and ranges for Room 30A.

Table 32.5. Room 30A ceramic mean dates and ranges by stratigraphic unit.

Stratum	Description	Ceramic Mean Date	Best Ceramic Range	Max Ceramic Range
B-1-2	Postoccupational fill	1183	1146-1219	1109-1256
F-1-3	Roof-fall	1136	1092-1181	1048-1225
H-1-4	Floor	1168	1139-1196	1110-1225

This finding is not surprising because the stratum comprises an original Chacoan roof (and associated materials) that was apparently reused by the later San Juan occupants. A ceramic mean date of 1136, a best range of 1092–1181, and maximum ceramic range of 1048–1225 indicate mixed deposits in F-1-3. If these earlier ceramic types are considered intrusive (and removed from the date calculation), the mean date becomes 1149 and the best range is 1105–1193. Excluding these earlier sherds adjusts the date range closer to our expectations for the deposition of this stratum.

An examination of the floor assemblage (H-1-4) shows only nine sherds present, including Mesa Verde B/w, Mancos B/w (Dogoszhi style), a few corrugated gray ware, and a few slipped white ware. Similar to the assemblage from stratum B-1-2, the number of typeable sherds from H-1-4 is not enough to provide confidence in the mean date, best range, and maximum ceramic range. Nevertheless, two sherds were used to produce the ceramic mean date of 1168, the best range of 1139–1196, and the maximum ceramic range of 1110–1225.

The dating of Room 30A by ceramic data is problematic due to mixing of earlier and later materials in the F-1-3 stratum, which contained the largest assemblage examined from the room. In addition, the small number of sherds present on the floor (H-1-4) and in the postoccupation fill (B-1-2) casts some doubt on the dates generated from those two strata. The scant ceramic chronometric data suggest that Room 30A dates from the middle 1100s to early 1200s. The lack of Mesa Verde style corrugated ceramics may support this determination as well as the high number of McElmo B/w ceramics. Architectural and other data from the room, however, suggest usage well into the mid-1200s.

Trade Ware Ceramics

From Room 30A, 77 ceramics (9% of the room assemblage) were trade ware or manufactured outside the Middle San Juan region. As shown in Figure 32.2, much of the trade ware came from the Chuska Valley and Northern San Juan sources. Only 17 percent of the nonlocal ceramics originated from the Cibola region to the south.

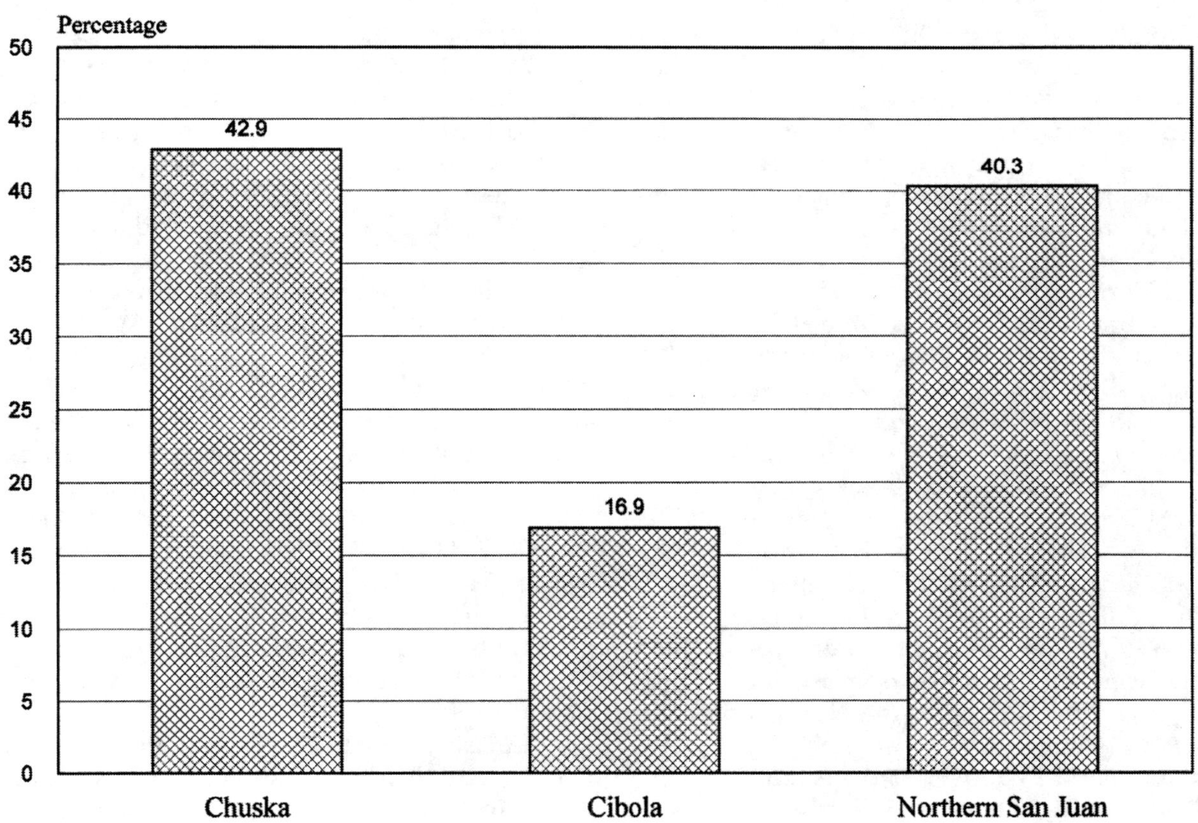

Figure 32.2. Distribution of trade ware ceramics from Room 30A.

Approximately 43 percent of the nonlocal ceramics were gray ware from the Chuska Valley. The 33 jar body sherds identified as Chuska Gray Ware consisted of 28 Blue Shale Corrugated body fragments, 1 Captain Tom Corrugated body sherd, and 4 corrugated body sherds of indeterminate type. The Blue Shale Corrugated body sherds were identified based on indented corrugations that were not as exuberantly corrugated as Newcomb Corrugated or as tightly spaced and finely executed as Hunter Corrugated. The presence of rim sherds would have been useful as supportive data for the type classification. None of the Blue Shale Corrugated sherds could be assigned to individual vessels with confidence, and they seemed to occur in the strata as sherds rather than broken vessels. All Chuska Gray Ware was recovered from stratum F-1-3, the roof-fall deposits.

F-1-3 also contained all of the Cibola trade ware ceramics, including gray, white, and White Mountain Red Ware. As shown in Figure 32.2, these sherds comprise 17 percent of the trade ware, including two gray ware, six white ware, and five red ware. The gray ware assemblage included one plain ware bowl rim and one polished gray jar body fragment. The white ware ceramics included two Gallup B/w and four slipped white ware jar fragments. Finally, the White Mountain Red Ware ceramics were mostly unidentifiable as to type, but included a greater variety of vessel forms. Of the four indeterminate White Mountain Red Ware sherds, one was a bowl fragment, one was from a canteen, one was a jar fragment, and the fourth was a fragment of a miniature necked jar. The single Wingate B/r bowl sherd was a body fragment.

Forty percent (n = 31) of the trade ware came from the Northern San Juan region, mostly recovered from stratum F-1-3 (roof-fall deposits); only one sherd was located in B-1-2 (postoccupational fill). The single sherd from B-1-2 was a corrugated gray jar fragment. Twenty-six corrugated jar body sherds were recovered from the roof-fall deposits, but similar to the Chuska Gray Ware, none of these corrugated sherds were from the same vessel. The white ware included four sherds from F-1-3 identified as Mesa Verde B/w bowl fragments (n = 2) and Pueblo II–III style B/w bowl fragments (n = 2). As described in Chapter 31, these Northern San Juan ceramics were differentiated from the locally produced pottery by differences in paste, temper, and slip characteristics.

In summary, trade ware from Room 30A consisted of Chuska, Cibola, and Northern San Juan ceramics, but with less variety than from Room 30W. All of the nonlocal pottery was recovered from strata F-1-3 (the majority) and B-1-2. The limited floor deposits from Room 30A did not contain any trade ware ceramics.

Locally Produced Ceramics

Locally produced pottery from Room 30A totaled 780 sherds (91% of the analyzed assemblage). These ceramics included both Northern San Juan and Cibola series pottery, identified as local based on the criteria discussed in Chapter 31. All of the strata analyzed yielded local Animas Variety pottery, of which 732 were classified as Northern San Juan and 48 were classified as Cibola. None of the sherds were identified as reconstructible vessels, and few of the sherds appeared to refit.

As shown in Table 32.4 and discussed in the Chronology section, all of the sherds from B-1-2 were Northern San Juan Animas Variety except for a single imported Northern San Juan corrugated. Three typeable sherds were identified—one McElmo B/w and two Mesa Verde B/w—hence the later ceramic dates for the postoccupational fill (B-1-2). The roof-fall deposits (F-1-3) contained a much greater variety of ceramic types, including Pueblo II and III typeable sherds, bringing the ceramic dates for the strata earlier. The majority of typeable ceramics from F-1-3, however, were identified as Mesa Verde B/w, McElmo B/w, and Chaco-McElmo B/w. As discussed in Chapter 31, the date range for Chaco-McElmo B/w produced in the Middle San Juan region is extended up to 1300 due to the number of Mesa Verde style designs identified on Chaco-McElmo vessels. Thus, the presence of local Chaco-McElmo, for which Toll and McKenna (1997) have suggested a terminal date of 1150 in Chaco, should not affect the dating of later deposits. (It may be useful in later analyses to adjust the dating of local Chaco-McElmo based on disparate McElmo and Mesa Verde design styles.) For the Chaco-McElmo sherds classified by style, 10 out of 12 were classed as McElmo style, 1 was Mesa Verde style, and 1 was not classed by style. Thus, use of the style classification in the mean ceramic dating for F-1-3 might have produced an earlier date based on the number of Chaco-McElmo sherds classed as McElmo style. Because we have just begun classification of style data for Chaco-McElmo, we do not (as yet) intend to subdivide the dating of the type based on design style without further data and analysis of stratigraphy.

An examination of slip application shows that all of the local Northern San Juan ceramics with washy slips included one Mancos B/w (Dogoszhi style), one Pueblo II–III style B/w, and one slipped white ware from stratum F-1-3. The majority (81.5%, n =

88) of the Northern San Juan Animas Variety white ware had thick-chalky slips, including most of the McElmo and Mesa Verde B/w sherds. Eleven sherds had thin slips and six sherds had no slip. Forty-four percent of the Cibola Animas Variety ceramics (n = 17) had washy slips and 28 percent (n = 11) had thin slips, as is typical of our expectations for pottery influenced by Chacoan-Cibola potters. The remaining 28 percent included six with thick-chalky slips, three with thick-crackly slips, and 2 with unknown slips. All but one of the washy-slipped Cibola ceramics were recovered from the roof-fall deposits (F-1-3). Thus, the local Northern San Juan and Cibola series ceramics were represented primarily by slip application expected for the tradition norms, with some exceptions that may indicate a mixing of technology and influence between the two traditions.

Of the 108 Northern San Juan Animas Variety white ware sherds, most (n = 68) were identified as Mesa Verde B/w and Pueblo II–III style B/w. This group of sherds profoundly influenced the mean date, best range, and maximum ceramic range calculations for Room 30A. In addition, Mancos B/w styles Black Mesa, Dogoszhi, and Sosi were identified in small numbers. McElmo B/w was also identified, but the early style (Early McElmo) of the type was lacking in Room 30A. Vessel forms were limited to bowls (n = 87) and jars (n = 21). All of the Mesa Verde B/w sherds were from bowls, and 12 bowl fragments and three jar sherds were McElmo B/w. The Mancos B/w ceramics were evenly divided between bowls and jars. The floor deposits (H-1-4) included two bowls and one jar fragment. The roof-fall (F-1-3), containing the majority of ceramics, included primarily Northern San Juan Animas Variety bowls (n = 81) and 20 jar fragments.

Gray ware ceramics identified as local Northern San Juan totaled 624 sherds—all from jars. The sample included 574 body fragments, 35 rims, 8 neck fragments, 2 neck-body joins, and 5 base fragments. Although the number of gray ware body fragments is large, none of these sherds grouped together as reconstructible vessels or even as enough of a vessel to assign a letter designation. A few of the rim sherds refit, however, and represented single vessels. All of the corrugated gray ware rim sherds were from the roof-fall deposits (F-1-3) and were classified as Pueblo II corrugated based on the eversion curvature of the neck and rim portion. Given the best ceramic date range of 1092–1181, it is clear that corrugated gray ware with a rim eversion between 0 and 30 degrees remained in production through the 1100s. Thus, classification of such sherds as Pueblo II style is not accurate.

Cibola Animas Variety ceramics from Room 30A totaled 38 sherds from strata F-1-3 (n = 37) and H-1-4 (n = 1). Chaco-McElmo B/w sherds represented the majority (32%) of the local Cibola assemblage. The other typeable sherds were Gallup B/w (n = 3) and Red Mesa B/w (n = 1). As shown in Table 32.4, the remaining ceramics were identified as Pueblo I–II style, Pueblo II–III style, Pueblo III style b/w, and painted or slipped white ware. The single slipped white ware from the floor (H-1-4) was a jar fragment. Stratum F-1-3 included a variety of vessel forms, including bowl, jar, and ladle fragments. The ladle fragment was not typeable, but was identified as Pueblo II–III style B/w. Nineteen jar fragments were analyzed from the roof-fall deposits (F-1-3), including 8 Chaco-McElmo B/w sherds and 11 sherds identified as Pueblo I–II style and Pueblo II–III style b/w, painted b/w, and slipped white ware. Bowl fragments from the roof-fall included more typeable sherds, including Chaco-McElmo B/w (n = 4), Gallup B/w (n = 3), and Red Mesa B/w (n = 1), along with nine sherds identified as Pueblo I–II style, Pueblo II–III style, and Pueblo III style b/w, and slipped white ware.

Ten local Cibola Gray Ware sherds were also identified in the roof-fall deposits (F-1-3). These jar fragments included corrugated, plain, and polished gray ware (see Table 32.4). As discussed in Chapter 31, Cibola Animas Variety white and gray ware sherds were identified based on paste, temper, and white ware slip differences. All of these gray ware sherds had local paste similar to the Northern San Juan ceramics, but had predominantly sand temper with lesser inclusions of shale, sherd, and, in one case, biotite mica.

Summary

The sample of ceramics analyzed from Room 30A clearly dates the room to the middle 1100s, but indicatets a mixed assemblage of earlier Chacoan trash in the predominantly Early San Juan phase trash deposit (F-1-3). Confidence in the ceramic mean date, best range, and maximum ceramic range for both the postoccupational fill (B-1-2) and the floor fill (H-1-4) was low due to the small number of sherds available for generating the dates. The ceramic mean dates and ranges suggest an occupation from the middle 1100s into the early-mid 1200s. Trade ware ceramics were limited to Chuska, Cibola, and Northern San Juan sources, including White Mountain Red Ware. Local ceramics were predominantly Northern San Juan, and only a small number of Cibola sherds were present. Similar to Room 30W, the small number of locally made Cibola Animas Variety ceramics suggests the presence of a few vessels compared to the much larger number of Northern San Juan Animas Variety ceramics. This trend again seems to suggest emulation of Cibola pottery or limited distribution of pottery produced at Salmon by Chacoan Cibola migrants. Other room assemblages may yield greater numbers of local Cibola pottery, suggesting occupation by Cibola migrants.

ROOM 30B

Room 30B is the western half of Room 30W, with Room 30A as the eastern half. The stratigraphy of the two small rooms is similar: six vertical units were identified in Room 30B. These units include post-occupational fill, roof-fall, and a floor unit. The substantial amount of corn remaining in the room indicates that it functioned as a corn storage room, in tandem with Room 30A (used for corn milling).

In total, 997 sherds were analyzed from two strata: F-1-3 and G-1-4. Stratum F-1-3 was identified as roof-fall containing 963 sherds, and G-1-4 was identified as floor fill with 34 sherds. Table 32.6 presents the ceramic tradition, variety, ware, and type data recorded for each stratum.

Ceramic Chronology

Ceramic mean dates, best ranges, and maximum ceramic ranges were generated for the two stratigraphic units using the ceramic types identified in Chapter 31 and the types identified in Table 32.6. The roof-fall stratum contained a substantial number of types associated with the Pueblo II period (see Table 32.6), including Kiatuthlanna B/w, Red Mesa B/w, Gallup B/w, and Mancos B/w (Mancos and Dogoszhi styles), along with untypeable sherds identified as Pueblo I–II style and Pueblo II–III style. The presence of these types helped produce an earlier ceramic mean date, best range, and maximum ceramic range than expected for this Secondary roof-fall layer. As shown in Table 32.7, the ceramic mean date is 1136, the range is 1094–1178, and the maximum ceramic range is 1052–1220. In contrast, the assemblage from the floor (G-1-4) generated a ceramic mean date of 1189, a best range of 1150–1229, and maximum ceramic range of 1111–1268, much later in time than the roof-fall. This finding suggests that the original Chacoan roof was used by later inhabitants, and subsequently collapsed, combining ceramics and other materials from both occupations. The floor assemblage was much smaller and included local Chaco-McElmo B/w, which appears to have been produced much later at Middle San Juan sites than in the Chaco Canyon region. With the identification of Mesa Verde style designs on locally produced Chaco-McElmo B/w pottery, it is likely that the type was produced into the 1200s. Mesa Verde B/w and McElmo B/w were also present in significant numbers on the floor of Room 30B.

Trade Ware Ceramics

From Room 30B, 80 sherds (8% of the room assemblage) were identified as trade ware (ceramics manufactured outside the Middle San Juan region). As shown in Figure 32.3, the majority of the trade ware had its origin in the Northern San Juan region, in contrast to the earlier occupation of Room 30W but more in line with Room 30A. In contrast to 30A, however, the percentage of Chuskan ceramics in 30B is much lower. The percentage of Cibola pottery for both 30A and 30B is consistent at approximately 16 percent. One sherd from the Kayenta region, a Citadel Polychrome, was identified in Room 30B.

Of the 45 Northern San Juan trade ware sherds, 28 were gray ware (27 corrugated gray body fragments and one polished gray body fragment). None of the corrugated jar sherds represented reconstructible vessels, but a few of the fragments did refit. The white ware sherds included 1 Mancos B/w (Dogoszhi style) and 5 Mesa Verde B/w, along with 11 other fragments classified as Pueblo I–II style B/w, Pueblo II–III style B/w, and slipped white ware. None of the white ware sherds represented reconstructible vessels, but there were both bowls and jars. As shown in Table 32.6, all of the Northern San Juan trade ware ceramics were located in the roof-fall deposits (F-1-3).

All 21 Chuskan sherds are Blue Shale Corrugated (n = 16) and corrugated body fragments (n = 5) from at least three jars. This collection of Chuska Gray Ware was recovered from the roof-fall deposits (F-1-3).

Cibola trade ware ceramics were also recovered from the roof-fall deposits, and none were present on the floor of Room 30B. As indicated in Table 32.6, the typeable sherds included Kiatuthlanna B/w, Gallup B/w, Reserve B/w, and a few indeterminate White Mountain Red Ware examples. Clearly, this is an assemblage that may all represent early to late Pueblo II pottery, further suggesting the mixing of deposits in the roof-fall stratum. As expected from the Cibola region, vessel forms are varied, including bowl, jar, seed jar, and mug fragments. The seed jar was identified as indeterminate White Mountain Red Ware and the mug base fragment was not typeable but was classified as Pueblo II–III style b/w.

Finally, the single Citadel Polychrome sherd from the Kayenta region was from the body portion of a jar. Of the trade ware from the roof-fall deposits,

Table 32.6. Ceramics from Room 30B stratigraphic units.

Stratum	Tradition	Variety	Ware	Ceramic Type	Total
F-1-3	Chuska	Trade ware	Gray	Blue Shale Corrugated*	16
				Corrugated gray	5
	Cibola	Animas	Gray	Plain gray	2
			White	Chaco-McElmo B/w*	3
				Pueblo I-II style B/w*	1
				Pueblo II-III style B/w*	3
				Red Mesa B/w*	1
				Slipped white	5
		Trade ware	Gray	Polished gray	1
			Red	Indeterminate White Mountain B/r	1
				Indeterminate White Mountain Red Ware	2
			White	Gallup B/w*	3
				Kiatuthlanna B/w*	1
				Pueblo II-III style B/w*	1
				Reserve B/w*	1
				Slipped white	3
	Kayenta	Trade ware	Red	Citadel Polychrome*	1
	Northern San Juan	Animas	Gray	Corrugated gray	660
				Indeterminate gray	1
				Plain gray	19
				Polished gray	2
				Pueblo II corrugated	12
			White	Early McElmo B/w*	1
				Mancos B/w (Mancos style)*	1
				Mancos B/w (Reserve style)*	1
				McElmo B/w*	35
				Mesa Verde B/w*	32
				Painted B/w	1
				Pueblo I-II style B/w*	1
				Pueblo II-III style B/w*	67
				Pueblo III style B/w*	1
				Slipped white	34
		Trade ware	Gray	Corrugated gray	27
				Polished gray	1
			White	Mancos B/w (Dogoszhi style)*	1
				Mesa Verde B/w*	5
				Pueblo I-II style B/w*	1
				Pueblo II-III style B/w*	1
				Slipped white	9
				Subtotal	963
G-1-4	Cibola	Animas	White	Chaco-McElmo B/w*	2
	Northern San Juan	Animas	Gray	Corrugated gray	14
				Plain gray	1
				Pueblo II corrugated	2
			White	McElmo B/w*	2
				Mesa Verde B/w*	8
				Pueblo II-III style B/w*	4
				Pueblo III style B/w*	1
				Subtotal	34
Total					997

* Types used to generate ceramic mean dates and ranges for Room 30B.

Table 32.7. Room 30B ceramic mean dates and ranges by stratigraphic unit.

Stratum	Description	Ceramic Mean Date	Best Ceramic Range	Max Ceramic Range
F-1-3	Roof-fall	1136	1094-1178	1052-1220
G-1-4	Floor fill	1189	1150-1229	1111-1268

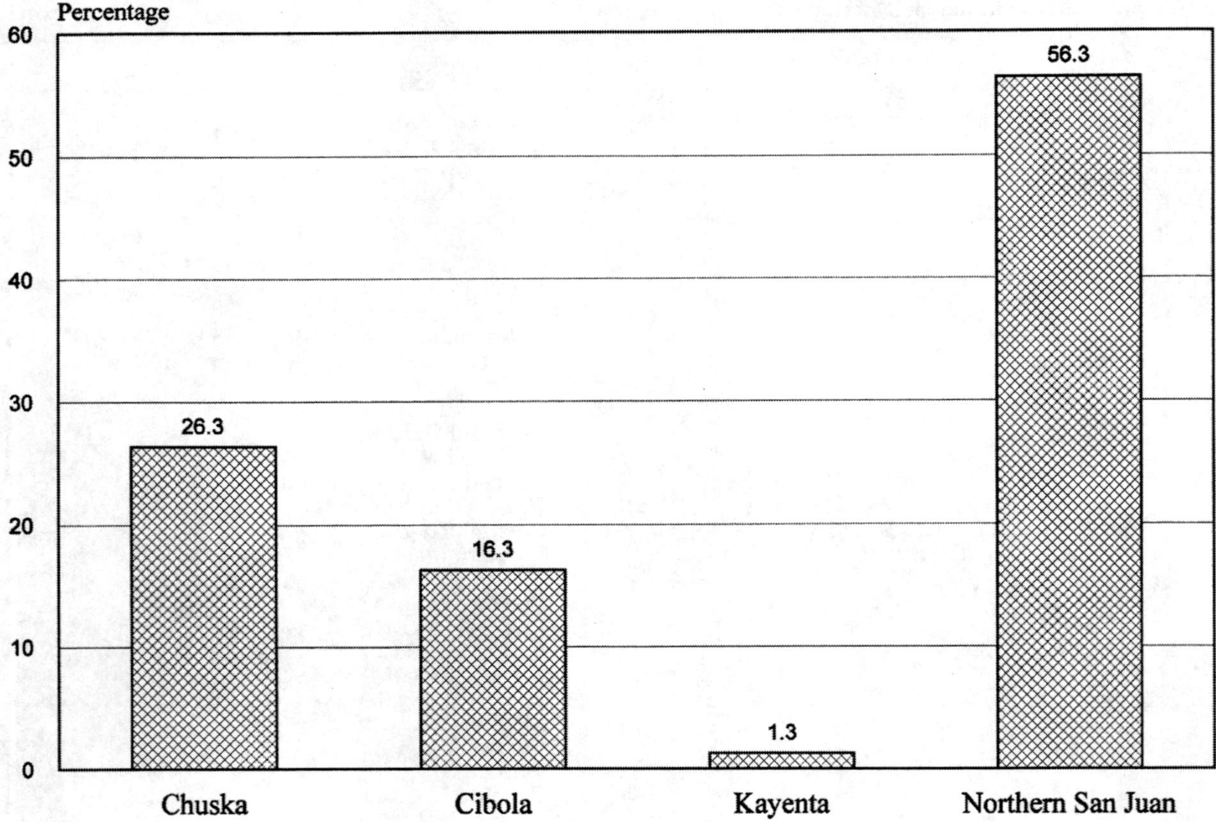

Figure 32.3. Distribution of trade ware ceramics from Room 30B.

the Citadel Polychrome sherd is one of the later ceramics, with a date of AD 1125–1200.

In summary, the trade ware from Room 30B was all recovered from the roof-fall deposits (F-1-3). Most of the nonlocal assemblage represents earlier ceramics dating to the Pueblo II period, indicating a mixed assemblage from the roof-fall. The majority of the nonlocal ceramics were from the Northern San Juan region, contrasting with the adjacent Room 30A, which contained almost equal amounts of Northern San Juan and Chuskan pottery.

Locally Produced Ceramics

Animas Variety ceramics from Room 30B were represented by an assemblage of 917 sherds; 900 were Northern San Juan and 17 were Cibola. As discussed in Chapter 31, locally produced pottery identified at Salmon and produced at other sites in the Middle San Juan, such as Aztec and the Tommy site, are characterized by high silt pastes with brown to yellow discoloration. The white wares have silty, grainy slips that are also frequently discolored to a yellowish tint. As shown in Table 32.6, Animas Variety ceramics were identified in both strata analyzed during the study. Also of note, only Animas Variety ceramics were located on the floor (G-1-4) of Room 30B. The later ceramic date for the floor (G-1-4) was influenced by the presence of local Mesa Verde B/w, McElmo B/w, and Chaco-McElmo B/w, as well as the absence of earlier Pueblo II ceramics.

Local Cibola ceramics were identified in both the roof-fall and floor strata. Fifteen of the sherds (83%) were located in the roof-fall, including one Red Mesa B/w and three Chaco-McElmo B/w. On the floor, however, only two local Cibola sherds, Chaco-McElmo B/w, were present. The two sherds from the floor were from different vessels, one from a jar and the other from a bowl. In the roof-fall, however, all of the typeable sherds were from bowls, and the assemblage included six bowl fragments and nine jar fragments.

In Room 30B, the distribution of slip application was more varied for the local Cibola ceramics. Of the 15 white ware sherds, there was almost equal representation of washy, thin, and thick-chalky slip coverage. Five examples had washy slips, including

Chaco-McElmo B/w (n = 1), Pueblo I–II and Pueblo II–III style b/w (n = 3), and slipped white ware (n = 1). Thin slips were identified on one Chaco-McElmo B/w and three slipped white ware sherds. Thick-chalky slips were represented on two Chaco-McElmo B/w, one Red Mesa B/w, and one slipped white ware. Finally, one Chaco-McElmo B/w and one Pueblo II–III style B/w were unslipped. The variability observed in Room 30B suggests integration of technology among potters representing local Cibola and Northern San Juan traditions.

An examination of Northern San Juan slip application, however, shows a different pattern with greater consistency in use of thick-chalky slips. Ninety percent of the local rock-tempered pottery had thick-chalky slips, corresponding with expected technological norms for Northern San Juan potters. The remaining 10 percent included four examples (not typeable) with washy slips, seven with thin slips, four with thick-crackly slips, and four with no slip. The consistency of the Northern San Juan slip application in Room 30B ceramics contrasts with the variability of local Cibola slip coverage. This finding suggests that local Middle San Juan potters were emulating Chaco pottery technology and style rather than local production by transplanted Chacoan potters.

The assemblage of Northern San Juan Animas Variety pottery comprised the majority (90%, n = 900) of ceramics from Room 30B. As expected, both gray and white wares are well represented, with 711 gray ware sherds and 189 white ware sherds. The gray ware sherds were disproportionately located in the roof-fall (F-1-3; see Table 32.6). Many of the 694 gray ware sherds in the roof-fall were from the same vessels, but none were of substantial size or continuity to identify as reconstructible. Twelve were classified as Pueblo II corrugated rims based on eversion measurements between 0 and 30 degrees. The majority (n = 660), however, were corrugated body sherds that were randomly refit, but not representative of any distinguishable vessels. Very few of the gray ware evidenced soot deposits, suggesting that they were not used for cooking; those with soot were most likely sooted as a result of postdepositional fires. Evaluation of soot deposits derived from cooking use is difficult with sherd assemblages due to the loss of contextual data regarding location of soot and oxidation patterns on the vessel. Soot may come to be present on a sherd through various processes, only one of which is cooking use; patterns of cooking use soot and oxidation are very specific to vessels and cooking processes (see Skibo 1992).

Seventeen gray ware sherds were recovered from the floor assemblage; these were identified as Pueblo II corrugated, corrugated gray, and plain gray (see Table 32.6). Similar to the roof-fall deposits, none of these sherds represented a complete or reconstructible vessel. Further, the lack of sooting on most of the sherds and lack of contextual vessel data precluded evaluation of cooking pot versus storage use. With Pueblo II corrugated sherds located in the same context as Mesa Verde B/w and McElmo B/w yielding a mean ceramic date of 1189, a best range of 1150–1229, and a maximum ceramic range of 1111–1268, the temporal significance of rim eversion in the Middle San Juan may not be as relevant as in other areas. The presence or absence of Mesa Verde style corrugated rims, however, may be the most temporally significant aspect of the local gray ware.

Local Northern San Juan White Ware totaled 189 sherds, including 174 from roof-fall deposits and 15 from the floor in Room 30B. From the roof-fall strata, the majority of the sherds were identified as Pueblo II–III style b/w, and thus were not typeable. McElmo B/w (n = 35) and Mesa Verde B/w (n = 32) were the two most abundant local white ware types from the roof-fall. Much smaller numbers of Early McElmo B/w, Mancos B/w (Mancos and Reserve styles), and other nontypeable ceramics were recovered from the roof-fall strata. Given the number of nonlocal ceramics identified as Pueblo II period types, the larger numbers of local McElmo and Mesa Verde B/w influenced the ceramic mean dating significantly.

With the exception of one jar sherd, all of the Mesa Verde B/w sherds were from bowls. In contrast, McElmo B/w sherds were evenly divided between bowls and jars, suggesting differences in vessel use patterns between the two white ware types. Clearly, the data from Room 30B suggest that Mesa Verde vessels were used primarily for serving and McElmo vessels had a greater variety of uses.

From the floor assemblage, the typeable sherds included only McElmo (n = 2) and Mesa Verde B/w (n = 8) sherds, along with five other nontypeable (Pueblo II–III and III style B/w) fragments. All of the typeable sherds and one Pueblo II–III style sherd were from bowls (n = 11), but only three nontypeable sherds were from jars.

Summary

Ceramics analyzed from Room 30B (the storage room partner to Room 30A) suggest final use of the room in the mid to late 1200s. The roof-fall, however, contains mixed deposits of Chacoan and San Juan age. All of the trade ware in Room 30B was located in the roof-fall deposits, and the floor assemblage consists of local Animas Variety ceramics. Most of the trade ware was earlier Pueblo II pottery originating from the Northern San Juan, Chuska, Cibola, and Kayenta regions.

ROOM 64W

Also known as Salmon's Tower Kiva, Room 64W is located in the center of the pueblo's east-west trending primary roomblock. Tree-ring dates indicate that the structure was built during Salmon's first construction episode at AD 1090 (see Reed, Chapter 12). Although the Tower Kiva was constructed during the Chacoan occupation of Salmon, most of the deposits within the structure reflect its reuse during the Secondary period. Because of a catastrophic fire during the Secondary occupation (see Akins 2005; P. Reed, Chapter 8), a considerable amount of pottery, perishables, tools, and other kiva equipment was abandoned in place. During excavation, 28 strata were defined; roughly half were associated with reuse of the Tower Kiva during the Secondary occupation.

Analysis of Room 64W ceramics focused on 431 sherds from eight stratigraphic units (Table 32.8). Most of the assemblage (n = 399) came from the F-1-6 Secondary roof-fall layer.

Ceramic Chronology

Ceramic mean dates, best ranges, and maximum ceramic ranges for each stratum in Room 64W were generated based on the formula and ceramic types identified in Chapter 31. Table 32.9 presents the ceramic types identified in Room 64W as well as the types used to produce ceramic mean dates and ceramic date ranges. Observations from the data in Table 32.9 include the absence of typeable sherds in postoccupational fill (B-3-4) and the presence of Chaco-McElmo B/w, both local and trade ware, in most of the strata. The roof-fall (F-1-6) contained the largest assemblage of sherds, including most of the trade ware from the Chuska, Cibola, and Mogollon regions, as well as the greatest variety of local ceramic types.

Table 32.8. Room 64W stratigraphic units and ceramics analyzed.

Stratum	Description	Total
B-3-4	Postoccupational fill	1
F-1-6	Roof-fall	399
L-1-9	Trench on kiva bench	3
L-2-10	Pilasters	5
L-4-12	Vent shaft and tunnel	5
D-1-13	Fill above floor	8
L-6-15	East foot drum	9
H-2-16	Chacoan floor	1
Total		431

As shown in Table 32.8, only two analyzed strata fall within the Chacoan period. The first is a trench on the kiva bench (L-1-9) with a ceramic mean date of 1100 and a best ceramic range of 1069–1131. The second is the fill above the Chacoan floor (D-1-13) with a ceramic mean date of 1125 and a best range of 1086–1164. All of the remaining strata either yielded no date or had best date ranges after 1100, indicating Chacoan to Early San Juan phase use of the kiva.

Ceramic Trade Ware

Ten ceramics (2.3% of the room assemblage) from Room 64W were identified as trade ware or manufactured outside the Middle San Juan region. As shown in Figure 32.4, the majority of the trade ware in this room had its origin in the Chuska Valley, a pattern not unexpected for deposits primarily of Chacoan age. Approximately 70 percent of the nonlocal ceramics were gray ware jar sherds from the Chuska Valley, including Blue Shale Corrugated (n = 4) and Newcomb Corrugated (n = 1), along with a banded body sherd and an indeterminate gray rim fillet. No white ware was identified. Chuskan ceramics were present in Strata F-1-6, the roof-fall, and L-6-15, the east foot drum.

Two Cibola tradition sherds were both identified as Chaco-McElmo B/w, one painted in McElmo style. One is from a jar; the other is a mug rim. These sherds represent vessels that originated in the San Juan Basin. The jar sherd came from stratum L-6-15 (the east foot drum), and the mug came from stratum L-4-12, the vent shaft and tunnel.

One sherd is from the northern Mogollon region. This sherd was identified as a Showlow Smudged bowl fragment from stratum F-1-6 (roof-fall).

In summary, trade ware was less common in Room 64W than in other rooms at Salmon, but does not reflect trade with culture areas that were not also represented in other rooms. Most significant seems to be the presence of Chuska ceramics only in the form of gray wares, whereas other rooms also included white wares. Chuskan-made gray wares may have remained a priority for kiva use even though they were less important overall at Salmon than they were in the San Juan Basin and Chaco Canyon. The Cibola sherds seem to be strictly from Secondary use of the kiva.

Table 32.9. Ceramics from Room 64W stratigraphic units.

Stratum	Tradition	Variety	Ware	Ceramic Type	Total
B-3-4	Northern San Juan	Animas	White	Slipped white	1
				Subtotal	1
F-1-6	Chuska	Trade ware	Gray	Banded gray	1
				Blue Shale Corrugated*	4
				Indeterminate gray	1
	Cibola	Animas	Gray	Corrugated gray	1
				Polished gray	2
			White	Chaco B/w*	1
				Chaco-McElmo B/w*	3
				Pueblo III style B/w*	1
				Puerco B/w*	1
				Reserve B/w*	1
	Mogollon	Not analyzed	Brown	Showlow Smudged*	1
	Northern San Juan	Animas	Gray	Corrugated gray	282
				Indeterminate gray	2
				Plain gray	9
				Polished gray	1
				Pueblo II corrugated	11
			White	Mancos B/w (Dogoszhi style)*	3
				Mancos B/w (Mancos style)*	2
				Mancos B/w (Sosi style)*	2
				McElmo B/w*	9
				McElmo/Mesa Verde B/w*	1
				Mesa Verde B/w*	12
				Pueblo II-III style B/w*	8
				Pueblo III style B/w*	13
				Subtotal	394
L-1-9	Cibola	Animas	White	Escavada B/w*	1
	Northern San Juan	Animas	Gray	Pueblo II corrugated	1
			White	McElmo B/w*	1
				Subtotal	3
L-2-10	Northern San Juan	Animas	Gray	Corrugated gray	5
				Subtotal	5
L-4-12	Cibola	Trade ware	White	Chaco-McElmo B/w*	1
	Northern San Juan	Animas	White	McElmo B/w*	3
				Mesa Verde B/w*	1
				Subtotal	5
D-1-13	Cibola	Animas	White	Chaco-McElmo B/w*	1
	Northern San Juan	Animas	Gray	Indeterminate gray	1
			White	McElmo B/w*	3
				Pueblo II-III style B/w*	3
				Subtotal	8
L-6-15	Chuska	Trade ware	Gray	Newcomb Corrugated*	1
	Cibola	Animas	White	Chaco-McElmo B/w*	3
				Pueblo III style B/w*	1
				Slipped white	1
		Trade ware	White	Chaco-McElmo B/w*	1
	Northern San Juan	Animas	Gray	Corrugated gray	1
				Plain gray	1
				Subtotal	9
H-2-16	Cibola	Animas	White	Chaco-McElmo B/w*	1
				Subtotal	1
Total					426

* Types used to generate ceramic mean dates and ranges for Room 64W.

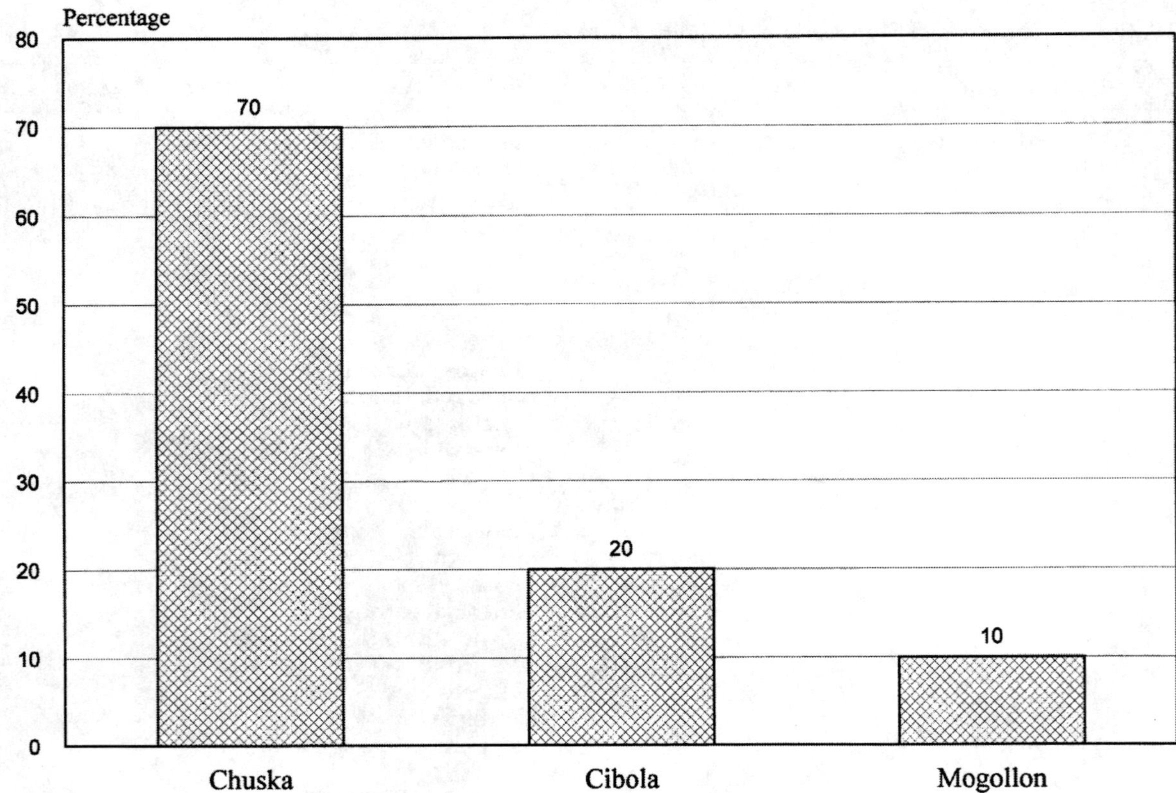

Figure 32.4. Distribution of trade ware ceramics from Tower Kiva (Room 64W).

Locally Produced Ceramics

Animas Variety ceramics, considered locally produced at Salmon or in the Middle San Juan region, were identified based on the criteria discussed in Chapter 31. These ceramics total 421 from Room 64W. Northern San Juan Animas Variety ceramics were present in all stratigraphic units analyzed except H-2-16, the Chacoan floor. Cibola Animas Variety was present in most of the stratigraphic units, but not in strata B-3-4 (postoccupational fill), L-2-10 (pilasters), or L-4-12 (vent shaft and tunnel). Northern San Juan Animas Variety ceramics totaled 398 sherds, including white and gray ware. Cibola Animas Variety ceramics totaled 18, also including white and gray ware.

As shown in Table 32.9, Pueblo III period ceramic types were common in this room, which should not be unexpected given that the kiva was used during both occupations. The floor (H-2-16), however, contained only one sherd—an Animas Variety Cibola Chaco-McElmo B/w bowl fragment. Although Pueblo III ceramic types are present in high quantities, Mesa Verde B/w itself makes up only 26.5 percent of the typeable Animas Variety white wares in Room 64W and only 25.5 percent of all typeable white wares in the room.

Slip application, one of the attributes examined as a means of tracking Cibola influence, shows relative consistency in the Room 64W assemblage, with 90.5 percent of the Northern San Juan Animas Variety white ware having thick-chalky slips. Other slip forms included three sherds with thick-crackly slips, one with a thin slip, one with indeterminate slip, and three with no slip. None had washy slip, which is sometimes seen in Animas Variety ceramics of the Northern San Juan tradition. Cibola Animas Variety slips were also typical; 46.7 percent had washy slips, but five sherds (33.3%) had thick-chalky slips, two had thin but not washy slips, and one had no slip. Thick slips on Animas Variety Cibola sherds are not limited to Pueblo III period types, nor are thin or washy slips on Animas Variety Northern San Juan sherds limited to Pueblo II period types. When examined by stratigraphic unit, the distribution of slip type on locally produced white wares shows no real pattern.

Northern San Juan Animas Variety white ware ceramics included a number of different vessel forms, such as bowls (n = 66), jars (n = 14), mugs (n =

3), and one that was indeterminate. Mug fragments included McElmo B/w and Mesa Verde B/w, and all three were recovered from stratum F-1-6. McElmo B/w was present in D-1-13 (fill above floor), F-1-6, L-1-9 (trench on kiva bench), and L-4-12. Mancos B/w, which was present only in F-1-6, included Dogoszhi, Sosi, and Mancos styles. Transitional McElmo–Mesa Verde B/w was present only in stratum F-1-6. Mesa Verde B/w was present in strata F-1-6 and L-4-12.

Northern San Juan Animas Variety gray ware from Room 64W totaled 314 sherds, including a number of sherds identified as refits or belonging to the same vessel. As discussed in Chapter 31, Animas Variety gray ware has characteristically coarsely crushed igneous (augite diorite) temper with frequent inclusions of sand and shale. Sherd temper is less common than in the nonlocal Northern San Juan Gray Ware. Types included untyped plain, polished, and corrugated gray body sherds from jars, as well as indeterminate gray rim fillets and some Pueblo II corrugated jar rims. Animas Variety gray ware was present in strata D-1-13, F-1-6, L-1-9, L-2-10, and L-6-15.

Cibola Animas Variety ceramics included both white ware (n = 15) and gray ware (n = 3). Both were identified by paste similarities with Northern San Juan Animas Variety ceramics, including high silt content and brown to yellow discoloration. Tempering material, however, consisted of various combinations of sand, shale, and sherd. Gray ware sherds were undiagnostic body sherds from corrugated jars and a polished bowl, all in stratum F-1-6.

Cibola Animas Variety white ware included Pueblo II ceramic types (Chaco, Escavada, Puerco, and Reserve B/w) as well as Pueblo III (Chaco-McElmo B/w in Early McElmo, McElmo, and Mesa Verde styles). Chaco-McElmo B/w was present in strata D-1-13, F-1-6, H-2-16, and L-6-15. Chaco, Puerco, and Reserve B/w were present only in stratum F-1-6, and Escavada B/w was present only in stratum L-1-9.

Summary

Room 64W, the Tower Kiva, was built during the Chacoan occupation of Salmon and used by later San Juan occupants. The ceramic mean dates, best ranges, and maximum ceramic ranges for the kiva (Table 32.10) show the temporal span in which the kiva was built and occupied. The trench on the kiva bench contained sherds providing a best range of 1069–1131, within the period of Chacoan construction and early use of the Tower Kiva. Ceramics from the floor fill above the Chacoan floor provided a best range of 1086–1164, also largely within the range of Chacoan and early San Juan use of the kiva. The remaining strata examined during the study, however, generated ceramic dates well within the early and late San Juan periods.

Trash fill stratum F-1-6 contained the largest amount of sherds, including Mesa Verde B/w and numerous Pueblo II types, suggesting a mixed fill situation. Trade ware sherds from the Cibola, Chuska, and Mogollon regions were present in most of the strata, but nonlocal wares from the Northern San Juan region were absent. Trade ware ceramics were less common in the Tower Kiva than in the other rooms examined during the study. The distribution of vessel forms in the sherd assemblage also showed less variability than in most of the other rooms.

ROOM 90W

Room 90W is located along Salmon's back wall and is part of the northernmost Chacoan room suite consisting of Rooms 92W, 91W, and 90W. The room was originally built during the Chacoan construction episode around AD 1090, with some repairs occurring at 1094. Room 90W was not divided into two smaller rooms during the San Juan occupation, as

Table 32.10. Room 64W ceramic mean dates and ranges by stratigraphic unit.

Stratum	Description	Ceramic Mean Date	Best Ceramic Range	Max Ceramic Range
B-3-4	Postoccupational fill	No date	No date	No date
F-1-6	Roof-fall	1160	1120-1201	1080-1241
L-1-9	Trench on kiva bench	1100	1069-1131	1038-1162
L-2-10	Pilasters	No date	No date	No date
L-4-12	Vent shaft and tunnel	1163	1132-1194	1101-1225
D-1-13	Fill above floor	1125	1086-1164	1047-1203
L-6-15	East foot drum	1154	1117-1192	1080-1229
H-2-16	Chacoan floor	1200	1150-1250	1100-1300

many of the Chacoan rooms at Salmon were. Twenty distinct stratigraphic units were identified during excavation of Room 90W, including postoccupational fill, structured trash, roof-fall, occupational fill, floor and floor contact deposits, artificial fill, construction debris, and feature fill. Although a Chacoan floor was identified during excavation, the floor from the San Juan period occupation could not be confirmed. The Chacoan floor had a hearth, suggesting that the room had some residential use, but its location in the second to last tier of rooms suggests storage use. The absence of other features and the lack of confirmation of a San Juan floor suggest use as storage during the San Juan period.

During the ceramic analysis, eight stratigraphic units were selected for examination, including postoccupational fill, trash fill above roof-fall, Secondary roof-fall, Chacoan trash deposits, and the Chacoan floor fill (Table 32.11). In total, 448 sherds were analyzed from Room 90W during the Salmon Research Initiative (Table 32.12). These ceramics were selected from roof-fall, floor fill, postoccupational contexts, and contexts identified as Chacoan trash.

Ceramic Chronology

Ceramic mean dates, best ranges, and maximum ceramic ranges were generated for each of the strata examined during the analysis based on the typeable ceramics and known temporal ranges of manufacture presented in Chapter 31. The typeable ceramics from each strata (see Table 32.12) were used to generate the mean dates presented in Table 32.13. The stratigraphic units are listed in Table 32.13 in order of excavation from the top strata down to the lowest strata examined during the ceramic study, identified as the Chacoan floor fill just above the floor surface.

Table 32.11. Room 90W stratigraphic units and ceramics analyzed.

Stratum	Description	Total
B-3-4	Postoccupational	5
C-1-6	Trash above roof-fall	21
C-2-7	Trash above roof-fall	151
F-2-9	Secondary roof-fall	167
C-3-10	Chacoan trash	57
C-4-11	Chacoan trash	4
G-1-11.5	Chacoan floor fill	1
H-1-12	Chacoan floor	42
Total		448

The uppermost stratum examined, postoccupational fill (B-3-4), generated a ceramic mean date of 1238, a best range of 1208–1269, and a maximum ceramic range of 1178–1299—within the Late San Juan phase. The assemblage from the stratum was small, but included only Mesa Verde B/w and St. Johns Polychrome, along with a few small sherds. Based on this handful of sherds, we infer that the B-3-4 stratum was deposited during the Late San Juan phase. Below the postoccupational fill, two trash deposits (C-1-6 and C-2-7) generated similar mean dates and ranges, suggesting that both deposit episodes occurred within a 70-year period. For C-1-6, the ceramic mean is 1189 with a best range of 1157–1221 and a maximum ceramic range of 1125–1253. For C-2-7, the mean date is 1181 with a best range of 1148–1213 and a maximum ceramic range of 1115–1246. Differences between the two strata, however, are significant. The highest trash deposit (C-1-6) had fewer typeable sherds with which to generate the mean date, best range, and maximum ceramic range (Table 32.12). Further, the assemblage from C-2-7 includes an array of Pueblo II types along with Mesa Verde B/w and White Mountain Red Ware types, indicating a highly mixed assemblage. The mean date of 1189 for C-1-6, then, represents an average of early and late types.

The Secondary roof-fall from a second-story Chacoan level that was originally interpreted as having Secondary occupation (Early San Juan phase) fill sitting on top provided a ceramic mean date of 1165, a best range of 1131–1200, and a maximum ceramic range of 1097–1234. The best range clearly falls within the Early San Juan phase. Ceramics from the roof-fall deposit (F-2-9), however, show mixing of Pueblo II and III types, including Kiatuthlanna B/w, Mancos B/w, Gallup B/w, and Escavada B/w, along with Mesa Verde and McElmo B/w. The gray ware was identified as Pueblo II corrugated and Pueblo II–III corrugated; however, 11 of 17 local corrugated rim sherds were classified as Pueblo II style based on rim eversion, again calling into question the temporal significance of gray ware rim typology.

Two Chacoan trash strata were examined from below the Secondary roof-fall: C-3-10 and C-4-11. These two strata produced different best ranges and maximum ceramic ranges, primarily due to small sample size issues for the lower stratum, C-4-11. As shown in Table 32.12, trash stratum C-3-10 contained 13 sherds used in the ceramic date calculations, including Red Mesa B/w, Mancos B/w (Mancos and Dogoszhi styles), and Gallup B/w representing Pueblo II period types. Mesa Verde B/w and St. Johns B/r were the only later types representing the

Table 32.12. Ceramics from Room 90W stratigraphic units.

Stratum	Tradition	Variety	Ware	Ceramic Type	Total
B-3-4	Cibola	Trade ware	Red	St. Johns Polychrome*	2
	Northern San Juan	Animas	White	Mesa Verde B/w*	1
	Not analyzed	Not analyzed	Not analyzed	Too small for analysis or exfoliated	2
				Subtotal	5
C-1-6	Chuska	Trade ware	White	Crumbled House B/w*	1
	Cibola	Animas	White	Pueblo III style B/w*	1
				Red Mesa B/w*	1
	Kayenta	Trade ware	Red	Indeterminate red	1
			White	Black Mesa B/w*	1
	Little Colorado	Trade ware	White	Padre B/w*	1
	Northern San Juan	Animas	White	Mancos B/w (Mancos style)*	1
				McElmo B/w*	3
				Mesa Verde B/w*	10
		Trade ware	White	Mesa Verde B/w*	1
				Subtotal	21
C-2-7	Chuska	Trade ware	Gray	Blue Shale Corrugated*	1
			White	Crumbled House B/w*	9
				Nava B/w*	1
				Pueblo I-II style B/w*	1
	Cibola	Animas	White	Chaco-McElmo B/w*	4
				Escavada B/w*	2
				Gallup B/w*	1
				Pueblo II-III style B/w*	2
		Trade ware	Red	Indeterminate White Mountain B/r	1
				St. Johns B/r*	4
				St. Johns Polychrome*	2
				Wingate Polychrome*	1
			White	Chaco B/w*	2
				Escavada B/w*	1
				Gallup B/w*	4
				Reserve B/w*	1
	Indeterminate	Indeterminate	Brown	Mud ware	1
	Kayenta	Trade ware	White	Sosi B/w*	2
	Little Colorado	Trade ware	White	Padre B/w*	1
	Mogollon	Trade ware	Brown	Showlow Red*	1
	Northern San Juan	Animas	Gray	Corrugated gray	6
				Indeterminate gray	1
				Pueblo II corrugated	2
				Pueblo II-III corrugated	53
			White	Cortez B/w (Kiatuthlanna style)*	1
				Mancos B/w (Dogoszhi style)*	1
				Mancos B/w (Mancos style)*	1
				Mancos B/w (Reserve style)*	1
				Mancos B/w (Sosi style)*	1
				McElmo B/w*	4
				Mesa Verde B/w*	31
				Painted B/w	2
				Pueblo II-III style B/w*	2
				Pueblo III style B/w*	1
		Trade ware	White	Mancos B/w (Dogoszhi style)*	1
				Mancos B/w (Sosi style)*	1
				Subtotal	151
F-2-9	Chuska	Trade ware	Gray	Blue Shale Corrugated*	7
			White	Taylor B/w (Sosi style)*	2
				Toadlena B/w (Sosi style)*	2
	Cibola	Animas	White	Chaco-McElmo B/w*	1
				Escavada B/w*	3
				Gallup B/w*	2
				Kiatuthlanna B/w*	2
				Pueblo II-III style B/w*	1
				Pueblo III style B/w*	1
				Slipped white	2
		Trade ware	Red	Puerco B/r*	1
				St. Johns B/r*	2
				St. Johns Polychrome*	2

Table 32.12 (continued)

Stratum	Tradition	Variety	Ware	Ceramic Type	Total
				Wingate B/r*	1
				Wingate Polychrome*	1
			White	Escavada B/w*	1
				Gallup B/w*	4
				Kiatuthlanna B/w*	1
				Pueblo I-II style B/w*	4
	Kayenta	Trade ware	Red	Indeterminate B/r	1
	Northern San Juan	Animas	Gray	Corrugated gray	26
				Plain gray	1
				Pueblo II corrugated	11
				Pueblo II-III corrugated	6
			White	Mancos B/w (Dogoszhi style)*	1
				Mancos B/w (Mancos style)*	2
				Mancos B/w (Puerco style)*	1
				Mancos B/w (Sosi style)*	3
				McElmo B/w*	9
				Mesa Verde B/w*	50
				Pueblo I-II style B/w*	1
				Pueblo II-III style B/w*	8
				Pueblo III style B/w*	2
				Slipped white	2
		Trade ware	Gray	Corrugated gray	2
			White	Mesa Verde B/w*	1
				Subtotal	167
C-3-10	Cibola	Animas	White	Pueblo I-II style B/w*	1
				Red Mesa B/w*	1
		Trade ware	Red	St. Johns B/r*	1
			White	Gallup B/w*	1
	Northern San Juan	Animas	Gray	Corrugated gray	24
				Plain gray	16
				Polished gray	1
				Pueblo II corrugated	2
			White	Mancos B/w (Dogoszhi style)*	1
				Mancos B/w (Mancos style)*	2
				Mesa Verde B/w*	3
				Pueblo II-III style B/w*	2
				Pueblo III style B/w*	1
				Slipped white	1
				Subtotal	57
C-4-11	Northern San Juan	Animas	Gray	Corrugated gray	1
				Plain gray	2
			White	Mesa Verde B/w*	1
				Subtotal	4
G-1-11.5	Northern San Juan	Animas	Gray	Corrugated gray	1
				Subtotal	1
H-1-12	Chuska	Trade ware	White	Nava B/w*	2
	Cibola	Trade ware	Gray	Chaco Corrugated (PII-PIII)	9
				Plain gray	1
	Northern San Juan	Animas	Gray	Corrugated gray	9
				Indeterminate gray	1
				Plain gray	10
				Polished gray	3
			White	Mancos B/w (Sosi style)*	2
				McElmo B/w*	2
				Pueblo II-III style B/w*	2
				Slipped white	1
				Subtotal	42
Total					448

* Types used to generate ceramic mean dates and ranges for Room 90W.

Table 32.13. Room 90W ceramic mean dates and ranges by stratigraphic unit.

Stratum	Description	Ceramic Mean Date	Best Ceramic Range	Max Ceramic Range
B-3-4	Postoccupational fill	1238	1208-1269	1178-1299
C-1-6	Trash fill above roof	1189	1157-1221	1125-1253
C-2-7	Trash fill above roof	1181	1148-1213	1115-1246
F-2-9	Secondary roof-fall	1165	1131-1200	1097-1234
C-3-10	Chacoan trash	1129	1092-1166	1055-1203
C-4-11	Chacoan trash	1240	*1210-1270	1180-1300
G-1-11.5	Chacoan floor fill	No date	No date	No date
H-1-12	Chacoan floor	1122	1086-1158	1050-1194

* Based on one Mesa Verde B/w sherd.

Pueblo III period. Thus, the ceramic mean date for stratum C-3-10 was 1129 with a best range of 1092–1166 and a maximum ceramic range of 1055–1203, falling within the period of Chacoan construction and occupation and Early San Juan phase occupation of the site. The lower stratum, C-4-11, produced a mean date of 1240, a best range of 1210–1270, and a maximum ceramic range of 1180–1300 based on the single Mesa Verde B/w sherd recovered from the trash deposit. Clearly, the confidence in a date based on one sherd is extremely low, and we suggest that the date does not represent the actual deposits in C-4-11.

Ceramic mean dates and ranges were not run for the Chacoan floor fill stratum G-1-11.5 because it contained only one corrugated gray sherd. The floor fill stratum (H-1-12) just below, however, contained 42 sherds, of which 8 were typeable and therefore useful for ceramic mean dating. These sherds (Table 32.12) were Nava B/w of the Chuska series and local ceramics Mancos B/w (Sosi style), McElmo B/w, and Pueblo II–III b/w. The resulting ceramic mean date was 1122, the best range was 1086–1158, and the maximum ceramic range was 1050–1194, corresponding with the construction and Chacoan occupation of the floor, as well as an Early San Juan occupation.

Ceramic Trade Ware

From Room 90W, 89 ceramics (20% of the room assemblage) were identified as trade ware or manufactured outside the Middle San Juan region. As shown in Figure 32.5, the majority of the trade ware from Room 90W had its origin in the Cibola region, suggesting Chacoan trade. Approximately 53 percent of the nonlocal ceramics were white and gray ware from the Cibola region. The gray ware ceramics were primarily Chaco Corrugated of both Pueblo II and Pueblo III time periods, as well as plain and corrugated body sherds. White ware includes predominantly Gallup B/w and lesser quantities of other Pueblo II types, Chaco B/w, Escavada B/w, Kiatuthlanna B/w, and Reserve B/w. Only three white ware sherds were from bowls (two Chaco B/w and one Gallup B/w); the rest were from jars. Cibola White Mountain Red Wares, including Puerco B/r, St. John's B/r and Polychrome, and Wingate B/r and Polychrome, were also present in high quantities. All White Mountain Red Ware sherds from this room were from bowls. Cibola tradition sherds came from levels B-3-4, C-2-7, F-2-9, C-3-10, and H-1-12, with the greatest concentrations in C-2-7 and F-2-9, strata identified as trash above roof-fall and Secondary roof-fall, respectively.

No vessel numbers or letters were assigned to the Cibola tradition sherds, but several pieces refit. These include two St. John's Polychrome, the only Cibola tradition sherds recovered from stratum B-3-4, and nine fragments of a Chaco Corrugated vessel, which along with one plain gray sherd comprised all of the Cibola tradition ceramics from stratum H-1-12. Neither group of refitted sherds was considered reconstructible vessels.

Chuska tradition ceramics, from the Chuska Valley, include both gray and white ware. Chuskan ceramics, which comprise 29 percent of the trade ware from Room 90W, were found in strata C-1-6, C-2-7, F-2-9, and H-1-12, with the greatest concentrations in strata C-2-7 and F-2-9. No vessel numbers or letters were assigned as none of the refitting sherds were considered reconstructible vessels. All gray ware came from jars identified as Blue Shale Corrugated (one rim from stratum C-2-7) or corrugated body sherds (n = 7) from stratum F-2-9. Identifiable Pueblo II white ware was all from stratum F-2-9, and included Sosi style from both Toadlena B/w (organic paint, two jar sherds) and Taylor B/w (mineral paint, two bowl sherds). Pueblo III types include

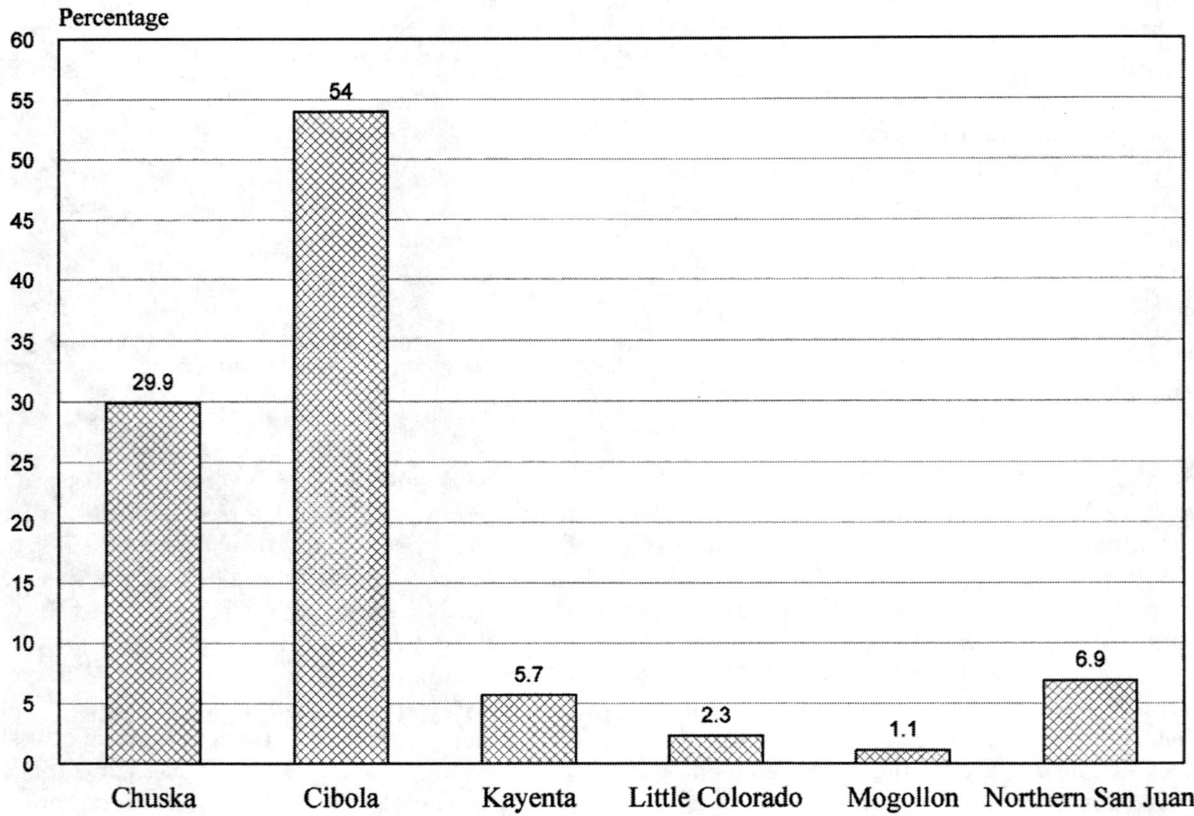

Figure 32.5. Distribution of trade ware ceramics from Room 90W.

Nava B/w (two bowl sherds from stratum H-1-12 and one bowl sherd from C-2-7), and Crumbled House B/w (nine bowl sherds from stratum C-2-7, seven of which are from the same vessel). Although most of the Chuska ceramics were located in areas of trash above roof-fall and Secondary roof-fall, two late white ware sherds came from the lowest floor fill, suggesting that all the fill layers may be mixed.

Nonlocal Northern San Juan ceramics were rare in Room 90W, totaling six sherds or 6.7 percent of the trade ware. Two sherds were corrugated gray jar body fragments, both from stratum F-2-9. Pueblo II period white ware was found only in stratum C-2-7: one Mancos B/w, Dogoszhi style bowl sherd, and one Mancos B/w, Sosi style jar rim sherd. The remaining two white ware sherds were Mesa Verde B/w and were found in strata C-1-6 (one bowl sherd) and F-2-9 (one bowl sherd). Based on the distribution of these sherds, the Northern San Juan sample was located only within the trash above roof-fall and the Secondary roof-fall. Thus, there is no real patterning to the distribution of these ceramics.

Five sherds from the Kayenta region were identified in Room 90W, including one indeterminate B/r bowl fragment from stratum F-2-9, two Sosi B/w bowl fragments from C-2-7, and one indeterminate red ware bowl fragment and one Black Mesa B/w bowl fragment from C-1-6. As with most of the other trade wares, these sherds were from strata identified as trash above the roof-fall and Secondary roof-fall. The Kayenta sherds comprised 5.6 percent of the trade wares.

Two sherds in Room 90W were trade ware from the Little Colorado region. Both were Padre B/w jar sherds; one was found in stratum C-1-6 and the other in C-2-7. These strata represent fill units from above the roof-fall. These sherds comprised 2.2 percent of the trade wares.

One Showlow Red bowl fragment from the northern Mogollon region came from stratum C-2-7. This stratum is a fill unit above the roof-fall.

In summary, although the locations from which trade wares were procured are varied, many are present in very low numbers. Cibola and Chuska tradition ceramics are present in relatively high numbers, in comparison to the Northern San Juan, Kayenta, Little Colorado, and Mogollon tradition trade wares. Very little patterning is observable, other than that some of the Cibola and Chuska tradition sherds came from Chacoan strata, specifically H-1-12, which is identified as Chacoan floor fill (see Table 32.12).

Locally Produced Ceramics

Animas Variety ceramics, considered locally produced at Salmon or in the Middle San Juan region, were identified based on the criteria discussed in Chapter 31. These ceramics total 358 from Room 90W. All stratigraphic units analyzed yielded Animas Variety ceramics of the Northern San Juan tradition, but only some had Animas Variety ceramics of the Cibola tradition. Northern San Juan Animas Variety ceramics totaled 333 sherds, including white and gray ware. Cibola Animas Variety ceramics, which were only white ware, totaled 25. A reconstructible partial vessel (Vessel D) consisting of 50 sherds is Northern San Juan, Animas Variety Pueblo II–III corrugated gray found in stratum C-2-7, the fill above the roof-fall.

No floors were identified in Room 90W, but one floor fill stratum was believed to represent the Chacoan occupation. Many identified strata included in the analysis were trash fill, and although some were associated with Chacoan rather than Secondary occupation, it is clear (see Table 32.12) that all of the trash and fill layers included ceramic types that belong to both Pueblo II and Pueblo III periods. Mesa Verde and McElmo types are present throughout the stratigraphy of this room, rather than only in the uppermost layers. Mesa Verde B/w by itself (n = 96) comprised approximately 53 percent of the Animas Variety white ware in this room.

Slip application, one of the attributes examined as a means of tracking Cibola influence, shows relative consistency in Room 90W among Cibola Animas Variety ceramics, with 48 percent (n = 12) having the expected washy slip, 20 percent (n = 5) with a thick-chalky slip, and 32 percent (n = 8) having a thin but not washy slip. Among Northern San Juan Animas Variety white ware, 15.9 percent (n = 25) have no slip, 51 percent (n = 80) have thick-chalky slips, 15.9 percent (n = 25) have thick-crackly slips, and 17.2 percent (n = 27) have thin slips. When examined by stratigraphic unit, the distribution of washy slips on local Northern San Juan sherds shows no real pattern other than being scattered throughout the Chacoan trash and in the Secondary roof-fall.

Northern San Juan Animas Variety white ware ceramics included a number of different vessel forms, such as bowls (n = 123), jars (n = 26), ladles (n = 2), mugs (n = 5), and kiva jars (n = 1). Both ladle fragments could only be identified as painted b/w, from stratum C-2-7. Four of the mug fragments were Mesa Verde B/w, two from stratum C-2-7 and two from stratum F-2-9. The remaining mug fragment was McElmo B/w from stratum C-1-6. The single kiva jar rim fragment was identified as Pueblo III style b/w from stratum C-2-7.

Northern San Juan Animas Variety gray ware from Room 90W totaled 176 sherds, including one reconstructible jar (Vessel D) from stratum C-2-7. As discussed in Chapter 31, Animas Variety gray ware has characteristically coarsely crushed igneous (augite diorite) temper with frequent inclusions of sand and shale. Sherd temper is less common than in the nonlocal Northern San Juan Gray Ware.

Cibola Animas Variety was identified by paste similarities with Northern San Juan Animas Variety ceramics, including high silt content and brown to yellow discoloration. Tempering material, however, consisted of various combinations of sand, shale, and sherd. Vessel forms were limited to bowls and jars, and included Kiatuthlanna, Red Mesa, Gallup and Escavada B/w ceramic types, as well as Chaco-McElmo B/w. As shown in Table 32.12, only 2 of the 25 Cibola Animas Variety ceramics came from the levels designated as Chacoan, even though many were Pueblo II types. They were recovered only from C-1-6, C-2-7, F-2-9, and C-3-10. Northern San Juan Animas Variety, however, was present throughout all the levels.

Summary

The ceramic dating for Room 90W follows a progression from late dates in the upper levels (a best range of 1208–1269 for most recent stratum) to earlier Chacoan dates and ranges for the floor fill. The only anomalous date within the strata occurred in stratum C-4-11, a trash deposit just above the floor fill that included only one Mesa Verde B/w sherd producing a best range of 1210–1270.

Trade ware ceramic included a range of types from the Cibola, Chuska, Kayenta, Northern San Juan, Little Colorado, and Mogollon regions. Cibola and Chuska ceramics were by far the most common trade ware identified in the Room 90W sample. The Cibola ceramics included white ware from the San Juan Basin and White Mountain Red Ware from further south near the Zuni area and into eastern Arizona.

The local pottery included both Animas Variety Cibola and Northern San Juan, identified by the paste, temper, and slip characteristics outlined in Chapter 31. Gray ware and white ware types were present. The gray ware ceramics included Pueblo II and Pueblo III corrugated, which at this point is undergoing revision and study concerning its temporal significance. Both Pueblo II and Pueblo III white ware ceramics were identified, including a range of style subdivisions for Mancos B/w, some that have later temporal significance than the Pueblo II styles. Mesa Verde B/w was a common type in Room 90W, and its presence influenced some of the later San Juan period date ranges for the room strata.

ROOM 100W

Room 100W, one of the largest rooms at Salmon, is the front (living and habitation) room for a Chacoan suite of rooms that included 100W, 97W, 101W, and 76W (see P. Reed, Chapter 8). The original Chacoan floor had numerous pits, hearths, and postholes, and a large corrugated vessel set into the floor. The room was abandoned during the Chacoan occupation, but was later used as a major trash repository during the Chacoan and Chacoan-Secondary transition. The room continued as a trash repository into the Secondary period until it was destroyed by fire. During excavation, nearly 80 strata were defined—the majority of Chacoan origin. San Juan deposits included a high roof-fall layer with structured trash below, but no floors were identified. The large number of features in the Chacoan deposits suggests that a diversity of activities took place in Room 100W and that it was probably a residential room. Tree-ring dates from dozens of samples suggest initial construction at 1090 during the first Chacoan construction phase. A tree-ring date at 1106 indicates later repair or remodeling of the room's roof. The stratigraphic sequence (Table 32.14) and ceramic data, however, indicate that the room was used either as a residence or as trash repository through the 1100s and into the late 1280s.

Table 32.14. Room 100W stratigraphic units and ceramics analyzed.

Stratum	Description	Total
N-1-3	Mixed roof-fall	4560
C-1-4	Trash deposits	441
C-2-5	Trash deposits	596
C-2-5.1	Trash deposits	67
C-2-5.3	Trash deposits	172
C-3-6	Trash deposits	227
C-7-12	Trash deposits	282
C-8-13	Trash deposits	112
C-9-14	Trash deposits	49
C-10-15	Trash deposits	23
C-11-16	Trash deposits	75
C-11-16.1	Trash deposits	5
C-11-16.2	Trash deposits	1
C-11-16.3	Trash deposits	5
C-12-17	Trash deposits	41
C-13-18	Trash deposits	23
H-1-19	Chacoan floor	35
I-1-19.5	Chacoan floor	6
CT-1-19.8	Trash deposits	2
L-5-25	Storage vessel in floor	11
L-7-27	Storage pit in floor	15
L-8-28	Posthole	1
I-3-36.5	Chacoan floor	1
L-22-46.1	Chacoan trash	7
L-23-47	Chacoan hearth	7
Total		6764

Ceramic Chronology

From the typeable ceramics identified and using the methodology discussed in Chapter 31 (sherds highlighted in Table 32.15), ceramic mean dates, best ranges, and maximum ceramic ranges were generated for each stratigraphic unit examined during the Salmon Research Initiative. The stratigraphic units in Table 32.15 are listed in order of excavation from the top Strata of Room 100 down to the bottom strata identified as a Chacoan hearth dug into the floor.

One of the initial observations from Table 32.15 is the predominance of later Pueblo III, Early and Late San Juan phase ceramics mixed with late Pueblo II ceramics in strata N-1-3, C-1-4, and C-2-5. These strata show mixed deposits, but the high number of Mesa Verde B/w, White Mountain Polychromes, and some Kayenta polychromes, and later Chuska Pueblo III wares such as Crumbled House Black-white, brought the ceramic mean dates, best ranges, and maximum ceramic ranges later in time. As shown in Table 32.16, stratum N-1-3 (the highest stratum examined) was a mixed roof-fall deposit that produced a ceramic mean date of 1182, a best range of 1144–1219, and a maximum ceramic range of 1106–1257. Although a small number of Pueblo II ceramics are present in this stratum, the significantly greater numbers of McElmo B/w (n = 101), Mesa Verde B/w (n = 183), and Pueblo III style B/w (local; n = 129) greatly influenced the late dating of N-1-3. The date and ranges for N-1-3 are expected given its location high in the room stratigraphy and the identification of this roof-fall layer as San Juan during the excavation phase.

Stratum C-1-4 also has mixed deposits, but the ceramic assemblage and mean date calculations show that the trash deposits in this layer are earlier than the mixed roof-fall N-1-3. As shown in Table 32.15, the presence of locally produced Mesa Verde B/w decreased from 183 sherds in N-1-3 to 49 sherds

Table 32.15. Ceramics from Room 100W stratigraphic units.

Stratum	Tradition	Variety	Ware	Ceramic Type	Total
N-1-3	Chuska	Trade ware	Gray	Blue Shale Corrugated*	14
				Gray Hills Banded*	1
				Indeterminate gray	2
				Newcomb Corrugated*	1
				Plain gray	1
				Polished gray	1
			White	Nava B/w*	4
				Pueblo II-III style B/w*	1
				Slipped white	3
				Toadlena B/w (Sosi style)*	3
	Cibola	Animas	Gray	Corrugated gray	1
				Plain gray	3
				Polished gray	1
			White	Chaco-McElmo B/w*	18
				Escavada B/w*	6
				Gallup B/w*	2
				Pueblo I-II style B/w*	1
				Pueblo II-III style B/w*	2
				Pueblo III style B/w*	4
				Red Mesa B/w*	1
				Reserve B/w*	1
				Slipped white	13
		Trade ware	Red	Indeterminate White Mountain B/r	5
				Indeterminate White Mountain Polychrome	1
				Indeterminate White Mountain Red Ware	7
				St. Johns B/r*	1
				St. Johns Polychrome*	6
				Wingate B/r*	2
				Wingate Polychrome*	10
			White	Chaco B/w*	3
				Chaco-McElmo B/w*	3
				Escavada B/w*	5
				Gallup B/w*	1
				Reserve B/w*	1
				Slipped white	4
	Indeterminate	Indeterminate	White	Slipped white	1
				Sosi style B/w*	1
	Kayenta	Trade ware	Red	Indeterminate polychrome	1
	Mogollon	Trade ware	Brown	Indeterminate	1
				Showlow Red*	3
				Showlow Smudged*	2
				Woodruff Brown	1
				Woodruff Red	2
	Northern San Juan	Animas	Gray	Banded gray	1
				Corrugated gray	3674
				Indeterminate gray	7
				Plain gray	23
				Polished gray	3
				Pueblo II corrugated	52
				Pueblo II-III corrugated	48
			White	Cortez B/w (Red Mesa style)*	1
				Early McElmo B/w*	5
				Mancos B/w (Black Mesa style)*	1
				Mancos B/w (Dogoszhi style)*	2
				Mancos B/w (Puerco style)*	1
				Mancos B/w (Reserve style)*	3
				Mancos B/w (Sosi style)*	3
				McElmo B/w*	101
				McElmo/Mesa Verde B/w*	22
				Mesa Verde B/w*	183
				Painted B/w	3
				Pueblo II-III style B/w*	44
				Pueblo III style B/w*	129
				Slipped white	84
		Trade ware	Gray	Corrugated gray	3
				Dolores Corrugated	1
				Indeterminate gray	2

Table 32.15 (continued)

Stratum	Tradition	Variety	Ware	Ceramic Type	Total
			White	Mancos B/w (Reserve style)*	1
				Mancos B/w (Sosi style)*	1
				McElmo B/w*	6
				McElmo/Mesa Verde B/w*	2
				Mesa Verde B/w*	3
				Pueblo II-III style B/w*	1
				Pueblo III style B/w*	2
				Slipped white	3
				Subtotal	4560
C-1-4	Chuska	Trade ware	White	Nava B/w*	1
				Toadlena B/w (Sosi style)*	1
	Cibola	Animas	White	Chaco-McElmo B/w*	9
				Escavada B/w*	1
				Gallup B/w*	2
				Reserve B/w*	2
		Trade ware	Red	Indeterminate White Mountain B/r	8
				Indeterminate White Mountain Polychrome	1
				Indeterminate White Mountain Red Ware	6
				Puerco B/r*	3
				St. Johns B/r*	10
				St. Johns Polychrome*	4
				Wingate B/r*	1
				Wingate Polychrome*	3
			White	Chaco-McElmo B/w*	2
				Escavada B/w*	2
				Gallup B/w*	3
				Pueblo I-II style B/w*	1
	Indeterminate	Indeterminate	White	Pueblo III style B/w*	2
				Slipped white	2
	Kayenta	Trade ware	Red	Medicine B/o*	1
			White	Dogoszhi B/w*	1
				Flagstaff B/w*	1
				Sosi B/w*	1
	Mogollon	Trade ware	Brown	Woodruff Smudged	1
	Northern San Juan	Animas	Gray	Corrugated gray	31
				Indeterminate gray	10
				Pueblo II corrugated	15
				Pueblo II-III corrugated	15
			White	Cortez B/w (Red Mesa style)*	1
				Early McElmo B/w*	6
				Mancos B/w (Dogoszhi style)*	11
				Mancos B/w (Mancos style)*	3
				Mancos B/w (Puerco style)*	1
				Mancos B/w (Reserve style)*	5
				Mancos B/w (Sosi style)*	13
				McElmo B/w*	112
				McElmo/Mesa Verde B/w*	4
				Mesa Verde B/w*	49
				Pueblo II-III style B/w*	1
				Pueblo III style B/w*	3
				Slipped white	1
		Trade ware	White	Mancos B/w (Dogoszhi style)*	2
				Mancos B/w (Mancos style)*	1
				Mancos B/w (Sosi style)*	1
				McElmo B/w*	19
				McElmo/Mesa Verde B/w*	1
				Mesa Verde B/w*	5
				Pueblo II-III style B/w*	1
	Not analyzed	Not analyzed	Gray	Corrugated gray	51
				Indeterminate gray body	3
			White	Pueblo III style B/w*	3
				Slipped white	4
				Subtotal	441
C-2-5	Chuska	Trade ware	White	Burnham B/w*	1
				Chuska B/w*	1
				Crumbled House B/w*	1

Table 32.15 (continued)

Stratum	Tradition	Variety	Ware	Ceramic Type	Total
				Nava B/w*	1
				Pueblo III style B/w*	1
				Taylor B/w (Puerco style)*	1
				Toadlena B/w (Black Mesa style)*	1
	Cibola	Animas	White	Chaco B/w*	1
				Chaco-McElmo B/w*	18
				Escavada B/w*	5
				Gallup B/w*	6
				Puerco B/w*	3
				Red Mesa B/w*	1
		Trade ware	Red	Indeterminate White Mountain B/r	26
				Indeterminate White Mountain Red Ware	13
				Puerco B/r*	2
				St. Johns B/r*	8
				Wingate B/r*	14
				Wingate Polychrome*	2
			White	Chaco B/w*	2
				Chaco-McElmo B/w*	9
				Escavada B/w*	3
				Gallup B/w*	5
	Indeterminate	Indeterminate	White	McElmo style B/w*	2
				Mesa Verde style B/w*	1
				Painted B/w	1
	Kayenta	Trade ware	Red	Citadel Polychrome*	1
				Indeterminate B/r	1
				Indeterminate polychrome	1
	Mogollon	Trade ware	Brown	Showlow Red*	5
				Showlow Smudged*	3
	Northern San Juan	Animas	Gray	Corrugated gray	26
				Indeterminate gray	15
				Plain gray	1
				Pueblo II corrugated	22
				Pueblo II-III corrugated	28
			White	Cortez B/w (Red Mesa style)*	1
				Early McElmo B/w*	12
				Mancos B/w (Black Mesa style)*	1
				Mancos B/w (Dogoszhi style)*	15
				Mancos B/w (Mancos style)*	5
				Mancos B/w (Puerco style)*	1
				Mancos B/w (Reserve style)*	5
				Mancos B/w (Sosi style)*	12
				McElmo B/w*	213
				McElmo/Mesa Verde B/w*	3
				Mesa Verde B/w*	54
				Pueblo II-III style B/w*	1
				Pueblo III style B/w*	5
				Slipped white	2
		Indeterminate	White	McElmo B/w*	2
		Trade ware	Gray	Indeterminate gray	2
				Mancos Corrugated	1
			Red	Deadmans B/r*	1
				Indeterminate B/r	1
				Transitional Bluff/Deadmans B/r*	1
			White	Mancos B/w (Dogoszhi style)*	2
				Mancos B/w (Reserve style)*	2
				Mancos B/w (Sosi style)*	5
				McElmo B/w*	14
				McElmo/Mesa Verde B/w*	1
				Mesa Verde B/w*	1
				Pueblo III style B/w*	1
				Subtotal	596
C-2-5.1	Cibola	Trade ware	Red	Indeterminate White Mountain B/r	1
				Indeterminate White Mountain Red Ware	3
				St. Johns B/r*	2
				St. Johns Polychrome*	1
			White	Snowflake B/w*	1

Table 32.15 (continued)

Stratum	Tradition	Variety	Ware	Ceramic Type	Total
	Mogollon	Trade ware	Brown	Tularosa Pattern Corrugated (smudged)*	1
	Northern San Juan	Animas	Gray	Corrugated gray	1
				Indeterminate gray	5
				Pueblo II corrugated	4
				Pueblo II-III corrugated	3
			White	Early McElmo B/w*	2
				Mancos B/w (Dogoszhi style)*	1
				McElmo B/w*	26
				McElmo/Mesa Verde B/w*	1
				Mesa Verde B/w*	11
				Pueblo III style B/w*	1
				Slipped white	1
		Trade ware	White	Mesa Verde B/w*	2
				Subtotal	67
C-2-5.3	Chuska	Trade ware	White	Nava B/w*	2
	Cibola	Animas	White	Chaco-McElmo B/w*	8
				Escavada B/w*	3
				Gallup B/w*	3
				Pueblo II-III style B/w*	1
				Puerco B/w*	1
		Trade ware	Red	Indeterminate White Mountain B/r	6
				Indeterminate White Mountain Red Ware	3
				Puerco B/r*	1
				St. Johns B/r*	1
				St. Johns Polychrome*	2
				Wingate B/r*	2
				Wingate Polychrome*	1
			White	Chaco-McElmo B/w*	2
				Gallup B/w*	1
	Northern San Juan	Animas	Gray	Corrugated gray	14
				Indeterminate gray	6
				Pueblo II corrugated	2
				Pueblo II-III corrugated	4
			White	Early McElmo B/w*	6
				Mancos B/w (Dogoszhi style)*	3
				Mancos B/w (Mancos style)*	1
				Mancos B/w (Puerco style)*	1
				Mancos B/w (Reserve style)*	1
				McElmo B/w*	41
				McElmo/Mesa Verde B/w*	9
				Mesa Verde B/w*	34
				Pueblo III style B/w*	4
		Trade ware	Gray	Dolores Corrugated	1
			White	Early McElmo B/w*	1
				McElmo B/w*	4
				Mesa Verde B/w*	3
				Subtotal	172
C-3-6	Chuska	Trade ware	Gray	Newcomb Corrugated*	1
			White	Brimhall B/w*	1
				Chuska B/w*	3
				Nava B/w*	1
	Cibola	Animas	White	Chaco-McElmo B/w*	10
				Escavada B/w*	4
				Gallup B/w*	7
				Puerco B/w*	3
		Trade ware	Red	Indeterminate White Mountain B/r	3
				Indeterminate White Mountain Red Ware	5
				Puerco B/r*	2
				St. Johns B/r*	6
				Wingate B/r*	2
			White	Chaco-McElmo B/w*	8
				Escavada B/w*	4
				Gallup B/w*	5
				Red Mesa B/w*	1
	Indeterminate	Indeterminate	Gray	Indeterminate gray body	1
	Kayenta	Trade ware	Red	Cameron Polychrome*	1

Table 32.15 (continued)

Stratum	Tradition	Variety	Ware	Ceramic Type	Total
	Mogollon	Trade ware	Brown	Showlow Smudged*	6
				Tularosa Pattern Corrugated (smudged)*	1
	Northern San Juan	Animas	Gray	Corrugated gray	5
				Indeterminate gray	9
				Pueblo II corrugated	5
				Pueblo II-III corrugated	17
			White	Cortez B/w (Red Mesa style)*	1
				Early McElmo B/w*	14
				Mancos B/w (Black Mesa style)*	1
				Mancos B/w (Dogoszhi style)*	5
				Mancos B/w (Mancos style)*	2
				Mancos B/w (Puerco style)*	2
				Mancos B/w (Reserve style)*	2
				Mancos B/w (Sosi style)*	10
				McElmo B/w*	56
				Mesa Verde B/w*	1
				Painted B/w	2
				Piedra B/w*	2
				Pueblo I-II style B/w*	4
		Trade ware	White	Cortez B/w (Red Mesa style)*	2
				Early McElmo B/w*	2
				Mancos B/w (Dogoszhi style)*	2
				Mancos B/w (Mancos style)*	1
				McElmo B/w*	6
				Pueblo I-II style B/w*	1
				Subtotal	227
C-7-12	Chuska	Trade ware	White	Nava B/w*	1
				Taylor B/w (Sosi style)*	1
				Toadlena B/w (Black Mesa style)*	1
				Toadlena B/w (Puerco style)*	1
	Cibola	Animas	White	Chaco-McElmo B/w*	11
				Gallup B/w*	2
				Pueblo I-II style B/w*	1
				Red Mesa B/w*	1
				Reserve B/w*	1
				Slipped white	3
		Trade ware	Red	Indeterminate White Mountain B/r	20
				Indeterminate White Mountain Red Ware	9
				St. Johns B/r*	3
				Wingate B/r*	4
			White	Chaco-McElmo B/w*	5
				Escavada B/w*	5
				Gallup B/w*	3
				Puerco B/w*	3
				Red Mesa B/w*	2
				Reserve B/w*	1
	Indeterminate	Indeterminate	Red	Indeterminate red	1
			Unfired	Indeterminate unfired vessel	2
			White	McElmo style B/w*	1
	Kayenta	Trade ware	Red	Cameron Polychrome*	3
				Citadel Polychrome*	1
			White	Dogoszhi B/w*	1
	Mogollon	Trade ware	Brown	Showlow Red*	3
				Showlow Smudged*	3
				Woodruff Smudged	1
	Northern San Juan	Animas	Gray	Corrugated gray	7
				Indeterminate gray	5
				Pueblo II corrugated	13
				Pueblo II-III corrugated	16
			White	Cortez B/w (Kiatuthlanna style)*	2
				Cortez B/w (Red Mesa style)*	2
				Early McElmo B/w*	11
				Mancos B/w (Black Mesa style)*	3
				Mancos B/w (Dogoszhi style)*	5
				Mancos B/w (Mancos style)*	1
				Mancos B/w (Reserve style)*	5

Table 32.15 (continued)

Stratum	Tradition	Variety	Ware	Ceramic Type	Total
				Mancos B/w (Sosi style)*	6
				McElmo B/w*	83
				Mesa Verde B/w*	8
				Slipped white	1
		Trade ware	Gray	Indeterminate gray	1
			Red	Deadmans B/r*	1
				Indeterminate B/r	1
			White	Cortez B/w (Red Mesa style)*	1
				Early McElmo B/w*	1
				Mancos B/w (Dogoszhi style)*	1
				Mancos B/w (Mancos style)*	2
				Mancos B/w (Reserve style)*	3
				McElmo B/w*	7
				Pueblo II-III style B/w*	1
				Pueblo III style B/w*	1
				Subtotal	282
C-8-13	Cibola	Animas	White	Chaco-McElmo B/w*	3
				Escavada B/w*	2
				Red Mesa B/w*	1
		Trade ware	Red	Indeterminate White Mountain B/r	4
				St. Johns B/r*	13
			White	Chaco-McElmo B/w*	2
				Escavada B/w*	1
				Gallup B/w*	3
				Kiatuthlanna B/w*	1
	Mogollon	Trade ware	Brown	Woodruff Brown	2
	Northern San Juan	Animas	Gray	Corrugated gray	1
				Indeterminate gray	7
				Pueblo II corrugated	2
				Pueblo II-III corrugated	8
			White	Mancos B/w (Dogoszhi style)*	6
				Mancos B/w (Mancos style)*	2
				Mancos B/w (Sosi style)*	3
				McElmo B/w*	38
				McElmo/Mesa Verde B/w*	1
				Piedra B/w*	2
				Pueblo III style B/w*	1
		Indeterminate	White	Early McElmo B/w*	1
		Trade ware	Gray	Indeterminate gray	2
			White	Cortez B/w (Red Mesa style)*	1
				McElmo B/w*	3
				Mesa Verde B/w*	2
				Subtotal	112
C-9-14	Cibola	Animas	White	Chaco-McElmo B/w*	1
				Slipped white	1
		Trade ware	Red	St. Johns B/r*	1
			White	Chaco B/w*	1
	Mogollon	Trade ware	Brown	Showlow Red*	1
				Showlow Smudged*	1
	Northern San Juan	Animas	Gray	Corrugated gray	2
				Pueblo II corrugated	3
			White	Early McElmo B/w*	1
				Mancos B/w (Dogoszhi style)*	1
				Mancos B/w (Mancos style)*	2
				Mancos B/w (Sosi style)*	2
				McElmo B/w*	17
		Trade ware	Gray	Banded gray	2
			Red	Bluff B/r*	1
				Indeterminate red	2
			White	Cortez B/w (Kiatuthlanna style)*	1
				Cortez B/w (Red Mesa style)*	1
				Early McElmo B/w*	1
				McElmo B/w*	7
				Subtotal	49

Table 32.15 (continued)

Stratum	Tradition	Variety	Ware	Ceramic Type	Total
C-10-15	Chuska	Trade ware	White	Chuska B/w*	2
	Cibola	Animas	White	Chaco-McElmo B/w*	1
				Gallup B/w*	3
		Trade ware	White	Gallup B/w*	2
	Kayenta	Trade ware	Red	Cameron Polychrome*	1
				Indeterminate red	1
	Northern San Juan	Animas	Gray	Corrugated gray	2
				Indeterminate gray	1
			White	Early McElmo B/w*	1
				Mancos B/w (Dogoszhi style)*	2
				Mancos B/w (Sosi style)*	6
				McElmo B/w*	1
				Subtotal	23
C-11-16	Chuska	Trade ware	Gray	Hunter Corrugated*	1
			White	Nava B/w*	3
	Cibola	Animas	White	Chaco-McElmo B/w*	7
				Puerco B/w*	1
		Trade ware	Red	Puerco B/r*	1
			White	Chaco B/w*	3
				Chaco-McElmo B/w*	10
				Escavada B/w*	3
				Pueblo I-II style B/w*	1
	Kayenta	Trade ware	Red	Tusayan B/r*	1
	Mogollon	Trade ware	Brown	Showlow Red*	4
	Northern San Juan	Animas	Gray	Corrugated gray	1
				Pueblo II corrugated	1
			White	Early McElmo B/w*	2
				Mancos B/w (Dogoszhi style)*	2
				Mancos B/w (Mancos style)*	1
				Mancos B/w (Sosi style)*	3
				McElmo B/w*	6
				Mesa Verde B/w*	1
		Trade ware	Gray	Mancos Corrugated	1
			Red	Indeterminate red	1
			White	Early McElmo B/w*	2
				Mancos B/w (Dogoszhi style)*	5
				Mancos B/w (Mancos style)*	1
				Mancos B/w (Sosi style)*	1
				McElmo B/w*	10
				McElmo/Mesa Verde B/w*	1
				Slipped white	1
				Subtotal	75
C-11-16.1	Northern San Juan	Animas	Gray	Pueblo II corrugated	1
				Pueblo II-III corrugated	1
		Trade ware	White	Early McElmo B/w*	2
				Mancos B/w (Sosi style)*	1
				Subtotal	5
C-11-16.2	Northern San Juan	Trade ware	White	McElmo B/w*	1
				Subtotal	1
C-11-16.3	Chuska	Trade ware	White	Chuska B/w*	1
	Cibola	Animas	White	Chaco-McElmo B/w*	2
		Trade ware	White	Gallup B/w*	1
	Northern San Juan	Trade ware	White	Mesa Verde B/w*	1
				Subtotal	5
C-12-17	Chuska	Trade ware	White	Toadlena B/w (Sosi style)*	1
	Cibola	Animas	White	Chaco B/w*	1
				Escavada B/w*	1
		Trade ware	Red	Indeterminate White Mountain B/r	1
			White	Chaco B/w*	1
				Escavada B/w*	1
				Gallup B/w*	2
	Northern San Juan	Animas	Gray	Corrugated gray	1
				Mancos Gray	3
				Pueblo II corrugated	2
				Pueblo II-III corrugated	7
			White	Mancos B/w (Dogoszhi style)*	1

Table 32.15 (continued)

Stratum	Tradition	Variety	Ware	Ceramic Type	Total
				Mancos B/w (Sosi style)*	8
				McElmo B/w*	3
				Mesa Verde B/w*	1
		Indeterminate	White	McElmo B/w*	1
		Trade ware	White	Early McElmo B/w*	1
				Mancos B/w (Dogoszhi style)*	1
				Mancos B/w (Mancos style)*	1
				Mancos B/w (Sosi style)*	2
				McElmo B/w*	1
				Subtotal	41
C-13-18	Chuska	Trade ware	White	Nava B/w*	1
	Cibola	Animas	White	Chaco B/w*	6
		Trade ware	White	Chaco B/w*	1
				Gallup B/w*	1
	Northern San Juan	Animas	Gray	Pueblo II corrugated	2
			White	Mancos B/w (Chaco style)*	4
				Mancos B/w (Sosi style)*	2
				McElmo B/w*	5
		Trade ware	White	Mancos B/w (Dogoszhi style)*	1
				Subtotal	23
H-1-19	Chuska	Trade ware	Gray	Hunter Corrugated*	2
	Northern San Juan	Animas	Gray	Corrugated gray	12
				Indeterminate gray	2
				Plain gray	3
				Pueblo II corrugated	4
			White	Early McElmo B/w*	4
				Mancos B/w (Sosi style)*	2
		Trade ware	White	Mancos B/w (Dogoszhi style)*	1
				McElmo B/w*	1
				Slipped white	4
				Subtotal	35
I-1-19.5	Chuska	Trade ware	Gray	Blue Shale Corrugated*	1
	Cibola	Animas	White	Slipped white	2
	Northern San Juan	Animas	Gray	Plain gray	1
				Pueblo II corrugated	1
			White	Mancos B/w (Dogoszhi style)*	1
				Subtotal	6
CT-1-19.8	Chuska	Trade ware	White	Chuska B/w*	1
	Cibola	Trade ware	White	Gallup B/w*	1
				Subtotal	2
L-5-25	Chuska	Trade ware	Gray	Indeterminate gray	8
	Northern San Juan	Animas	Gray	Banded gray	1
			White	Early McElmo B/w*	1
				McElmo B/w*	1
				Subtotal	11
L-7-27	Cibola	Animas	White	Escavada B/w*	1
		Trade ware	White	Escavada B/w*	1
	Mogollon	Trade ware	Brown	Woodruff Smudged	6
	Northern San Juan	Animas	Gray	Corrugated gray	4
				Pueblo II corrugated	1
			White	McElmo B/w*	1
		Trade ware	Red	Indeterminate red	1
				Subtotal	15
L-8-28	Northern San Juan	Animas	White	Mancos B/w (Sosi style)*	1
				Subtotal	1
I-3-36.5	Northern San Juan	Animas	Gray	Corrugated gray	1
				Subtotal	1
L-22-46.1	Northern San Juan	Animas	Gray	Indeterminate gray	3
				Pueblo II corrugated	4
				Subtotal	7
L-23-47	Northern San Juan	Animas	Gray	Indeterminate gray	2
				Pueblo II corrugated	5
				Subtotal	7
Total					6764

* Types used to generate ceramic mean dates and ranges for Room 100W.

Table 32.16. Room 100W ceramic mean dates and ranges by stratigraphic unit.

Stratum	Description	Ceramic Mean Date	Best Ceramic Range	Max Ceramic Range
N-1-3	Mixed roof-fall	1182	1144-1219	1106-1257
C-1-4	Trash deposits	1160	1126-1194	1092-1228
C-2-5	Trash deposits	1148	1115-1182	1082-1215
C-2-5.1	Trash deposits	1176	1142-1210	1108-1244
C-2-5.3	Trash deposits	1173	1141-1205	1109-1237
C-3-6	Trash deposits	1109	1076-1142	1043-1175
C-7-12	Trash deposits	1127	1094-1161	1061-1194
C-8-13	Trash deposits	1138	1104-1172	1070-1206
C-9-14	Trash deposits	1119	1086-1152	1053-1185
C-10-15	Trash deposits	1085	1053-1117	1021-1149
C-11-16	Trash deposits	1122	1093-1151	1064-1180
C-11-16.1	Trash deposits	1088	1069-1106	1050-1125
C-11-16.2	Trash deposits	1163	*1131-1194	1099-1226
C-11-16.3	Trash deposits	1153	1115-1192	1077-1230
C-12-17	Trash deposits	1092	1061-1122	1030-1153
C-13-18	Trash deposits	1167	1089-1141	1011-1219
H-1-19	Chacoan floor	1110	1085-1135	1060-1160
I-1-19.5	Chacoan floor	1098	1059-1136	1020-1175
CT-1-19.8	Trash deposits	1063	1031-1094	999-1126
L-5-25	Storage vessel in floor	1113	1088-1138	1063-1163
L-7-27	Storage pit in floor	1088	1056-1119	1024-1151
L-8-28	Posthole	1063	*1031-1094	999-1126
I-3-36.5	Chacoan floor	No date	No date	No date
L-22-46.1	Chacoan trash	No date	No date	No date
L-23-47	Chacoan hearth	No date	No date	No date

* Based on one typeable sherd.

in C-1-4, a 74 percent difference between the two strata. Although the occurrence of White Mountain Red Ware remained roughly the same, the difference in Mesa Verde B/w frequencies clearly contributed to the earlier best range for C-1-4. The mean ceramic date for C-1-4 is 1160 and the best range is 1126–1194, suggesting that deposition of the stratum began at the Chacoan to Early San Juan transition.

Showing yet earlier deposits, C-2-5 contained a significant amount of Pueblo II ceramics and Early McElmo B/w. On the other hand, the numbers of Mesa Verde B/w, White Mountain Red Ware, Chaco-McElmo B/w (Animas Variety; dating later than the Cibola series), and Crumbled House B/w influenced the dating of stratum C-2-5 (see Table 32.15). The resulting ceramic mean date was 1148, the best range was 1115–1182, and the maximum ceramic range was 1082–1215 (see Table 32.16).

Trash stratum C-2-5 was subdivided into C-2-5.1 and C-2-5.3 as a means of segregating natural layers identified within the overall stratum. Sixty-seven sherds were recovered from stratum C-2-5.1 and 172 sherds were recovered from C-2-5.3. Stratum C-2-5.1 was unusual in that its assemblage consisted of only Cibola trade ware, Mogollon trade ware, Northern San Juan trade ware, and Animas Variety Northern San Juan ceramics; Cibola Animas Variety and Chuska trade ware were completely absent from the assemblage. White Mountain Red Ware included St. Johns B/r and Polychrome, but the only other Cibola trade ware was a single Snowflake B/w. The Mogollon trade ware was a single Tularosa Patterned Corrugated Smudged rim sherd. The Northern San Juan trade ware included two Mesa Verde B/w sherds, and the local Northern San Juan assemblage included Early McElmo B/w and Mancos B/w (Dogoszhi style), but lacked any other Pueblo II ceramics. McElmo and Mesa Verde B/w appeared to dominate the ceramics from stratum C-2-5.1. Thus, the ceramic mean date was 1176, the best range was 1142–1210, and the maximum ceramic range was 1108-1244.

This same pattern in terms of producing later mean dates but having a somewhat different outcome also applies to the next lower stratum, C-2-5.3. Trade ware included Chuska, Cibola, and Northern San Juan; no Mogollon Brown Ware was identified. Chuska trade ware included Nava B/w. White Mountain Red Ware was represented by all of the Wingate and St. John types. Cibola trade ware included Gallup and Chaco-McElmo B/w, and Northern San Juan trade ware included Dolores Corrugated, Early McElmo B/w, McElmo B/w, and Mesa Verde B/w. Local ceramics comprised both Northern San Juan and Cibola, yielding an assemblage of Early McElmo B/w, Mancos B/w (numerous styles), McElmo B/w, McElmo–Mesa Verde B/w, Mesa Verde B/w, Pueblo II corrugated, Pueblo II–III corrugated, and Chaco-McElmo, Gallup, and Escavada B/w. The types and frequencies tend to show a mixed assemblage, but the Mesa Verde, local Chaco-McElmo, and White Mountain Red Ware appear to influence the ceramic dating. A ceramic mean date of 1173, a best range of 1141–1205, and maximum ceramic range of 1109–1237 were generated. Both C-2-5.1 and C-2-5.3 appear as late mixed deposits in the middle of earlier trash, for which the stratum above dates roughly 30 years earlier and the stratum below dates 64 years earlier when the mean dates are subtracted.

The assemblage from C-3-6, trash deposit, contained greater numbers of Pueblo II ceramics than the higher strata discussed above. Of significance (see Table 32.15) is the presence of Chuska B/w and Nava B/w of the Chuska series, the presence of Puerco B/r (the earliest of the White Mountain Red Wares), the absence of White Mountain Polychromes, the presence of Pueblo II Cibola, and representation of all the substyles of Mancos B/w, along with Early McElmo. This trend and the near absence of Mesa Verde B/w (n = 1) brought the ceramic date calculations much earlier. A ceramic mean date of 1109, a best range of 1076–1142, and a maximum ceramic range of 1043–1175 were produced for stratum C-3-6. The trash from this stratum clearly falls within the Chacoan period of initial construction at Salmon (with some later sherds present).

The next trash stratum, C-7-12, contained a large assemblage of 282 sherds for analysis (Table 32.15). Trade ware included Pueblo II types from the Chuska Valley, White Mountain Red Ware, Cibola Pueblo II types and Chaco-McElmo B/w, Tusayan polychromes from the Kayenta region, Showlow and Woodruff brown ware from the Mogollon region, Deadman's B/r of the San Juan Red Ware series, numerous Pueblo II types, and McElmo B/w from the Northern San Juan. The local Animas Variety ceramics included a small number of Cibola White Ware sherds, such as Chaco-McElmo, Gallup, Reserve, and Red Mesa B/w. The majority of the local ceramics, Northern San Juan, included Pueblo II corrugated, Pueblo II–III corrugated, both styles of Cortez B/w, significant numbers of Early McElmo B/w, almost all of the Mancos style, a large number of McElmo B/w sherds, and a handful of Mesa Verde sherds. Although there appears to have been some mixing of deposits (i.e., Mesa Verde B/w and Tusayan polychromes present), this stratum exhibits minimal mixing compared to later strata (e.g., C-3-6). With the typeable ceramics and their known dates of manufacture, a ceramic mean date of 1127, a best range of 1094–1161, and a maximum ceramic range of 1061–1194 were generated for C-7-12 (see Table 32.16).

Stratum C-8-13, a trash deposit, contained 112 ceramics including local and trade ware sherds. As shown in Table 32.15, the Pueblo II trade ware included Kiatuthlanna B/w, Gallup B/w, and Escavada B/w of the Cibola series, Woodruff Brown of the Mogollon series, and Cortez B/w (Red Mesa style) of the Northern San Juan series. Early and late Pueblo III trade ware ceramics identified in stratum C-8-13 were St. Johns B/r of the White Mountain Red Ware series, Chaco-McElmo B/w of the Cibola series, and McElmo and Mesa Verde B/w of the Northern San Juan series. The local ceramics included Cibola Red Mesa and Escavada B/w representing the Pueblo II period, and Chaco-McElmo B/w representing the Pueblo III period. Table 32.15 shows the distribution of local Northern San Juan ceramics, including Piedra B/w (a Pueblo I type), Mancos B/w (a number of styles), and a larger number of McElmo B/w. The absence of Mesa Verde B/w, however, is noticeable and significant in generating the ceramic dates. Similar to most of the strata, gray ware rims were identified as Pueblo II corrugated or Pueblo II–III corrugated. Based on these ceramics and the date ranges presented in Chapter 31, a ceramic mean date of 1138, a best range of 1104–1172, and a maximum ceramic range of 1070–1206 were generated.

The next (lower) trash deposit (C-9-14) contained 49 sherds that were analyzed. As with other strata, most ceramics were gray ware body or white ware sherds that could not be typed and were not analyzed. Trade ware from C-9-14 included St. Johns B/r of the White Mountain Red Ware series, Chaco B/w of the Cibola series, and a much larger assemblage from the Northern San Juan series. Northern San Juan ceramics included Bluff B/r and Cortez B/w (Kiatuthlanna style) dating to the late Pueblo I and early Pueblo II periods, Cortez B/w (Red Mesa style) dating to the early Pueblo II period, Early McElmo B/w, and McElmo B/w. Local ceramics included Chaco-McElmo B/w, Mancos B/w (a number of styles), Early McElmo B/w, and a larger number of McElmo B/w. The large number of McElmo B/w itself is influential in the mean date calculations, but the combined numbers of individual sherds from the Pueblo II types clearly offset the Early San Juan phase predominance of McElmo ceramics. Thus, the ceramic mean date for C-9-14 was 1119, the best range was 1086–1152, and the maximum ceramic range was 1053–1185, all indicating usage during (and after) the construction period for Salmon.

Stratum C-10-15 contained only 23 sherds that we considered typeable. The trade ware included Chuska B/w, Gallup B/w, and Cameron Polychrome. Local ceramics including both Cibola and Northern San Juan sherds included Gallup and Chaco-McElmo B/w, Mancos B/w (Sosi and Dogoszhi styles), Early McElmo B/w, and McElmo B/w. There were no typeable corrugated rims in the assemblage. Most of the ceramics from C-10-15 are late Pueblo II types, with a few Early San Juan phase ceramics included. The ceramic mean date for the stratum was 1085, the best range was 1053–1173, and the maximum ceramic range was 1021–1149. Thus, much of the ceramic range falls within the Chacoan period.

Stratum C-11-16, a trash deposit, contained 75 sherds analyzed during the study. This stratum also included some mixed deposits of Pueblo II and some later Pueblo III types. Pueblo II trade ware included Puerco B/r of the Cibola series, Tusayan B/r from the Kayenta region, Showlow Red of the Mogollon region, and Early McElmo B/w and Mancos B/w (Dogoszhi, Mancos, and Sosi styles) of the Northern San Juan series. Local Pueblo II types included examples of Chaco and Escavada B/w, Early McElmo B/w, and Mancos B/w (Dogoszhi, Mancos, and Sosi styles). Pueblo III types included Hunter Corrugated and Nava B/w of the Chuska series, Chaco-McElmo B/w of the Cibola series, and McElmo B/w and McElmo–Mesa Verde B/w of the Northern San Juan series. Local Pueblo III types included Chaco-McElmo B/w, McElmo B/w, and Mesa Verde B/w. Gray ware sherds were typed as Pueblo II corrugated. Based on these ceramics, a mean ceramic date of 1122, a best range of 1093 to 1151, and a maximum ceramic range of 1064–1180 were generated. The Pueblo II ceramics brought the best range low enough to fit within the Chacoan occupation of Salmon, but the primary best range for the stratum appears to fall within the Early San Juan period.

Lower-level trash deposits below C-11-16 were subdivided into three strata: C-11-16.1, C-11-16.2, and C-11-16.3. These three trash strata contained few typeable sherds, providing low confidence in the ceramic mean date, best range, and maximum ceramic range calculations. C-11-16.1 contained a total of five sherds meeting our criteria for analysis, including one Pueblo II corrugated and one Pueblo II–III corrugated of local origin, and two Early McElmo B/w and one Mancos B/w (Sosi style) of Northern San Juan trade ware origin. This group of ceramics yielded a ceramic mean date of 1088, a best range of 1069–1106, and a maximum ceramic range of 1050–1125 within the full range of Chacoan occupation and initial construction. C-11-16.2, on the other hand, contained only one sherd—a nonlocal McElmo B/w—which by itself produced a mean ceramic date of 1163, a best range of 1131–1194, and a maximum ceramic range of 1099–1226. Based on a single sherd, the date is questionable. Finally, stratum C-11-16.3 contained five typeable sherds: one Chuska B/w from the Chuska Valley, one Gallup B/w from the Cibola region, one Mesa Verde B/w from the Northern San Juan region, and two local Chaco-McElmo B/w sherds. From this small group of sherds, a mean ceramic date of 1153, a best range of 1115–1192, and a maximum ceramic range of 1077–1230 were generated. This mixed group of ceramics was influenced by the small sample size resulting from our strategy of examining only typeable ceramics from the trash layers. Thus, the ceramic dates from these three strata are questionable and have low confidence.

Stratum C-12-17 contained 41 typeable sherds examined during the study, including trade ware from the Chuska Valley, the Cibola San Juan Basin area, and the Northern San Juan region. Most of the ceramics were late Pueblo II types (Table 32.15), including Toadlena B/w (Sosi style), Chaco B/w, Escavada B/w, Gallup B/w, Mancos (Dogoszhi, Sosi, and Mancos styles), and Pueblo II corrugated and Pueblo II–III corrugated (although there is evidence to suggest that both these types extend into the Pueblo III period). Pueblo III types included lesser amounts of McElmo and Mesa Verde B/w. As a result, the ceramic date calculations reflect the low numbers and absence of other Pueblo III types with a mean date of 1092, a best range of 1061–1122, and a maximum ceramic range of 1030–1153.

C-13-18, a trash deposit stratum just above Chacoan floor fill H-1-19, yielded an assemblage of 23 typeable sherds (Table 32.15). Trade ware ceramics included a small number from the Chuska Valley, the Cibola San Juan Basin, and the Northern San Juan region. Most of the ceramics were of local origin. Pueblo II types included Chaco B/w, Gallup B/w, and Mancos B/w (Dogoszhi and Sosi styles). Pueblo III types included Nava and McElmo B/w. A ceramic mean date of 1167, a best range of 1089–1141, and a maximum ceramic range of 1011–1219 were generated, falling in line with the early occupation of Salmon and extending into the Early San Juan phase.

The first Chacoan floor unit, H-1-19, contained 35 typeable sherds, which included trade ware from the Chuska Valley and the Northern San Juan region. Pueblo II types included Early McElmo B/w and Mancos B/w (Dogoszhi and Sosi styles). Pueblo III types included Hunter Corrugated and McElmo B/w. Typeable local corrugated rims included Pueblo II corrugated. This group of typeable pottery produced a ceramic mean date of 1110, a best range of 1085–1135, and a maximum ceramic range of 1060–1160. These dates indicate floor fill dating to the time of construction of Room 100W and probably later into the Early San Juan period.

The Chacoan floor surface itself (I-1-19.5) below the floor level (H-1-19) contained six sherds: Blue Shale Corrugated from the Chuska Valley, a local Cibola slipped white sherd, and local Northern San Juan plain gray, Pueblo II corrugated, and Mancos B/w (Dogoszhi style). This small group of sherds generated a ceramic mean date of 1098, a best range of 1059–1136, and a maximum ceramic range of 1020–1175.

Two typeable sherds were identified from the trash stratum below the Chacoan floor surface (CT-1-19.8): one Chuska B/w from the Chuska Valley and one Gallup B/w from the Cibola area. A ceramic mean date of 1063, a best range of 1031–1094, and a maximum ceramic range of 999–1126 were generated by the two sherds; based on only two sherds, this date is tentative. Nevertheless, the best range falls well within the construction period for Room 100W.

Stratum L-5-25 was assigned to Feature 5001, a storage vessel set into the Chacoan floor (I-1-19.5). Eleven sherds were associated with the storage vessel: eight Chuska indeterminate gray ware, one local banded gray ware, one local Early McElmo B/w, and one McElmo B/w were identified. This small group of sherds provided a ceramic mean date of 1113, a best range of 1088–1138, and a maximum ceramic range of 1063–1163. Given that these dates were based only on the Early McElmo and McElmo B/w sherds, the ceramic dates are of low confidence.

Feature 5006 (stratum L-7-27) was a storage pit in the Chacoan floor (I-1-19.5) that contained 15 sherds. Most are trade ware, including Escavada B/w of the Cibola series, Woodruff Brown of the Mogollon region, and an indeterminate San Juan Red Ware. Local ceramics included Escavada B/w, McElmo B/w, corrugated gray, and Pueblo II corrugated. The ceramic mean date, best range, and maximum ceramic range were based on three sherds, Escavada B/w and McElmo B/w, providing a low level of confidence. Nevertheless, the ceramic mean date is 1088, the best range is 1056–1119, and the maximum ceramic range is 1024–1151, falling within the Chacoan period of construction and occupation by Chacoan occupants.

A posthole (stratum L-8-28) contained one locally produced Mancos B/w (Sosi style) sherd, yielding a ceramic mean date of 1063, a best range of 1031–1094, and a maximum ceramic range of 999–1126. Clearly, ceramic dating based on a single sherd is questionable. The mean date is early but the latter part of the best range falls within the primary construction sequence for Room 100W and the pueblo as a whole.

As shown in Table 32.15, the next lowest Chacoan floor (I-3-36.5), the trash deposit below (L-22-46.1), and the Chacoan hearth (L-23-47) contained no typeable ceramics. Thus, ceramic mean dates, best ranges, and maximum ceramic ranges were not generated for these proveniences.

In summary, ceramic mean dates for Room 100W show a progression from the latest occupation of the room in the upper levels down to the lowest level strata at one of the Chacoan floors (I-1-19.5). Evidence of mixing occurs in some of the trash deposits, but in most cases the presence of later ceramics does not significantly skew the mean dates. The distribution of types and the ceramic mean dates show that Room 100W was primarily a Chacoan room with a later San Juan occupation in the highest strata.

Ceramic Trade Ware

In Room 100W, 676 ceramics (9.4% of the room assemblage) were identified as trade ware or manufactured outside the Middle San Juan region. As shown in Figure 32.6, the majority of the trade ware in this room had its origin in the Cibola region, suggesting Chacoan trade. Approximately 51 percent of the nonlocal ceramics were white and red wares from the Cibola region. The white ware consists predominantly of Chaco-McElmo B/w; also present are other Pueblo II types such as Chaco, Escavada, Gallup, Kiatuthlanna, Red Mesa, Puerco, Reserve, and Snowflake B/w. A number of vessel forms are included in the white ware assemblage. Cibola White Mountain Red Ware was also present in high quantities, including all the expected types: Puerco B/r, St.

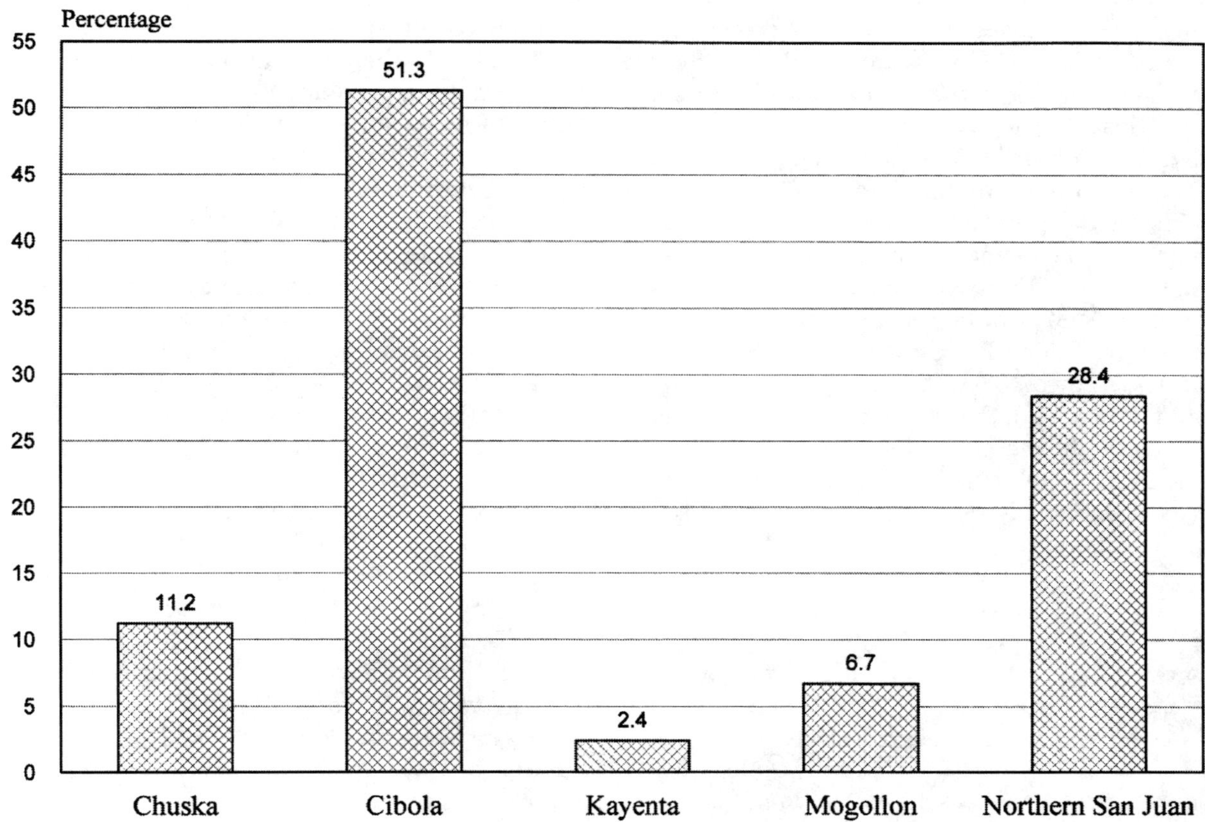

Figure 32.6. Distribution of trade ware ceramics from Room 100W.

John's B/r and Polychrome, and Wingate B/r and Polychrome. All typeable White Mountain Red Ware sherds are from bowls. However, two sherds in the indeterminate White Mountain Red Ware category are from a jar and a pinch pot.

No vessel numbers or letters were assigned to the Cibola tradition sherds; however, a number of pieces refit or belong to the same vessel. Vessel forms in Cibola white ware include bowls (n = 267), jars (n = 62), ladles (n = 12), mugs (n = 3), pitchers (n = 2), one olla, and one pinch pot. The pinch pot fragment is from either an unslipped and undecorated red ware or a misfired gray ware. The olla fragment is from a misfired Escavada B/w vessel. The two refitting sherds from a pitcher represent an Escavada B/w vessel that had a strap handle; after the handle broke off, the attachments were ground smooth. Two sherds are from a Chaco-McElmo B/w mug, painted in Mesa Verde style. One sherd is from a Gallup B/w mug and so is probably more likely to be a tall pitcher-mug than the short mugs seen in Pueblo III assemblages. One ladle sherd is Gallup B/w; the other 11 are Chaco-McElmo B/w in McElmo and Early McElmo styles. The pinch pot and pitcher both came from stratum C-7-12. The olla sherd came from stratum C-11-16. The Chaco-McElmo mug also came from C-11-16, but the Gallup B/w mug came from C-1-4. Four Chaco-McElmo B/w ladle pieces, all belonging to the same ladle, came from C-2-5. Six ladle sherds, representing two different Chaco-McElmo B/w ladles, came from C-3-6. One is Early McElmo style, the other McElmo style. The Gallup B/w ladle fragment came from C-10-15, and one final Chaco-McElmo B/w ladle fragment, painted in McElmo style, came from C-11-16.

Nonlocal Northern San Juan ceramics totaled 194, or 28.4 percent of the trade wares in Room 100W. This is the largest concentration of nonlocal Northern San Juan ceramics in any of the rooms that were analyzed during this project at Salmon. These ceramics included gray, white, and red wares. Gray ware sherds (n = 16) were identified as Mancos and Dolores Corrugated, as well as a number of indeterminate body sherds that included banded, corrugated, and plain surfaces. Red ware sherds (n = 10) were identified as Bluff B/r (from C-9-14), Deadman's B/r (from C-2-5 and C-7-12), and Transitional Bluff-Deadman's B/r (from C-2-5).

Indeterminate red ware sherds were also present in a number of strata, all trash layers except for the storage pit (L-7-27.3). White ware sherds (n = 168) came from bowls, jars, ladles, and a mug. The mug, which is Mesa Verde B/w, was recovered from stratum C-1-4. The ladles include Mancos B/w, Sosi style from C-11-16.1, Early McElmo B/w from C-3-6, and McElmo B/w from C-7-12 and C-11-16. Ceramic types seen on jars include Cortez B/w, Red Mesa style, Mancos B/w (Dogoszhi, Mancos, Reserve, and Sosi styles), and McElmo B/w. Ceramic types seen on jars include Cortez B/w, Kiatuthlanna and Red Mesa styles, Mancos B/w (Dogoszhi, Mancos, Reserve, and Sosi styles), Early McElmo B/w, McElmo B/w, Transitional McElmo–Mesa Verde B/w, and Mesa Verde B/w. Northern San Juan white ware was recovered from N-1-3, H-1-19, and every C stratum, but not from the Chacoan floor or any of the features.

Chuska tradition ceramics, from the Chuska Valley, include both gray and white ware (n = 72). Chuskan ceramics, which make up 11.2 percent of the trade ware in Room 100W, were found in stratum N-1-3, most of the C strata, and H-1-19, I-1-19.5, CT-1-19.8, and L-5-25. These include the upper Chacoan floor, a storage vessel set into the floor, and the Chacoan floor fill. The greatest concentration is in stratum N-1-3, the roof-fall. No vessel numbers or letters were assigned as none of the refitting sherds were considered reconstructible vessels. All gray ware (n = 32) came from jars and included Blue Shale Corrugated, Gray Hills Banded, Hunter Corrugated, and Newcomb corrugated, as well as body sherds that could only be identified as plain, polished, or indeterminate gray rim fillets. Most gray ware came from stratum N-1-3, but C-3-6 contained one Newcomb Corrugated, C-11-16 contained one Hunter Corrugated, H-1-9 contained two Hunter Corrugated, I-1-19.5 contained one Blue Shale Corrugated, and L-5-25 contained eight indeterminate gray sherds. Identifiable Pueblo II white ware included both organic- and mineral-painted ceramic types, including Brimhall B/w, Burnham B/w, Chuska B/w, Taylor B/w (Puerco and Sosi styles), and Toadlena B/w (Black Mesa, Puerco, and Sosi styles). Pueblo III white ware included both Nava B/w and Crumbled House B/w. Vessel forms included a seed jar fragment that could only be identified as Pueblo II-Pueblo III B/w from stratum N-1-3, a Crumbled House B/w ladle from stratum C-2-5, jars (n = 11), and bowls (n = 27). White ware was distributed throughout most C strata, but was also found in CT-1-19.8 (one Chuska B/w) and N-1-3 (diagnostic types were two Toadlena B/w, Sosi style sherds and four Nava B/w sherds). No Chuskan white ware came from Chacoan floors, features, or fill layers.

In total, 45 sherds are attributed to the northern Mogollon region, making up 6.7 percent of the trade ware in Room 100W. Mogollon types include Showlow Red, Showlow Smudged, Tularosa Pattern Corrugated with smudged interior, Woodruff Brown, Woodruff Red, and Woodruff Smudged. No vessel numbers or letters were assigned as none of the refitting sherds or sherds from the same vessel were considered reconstructible. Two Showlow Red sherds came from jars, possibly representing the same vessel. All other sherds came from bowls. Showlow Red was found in strata N-1-3, C-2-5, C-7-12, C-9-14, and C-11-16. Showlow Smudged was found in strata N-1-3, C-2-5, C-3-6, C-7-12, and C-9-14. Tularosa Pattern Corrugated was found in Strata C-2-5.1 and C-3-6. Woodruff Brown was found in N-1-3 and C-8-13. Woodruff Red was found only in stratum N-1-3. Woodruff Smudged was found in C-1-4, C-7-12 and L-7-27. Stratum L-7-27 was a storage pit in the upper Chacoan floor, stratum I-1-19.5.

Kayenta trade wares totaled 17, or 2.4 percent of the trade ware in Room 100W. This is a greater number of Kayenta sherds than in any other room studied during this research at Salmon. Most of these sherds were red ware, including Cameron Polychrome, Citadel Polychrome, Medicine Black-on-orange, and Tusayan B/r, along with indeterminate plain and decorated red wares. All of the red ware sherds are from bowls. Kayenta white wares included two Dogoszhi B/w jar sherds, one Flagstaff B/w bowl sherd with a ground edge, and one Sosi B/w bowl sherd. Stratum C-1-4 contained all three white ware types, and C-7-12 also contained a second Dogoszhi B/w sherd.

In summary, most of the trade ware was recovered from one of the many trash deposits (C strata) or from the roof-fall (stratum N-1-3). Cibola and Northern San Juan tradition ceramics are present in high numbers, in comparison to other rooms in the sample where Northern San Juan ceramics were rare or even nonexistent. Chacoan levels that included trade ware are H-1-19, I-1-19.5, CT-1-19.8, L-5-25, and L-7-27. Stratum H-1-19, the Chacoan floor fill, contained two Chuskan Hunter Corrugated sherds and six Northern San Juan sherds: four slipped white, one Mancos B/w (Dogoszhi style), and one McElmo B/w. Stratum I-1-19.5, the Chacoan floor, contained one Chuskan Blue Shale Corrugated sherd. Stratum CT-1-19.8, which is not identified, contained one Chuska B/w sherd and one Cibola Gallup B/w sherd. Stratum L-5-25, a storage vessel inset into the floor, contained (or was made up of) eight Chuskan indeterminate gray sherds. Stratum L-7-27, a storage pit in the floor, contained one Cibola Escavada B/w sherd, six Mogollon Woodruff Smudged sherds, and one Northern San Juan indeterminate Red sherd. Nearly all are Pueblo II period ceramics, as would be expected in the Chacoan strata. Curiously, none of the trade wares are associated with the lower Chacoan floor (stratum I-3-36.5) or any of the trash or features associated with it.

Locally Produced Ceramics

Animas Variety ceramics, produced locally at Salmon or at other sites in the Middle San Juan region, were identified based on the criteria discussed in Chapter 31. These ceramics total 6367 from Room 100W. Unlike other rooms examined during the study, not all stratigraphic units analyzed contained Animas Variety ceramics of both Cibola and Northern San Juan traditions. Cibola Animas Variety ceramics were absent from nine strata—C-2-5.1 (trash deposit), C-11-16.1 (trash deposit), C-11-16.2 (trash deposit), H-1-19 (Chacoan floor fill), L-5-25 (vessel in floor), L-8-28 (posthole), I-3-36.5 (Chacoan floor), L-22-46.1 (trash deposit), and L-23-47 (hearth). Neither Cibola nor Northern San Juan Animas Variety ceramics were present in stratum C-11-16.3, a trash deposit. From the sherd assemblage, one partial Mesa Verde B/w bowl was identified in stratum N-1-3, mixed roof-fall in the uppermost deposits of Room 100W.

As shown in Table 32.16, the mean ceramic dates for the top five strata examined range within the 1100s, indicating an occupation (N-1-3, roof-fall) and trash deposits (C-1-4, C-2-5, C-2-5.1, C-1-5.3) in the Early San Juan phase and possibly into the Late San Juan phase. Below these deposits, the lower strata are primarily Chacoan and into the Early San Juan phase with some mixing, but the lower Chacoan floor fill (H-1-19), floor (I-1-19.5), and below floor trash (CT-1-19.8) clearly date within the Chacoan period. The distribution of Animas Variety types influenced the dating of these strata significantly due to the high frequency of these types throughout the deposits of Room 100W.

The upper strata dating to the Early San Juan phase contained abundant Mesa Verde B/w and McElmo B/w pottery, particularly in stratum N-1-3. The frequency of Mesa Verde B/w in the roof-fall deposit and the number of McElmo and earlier Pueblo II types suggests mixing of deposits in this roof-fall layer. With 183 Mesa Verde B/w sherds and a partial vessel, this strata probably contained the largest assemblage of Mesa Verde pottery identified during the study. Just below the roof, the number of Mesa Verde B/w sherds decreased to 49 and the number of McElmo B/w stayed relatively the same, suggesting that the Mesa Verde sherds in the roof-fall deposits may have been dumped there in a trash deposit episode.

Pueblo II local Northern San Juan ceramics are well represented even in the high strata, such as C-2-5, with Early McElmo B/w and Mancos B/w (numerous styles; Table 32.15). Farther down into the Room 100W deposits, Pueblo II types became more abundant and the frequency of McElmo B/w decreased, coinciding with the earlier ceramic mean dates and best ranges for these strata (C-8-13, C-9-14, C-10-15, and C-11-16). Closer to the Chacoan floor (I-1-19.5) there is a clear decrease in McElmo B/w and a predominance of Pueblo II types. Throughout Room 100W, local gray ware is consistently Pueblo II or Pueblo II–III corrugated.

Room 100W produced a wide variety of Northern San Juan Animas Variety vessel forms, including bowls (n = 1345), jars (n = 4748), ladles (n = 64), mugs (n = 6), seed jars (n = 2), miniatures (n = 1), flute fragments (n = 1), and indeterminate forms (n = 4). Gray ware vessel forms were mostly jars, but some of the polished gray ware was identified as bowls and may have originated from painted vessels. Bowls represent 78 percent (n = 1341) of the white ware assemblage, and jars represent 17.5 percent (n = 301). Bowls and jars were scattered throughout the strata, but mugs were identified in strata N-1-3 (San Juan roof-fall deposit), C-2-5 (trash deposit), and C-2-5.3 (trash deposit). The two mugs from the San Juan roof-fall deposit are Mesa Verde B/w and Pueblo III style B/w. From the trash deposit, one mug fragment is a Mancos B/w (Dogoszhi style) and the other is a McElmo B/w. Both seed jar fragments are McElmo B/w; one is from the San Juan roof-fall deposit and the other is from trash deposit C-7-12. Ladle fragments, which were scattered throughout Room 100 (San Juan roof-fall deposits and trash strata), include Mancos B/w, Early McElmo B/w, McElmo B/w, and McElmo–Mesa Verde B/w.

Most of Room 100W's Northern San Juan Animas Variety White Ware has thick-chalky slips (81%, n = 1,398). The remaining 11 percent exhibits thick crackly (n = 151), thin (n = 55), washy (n = 89), indeterminate (n = 1), or no slip (n = 25). Slip application was analyzed to examine the influence of Cibola technological attributes on local pottery. Mesa Verde B/w sherds had either thick chalky, thick crackly, or no slip; thin or washy slips were not identified on Mesa Verde sherds. All of the Pueblo II types and McElmo B/w had thin and washy slips as well as thick chalky, thick crackly, and no slip. Thus, it would appear that Cibola slip application was more influential for Pueblo II and McElmo B/w than for Mesa Verde B/w in the Room 100W assemblage.

Cibola Animas Variety ceramics included 191 sherds, of which 5 were gray ware and 191 were white ware. Both ware categories were identified by paste similarities with Northern San Juan Animas Variety ceramics, including high silt content and brown to yellow discoloration. Tempering material, however, consisted of various combinations of sand, shale, and sherd. The five gray ware sherds included one corrugated gray, three plain gray, and one polished gray, all from the San Juan roof-fall deposit.

White ware included all of the typeable ceramics in the local sequence scattered throughout Room 100W strata, with the exception of C-2-5.1, C-11-16.1, C-11-16.2, H-1-19, CT-1-19.8, L-5-25, L-8-28, I-3-36.5, L-22-46.1, and L-23-47 (see Table 32.14). Chaco-McElmo B/w was the most common local Cibola type, comprising 46 percent of the assemblage (n = 88). It was identified in the San Juan roof-fall deposits and scattered throughout the trash deposits but was not located on the Chacoan floor or floor deposits. Eight local Chaco B/w sherds were identified in the C-2-5 trash deposit and in the two trash deposit strata above the Chacoan floor fill and floor, C-12-17 and C-13-18. The remaining local Cibola White Ware included Red Mesa B/w (n = 4), Gallup B/w (n = 27), Escavada B/w (n = 23), Puerco B/w (n = 8), and Reserve B/w (n = 4), along with slipped white and Pueblo I–II style, Pueblo II–III style, and Pueblo III style B/w.

For such a small assemblage, the types of vessel forms were varied, including bowls, jars, ladles, ollas, mugs, seed jars, and an effigy/figurine. Bowls were the most common form, comprising 60 percent (n = 114) of the Cibola Animas Variety White Ware assemblage, followed by jars at 33 percent (n = 63). The remaining 7 percent included six ladle fragments, two mug fragments, four olla fragments, one seed jar rim, and one effigy/figurine fragment. The bowls and jars are scattered throughout the Room 100W strata, but the olla rim fragment was located in the San Juan roof-fall deposit and the remaining special forms (mugs, ladles, seed jar, and effigy/figurine) were scattered throughout the trash deposits. The effigy/figurine was identified as Escavada B/w. The mug was identified as Chaco-McElmo B/w. The seed jar was identified as Puerco B/w, a common form for the type. The ladles included Red Mesa B/w, Escavada B/w, and Chaco-McElmo B/w.

In contrast to the local Northern San Juan White Ware, the local Cibola ceramics had a high number of sherds with washy slips (45%, n = 86); this is typical of Cibola ceramics produced in the San Juan Basin and would be expected for emulation by Northern San Juan potters or for Chacoan migrants recreating their own pottery in the Middle San Juan. The number of local Cibola White Ware sherds with thick-chalky slips, however, is equally high at 32 percent (n = 61), which gives the impression that either local Northern San Juan potters were applying their own technology to sand-tempered pottery or Chacoan migrants were borrowing Northern San Juan technology. The remaining 23 percent included sherds having thick-crackly (n = 12, more similar to Northern San Juan), thin (n = 29, more similar to Cibola), or no slip (n = 3).

Summary

Most of the ceramics from Room 100W are local, but they were not present in all strata. Some of the room strata with small numbers of sherds included only trade ware. Ceramic mean dates, best ranges, and maximum ceramic ranges indicate that the San Juan roof-fall deposit N-1-3 dated to the Early San Juan phase and that possibly the large number of Mesa Verde B/w sherds were a later intrusion through trash deposition. The consistency in numbers of McElmo B/w from the San Juan roof-fall deposit down through the following several trash strata seems to support this supposition. Below the first several layers of trash deposition, however, the frequency of McElmo B/w tails off, and the number of Pueblo II ceramics increases to bring the ceramic mean dates, best ranges, and maximum ceramic ranges in line with a Chacoan occupation for the trash fill above the Chacoan floor fill and floor. The variety of vessel forms in Room 100W clearly shows that the room had special use. Trade ware in the room also was variable, including ceramics from the Chuska, Cibola, Kayenta, Northern San Juan, and Mogollon regions, as well as one of the few Tularosa Patterned Corrugated Smudged sherds identified in the study.

ROOM 123W

Room 123W is part of a Chacoan room suite, including Rooms 124, 127, and possibly 128, located in the southernmost tier of rooms. Room 123W had a Chacoan floor with evidence of Secondary intrusion for burial purposes. During the late San Juan occupation, the room was subdivided into two smaller rooms, 123A and 123B. During excavation, 28 strata were identified in the room, including postoccupational fill, structured trash, occupational fill, feature fill, and construction debris. In total, 146 sherds from five strata were chosen for the ceramic re-analysis (Table 32.17). These ceramics were selected from mixed trash, mixed occupational fill unit, a Chacoan floor, and mixed trash fill under the Chacoan floor.

Table 32.17. Room 123W stratigraphic units analyzed.

Stratum	Description	Total
G-1-1	Mixed occupational fill	27
I-1-2	Chacoan floor	41
C-1-3	Mixed trash	1
J-1-3	Mixed trash fill under Chacoan floor	46
C-2-8	Mixed trash	31
Total		146

Ceramic Chronology

Ceramic mean dates, best ranges, and maximum ceramic ranges were calculated for the five selected strata using the procedure and ceramic manufacturing dates for typeable ceramics discussed in Chapter 31. The top stratum examined during the study was G-1-1, mixed occupation fill associated with the Chacoan floor (I-1-2). Stratum G-1-1 contained 27 sherds, including locally produced Northern San Juan and Cibola ceramics and White Mountain Red Ware. The only trade ware, a St. Johns B/r, is a Pueblo III type. The local ceramics included Escavada B/w, McElmo B/w, Pueblo II–III B/w, and Pueblo III B/w. A ceramic mean date for the stratum was 1150 and the best range was 1109–1191—within the Early San Juan period (Table 32.18).

The Chacoan floor (I-1-2) contained 41 sherds, all of which were locally produced. Typeable ceramics included Escavada B/w, Reserve B/w, and Pueblo II–III style B/w. This small group of six sherds produced a ceramic mean date of 1096 and a best range of 1056–1135, corresponding with the Chacoan occupation of the room.

The trash deposits below the Chacoan floor, however, yielded later ceramic dates due to their mixed trash context. Forty-six sherds were analyzed from stratum J-1-3, including trade ware from the Chuska, Cibola, and Mogollon regions. These types included Blue Shale Corrugated from the Chuska Valley, Chaco-McElmo B/w and Puerco B/w from the Cibola region, Wingate B/r from the Zuni and eastern Arizona areas, and Woodruff Smudged from the Mogollon region. Local Cibola pottery included Escavada B/w, Gallup B/w, Puerco B/w, and Chaco-McElmo B/w. Local gray ware was identified as Pueblo II corrugated and Pueblo II–III corrugated, but their usefulness as temporal indicators is questionable and needs further study in the Middle San Juan region. Finally, local Northern San Juan white ware included Mancos B/w (Dogoszhi and Puerco styles), Early McElmo B/w, McElmo B/w, and Mesa Verde B/w. This stratum produced a ceramic mean date of 1131, a best range of 1096-1166, and a maximum ceramic range of 1061–1201. The beginning best range for J-1-3 just below the Chacoan floor is exactly 40 years later than the 1166 date.

Below J-1-3 is another trash deposit (C-1-3) that yielded only one typeable sherd, a McElmo B/w. Based on this single sherd, a ceramic mean date of 1150, a best range of 1113–1188, and a maximum ceramic range of 1076–1225 were generated. It should be noted that a ceramic mean date and ranges based on a single sherd are tentative.

The final trash deposit examined was C-2-8, containing 31 sherds. Trade ware was identified from the Chuska, Cibola, and Kayenta regions, including Blue Shale Corrugated, Chuska B/w, Nava B/w, Chaco-McElmo B/w, indeterminate White Mountain Red Ware, and Citadel Polychrome. Local Cibola and Northern San Juan ceramics included Escavada and Chaco-McElmo B/w, Pueblo II corrugated, Mancos B/w (Dogoszhi style), McElmo B/w, and Mesa Verde B/w. From the frequency and combination of these typeable ceramics in stratum C-2-8, a ceramic mean date of 1145, a best range of 1107–1182, and a maximum ceramic range 1069–1220 were calculated. The ceramic mean dates and ranges from Room 123W cluster mostly in the Early San Juan phase, with the exception of the Chacoan floor and the subfloor trash deposit.

Table 32.18. Room 123W ceramic mean dates and ranges by stratigraphic unit.

Stratum	Description	Ceramic Mean Date	Best Ceramic Range	Max Ceramic Range
G-1-1	Mixed occupational fill	1150	1109-1191	1068-1232
I-1-2	Chacoan floor	1096	1056-1135	1016-1175
J-1-3	Mixed trash fill under Chacoan floor	1131	1096-1166	1061-1201
C-1-3	Mixed trash	1150	1113-1188*	1076-1225
C-2-8	Mixed trash	1145	1107-1182	1069-1220

*Based on one McElmo B/w sherd.

Ceramic Trade Ware

From Room 123W, 15 ceramics (10.3% of the room assemblage) were identified as trade ware or manufactured outside the Middle San Juan region. As shown in Figure 32.7, most of the trade ware from Room 123W had its origin in the Chuska Valley, a pattern not unexpected for deposits primarily of Chacoan age. Approximately 46.7 percent (n = 7) of the nonlocal ceramics were white and gray ware from the Chuska Valley. The gray ware ceramics, which are all jar rims, include Blue Shale Corrugated (n = 2) and indeterminate gray (n = 2). White ware includes only organic-painted types: one Chuska B/w bowl body sherd and two Nava B/w bowl rim sherds. The predominance of organic-painted Chuska white wares in Room 123W correlates with the overall trend at Salmon, for which organic-painted Chuska wares were more commonly imported than mineral types. Chuskan ceramics were recovered from strata C-2-8 and J-1-3, both trash layers but one from under the identified Chacoan floor.

Cibola ceramics included white ware from the San Juan Basin and White Mountain Red Ware from the central New Mexico and Arizona region. As shown in Figure 32.7, the combined Cibola group represents 40 percent (n = 6) of the trade ware identified in Room 123W. White Mountain RedWare included one sherd each of St. John's B/r, Wingate B/r, and indeterminate red. All Cibola red wares are bowl fragments. White ware included one Puerco B/w jar body sherd and two Chaco-McElmo B/w bowl sherds, from a rim and a body. Cibola trade wares were distributed throughout strata C-2-8, G-1-1, and J-1-3; these layers include trash fill and occupational fill.

One trade ware sherd was from the Kayenta region, identified as Citadel Polychrome. This bowl rim sherd was found in stratum C-2-8. One trade ware sherd was from the northern Mogollon region, identified as a Woodruff Smudged bowl body sherd. This sherd came from stratum J-1-3.

In summary, the trade ware ceramics in Room 123W are dominated by Chuska and Cibola tradition sherds, which are present in nearly equal amounts. Other traditions are present, but clearly held less importance as shown by their low numbers. However, none of the trade wares were found in contact with the Chacoan floor. No pattern is evident in the mixed fill strata. Very unexpectedly, there is no Northern San Juan trade ware in this room at all. All Northern San Juan tradition ceramics are Animas Variety.

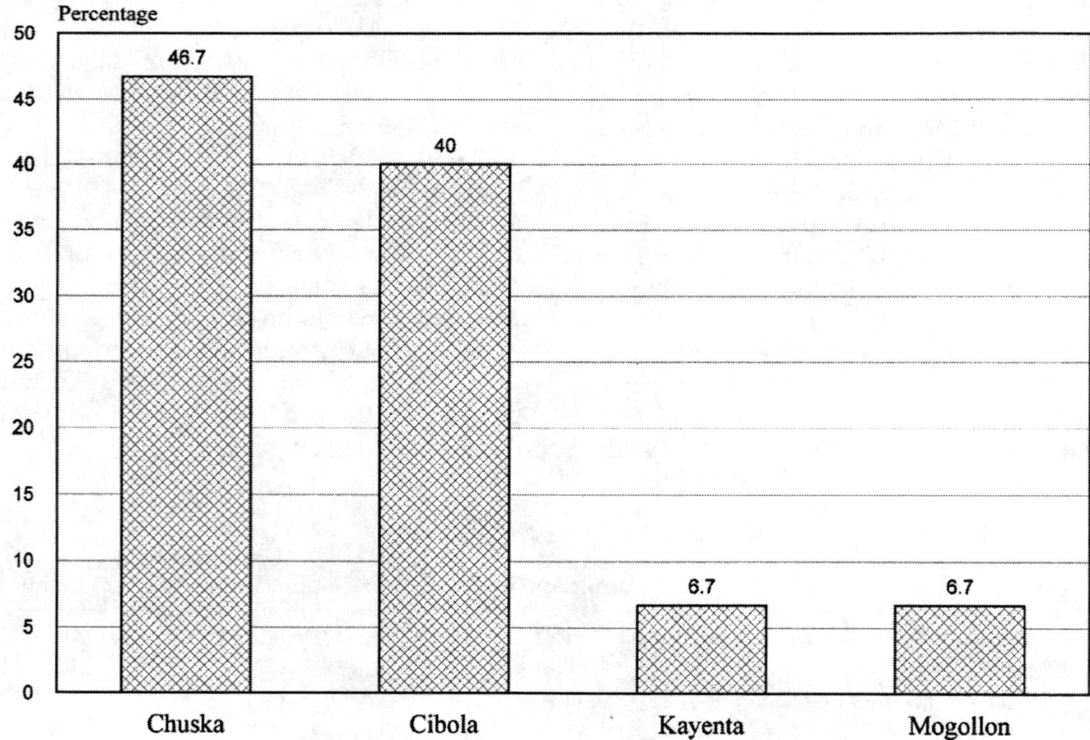

Figure 32.7. Distribution of trade ware ceramics from Room 123W.

Locally Produced Ceramics

Animas Variety ceramics, considered locally produced at Salmon or in the Middle San Juan region, were identified based on the criteria discussed in Chapter 31. These ceramics total 131 from Room 123W. Animas Variety ceramics from the Cibola tradition were present in strata C-2-8, G-1-1, I-1-2, and J-1-3. Animas Variety ceramics from the Northern San Juan tradition were present in all stratigraphic units analyzed in this room. All 24 Cibola Animas Variety ceramics are white ware types, whereas the 107 Northern San Juan Animas Variety ceramics include both gray and white wares. No vessel numbers or letters were assigned to Animas Variety ceramics in Room 123W, and none were identified as reconstructible although several items refit or belong to the same vessel.

As shown in Table 32.19, Pueblo III ceramic types were not restricted to the upper mixed fill layers, but were not present on the Chacoan floor (I-1-2). Mesa Verde B/w itself makes up only 7.5 percent of the white ware (n = 6).

Slip application, one of the attributes examined as a means of tracking Cibola influence, shows mixing of technologies in Room 123W among Cibola Animas Variety ceramics, with 50 percent (n = 12) having the expected washy slip, 37.5 percent (n = 9) with a thick-chalky slip, 4.2 percent (n = 1) with a thin but not washy slip, and 8.3 percent (n = 2) with no slip at all. Among Northern San Juan Animas Variety white ware, 3.8 percent (n = 2) have no slip, 81.1 percent (n = 43) have a thick-chalky slip, 13.2 percent (n = 7) a thin slip, and 1.9 percent (n = 1) a washy slip. This is a classic example of how Animas Variety ceramics exhibit "mix-and-match" technological attributes. The Northern San Juan Animas Variety sherd with a washy slip is from stratum J-1-3. Cibola Animas Variety sherds with thick-chalky slips are found in strata C-2-8, I-1-2, and J-1-3.

Northern San Juan Animas Variety white ware ceramics represent a number of different vessel forms, including bowls (n = 37), jars (n = 59), seed jars (n = 5), ladles (n = 4), one miniature fragment, and one olla fragment. All the seed jar sherds refit and were made from Mancos B/w, Puerco style, recovered from stratum J-1-3. The olla sherd could not be identified beyond slipped white; it was recovered from the Chacoan floor, stratum I-1-2. The miniature sherd is from a polished gray bowl, recovered from stratum J-1-3. Ladles are made from Early McElmo B/w (J-1-3), Mesa Verde B/w (C-2-8), and Pueblo II–III B/w (strata G-1-1 and J-1-3).

Northern San Juan Animas Variety gray ware from Room 123W totaled 54 sherds, including the polished gray miniature bowl sherd described above, a number of corrugated gray body sherds, an indeterminate gray rim fillet, and rim fragments that could be classified as either Pueblo II or Pueblo II–III corrugated gray. Animas Variety gray ware was recovered from strata C-2-8, G-1-1, I-1-2, and J-1-3. As discussed in Chapter 31, Animas Variety gray ware characteristically has coarsely crushed igneous (augite diorite) temper with frequent inclusions of sand and shale. Sherd temper is less common than in the nonlocal Northern San Juan Gray Ware.

Cibola Animas Variety pottery in Room 123W was exclusively white ware (n = 24). It was identified by ceramic paste similar to that of the Northern San Juan Animas Variety ceramics, including high silt content and brown to yellow discoloration. Tempering material consisted of various combinations of sand, shale, and sherd. Identifiable types in the four strata from which Animas Variety Cibola sherds were recovered included both Pueblo II and Pueblo III types. Vessel forms were limited to bowls and jars. Several Chaco-McElmo B/w sherds were recovered from stratum C-2-8; three of these could be identified as McElmo style. One Escavada B/w was also found. One Escavada B/w sherd was found in stratum G-1-1. In stratum I-1-2, identifiable types were Escavada B/w and Reserve B/w. In stratum J-1-3, identifiable types were Escavada, Gallup, and Puerco B/w, and several Chaco-McElmo B/w sherds, one of which was painted in McElmo style.

Summary

The ceramics examined from Room 123W show primarily an Early San Juan phase occupation with a Chacoan floor (stratum I-1-2) and mixed subfloor trash deposit (J-1-3). Trade ware from the Chacoan occupation was identified as Chuska, Cibola, and Mogollon. The San Juan phase deposits were mixed occupational (G-1-1) and lower trash deposits (C-1-3 and C-2-8). Trade ware from the San Juan phase strata included Cibola, Chuska, Kayenta, and White Mountain Red Ware. Room 123W lacked trade ware from the Northern San Juan region. Chacoan and Early San Juan phase mixed deposits include Pueblo II and Pueblo II–III corrugated, providing little means of segregating the corrugated pottery into meaningful temporal sequences.

ROOM 123A

As noted, the abandonment and subsequent division of Room 123W in the late twelfth or early

Table 32.19. Ceramics from Room 123W stratigraphic units.

Stratum	Tradition	Variety	Ware	Ceramic Type	Total
G-1-1	Cibola	Animas	White	Escavada B/w*	1
				Pueblo II-III style B/w*	1
		Trade ware	Red	St. Johns B/r*	1
	Northern San Juan	Animas	Gray	Corrugated gray	3
				Pueblo II-III corrugated	12
			White	McElmo B/w*	6
				Pueblo II-III style B/w*	1
				Pueblo III style B/w*	2
				Subtotal	27
I-1-2	Cibola	Animas	White	Escavada B/w*	2
				Reserve B/w*	2
				Slipped white	4
	Northern San Juan	Animas	Gray	Corrugated gray	30
			White	Pueblo II-III style B/w*	2
				Slipped white	1
				Subtotal	41
J-1-3	Chuska	Trade ware	Gray	Blue Shale Corrugated*	1
				Indeterminate gray	1
			White	Nava B/w*	1
	Cibola	Animas	White	Chaco-McElmo B/w*	3
				Escavada B/w*	1
				Gallup B/w*	1
				Pueblo III style B/w*	1
				Puerco B/w*	1
		Trade ware	Red	Wingate B/r*	1
			White	Chaco-McElmo B/w*	1
				Puerco B/w*	1
	Mogollon	Trade ware	Brown	Woodruff Smudged	1
	Northern San Juan	Animas	Gray	Corrugated gray	1
				Indeterminate gray	1
				Polished gray	1
				Pueblo II corrugated	1
				Pueblo II-III corrugated	1
			White	Early McElmo B/w*	4
				Mancos B/w (Dogoszhi style)*	1
				Mancos B/w (Puerco style)*	6
				McElmo B/w*	8
				Mesa Verde B/w*	4
				Pueblo II-III style B/w*	4
				Subtotal	46
C-1-3	Northern San Juan	Animas	White	McElmo B/w*	1
				Subtotal	1
C-2-8	Chuska	Trade ware	Gray	Blue Shale Corrugated*	1
				Indeterminate gray	1
			White	Chuska B/w*	1
				Nava B/w*	1
	Cibola	Animas	White	Chaco-McElmo B/w*	6
				Escavada B/w*	1
		Trade ware	Red	Indeterminate White Mountain Red Ware	1
			White	Chaco-McElmo B/w*	1
	Kayenta	Trade ware	Red	Citadel Polychrome*	1
	Northern San Juan	Animas	Gray	Pueblo II corrugated	4
			White	Early McElmo B/w*	2
				Mancos B/w (Dogoszhi style)*	1
				McElmo B/w*	4
				Mesa Verde B/w*	2
				Pueblo II-III style B/w*	4
				Subtotal	31
Total					146

* Types used to generate ceramic mean dates and ranges for Room 123W.

thirteenth century resulted in two smaller rooms; 123A is the northern room. Six strata were identified in Room 123A, including postoccupational layers, roof-fall, structured trash, and a floor complex (H-1-5/I-1-6). Room 123A had three identified features: two milling bins associated with the floor complex and the cobble-mortar wall that divided it from 123B. The room evidently functioned as a milling facility, and perhaps for corn storage as well. Ceramics from Room 123A were minimal, including only eight sherds, all belonging to the same bowl. This bowl, a Northern San Juan Animas Variety Transitional McElmo–Mesa Verde B/w vessel, was recovered from stratum C-1-4. When partly reconstructed, the sherds show an unusual banded design.

ROOM 123B

Room 123B is the southern part of the original 123W. Three strata were recorded in Room 123B: two postoccupational layers and a structured trash deposit. Excavation work ceased in the room early, and the lower levels were never excavated. Ceramics from Room 123B totaled 157, all from a single stratigraphic layer, B-1-2, described as a San Juan stratum. The typeable ceramics (Table 32.20) generated a ceramic mean date of 1169, a best range of 1134–1203, and a maximum range of 1099–1238. These dates indicate an Early-Late San Juan occupation.

Ceramic Trade Ware

From Room 123B, 17 ceramics (10.8% of the room assemblage) were identified as trade ware or were manufactured outside the Middle San Juan region. As shown in Figure 32.8, most of the trade ware from Room 123B is from the Cibola region. This is in direct contrast with the trade ware in this room from the earlier occupation, for which Chuska and Cibola trade ware was present in nearly equal amounts.

Approximately 52.9 percent (n = 9) of the nonlocal ceramics were Cibola White Ware and White Mountain Red Ware. The White Mountain Red Ware from the central New Mexico and Arizona region included St. John's Polychrome, as well as a number

Table 32.20. Ceramics from Room 123B stratigraphic units.

Stratum	Tradition	Variety	Ware	Ceramic Type	Total
B-1-2	Chuska	Trade ware	Gray	Newcomb Corrugated*	1
			White	Nava B/w*	1
	Cibola	Animas	White	Chaco-McElmo B/w*	4
				Escavada B/w*	2
				Pueblo II-III style B/w*	1
				Slipped white	1
		Trade ware	Red	Indeterminate White Mountain B/r	2
				Indeterminate White Mountain Red Ware	1
				St. Johns Polychrome*	3
			White	Gallup B/w*	1
				Pueblo II-III style B/w*	1
				Puerco B/w*	1
	Kayenta	Trade ware	Red	Indeterminate B/r	1
	Mogollon	Trade ware	Brown	Showlow Red*	1
				Woodruff Brown	2
				Woodruff Smudged	2
	Northern San Juan	Animas	Gray	Corrugated gray	4
				Indeterminate gray	3
				Plain gray	2
				Pueblo II corrugated	24
				Pueblo II-III corrugated	6
			White	Early McElmo B/w*	8
				Mancos B/w (Dogoszhi style)*	6
				Mancos B/w (Puerco style)*	1
				Mancos B/w (Reserve style)*	2
				Mancos B/w (Sosi style)*	3
				McElmo B/w*	22
				McElmo/Mesa Verde B/w*	8
				Mesa Verde B/w*	25
				Pueblo II-III style B/w*	6
				Pueblo III style B/w*	11
		Indeterminate	White	Pueblo II-III style B/w*	1
				Subtotal	157
Total					157

* Types used to generate ceramic mean dates and ranges for Room 123B.

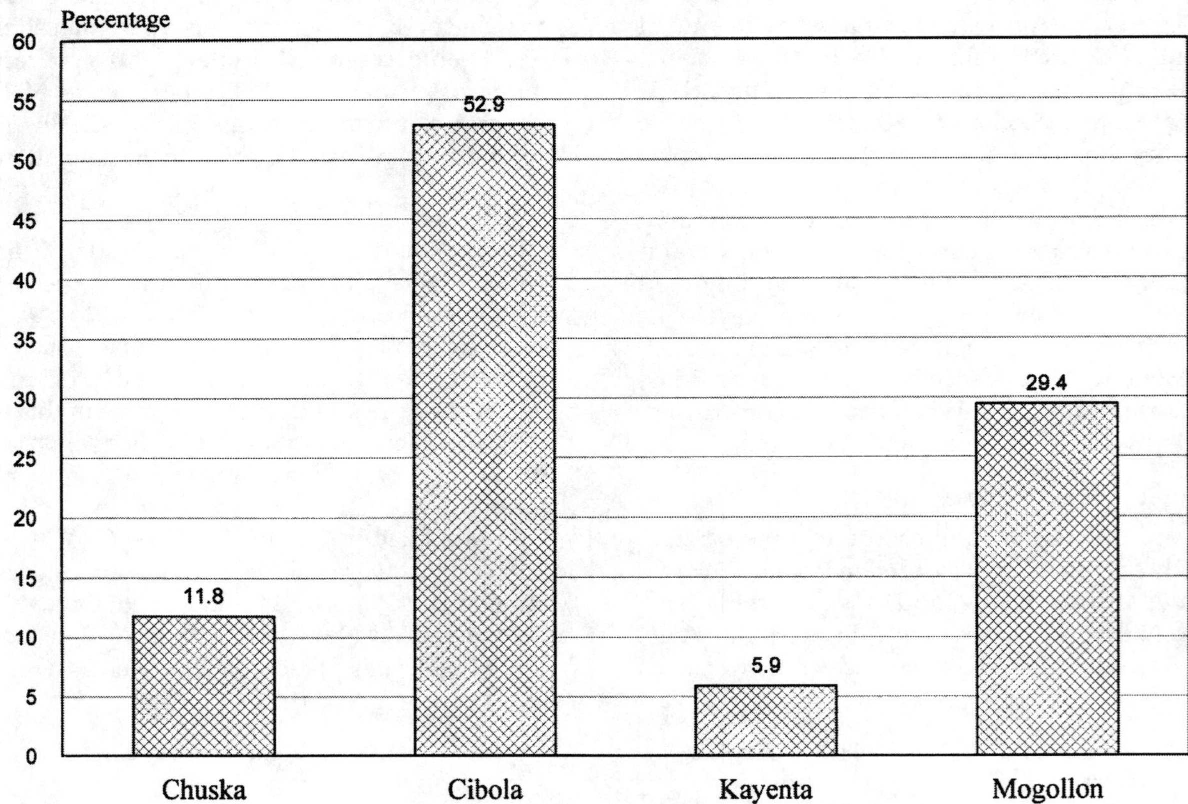

Figure 32.8. Distribution of trade ware ceramics from Room 123B.

of indeterminate b/r and plain red sherds. All of the White Mountain Red Ware sherds are from bowls. Identifiable Cibola White Ware types were a Puerco B/w bowl sherd and a Gallup B/w jar sherd.

The second most common trade wares during the Secondary occupation of Room 123B were northern Mogollon brown ware. Five sherds (29.4% of the trade ware) were Showlow Red, Woodruff Brown, and Woodruff Smudged. These sherds were all bowl fragments.

No vessel numbers or letters were assigned to trade ware from Room 123B. Nevertheless, two St. John's Polychrome sherds are from the same vessel, and the two Woodruff Smudged sherds refit.

Two sherds were from the Chuska Valley. One was a Newcomb corrugated jar rim and the other was a Nava B/w bowl body sherd. One sherd was from the Kayenta region, an indeterminate B/r bowl fragment.

In summary, the evolution of Room 123 suggests that during later times the trade focus moved away from Chuskan ceramics and toward Mogollon ceramics, although ties were not entirely severed with the Chuska region. It is interesting that Cibola ceramics remained relatively important throughout both time periods, although locally produced ceramics in the assemblage outweigh the number of imported ceramics by far. Curiously, there is still no Northern San Juan trade ware present in this room, even during the later occupation.

Locally Produced Ceramics

Animas Variety ceramics, considered locally produced at Salmon or in the Middle San Juan region, were identified based on the criteria discussed in Chapter 31. These ceramics totaled 139 from Room 123B. Both Cibola and Northern San Juan Animas Variety ceramics were present, but all nine Cibola Animas Variety ceramics were white ware types, whereas the 131 Northern San Juan Animas Variety ceramics included gray and white ware. No vessel numbers or letters were assigned to Animas Variety ceramics in Room 123B, and none were identified as reconstructible although several items refit or belong to the same vessel.

As shown in Table 32.20, Pueblo III ceramic types dominate the Animas Variety assemblage from this room, although some mixing with Pueblo II ceramic types is apparent. Mesa Verde B/w itself makes up only 25 percent of the white ware (n = 25), but McElmo B/w sherds are nearly as numerous, and late period ceramic types from other traditions are present as well.

Slip application, one of the attributes examined as a means of tracking Cibola influence, shows some variability in Room 123B among Cibola Animas Variety ceramics. Most of the ceramics, however, had washy or thin slips; 37.5 percent (n = 3) had the expected washy slip and 37.5 percent (n = 3) had a thin but not washy slip. A smaller group had slips more typical of Northern San Juan ceramics: 12.5 percent (n = 1) with a thick-chalky slip and 12.5 percent (n = 1) with a thick-crackly slip. Among Northern San Juan Animas Variety white ware, 3.3 percent (n = 3) have no slip, 85.9 percent (n = 79) have a thick-chalky slip, 5.4 percent (n = 5) have a thin slip, and 5.4 percent (n = 5) have a washy slip. This is another classic example of how Animas Variety ceramics exhibit mix-and-match technological attributes from ceramic traditions.

Northern San Juan Animas Variety white ware ceramics comprise bowls (n = 78), jars (n = 109), seed jars (n = 2), and ladles (n = 2). One seed jar sherd is Mancos B/w (Dogoszhi style) and the other is McElmo B/w. One ladle sherd is Mancos B/w (Dogoszhi style), and the other is not typeable.

Northern San Juan Animas Variety gray ware from Room 123B totaled 39 sherds, including corrugated and plain gray body sherds, indeterminate gray rim fillets, and rim fragments that could be classified as either Pueblo II or Pueblo II–III corrugated gray. As discussed in Chapter 31, Animas Variety gray ware has coarsely crushed igneous (augite diorite) temper with frequent inclusions of sand and shale. Sherd temper is less common than in the nonlocal Northern San Juan Gray Ware.

Cibola Animas Variety pottery in Room 123B was exclusively white ware (n = 8). It was identified by paste similarities with Northern San Juan Animas Variety ceramics, including high silt content and brown to yellow discoloration. Tempering material consisted of various combinations of sand, shale, and sherd. Vessel forms included bowls, jars, ladles, and ollas. Identifiable types were one Chaco-McElmo B/w (McElmo style) bowl sherd, two Chaco-McElmo B/w (McElmo style) jar sherds, one Escavada B/w jar sherd, one Escavada B/w ladle sherd, and one Chaco-McElmo B/w olla sherd.

Summary

The single stratum (B-1-2) from Room 123B contained 157 ceramics analyzed during the study. Based on the typeable ceramics the postoccupational strata dates to the Early-Late San Juan period, with a ceramic mean date of 1169 and a maximum range of 1099–1238. Trade ware included Chuska, Cibola, White Mountain Red Ware, Kayenta, and Mogollon ceramics. Local pottery included a number of Pueblo II ceramic types, but the number of McElmo and Mesa Verde ceramics kept the mean dates in the Early San Juan phase. The number of Mancos B/w, Gallup B/w, and Newcomb Corrugated sherds suggests a mixed assemblage.

ROOM 127W

Room 127W is part of the original Chacoan room suite that includes Rooms 124W, 123W, and possibly 128W, located in Salmon's southeast sector. Room 127W was evidently constructed as part of Salmon's initial construction episode around AD 1090. Later, the San Juan occupants added a small kiva (designated 127A) to the northern half of the room. Room 127W produced Chacoan floors with evidence of considerable Secondary intrusion for burial purposes. A later Secondary floor and an associated burned roof-fall stratum indicates use of the room for food preparation (milling), particularly on the second-story floor. After its initial destruction by fire during the San Juan occupation, the room was converted into a very small kiva with an extended southern ventilator shaft and recess. The kiva was finally destroyed by fire in the AD 1280s or 1290s.

Fifteen of the 46 strata identified in Room 127W were examined during the ceramic re-analysis (Table 32.21). In total, 2776 sherds were analyzed from Room 127W during the Salmon Research Initiative (Table 32.22). These ceramics were from roof-fall, various trash deposits, several hearths, a San Juan

Table 32.21. Room 127W stratigraphic units and ceramics analyzed.

Stratum	Description	Total
C-1-3	Trash deposit	119
F-1-4	Roof -fall deposit	1925
H-1-5	Floor deposit	558
I-1-6	Floor	79
C-3-7	Trash deposit	41
L-1-8	Burial	4
L-3-11.7	Hearth	3
L-4-12	Hearth	8
L-8-20	Burial	4
L-9-21	Hearth	3
L-10-22	Hearth	1
L-12-26	Burial	2
L-16-31	Hearth	1
I-3-32	Lower Chacoan floor	25
L-19-39	Ritual feature	1
Total		2774

Table 32.22. Ceramics from Room 127W stratigraphic units.

Stratum	Tradition	Variety	Ware	Ceramic Type	Total
C-1-3	Chuska	Trade ware	Gray	Blue Shale Corrugated*	2
			White	Chuska B/w*	1
	Cibola	Animas	White	Chaco-McElmo B/w*	2
				Gallup B/w*	1
				Red Mesa B/w*	1
		Trade ware	Red	Indeterminate White Mountain B/r	1
				Indeterminate White Mountain Red Ware	1
				Puerco B/r*	1
				St. Johns B/r*	1
				St. Johns Polychrome*	3
				Wingate Polychrome*	1
			White	Chaco-McElmo B/w*	1
				Gallup B/w*	2
	Northern San Juan	Animas	Gray	Corrugated gray	27
				Plain gray	3
				Pueblo II corrugated	27
				Pueblo II-III corrugated	1
			White	Mancos B/w (Sosi style)*	1
				McElmo B/w*	15
				Mesa Verde B/w*	21
				Pueblo II-III style B/w*	4
		Trade ware	White	Pueblo II-III style B/w*	2
				Subtotal	119
F-1-4	Chuska	Trade ware	Gray	Blue Shale Corrugated*	9
				Newcomb Corrugated*	3
				Plain gray	1
			White	Brimhall B/w*	1
				Painted B/w	1
				Pueblo II-III style B/w*	1
				Toadlena B/w (Puerco style)*	1
				Toadlena B/w (Sosi style)*	1
	Cibola	Animas	Gray	Corrugated gray	6
				Plain gray	6
				Polished gray	2
			White	Chaco-McElmo B/w*	8
				Escavada B/w*	3
				Gallup B/w*	1
				Pueblo II-III style B/w*	3
				Pueblo III style B/w*	1
				Red Mesa B/w*	2
				Reserve B/w*	3
				Slipped white	12
		Trade ware	Gray	Plain gray	4
				Polished gray	1
			Red	Indeterminate White Mountain B/r	2
				Indeterminate White Mountain Polychrome	1
				Indeterminate White Mountain Red Ware	3
				St. Johns B/r*	2
				St. Johns Polychrome*	1
				Wingate B/r*	1
			White	Chaco-McElmo B/w*	7
				Gallup B/w*	4
				Red Mesa B/w*	1
				Slipped white	2
	Kayenta	Trade ware	White	Pueblo II-III style B/w	1
	Mogollon	Trade ware	Brown	Showlow Corrugated Smudged*	1
				Showlow Smudged*	2
				Woodruff Smudged	2
	Northern San Juan	Animas	Gray	Corrugated gray	1442
				Indeterminate gray	1
				Plain gray	26
				Polished gray	3
				Pueblo II corrugated	118
				Pueblo II-III corrugated	16
			White	Early McElmo B/w*	3
				Mancos B/w (Black Mesa style)*	3

Table 32.22 (continued)

Stratum	Tradition	Variety	Ware	Ceramic Type	Total
				Mancos B/w (Dogoszhi style)*	2
				Mancos B/w (Puerco style)*	2
				Mancos B/w (Reserve style)*	2
				Mancos B/w (Sosi style)*	1
				McElmo B/w*	22
				Mesa Verde B/w*	57
				Pueblo I-II style B/w*	1
				Pueblo II-III style B/w*	48
				Pueblo III style B/w*	2
				Slipped white	76
				Subtotal	1925
H-1-5	Chuska	Trade ware	White	Toadlena B/w (Sosi style)*	1
	Northern San Juan	Animas	Gray	Corrugated gray	386
				Pueblo II corrugated	151
				Pueblo II-III corrugated	14
			White	Early McElmo B/w*	1
				McElmo B/w*	1
				McElmo/Mesa Verde B/w*	2
				Mesa Verde B/w*	1
				Slipped white	1
				Subtotal	558
I-1-6	Chuska	Trade ware	Gray	Blue Shale Corrugated*	1
	Cibola	Animas	White	Slipped white	2
		Trade ware	Red	St. Johns B/r*	1
	Northern San Juan	Animas	Gray	Corrugated gray	56
				Indeterminate gray	1
				Plain gray	6
			White	McElmo B/w*	6
				Mesa Verde B/w*	2
				Pueblo II-III style B/w*	3
				Slipped white	1
				Subtotal	79
C-3-7	Cibola	Animas	White	Gallup B/w*	1
		Trade ware	Red	Indeterminate White Mountain Red Ware	1
	Mogollon	Trade ware	Brown	Woodruff Smudged	1
	Northern San Juan	Animas	Gray	Corrugated gray	2
				Plain gray	16
				Pueblo II corrugated	9
			White	Mancos B/w (Sosi style)*	1
				McElmo B/w*	1
				McElmo/Mesa Verde B/w*	2
				Mesa Verde B/w*	2
				Pueblo II-III style B/w*	4
				Slipped white	1
				Subtotal	41
L-1-8	Cibola	Trade ware	Red	Indeterminate White Mountain Polychrome	1
	Northern San Juan	Animas	White	Mancos B/w (Dogoszhi style)*	1
				McElmo B/w*	1
				Pueblo II-III style B/w*	1
				Subtotal	4
L-3-11.7	Northern San Juan	Animas	White	McElmo B/w*	3
				Subtotal	3
L-4-12	Cibola	Trade ware	White	Chaco-McElmo B/w*	2
	Northern San Juan	Animas	White	McElmo B/w*	2
				Mesa Verde B/w*	4
				Subtotal	8
L-8-20	Cibola	Trade ware	White	Reserve B/w*	3
	Northern San Juan	Animas	Gray	Corrugated gray	1
				Subtotal	4
L-9-21	Northern San Juan	Animas	Gray	Pueblo II corrugated	3
				Subtotal	3
L-10-22	Northern San Juan	Animas	White	Mesa Verde B/w*	1
				Subtotal	1
L-12-26	Mogollon	Trade ware	Brown	Woodruff Brown	1
	Northern San Juan	Animas	Gray	Corrugated gray	1
				Subtotal	2

Table 32.22 (continued)

Stratum	Tradition	Variety	Ware	Ceramic Type	Total
L-16-31	Cibola	Trade ware	Red	St. Johns B/r*	1
				Subtotal	1
I-3-32	Cibola	Animas	White	Gallup B/w*	3
		Trade ware	Red	Wingate B/r*	1
			White	Gallup B/w*	1
	Northern San Juan	Animas	Gray	Corrugated gray	16
				Plain gray	1
			White	McElmo B/w*	2
				Pueblo II-III style B/w*	1
				Subtotal	25
L-19-39	Northern San Juan	Animas	White	McElmo B/w*	1
				Subtotal	1
Total					2774

*Types used to generate ceramic mean dates and ranges for Room 127W.

period floor, a Chacoan floor, a ritual feature, and three burials.

Ceramic Chronology

Of the 15 strata from Room 127W examined during the ceramic study, the highest-level stratum was C-1-3, a trash deposit containing 119 sherds. Trade ware included Chuska, Cibola, and Northern San Juan ceramics. The Chuska pottery included Blue Shale Corrugated and Chuska B/w, primarily late Pueblo II types. The nonlocal Cibola ceramics were Gallup B/w, a Pueblo II type, and Chaco-McElmo B/w, an early Pueblo III type. Also included in the Cibola series were the White Mountain Red Ware ceramics Puerco B/r, Wingate Polychrome, St. Johns B/r, and St. Johns Polychrome, primarily Pueblo III types. The local ceramics included a mix of Pueblo II and Pueblo III pottery, as shown in Table 32.22. The resulting ceramic mean date is 1173, the best range is 1137–1208, and the maximum ceramic range is 1101–1244, well within the Early-Late San Juan phase (Table 32.23).

The next stratum down (F-1-4), roof-fall deposit, contained 1925 ceramics which were completely analyzed. Trade ware included Chuska, Cibola, Kayenta, and Mogollon ceramics. All of the Chuska ceramics were late Pueblo II, including Blue Shale Corrugated and Brimhall, Newcomb, and Toadlena B/w. With the exception of Chaco-McElmo B/w, the Cibola trade ware sherds were the Pueblo II types Gallup and Red Mesa B/w. The White Mountain Red Ware ceramics, on the other hand, were predominantly Pueblo III types Wingate B/r, St. Johns B/r, and St. Johns Polychrome. Local ceramics included a number of Mancos B/w sherds, but the predominant types were McElmo and Mesa Verde B/w. The mixed, yet predominantly Pueblo III assemblage generated a ceramic mean date of 1148, a best range of 1111–1186, and a maximum ceramic range of 1074–1223, indicating an Early-Late San Juan phase occupation.

The highest-level floor deposit, H-1-5, also indicates an Early San Juan phase occupation. Although 558 sherds were present in the floor deposit, the ceramics were either locally produced or imported from the Chuska Valley. Chuska Valley sherds included only one Toadlena B/w. The remaining ceramics were all locally produced Northern San Juan types of predominantly Pueblo II corrugated or Pueblo II–III corrugated, which are not confidently dated at this time in the Middle San Juan region. The local white ware included a handful of Early McElmo, McElmo, McElmo–Mesa Verde, and Mesa Verde B/w. Thus, the ceramic mean was calculated at 1155, the best range at 1132–1177, and the maximum ceramic range at 1109–1200, largely within the Early San Juan phase.

The floor (I-1-6) immediately below H-1-5 contained an assemblage of 79 sherds that were completely analyzed during the study (Table 32.22). Typeable trade ware included Blue Shale Corrugated and St. Johns B/r. Typeable local ceramics are McElmo B/w and Mesa Verde B/w. Most are corrugated gray ware. This small assemblage of typeable sherds generated a ceramic mean date of 1155, a best range of 1115–1195, and a maximum ceramic range of 1075–1235 for the Early San Juan phase floor.

Below the floor was a trash deposit (C-3-7) containing 41 sherds analyzed during the study. Trade ware ceramics were confined to Cibola White Mountain Red Ware and Mogollon sherds, including indeterminate White Mountain Red Ware and Woodruff Smudged. All of the remaining sherds were local, including Gallup B/w, Mancos B/w (Sosi style),

Table 32.23. Room 127W ceramic mean dates and ranges by stratigraphic unit.

Stratum	Description	Ceramic Mean Date	Best Ceramic Range	Max Ceramic Range
C-1-3	Trash deposit	1173	1137-1208	1101-1244
F-1-4	Roof-fall deposit	1148	1111-1186	1074-1223
H-1-5	Floor deposit	1155	1132-1177	1109-1200
I-1-6	Floor	1155	1115-1195	1075-1235
C-3-7	Trash deposit	1141	1106-1176	1071-1211
L-1-8	Burial	1115	1077-1153	1039-1191
L-3-11.7	Hearth	1150	1113-1188	1076-1225
L-4-12	Hearth	1189	1161-1216	1133-1244
L-8-20	Burial	1125	1088-1163	1051-1200
L-9-21	Hearth	No date	No date	No date
L-10-22	Hearth	1240	1210-1270	1180-1300
L-12-26	Burial	No date	No date	No date
L-16-31	Hearth	1238	1206-1269	1174-1301
I-3-32	Lower Chacoan floor	1099	1065-1134	1031-1168
L-19-39	Ritual Feature	1150	1113-1188	1076-1225

McElmo B/w, McElmo–Mesa Verde B/w, and Mesa Verde B/w. As shown in Table 32.22, the majority of the pottery from the C-3-7 trash deposit was corrugated gray, plain gray, and Pueblo II corrugated. The mean ceramic date was 1141 and the best range was 1106–1176, falling within the Early San Juan phase.

Several burials were placed into trash in Room 127W, including L-1-8, L-8-20, and L-12-26 (Table 32.22). Several hearths and a ritual feature also had ceramics that were studied. Sherds associated with these features were few in number, producing questionable or low-confidence mean dates or no dates at all. L-1-8, a burial, included four sherds, an indeterminate White Mountain Red polychrome, local Mancos B/w (Dogoszhi style), local McElmo B/w, and local Pueblo II–III style B/w. The resulting ceramic mean date was 1115, the best range was 1077–1153, and the maximum ceramic range was 1039–1191, suggesting a Chacoan period or Early San Juan phase burial. L-3-11.7, a hearth, included three local McElmo B/w sherds, yielding a low confidence ceramic mean date of 1150, a best range of 1113–1188, and a maximum ceramic range of 1076–1225. L-4-12, a hearth, included eight sherds—two Cibola trade ware Chaco-McElmo B/w, two local McElmo B/w, and four local Mesa Verde B/w—all of which yielded a ceramic mean date of 1189, a best range of 1161–1216, and a maximum ceramic range of 1133–1244. These dates fall in the later half of the Early San Juan phase and the early decades of the Late San Juan phase. The burial in L-8-20 included four sherds, one local corrugated gray and three Cibola trade ware Reserve B/w ceramics, providing a mean ceramic date of 1125, a best range of 1088–1163, and a maximum ceramic range of 1051–1200, falling within the period of Chacoan occupation and also within the first half of the Early San Juan phase. The hearth in L-9-21 contained three local Pueblo II corrugated rim sherds, providing no ceramic date information. The hearth in L-10-22 contained one local Mesa Verde B/w sherd, yielding a low-confidence ceramic mean date of 1240, a best range of 1210–1270, and a maximum ceramic range of 1180–1300. L-12-26, a burial, contained one local corrugated gray sherd and one Woodruff Brown sherd, both of which provide no chronometric data for the burial feature. Finally, the L-16-31 hearth contained one St. Johns B/r sherd, providing a low-confidence ceramic mean date of 1238, a best range of 1206–1269, and a maximum ceramic range of 1174–1301.

The lower Chacoan floor (I-3-32) contained 25 sherds, of which the majority are local corrugated and plain gray. Trade ware included Wingate B/r and Cibola Gallup B/w. Local white ware included Gallup B/w, McElmo B/w, and Pueblo II–III style b/w. The resulting ceramic mean date for the floor was 1099, the best range was 1065–1134, and the maximum ceramic range was 1031–1168, including the period during the initial construction and occupation by Chacoan people and the Early San Juan phase occupation as well.

The ritual feature (L-19-39) below the Chacoan floor was also examined, yielding one local McElmo B/w sherd. The resulting ceramic mean date was

1150 and the best range was 1113–1188, within the Early San Juan phase occupation.

In summary, the occupation and trash deposits of Room 127W are primarily Early San Juan phase, although some of the trash deposits appear mixed with earlier Chacoan trash. The lower Chacoan floor and the burial (Feature 115, L-8-20) are the two features in Room 127W that clearly date or at least have a mean best range, of which the early portion falls within the Chacoan occupational period.

Ceramic Trade Ware

From Room 127W, 84 ceramics (3% of the room assemblage) were identified as trade ware or manufactured outside the Middle San Juan region. As shown in Figure 32.9, the majority of the trade ware (n = 51) from Room 127W had its origin in the Cibola region, suggesting Chacoan trade. Approximately 60.7 percent of the nonlocal ceramics were gray and white ware from the San Juan Basin. The gray ware ceramics are plain and polished gray sherds, but none were diagnostic types. White wares are mostly Chaco-McElmo B/w (n = 10) and Gallup B/w (n = 7), but a few others were identified, including Red Mesa and Reserve B/w. Most sherds are from bowls, except for five Gallup B/w jar sherds and four Chaco-McElmo B/w mug fragments. White Mountain Red Wares were also present in high quantities (n = 23) and include a number of indeterminate b/r, polychrome, and plain red sherds, as well as St. John's B/r and Polychrome and Wingate B/r and Polychrome. Four sherds come from jars; the rest are from bowls. Cibola tradition sherds come from strata C-1-3, C-3-7, F-1-4, I-1-6, I-3-32, L-16-31, L-1-8, L-4-12, and L-8-20, with the greatest concentration in F-1-4, the roof-fall deposit. No Cibola sherds were recovered from the San Juan occupation floor, but one Wingate B/r and one Gallup B/w sherd came from the Chacoan floor (stratum I-3-32). Some levels had as few as one Cibola sherd in them. One St. John's B/r sherd was associated with hearth L-16-31, and one indeterminate White Mountain Polychrome sherd was associated with burial L-1-8.

No vessel numbers or letters were assigned to the Cibola tradition sherds; however, several pieces that refit are present. These include two St. John's Polychrome sherds from stratum C-1-3, three reconstructed Reserve B/w sherds from L-8-20 (a burial), three Gallup B/w sherds from F-1-4, the four Chaco-McElmo B/w mug fragments in F-1-4 that are painted in McElmo style, two Chaco-McElmo B/w sherds in F-1-4 that are painted in Early McElmo style, and two reconstructed Chaco-McElmo B/w sherds in L-4-12 (a hearth).

Chuska tradition ceramics, from the Chuska Valley, include both gray and white ware. As shown in Figure 32.9, Chuskan ceramics make up 27.4 percent of the trade ware in Room 127W (n = 23) and were found in strata C-1-3, F-1-4, H-1-5, and I-1-6, with the greatest concentration in F-1-4, the Early San Juan roof-fall deposits. No vessel numbers or letters were assigned, as none of the sherds refit or no sherds belonging to the same vessel were identified. All gray ware, which came from jars, was identified as Blue Shale Corrugated (present in all three strata) or Newcomb Corrugated (found only in F-1-4). Identifiable Pueblo II white ware came from strata C-1-3 (Chuska B/w), F-1-4 (Brimhall B/w and Toadlena B/w in both Puerco and Sosi styles), and H-1-5 (Toadlena B/w, Sosi style), showing a weak preference for organic-painted vessels over mineral-painted vessels. No Pueblo III types were identified. One Toadlena B/w, Sosi style bowl body sherd and one Blue Shale Corrugated jar body sherd came from the San Juan floor and floor deposit strata.

Seven sherds (8.3%) are from the northern Mogollon region. All came from bowls, represented by Showlow Smudged, Showlow Corrugated Smudged, Woodruff Brown, and Woodruff Smudged. Woodruff Smudged was found in strata C-3-7 and F-1-4. Showlow Smudged and Showlow Corrugated Smudged were found in F-1-4, and Woodruff Brown was found in L-12-26 (a burial).

Only two sherds represent nonlocal Northern San Juan ceramics (2.4%). Both are from the same vessel, which could not be conclusively typed beyond Pueblo II–III b/w; they came from stratum C-1-3.

One sherd is from the Kayenta region (1.2%), an inconclusively typed Pueblo II–III style b/w sherd from stratum F-1-4.

The preponderance of Cibola and Chuska trade wares over any other kind of imported ceramic is expected for the Chacoan period, although it is somewhat surprising that Northern San Juan trade wares are not present in greater quantities. Trade wares that were included with San Juan occupation burials were restricted to Cibola and Mogollon ceramics. The only trade ware found on the later period floor was a Chuskan sherd identified as a Pueblo II type, while two Cibola sherds were found on the Chacoan floor. Most ceramics came from the roof-fall stratum, so it is not surprising that most of the trade wares also came from F-1-4.

Locally Produced Ceramics

Animas Variety ceramics, considered locally produced at Salmon or in the Middle San Juan region,

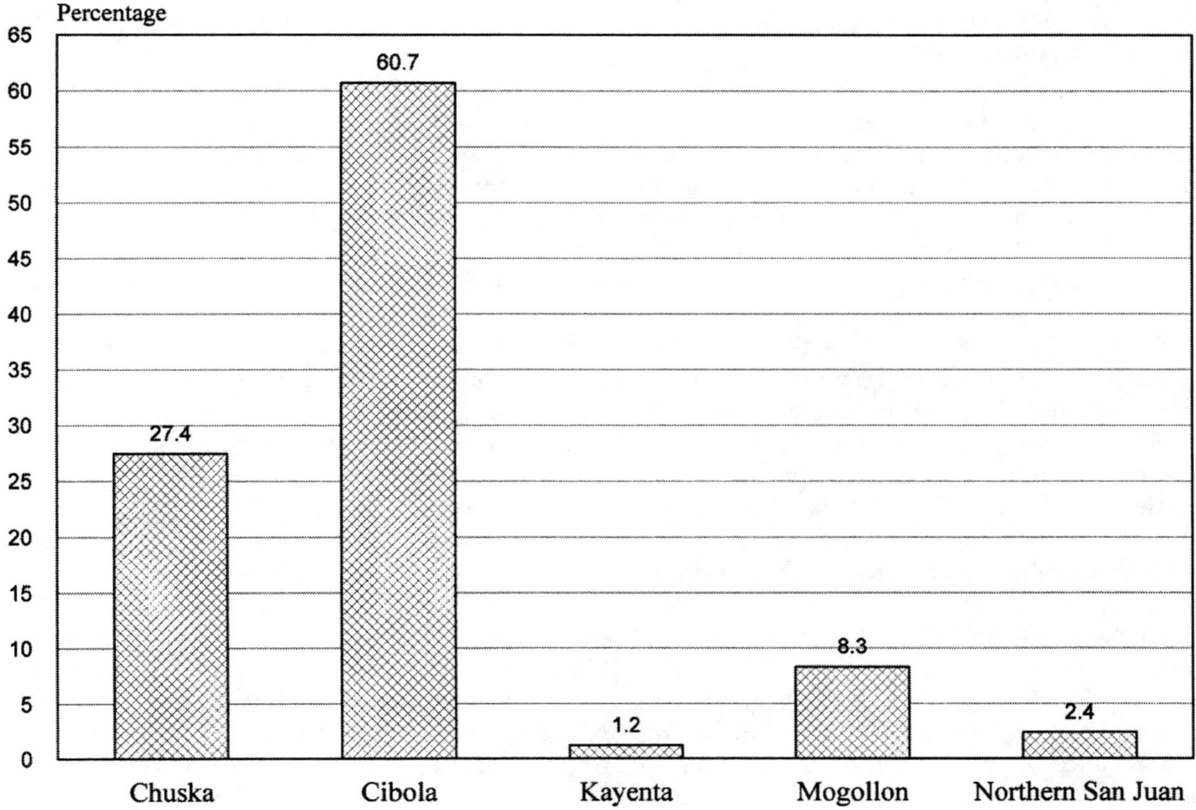

Figure 32.9. Distribution of trade ware ceramics from Room 127W.

were identified based on the criteria discussed in Chapter 31. These ceramics total 2692 from Room 127W (see Table 32.22). All stratigraphic units analyzed yielded Animas Variety ceramics of the Northern San Juan tradition, but only some had Animas Variety ceramics of the Cibola tradition. None of the burial levels contained Cibola Animas Variety ceramics, although some did contain Cibola trade ware ceramics, and all contained at least one Northern San Juan Animas Variety sherd. Northern San Juan Animas Variety ceramics totaled 2635 sherds, including white and gray ware. Cibola Animas Variety ceramics totaled 57, with both white and gray ware. No vessel numbers or letters were assigned, although a number of sherds are recorded as having refitting pieces or fragments that belong to the same vessel.

Identifiable types found on the upper floor (H-1-5) from the Northern San Juan Animas Variety include one Mesa Verde B/w, two Transitional McElmo–Mesa Verde B/w that refit, one McElmo B/w, and one Early McElmo B/w. The 386 corrugated gray sherds found in association represent several different vessels. Identifiable types found on the lower Chacoan floor (I-3-32) include three Cibola Animas Variety Gallup B/w sherds, as well as Northern San Juan Animas Variety McElmo B/w (n = 2) and 16 corrugated gray sherds that represent several different vessels. Pueblo III ceramic types are spread throughout the levels in the room, although there is no Mesa Verde B/w on the Chacoan floor. Mesa Verde B/w by itself (n = 88) makes up 12.8 percent of the Animas Variety white ware in this room.

Slip application, one of the attributes examined as a means of tracking Cibola influence, shows relative consistency in Room 127W among Cibola Animas Variety ceramics, with 39.5 percent (n = 17) having the expected washy slip, 32.6 percent (n = 14) with a thick-chalky slip, 9.3 percent (n = 4) with a thick-crackly slip, 2.3 percent (n = 1) with no slip, and 16.3 percent (n = 7) having a thin but not washy slip. Among Northern San Juan Animas Variety white ware, 3.6 percent (n = 11) have no slip, 87.6 percent (n = 269) have thick-chalky slips, 1 percent (n = 3) have thick-crackly slips, 7.2 percent (n = 22) have thin slips, and 0.7 percent (n = 2) have washy slips. When examined by stratigraphic unit, the distribution of washy slips on local Northern San Juan sherds is found only in stratum C-1-3, and non-washy slips on Cibola sherds are found mainly in F-1-4. Other strata contain Cibola white ware sherds, nearly all of which have washy slips.

Northern San Juan Animas Variety white ware ceramics included a number of different vessel forms, such as bowls (n = 250), jars (n = 52), two miniatures, one ladle, one mug, and one seed jar. Both fragments from miniatures are identified as McElmo B/w from stratum C-1-3. The ladle fragment could only be identified as Pueblo II–III b/w from stratum F-1-4. The mug fragment was McElmo B/w from stratum F-1-4. The seed jar fragment was McElmo B/w from stratum C-1-3. Burial L-1-8 contained a bowl fragment as well as two jar fragments, but hearths L-3-11.7, L-4-12, and L-10-22 and ritual feature L-19-39 contained only bowl fragments of this ceramic tradition and variety. The Chacoan floor, stratum I-3-32, also contained only bowl fragments, but the San Juan floor (I-1-6) contained both jar and bowl fragments.

Northern San Juan Animas Variety gray ware from Room 127W totaled 2328 sherds, including many observances of sherds that refit or belong to the same vessel. As discussed in Chapter 31, Animas Variety gray ware has coarsely crushed igneous (augite diorite) temper with frequent inclusions of sand and shale. Sherd temper is less common than in the nonlocal Northern San Juan Gray Ware.

Cibola Animas Variety white ware was identified by paste similarities with Northern San Juan Animas Variety ceramics, including high silt content and brown to yellow discoloration. Tempering material consisted of various combinations of sand, shale, and sherd. Vessel forms were limited to bowls (n = 14), jars (n = 27), and mugs (n = 2). The two mug sherds were both Chaco-McElmo B/w, painted in McElmo style; one came from stratum C-1-3 and the other from F-1-4. Other identified types included Reserve, Red Mesa, Gallup, and Escavada B/w. As shown in Table 32.22, only 3 of the 43 Cibola Animas Variety ceramics came from the Chacoan floor (I-3-32), even though many were Pueblo II types. They were recovered from strata C-1-3, C-3-7, F-1-4, and I-1-6 (the San Juan floor). Northern San Juan Animas Variety, however, was present throughout all the levels, including the burials.

Cibola Animas Variety gray ware from Room 127W totaled only 14 sherds, none of which were assigned to diagnostic types. All of the Cibola Animas Variety gray ware came from stratum F-1-4; it consists of corrugated, plain, and polished vessel fragments. Crushed sherd in temper was not always present, but sand, shale, sandstone, and various combinations thereof were typical tempers. Animas Variety gray ware identification relied especially on silt and discoloration characteristics because the tempering material was often so similar to Cibola Gray Ware from the San Juan Basin.

Patterns can be seen in the distribution of ceramic traditions, regardless of type. Chuska tradition trade wares were found only in strata C-1-3 (San Juan trash deposit), F-1-4 (mixed roof-fall deposit), H-1-5 (San Juan floor deposit), and I-1-6 (San Juan occupation floor). Cibola tradition trade ware was found alone in hearth L-16-31, as well as in burials L-1-8 and L-8-20 and hearth L-4-12. Cibola tradition trade wares were found in combination with Cibola Animas Variety ceramics in C-1-3, C-3-7 (a trash deposit that occurred between final use of the Chacoan floor and placement of burials beneath the San Juan floor), F-1-4, I-1-6, and I-3-32 (the Chacoan floor). Mogollon trade wares were found in C-3-7, F-1-4, and burial L-12-26. Kayenta trade wares were found only in stratum F-1-4. Northern San Juan trade ware was never found alone but was found in combination with Northern San Juan Animas Variety ceramics in stratum C-1-3. Northern San Juan Animas Variety ceramics were found in C-3-7, F-1-4, H-1-5, I-1-6, and I-3-32 and in burials L-12-26, L-1-8, and L-8-20 and hearth L-4-12. Northern San Juan Animas Variety ceramics were found alone in hearths L-3-11.7, L-9-21, and L-10-22 and ritual feature L-19-39. It is interesting that although Northern San Juan Animas Variety ceramics were present in every burial, often in combination with trade wares, Cibola Animas Variety was never included in a burial. It is also interesting that the ceramic traditions found on the two floors differ only in the addition of Chuska ceramics on the San Juan floor. Mogollon trade wares appear to have gained importance by the later periods of use in Room 127W.

Summary

Ceramic mean dates for Room 127W indicate usage during the Early and Late San Juan occupations, with mixed trash strata beneath. All of the burials and hearths are Early-Late San Juan, with the exception of L-1-8, which may represent a Chacoan interment, and L-10-22 which dates to the Late San Juan phase. Based on sherd data with few ceramic items to produce mean dates, however, some of the burial dates have a low confidence level. The lower level Chacoan floor, on the other hand, clearly dates to the Chacoan period, with a mean best range of 1064–1134. A wide variety of trade ware was present in Room 127W, including Chuska, Cibola, White

Mountain Red Ware, Northern San Juan, Kayenta (Tusayan), and Mogollon wares. Local ceramics included gray ware and white ware in a variety of Pueblo II and Pueblo III types.

CONCLUSION

The analysis of the ceramic sample for the Salmon study produced a database of 14,213 sherds from six rooms. Selection of the six rooms was made based on their potential for Chacoan trash and floor deposits. It was also useful to sort through the upper levels of the rooms and the mixed trash deposits as we explored the differences between local and nonlocal ceramic traditions. Each room had its own character regarding the trade ware ceramics contained in the assemblage and the distribution of local ceramic types comprising the Cibola or Northern San Juan traditions.

As an alternative to factor analysis for generating ceramic dates, we calculated mean ceramic dates, best ranges, and maximum ceramic ranges (see Chapter 30. These dates were an integral part of the analysis presented here. For each stratum examined during the study, a ceramic mean date, best range, and a maximum ceramic range was calculated based on the typeable ceramics identified from the stratum. In some of the mixed trash fill context in which the McElmo B/w or Mesa Verde B/w were known to be intrusive, experiments with excluding intrusive ceramic types from mean calculations generally changed the mean date and best range by only 10 years or so. In these circumstances, the universe of typeable sherds comprising the date calculation was generally over 100, providing a large number of ceramics with which to redistribute the weight of the mean after removing sherds from the calculation. One of the major difficulties involved having too few sherds to run the mean date calculations, such as occurred in Room 100W or 127W in the features at floor level. In those cases, the number of sherds and the limitations of the date, best range, and maximum ceramic range are indicated.

In some ways, the first phase of ceramic analysis for the Salmon Research Initiative reported here was a means of testing our analysis strategies on a sample of the ceramic artifacts from Salmon. In many cases we used revised manufacturing date ranges for some ceramic types (see L. Reed and Goff 2003) and a local type chronology that we developed for the Northern San Juan and Cibola ceramics to generate ceramic mean dates, best ranges, and maximum ceramic ranges for the room strata. One of the difficulties faced was the paucity of tree-ring dates or other absolute chronometric dates available for various time periods other than initial construction phases, significant rebuilding episodes, or repairs to roof materials. As a result, chronology and manufacturing date ranges for local ceramic types were more reliant upon their association with trade ware ceramics than wspecific absolute dated contexts. Although Franklin (1980a; Chapter 23, this volume) applied factor analysis to generate factor scores to stratify ceramic samples by occupational period, the factor analysis and ceramic mean date calculation results are not comparable without a great deal of ceramic data examination. It appears, however, that the ceramic mean date, best range, and maximum ceramic range technique and the ceramic chronology used to generate the dates worked well in the room and strata temporal examination study. The temporal data generated during this study also fit well with the general strata period and phase designations assigned during the original Salmon project. For the most part, all of the Chacoan floor fill, floors, and trash fill generated best ranges for which the first half or quarter of the range fell within the late decades of the 1100s, coinciding with the construction and early occupation of Salmon.

Trade ware for the Salmon assemblage had its origins from north, south, and west of the Middle San Juan region. From the north, 25 percent of the trade ware from the Salmon sample originated from the Northern San Juan region. Differentiation of these ceramics from the local Northern San Juan tradition was based on temper type, temper preparation, paste differences, and, in many cases, slip differences. White ware ceramic types from the region began with Cortez B/w (Kiatuthlanna style) and went through the entire sequence to Mesa Verde B/w. Gray ware types included Mancos and Dolores Corrugated. Red ware included Bluff B/w, Deadman's B/r, and a transitional Bluff/Deadmans example.

From the south, trade ware was identified as 26 percent White Mountain Red Ware, 19.5 percent Cibola, and 6 percent Mogollon. White Mountain Red Ware included primarily Pueblo III types, St. Johns Polychrome, St. Johns B/w, Wingate Polychrome, and Wingate B/r. Very few sherds of Puerco B/r, associated more with the late Pueblo II assemblage, were identified. Cibola white ware comprised most of the trade ware from the San Juan Basin and included the full range of ceramic types beginning with Kiatuthlanna B/w. Mogollon pottery included Showlow Red and Smudged, some Woodruff, and a small number of Tularosa Patterned Corrugated Smudged. Combined as a group, however, trade ware ceramics from the south were an important component of the Salmon assemblage and involvement in regional networks.

West to southwest trade included ceramics from the Chuska Valley, Kayenta region, and Little Colorado region. Chuska ceramics comprised 21 percent of the trade ware identified in the Salmon sample, most of which was gray ware. The white ware assemblage included predominantly organic-painted ceramics, even for the Pueblo II ceramics. Kayenta ceramics included red and white ware comprising just over 2 percent of the trade ware; two-thirds of the Kayenta pottery was Tusayan Red Ware. Less than 0.05 percent of the trade ware was identified as Little Colorado White Ware.

The distribution of trade ware was not equal among the Salmon rooms, but rather some rooms contained the full contingent of trade ware and some rooms lacked specific ceramic traditions. Rooms 30W, 100W, and 127W contained representative ceramics from all of the trade ware traditions. The two later San Juan rooms built above the Chacoan Room 30W lacked specific trade ware. Room 30A contained only Chuska, Cibola, and Northern San Juan ceramics, lacking Mogollon and Kayenta pottery. Room 30B, the storage room partner to 30A, contained Chuska, Cibola, and Northern San Juan, but did in contrast contain Kayenta Tusayan Red Ware. Thus, the size of the sherd assemblage may have influenced the types of ceramics identified in certain rooms, but clearly some of the smaller rooms and smaller assemblages (30A and 30B) contained significant amounts of trade ware.

One of the goals during the analysis was to bring clarity to the identification and classification of locally produced (Animas Variety) pottery at Salmon. With the temper, paste, and slip characteristics identified in contrast to the nonlocal Northern San Juan and Cibola pottery, the technological signature of the local ceramics became clear. Representative samples of local white and gray ware ceramics were present in all Salmon rooms. As discussed in Chapter 31, the full white and gray ware type sequence for Northern San Juan Animas Variety ceramics is present in the Salmon sample. For Cibola Animas Variety, however, gray ware is extremely rare, but the full white ware type sequence is present in a local form. All Salmon rooms except 123A have Cibola Animas Variety pottery. Of the combined locally made pottery identified in the Salmon sample (n = 12,893), less than 4 percent was identified as Cibola Animas Variety. Given the possibility of Chacoan families living at Salmon for a few generations and producing their own pottery, 480 sherds from six rooms does not constitute an assemblage large enough at this stage of the study to consider migration. It is maybe more likely that local Northern San Juan potters were emulating Chacoan pottery for specific purposes. Greater consideration of the data presented here and analysis from study of additional rooms may provide more data with which to address this specific research issue.

Chapter 33

TRENDS IN SALMON PUEBLO CERAMICS

By Lori Stephens Reed

The analysis of more than 14,000 sherds from six rooms at Salmon seems minor compared to the overwhelming number of ceramics excavated from the original work and the research undertaken at the site more than a quarter-century ago. Since that time, however, there have been significant changes to ceramic analysis and the technology used to obtain data from sherds and whole or reconstructible pots. Thus, the Salmon Research Initiative included a ceramic analysis of six rooms from which a sample was selected to explore several research issues. Foremost among these were identification of Chacoan contexts and refinement of the ceramic typology and chronology for each room. Identifying the production of local pottery and the unique signature of ceramics produced in the Middle San Juan region was a priority for the Salmon analysis, following research begun at the Tommy site.

MIDDLE SAN JUAN TYPOLOGY AND LOCAL PRODUCTION

One of the most important accomplishments of our reanalysis consisted of reevaluating local production at Salmon and in the Middle San Juan region and formulating a working typology. For most of the archaeological history of the Middle San Juan region, ceramics have been identified and classified using typologies developed in regions outside the Animas, San Juan, and La Plata River valleys (e.g., Franklin 1980a; Mills 1991; Morris 1924, 1928). Of course, given the crushed rock temper in the Middle San Juan ceramics, the local pottery does belong in the Northern San Juan tradition, but the variation in crushed diorite and clay resources used to produce the Middle San Juan ceramics contrasts with pottery from the north, so a geographically and resource distinct variety is justifiably appropriate. Thus, through research of ceramics at the Tommy site, Salmon, and Aztec, an Animas Variety of the Northern San Juan series was established.

A second minor local tradition was identified based on the use of local clay resources, the addition of sand, shale, or sherd temper, and the use of silty clay for slips. This minor local tradition was identified as the Animas Variety of the Cibola series. As discussed in Chapter 31, numerous sherds and whole vessels (initially from the Aztec Collection in New York) exhibited local paste characteristics, sand (with shale or sherd) temper, and washy to thick slips applied with clays of an extremely silty consistency. In the early analysis of the Tommy site, these ceramics were classified as Cibola from the San Juan Basin, but through time, it became clear that these ceramics were more similar to local Middle San Juan pottery. Also, the same washy, silty slips were noted on some Northern San Juan Animas Variety ceramics as well. Thus, analysis methodology and ceramic classification for the Middle San Juan had changed prior to the Salmon Research Initiative and the Aztec analyses to capture this variability and the possibility of local Cibola ceramic production.

The ceramic assemblage from Salmon was critical in recognizing and classifying the Animas Varieties, but data sets from other sites contributed as well. Data from Aztec were accumulated by means of three projects: one was an analysis of 55 whole pots curated at the American Museum of Natural History in New York City (L. Reed et al. 2005), the second was an analysis of 28,155 ceramics from several rooms at Aztec (Reed and Myers 2005), and the third was an analysis of 1934 sherds from several rooms at Aztec as part of the Salmon Research Initiative (these data will be published as part of the National Science Foundation grant phase).

Ceramic research at the Tommy site has been ongoing since 2000, and the data have been presented at several conferences (e.g., L. Reed 2004) and in one publication (L. Reed 2005a). Assemblages from the Salmon Research Initiative and the Tommy site have provided the baseline data from which both the Northern San Juan Animas Variety and the Cibola Animas Variety have been established.

Most of the assemblage from Salmon consists of local Northern San Juan Animas Variety ceramics (see Chapter 32). Of the local pottery identified in the Salmon sample (12,893 sherds), 96 percent was tempered with augite diorite, either as the only temper material or in combination with sand, shale, unidentified crushed rock, sherd, or another minor material. Only 4 percent of the local pottery was identified as Cibola Animas Variety, which does not apparently support the research hypothesis of Chacoan potters residing at Salmon. Another interpretation of these data would be emulation of Chacoan ceramics by local potters.

All of the rooms, except 123A, contained as few as 8 and as many as 196 Cibola Animas Variety sherds, but there were no clear concentrations of these ceramics, and none represented individual pots. Of course, these data are based on only six rooms, two of which are ceremonial (100W and 64W). Analysis of ceramics from additional household rooms is required to fully address the issue of Chacoan residence at Salmon and the identification of concentrations of Cibola Animas Variety ceramics in household contexts.

PHASE SEQUENCES AND CERAMIC DISTRIBUTIONS

Ceramic mean dates and ranges were calculated for each room and stratigraphic unit (see Chapter 32) to provide temporal control in the absence of absolute chronometric data. This method proved critical in evaluating each room stratum as a horizontal sequence of ceramic layers in which mean dates were quickly calculated and examined for obviously out of sequence strata. The ceramic mean ranges also provided a proxy for developing ceramic groups for each occupational phase recognized at Salmon. Data from Room 100 proved the most useful in developing ceramic groups for each phase due to the evidence for numerous Chaco period strata in the lowest depths of the room and the subsequent stratigraphy with ceramic assemblages fitting anticipated type frequencies based on temporal fall-off rates. For example, numerous strata in the lowest depths of Room 100 contained similar frequencies of ceramic types with no typeable intrusive types such as Mesa Verde B/w or Pueblo III White Mountain Red Wares. As described for each of the phases below, the percentage of temporally intrusive ceramic types and the percentage of fully developed McElmo B/w and Mesa Verde B/w in their respective phases of dominance were primary factors in isolating representative ceramic groups and out of sequence stratigraphic levels.

The distribution of white and red ware within each stratigraphic level of Room 100 was examined in detail to identify patterning in ceramic types among contiguous strata. As frequencies and percentages in white and red ware ceramics changed between contiguous strata, suggesting a temporal shift, these breaks in patterning were noted, and a new group of ceramic types was generated for that stratum along with the subsequent strata above. If the new pattern continued, it was classified as a new ceramic group. In all cases, the new ceramic groups contained significant shifts in the frequency and percentage of locally produced ceramics and trade ware. From the lowest levels to the highest deposits of Room 100, classification of four ceramic groups was accomplished. These groups include a Chaco period ceramic group, an Early San Juan ceramic group, a Transitional Early-Late San Juan ceramic group, and a Late San Juan phase ceramic group. Not all of the stratigraphic levels within Room 100, however, fit this ceramic group model. There were strata containing too few sherds to confidently evaluate placement or strata containing confusing ceramic distributions that could be interpreted as mixed deposits. Also, the absence of whole vessel data from the evaluation of floor assemblages during this treatment of the ceramic data hindered the ceramic group model to some extent.

Consistency in the percentage of McElmo and Mesa Verde B/w ceramics was the primary criteria for placing contiguous stratigraphic levels into one of the three ceramic groups. Lower level strata containing less than 35 percent McElmo B/w and McElmo style types (e.g., Nava B/w, Chaco-McElmo B/w) and significantly higher percentages of Pueblo II ceramic types (e.g., Mancos B/w, Gallup B/w, Escavada B/w) were identified as Chaco period contexts. Stratigraphic levels containing between 45 and 65 percent McElmo B/w and McElmo style types along with lower percentages of Pueblo II ceramic types were identified as Early San Juan phase contexts. Rooms 30W, 64W, 100W, and 127W had a small number of strata classified as Chaco/ Early San Juan due to possible mixing of deposits or assemblages with too few sherds to adequately evaluate the phase. An actual Early-Late San Juan phase assemblage was identified in Room 100 based on two strata (C-2-5.1 and C-2-5.3) having almost equal percentages of McElmo B/w (40%) and Mesa Verde B/w (35%). The legitimacy of this transitional phase will be tested further with future analysis at Salmon and Aztec. Room 127 (F-1-4 roof-fall, H-1-5 floor) contained an Early-Late San Juan assemblage as well. Finally, Late San Juan phase strata are identified by assemblages containing greater than 60 percent Mesa Verde B/w and Mesa Verde style types (e.g., Crumbled House B/w and locally produced Chaco-McElmo B/w with Mesa Verde style designs). The representative ceramic types and their distributions for each phase are presented below in the phase trend discussions.

As expected, most of the stratigraphic levels contained small numbers of ceramics determined as intrusive from earlier time periods, such as Piedra B/w, Kiatuthlanna B/w, Cortez B/w, and Red Mesa B/w. In most cases, these sherds occurred in Chacoan contexts (dating after AD 1090 at Salmon) and were represented by a single sherd or a single worked sherd possibly collected as a curated item. Given the propensity of potters to replicate earlier design styles on McElmo B/w, it is not unreasonable to speculate that these earlier sherds were collected to copy design motifs. In the same respect, some Early San Juan phase contexts contained small numbers of intrusive ceramics from the Late San Juan phase occupation that could have been moved down by various postdepositional processes. Finally, there were contexts for which the combination and distribution of ceramic types were of clearly mixed origin. For example, the ceramics on the floor of Room 30B clearly represent a Late San Juan phase assemblage with more than 60 percent Mesa Verde B/w, 16 percent McElmo B/w, and 16 percent Chaco-McElmo B/w. This distribution of ceramics correlates well with the original interpretation of the later addition of two second-story rooms above Room 30W. The roof-fall of Room 30B (F-1-3), however, shows a mixed assemblage of equal percentages of Mesa Verde and McElmo B/w, a small number of Chaco-McElmo B/w, and a small number of Pueblo II types. In contrast to the Late San Juan phase floor assemblage, the roof-fall suggests a Transitional Early-Late San Juan assemblage, but it may be more prudent to assume mixing of actual roof deposits with trash from an earlier context. Thus, both the stratigraphic level itself and the subsequent level must be taken into account as the ceramic group model is applied.

LATE PUEBLO II CERAMIC TRENDS

Because Salmon was built and occupied in the last decades of the 1000s, identifying Chaco period contexts in the six rooms selected for this study is more a matter of degree than kind. Or, in other words, the ceramic types present in Early San Juan phase contexts are many of the same ones present in the Chacoan contexts. The difference lies in the distribution of the types and what percentage McElmo B/w comprises the assemblage in question. By the last early decades of the 1100s, potters at Salmon and other sites in the Middle San Juan region were in, and probably through, a transition from Mancos B/w and its various design styles, to an early version of McElmo B/w, and into a fully developed version of what ceramic analysts call McElmo B/w. As interpreted from the results of this study, the frequency of Early McElmo B/w suggests that the type represented a short-lived transition between Mancos B/w and a fully developed McElmo B/w. It should be noted, however, that its presence in both Chacoan and Early San Juan contexts might be the result of continued variation in McElmo B/w. Its presence in Chacoan occupations at both Salmon and Aztec, however, suggests that it probably first represented a transition in design style, layout, rim thickening, and rim decoration changes. In Chacoan era contexts at Salmon, this early style of McElmo B/w represents almost 4 percent of the assemblage. At the same time that McElmo B/w was produced at Salmon during the Chacoan period, potters continued to produce Late Pueblo II types, such as the various styles of Mancos B/w and the local version of Cibola pottery, such as Gallup B/w and Escavada B/w, that was made in small numbers. As shown in Table 33.1, dominant ceramic types remain Dogoszhi, Chaco, and Sosi style ceramics of the Late Pueblo II period along with McElmo style ceramics that would indicate an Early Pueblo III time period. The distribution of these types, however, shows that Pueblo II types comprise an average of 51 percent, and the McElmo style ceramics comprise an average of 39 percent of the Chaco period strata. Intrusive ceramics are more commonly single fragments of Red Mesa B/w, Kiatuthlanna B/w, Newcomb B/w, or Cortez B/w, but even rarer in the Chaco period strata are intrusive fragments of Mesa Verde B/w.

Most of the rooms studied contained Chacoan floors and fill—including Room 30W, the bench above the floor in Room 64W (Tower Kiva), the Chacoan floor of Room 90W, the Chacoan floor of Room 123W, and the Chacoan floor of Room 127W. As already identified, Room 100W had the best stratigraphy of Chacoan period deposits, along with Room 30W, which has clear assemblages from the first-story floor, roof, and four subsequent trash levels. Based on the sherd data alone, Room 64W shows significant mixing in the lower levels, or in a more explanatory interpretation, the data show the long period of use the Tower Kiva represents at Salmon. Thus, the Early Bonito phase stratigraphy expected from its early construction at the site is obscured by the continual use. The trench on the kiva bench of Room 64W, however, does appear to date to the Early Bonito phase based on the ceramic

Table 33.1. Ceramic group for Chaco period contexts at Salmon.

Ceramic Tradition	Variety/Origin	Ceramic Types
Northern San Juan	Animas	Dominant: McElmo B/w, Mancos B/w (Sosi style), McElmo B/w (Early style), Mancos B/w (Dogoszhi style), Pueblo II corrugated, Pueblo II-III corrugated Minor: Mancos B/w (Mancos, Chaco, Puerco, Reserve, & Black Mesa styles),
Cibola	Animas	Dominant: Chaco-McElmo B/w (Early McElmo and McElmo styles), Chaco B/w, Gallup B/w, Escavada B/w Minor: Puerco B/w, Reserve B/w
Northern San Juan	Nonlocal	Dominant: McElmo B/w, Mancos B/w (Dogoszhi style) Minor: Mancos B/w (Mancos & Sosi styles), Early McElmo B/w, Mancos Corrugated
Cibola	Nonlocal	Dominant: Chaco-McElmo B/w (Early McElmo and McElmo styles), Chaco B/w, Gallup B/w, Escavada B/w Minor: Puerco B/w, Red Mesa B/w
Cibola: White Mtn. Red Ware	Nonlocal	Minor: Puerco B/r, Wingate B/r
Chuska	Nonlocal	Dominant: Chuska B/w, Nava B/w, Toadlena B/w (Sosi & Reserve styles), Newcomb B/w, Blue Shale Corrugated, Hunter Corrugated, Newcomb Corrugated
Kayenta	Nonlocal	Minor: Sosi B/w, Tusayan B/r, Medicine B/o,
Mogollon	Nonlocal	Minor: Showlow Red, Showlow Smudged, Woodruff Smudged

data. The single Chaco-McElmo B/w Animas Variety sherd on the floor of Room 64W does not provide much information concerning dating except for either the Chaco period or Early San Juan phase. Room 90W evidenced Early Bonito phase ceramics on the first-story floor (H-1-12), but immediately above the floor and a few questionable trash levels, the deposits sampled were clearly Late San Juan phase with more than 55 percent Mesa Verde B/w.

Room 100W contained the greatest number of Early Bonito phase strata (16 in the sample), beginning with two Chacoan floors (I-1-19.5 and I-3-36.5), their associated features, floor fill, and subsequent trash deposits (C-10-15 through C-13-18). All of these strata either lacked McElmo B/w and contained only Early McElmo B/w or contained anywhere between 5 and 28 percent McElmo B/w. As described in Chapter 31, Early McElmo B/w may have one or two of the McElmo style characteristics, but it does not entirely fit the type description and in most cases has attributes similar to Mancos B/w.

Room 123W had a small number of typeable ceramics on the Chacoan floor, indicating a Chaco period component. The stratum immediately below the floor designated a mixed trash layer contained one typeable McElmo B/w sherd representing either a Chaco period or Early San Juan phase stratum. Thus, the strata from Room 123W show the potential for more mixed deposits than clearly Chacoan occupation strata. The fill above the floor appears to represent Early San Juan phase deposits.

The Chacoan floor (I-3-32) in Room 127W dates to the Chacoan occupation based on a small number of typeable sherds. Strata above the floor, however, contain significantly greater numbers of McElmo B/w and Mesa Verde B/w, indicating later deposits into the Early and Late San Juan phases.

Rooms 30A, 30B, 123A, and 123B contained no evidence of Chacoan period strata. All of the ceramics from these three rooms, particularly the floors, were associated with Early and Late San Juan phase occupations.

As shown in Figure 33.1, the Chacoan assemblage from Salmon consists of 76.6 percent locally produced pottery, with roughly 9 percent of the trade ware originating from the Chaco Cibola region. One percent of the Cibola trade ware is White Mountain Red Ware from the Zuni region and farther west and south. The most notable pattern, however, is the low percentage of Chuska pottery imported into Salmon (4.8%); this pattern is not unusual for the Middle San Juan area. At the Tommy site, which spans a temporal period roughly from early Pueblo II to early Pueblo III, Chuska ceramics comprise only 14 percent of the assemblage. Compared to sites in Chaco Canyon (Toll 1991; Toll and McKenna 1997) and in other parts of the San Juan Basin (e.g., Mills et al. 1993; Toll et al. 2001), these percentages are extremely low and do not indicate the same type of trade and interaction relationships for the Middle San Juan that occurred for most of the San Juan Basin. Northern San Juan trade ware represents 3.8

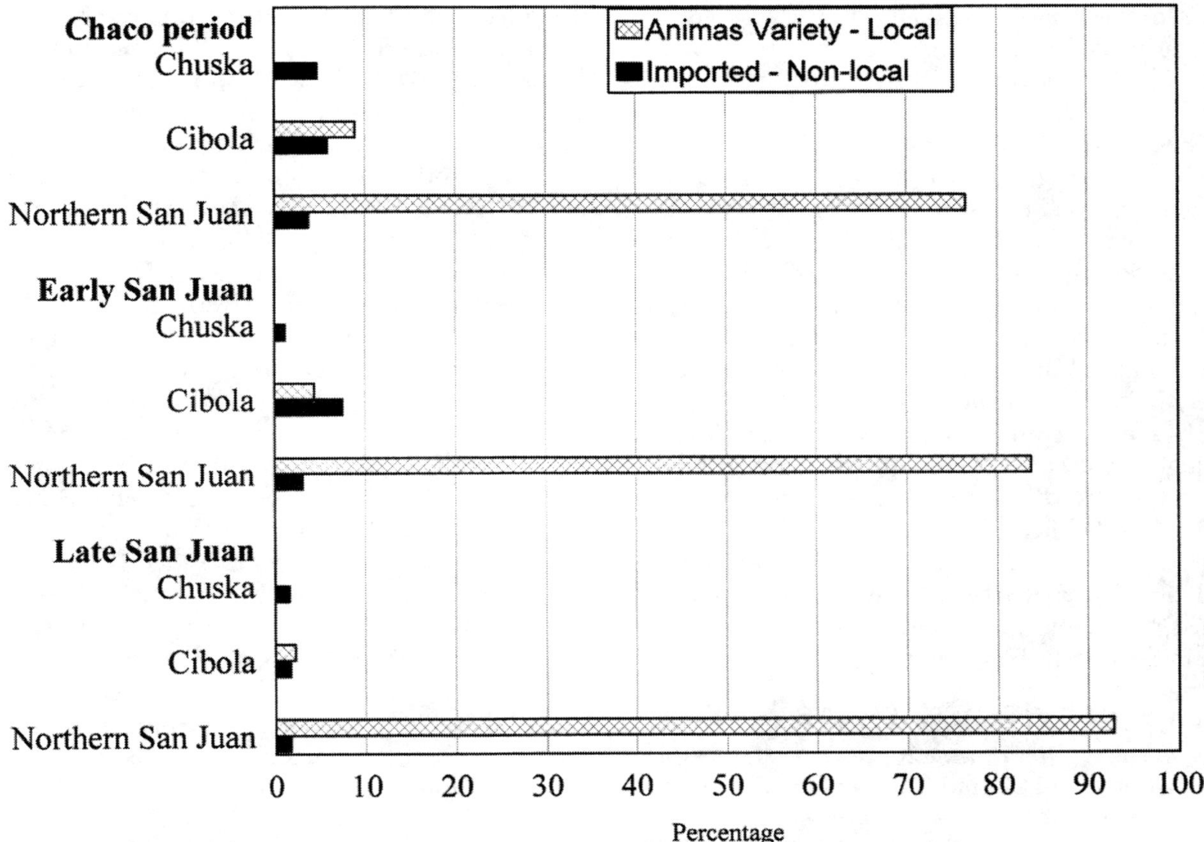

Figure 33.1. Distribution of ceramics at Salmon by variety and occupational period.

percent of the Chacoan period assemblage at Salmon, indicating trade relationships to the north but not as extensive as expected. Although not shown in Figure 33.1, percentages of less than 1 percent are represented by ceramics from the Kayenta and Mogollon regions.

The local Northern San Juan portion of the late Pueblo II assemblage includes the expected ceramic types. The majority (40%) of the typeable white ware ceramics was identified as Mancos B/w (Black Mesa, Dogoszhi, Mancos, Reserve, and Sosi styles); most are Sosi style. McElmo B/w also represents 40 percent of the combined Chaco period assemblage. Early McElmo B/w comprises a much smaller percentage of the overall assemblage than expected (6%, 16 sherds), but its origin and function may require further research. Gray ware includes Mancos Gray, Pueblo II corrugated, and Pueblo II–III corrugated. As mentioned in Chapter 32, the temporal significance of the corrugated rims from Salmon and other sites in the Middle San Juan requires more study. None of the corrugated rims examined from the six rooms were identified as Mesa Verde Pueblo III corrugated, but both Pueblo II and Pueblo II–III corrugated rims were present in all temporal contexts. Thus, my interpretation, at this point, is that rim eversion between 0 and 60 degrees may date between 1080 and the early 1200s, and Mesa Verde Pueblo III corrugated rim eversions greater than 60 degrees were likely not present in the Middle San Juan area until the late decades of the 1200s. More data and whole vessel assemblages are required to fully address this issue and to provide a more confident interpretation of the temporal trend. Mills's (1991) analysis of the Pueblo III occupation of the Box B site shows that Mesa Verde Pueblo III corrugated vessels with extremely everted rims were present in that assemblage, further suggesting a later 1200s transition to Mesa Verde style corrugated jars.

With the exception of Room 30W, Chaco-McElmo B/w (both locally produced and imported from the Chaco Cibola region) was monitored for design style variation. In Chaco period contexts, Chaco-McElmo B/w was consistently classified as either Early McElmo style or McElmo style correlating with the temporal placement of the overall assemblage. As indicated below for the Late San Juan phase, locally produced Chaco-McElmo B/w, although occurring in small numbers, eventually began to transition into Mesa Verde style designs.

In summary, the Chaco period strata at Salmon are characterized by a wide variety of ceramic types including a primary local tradition of Northern San Juan Animas Variety, a minor local tradition of Cibola Animas Variety, and trade ware from the Chuska, Mesa Verde (Northern San Juan), Chaco Cibola, Kayenta, Zuni (White Mountain Red Ware), and Mogollon (Showlow/Woodruff) regions. With the recognition of small numbers of intrusive ceramics from earlier and later time periods within Chaco period strata, ceramic mean dates and typological patterning in the data were employed to produce a ceramic group representing this time period in the Middle San Juan.

EARLY SAN JUAN PHASE CERAMIC TRENDS

The early San Juan phase represents occupation of Salmon between 1125 and 1200. Single-component early San Juan phase strata are present in Rooms 30W, 64W (Tower Kiva), 100W, 123W, and 127W. These strata include trash deposits, roof-fall, floor fill, floors, and burials. Based on the distribution of ceramic types and the calculation of ceramic mean dates to some extent, an Early San Juan ceramic group is presented in Table 33.2. Many of the same ceramic types are found in Early San Juan phase contexts at Salmon that are listed above for the Chacoan occupations. The difference is the distribution of these ceramics types and the shift in local production from what archaeologists see as type variability to stylistic variability within a single type—McElmo B/w. In contrast to the earlier Chacoan contexts, McElmo B/w and McElmo style ceramics in general (e.g., Nava B/w and Chaco-McElmo B/w) increase to 53 percent within the combined Early San Juan dataset. Pueblo II ceramic types, such as Mancos B/w (all styles), Gallup B/w, Escavada B/w, and Chuska B/w, among others, decrease to 21 percent. As discussed above, the possibility of a transitional type between Mancos B/w and McElmo B/w was classified as Early McElmo B/w or early style McElmo B/w during the analysis. The occurrence of the early style remains at roughly 4 percent in Early San Juan contexts just as it was represented in Late Bonito phase strata. Although most of the Early San Juan strata contained no evidence of Mesa Verde B/w or at the most one or two sherds, some strata designated Early San Juan, occurring just below Late San Juan phase floors, contained higher numbers of Mesa Verde B/w. Evaluation of ceramic distributions and context allowed for inclusion of most of these strata into the Early San Juan phase designation, while others were placed into a more ambiguous Early-Late San Juan strata designation. In most cases, my phase classifications fit well with the original Salmon period classes of Intermediate or Intermediate/Secondary; for others, I was able to clarify combined designations in the original study. Nevertheless, problems of postdepositional processes between strata of varying time periods and the basic numbers game in splitting hairs among individual strata based on distributions of ceramic types resulted in Mesa Verde B/w comprising 13 percent of the combined Early San Juan phase assemblage.

As for actual strata identified as Early San Juan phase, Room 30W contained a single stratum of room fill (G-1-3) above a probable Chacoan floor (I-1-5). Room 64W, the Tower Kiva, had two strata designated as Early San Juan phase. The vent shaft and tunnel (L-4-12) and the fill above the Chacoan floor (D-1-13) contained typeable ceramics identified as McElmo B/w and Chaco-McElmo B/w, along with other unclassified sherds and one Mesa Verde B/w from the vent shaft and tunnel. Room 100W included the best set of contiguous strata dating to the Early San Juan phase and was the model for the ceramic group. Early San Juan strata from Room 100W were trash fill deposits (C-1-4, C-2-5, C-3-6, C-7-12, C-8-13, and C-9-14) overlying Chacoan trash fill above the Chacoan floor. Room 123W has two strata fitting the Early San Juan group. Fill deposits (G-1-1) above the Chacoan floor contain 75 percent McElmo B/w, but the typeable assemblage is small. The second trash strata, C-2-8, is problematic due to its horizontal location below the Chacoan floor and, although it fits to ceramic group pattern for Early San Juan, C-2-8 is more likely a mixed deposit of trash. Finally, Room 127W contained one Early San Juan strata, I-1-6, a floor yielding a typeable assemblage of 67 percent McElmo B/w. The fill and roof-fall associated with the Early San Juan floor probably date to the proposed Transitional Early-Late San Juan phase based on the almost equal percentages of McElmo and Mesa Verde B/w and the small number of St. Johns Polychrome and St. Johns B/r ceramics.

Looking again at Figure 33.1, shifts in local production and exchange are evident from the Chacoan period to the Early San Juan occupation of Salmon. First, importation of Chuska ceramics decreases noticeably with the Early San Juan assemblage. The

Table 33.2. Ceramic group for Early San Juan phase contexts at Salmon.

Ceramic Tradition	Variety/Origin	Ceramic Types
Northern San Juan	Animas	Dominant: McElmo B/w, Mancos B/w (Sosi and Dogoszhi styles), McElmo B/w (Early style), Pueblo II corrugated, Pueblo II-III corrugated Minor: Mancos B/w (Mancos style), Mancos B/w (Puerco style), Mancos B/w (Reserve style), McElmo/Mesa Verde B/w
Cibola	Animas	Dominant: Chaco-McElmo B/w (McElmo style), Gallup B/w, Escavada B/w Minor: Puerco B/w, Reserve B/w, Chaco B/w
Northern San Juan	Nonlocal	Dominant: McElmo B/w Minor: McElmo B/w (Early style), Mancos B/w (Sosi, Dogoszhi, Reserve, Mancos styles), McElmo/Mesa Verde B/w, Mesa Verde B/w
Cibola	Nonlocal	Dominant: Chaco-McElmo B/w (McElmo & Early styles), Gallup B/w, Escavada B/w Minor: Chaco B/w, Reserve B/w, Puerco B/w
Cibola: White Mtn. Red Ware	Nonlocal	Minor: Wingate B/r, Wingate Polychrome, St. Johns Polychrome, Puerco B/r
Chuska	Nonlocal	Minor: Chuska B/w, Nava B/w, Blue Shale Corrugated, Newcomb Corrugated, Brimhall B/w, Toadlena B/w (Sosi, Puerco & Black33.1. erco styles)
Kayenta	Nonlocal	Minor: Dogoszhi B/w, Flagstaff B/w, Cameron Polychrome, Citadel Polychrome
Mogollon	Nonlocal	Minor: Showlow Smudged, Showlow Red, Showlow Corrugated Smudged, Tularosa Patterned Corrugated (smudged interior), Woodruff Brown, Woodruff Smudged

percentage of Chuska pottery decreases from almost 5 percent to just over 1 percent by the middle 1100s. This decrease is most noticeable in frequency of the gray ware, but the number of Chuska B/w and Nava B/w remains relatively consistent. The continued decrease of imported trade ware coincided with the general Pueblo III trend of localization and the collapse of regional trade networks associated with the Chacoan system. Smaller numbers of Pueblo II Chuska White Ware present in the Early San Juan assemblage include Brimhall, Taylor, and Toadlena Black-on-whites. Only a handful of Chuska Gray Ware sherds were identified, all of which include Newcomb and Blue Shale Corrugated.

Cibola trade ware increases to 13 percent in the Early San Juan phase from its maximum of 6 percent in the late Pueblo II Chacoan contexts. Although unexpected given the breakdown of the Chacoan system by the late 1000s, this increase is deceiving given the inclusion of White Mountain Red Ware with the Cibola tradition. Nine percent of the Cibola trade ware during the Early San Juan phase is due to a greater number of White Mountain Red Ware coming into Salmon from the Zuni region and areas farther south and west. Only 4 percent of the Cibola ceramics are actually trade ware from the Chaco Cibola region, indicating a slight decrease from the 6 percent of the preceding Chacoan period at Salmon. Chaco-McElmo B/w is the most common type, followed by Gallup and Escavada B/w. St. Johns B/r and Wingate B/r are the most common White Mountain Red Ware types, followed by only a small number of St. Johns and Wingate Polychromes and Puerco B/r. The trend by the Early San Juan phase is a clear dropoff in Chaco Cibola ceramics and a noted increase in trade ware from the White Mountain Red Ware producing region.

The distribution of Northern San Juan trade ware remains relatively stable from the Chaco period through the Early San Juan phase, as shown in Figure 33.1. As expected, almost 75 percent of the white ware imported from the north was McElmo B/w. The remaining ceramics include various styles of Mancos B/w (see Table 33.2). Gray ware ceramics include only a handful of corrugated body sherds and a Mancos gray rim. Although the nonlocal Northern San Juan assemblage is small, it is clearly diverse, reflecting the range of types available through trade to the Salmon residents.

Similar to the Chacoan occupation, trade wares from the Kayenta and Mogollon regions were present as well. Although not shown in Figure 33.1, pottery from the Kayenta region comprises just less than 1 percent, and from the Mogollon region 1.5 percent of the Early San Juan assemblage.

Most of the ceramics in the six-room Salmon assemblage from Early San Juan phase contexts are local Northern San Juan Animas Variety. The local pottery includes gray and white ware, of which the gray ware comprises 70 percent (n = 2762) of the assemblage. Typeable gray ware rims include Pueblo II corrugated and Pueblo II–III corrugated. McElmo B/w dominates the local igneous-tempered white ware at 42 percent but varies within individual strata from 35 to 75 percent. Other white ware types, such as Mancos B/w and its various styles are present but comprise no more than 4 percent in any given type category. The primary trend in the local ceramics during the Early San Juan phase is the dominance of McElmo B/w.

The local Cibola Animas Variety ceramics show a decrease in frequency in the Early San Juan phase. Local sand-tempered gray ware—uncommon in all temporal phases at Salmon—is represented in the early San Juan contexts by seven corrugated sherds from Rooms 64W and 127W. The local white ware includes all of the Pueblo II types, but most of the local Cibola ceramics are Chaco-McElmo B/w (53% of the local Cibola white ware). As recorded in the comments for the analysis, most of the Chaco-McElmo B/w sherds have either Early McElmo or McElmo style designs. Only 7 of the 55 Chaco-McElmo sherds exhibit Mesa Verde style designs, correlating with the presence of local Mesa Verde B/w in some of the Early San Juan phase contexts.

In summary, the Early San Juan phase contexts yielded ceramics dating primarily to the early Pueblo III period. The assemblage is dominated by McElmo style ceramics, such as local McElmo B/w, Northern San Juan McElmo B/w, and Chaco-McElmo B/w, both local Animas Variety and Cibola traditions. Numerous Pueblo II ceramics are present, but they are clearly part of the general decrease expected for earlier ceramic types. Trade ware continued to decrease from the Chaco period, but shifts in red ware imports were solidly in place by the Early San Juan phase, with greater numbers of ceramics coming in from the White Mountain Red Ware production area to the south.

EARLY-LATE SAN JUAN PHASE CERAMIC TRENDS

A small number of strata were classified temporally as Early-Late San Juan phase due primarily to ceramic assemblages having equal numbers of McElmo and Mesa Verde B/w, suggesting that these contexts might be transitional. Due to the tentative definition of this transitional phase, the small number of strata representing the proposed phase, and the need for further testing of its legitimacy and existence, data are not provided in Figure 33.1 and a formal ceramic group is not presented. Early-Late San Juan phase strata were identified in Rooms 100W and 127W. These strata include trash deposits, roof-fall, and a floor.

In Room 100W, two strata of trash deposits (C-2-5.1 and C-2-5.3) were identified as transitional Early-Late San Juan based on the presence of 65 percent Early San Juan phase and 35 percent Late San Juan phase pottery in C-2-5.1 and 59 percent Early San Juan phase pottery and 41 percent Late San Juan phase pottery in C-2-5.3. As indicated, most of this distinction is based on percentages of McElmo and Mesa Verde B/w, but the presence of Nava B/w, early styles of Chaco-McElmo B/w, and Early McElmo B/w contributes to the overall percentage of Early San Juan pottery. Similarly, percentages of St. Johns and Wingate Polychromes contribute to the overall percentage of Late San Juan pottery. It should be noted, however, that these two strata occur in the upper levels of Room 100W, but the two terminal trash strata (C-1-4 and C-2-5) just above these two possible transitional phase strata have Early San Juan assemblages.

Three strata in Room 127W, including a contiguous sequence of floor, roof-fall, and trash deposit strata (H-1-5, F-1-4, and C-1-3), were classed as transitional Early-Late San Juan. The floor stratum (H-1-5) contained a small assemblage of typeable sherds, but the concentration of transitional McElmo–Mesa Verde B/w, McElmo B/w, and Mesa Verde B/w suggests potential for a temporally transitional provenience. Also, the roof-fall (F-1-4) contained 32 percent Early San Juan pottery and 45 percent Late San Juan pottery, along with various Pueblo II types that probably represent intrusive sherds. Trash deposits above the roof-fall (C-1-3) contained 37 percent Early San Juan pottery and 51 percent Late San Juan pottery, along with a handful of earlier Pueblo II sherds probably representing intrusive fragments.

Although not shown in Figure 33.1, the percentages of ceramic traditions represented in the assemblage are within the range of variation shown for the Early and Late San Juan phases. Chuskan pottery in the transitional assemblage is almost 1 percent, including Blue Shale Corrugated, Newcomb Corrugated, Nava B/w, and a few Chuska and Toadlena B/w as intrusive Pueblo II sherds. Blue Shale Corrugated is the most abundant Chuska type correlating with the local production trend at Salmon of Pueblo II style corrugated ceramics extending into the late Pueblo III period. The lack of Crumbled House B/w in the Chuska assemblage might be due to small sample size for contexts dating to this probably short-lived transitional phase.

Cibola trade ware also decreased from the earlier periods to roughly 2 percent, following a downward trend. White Mountain Red Ware from the Zuni and east-central Arizona areas represents 67 percent of the Cibola trade ware, continuing the overall decrease in ceramics from the Chaco Cibola region. The full range of red ware types is present, including Puerco B/r, Wingate B/r, Wingate Polychrome, St. Johns B/r, and St. Johns Polychrome—these two polychrome types represent most of the red ware.

Kayenta and Mogollon ceramics combined comprise less than 1 percent of the transitional assemblage. Unlike the earlier phase assemblages, only one unidentified Pueblo II–III style B/w Kayenta sherd was identified. Although smaller in number, the Mogollon ceramics retain the same distribution of types with Showlow Smudged, Showlow Corrugated, Woodruff Smudged, and Tularosa Patterned Corrugated (smudged).

Nonlocal Northern San Juan ceramics represent less than 1 percent of the transitional assemblage as well. McElmo B/w and Mesa Verde B/w are the dominant types imported from the north, along with Dolores Corrugated and Early McElmo B/w.

A continued increase in locally produced ceramics is the most notable trend in the transitional Early-Late San Juan phase assemblage. The Animas Variety of Northern San Juan pottery comprises 94 percent of the typeable ceramics. Cibola Animas Variety ceramics, however, decrease to roughly 2 percent of the assemblage, continuing the overall trend of decreasing production of local sand and sand/sherd-tempered pottery with predominantly washy slips. Locally produced corrugated gray ware shows a continued absence of rim and neck profiles with greater than 60° eversion, typical of Mesa Verde style corrugated pottery of the Northern San Juan region. The absence of Pueblo III Mesa Verde style corrugated in contexts extending into the early 1200s suggests that production of Mesa Verde style corrugated jars may have been a later 1200s occurrence at sites in the Middle San Juan area. Animas Variety McElmo B/w and Mesa Verde B/w dominate the transitional assemblage in almost equal numbers, and the remaining white ware includes only a handful of Early McElmo B/w and Pueblo II ceramics.

Chaco-McElmo B/w dominates the Cibola Animas Variety sherds at 34 percent, with both McElmo and Mesa Verde styles represented. The remaining ceramics were either untypeable or Pueblo II types probably representing intrusive sherds. Although produced in small numbers, the occurrence of locally made Chaco-McElmo B/w into the 1200s with Mesa Verde style designs is noteworthy at Salmon.

In summary, the various strata identified as transitional Early-Late San Juan phase appear to correlate well with an expected assemblage configuration for the late 1100s and early 1200s. McElmo and Mesa Verde B/w ceramics dominate the assemblages from these contexts and White Mountain Red Ware shows increased frequency. Trade ware from the Chuska Valley and most of the other regions decreased, correlating with the shift in trade networks commensurate with the reorganization of the Chacoan system and a more localized social and economic network.

LATE SAN JUAN PHASE CERAMIC TRENDS

From the six rooms analyzed during the Salmon Research Initiative, the main focus was to identify rooms with Chacoan period occupation strata. The upper levels and second-story occupations of most of the rooms, however, had Late San Juan phase strata and occupations, providing a significant amount of data to examine late Pueblo III trends at Salmon. As discussed earlier, the criteria for recognizing a Late San Juan ceramic group (Table 33.3) were based on the dominance of Mesa Verde B/w ceramics, lower numbers of McElmo B/w ceramics, and greater numbers of White Mountain Red Ware. Rooms 30A, 30B, 30W, 90W, 100W, and 127W contained strata dating to the Late San Juan phase.

Rooms 30A and 30B are smaller second-story rooms built over the larger Chacoan period Room 30W. Both of these rooms date to the Late San Juan phase with assemblages dominated by Mesa Verde B/w. The floor (H-1-4), roof-fall (F-1-3), and post-occupational fill (B-1-2) of Room 30A all contained more than 45 percent Mesa Verde B/w in the typeable ceramic assemblage. The floor fill (G-1-4) and roof-fall (F-1-3) of Room 30B contained almost the same distribution of Mesa Verde B/w as Room 30A, indicating the rooms were contemporaneously occupied. The floor stratum of Room 30B, in particular, contained 67 percent Mesa Verde B/w from the typeable assemblage.

One stratum from Room 30W, the final occupational roof-fall (F-1-2), was classed as Late San Juan phase based on the presence of 46 percent Mesa Verde B/w. This temporal designation might be problematic based on the room fill (G-1-3) stratum below designated as Early San Juan phase, but the high number of Mesa Verde B/w ceramics on the roof may be an indication of later use. Nevertheless, a Late San Juan phase designation based on the ceramic group model correlates with the original interpretation of the roof-fall as Secondary occupation.

Four strata from Room 90W were designated as Late San Juan phase, including roof-fall (F-2-9) above

Table 33.3. Ceramic group for Late San Juan phase contexts at Salmon.

Ceramic Tradition	Variety/Origin	Ceramic Types
Northern San Juan	Animas	Dominant: Mesa Verde B/w, McElmo B/w, McElmo/Mesa Verde B/w, Pueblo II corrugated, Pueblo II-III corrugated
Cibola	Animas	Dominant: Chaco-McElmo B/w (all styles) Minor: Gallup B/w, Escavada B/w, Reserve B/w
Northern San Juan	Nonlocal	Dominant: McElmo B/w Minor: McElmo B/w (Early style), Mancos B/w (Sosi, Dogoszhi, Reserve, Mancos styles), McElmo/Mesa Verde B/w, Mesa Verde B/w
Cibola		Minor: Chaco-McElmo B/w (all styles), Gallup B/w, Chaco B/w, Escavada B/w, Reserve B/w
Cibola: White Mtn. Red Ware	Nonlocal	Minor: St. Johns Polychrome, St. Johns B/r, Wingate B/r, Wingate Polychrome, Puerco B/r
Chuska	Nonlocal	Minor: Crumbled House B/w, Blue Shale Corrugated, Nava B/w
Kayenta	Nonlocal	Minor: Sosi B/w, Cameron Polychrome, Citadel Polychrome
Little Colorado	Nonlocal	Minor: Padre B/w
Mogollon	Nonlocal	Minor: Showlow Smudged, Showlow Red, Woodruff Brown, Woodruff Red

the Chacoan floor fill and trash deposits, trash fill strata above the roof (C-1-6 and C-2-7), and the post-occupational fill (B-3-4). Ceramic mean date and range calculations clearly indicate that these strata date into the AD 1200s. The roof-fall stratum contained a relatively large sample of 92 typeable ceramics, including 54 percent Mesa Verde B/w and 16 percent additional Pueblo III types (St. Johns B/r, St. Johns Polychrome, Wingate B/r, Wingate Polychrome, Animas Variety Chaco-McElmo B/w, and Animas Variety McElmo B/w). Both trash fill strata contain between 16 and 28 percent probable intrusive sherds from earlier Chacoan and Early San Juan phase deposits or, in other words, Pueblo II ceramic types. Most ceramics from the stratum C-2-7, however, are late Pueblo III sherds representing 72 percent of the typeable assemblage, including Mesa Verde B/w, Crumbled House B/w, McElmo B/w, Nava B/w, Padre B/w, St. Johns B/r, St. Johns Polychrome, and Wingate Polychrome. Stratum C-1-6 contained 63 percent Mesa Verde B/w and Crumbled House B/w, along with McElmo B/w and Padre B/w. Finally, the postoccupational fill from Room 90W contained a small typeable assemblage of one Mesa Verde B/w and two St. Johns Polychrome sherds.

The terminal roof-fall stratum from Room 100W was classed as Late San Juan phase based on 52 percent of the typeable assemblage identified as Mesa Verde B/w, McElmo–Mesa Verde B/w, St. Johns B/r, St. Johns Polychrome, and Animas Variety Chaco-McElmo B/w (Mesa Verde style). McElmo B/w comprises 24 percent of the typeable assemblage, along with a small number of Nava B/w and Animas Variety Chaco-McElmo B/w (McElmo style) sherds. As expected, just over 12 percent of the typeable ceramics are Pueblo II types that are probably intrusive.

All of the Late San Juan phase proveniences identified from Room 127W are hearths. Three hearths (L-4-12, L-10-22, and L-16-31) were classed as Late San Juan based on the small number of sherds associated with their remains. Hearth L-4-12 contained eight associated sherds, including two nonlocal Chaco-McElmo B/w, two local McElmo B/w, and four local Mesa Verde B/w. Hearth L-10-22 was associated with an Animas Variety Mesa Verde B/w sherd. Hearth L-16-21 was associated with a single St. Johns Polychrome fragment.

Examination of the combined Late San Juan gray ware assemblage shows a continued trend toward local production of jars with rim and neck eversion of less than 60°. All of the gray ware rim fragments were typed as either Pueblo II or Pueblo II–III corrugated. This trend at Salmon stands in contrast to the assemblage from the Box B site (Mills 1991) from which the Pueblo III component yielded significant numbers of gray ware jars identified as locally made Mesa Verde Corrugated with rim eversion greater than 60°. The absence of Mesa Verde style corrugated jars in the Salmon rooms examined during this study is intriguing and may provide some indication of cultural ties, pottery tradition heritage, and variability in exchange patterns at individual site levels in the Middle San Juan. At the time of the Box B analysis, many of the temper and paste nuances that were used during the current Salmon study were not yet realized. Thus, many of the Mesa Verde Corrugated jars from Box B could be imported from the Northern San Juan (Mesa Verde) region. A detailed binocular temper and paste study, along with petrographic and geochemical analyses, would be beneficial given the new data generated from Salmon, Aztec, and the Tommy site.

Trade ware from the Late San Juan phase assemblage shows a decrease, continuing the decline from the Chacoan period during which imported ceramics were the most abundant. As shown in Figure 33.1, all trade ware traditions decrease significantly. The percentage of Chuskan trade ware appears to remain roughly the same, but approximately half of the Chuskan ceramics identified in Late San Juan contexts are intrusive Pueblo II types. Thus, there was a decrease in ceramic trade from the Chuska Valley sites. Crumbled House B/w and Nava B/w continue to occur in Late San Juan phase contexts, but the percentage is smaller than Chuskan ceramics from earlier time periods. Given the trend toward continued production of Pueblo II and Pueblo II–III style corrugated jars at Chuska Valley sites (Reed and Goff 2003), the presence of Blue Shale Corrugated in Late San Juan phase contexts must be assumed as a temporally appropriate association. Although the presence of Chuskan pottery in the Middle San Juan does not appear to have reached nearly the levels of that at Chaco Canyon or other San Juan Basin sites, the trend toward decreased Chuskan imports through time is evident.

Cibola ceramics from Late San Juan phase contexts are predominantly White Mountain Red Ware, comprising 68 percent of the typeable assemblage. Most of the sherds were unidentified fragments of b/r and polychrome bowls, but St. Johns Polychrome was the most abundant type. The remaining Cibola sherds are Pueblo II types considered intrusive within the late Pueblo III contexts.

Although not shown in Figure 33.1, ceramics from the Kayenta and Mogollon regions comprise just over 1 percent of the Late San Juan assemblage. Kayenta types include Citadel Polychrome, Cameron Polychrome, Flagstaff B/w, and Dogoszhi B/w. Mogollon types include the same group of brown and red wares found in the earlier assemblages—Showlow Red, Showlow Smudged, Woodruff Brown, Woodruff Smudged, and Tularosa Patterned Corrugated (smudged). Given the dates for the Showlow types, it is assumed these sherds are intrusive earlier Chacoan to Early San Juan phase types.

Almost 2 percent of the typeable assemblage was identified as Northern San Juan trade ware, showing a decrease by about half from the Early San Juan phase. Dolores Corrugated is the only gray ware type present in the Late San Juan contexts. Mesa Verde B/w, transitional McElmo–Mesa Verde B/w, and McElmo B/w are the imported white ware ceramics, although Mesa Verde and McElmo B/w sherds occur in almost equal numbers. The few Northern San Juan Pueblo II sherds present in Late San Juan contexts are considered intrusive along with the small percentage of other Pueblo II ceramics that seem to occur as a part of all contexts across the site.

As expected for the late occupation at Salmon, local production of rock-tempered pottery increased, but production of local Cibola pottery decreased (Figure 33.1). As already mentioned, all of the gray ware rim sherds were classified as Pueblo II and Pueblo II–III corrugated based on the degree of rim eversion in relation to the curvature of the neck. Animas Variety Mesa Verde B/w dominates the Late San Juan typeable ceramics, representing 58 percent. Thirty-one percent of the typeable assemblage is McElmo B/w and only 4 percent is transitional McElmo–Mesa Verde B/w. The remaining 7 percent includes Mancos B/w (all styles) and a few Early McElmo B/w sherds, representing the overlay of Pueblo II and early Pueblo III ceramics that appears in all of the Salmon strata. Animas Variety Cibola pottery from the Late San Juan phase strata includes 43 percent Pueblo II types that are considered intrusive. The remaining 57 percent of the typeable assemblage is Chaco-McElmo B/w. Many of these sherds are likely associated with the Late San Juan phase occupation, given that 24 percent of them have Mesa Verde style designs. The implications of local production of Chaco-McElmo B/w with its distinctive washy slips and Mesa Verde style designs bears significance in the context of Chacoan people living at Salmon and the continuation of Chacoan ancestral ties or ceremonialism.

CONCLUSION

During this phase of the Salmon Research Initiative, the focus was on refining the typology, finetuning the recognition of local production, developing a local chronology for the ceramics, and recognizing the temporal variation in the Salmon assemblage. Through analysis of a sample of ceramics from six rooms, two of which were ceremonial, Chacoan deposits were recognized and confirmed with the original Salmon analyses, and variation in local production signatures were confirmed using a binocular microscope. Also, a local variant of Cibola White Ware was identified at

Salmon, further confirming analysis results at the Tommy site and Aztec.

This study is merely the beginning of ceramic research in the Middle San Juan region. As in most research projects, this study opened more doors and provided more research questions to pursue during future studies. There is more field reconnaissance and analysis to be done with the raw material and with refire, petrographic, and geocompositional studies. Also, with only six rooms analyzed using the updated approach presented in Chapters 30 and 31 and the ceramic groups presented in this chapter, there is more analysis to undertake with additional identification of local Cibola pottery. Identification of Chacoan migrants and households at Salmon will require additional analysis of household rooms at Salmon with the focus on recognizing Chacoan Cibola technology that used local Middle San Juan resources. The local gray ware ceramics require additional attention as well, with the focus on rim eversion as a chronometric tool and on tracking the types of corrugation through time. As Franklin (1980a) indicated in his original analysis, there was a shift in corrugation style with the later Pueblo III contexts to an obliterated corrugated that needs to be explored more fully.

Although not presented in this phase of the study, differences in geocompositional signatures of clays from the Middle San Juan region (Kirtland/Fruitland, San Jose, and Nacimiento Formation) and the predominant Menefee Formation clays of the Chaco Cibola region are evident with use of the inductively coupled plasma emission spectroscopy (ICP) technique (Hensler and Reed 2005). Ceramics from Salmon, Aztec, and the Tommy site tempered with sand or sand and sherd were well matched with Middle San Juan clays, and ceramics imported from the Chaco Cibola region were well matched with Cibola region clays. Thus, the technique worked well with the predominantly sand-tempered ceramics and in our preliminary studies showing local production of Animas Variety Cibola pottery in the Middle San Juan region correlating with the preparation and application of washy slips by local potters. Application of ICP with the rock-tempered ceramics, however, indicated a much more complex situation of igneous temper effects on the clay signatures, producing a lack of clustering in the data. Although petrographic analysis has shown differences in the diorites used for temper between the Middle San Juan Animas Variety and Northern San Juan (Mesa Verde) ceramics, the subtle variability in the mineralogy of these diorites may be enough to throw off statistical clustering of ICP data, for which only 12 chemical elements are measured. The overall issue in choosing ICP over a more precise technique, such as instrumental neutron activation analysis (INAA), was the extensive ICP dataset available for ceramics from sites in the Chaco Cibola region, which we were most interested in for comparative analyses (see Hensler 1999, 2002; Zedeño et al. 1993). To gain a better understanding of resource selection and use in the Middle San Juan, as well as the extent of imported ceramics from both the Cibola and Northern San Juan regions, a refocus of techniques to include INAA is planned for ongoing studies at Salmon and other sites. Results and interpretations from all techniques will be reported with future publications.

Complexity and variability are probably appropriate descriptive terms for the ceramics from Salmon, along with those from Aztec and the Tommy site. Although there is a coherent Animas Variety tradition and superficially a Mancos B/w bowl is still a Mancos B/w bowl, there are nuances to the ceramics from each site, the resources selected, and the way in which local potters processed and used those resources. For example the mixing of mineral and organic paints appears to have been more common during the Chacoan period, and organic paint was possibly used earlier on Mancos B/w ceramics at Salmon and other Middle San Juan sites than in other regions. The potential for ancestral ties to Pueblo I Upper San Juan peoples in the Animas and La Plata valleys may have influenced the use of organic pigments on Pueblo II ceramics in the Middle San Juan region. The variability in slip preparation and application evident on both local Cibola and Northern San Juan vessels suggests either influence by Cibola technology or the presence of actual Cibola potters at Salmon and possibly other sites in the Middle San Juan. Although the original Salmon ceramic analysis and the reexamination of ceramics from a small number of rooms is now published in this volume, these data and interpretations merely address a few questions and open the door to a multitude of new ones.

REFERENCES CITED

Abel, Leland J.
1955 *Pottery Types of the Southwest: San Juan Red Ware, Mesa Verde Gray and White Ware, San Juan White Ware.* Museum of Northern Arizona Ceramic Series 3. Northern Arizona Society of Science and Art, Flagstaff.

Adams, Karen R.
1980 *Pollen, Parched Seeds, and Prehistory: A Pilot Investigation of Prehistoric Plant Remains from Salmon Ruin, a Chacoan Pueblo in Northwestern New Mexico.* Contributions in Anthropology 9. Eastern New Mexico University, Portales.

2005 Subsistence and Plant Use Among the Chacoan and Secondary Occupations at Salmon Ruin. In *Salmon Ruins: Chacoan Outlier and Thirteenth-Century Pueblo in the Middle San Juan Region,* edited by P. F. Reed. Ms. in review, University of Utah Press, Salt Lake City.

Adams, Rex K.
1980 The Codex of Salmon Ruin Stratigraphy. In *Investigations at the Salmon Site: The Structure of Chacoan Society in the Northern Southwest,* edited by C. Irwin-Williams and P. Shelley, Appendix 4.1. Unpublished report submitted to funding agencies. On file, Salmon Ruins Library, Bloomfield, New Mexico.

Allen, W. L., and J. B. Richardson III
1971 The Reconstruction of Kinship from Archaeological Data: The Concepts, the Methods, and the Feasibility. *American Antiquity* 36:41–53.

Anderberg, M. R.
1973 *Cluster Analysis for Applications.* Academic Press, New York.

Arany, L.
1978 Functional Analysis of Culinary Ware, Starting with Room 33W, Salmon Ruin. Ms. on file, Salmon Ruins Library, Bloomfield, New Mexico.

Baltz, E. H.
1967 *Stratigraphic and Regional Tectonic Implications of Part of the Upper Cretaceous and Tertiary Rocks, East-Central San Juan Basin, New Mexico.* USGS Professional Paper 552. U.S. Geological Survey, Washington, D.C.

Baltz, E. H., S. F. Ash, and R. Anderson
1966 *History of Nomenclature and Stratigraphy of Rocks Adjacent to the Cretaceous-Tertiary Boundary, Western San Juan Basin, New Mexico.* USGS Professional Paper 524-D. U.S. Geological Survey, Washington, D.C.

Bennett, M. Ann
1974 *Basic Ceramic Analysis.* Contributions in Anthropology 6(1). Eastern New Mexico University, Portales.

Bice, Richard A.
1983 The Sterling Site–An Initial Report. In *Collected Papers in Honor of Charlie R. Steen,* edited by N. Fox, pp. 49–86. Papers of the Archaeological Society of New Mexico 8. Albuquerque Archaeological Society Press, Albuquerque.

Binford, L. R.
1962 Archaeology As Anthropology. *American Antiquity* 28:217–225.

1972 *An Archaeological Perspective.* Seminar Press, New York.

Blinman, Eric
1988 Justification and Procedures for Ceramic Dating. In *Dolores Archaeological Program: Supporting Studies: Additive and Reductive Technologies,* compiled by E. Blinman, K. Phagan, and R. Wilshusen, pp. 501–544. Bureau of Reclamation Engineering and Research Center, Denver.

Blinman, Eric, and C. Dean Wilson
1989 Mesa Verde Region Ceramic Types. Paper Prepared for NMAC Ceramic Workshop, Red Rock State Park, New Mexico.

1994 Ceramic Analysis. In *Excavations Along the Arkansas Loop Pipeline Corridor, Northwestern New Mexico,* edited by L. Honeycutt and J. Fetterman, pp. 29-1 to 29-15. Woods Canyon Archaeological Consultants, Yellow Jacket, Colorado.

Bradley, Suzanne
1979 *Salmon Ruin: West End Ceramics.* Master's thesis, Department of Anthropology, University of Denver.

Breternitz, David A.
1966 *An Appraisal of Tree-Ring Dated Pottery in the Southwest.* Anthropological Papers of the University of Arizona 10. University of Arizona Press, Tucson.

Breternitz, David A., Arthur H. Rohn, Jr., and Elizabeth A. Morris
1974 *Prehistoric Ceramics of the Mesa Verde Region.* Museum of Northern Arizona Ceramic Series 5. Northern Arizona Society of Science and Art, Flagstaff.

Bunzel, Ruth
1929 *The Pueblo Potter*. Columbia University Press, New York.

Carlson, Roy L.
1970 *White Mountain Redware: A Pottery Tradition of East-Central Arizona and Western New Mexico*. Anthropological Papers of the University of Arizona 19. University of Arizona Press, Tucson.

Carpenter, Andrea J.
2005 Petrographic Analysis of Ceramics from Aztec and Salmon Ruins. Unpublished report on file at Animas Ceramic Consulting, Farmington, New Mexico.

Chapman, K. M.
1938 *The Pottery of Santo Domingo Pueblo*. Laboratory of Anthropology, Museum of New Mexico, Santa Fe.
1970 *The Pottery of San Ildefonso Pueblo*. School of American Research Monograph Series 28. Santa Fe.

Christenson, Andrew L.
1994 A Test of Mean Ceramic Dating Using Well-Dated Kayenta Anasazi Sites. *Kiva* 59:297–317.

Colton, Harold S.
1955 *Wares 8A, 8B, 9A, 9B, Tusayan Gray and White Ware, Little Colorado Gray and White Ware*. Museum of Northern Arizona Ceramic Series 3A. Northern Arizona Society of Science and Art, Flagstaff.
1956 *Wares 5A, 5B, 6A, 6B, 7A, 7B, 7C, San Juan Red Ware, Tsegi Orange Ware, Homolovi Orange Ware, Winslow Orange Ware, Awatovi Yellow Ware, Jeddito Yellow Ware, Sichomovi Red Ware*. Museum of Northern Arizona Ceramic Series 3C. Northern Arizona Society of Science and Art, Flagstaff.

Colton, Harold S., and Lyndon L. Hargrave
1937 *Handbook of Northern Arizona Pottery Wares*. Museum of Northern Arizona Bulletin 11. Northern Arizona Society of Science and Art, Flagstaff.

Conrad, Geoffrey W.
1977 Chiquitoy Viejo: An Inca Administrative Center in the Chicama Valley, Peru. *Journal of Field Archaeology* 4:1–18.

Cook, Edward R., Connie A. Woodhouse, C. Mark Eakin, David M. Meko, and David W. Stahle
2004 Long-Term Aridity Changes in the Western United States. *Science* 306:1015–1018.

Costin, Cathy Lynne
1991 Craft Specialization: Issues in Defining, Documenting and Explaining the Organization of Production. *Archaeological Method and Theory*, vol. 3, edited by M. B. Schiffer, pp. 1–56. University of Arizona Press, Tucson.

Cronin, C.
1962 An Analysis of Pottery Design Elements Indicating Possible Relationships Between Three Decorated Types. In *Chapters in the Prehistory of Eastern Arizona I*, by P. S. Martin, J. B. Rinaldo, W. A. Longacre, C. Cronin, L. G. Freeman, Jr., and J. Schoenwetter, pp. 105–114. Fieldiana: Anthropology 53(1). Field Museum of Natural History, Chicago.

Dean, Jeffrey S.
1988 A Model of Anasazi Behavioral Adaptation. In *The Anasazi in a Changing Environment*, edited by G. Gumerman, pp. 25–44. Cambridge University Press, Cambridge.

Deetz, J. F.
1965 *The Dynamics of Stylistic Change in Arikara Ceramics*. Illinois Studies in Anthropology 4. University of Illinois Press, Urbana.

DeGarmo, Glen D.
1975 *Coyote Creek, Site 01: A Methodological Study of a Prehistoric Pueblo Population*. Ph.D. dissertation, University of California, Los Angeles. University Microfilms, Ann Arbor.

Dozier, E.
1965 Southwestern Social Units and Archaeology. *American Antiquity* 31:38–47.

Drennan, Robert D.
1996 *Statistics for Archaeologists: A Commonsense Approach*. Plenum Press, New York.

Dumond, D. E.
1977 Science in Archaeology: The Saints Go Marching In. *American Antiquity* 42:330–349.

Durand, Kathy Roler, and Stephen R. Durand
2005 Faunal Exploitation in the Chacoan World. In *Salmon Ruins: Chacoan Outlier and Thirteenth-Century Pueblo in the Middle San Juan Region*, edited by P. F. Reed. Ms. in review, University of Utah Press, Salt Lake City.

Dykeman, Douglas D., and Kristin Langenfeld
1987 *Prehistory and History of the La Plata Valley, New Mexico*. Contributions to Anthropology Series 891. San Juan County Archaeological Research Center and Library, Bloomfield, New Mexico.

Eddy, Frank W.
1966 *Prehistory in the Navajo Reservoir District, Northwestern New Mexico*. Museum of New Mexico Papers in Anthropology 15. Museum of New Mexico Press, Santa Fe.

Fassett, J. E., and J. S. Hinds
1971 *Geology and Fuel Resource of the Fruitland Formation and Kirtland Shale of the San Juan Basin, New Mexico and Colorado*. USGS Professional Paper 676. U.S. Geological Survey, Washington, D.C.

Franklin, Hayward H.

1975a Analysis of Ceramics Found on the Chaco North Road by Pierre Morenon. Ms. on file, Salmon Ruins Library, Bloomfield, New Mexico.

1975b Analysis of Ceramics from Sites Adjacent to the Chacoan North Road. Ms. on file, Salmon Ruins Library, Bloomfield, New Mexico.

1978 A Comparison of Ceramic Counts from Salmon and Aztec Ruins. *Pottery Southwest* 5(3).

1979a A Preliminary Refiring of Clays from the Vicinity of Salmon Ruin. In *San Juan Valley Archaeological Resource Development Program: Final Report for the Four Corners Commission 1978–1979*, edited by C. Irwin-Williams. On file, Salmon Ruins Library, Bloomfield, New Mexico.

1979b Refiring of Cibola and Chuska Whitewares from Salmon Ruin. In *San Juan Valley Archaeological Resource Development Program: Final Report for the Four Corners Commission, 1978–1979*, edited by C. Irwin-Williams. Ms. on file, Salmon Ruins Library, Bloomfield, New Mexico.

1979c Refiring of Corrugated Sherds from Chaco Canyon. Ms. on file, Salmon Ruins Library, Bloomfield, New Mexico.

1979d Refiring of Culinary Wares from Salmon Ruin. In *San Juan Valley Archaeological Resource Development Program: Final Report for the Four Corners Commission, 1978–1979*, edited by C. Irwin-Williams. Ms. on file, Salmon Ruins Library, Bloomfield, New Mexico.

1979e Refiring Analysis of Sherds from Morris 41, La Plata River. Ms. on file, Salmon Ruins Library, Bloomfield, New Mexico.

1980a Salmon Ruin Ceramics Laboratory Report. In *Investigations at the Salmon Site: The Structure of Chacoan Society in the Northern Southwest*, vol. II, edited by C. Irwin-Williams and P. H. Shelley, part 5, pp. 1–583. Unpublished report submitted to funding agencies. On file, Salmon Ruins Library, Bloomfield, New Mexico.

1980b Stylistic Relationships Between Mesa Verde B/w and the White Mountain Redwares. Paper presented at the annual meeting of the Society for American Archaeology, Philadelphia. On file, Salmon Ruins Library, Bloomfield, New Mexico.

Franklin, Hayward H., and Peter McKenna

2004 Sterling Site Ceramics—A Progress Report. Paper presented at the Salmon Working Conference, Farmington, New Mexico, April 2004.

Freeman, L. G., Jr., and J. A. Brown

1964 Statistical Analysis of Carter Ranch Pottery. In *Chapters in the Prehistory of Eastern Arizona II*, by P. S. Martin, J. B. Rinaldo, W. A. Longacre, L. G. Freeman, Jr., J. A. Brown, R. H. Hevly, and M. E. Cooley, pp. 125–154. Fieldiana: Anthropology 55. Field Museum of Natural History, Chicago.

Goetze, Christine E., and Barbara J. Mills

1993 Ceramic Chronometry. In *Across the Colorado Plateau: Anthropological Studies for the Transwestern Pipeline Expansion Project, vol. 16: Interpretation of Ceramic Artifacts*, edited by B. J. Mills, C. E. Goetze, and M. N. Zedeño, pp. 87–150. Office of Contract Archaeology and Maxwell Museum of Anthropology, University of New Mexico, Albuquerque.

Goff, Joell, and Lori Stephens Reed

1998 Classification Criteria for Temper, Generic Ceramic Types, and Specific Ceramic Types. In *Pipeline Archaeology 1990–1993: The El Paso Natural Gas North System Expansion Project, New Mexico and Arizona*, by L. S. Reed, J. Goff, and K. N. Hensler, pp. 2-1 to 2-74. Western Cultural Resources Management, Inc., Farmington, New Mexico.

Gomolak, Andrew R.

1980 Another Cheap Shot at Normative Thought. Paper Presented at the 1980 Annual Meeting of the New Mexico Archaeological Council and the New Mexico Archaeological Society, Albuquerque.

Grebinger, Paul

1973 Prehistoric Social Organization in Chaco Canyon, New Mexico: An Alternative Reconstruction. *The Kiva* 39:3–23.

Guthe, C. E.

1925 *Pueblo Pottery Making at the Village of San Ildefonso.* Papers of the Phillips Academy, Southwestern Expedition 2. Yale University, New Haven.

Hawley, F. M.

1936 *Field Manual of Prehistoric Pottery Types.* University of New Mexico Anthropology Series 1(4). Albuquerque.

Hayes, Alden C.

1964 *Archaeological Survey of Wetherill Mesa, Mesa Verde National Park, Colorado.* Research Series 7A. National Park Service, Washington, D.C.

1998 *Two Raven House: Wetherill Mesa Excavations, Mesa Verde National Park – Colorado.* Mesa Verde Museum Association, Mesa Verde National Park, Colorado.

Hayes, Alden C., and J. A. Lancaster

1975 *Badger House Community, Mesa Verde National Park.* Research Series 7E. National Park Service, Washington, D.C.

Hayes, Alden C., David M. Brugge, and W. James Judge

1981 *Archaeological Surveys of Chaco Canyon, New Mexico.* Publications in Archeology 18A, National Park Service, Washington, D.C.

Hays-Gilpin, Kelley, and Eric van Hartesveldt (editors)
1998 *Prehistoric Ceramics of the Puerco Valley: The 1995 Chambers-Sanders Trust Lands Ceramic Conference.* Ceramic Series 7. Museum of Northern Arizona, Flagstaff.

Hill, James H.
1968 Broken K Pueblo: Patterns of Form and Function. In *New Perspectives in Archaeology,* edited by S. R. Binford and L. R. Binford, pp. 103–142. Aldine, Chicago.

1978 Individuals and their Artifacts: An Experiment in Archaeology. *American Antiquity* 43:245–257.

1970 Broken *K Pueblo: Prehistoric Social Organization in the American Southwest.* Anthropological Papers of the University of Arizona 18. University of Arizona Press, Tucson.

Hodson, F. R.
1970 Cluster Analysis and Archaeology: Some New Developments and Applications. *World Archaeology* 1(3):297–320.

Horn, Jonathan C., Jerry Fetterman, and Linda Honeycutt (compilers)
2003 *The Rocky Mountain Expansion Loop Pipeline Data Recovery Project, vol. 2: New Mexico Technical Site Reports.* Alpine Archaeological Consultants, Inc., Montrose, Colorado and Woods Canyon Archaeological Consultant, Inc., Yellow Jacket, Colorado.

Hurlburt, C. S., Jr., and C. Klein
1977 *Manual of Mineralogy: After Dana.* Wiley, New York.

Hyslop, John
1984 *The Inka Road System.* Academic Press, Orlando.

Irwin-Williams, Cynthia
1972 *The Structure of Chacoan Society in the Northern Southwest, Investigations at the Salmon Site – 1972.* Contributions in Anthropology 4(3). Eastern New Mexico University, Portales.

1977 Investigations at the Salmon Site: The Structure of Chacoan Society in the Northern Southwest. Research proposal submitted to the National Science Foundation. Ms. on file, Salmon Ruins Library, Bloomfield, New Mexico.

Irwin-Williams, Cynthia, and Phillip H. Shelley (editors)
1980 *Investigations at the Salmon Site: The Structure of Chacoan Society in the Northern Southwest.* 4 vols. Unpublished report submitted to funding agencies. On file, Salmon Ruins Library, Bloomfield, New Mexico.

Judd, N. M.
1954 *The Material Culture of Pueblo Bonito.* Smithsonian Miscellaneous Collections 123. Smithsonian Institution, Washington, D.C.

1959 *Pueblo del Arroyo, Chaco Canyon, New Mexico.* Smithsonian Miscellaneous Collections 133(1). Smithsonian Institution, Washington, D.C.

1964 *The Architecture of Pueblo Bonito.* Smithsonian Miscellaneous Collections 147(1). Smithsonian Institution, Washington, D.C.

Judge, W. James
1979 The Development of a Complex Ecosystem in the Chaco Basin, New Mexico. In *Proceedings of the First Conference on Scientific Research in the National Parks,* vol. II, edited by R. M. Linn, pp. 901–906. Transactions and Proceedings Series 5. National Park Service, Washington, D.C.

Klecka, W. R.
1975 Discriminant Analysis. In *Statistical Package for the Social Sciences,* edited by N. H. Nie et al., pp. 434–467. McGraw-Hill, New York.

Kincaid, Chris (editor)
1983 *Chaco Roads Project Phase I: A Reappraisal of Prehistoric Roads in the San Juan Basin, 1983.* Bureau of Land Management, New Mexico State Office, Albuquerque.

Kruskal, J., and M. Wish
1978 *Multidimensional Scaling.* Sage University Paper Series on Quantitative Applications in the Social Sciences 07-011. Sage Publications, Beverly Hills.

Lekson, S., and C. Cameron
1975 Artifact Assemblages at the Salmon Site: A Trial Formulation on Material from Living Floor Contexts. Ms. on file, Salmon Ruins Library, Bloomfield, New Mexico.

Longacre, W. A.
1966 Changing Patterns of Social Integration: A Prehistoric Example from the American Southwest. *American Anthropologist* 68(1):94–102.

1970 *Archaeology as Anthropology: A Case Study.* Anthropological Papers of the University of Arizona 17. University of Arizona Press, Tucson.

Lyons, T. R.
1973 Archaeological Research Strategies: The Chaco Canyon Road Survey. Ms. on file, Salmon Ruins Library, Bloomfield, New Mexico.

Marshall, Michael P., John R. Stein, Richard W. Loose, and Judith E. Novotny
1979 *Anasazi Communities of the San Juan Basin*. Public Service Company of New Mexico and the Historic Preservation Bureau, State of New Mexico.

Martin, Paul S., and John B. Rinaldo
1950 *Turkey Foot Ridge Site: A Mogollon Village, Pine Lawn Valley, Western New Mexico*. Fieldiana: Anthropology 38(2). Field Museum of Natural History, Chicago.

McNeil, Jimmy D.
1986 *Ornaments of Salmon Ruin, San Juan County, New Mexico*. Master's thesis, Department of Anthropology, Eastern New Mexico University, Portales.

Mills, Barbara J.
1991 Ceramics from the Box B Site. In *Archaeology of the San Juan Breaks, The Anasazi Occupation*, edited by P. Hogan and L. Sebastian, pp. 51–88. Office of Contract Archeology, University of New Mexico, Albuquerque.

Mills, Barbara J., Andrea J. Carpenter, and William Grimm
1997 Sourcing Chuskan Ceramic Production: Petrographic and Experimental Analyses. *Kiva* 62(3):261–282.

Mills, Barbara J., Christine E. Goetze, and Maria Nieves Zedeño
1993 *Across the Colorado Plateau: Anthropological Studies for the Transwestern Pipeline Expansion Project, vol. 16: Interpretation of Ceramic Artifacts*. Office of Contract Archaeology and Maxwell Museum of Anthropology, University of New Mexico, Albuquerque.

Morenon, E. Pierre
1975 Chacoan Roads and Adaptation: How a Prehistoric Population Can Define and Control its Social and Natural Environment. In *The Structure of Chacoan Society in the Northern Southwest, Investigations at the Salmon Site, 1974–1975*, edited by C. Irwin-Williams, pp. 187–200. Ms. on file, Salmon Ruins Museum, Bloomfield, New Mexico.

1977 A View of the Chacoan Phenomenon from the "Backwoods": A Speculative Essay. Ms. on file, Salmon Ruins Library, Bloomfield, New Mexico.

Morris, Craig
1982 The Infrastructure of Inca Control in the Peruvian Central Highlands. In *The Inca and Aztec States, 1400–1880*, edited by G. Collier, R. Rosaldo, and J. Wirth, pp. 153–171. Academic Press, New York.

Morris, Craig, and Donald E. Thompson
1985 *Huanuca Pampa*. Thames and Hudson, New York.

Morris, Earl H.
1919 *The Aztec Ruin*. Anthropological Papers 26(1). American Museum of Natural History, New York.

1921 *The House of the Great Kiva at the Aztec Ruin*. Anthropological Papers 26(2). American Museum of Natural History, New York.

1924a *Burials in the Aztec Ruin*. Anthropological Papers 26(3). American Museum of Natural History, New York.

1924b *The Aztec Ruin Annex*. Anthropological Papers 26(4). American Museum of Natural History, New York.

1928 *Notes on Excavations in the Aztec Ruin*. Anthropological Papers 26(5). American Museum of Natural History, New York.

1939 *Archaeological Studies in the La Plata District*. Publication 519. Carnegie Institution of Washington, D.C.

Museum of Northern Arizona
1958 *Cibola Whiteware Conference, 1958*, edited by H. S. Colton. Museum of Northern Arizona, Flagstaff.

1959 *Second Southwestern Ceramic Seminar (White Mountain Redware, Siwanna Redware)*. Museum of Northern Arizona, Flagstaff.

Peckham, S., and J. Wilson
1965 Chuska Valley Ceramics. Ms. on file, Salmon Ruins Library, Bloomfield, New Mexico.

1967 Archaeological Survey of the Chuska Valley and Chaco Plateau, New Mexico, part II: Survey. Ms. on file, Salmon Ruins Library, Bloomfield, New Mexico.

Powers, Robert P., William B. Gillespie, and Stephen H. Lekson
1983 *The Outlier Survey: A Regional View of Settlement in the San Juan Basin*. Reports of the Chaco Center 3. Division of Cultural Research, National Park Service, Albuquerque.

Priesnitz, J.
1979 *A Preliminary Investigation of Organizational Loci at Salmon Ruin, a Chacoan Outlier in Northwestern New Mexico*. Master's thesis, Department of Anthropology, Eastern New Mexico University, Portales.

Reed, Lori Stephens
1993 Review of Northern Anasazi Ceramic Styles: A Field Guide for Identification, edited by W. A. Lucius and D. A. Breternitz. *Pottery Southwest* 20:9–10.

2005 Ceramics of the Middle San Juan Region: A Medley of Cibola, San Juan, and Local Traditions. In *Salmon Pueblo: Chacoan Outlier and Thirteenth-Century Pueblo in the Middle San Juan Region*, edited by P. F. Reed. Ms. in review, University of Utah Press, Salt Lake City.

2006 Ceramic Analysis Results. In *The Manuel Canyon Settlement Patterns Inventory: Archaic, Early Anasazi, Navajo, and Historic Occupations in Northwestern New Mexico*, assembled by E. M. Kotyk, pp. 13–1 to 13–30. Research Papers in Anthropology 11. Cultural Resources Management Program, San Juan College, Farmington, New Mexico. In preparation, expected 2006.

Reed, Lori Stephens, and Joell Goff
2003 A Reappraisal of the Chronology of the Chuska Pottery Sequence. In *Anasazi Archaeology at the Millennium: Proceedings of the Sixth Occasional Anasazi Symposium*, edited by P. F. Reed, pp. 97–110. Center for Desert Archaeology, Tucson.

Reed, Lori Stephens, and Tori L. Myers
2005 Ceramic Artifacts from the 1984 Aztec Ruin Excavation Project. Draft report submitted to Aztec Ruins National Monument, National Park Service, Aztec, New Mexico. Technical Report No. ACC-2005-01, Animas Ceramic Consulting, Inc., Farmington, New Mexico.

Reed, Lori Stephens, Joell Goff, and Kathy Niles Hensler
1998 *Exploring Ceramic Production, Distribution, and Exchange in the Southern Chuska Valley: Analytical Results from the El Paso Natural Gas North System Expansion Project*. Pipeline Archaeology 1990–1993: The El Paso Natural Gas North System Expansion Project, New Mexico and Arizona, Vol. XI. Technical Report WCRM (F)035, Western Cultural Resource Management, Farmington, New Mexico.

Reed, Lori Stephens, Kathy Niles Hensler, and Andrea J. Carpenter
2001a Tracking the Trachyte: Origins and Development of Chuska Pottery Technology. Paper presented at the 66th annual meeting of the Society for American Archaeology, New Orleans.

2001b Tommy Site Ceramic Sourcing Study. In *Special Ceramic Studies: Totah Archaeological Project Field School*, by San Juan College Cultural Resources Management Program and Animas Ceramic Consulting, Inc. Submitted to State of New Mexico Historic Preservation Division in fulfillment of New Mexico Historic Preservation Grant 35-00-15334.02. 2000-SJC-133, San Juan College Cultural Resource Management Program, Farmington, New Mexico.

Reed, Lori Stephens, Jim Railey, Chris Turnbow, Hector Neff, and Andrea Carpenter
2000 Identifying Local Pottery Production at the Power Site: An Early Pithouse Period Habitation in the Burro Mountains, New Mexico. In *Mogollon Archaeology: Collected Papers from the Eleventh Mogollon Conference, 20th Anniversary: 1980–2000*, edited by Patrick H. Beckett, pp. 165–188. Coas Publishing and Research, Las Cruces, New Mexico.

Reed, Paul F.
1999 Chronometric Dating. In *Anasazi Community Development in Cove–Redrock Valley: Archaeological Excavations Along the N33 Road in Apache County, Arizona*, edited by P. F. Reed and K. N. Hensler, pp. 903–912. Navajo Nation Papers in Anthropology 33. Navajo Nation Archaeology Department, Window Rock, Arizona.

2004 *The Puebloan Society of Chaco Canyon*. Greenwood Press, Westport, CT.

2005 Salmon Pueblo As a Ritual and Residential Chacoan Great House. In *Salmon Pueblo: Chacoan Outlier and Thirteenth Century Pueblo in the Middle San Juan Region*, edited by P. F. Reed. Ms. in review, University of Utah Press, Salt Lake City.

Reeside, J. B.
1924 *Upper Cretaceous and Tertiary Formations of the Western Part of the San Juan Basin of Colorado and New Mexico.* USGS Professional Paper 134. U.S. Geological Survey, Washington, D.C.

Rice, Prudence, M.
1987 *Pottery Analysis: A Sourcebook*. University of Chicago Press, Chicago.

Rinaldo, John B.
1959 *Foote Canyon Pueblo, Eastern Arizona*. Fieldiana: Anthropology 49(2). Field Museum of Natural History, Chicago.

Rinaldo, John B., and Elaine A. Bluhm
1956 *Late Mogollon Pottery Types of the Reserve Area*. Fieldiana: Anthropology 36(7). Field Museum of Natural History, Chicago.

Rohn, Arthur H.
1965 Postulation of Socio-Economic Groups from Archaeological Evidence. In *Contributions of the Wetherill Mesa Archaeological Project*, assembled by D. Osborne, pp. 65–69. SAA Memoir 19. Society for American Archaeology, Washington, D.C.

1971 *Mug House*. Archeological Research Series 7-D. National Park Service, Washington, D.C.

1977 *Cultural Change and Continuity on Chapin Mesa*. Regents Press of Kansas, Lawrence.

Rose, Janet
1979 A Palynological Study of Rooms 82W and 62W at Salmon Ruin, New Mexico. Ms. on file, Salmon Ruins Library, Bloomfield, New Mexico.

Schiffer, M. B.
1976 *Behavioral Archaeology*. Academic Press, New York.

Schreiber, Katharina J.
1987 Conquest and Consolidation: A Comparison of the Wari and Inka Occupations of a Highland Peruvian Valley. *American Antiquity* 52(2):266–284.

Sekaquapetwa, Emory, and Dorothy Washburn
2003 Metaphors of Meaning in the Awatovi Murals. Museum of Northern Arizona for the Hopi Mural Project. Ms. in possession of authors.

2004 They Go Along Singing: Reconstructing the Hopi Past from Ritual Metaphors in Song and Image. *American Antiquity* 69:457–486.

Shelley, Phillip H.
1983 *Lithic Specialization at Salmon Ruin, San Juan County, New Mexico.* Ph.D. dissertation, Washington State University, Pullman. University Microfilms, Ann Arbor.

Shepard, Anna O.
1939 Technology of La Plata Pottery. In *Archaeological Studies in the La Plata District, Southwestern Colorado and Northwestern New Mexico,* edited by E. H. Morris, pp. 249–287. Publication 519. Carnegie Institute of Washington, D.C.

1965 *Ceramics for the Archaeologist.* Publication 609. Carnegie Institution of Washington, D.C.

Skibo, James M.
1992 *Pottery Function: A Use-Alteration Perspective.* Plenum Press, New York.

Skibo, James M., and Eric Blinman
1999 Exploring the Origins of Pottery on the Colorado Plateau. In *Pottery and People: A Dynamic Interaction,* edited by J. M. Skibo and G. M. Feinman, pp. 171–183. University of Utah Press, Salt Lake City.

South, Stanley
1977 *Method and Theory in Historical Archaeology.* Academic Press, New York.

Stanislawski, M. B.
1973 Ethnoarchaeology and Settlement Archaeology. *Ethnohistory* 20(4):375–392.

1977 The Ethnoarchaeology Hopi and Hopi-Tewa Pottery Making: Styles of Learning. In *Experimental Archaeology,* edited by D. Ingersoll, J. E. Yellen, and W. Macdonald, pp. 378–408. Columbia University Press, New York.

Stein, John R., and Peter J. McKenna
1988 *An Archaeological Reconnaissance of a Late Bonito Phase Occupation Near Aztec Ruins National Monument, New Mexico.* Southwest Cultural Resources Center, National Park Service, Santa Fe.

Swannack, Jervis D., Jr.
1969 *Big Juniper House, Wetherill Mesa Excavations, Mesa Verde National Park – Colorado.* Research Series 7C. National Park Service, Washington, D.C.

Thomas, D. H.
1976 *Figuring Anthropology.* Holt, Rinehart, and Winston, New York.

1978 The Awful Truth About Statistics in Archaeology. *American Antiquity* 43(2):231–244.

Toll, H. Wolcott, III
2001 Making and Breaking Pots in the Chaco World. *American Antiquity* 66:56–78.

2005 The La Plata, the Totah, and the Chaco: Variations on a Theme. In *Salmon Ruins: Chacoan Outlier and Thirteenth-Century Pueblo in the Middle San Juan Region,* edited by P. F. Reed. Ms. in review, University of Utah Press, Salt Lake City.

Toll, H. Wolcott, III, and Peter J. McKenna
1992 The Rhetoric and the Ceramics: Discussion of Types, Functions, Distributions and Sources of the Ceramics of 29SJ 627. In *Excavations at 29SJ 627, Chaco Canyon, New Mexico,* vol. II, edited by F. J. Mathien, pp. 37–248. Reports of the Chaco Center 11. National Park Service, Santa Fe.

1997 Chaco Ceramics. In *Ceramics, Lithics, and Ornaments of Chaco Canyon: Analyses of Artifacts from the Chaco Project, 1971–1978,* edited by Joan Mathien, pp. 17–530. Publications in Archeology 18G. National Park Service, Santa Fe.

Toll, H. Wolcott, Eric Blinman, and C. Dean Wilson
2001 Chaco in the Context of Ceramic Regional Systems. In *Anasazi Regional Organization and the Chaco System,* edited by D. Doyel, pp. 147–158. Anthropological Papers 5. Maxwell Museum of Anthropology, University of New Mexico, Albuquerque.

Van West, Carla R., and Jeffrey S. Dean
2000 Environmental Characteristics of the AD 900–1300 Period in the Central Mesa Verde Region. *Kiva* 66:19–44.

Vivian, Gordon, and T. W. Mathews
1964 *Kin Kletso: A Pueblo III Community in Chaco Canyon, New Mexico.* Technical Series 6(1). Southwest Monuments Association, Globe, Arizona.

Vivian, R. Gwinn
1970 An Inquiry into Prehistoric Society in Chaco Canyon. In *Reconstructing Prehistoric Pueblo Societies,* edited by W. A. Longacre, pp. 59–83. University of New Mexico Press, Albuquerque.

Warren, A. H.
1967 Petrographic Analyses of Pottery and Lithics. In *An Archaeological Survey of the Chuska Valley and the Chaco Plateau, New Mexico. Part 1, Natural Science Studies,* by A. H. Harris, J. Schoenwetter, and A. H. Warren. Museum of New Mexico Research Records 4. Santa Fe.

1974 Progress Report for Summer of 1974. Ms. on file, Salmon Ruins Library, Bloomfield, New Mexico.

1975a Notes of the Surface Collection at ENM 5108, July, 1975. Ms. on file, Salmon Ruins Library, Bloomfield, New Mexico.

1975b Notes on the Tempering Materials of the Pottery of LA 8846, the Salmon Pueblo. Ms. on file, Salmon Ruins Library, Bloomfield, New Mexico.

Washburn, Dorothy K.

1977 *A Symmetry Analysis of Upper Gila Area Ceramic Design*. Papers of the Peabody Museum of Archaeology and Ethnology 68. Harvard University, Cambridge.

1980 The Mexican Connection: Cylinder Jars from the Valley of Oaxaca. In *New Frontiers in the Archaeology and Ethnohistory of the Greater Southwest*, edited by C. Riley and B. Hedrick, pp. 70–85. Transactions of the Illinois State Academy of Science 72(4).

1983 Symmetry Analysis of Ceramic Design: Two Tests of the Method on Neolithic Material from Greece and the Aegean. In *Structure and Cognition in Art*, edited by D. Washburn, pp. 138–164. Cambridge University Press, Cambridge.

1986 Symmetry Analysis of Yurok, Karok, and Hupa Indian Basket Designs. *Empirical Studies of the Arts* 4(1):19–45.

1987 The Neighbor Factor: Basket Designs in Northern and Central California. *Journal of California and Great Basin Anthropology* 9(2):146–173.

1990 Style, Classification, and Ethnicity: Design Categories on Bakuba Raffia Cloth. *Transactions of the American Philosophical Society* 80(3).

1991 Southern Laotian Textiles: Relationships Between Pattern Structure and Weaving Technology. *Ars Textrina* 15:35–66.

1999 Perceptual Anthropology: The Cultural Salience of Symmetry. *American Anthropologist* 101(3):547–562.

2001 Remembering Things Seen: Experimental Approaches to the Process of Information Transmittal. *Journal of Archaeological Method and Theory* 8(1):67–99.

2002 The Cultural Salience of Symmetry. In *Symmetry 2000*, edited by I. Hargittai and T. Laurent, pp. 429–444. Wenner-Gren vol. 80. Portland Press, London.

2004 Symmetry Analysis of Ica Valley Ceramics: Insights into Ica-Inca Interactions. In *Symmetry Comes of Age*, edited by D. K. Washburn and D. W. Crowe, pp. 215–231. University of Washington Press, Seattle.

2005 The Position of Salmon Ruins in the Middle San Juan AD 1000–1300: A Perspective from Ceramic Design Structure. In *Salmon Pueblo: Chacoan Outlier and Thirteenth-Century Pueblo in the Middle San Juan Region*, edited by P. F. Reed. Ms. in review, University of Utah Press, Salt Lake City.

Washburn, Dorothy K., and Donald W. Crowe

1988 *Symmetries of Culture: Theory and Practice of Plane Pattern Analysis.* University of Washington Press, Seattle.

Washburn, Dorothy K., and Donald W. Crowe (editors)

2004 *Symmetry Comes of Age: The Role of Pattern in Culture.* University of Washington Press, Seattle.

Washburn, Dorothy, and Diane Humphrey

2001 Symmetries in the Mind: Production, Perception, and Preference for Seven One-Dimensional Patterns. *Visual Arts Research* 27(2):57–68.

Washburn, Dorothy K., and R. G. Matson

1985 Use of Multidimensional Scaling to Display Sensitivity of Symmetry Analysis of Patterned Design to Spatial and Chronological Change: Examples from Anasazi Prehistory. In *Decoding Prehistoric Ceramics*, edited by B. Nelson, pp. 75–101. Southern Illinois University Press, Carbondale.

Webster, Laurie D.

2005 A Preliminary Assessment of Perishable Relationships Between Chaco, Salmon, and Aztec. In *Salmon Ruins: Chacoan Outlier and Thirteenth-Century Pueblo in the Middle San Juan Region*, edited by P. F. Reed. Ms. in review, University of Utah Press, Salt Lake City.

Whalley, Lucy A.

1980 *Chacoan Ceramic Exchange in the Middle San Juan Area, A.D. 900–1300.* Master's thesis, Department of Anthropology, Eastern New Mexico University, Portales.

Wheelbarger, Linda

2005 Puebloan Communities on the South Side of the Middle San Juan River. In *Salmon Ruins: Chacoan Outlier and Thirteenth-Century Pueblo in the Middle San Juan Region*, edited by P. F. Reed. Ms. in review, University of Utah Press, Salt Lake City.

Wilshusen, Richard H., and C. Dean Wilson

1995 Reformatting the Social Landscape in the Late Pueblo I–Early Pueblo II Period: The Cedar Hill Data in Regional Context. In *The Cedar Hill Special Treatment Project: Late Pueblo I, Early Navajo, and Historic Occupations in Northwestern New Mexico*, compiled by R. H. Wilshusen, pp. 43–80. Research Papers 1. La Plata Archaeological Consultants, Dolores, Colorado.

Wilson, C. Dean

1985 *Refiring Analysis of San Juan Wares from Salmon Ruin and the Vicinity.* Master's thesis, Department of Anthropology, Eastern New Mexico University, Portales.

1996 Ceramic Pigment Distributions and Regional Interactions: A Re-examination of Interpretations in Shepard's "Technology of La Plata Pottery." *Kiva* 62:83–102.

Windes, Thomas C.

1977 Typology and Technology of Anasazi Ceramics. In *Settlement and Subsistence Along the Lower Chaco River: The CGP Survey,* edited by C. A. Reher, pp. 279–370. University of New Mexico Press, Albuquerque.

1980 Tests and Excavations at the Pueblo alto Complex, 1974–1979. Data Appendices. Ms. on file, Chaco Archives, National Park Service, Albuquerque, New Mexico.

1985 Chaco-McElmo Black-on-White. In *Prehistory and History in the Southwest. Collected Papers in Honor of Alden C. Hayes,* edited by N. Fox, pp. 19–42. Papers of the Archaeological Society of New Mexico 11. Ancient City Press, Santa Fe.

1987 *Investigations at the Pueblo Alto Complex, Chaco Canyon, New Mexico, 1975–1979.* Publications in Archaeology 18F. National Park Service, Santa Fe.

Windes, Thomas C., and Peter J. McKenna

1989 Cibola Whiteware and Cibola Grayware: The Chaco Series. Paper prepared for NMAC Ceramic Workshop, Red Rock State Park, New Mexico.

Wood, J. J.

1974 A Computer Program for Hierarchical Cluster Analysis. *Newsletter of Computer Archaeology* 9(4):1–11.

Zaslow, Bert

1977 *Pattern Mathematics and Archaeology.* Anthropological Research Papers 2. Arizona State University, Tempe.

1981 *Pattern Dissemination in the Prehistoric Southwest and Mesoamerica.* Anthropological Research Papers 25. Arizona State University, Tempe.